THE COLUMBIA DOCUMENTARY HISTORY OF AMERICAN WOMEN SINCE 1941

THE COLUMBIA DOCUMENTARY HISTORY OF

AMERICAN WOMEN SINCE 1941

EDITED BY
HARRIET SIGERMAN

 COLUMBIA UNIVERSITY PRESS / NEW YORK

COLUMBIA UNIVERSITY PRESS

Publishers Since 1893

New York   Chichester, West Sussex

Copyright © 2003 Columbia University Press

All rights reserved

Every effort has been made to trace copyright holders and
give proper credit for all copyrighted material used in this
book. The editor regrets if there are any oversights. The
publisher will be pleased to hear from any copyright holders
not acknowledged in this edition.

Library of Congress Cataloging-in-Publication Data
The Columbia documentary history of American women
      since 1941 / edited by Harriet Sigerman.
           p.   cm.
      Includes bibliographical references and index.
      ISBN 0-231-11698-5 (alk. paper)
           1. Women—United States—History—20th century—
   Sources. 2. Women's rights—United States—History—
   Sources. 3. Feminism—United States—History—Sources.
   I. Sigerman, Harriet.

HQ1420.C65 2003
305.4'0973'0904—dc21   2002041395

Columbia University Press books are printed
on permanent and durable acid-free paper.
Designed by Lisa Hamm
Composed by William Meyers
Printed in the United States of America
c 10 9 8 7 6 5 4 3 2 1

To a new generation of scholars in women's history

CONTENTS

ACKNOWLEDGMENTS

Beyond the author's work, every book reflects the collective efforts of several dedicated and talented individuals. James Warren, executive editor at Columbia University Press, first suggested the idea for this book and then waited patiently for the manuscript. Plaegian Alexander, assistant editor, was extremely helpful in answering questions pertaining to permissions. I also wish to thank Susan Heath, freelance manuscript editor, for her excellent copyediting, and Susan Pensak, senior manuscript editor at Columbia University Press, for shepherding the manuscript through its many stages to a finished book. Finally, my husband, Jay L. Banks, with grace and good humor, cheered me on through the lengthy process of bringing this book to fruition.

THE COLUMBIA DOCUMENTARY HISTORY OF
AMERICAN WOMEN SINCE 1941

The second half of the twentieth century was a pivotal period of change and resistance, progress and backlash for American women. From the Hoover vacuum cleaner to the fax machine, from the pill to a bewildering array of assisted reproductive techniques, from Rosie the Riveter to Martha Stewart and Hillary Rodham Clinton, American women have grappled with a dizzying rate of social and economic change and the many ways in which that velocity of change has contributed to redefining conceptions of gender.

Over the past half century, American women have played a vital role in a world war and in several smaller wars and regional conflicts, not only as medical and administrative personnel but as soldiers in combat; reignited a movement for their own social and political equality and, in the process, sparked a social revolution; moved into the workforce in much greater numbers, including the highest levels of corporate power and academic and professional achievement; and also rediscovered their own history and created a new academic discipline—that of women's history.

This collection of documents seeks to chronicle the exciting and tumultuous recent history of American women, beginning with our nation's entry into World War II. That war is a watershed event in American history and, in particular, for American women. For the nation as a whole, the war helped to pull the country out of the worst economic depression it had ever known and catapulted the United States onto the world stage as a political and economic superpower. For American women, the war offered greater employment opportunities and, without undermining long-standing beliefs about women's and men's separate and distinct gender roles, accelerated trends already set into motion to give women more choices in their lives. These trends included increased employment opportunities, which led to greater economic and personal independence; public approval to combine work with marriage and motherhood; and greater access to higher education.

The war paved the way for American women's increased entry into the public realm, both as workers and as citizens rallying to the crisis. In 1944, at the peak of war production, almost one in three women defense workers had previously been a full-time homemaker. For the first time in American history, the number of married women workers surpassed that of single women workers. Although American women did not achieve equal pay or working conditions and did not change public attitudes, including those of women, about traditional expectations for women's lives, the war helped women move into a more public arena and, as many of the documents in chapter 1 illustrate, to develop confidence in their skills and abilities and recognition of their contribution to the nation's victory. World War II seems a fitting start, then, for a document collection that focuses on recent American women's history.

Chapter 2 unfolds the contradictions and cultural tensions of the immediate postwar period, from women's determination to continue working outside the home in an era of intense social pressure to marry and bear large families to the remarkable variety of social and political activism that women spearheaded during an acute period of social conformity and political conservatism. This chapter aims to shatter stereotypes of the 1950s as the somnolent or gray decade and demonstrate the varieties of American women's social and political activism. The emblematic stereotype of the white middleclass suburban housewife masks the diverse ways in which women conducted their personal and public lives. In trade unions, the peace movement, civil rights, and civic reform, women initiated social change and were increasingly more visible in public affairs. Some of the most courageous female activists in the civil rights and peace movements marched and spoke out during these years, including Rosa Parks and Fannie Lou Hamer; the young mothers of Women Strike for Peace, who protested the proliferation of nuclear weapons; and Lillian Smith, a white journalist from the South who publicly condemned racism and segregation in numerous articles and books. But American women's activism was not limited to civil rights, the peace movement, or bread-and-butter issues. Margaret Chase Smith, the only female senator in the United States Senate, courageously spoke out against the bullying tactics of right-wing senator Joseph McCarthy during the anti-Communist hysteria of the early 1950s, and throughout that decade Rachel Carson, a marine biologist, wrote urgently and eloquently about the destruction of the environment by technology and industry. Her early exhortations to protect the beauty of the natural world helped inspire the environmental movement of a decade later.

Chapter 3 focuses on the rebirth of feminism and the historic changes it created in the lives of both women and men. With the resurgence of the women's movement came an extraordinary outpouring of ideas and visions for women's lives. The documents in this chapter will introduce readers to the rich strands of feminist thinking and also to the ways in which women embraced or disavowed the movement. The feminist writings by women of color offer some of the most challenging and creative writing within the feminist movement because of their early and astute understanding that race and class are inextricably linked to their struggles as women. These thinkers invigorated feminist praxis with a complex, multilayered analysis of social and political change and also infused it with a personal quality that spoke across class and ethnic lines. In their work they celebrated the wellsprings of strength, pride, and creativity possessed by their mothers and other female relatives. This celebration of womanhood and the desire to explore generational links among women was a distinct hallmark of feminist writing throughout the 1970s and early 1980s and found a highly responsive readership.

Feminist thinking also extended to the church and synagogue and to the therapist's office. The selections pertaining to feminist spirituality demonstrate feminist ways of reinterpreting traditional rituals and beliefs in order to rectify the exclusion or distortion of women's experience and points of view. Although some of these selections perhaps reached a small readership, the spirit of their writings—the attempt to recover and reaffirm the experiences of women on their own terms and not through the values and standards established by men—reverberated in less ideological ways among the larger community of American women.

The last three chapters look at changes in women's lives over the past quarter century, since the early 1980s, when the goals and ideas of sexual equality were percolating throughout mainstream American culture. Chapters 4 and 5 examine the reverberations of the women's movement upon women's lives: how women handled the delicate balancing act between paid work outside the home and domestic responsibilities at home; the impact of a new and powerful radical right grassroots movement, which challenged the tenets of feminism and sought a return to a traditional nuclear family, with a breadwinning husband and a wife and mother at home full time ; the critical impact of these fundamentalist ideas on women's hard-won reproductive freedoms; and the significant public policies of the Reagan/Bush and Clinton administrations that

4

hampered as well as promoted women's ability to combat gender discrimination and seek lives of greater personal independence and professional accomplishment. Chapter 6 presents documents that revisit some old problems of workplace equality and offer new and thought-provoking visions for women's lives in the new millennium.

Four major themes run through postwar American women's history and also inform the choice of documents in this anthology. The first theme is the ever-changing conception of gender and its role in stretching or limiting women's access to power and in framing the choices that women and men make in their work and family lives and their relation to the state. After World War II traditional ideas about women's primary domestic role helped to restrict women's access to the jobs they had held during the war, and in the early postwar years the kinds of jobs available to women were mostly in the "pink-collar ghetto" as secretaries, clerks, saleswomen, teachers, bank tellers, and waitresses. But, as they have throughout American history, women quickly learned to use these traditional ideas about gender to carve out a more public role for themselves. The determined activists of Women Strike for Peace, for example, based their activism on their mission as mothers to protect their children from nuclear annihilation. As Blanche Posner, a member of Women Strike for Peace, declared during a hearing before the House Committee on Un-American Activities in 1962, "You don't quite understand the nature of this movement. [It] was inspired and motivated by mothers' love for children. . . . When they were putting their breakfasts on the table, they saw not only the wheaties and milk, but they also saw strontium 90 and iodine 131."*

Gender is a mutable concept that interacts with social, economic, and political change. Ideas about gender have shaped social welfare legislation, economic policy, attitudes and expectations about marriage and sexuality, and a host of other social and political issues, and historians continue to probe how gender expectations both respond to and influence changing social and economic conditions and cultural mores.

Closely related to the changing meaning of gender is the complex connection between personal issues and their political implications. When women in their consciousness-raising groups, in the 1960s and 1970s, declared that the "personal is political," they touched upon a motif that runs throughout late-

---

* Blanche Posner, "Testimony before the House Committee on Un-American Activities," *Hearings: Communist Activities in the Peace Movement, December 11–13, 1962* (Washington, D.C.: Government Printing Office, 1963, p. 2201).

twentieth-century American women's history. Personal issues such as sexuality, choice of work, and consumption patterns have always been freighted with political implications. But one of the achievements of the women's movement has been to articulate these political implications more clearly, if not occasionally more passionately, and to do battle in the legal system, on the streets, in the legislatures, and in the court of public opinion to redress sexual inequality in all its forms. The exposure of sexual abuse and harassment in the home and workplace as well as the emergence of separate women's institutions such as health clinics and shelters, coffee houses, bookstores, publishing houses, and a thriving gay and lesbian rights movement reflect a desire to dismantle not only the political barriers but the modes of behavior that have encoded women's subordinate social and political role. Housework, child rearing, sexuality, etiquette, and even language became, under the microscope of consciousness-raising groups and, later, the occasionally abstruse analyses of academic historians, political issues that laid bare the unequal power relations, ingrained social attitudes, and inequitable government policies that impeded women's road to equality.

Taking a cue from the strategies and accomplishments of the civil rights movement, feminists achieved major legislative victories in the 1960s and 1970s and managed to prick public awareness. In the process they engendered a spirited public debate over cultural values, which helped to expose the political underpinnings of personal ideas and opinions and continues unabated to this day. The inflammatory statements and apocalyptic claims by opponents of the Equal Rights Amendment (ERA) during the 1970s and early 1980s, the ongoing battle for safe, legal abortion, and the evisceration of the civil rights of gays and lesbians reflect the lengths to which it is possible to go to defend a particular conception of gender relations and public morality. Whether women embraced all or part of the feminist agenda for social and political equality, or completely disavowed the movement, they simply could not avoid coming into contact with its ideas, if only in the popular media, and they spoke out freely and in venues available to the historian.

The third theme reflects an enduring concern among feminist historians: to find the common threads of women's historical experience amidst a deluge of evidence and argument about difference. The traditional categories of gender, race, and class have now made room for a raft of other conceptions of difference—regional and religious differences, sexual persuasion, physical disablement, and life-cycle differences. Just as feminist historians grapple with the impact of such differences in assessing women's historical experience,

I would argue—and this document collection will demonstrate—that part of the odyssey of twentieth-century American women has been toward recognizing and then uniting around such differences for mutual strength, pride, and empowerment. Black, Hispanic, Asian American, and other women from a variety of cultural backgrounds and religious outlooks, older women, blue-collar as well as professional women, and others have all discovered—or, more accurately rediscovered, since institution-building has always been integral to American women's historical experience—the power of organizing around and articulating their common concerns and interests as members of a self-defined group. Although these "tribal allegiances" have often led to fractious relations among women in and out of the women's movement over priorities and strategies for improving women's lives, they have expanded and enriched the scope of women's concerns and have empowered women to achieve important goals, be it more equitable workplace benefits or more research on breast cancer.

Finally, although the assertion of identity differences has conspired to shatter notions of a common sense of sisterhood, other forces—social, political, economic, and technological—have brought most American women increasingly into the public arena as wage earners, business leaders, political figures, and activists. Greater educational and economic opportunities, the changing demographics of marriage and family size, and the reemergence of single working women have demonstrated that the family and the state exert less control over women's lives than in any other period of American history. The notion of a "woman's sphere" is far less prevalent and influential in public discourse and social policy than it was a century ago. Yet gender continues to exert a not-so-subtle influence over women's life choices, presenting new opportunities as well as resurrecting old problems. Although women's employment opportunities and income have risen dramatically from the 1940s to the new millennium, their *overall* economic well-being—measured by income and leisure time—has not, compared to that of men. In two-income families, women still shoulder most of the domestic and child-rearing responsibilities. And the increase in the number of divorced women with children has also increased women's financial responsibility for their children—while they continue to earn less than men.

And though more American women than ever before now hold professional positions with incomes above $50,000 a year, many women continue to work in traditionally female occupations that offer little opportunity for advancement, such as bank tellers, bookkeepers, cashiers, secretaries, telephone operators, waitresses, domestics, and child-care and garment workers. These sex-segregated jobs are resistant to affirmative action policies that are intended to give women access to positions that had previously been filled only by white men. Affirmative action and other equal-opportunity programs benefit only those women who have the skills, credentials, and education to move into positions previously closed to women.

THE DOCUMENTS in this collection bring together a rich diversity of voices, viewpoints, and sources, from court cases, political tracts, and legislation that has significantly affected women's lives to personal letters, oral histories, interviews, and articles and speeches. Some of the documents were intended for public consumption; others were not. But together they stitch a complex and compelling portrait of American women's lives over the last half century. Their authors speak with passion and power, and even the most private letters offer a glimpse of the impact of public events on private lives and demonstrate that every person plays a part in shaping historical change. The range of documents included here also emphasizes the importance of uncovering both the public and private aspects of women's lives in understanding women's historical experience. Sexual mores, women's attitudes toward marriage and childbirth, even the fashion trends of an era, have an impact on political, social, and economic behavior and contribute to the dynamics of historical change.

The choice of documents is highly selective; another historian would no doubt have made different choices. I believe that my choices represent the major events, social and political changes, and cultural preoccupations of the postwar period, and I have endeavored to offer a cross-section of voices and opinions from the writings of well-known women as well as the accounts of ordinary women from a variety of regional, ethnic, class, and religious backgrounds. The documents are intended to demonstrate the many ways that women have helped to shape postwar America as workers, political leaders and community builders, authors and activists, homemakers, and citizens. I believe, as do the vast majority of other scholars of women's history, that ordinary people create historical change as much, if not more than, political and other public figures, and that women's historical experience is made up of a plurality of voices.

Each chapter begins with a brief introduction that sets the historical context and themes of the documents, and headnotes precede each document to provide specific information and point out the significance of the document.

As readers delve into this collection, I hope they will keep in mind two historiographical questions, the first of which is particularly germane to using a collection of primary documents: what is the relationship between prescriptive literature—the literature of sermons, speeches, articles, self-help books, and other forms of discourse that prescribe conduct and values—to the corresponding social reality? To what extent do ideological definitions of womanhood reflect or diverge from the historical reality? For example, Adlai Stevenson's exhortations to the 1955 graduating class of Smith College to use their education to inspire their husbands and sons or Marynia Farnham and Frederick Lundberg's criticism of women who want to "compete" with their husbands by pursuing paid employment were delivered in an era that enshrined home, family, and motherhood in public discourse, but the social reality was often quite different. Women entered the labor force more rapidly than ever before and also engaged in social protest. But, as I have already indicated, they often justified their paid employment and social activism by relying on a domestic ideology of promoting their families' welfare. Hence, though the reality of women's lives belied the cozy ideal of a mother who spent her days cooking, sewing, and chauffering her children around in the family station wagon, the ideology helped to fuel women's social activism and motivation to seek paid employment. The relationship between prescription and actual behavior is complex and is an inherent part of historical change.

Second, I would like readers to reassess how they define progress, especially in regard to women's lives. This question is particularly relevant to the study of postwar women's lives. Starting in the latter part of the twentieth century, women have clearly gained more educational and professional opportunities and have achieved a larger measure of social and political equality. More women have moved into the highest echelons of corporate power, and many others hold public office at all levels of government. But which women are we talking about? During the mid-1990s, educated middle- and upper-class women clearly benefited from a booming economy and more employment opportunities in the technology sector, while factory jobs diminished for less educated women and more stringent government social welfare policies greatly hurt women in need. Violence against women continues to be one of the fastest-growing forms of crime, and all American women are at risk of losing important reproductive freedoms. Women continue to work after marriage and motherhood, but, relative to men, their amount of leisure time continues to diminish because they still assume primary responsibility for housekeeping and child care—"the second shift," as Arlie Hochschild terms it. What are the barometers of progress and how do they apply to women across the spectrum of class and ethnic differences? These are questions that occupy historians and other scholars of women's history and continue to resonate in people's lives.

CHAPTER 1

WARRIORS ON THE HOMEFRONT: AMERICAN WOMEN AND WORLD WAR II

On October 21, 1945, Edith Speert, a director of a federally sponsored day-care center for children of working mothers, wrote her husband, Victor, who was stationed overseas, "I must admit I'm not exactly the same girl you left—I'm twice as independent as I used to be and . . . I've been living exactly as *I* want to . . . I do as I damn please. As a whole, I don't think my changes will [a]ffect our relationship, but I do think you'll have to remember that there are some slight alterations in me."[1] For Speert and millions of other American women, U.S. entry into World War II meant not only the anguish of sending beloved husbands, fathers, sons, and brothers to Europe and the Pacific theater to fight in a brutal and technologically sophisticated war, it also meant dramatic changes in their own lives, such as working outside of the home for the first time, learning how to be self-reliant, and, if they were married, taking charge of family affairs and finances. It also meant, as Edith Speert admits, enjoying a newfound freedom and independence.

Historians continue to debate the extent to which World War II was a turning point in American women's lives: did the influx of women into the labor market, for example, and especially into untraditional kinds of jobs transform traditional views of women as wives and mothers into women as workers? Or did the emergence of Rosie the Riveter—the image of a young muscular female worker in overalls and kerchief emblazoned on posters, magazine covers, and other media—simply reflect a new spin on an old theme: that Rosie was the same prewar woman who cooked, cleaned, cared for her family, and now did her patriotic duty to help defeat the Nazis and preserve democracy throughout the world?

There is truth to both perspectives. World War II helped to accelerate an already growing trend of older, married women into the work force and into untraditional positions, while drawing on deeply ingrained views of women as nurturers and helpmeets to justify that growing trend. Prior to the war, most women expected to marry, have children, and devote their time and energy to their families with perhaps some volunteer work on the side. But the war required new tasks and new sacrifices.

When the Japanese invaded Pearl Harbor on December 7, 1941, Americans were still grappling with the social and economic hardships of the Depression. Although the New Deal had put some people back to work and had pumped money into the economy, average wages remained stubbornly below those of 1929 and the unemployment rate continued to be high. Only in the feverish crisis of war did the nation finally solve its immediate economic problems. The war created new and higher-paying jobs for both women and men and lifted the American economy out of its persistent malaise. In 1940 the average worker was making $754 a year; four years later, in 1944, average yearly earnings had risen to $1,289. During the Depression more than half of all Americans lived below the poverty line; by the end of the war, just over one-third were poor, and the incomes of another third qualified as middle-class.[2]

Most American women benefited from this booming wartime economy. The proportion of women who were employed increased from 25 percent at the beginning of the war to 36 percent by the end—an increase that surpassed that of the previous four decades. Female war workers were highly praised in popular culture, and Rosie the Riveter became a national symbol of patriotism. Women worked in shipyards, aircraft plants, munitions factories, and other war-related industries. They also worked as nurses, nurse's aides, and for the Red Cross and in civilian positions in government agencies and on military bases. About 350,000 women joined the military as WACs (Women's Air Corps), WAVEs (Women Accepted for Voluntary Emergency Service), SPARs (Coast Guard Women's Reserves) or served in the MCWR (Marine Corps Women's Reserve), the ANC (Army Nurse Corps), and the NNC (Navy Nurse Corps). They proved themselves capable of doing dangerous and highly skilled military reconaissance work, as Jacqueline Cochran's oral history on pp. 76–79 attests.

During war, as in peacetime, American women's ethnic and class background and where they lived largely determined what kind of work they did and what economic benefits they reaped. As Christina Fanny Hill declares in her oral history in this chapter, "Hitler" finally got black women "out of the white folks' kitchen"—that is, the war opened up more employment opportunities for African American women beyond domestic service. But, as Hill's wartime experience also shows, discrimination continued to limit black women's ability to move into more skilled and better-paying factory positions.

Since the Revolution, American women had always worked directly for the military as nurses, cooks, seamstresses, laundresses, and later as clerical workers and even spies. In the Civil War, some four hundred Union and Confederate women even disguised themselves as men and fought in combat. In World War I more than ten thousand women served in the navy and marine corps, and several thousand women performed civilian clerical and communications tasks for U.S. forces in France. But American women's work during World War II was both quantitatively and qualitatively different: women in the armed forces served in every capacity except for combat and attained permanent regular status in the military; more women were employed in civilian and military war-related work, many in nontraditional factory and industrial jobs; and more married and older women worked than ever before. Indeed, for the first time, the majority of women workers were married, and one-third of the new female work force had children under age fourteen. Galvanized by military crisis, women's wartime work accelerated long-range trends in the kinds of jobs available to women and also dramatically changed the nature of women's wage-earning work. Although some of these advances were halted in the postwar era, women's employment patterns underwent significant change during the war years—setting the stage for a later generation's demand for equal employment opportunities.

While the economic crisis of the 1930s stigmatized working women—especially married working women, who were accused of stealing jobs from able-bodied men—the military crisis of the 1940s now encouraged and even pressured women to work in order to ease the labor shortage resulting from the massive numbers of men who joined the military. Between 1940 and 1945 the female labor force grew by more than 50 percent. The percentage of all women employed rose from 27.6 to 37 percent, and three-fourths of the new female workers were married.[3] Women went to work for a variety of reasons: to supplement their husbands' military salaries, especially when goods such as food and clothing became more expensive during wartime shortages and rationing; for the adventure or the social and financial independence that work offered; to express their patriotism; or to take advantage of higher salaries in war-related industries. As Lillian Hatcher, the first black woman to be hired by the Detroit auto industry as a factory worker instead of a domestic or cafeteria worker, explained, "I was working not for patriotic reasons; I was working for the money. The 97 cents an hour was the greatest salary that I had earned."[4] In contrast, a female worker in a rubber plant had different but equally compelling reasons for working: "Every time I test a batch of rubber,

I know it's going to help bring my three sons home quicker."[5] Juanita Loveless, a war worker whose oral history is included in this chapter, later explained, "What attracted me [to factory work] was not the money and it was not the job, because I didn't even know how much money I was going to make. But the ads . . . 'Do Your Part,' 'Uncle Sam Needs You,' 'V for Victory!' I got caught up in that patriotic 'Win the War, Help the Boys.'"[6]

Initially, however, women were not welcomed back into the labor force. Before the Japanese invasion of Pearl Harbor, the U.S. government and private industry began to gear up for production of war materials as the Nazi juggernaut swept through Europe, and employers fully intended to hire men for most of the new military manufacturing jobs. The War Department even issued a directive that defense producers "should not be encouraged to utilize women on a large scale until all available male labor in the area has first been employed."[7] In fact, thousands of women were laid off as plants that produced civilian goods retooled for war production and employers hired men for the new defense jobs.

Not until mid-1942—almost a year after the United States entered the war—did the government and private employers launch a concerted campaign to recruit women workers. Under the direction of the War Manpower Commission (WMC) and Office of War Information (OWI), two agencies dedicated to mobilizing support and labor for the war, Americans were bombarded in print and on radio with slogans and images that linked women's wartime work with victory. In 1943 the WMC introduced the idea that women could save lives by going to work to help end the war sooner and issued this slogan: "The More Women at Work, the Sooner We'll Win." Any work that freed a man to go overseas and fight or that contributed directly to the war effort, such as munitions work, aircraft assembly, or ship construction, became a socially sanctioned form of activity for women. Government propaganda even appealed to men to encourage their wives to take war jobs. One poster showed a woman worker and her husband standing in front of an American flag, the banner proclaiming, "I'm proud . . . my husband *wants* me to do my part." Although most women did not work in factories or in the armed services, the woman in the factory—the Rosies working to protect their men—dominated the wartime media, thus conveying the message that a woman in overalls was as acceptable

---

* Blanche Posner, "Testimony before the House Committee on Un-American Activities," *Hearings: Communist Activities in the Peace Movement, December 11–13, 1962* (Washington, D.C.: Government Printing Office, 1963, p. 2201).

as a woman in an apron, at least during times of crisis. This and other wartime images that appealed to women's patriotism or their desire to earn an income encouraged women to enter the work force.

The federal government became the largest employer, hiring nearly a million women for civilian office jobs and positions as mechanics and press, crane, and tractor operators. The armed forces also recruited women. One thousand civilian female pilots enlisted in the Women's Airforce Service Pilots (WASP); 140,000 women joined the Women's Army Corps (WAC); 100,000 entered the navy as WAVES (Women Accepted for Voluntary Emergency Service); and others joined the marines and coast guard. A few women were commissioned as army and navy doctors, and 76,000 more served as nurses. Military nurses served in every theater of the war, often right behind the front lines. They accompanied American troops in major Allied invasions of Italy, North Africa, and France, digging their own fox holes, enduring harsh field conditions, and caring for the wounded under enemy fire. And, as Betty Basye Hutchinson, a nurse in an orthopedic ward for severely wounded and disfigured soldiers, recounts in this chapter, nurses at home and on the battlefield soon disabused themselves of any romantic notions about war as they cared for patients mangled in battle.

But women's military duties nonetheless reflected the traditional gender-based divisions, and inequality, of work and wages within civilian society. Most WAVEs and WACs performed clerical or hospital tasks—the work they normally did in civilian life—and civilian and military propaganda extolled the "precision work at which women are so adept" and "the comfort and attention that only a woman can fill" in endeavoring to prove that military women did not lose their femininity or gentility. And while military men were supplied with contraceptives, mainly to prevent the spread of venereal disease, military women did not receive birth control and were punished more severely than men for any illicit sexual activity.[8]

Despite these persistent barriers to full equality, military service expanded women's personal and professional horizons; some women reenlisted after the war and pursued lifelong careers in the military. Whether they served at home or abroad, women learned new skills and acquired greater self-confidence and self-respect for their ability to rise to the many challenges of military service. The pride that Jacqueline Cochran expresses in describing women pilots' willingness to take on more dangerous tasks than male pilots reflects the satisfaction that many military women derived from testing their limits and doing untraditional work. But for all military women the expansive opportunities that military service offered were limited by the government's, and also the public's, persistent desire to preserve prewar gender roles and images. American society, even during wartime, still viewed women's essential role as wife and mother.

In industry as well women made significant strides by performing rigorous physical and technical tasks that were once considered "men's work." The largest increase in female employment was in manufacturing. Over the course of the war, more than 2.5 million women—an increase of 140 percent—worked in manufacturing, mostly in defense-related industries. Despite the long hours and arduous, often tedious work, factory jobs were appealing because of the higher wages they offered. Female factory hands earned $40.35 a week assembling B-29 bombers, building tanks and warships, and making ammunition. By 1943 half of the workers at major factories such as Boeing's enormous Seattle, Washington, plant were women. The large numbers of women who worked in war-related industries forced factories to retool workplace policies and facilities to accommodate women. Susan Laughlin's recollections of her experiences as a women's counselor in a large Lockheed aircraft plant in Los Angeles reveal how unprepared industry was to cope with the needs of women workers and the resulting hostility of male workers. Magazine articles about women in industry and how-to guides for getting or keeping a job in a wartime factory, such as the one featured in this chapter, abounded to meet the growing influx of women into wartime industrial work.

Women also worked as lumberjacks, train conductors, and surface miners. The wages they earned were a significant increase over the average weekly wage of $24.50, which they had made in low-paying nonunion jobs in laundries, department stores, restaurants, and hotels before the war.[9] Moreover, the federal government, through the National War Labor Board (NWLB), finally espoused the principle of equal pay for equal work by male and female workers. Although the results of this policy were modest—mostly favoring women who directly replaced men but leaving intact wage inequalities in departments and companies that had always paid women less—it encouraged private companies to abolish wage disparities, and it also put the power of the federal government behind the principle of equal pay for equal work.

A substantial number of married women, especially those with young children, did not work. They found other ways to contribute to the war effort, however. Many did volunteer work for the Red Cross, the United Service Organizations (USO), and other groups, and homemakers everywhere planted Victory Gardens to increase the supply of food; learned how to substitute other ingredients for butter and sugar, which were often in short supply because of the military's demand for such luxuries; and saved kitchen fats and grease to contribute to military uses.

Although the government and most employers tried to discourage women with young children from working, both the federal government and the private sector attempted to address the double burden of the working mother who labored forty-eight hours a week in an office or factory and then had to care for her home and children, especially when husbands were stationed long distance. The government urged stores and businesses to increase shopping hours and develop programs that provided prepared foods to serve at home. In addition, the government expanded day-care services that had been started during the Depression to care for the children of Works Project Administration (WPA) workers. In 1942 these same nurseries accepted the children of defense workers, and a year later the government developed more child-care centers. The program eventually cared for 130,000 children in more than three thousand centers with funding provided by the Lanham Act, passed in 1943. Although it was viewed as a stopgap emergency war measure—not a long-term necessity to help working mothers—and reached only a small percentage of the children of working mothers, the Lanham Act was highly significant; for the first time in the nation's history, the federal government took measures to ease the domestic burdens of working mothers. A few private companies also provided on-site day-care centers for employed children; installed shopping, laundry, and repair services; and provided prepared meals that workers could purchase and take home.

But just as the government and public were concerned about military women losing their femininity while doing a man's job, civilian employers were also eager to show that their female workers, though garbed in overalls and wielding a blowtorch, were as fresh and pretty as ever. Rosie the Riveter showed up in advertisements by civilian companies as well—but usually with long, dark eyelashes, manicured fingernails, and a polkadotted kerchief pertly tied around her head. She was young and strong but also pleasing to look at. The propaganda film *Glamour Girls of '43* even compared industrial work to domesticity: "Instead of cutting the lines of a dress, this woman cuts the pattern of aircraft parts. Instead of baking a cake, this woman is cooking gears to reduce the tension in the gears after use. . . . After a short apprenticeship, this woman can operate a drill press just as easily as a juice extractor in her own kitchen."[10]

As in the armed forces, black women were relegated to the lowliest, most dangerous jobs in wartime industries. In airplane assembly plants, they worked in the "dope rooms," breathing in poisonous glue fumes, while white women worked in well-ventilated sewing rooms. Wartime needs did not break down discrimination. Even the War Department promoted discrimination when it advertised for "competent, white female help in the Pentagon Cafeterias and Dining Rooms." And it looked the other way when companies with which it contracted for war materiel refused to hire black women.[11] But this discrimination did not undermine black women's pride in the historic role they were playing, both in the war and on behalf of the all black Americans. The National Council of Negro Women, a major African American women's organization, issued a pamphlet with a War Worker's Pledge: "I shall never for a moment forget that thirteen million Negroes believe in me and depend on me. . . . I am a soldier on the Home Front and I shall keep the faith."[12]

In the professions as well, women, especially white women, made inroads in replacing a growing shortage of male workers. A severe teacher shortage forced school boards across the country to end their ban against hiring married women, and colleges accepted women in math, science, and engineering programs. Medical schools, reluctant at first to accept female candidates because they wanted to train male doctors for military duty, accepted more female candidates as the war progressed and fewer male candidates became available. Black women in particular benefited from the wartime shortage of nursing. Before the war only forty-two of the twelve hundred nursing schools nationwide admitted blacks, and most of these were segregated. In 1943 Congress passed an act to establish the Cadet Nurse Corps, which provided tuition assistance for nursing education. Black women took full advantage of this opportunity and also gained admission for the first time into once-segregated programs at large city hospitals such as New York City's Bellevue and Philadelphia's General.

One group of women, however, did not benefit from the war effort: Japanese American women. The bombing of Pearl Harbor unleashed a wave of hostility toward Japanese Americans—many of whom had quietly lived and prospered in this country for generations—especially along the West Coast. The day after Japanese planes attacked Pearl Harbor, the FBI began to arrest Japanese community leaders who were believed to hold strongly pro-Japanese sentiments. On February 19, 1942, President Franklin Delano Roosevelt signed an executive order that authorized the removal of these citizens and their American-born children from their homes and into makeshift, prisonlike camps in California, Washington, Utah, Arizona, Colorado, Wyoming, Idaho, and Arkansas, where their activities could be monitored. Families usually had only one week to put their affairs in order, close down businesses, sell or store what they could not carry with them, and say good-bye to friends and associates. In many instances they had no choice but to sell businesses and precious heirlooms for a fraction of their value.

As Yoshika Uchido recalls in the selection from her memoir, and as the letters of Sonoko Shigezo reveal, camp life was crude and harsh, and severely disrupted family unity. As many as eight people lived in one twenty-by-twenty-foot room in a barracks divided into four to six sparsely furnished rooms. Shower and latrine facilities were communal and afforded no privacy, and everyone ate in large, noisy mess halls. Because of varying work assignments and hours, families seldom had the opportunity to eat together. Barbed wire and armed guards surrounded the camps.

While the war boosted the economy, it also quickened the rate of marriage. Between 1940 and 1943 the number of marriages skyrocketed. War brides faced many challenges, not the least of which was shuttling from one military base to another as their husbands were transferred around the country. A reporter for the *New York Times Magazine* described these young women as "wandering members of a huge unorganized club" who shared the travails of life on a military base or in a cramped apartment nearby.[13] Many newly married women enjoyed precious little time with their soldier husbands before their men were shipped overseas. Their pride in knowing that their husbands were serving their country was often overshadowed by their loneliness and longing for their spouses and by deeply disconcerting fears over their safety. The selection of letters by wives and mothers, starting on p. 65, attests to the anguish of sending husbands, sons, brothers, and other close relatives off to war.

But the war also toughened young married women on the homefront as profoundly as it changed their husbands on the battlefield. Whether they worked in a factory or stayed home full-time, women faced hardships and difficult decisions without their husbands' assistance. Many women endured pregnancy and childbirth while husbands were thousands of miles away. They made major family decisions on their own, and they learned how to cope with shortages of food and other goods. In the process they found new reserves of strength and independence, and they had no better champion and role model than Eleanor Roosevelt. In her syndicated newspaper column, "My Day," Roosevelt praised the strength and resourcefulness of American women and urged the nation to make even greater use of their talents in the postwar period. She tried to reach out to her readers as if she were enjoying a cup of coffee with the American people, and both men and women avidly read her column.

When Allied victory became imminent, the demobilization of American women from the work force turned swift and unrelenting. Both employers and colleges gave preference to returning male veterans. In manufacturing, one out of every four women was let go from factory jobs in the three-month period of June to September 1945. Those who remained in the labor force were pushed into traditional female jobs in the clerical, sales, and service sector, where they earned less and enjoyed fewer on-the-job benefits and protections. Similarly, by 1946 colleges turned down thousands of qualified female applicants to make room for veterans who were taking advantage of the new GI bill, which paid their college tuition and expenses. Female veterans also took advantage of these benefits, but they represented a fraction of the veterans educated under the GI bill.

World War II temporarily redefined social norms for appropriate women's work and roles. For a brief period women had access to traditionally male jobs, higher pay, and more equal wages. And through performing nontraditional work that was physically challenging and regarded by the public as necessary and useful, many American women gained greater pride and confidence in their talents and abilities. As Betty Jeanne Boggs, who had aspired to join the air force but worked instead in an aircraft plant installing and repairing wing flaps, observed of her experiences, "The war work, I think, showed me that a woman could work in different jobs other than say an office, which you ordinarily expect a woman to be in. . . . It opened up another field of thought, another viewpoint on life in general."[14]

But the new viewpoint was born out of the crisis of war, and translating it into new policies and initiatives to expand women's personal and professional options did not survive victory and the postwar return to normalcy. The wartime need for women's labor created a climate that favored women's public visibility and activity—for the benefit of their country, however, and not for personal satisfaction or gain. It did not undermine longstanding social beliefs about men's and women's separate social roles. Yet the war accelerated trends that were giving women more choices in their lives: it expanded employment opportunities, thus giving women access to jobs they would not have considered before; sanctioned paid employment for wives and mothers; and offered greater access to higher education. These significant social and economic advances proved to be a potent undertow to the postwar tide of social pressures pulling women back to the home and to full-time domesticity.

NOTES

1. Quoted in Judy Barrett Litoff and David Smith, eds., *Since You Went Away: World War II Letters from American Women on the Homefront* (New York: Oxford University Press, 1991), p. 157.
2. Susan M. Hartmann, *American Women in the 1940s: The Home Front and Beyond* (Boston: Twayne, 1982), p. 4.
3. Ibid., p. 21.
4. Quoted in Elaine Tyler May, "Pushing the Limits," in Nancy Cott, ed., *No Small Courage: A History of Women in the United States* (New York: Oxford University Press, 2000), p. 482.
5. Quoted in Hartmann, *American Women in the 1940s*, p. 79.
6. Quoted in Sherna Berger Gluck, ed., *Rosie the Riveter Revisited* (Boston: Twayne, 1987), p. 135.
7. Hartmann, *American Women in the 1940s*, p. 54.
8. May, "Pushing the Limits," p. 486.
9. Ibid., p. 476.
10. Quoted in Elaine Tyler May, *Pushing the Limits: American Women, 1940–1961* (New York: Oxford University Press, 1994), p. 25.
11. Hartmann, *American Women in the 1940s*, p. 80.
12. Quoted in Gluck, *Rosie the Riveter Revisited*, p. 12.
13. Quoted in Litoff and Smith, *Since You Went Away*, p. 65.
14. Quoted in Gluck, *Rosie the Riveter Revisited*, p. 123.

"WE WANT TO LIVE, NOT MERELY EXIST"
A BLACK WOMAN'S LETTER TO FDR

During the Depression, New Deal relief policies discriminated against African Americans, either by paying them smaller benefits or wages than those paid to whites or, in the South, by denying them benefits altogether. But blacks viewed President Franklin Roosevelt as a friend and believed that he would be sympathetic to their plight. In the following letter, written on the eve of America's entry into World War II, a young African-American wife boldly appeals to Roosevelt to find a solution to her husband's inability to secure better-paying work because of prejudice. As American involvement in the war became increasingly unavoidable, she courageously reminds FDR of the injustice of sending black men off to war to defend and even die for a country that won't permit them to enjoy a decent way of life. Indeed, the experience of fighting against Fascism in Europe galvanized blacks to demand a new level of equality and justice at home in the postwar years.

SOURCE: WPA Collection, Moorland-Spingarn Research Center, Howard University, Washington, D.C.

Chicago, Illinois
Feb. 16, 1941

Dear President Roosevelt:

I really don't know exactly how to begin this letter to you. Perhaps I should first tell you who I am. I am a young married woman. I am a Negro. . . . I believe that you are familiar with the labor situation among the Negroes, but I want you to know how I and many of us feel about it and what we expect of you.

My husband is working for the W.P.A. doing skilled labor. Before he started on this we were on relief for three months. We were three months trying to get relief. While trying to obtain relief I lost my unborn child. I believe if I had sufficient food this would not have happened. My husband was perfectly willing to work but could not find it. Now I am pregnant again. He is working at Tilden Tech. School where there are more white than colored. Every month more than one hundred persons are given private employment and not one of them are colored. It isn't that the colored men are not as skilled as the white, it is the fact that they are *black* and therefore *must not* get ahead.

We are citizens just as much or more than the majority of this country. . . . We are just as intelligent as they. This is suppose to be a free country regardless of color, creed or race but still *we* are slaves. . . . Won't you help us? I'm sure you can. I admire you and have very much confidence in you. I believe you are a real Christian and non-prejudice. I have never doubted that you would be elected again. I believe you can and must do something about the labor conditions of the Negro.

Why must our men fight and die for their country when it won't even give them a job that they are fitted for? They would much rather fight and die for their families or race. Before it is over many of them might. We did not ask to be brought here as slaves, nor did we ask to be born black. We are real citizens of this land and must and *will* be recognized as such! . . . If you are a real Christian you can not stand by and let these conditions exist.

My husband is young, intelligent and very depressed over this situation. We want to live, not merely exist from day to day, but to live as you or *any* human being desires to do. We want our unborn children to have an equal chance as the white. We don't want them to suffer as we are doing now because of race prejudice. My husband is 22 and I am 18 years of age. We want to own just a comfortable home by the time he reaches his early thirties. Is that asking too much? But how can we do that when the $26 he makes every two weeks don't hardly last the two weeks it should. I can manage money rather well but still we don't have the sufficient amount of food or clothes to keep us warm. . . .

I would appreciate it very much if you would give this letter some consideration and give me an answer. I realize that you are a very busy person and have many problems but please give this problem a little thought also.

I will close thanking you in advance.

Sincerely and hopefully yours

Mrs. Henry Weddington
WPA Box, Howard University,
Washington, D.C.

Economic necessity was not the only reason why women worked during the war. A strong sense of patriotism also drew them into the work force, especially into jobs that directly promoted the war effort, such as aircraft assembly and weapons manufacturing. In the following excerpt, Juanita Loveless recalls how patriotic ads and other publicity devices inspired her to leave a well-paying job as a gas station mechanic to work for Vega Aircraft, a division of Lockheed.

But Juanita Loveless also knew the darker side of war. Her father was scarred physically and mentally by having been exposed to nerve gas in World War I, and her uncle lost a leg in the same war. As a child growing up in Childress, Texas, she saw many homeless veterans of World War I with severe and disfiguring wounds. She witnessed firsthand how war could destroy the body and the spirit.

Growing up in an impoverished household, Juanita Loveless had to fend for herself from an early age. She worked as a domestic, farm laborer, and clerk before coming to Los Angeles in 1941. After working as an auto mechanic for six months, she went to work at Vega. Although the work was quite monotonous at first, she quickly moved up the ranks. She worked in different parts of the plant, acquiring new mechanical skills but also enduring extremely hazardous work conditions.

Juanita Loveless worked not only at Vega but at other jobs on the side. Her experience illustrates how open and fluid the job market was—for white women in particular—because of the shortage of men available. She also offers a vivid recollection of leisure-time activities for young single women and describes a culture of seemingly greater acceptance toward homosexuality. Her account is a rich, textured glimpse into life on the homefront for young, urban working women.

SOURCE: Sherna Berger Gluck, ed., *Rosie the Riveter Revisited* (Boston: Twayne, 1987), pp. 133–43. Reprinted by permission of Sherna Berger Gluck.

I GOT A JOB in the post exchange [at Fort Sill in Oklahoma]. That was in 1941. I was there about six months before the war started. All hell broke loose on the seventh of December. We were told to evacuate the barracks and find quarters in town. It was general confusion. Everybody was leaving to go to Seattle or California.

I came out here. In those days they had drivers' cars who came back and forth. You'd pay something like ten dollars or fifteen dollars. There were six or seven passengers and we were stacked on top of each other. They dropped us off in a hotel downtown and we were to wait in the lobby. We waited and he never came back. I had four or five dollars, a coat and the clothes on my back, and that was it. He took my luggage, my pictures, everything—the little souvenirs a young girl has. But every place I'd turn, someone was there to help me. Maybe it was my youth. . . .

So that's how I really got started in that first crucial two weeks. Then for food, I went to Thrifty Drugs and got a grilled cheese sandwich and a Coke for a dime, or an egg salad sandwich and a Coke. I lived on one meal a day for a week. That's my first early memory of being totally and completely alone in California.

I didn't know what to do: no experience and I was under age. So I walked to the bowling alley and I got a job as a pinsetter. I was working for tips, setting up pins, but I couldn't take that. It was too noisy. I stayed two days. Then I went to work at a gas station.

The first gas station I worked at was paying me sixteen dollars a week, Mueller Brothers, on Sunset Boulevard. They had a black comedian who greeted everyone. It was a gimmick. I walked over there and said I was interested in working. Fifteen minutes later I was filling tanks with gas. I had no experience, but I learned as I went along. They didn't want to pay me very much money. Then someone came into the gas station and recruited me: "Look, we'd like to have you. How much are you making here?" And I said, "Sixteen dollars," and they said, "We'll give you eighteen dollars. Come work for us."

So I went to work for Kreager Oil Company, which was better. They gave me a uniform everyday and soap to wash the grease off my hands, and they taught me how to do batteries. It was very simple, very easy: check the oil, wipe the windshield, put the gas in, get the money, get the coupon.

I worked for six months and everyday someone came in saying, "Do you want a job?" My head was going crazy. They were recruiting for any kind of work you wanted. Newspapers, just splashed everywhere: "Help Wanted," "Help Wanted," "Jobs," "Jobs," "Jobs." Propaganda on every radio station: "If you're an American citizen, come to gate so-and-so"—at Lockheed or at the shipyards in San Pedro. And they did it on the movie screens when they'd pass the collection cans. You were bombarded.

They were begging for workers. They didn't care whether you were black, white, young, old. They didn't really care if you could work. It got even worse in '43. I worked two jobs for a long time. I had so much work offered to me and I was not even qualified—I just had the capability of learning very fast.

Within three weeks of coming to California my mind was dazzled with all the offers I had. Before the war, in Oklahoma City and in California, I'd ask people if I could get a job and they'd say: "Well, you're not old enough." But here I didn't even have to look. I was having people approach me six to ten times a day—RCA Victor wanted me to come work for them; Technicolor said they'd train me.

Actually what attracted me—it was not the money and it was not the job because I didn't even know how much money I was going to make. But the ads—they had to be bombardments: "Do Your Part," "Uncle Sam Needs You," "V for Victory." I got caught up in that patriotic "win the war," "help the boys." The partiotism [sic] that was so strong in everyone then.

Anyhow, Vega Aircraft was the first one I learned about. Someone came in two or three times to the station to get me to come to the application office. One day I said, "I'll be off tomorrow and I'll go and fill out papers." I called this girl I had met and we went together. We both went for the same job, but she was immediately hired for a more educated job because she had finished high school. I went on the assembly line. . . .

Let me see if I can describe my first impression—which later wasn't the truth. It was like you were walking into a big, huge cavernous barn, just like a huge hangar; dead white from the huge, tremendous lights. On platforms—saw-jacks I would call them—they had poles and shelves and pieces and parts of planes. The first thing I noticed was that all the men were instructors. Most of the workers were men. I saw very few women. Even the bench I worked on, there were six or eight young boys, eighteen or nineteen years old, and myself, and two or three middle-aged women.

It was very dull, very boring. The first day I thought, "Oh, this is ridiculous. I have to set here for three weeks on this bench?" What we did was we learned to buck and then we learned to rivet. I set there for three or four hours that first day and I picked up the rivet gun: "You show me once and I'll do it for you." The bucking, you have a bar. I said, "What's to learn here? Look at my hands. I've been working as a grease monkey. I could do this. I don't have to set here and train." I learned very fast.

I went into the shell the next day. First I went inside and I bucked, and then I went outside and I riveted. I was working with real seasoned workable men and it was so easy. We did strip by strip, the whole hull. We used strips of like cheesecloth and paste that had to go on the inside and across the seam. I had to do that. Then, as the riveter outside riveted, I was inside bucking. It would be like a sewing machine, you just sort of have to go along with them.

I stayed there maybe six weeks, and I worked on all parts of it, up in the wings. One by one, day by day, new faces. I would say within six months there were maybe twenty or thirty men left in Department 16 where maybe there had been fifteen hundred. One by one they disappeared. I'd have a group leader one day and two or three days later he was gone. Leadman, two or three days later he was gone. There were men in the tool crib and one by one they disappeared.

As they recruited more and more women, men with deferments were the ones that actually remained to work. Even a lot of the young women working would disappear, going into the service. I made friends with four or five girls that became WACS and WAVES and nurses. It was very more difficult to keep friends, because they came and they went so fast.

By late '42 we had very few men left. They were gradually replaced by women and blacks. When the blacks started coming in, suddenly I was jerked off my nice little wing section and I was sent over to the training area, which was at the far end of the huge plant. The first day I picked a young man who was nineteen years old, Stan—I can't remember his full name, but today he is a musician and you see him on television in the Les Brown Orchestra—and four or five other blacks, men and women. I worked with training them the first day, the second day, the third day. They just couldn't get it. Stan, he'd fall asleep, he wouldn't work. I gave up. I went to my group leader and said, "I have to either transfer or I'm quitting."

So I got out of that assembly and went into final assembly, thank God, or I would never have stayed. I thought, "I really have got it made now." Only it was just as bad or worse, in a sense, because the heat and my getting up into those wings. I used to carry a crawl light with me, and I'd lay up there and I'd wait and wait for my partner on the outside. I had no way of knowing what's going on outside. I can't tell you how many times I'd lay there, and a drill or something would come through and nick me in the leg. Carelessness on the outside part and they'd missed the mark. Two or three of my very vivid experiences was climbing out of the wings of those planes, sweating, hot and dirty, finding whoever was supposed to be working with me sound asleep. I'd give them a good kick in the ass.

Then I transferred again. I went into the wiring and cockpit section and I loved it. But sometime during this work with chemicals and metals I got a skin disease. It started out on my arm. . . .

At the same time I worked in the aircraft, I also worked for a record-cutting company; we'd cut records and make tape recordings for the servicemen to send back home. I also worked for a fellow in Glendale who had a storage garage. As the young men were going to war, they would store their cars with him. He hired me to come over and take each car out every other day or so and put a few miles on it to keep up the engine, and I'd check the water, check the tires, check the oil, and sometimes lubricate them. He wasn't paying me very much, but I got gas coupons and I'd take a car occasionally to work.

I had so much work sometimes, I wouldn't even go back for my money. Sometimes they'd just mail me a check and I'd think, "Gee, now where was this?" At one period of time I had six or eight checks laying in my dresser drawer that I hadn't even cashed. I simply didn't know how to handle money. The first paycheck I got in aircraft was more money than I'd ever seen in my life. I didn't even know what to do with it. I didn't have a bank account. You couldn't buy anything much.

But we'd hang out in drive-ins or the bowling alleys. And we went to places like the Hangover, Tropics, Knickerbocker Hotel, Blackouts, Garden of Allah, Har 'O Mar, the Haig on Wilshire. I was going into bars and drinking. One of my favorites was the Jade on Hollywood Boulevard. Another was the Merry-Go-Round on Vine Street. When Nat King Cole sat at the piano and sang, he wasn't even known and the piano bar went round. This was long before I ever reached twenty-one.

Most of the fellows that I knew, by 1943 were gone in three days or a week. I mean they were just gone! The next thing you'd get a letter with just a PO number. "Can't tell you where I am, but will see you when I come back." The song that was very popular then was "I'll Be Seeing You." I think it was symbolic of that time. "I'll Be Seeing You," not when, where, how, or if.

Then I began to see boys coming back. One fellow I'd gone with in 1942, I got off the bus and I'm walking home and I heard: "tap, tap, tap." I turned around and looked and I thought: "Gee, a solider in uniform with a cane." I turned back again and I said, "My God, it's Dick." Still in uniform. He came home blind. That was my very first shock, seeing him come back blind. He could see just a little, but later became totally blind—at twenty-three years! There were two or three other fellows I had known at the bowling alley who I went with, my age. When I began to see them coming back like this, it really did something to me. . . .

By 1944 a lot of people were questioning the war. "Why the hell are we in it?" We were attacked by the Japanese and were fighting to defend our honor. But still, this other side had the Cadillacs and the "I can get it for you wholesale." They suddenly owned all the mom-and-pop stores and suddenly owned all the shoe factories. The rumblings began with that—and the discontent.

It raced through the plant, through the bowling alleys, through all the places where the young people got together. We began to break away from the older generation. We said, "Well, they brought the war on." I think when we actually began to see the boys come home in late 1943, 1944—those that had been injured had started coming back—then the rumbles grew into roars, and the young people thought maybe they were being led into this. Maybe if we would stop working so hard, they would end the war. There was also rumors that they were holding Patton back and that they were prolonging the war. That was what got us!!

I got an aversion to making anything that would hurt anybody. But I probably wouldn't have stayed in aircraft, anyway, because my skin disease got worse. It started out like a psoriasis patch and it scaled and I scratched, and I got it on my arms, my neck, my face, everyplace where I was exposed. But I had a change of heart again when I heard that my brother had been injured. I went to work for Hartman making small parts, bench work, which I hated. I stayed there about three months and I said, "This is no good. I can't do this. I've been too active and I've been a racehorse too long." I used to run up and down that plant and it must have been a mile long from one end to another.

But I felt I ought to do something to contribute. Then I reasoned with myself that I was buying war bonds, that's enough, and I'm a member of the USO. I'm doing my share! I would never have stayed as long as I did if I hadn't been motivated by the fact that in my mind war was hell. I could visualize it, but I wanted to black out some of it. I never went to see a war picture and I never wanted to read a newspaper. I never wanted to know what was going on. Maybe the older people did, but the young people didn't want to hear about what was happening in the war; they just wanted to know we were winning.

The workers in aircraft hated it. I don't care whether they worked on the assembly or the training bench, the cockpit or in the wings or the tail; whether they riveted, wired, or were the managers or group leaders; whether they were in the final assembly—I have yet to meet one who really enjoyed it. The final assembly was the best job of all because you got out of the heat and you got out of the noise. The heat and the noise, I don't know how I ever lived through it. And I've kept in touch with two or three of the women that I worked with, and most of them have tremendous hearing problems. Most of them say it came from that noise.

I would never do it again! Never, ever!!! I don't think any other woman would either. They might say they would, but no, I don't think if most women would really be truthful with you, they enjoyed working or would have stayed in it if they hadn't really been motivated by patriotism or actually having a member of the family in the war. . . .

A GUIDEBOOK FOR WOMEN WAR WORKERS:
WANTED, WOMEN IN WAR INDUSTRY
LAURA NELSON BAKER

With the demand for women factory workers in war-related industries soaring, it was not surprising that a how-to book for getting a job in a factory should appear on the market. Following are excerpts from a comprehensive guide that prepares the potential female factory worker for everything from her initial interview to balancing her job at the factory with her domestic responsibilities. The author is eager to emphasize the vital contribution that factory women can make to the war effort, but she is not above indulging in some traditional stereotypes about women's behavior and concerns—notably, that they are preoccupied with their appearance and take direction easily, especially from men.

SOURCE: From Laura Nelson Baker, *Wanted: Women in War Industry* (New York: Dutton, 1943), pp. 67–75, 89–91. Renewed copyright © 1971 by Laura Nelson Baker. Used by permission of Dutton, a division of Penguin Putnam Inc.

CHAPTER 8

What the Well Dressed Worker Wears

There is hardly a woman who is considering going to work in a factory, or is about to go to work in one, who isn't going to ask, and perhaps a little tremulously, "But what shall I wear?"

You must admit, for it is a well established fact, that you are a vain creature. And all the factory jobs in the country, whatever their other compensations, would not appeal to you if you had to appear before your fellow workers wearing some "simply horrid looking thing!"

It has been proved in some cases by sad experience, that the wrong kind of clothing can be one of the greatest dangers to any factory worker; for that reason we have come to be familiar with the term "safety clothing." The designers of the uniforms, slacks, overalls, coveralls, caps, and shoes that the well-dressed factory worker will wear are in the majority of instances, themselves women, and are fully aware of what will appeal to milady's eye and what will not. So safety clothing is not without the color, design, and attractiveness that women demand.

There are, of course, certain requirements for work clothes which hold good in almost any factory:

1. They must not be so tight as to hinder free movement nor so loose that they get caught in moving machinery.
2. They may have pockets only when they are not a hazard and even then they are limited to certain types.
3. Some sort of safety cap or head covering must be worn wherever there is any danger of hair getting caught in moving parts.
4. Workers must have well-fitted shoes which completely cover the foot, with extra protection if necessary.
5. Absolutely no jewelry may be worn, not even rings or watches.

In most factories there is no hard and fast rule about uniforms other than those rules which are made for your protection. In some plants the girls wear slacks, in some dresses, in some coveralls. Many plants have uniforms made up in suitable material and pleasing colors and sell them to the women at cost. If you are to work in such a factory, you have an advantage because these uniforms, and the caps that often go with them, have been designed after painstaking research for the best in safety, convenience, wearability, comfort, cleanliness and coolness.

Consider your feet first. Much fatigue and nervousness can be laid to badly fitting shoes. Much of the work in a modern war factory must be done standing or walking from one part of the plant to another, and cramped toes are not going to help either your efficiency or your disposition. Too much cannot be said about the importance of good shoes in a production job. If your shoes do not fit properly, it will not be just your feet that suffer, but the muscles of your legs and back, and you will feel a general lessening of energy.

Shoes should be long enough so that the ball of the foot fits into the tread of the shoe. They should be wide enough so that the toes are allowed to spread naturally, and yet fit snugly around the heel and instep. No two-inch heels here, my dear, but ones that are low and wide. High heels can be the direct cause of a fall, as can thin or worn soles. Toeless shoes are taboo in any factory. Some require safety shoes with reinforced toes. These special shoes are now made of a light weight material and you will be wise to wear them, required or no, particularly if you use a foot in operating a machine or if there is any danger of heavy objects falling on your feet. For certain kinds of work there are other types of special shoes. For women working with glass, for instance, a foot protector made of chrome leather with a piece of aluminum curved to fit the top of the foot has been designed. In plants where workers handle acids, or where conditions of great heat or moisture exist, wooden-soled shoes are worn.

In spite of their vanity and pride in appearance, women workers have let their better sense rule in most cases. At the Todd Shipyards in New York, they refused to wear the shoes that came in a special shipment from the Middle West. "The soles aren't heavy enough. And we want high shoes like the men, to protect our ankles. And steel toes!" So heavy, bulky men's work shoes were bought, in the smallest sizes obtainable, and fitted with arch pads to protect the women's higher arched feet. The women want, first of all, to do their jobs in the best possible way. . . .

CHAPTER 6

Work in a Factory and Like It!

You are an employee of a war industry! Beginning today, you will be working toward American victory. This morning, and every morning hereafter you are going to be walking up to these same gates, passing these same guards, mingling with these same fellow-workers, entering this same plant, and taking your place at your work-bench or machine proudly. This morning, your first, it is all very strange to you. You realize quite suddenly that you don't really even know just what the inside of a large industrial plant looks like. But you will soon find out!

The guards at the entrance to the well-patrolled plant grounds stop you. You are apt to think, perhaps, that they are rather a nosey lot. Who are you? What is your business there? You take out your job-appointment papers saucily and flaunt them in their faces to justify your presence there. Strangers to you yet, but it gives you a deep satisfying feeling to know that in a week, or perhaps two, they might even be saying "Hi" to you as you hurry by in the morning. There is a bond that holds these workers of Uncle Sam's together. You feel it already. These women filing through with you don't treat you as if you were "new here," but smile at you in a friendly sort of way. Girls in overalls, in coveralls, in dresses, some swinging lunch boxes. They mingle with the men and talk and laugh; evidently none of them comes to work grudgingly. Sure you're excited. Why shouldn't you be? Your first day at work!

Once past the guards, across the grounds, and inside the door, you find yourself in the capable hands of a receptionist who hustles you off to the man who hired you.

Every new employee is fingerprinted and photographed before he begins work and all prints are filed in the office of the plant. If it makes you feel like a criminal, remember that this careful investigation is for your protection and personal safety as well as the protection of plant and materials. It is a weapon against sabotage in the plant, sabotage that endangers your life along with all the other occupants of the building.

The fingerprinting over, some one will probably talk to you about what is generally termed "sharing your rights." This is a matter of arranging transportation for you if you have no car to drive and the plant is not easily accessible to bus or street car, or arranging passengers for you if you do drive. You will be told how to get the proper ration of gas for your needs and given instructions about tires and care of your car. Some one will show you a time card and the proper way to punch it, will explain to you just what safety clothing is necessary for your particular job and how you go about securing it. . . .

It is a tremendously exciting thing to walk down one of the innumerable aisles of an American defense plant, between rows of work people, some of whom have time to look up and smile and some of whom must necessarily keep their eyes on their work, to come to a stop beside your particular machine or work bench or tool, and know that from now on, you will be an integral part of an enormous industrial hum. America is at work and you are at work. You are part of your country in a way you probably have never quite been before.

Women seem to put forth their best efforts if they are permitted to take their place alongside men. They feel they have been granted a certain recognition and they will do everything they can to live up to it.

In the past, men seemed to object to women working with them or under them, but the more they have seen of the modern woman worker, the weaker have grown their objections. Women have certain characteristics that are a distinct advantage in learning a job. They generally do not try to appear clever, and, as a rule, do not mind being told in detail exactly how to do something. In many cases, women have been found to work better under male supervision, though some plant superintendents have discovered that women work better together with no men around at all.

Certain prejudices against women still exist in the minds of some plant managers and superintendents. They say that mixing men and women in a shop will ruin morale; that men do not like to have women around. Closer investigation proves that the plant managers who made these protests actually had very few women in their factories. In factories where a large number of women were employed, no mention of disciplinary problems came up at all.

An equally false generalization is the contention that women have no mechanical ability, interest, or aptitude. In some plants, where women are given responsibility, they set up their own machines. In England, where the employment of women has long been a necessity, women are setting up and operating machines—jobs supposedly impossible for them to do—with no special help. This independence on the part of the women workers has forced respect from the men they work under or with, and makes the general atmosphere harmonious.

Other protests are made. One of them is that to employ women on jobs involving any hazards is bad because injuries to women are regarded with greater concern by the public and are, therefore, likely to arouse criticism of the plant. British experience, however, has shown a decreasing accident rate on certain machine jobs where women have replaced men. It is possible that that eye for detail generally possessed by a woman makes her more cautious and careful.

These objections naturally grow weaker with the increasing necessity of having women workers. Since they are based largely on tradition and fear of innovation, it is as well that we are being freed from them. There are, of course, many hazards in production work, for both men and women, and you should recognize them before you begin your work. It has been found that most accidents are directly traceable to carelessness, and very few of them are inevitable.

A more difficult prejudice to overcome is the notion that woman's place is in the home. In the days when the home was itself a busy, crowded place where some of the necessities, such as clothes, were even manufactured, a woman was perhaps indispensable. But times and homes have changed, and with them, traditional ideas about women are changing too. A woman's place has come to be the one where she is most happy and useful, and for many that means a job in industry.

Of course, many of the married women who are going into industry have children, and theirs is a special problem that only now is being partially solved. Most of us realize that the domestic servant has practically disappeared from American life, at least for the duration. Uncle Sam needs former household workers in his factories and they, in turn, need the better wages and the job improvement a factory offers. It is possible that the day will come when domestic work will be recognized as the worthwhile occupation it could be, and will be paid and respected accordingly, but until that day, the woman who goes to work in a factory cannot depend on getting someone in to do her housework.

What can the mothers who work in a factory do about their homes? Believe it or not, most of them take care of both jobs and do them well! One woman who works on the assembly line of an electrical-equipment plant has four children ranging from seven to fifteen, plus a husband who operates a gas station. Five separate times during the day she must have meals on the table ready to be eaten. She and her husband have breakfast early and she leaves food prepared for the children so they can get the extra sleep their growing bodies need. She lives close to work and so comes home for a hot lunch with the children. Then at six, they have their regular family dinner, and another dinner must be ready for the father who cannot leave his gas station until nine-thirty. Besides that, she packs lunches for her husband who cannot come home at noon. The family does its own work entirely, washing and ironing included.

How does she manage it? Chiefly, it is a matter of organization and co-operation of every member of the household. . . .

If you are the mother of a family and hold a factory job too, you have a right to be proud of yourself. It is no simple task to hold down two jobs and not neglect either of them, and yet women are doing it every day, simply because they must. Here are some hints that will help you to do it:

1. Budget your time as well as your money by planning every day and minute.
2. Learn to be resourceful, willing to adopt new ways, to adjust your life to those changes which cannot be avoided. After all, in spite of your two jobs, life is still easier for you than for any of your men who may be out on the firing line.
3. Use modern conveniences whenever possible. It is not always economical to do your own washing, particularly if the extra labor robs you of efficiency on your war job.
4. Eliminate non-essential duties and activities unless you are a superwoman and can manage everything. There will be time after the war for doing many things.
5. If you have older children, teach them to help. The busier they are, the happier they will be, and the less likely to move toward the juvenile delinquency rolls.

6. Call on older relatives, who are probably not busy and have had to feel useless for many years, to help you. Co-operate with your neighbors in the care of children.

7. Condense your living quarters if you can. It saves both housework and fuel. This does not mean living in unhealthily crowded quarters; that would be the opposite of economy.

8. Not all quickly cooked food is poor food. Modern science has done a lot to cut down the hours of meal preparation. It is old-fashioned and foolish to be prejudiced against ready-to-serve foods.

"HITLER WAS THE ONE THAT GOT US OUT
OF THE WHITE FOLKS' KITCHEN"
FANNY CHRISTINA HILL

For many black women, World War II was a turning point in a more personal sense: the proliferation of jobs in the defense industry, along with President Franklin Roosevelt's executive order prohibiting discrimination in hiring, enabled black women to find better-paying work than domestic service. In fact, Fanny Christina Hill, whose oral history follows, was fond of saying that Hitler was "the one that got us out of the white folks' kitchen." She was not exaggerating. In Los Angeles in 1940, for example, more than 55 percent of women of color were domestic servants because other forms of employment were closed to them. By 1950, that figure was down to 40 percent.* Tina Hill's story reflects both the economic opportunities created by wartime defense work and the prejudice that blacks still faced on the job.

Born in rural Texas, she had to drop out of school during the Depression to help support her family. Eager to make more money, she struck out on her own and moved to a small town in Texas, where she worked as a domestic. Unhappy with this choice of work and lacking any other skills, she headed for California with less than ten dollars to her name. She worked at several jobs, including domestic service and waitressing, before applying for a position at North American Aviation; in response to pressure from local civil rights groups and the United Auto Workers union (UAW), North American hired more black workers than any other aircraft plant. Christina Hill's story is a riveting account of the opportunities that black women enjoyed during the war as well as the racial barriers that still prevented them from moving up the occupational structure.

SOURCE: Sherna Berger Gluck, ed., *Rosie the Riveter Revisited* (Boston: Twayner, 1987), pp. 37–44. Reprinted by permission of Sherna Berger Gluck.

I DON'T REMEMBER what day of the week it was, but I guess I must have started out pretty early that morning. When I went there [to apply for a job], the man didn't hire me. They had a school down here on Figueroa and he told me to go to the school. I went down and it was almost four o'clock and they told me they'd hire me. You had to fill out a form. They didn't bother too much

---

* Sherna Berger Gluck, ed., Rosie the Riveter Revisited (Boston: Twayne, 1987), p. 24.

about your experience because they knew you didn't have any experience in aircraft. Then they give you some kind of little test where you put the pegs in the right hole.

There were other people in there, kinda mixed. I assume it was more women than men. Most of the men was gone, and they weren't hiring too many men unless they had a good excuse. Most of the women was in my bracket, five or six years younger or older. I was twenty-four. There was a black girl that hired in with me. I went to work the next day, sixty cents an hour.

I think I stayed at the school for about four weeks. They only taught you shooting and bucking rivets and how to drill the holes and to file. You had to use a hammer for certain things. After a couple of whiles, you worked on the real thing. But you were supervised so you didn't make a mess.

When we went into the plant, it wasn't too much different than down at the school. It was the same amount of noise; it was the same routine. One difference was there was just so many more people, and when you went in the door you had a badge to show and they looked at your lunch. I had gotten accustomed to a lot of people and I knew if it was a lot of people, it always meant something was going on. I got carried away: "As long as there's a lot of people here, I'll be making money." That was all I could ever see.

I was a good student, if I do say so myself. But I have found out through life, sometimes even if you're good, you just don't get the breaks if the color's not right. I could see where they made a difference in placing you in certain jobs. They had fifteen or twenty departments, but all the Negroes went to Department 17 because there was nothing but shooting and bucking rivets. You stood on one side of the panel and your partner stood on this side, and he would shoot the rivets with a gun and you'd buck them with the bar. That was about the size of it. I just didn't like it. I didn't think I could stay there with all this shooting and a'bucking and a'jumping and a'bumping. I stayed in it about two or three weeks and then I just decided I did *not* like that. I went and told my foreman and he didn't do anything about it, so I decided I'd leave.

While I was standing out on the railroad track, I ran into somebody else out there fussing also. I went over to the union and they told me what to do. I went back inside and they sent me to another department where you did bench work and I liked that much better. You had a little small jig that you would work on and you just drilled out holes. Sometimes you would rout them or you would scribe them and then you'd cut them with a cutters.

I must have stayed there nearly a year, and then they put me over in another department, "Plastics." It was the tail section of the B-Bomber, the Billy

Mitchell Bomber. I put a little part in the gun-sight. You had a little ratchet set and you would screw it in there. Then I cleaned the top of the glass off and put a piece of paper over it to seal it off to go to the next section. I worked over there until the end of the war. Well, not quite the end, because I got pregnant, and while I was off having the baby the war was over.

Tina stayed at North American for almost two years during the war. Her description of housing and daily life underscores wartime conditions and is also a reminder of the extent to which northern cities, too, were still segregated in the 1940s.

NEGROES RENTED ROOMS quite a bit. It was a wonderful thing, 'cause it made it possible for you to come and stay without a problem. My sister and I was rooming with this lady and we was paying six dollars a week, which was good money, because she was renting the house for only twenty-six dollars a month. She had another girl living on the back porch and she was charging her three dollars. So you get the idea.

We were accustomed to shacking up with each other. We had to live like that because that was the only way to survive. . . .

In the kitchen everybody had a little place where he kept his food. You had a spot in the icebox; one shelf was yours. You bought one type of milk and the other ones bought another type of milk, so it didn't get tangled up. But you didn't buy too much to have on hand. You didn't overstock like I do today. Of course, we had rationing, but that didn't bother me. It just taught me a few things that I still do today. It taught me there's a lot of things you can get along without. I liked cornbread a lot—and we had to use Cream of Wheat, grits, to make cornbread. I found out I liked that just as well. So, strange as it may seem, I didn't suffer from the war thing.

I started working in April and before Thanksgiving, my sister and I decided we'd buy a house instead of renting this room. The people was getting a little hanky-panky with you; they was going up on the rent. So she bought the house in her name and I loaned her some money. The house only cost four thousand dollars with four hundred dollars down. It was two houses on the lot, and we stayed in the little small one-bedroom house in the back. I stayed in the living room part before my husband came home and she stayed in the bedroom. I bought the furniture to go in the house, which was the stove and refrigerator, and we had our old bedroom sets shipped from Texas. I worked the day shift and my sister worked the night shift. I worked ten hours a day for five days a week. Or did I work on a Saturday? I don't remember, but I know it was ten hours a day. I'd get up in the morning, take a bath, come to the kitchen, fix my lunch—I always liked a fresh fixed lunch—get my breakfast, and then stand outside for the ride to come by. I always managed to get someone that liked to go to work slightly early. I carried my crocheting and knitting with me.

You had a spot where you always stayed around, close to where you worked, because when the whistle blew, you wanted to be ready to get up and go to where you worked. The leadman always come by and give you a job to do or you already had one that was a hangover from the day before. So you had a general idea what you was going to do each day.

Then we'd work and come home. I was married when I started working in the war plant, so I wasn't looking for a boyfriend and that made me come home in the evening. Sometimes you'd stop on the way home and shop for groceries. Then you'd come home and clean house and get ready for bed so you can go back the next morning. Write letters or what have you. I really wasn't physically tired.

Recreation was Saturday and Sunday. But my sister worked the swing shift and that made her get up late on Saturday morning, so we didn't do nothing but piddle around the house. We'd work in the garden, and we'd just go for little rides on the streetcar. We'd go to the parks, and then we'd go to the picture show downtown and look at the newsreel: "Where it happens, you see it happen." We enjoyed going to do that on a Sunday, since we was both off together.

We had our little cliques going; our little parties. Before they decided to break into the white nightclubs, we had our own out here on Central Avenue. There were a ton of good little nightclubs that kept you entertained fairly well. I don't know when these things began to turn, because I remember when I first came to Los Angeles, we used to go down to a theater called the Orpheum and that's where all the Negro entertainers as well as whites went. We had those clip joints over on the east side. And the funniest thing about it, it would always be in our nightclubs that a white woman would come in with a Negro man, eventually. The white man would very seldom come out in the open with a black woman. Even today. But the white woman has always come out in the open, even though I'm sure she gets tromped on and told about it. . . .

Some weeks I brought home twenty-six dollars, some weeks sixteen dollars. Then it gradually went up to thirty dollars, then it went up a little bit more and a little bit more. And I learned somewhere along the line that in order to make a good move you gotta make some money. You don't make the same amount everyday. You have some days good, sometimes bad. Whatever you make you're supposed to save some. I was also getting that fifty dollars a month from my husband and that was just saved right away. I was planning on buying a home and a car. And I was going to go back to school. My husband came back, but I never was laid off, so I just never found it necessary to look for another job or to go to school for another job. . . .

I worked up until the end of March and then I took off. Beverly [her daughter] was born the twenty-first of June. I'd planned to come back somewhere in the last of August. I went to verify the fact that I did come back, so that did go on my record that I didn't just quit. But they laid off a lot of people, most of them, because the war was over.

It didn't bother me much—not thinking about it jobwise. I was just glad that the war was over. I didn't feel bad because my husband had a job and he also was eligible to go to school with his GI bill. So I really didn't have too many plans—which I wish I had had. I would have tore out page one and fixed it differently; put my version of page one in there.

I went and got me a job doing day work. That means you go to a person's house and clean up for one day out of the week and then you go to the next one and clean up. I did that a couple of times and I discovered I didn't like that so hot. Then I got me a job downtown working in a little factory where you do weaving—burned clothes and stuff like that. I learned to do that real good. It didn't pay too much but it paid enough to get me going, seventy-five cents or about like that.

When North American called me back, was I a happy soul! I dropped that job and went back. That was a dollar an hour. So, from sixty cents an hour, when I first hired in there, up to one dollar. That wasn't traveling fast, but it was better than anything else because you had hours to work by and you had benefits and you come home at night with your family. So it was a good deal.

It made me live better. I really did. We always say that Lincoln took the bale off of the Negroes. I think there is a statue up there in Washington, D.C., where he's lifting something off the Negro. Well, my sister always said—that's why you can't interview her because she's so radical—"Hitler was the one that got us out of the white folks' kitchen." . . .

But [blacks] had to fight. They fought hand, tooth, and nail to get in there. And the first five or six Negroes who went in there, they were well educated, but they started them off as janitors. After they once got their foot in the door and was there for three months—you work for three months before they say you're hired—then they had to start fighting all over again to get off of that broom and get something decent. And some of them did.

But they'd always give that Negro man the worst part of everything. See, the jobs have already been tested and tried out before they ever get into the department, and they know what's good about them and what's bad about them. They always managed to give the worst one to the Negro. The only reason why the women fared better was they just couldn't quite give the woman as tough a job that they gave the men. But sometimes they did.

I can't exactly tell you what a tough job would be, but it's just like putting that caster on that little stand there. Let's face it, now you know that's light and you can lift that real easy, but there are other jobs twice as heavy as that. See, the larger the hole is, the thicker the drill, which would take you longer. So you know that's a tougher job. Okay, so they'd have the Negro doing that tough drilling. But when they got to the place where they figured out to get a drill press to drill that with—which would be easier—they gave it to a white person. So they just practiced that and still do, right down to this day. I just don't know if it will ever get straight.

There were some departments, they didn't even allow a black person to walk through there let alone work in there. Some of the white people did not want to work with the Negro. They had arguments right there. Sometimes they would get fired and walk on out the door, but it was one more white person gone. I think even to this very day in certain places they still don't want to work with the Negro. I don't know what their story is, but if they would try then they might not knock it.

But they did everything they could to keep you separated. They just did not like for a Negro and a white person to get together and talk. Now I am a person that you can talk to and you will warm up to me much better than you can a lot of people. A white person seems to know that they could talk to me at ease. And when anyone would start—just plain, common talk, everyday talk—they didn't like it.

I know I had several leadmen—it's a lot of work if you're a lead; a lot of paperwork to do. You know yourself if anybody catches on and learns good, you kinda lean towards that person and you depend on them. If you step out for a few minutes, you say, "If anybody come in here looking for me, find out what they want and if you can, help them." You start doing like that and if you find out he's doing a good job at it, you leave that work for them to do. But they didn't like that at all. Shoot, they'd get rid of that leadman real quick.

And they'd keep you from advancing. They always manage to give the Negroes the worst end of the deal. I happened to fall into that when they get ready to transfer you from one department to the next. That was the only thing that

I ever ran into that I had to holler to the union about. And once I filed a complaint downtown with the Equal Opportunity.

The way they was doing this particular thing—they always have a lean spot where they're trying to lay off or go through there and see if they can curl out a bunch of people, get rid of the ones with the most seniority, I suppose. They had a good little system going. All the colored girls had more seniority in production than the whites because the average white woman did not come back after the war. They thought like I thought: that I have a husband now and I don't have to work and this was just only for the war and blah, blah, blah. But they didn't realize they was going to need the money. The average Negro was glad to come back because it meant more money than they was making before. So we always had more seniority in production than the white woman.

All the colored women in production, they was just one step behind the other. I had three months more than one, the next one had three months more than me, and that's the way it went. So they had a way of putting us all in Blueprint. We all had twenty years by the time you got in Blueprint and stayed a little while. Here come another one. He'd bump you out and then you went out the door, because they couldn't find nothing else for you to do—so they said. They just kept doing it and I could see myself: "Well, hell, I'm going to be the next one to go out the door!"

So I found some reason to file a grievance. I tried to get several other girls: "Let's get together and go downtown and file a grievance" [a discrimination complaint with the Equal Opportunities Employment Commission]. I only got two girls to go with me. That made three of us. I think we came out on top, because we all kept our jobs and then they stopped sending them to Blueprint, bumping each other like that. So, yeah, we've had to fight to stay there. . . .

Beatrice Morales Clifton, of Mexican ancestry, grew up in San Bernardino, California, and, as the youngest of four children, lived a somewhat protected life. She had already married twice and was a mother of four when she started her first job at Lockheed Aircraft in Burbank, California. She had never thought about working until she sought a job for an adopted niece in the aircraft industry. As it turned out, her niece was too young, but the recruiter corraled Clifton instead. Despite her husband's objections about having a working wife, she joined Lockheed. "Why I took Lockheed, I don't know," she later recalled. "But I just liked that name."

The work at Lockheed was her first sojourn in the world on her own without her husband, and though she was easily intimidated at first and flinched from criticism, she soon gained skill and confidence and excelled at her work. She enjoyed earning her own money and contributing to the family's standard of living, until one of her children became severely ill and she quit to take care of him. Her job at Lockheed had given her a taste for working outside of the home and earning her own money, however, and she went back to work, first at odd jobs and then once again at Lockheed. Her account illustrates both the struggles that women faced in trying to hold on to their jobs or return to the work force in the postwar years and the strategies they used to advance in their work.

SOURCE: Sherna Berger Gluck, ed., *Rosie the Riveter Revisited*, Boston: Twayne, 1987; pp. 208–13. Reprinted by permission of Sherna Berger Gluck.

I'D NEVER THOUGHT about working. My brother at that time had separated from his wife, and he had an adopted girl. His wife remarried and the stepfather didn't like the girl. We considered that girl like ours because my mother had gotten her when I was a kid. She used to take care of children from the Welfare, and she got that baby when she was six months old. She gave it to my brother because he didn't have no children. He brought that girl to me and says, "I'll have her stay with you and I'll give you some money every week." She was sixteen or fifteen and she wanted a job.

They had these offices everywhere in Pasadena, of aircraft. I went in there to try and get her something, but they said, "We've got aircraft work right now for

---

* Quoted in Gluck, ibid., p. 209.

everybody, except she's too young." He says, "Why don't you get it?" I said, "Me?" He said, "Yeah, why don't you get the job?" I said, "Well, I don't know." But the more I kept thinking about it, the more I said, "That's a good idea." So I took the forms and when I got home and told my husband, oh! he hit the roof. He was one of those men that didn't believe in the wife ever working; they want to be the supporter. I said, "Well, I've made up my mind. I'm going to go to work regardless of whether you like it or not." I was determined.

My family and everybody was surprised—his family. I said, "Well, yeah, I'm going to work." "And how does Julio feel?" "He doesn't want me to, but I'm going anyway." When he saw that, he just kept quiet; he didn't say no more. My mother didn't say nothing because I always told her, "Mother, you live your life and I live mine." We had that understanding. When I decided to go to work, I told her, "I'm going to go to work and maybe you can take care of the children." She said, "Yeah."

The intensity of emotions Bea felt on that day some forty years ago when she first walked through the doors of Lockheed was communicated through her demeanor as well as her words. She crouched in mock meekness and whispered hesitatingly, feigning fear.

I FILLED OUT the papers and everything and I got the job. Why I took Lockheed, I don't know, but I just liked that name. Then they asked me, "Do you want to go to Burbank, to Los Angeles?" I said, "I don't know where Burbank is." I didn't know my way around. The only way that I got up to Los Angeles was with Julio driving me there. I said, "Well, Los Angeles. The streetcar passes by Fair Oaks, close to where I live, and that drops me off in front."

To me, everything was new. They were doing the P-38s at that time. I was at Plant 2, on Seventh and Santa Fe. It was on the fifth floor. I went up there and saw the place, and I said, "Gee———." See, so many parts and things that you've never seen. Me, I'd never seen anything in my whole life. It was exciting and scary at the same time.

They put me way up in the back, putting little plate nuts and drilling holes. They put me with some guy—he was kind of a stinker, real mean. A lot of them guys at the time resented women coming into jobs, and they let you know about it. He says, "Well, have you ever done any work like this?" I said, "No." I was feeling just horrible. Horrible. Because I never worked with men, to be with men alone other than my husband. So then he says "You know what you've got in your hand? That's a rivet gun." I said, "Oh." What could I answer? I was terrified. So then time went on and I made a mistake. I messed up something, made a ding. He got so irritable with me, he says, "You're not worth the money Lockheed pays you."

He couldn't have hurt me more if he would have slapped me. When he said that, I dropped the gun and I went running downstairs to the restoom, with tears coming down. This girl from Texas saw me and she followed me. She was real good. She was one of these "toughies"; dressed up and walked like she was kind of tough. She asked me what was wrong. I told her what I had done and I was crying. She says, "Don't worry." She started cussing him. We came back up and she told them all off.

I was very scared because, like I say, I had never been away like that and I had never been among a lot of men. Actually, I had never been out on my own. Whenever I had gone anyplace, it was with my husband. It was all building up inside of me, so when that guy told me that I wasn't worth the money Lockheed paid me, it just came out in tears.

At the end of that first day, I was so tired. I was riding the streetcar and I had to stand all the way from Los Angeles clear to Pasadena. When I got home, the kids just said, "Oh, Mom is here." My husband, he didn't have very much to say, 'cause he didn't approve from the beginning. As time went on, his attitude changed a little, but I don't think he ever really, really got used to the idea of me working. But he was a very reserved man. He wasn't the type of guy that you'd sit down and you'd chatter on. Like me, I'm a chatterbox. You had to pull the words out of him. . . .

They had a union, but it wasn't very strong then. It wasn't like it is now. But I joined. I joined everything that they told me. Buck of the Month, everything. And they gave me a list of the stuff that I would be needing. At that time they used to sell you your tools and your toolboxes through Lockheed. So I bought a box. I bought the clothing at Sears. It was just a pair of pants and a blouse. To tell you the truth, I felt kind of funny wearing pants. Then at the same time, I said, "Oh, what the heck." And those shoes! I wasn't used to low shoes. Even in the house, I always wore high heels. That's how I started.

As time went on, I started getting a little bit better. I just made up my mind that I was going to do it. I learned my job so well that then they put me to the next operation. At the very first, I just began putting little plate nuts and stuff like that. Then afterwards I learned how to drill the skins and burr them. Later, as I got going, I learned to rivet and buck. I got to the point where I was very good.

I had a Mexican girl, Irene Herrera, and she was as good a bucker as I was a riveter. She would be facing me and we'd just go right on through. We'd go one side and then we'd get up to the corner and I'd hand her the gun or the bucking bar or whatever and then we'd come back. Her and I, we used to have a lot of fun. They would want maybe six or five elevators a day. I'd say, "let's get with it." We worked pretty hard all day until about 2:00. Then we would slack down.

I had a lot of friends there. We all spoke to each other. Most of them smoked, and we'd sit in the smoking areas out there in the aisle. Then, some of the girls—on the next corner there was a drugstore that served lunches. There was a white lady, she used to go, and Irene would go. We'd talk about our families and stuff like that.

Irene stayed on that same operation. I don't know why I got a chance to learn all the other jobs, but I learned the whole operation until I got up to the front, the last step. They used to put this little flap with a wire, with a hinge. I had to have that flap just right so that it would swing easy without no rubbing anywhere. I used to go with a little hammer and a screwdriver and knock those little deals down so that it would be just right. That guy that I used to work with helped me, teached me how to do it, and I could do it just like him.

New people would come in, and they would say, "You teach them the job. You know all the jobs." Sometimes it would make me mad. I'd tell them, "What the heck, you get paid for it. You show them the job." But I would still show them.

Then, like that leadperson, they'd say, "Look at her now. You should have seen her a year ago when she first came in. You'd go boo and she'd start crying. Now she can't keep her mouth shut." I figured this is the only way you're going to survive, so I'm going to do it.

I was just a mother of four kids, that's all. But I felt proud of myself and felt good being that I had never done anything like that. I felt good that I could do something, and being that it was war, I felt that I was doing my part.

I went from 65 cents to $1.05. That was top pay. It felt good and, besides, it was my own money. I could do whatever I wanted with it because my husband, whatever he was giving to the house, he kept on paying it. I used to buy clothes for the kids; buy little things that they needed. I had a bank account and I had a little saving at home where I could get ahold of the money right away if I needed it. Julio never asked about it. He knew how much I made; I showed him. If there was something that had to be paid and I had the money and he didn't, well, I used some of my money. But he never said, "Well, you have to pay because you're earning money." My money, I did what I wanted.

I started feeling a little more independent. Just a little, not too much, because I was still not on my own that I could do this and do that. I didn't until after. Then I got really independent. . . .

I got home and my mother told me, she says, "Gerry is very sick. He's got a lot of fever and it won't go down." I never thought of having a family doctor, so I had to call the police station and they sent me this doctor that was real nice. He started giving him shots and that's what brought him out. It was pneumonia and he was very sick for quite a long time.

My husband, right away, he jumped: "You see, the kids are like this because you're not here." My mother was there, but he blamed everything on me. We got into a little bit of an argument on account of that, and then I said, "Okay, I'll quit." I didn't want to, but I said my boy comes first. Afterwards, I realized I could have gone on a leave of absence. But I wasn't too familiar with all that, so I just panicked and quit.

When I quit, I just took over the same as I was before—taking care of my kids. Well, it was kind of quiet and I wasn't too satisfied. That's why I started looking to go to work. I had already tasted that going-out business and I wasn't too satisfied. I stayed home about a year or so, and then I took a little job at Joyce; they used to make shoes. It was walking distance from where I lived. I would get the packages of leather already cut and mark the shoes with a marking machine and put them in pairs and put them on the belt so the stitchers could sew them.

I worked there about a year. Then my husband told me, "Well, if you're going to be working, why don't you work with me?" There was this man that got sick—he was a janitor—so they gave me his theater. My husband would help me. He would get the biggest mopping and the windows. I would do mostly the auditorium—sweep it and vacuum. We would do his job and my job together. They were giving me a hassle. It was union and they didn't want me to join the union. I would be working on a permit with the union, and I said, "Well, if I can work on a permit, why can't I work as a member?" I finally said, "Look, go jump in the lake." So I quit.

I was already thinking of Lockheed. I wasn't satisfied. I felt myself alone and I said, "Oh, I can't do this; I can't stay here." In 1950 I wrote to Lockheed asking them if they had a job for me because I knew that they were still taking people. They wrote and told me that they weren't taking any women, but that they would the following year. The next year, the minute I received that telegram, I headed for Lockheed. . . .

"I FELT DEGRADED, HUMILIATED, AND OVERWHELMED"
YOSHIKO UCHIDA

The attack on Pearl Harbor signaled the beginning of another form of war—a war against Japanese American citizens, who were herded into relocation camps throughout the country. Forced to leave their homes and businesses and travel by crowded train or bus to remote outposts, many Japanese American citizens lost farms and businesses that they had diligently built up over the years. As this account by Yoshika Uchida, an American-born citizen from a successful, assimilated middle-class Japanese family shows, conditions in the camps were miserable: entire families shared one small room; cooking and bathing facilities were primitive; and the cramped living arrangements became a breeding ground for chicken pox, measles, and other potentially fatal diseases. Barbed wire and military guards surrounded many camps, and families had precious little privacy. For several months Uchida and her parents and sister shared a horse stall with another family; then they lived in a transport center before being relocated yet again. In the following selection she describes the indignities and material deprivation of their lives there, especially for her mother, who bore the ordeal with sad, quiet dignity. Within these crude prisonlike conditions, however, some young Japanese women learned new skills, acquired an education, and managed to distance themselves from restrictive cultural traditions governing Japanese American women's lives. Uchida, a student at the University of California at Berkeley, was assigned to teach a second-grade class. Although she lacked the formal skills and experience, she quickly learned to rely on her own instincts and decided to pursue a teaching career after the war. She also describes recreational diversions such as attending dances and art class. But these fleeting pleasures could not compensate for the degrading reality of being uprooted from her home and being treated as a potential enemy in her own country.

SOURCE: Yoshiko, Uchida, *Desert Exile* (Seattle: University of Washington Press, 1982) pp. 69–71, 75, 88–9, 96–7. Courtesy of the Bancroft Library, University of California, Berkeley.

AS THE BUS PULLED UP to the grandstand, I could see hundreds of Japanese Americans jammed along the fence that lined the track. These people had arrived a few days earlier and were now watching for the arrival of friends or had come to while away the empty hours that had suddenly been thrust upon them.

As soon as we got off the bus, we were directed to an area beneath the grandstand where we registered and filled out a series of forms. Our baggage was inspected for contraband, a cursory medical check was made, and our living quarters assigned. We were to be housed in Barrack 16, Apartment 40. Fortunately, some friends who had arrived earlier found us and offered to help us locate our quarters.

It had rained the day before and the hundreds of people who had trampled on the track had turned it into a miserable mass of slippery mud. We made our way on it carefully, helping my mother who was dressed just as she would have been to go to church. She wore a hat, gloves, her good coat, and her Sunday shoes, because she would not have thought of venturing outside our house dressed in any other way.

Everywhere there were black tar-papered barracks that had been hastily erected to house the 8,000 Japanese Americans of the area who had been uprooted from their homes. Barrack 16, however, was not among them, and we couldn't find it until we had traveled half the length of the track and gone beyond it to the northern rim of the race-track compound.

Finally one of our friends called out, "There it is, beyond that row of eucalyptus trees." Barrack 16 was not a barrack at all, but a long stable raised a few feet off the ground with a broad ramp the horses had used to reach their stalls. Each stall was now numbered and ours was number 40. That the stalls should have been called "apartments" was a euphemism so ludicrous it was comical.

When we reached stall number 40, we pushed open the narrow door and looked uneasily into the vacant darkness. The stall was about ten by twenty feet and empty except for three folded Army cots lying on the floor. Dust, dirt, and wood shavings covered the linoleum that had been laid over manure-covered boards, the smell of horses hung in the air, and the whitened corpses of many insects still clung to the hastily white-washed walls.

High on either side of the entrance were two small windows which were our only source of daylight. The stall was divided into two sections by Dutch doors worn down by teeth marks, and each stall in the stable was separated from the adjoining one only by rough partitions that stopped a foot short of the sloping roof. That space, while perhaps a good source of ventilation for the horses, deprived us of all but visual privacy, and we couldn't even be sure of that because of the crevices and knotholes in the dividing walls.

Because our friends had already spent a day as residents of Tanforan, they had become adept at scrounging for necessities. One found a broom and swept the floor for us. Two of the boys went to the barracks where mattresses were being issued, stuffed the ticking with straw themselves, and came back with three for our cots.

Nothing in the camp was ready. Everything was only half-finished. I wondered how much the nation's security would have been threatened had the Army permitted us to remain in our homes a few more days until the camps were adequately prepared for occupancy by families.

By the time we had cleaned out the stall and set up the cots, it was time for supper. Somehow, in all the confusion, we had not had lunch, so I was eager to get to the main mess hall which was located beneath the grandstand.

The sun was going down as we started along the muddy track, and a cold piercing wind swept in from the bay. When we arrived, there were six long weaving lines of people waiting to get into the mess hall. We took our place at the end of one of them, each of us clutching a plate and silverware borrowed from friends who had already received their baggage.

Shivering in the cold, we pressed close together trying to shield Mama from the wind. As we stood in what seemed a breadline for the destitute, I felt degraded, humiliated, and overwhelmed with a longing for home. And I saw the unutterable sadness on my mother's face.

This was only the first of many lines we were to endure, and we soon discovered that waiting in line was as inevitable a part of Tanforan as the north wind that swept in from the bay stirring up all the dust and litter of the camp.

Once we got inside the gloomy cavernous mess hall, I saw hundreds of people eating at wooden picnic tables, while those who had already eaten were shuffling aimlessly over the wet cement floor. When I reached the serving table and held out my plate, a cook reached into a dishpan full of canned sausages and dropped two onto my plate with his fingers. Another man gave me a boiled potato and a piece of butterless bread.

With 5,000 people to be fed, there were few unoccupied tables, so we separated from our friends and shared a table with an elderly man and a young family with two crying babies. No one at the table spoke to us, and even Mama could seem to find no friendly word to offer as she normally would have done. We tried to eat, but the food wouldn't go down. . . .

About one hundred feet from our stable were two latrines and two washrooms for our section of camp, one each for men and women. The latrines were crude wooden structures containing eight toilets, separated by partitions, but having no doors. The washrooms were divided into two sections. In the front section was a long tin trough spaced with spigots of hot and cold water where we washed our faces and brushed our teeth. To the rear were eight showers, also separated by partitions, but lacking doors or curtains. The showers were difficult to adjust and we either got scalded by torrents of hot water or shocked by an icy blast of cold. Most of the Issei were unaccustomed to showers, having known the luxury of soaking in deep pine-scented tubs during their years in Japan, and found the showers virtually impossible to use. . . .

Three weeks after we had entered Tanforan, registration was held for school children aged six to eighteen, who by then were anxious to have some orderly routine to give substance to their long days. Four schools for grades one through three were opened in various sections of the camp and an internee teacher with elementary school credentials was in charge of each one. I was assigned to assist at one of these schools and our first classes were held on May 26. When I arrived at the school barrack at 8:30 A.M., the children were already clamoring to get in. Our first day went remarkably well, although we had no supplies or equipment for teaching and all we could do was tell stories and sing with the children.

Classes were soon separated by grade, and because of the shortage of credentialed teachers, I was placed in charge of a second grade class. We taught classes in the morning and attended meetings in the afternoon, not only to plan lessons for the next day, but to put in our time for a forty-four-hour week. The day I took over my second grade, however, I had to dismiss the children early because the building we used was also occupied by the Buddhist church on Sundays and was needed that day for the first funeral to take place in camp.

Although I had acquired some experience as an assistant, when I was on my own, my methods were of necessity empirical, and I taught mostly by instinct. The children, however, were affectionate and devoted, and it didn't take them long to discover where I lived. Each morning I would find a covey of them clustered in front of my stall, and, like the Pied Piper, I would lead them to the school barrack. When school was over, many would wait until I was ready to leave and escort me back home.

I loved teaching and decided I would like to work for a teaching credential, for I now had received my degree from the university. My classmates and I had missed commencement by two weeks and my diploma, rolled in a cardboard container, had been handed to me in my horse stall by the Tanforan Mailman. The winner of the University Medal that year was a Nisei who also missed commencement because, as the president of the university stated at the ceremonies, "his country has called him elsewhere." . . .

After three months of communal living, the lack of privacy began to grate on my nerves. There was no place I could go to be completely alone—not in the washroom, the latrine, the shower, or my stall. I couldn't walk down the track without seeing someone I knew. I couldn't avoid the people I didn't like or choose those I wished to be near. There was no place to cry and no place to hide. It was impossible to escape from the constant noise and human presence. I felt stifled and suffocated and sometimes wanted to scream. But in my family we didn't scream or cry or fight or even have a major argument, because we knew the neighbors were always only inches away. . . .

Although we worked hard at our jobs to keep Tanforan functioning properly, we also sought to forestall the boredom of our confinement by keeping busy in a number of other ways. My sister and I both took first aid classes and joined the church choir, which once collaborated with the Little Theater group to present the works of Stephen Foster, complete with sets that featured a moving steamboat. We also went to some of the dances where decorations festooned the usually bleak hall at the grandstand and music was provided by a band made up of internee musicians. When I had time, I also went to art class and did some paintings so I would have a visual record of our life at Tanforan. I was surprised and pleased one day when I went to a hobby show and saw a second place red ribbon pinned to one of my paintings.

"SAYING 'NO' WAS THE ONLY WAY YOU COULD BECOME A WAVE"
MARY MEIGS

Despite the freedom to express their sexual preferences in wartime social venues, such as bars, dance halls, and private homes (see a description of these activities in Juanita Loveless's oral history on p. 26), lesbians in the military carefully kept their sexual orientation concealed from superior officers and heterosexual comrades. Mary Meigs, who later became a painter and writer in Cape Cod, Massachusetts, describes both the pleasure and freedom that lesbian military women found in each other's company and the fear and suspicion they harbored toward those who could "out" them. Her recollections also shed light on the privileges of secrecy that lesbian officers enjoyed by virtue of their elite position.

SOURCE: Yvonne M. Klein, ed., *Beyond the Home Front: Women's Autobiographical Writings of the Two World Wars* (New York: New York University Press, 1997), pp. 158–60. Reprinted by permission of New York University Press.

WITH OUR EYES reverently fixed on Old Glory hanging beside the interrogating officer, each of us said, "No," to his perfunctory question, "Are you a homosexual?" Don't tell is still the law in the USA, and it takes a very courageous woman like Gretta Cammermeyer to risk her career by saying, "I'm a lesbian." For me in 1943, "No" was not quite an outright lie. I had not yet engaged in the sexual activity classified as "homosexual" and I did not yet think of myself as a lesbian, yet I knew perfectly well that saying "No" was the only way you could become a WAVE.

MY SISTER-TRAINEES, many of whom could have said yes, had evidently made the same prudent decision. We were billeted in the wonderful old Northampton Inn where the peacetime staff still ran the kitchen and dining-room (we were served lobster thermidor for our farewell dinner). I was keenly aware of the vibrations of suppressed sexuality between officers and trainees and among the trainees themselves. We were assigned eight to a room which was crowded with four double-decker bunks. Above me was a woman ambiguously named Preston; she had a caressing Mississippi accent and curly hair that sprouted defiantly in every direction from under the confines of her WAVE hat. After lights-out I heard a stealthy sound as some of my roommates climbed into upper bunks, or occupants of upper banks climbed down. The sound of giggles and cautious movements was accompanied by the whispered confidences of straight WAVES who had changed bunks in order to talk. It surprises me still that the straight WAVES didn't squeal on us. I, too, climbed up to Preston's welcoming arms one night, was surprised by the ardour with which she wrapped them around me, and wriggled out and down. I had conjured up the spectre of an officer-on-watch bursting in, and of our subsequent dishonorable discharge.

When I graduated as an Ensign, I was assigned to the Bureau of Communications (BuComm) in Washington, DC, where I was aware only of WAVES who took themselves and their patriotic duty with appropriate seriousness. I was transferred after a period of incompetence to the Bureau of Personnel (BuPers) across the Potomac, to the Artists' Unit. The Post Office Department where I worked in BuComm was run by a crusty sergeant who shouted at us in the time-honored male way; now I was with compatible artists and writers, with civilian hearts unchanged by their uniforms. I fell in love with a russet-haired lesbian WAVE who gave me my first lesson in sex. I also fell in love with a WAVE lieutenant whom I passed sitting at her desk every time I walked up the corridor. When a round-eyed, round-faced sailor gave me an envelope with, inside, a big studio photograph of my WAVE lieutenant, of her twinkling eyes and smiling mouth, I felt discomfited and uneasy. Was this a way of saying, "I know, and can denounce you at any time?" or (but this only occurred to me recently) was he telling me that he was gay and understood why I stopped so often in front of the WAVE lieutenant's desk? The necessity for secrecy made us suspicious of everybody. I shunned the sailor with the round eyes, and would look away when we passed each other, for I read a kind of sly suggestiveness in his face. "We're buddies, you and I," it said. I was glad when I fell in love with men, too, even if these loves were never consummated. The russet-haired WAVE fell in love with a succession of sailors and was briefly married to one of them. It was standard practise for lesbians to hint at male lovers in their lives or claim to be mourning a lover who had been killed in the war.

The spy system in the services got underway when the mother of an enlisted WAAC surprised her daughter in bed with her lesbian lover and sounded the alarm. Enlisted lesbians who took the risk of sleeping together in barracks were likely to be denounced by informers, whereas officers, who lived in houses and apartments were neither identified as lesbians nor denounced. In this time before the feminist revolution, I was politically ignorant and had never thought about injustices to women based on class differences. When one of the

WAVE typists in my BuComm unit suddenly lashed out at me with, "You treat me like the ground under your feet!" I thought she was angry because I seemed to ignore her existence. It didn't occur to me until years later that she probably thought I'd ignored her existence because I was an upper-class snob.

The majority of WAVE officers were college-educated or had teaching degrees. They had more privileges, more freedom, and more power than enlisted women; their relations with male officers were more friendly and informal. WAVE officers were sometimes tempted to take advantage of a system that took their superiority for granted. The typist in BuComm had probably already suffered from this licensed sense of superiority, and my own attitude was the last straw.

Many of my recollections of being a WAVE in World War II are embellished by hindsight. I had then both a sense of superiority without foundation and a craven fear of my superiors, whether they were men or women. It was good judgement on someone's part not to assign me to top priority work that required total loyalty to the war effort. One of my lesbian friends now is an ex-WAVE who had a top-secret job in the intelligence structure essential to the ultimate dropping of Little Boy.*

I am thankful that my own work entailed nothing more deadly than revising a cookbook for enlisted men on aircraft-carriers.

---

* *Author's note:* The atomic bomb dropped on Hiroshima.

"I BELIEVE THE WAR WAS THE BEGINNING OF MY SEEING THINGS"
PEGGY TERRY

Peggy Terry grew up in the small town of Paducah, Kentucky, and worked at a shell-loading plant in a nearby town during the war. For her, the war meant a steady income and she honestly admits, "It didn't occur to us that we were making these shells to kill people." Nor did she or her coworkers question the potential health hazards of their work environment. Terry's account poignantly reveals the impact of the war on both her and her husband. The war was the beginning of her "seeing things"—of questioning long-held religious beliefs and political ideas—and, as her brief description of her husband's abusive behavior toward her and her children reveals, of the violence and trauma of war that lingered over people's lives long after V-day celebrations had ended.

SOURCE: Copyright © 1992. *Race: How Blacks and Whites Think and Feel About the American Obsession* by Studs Terkel. Reprinted by permission of the New Press.

THE FIRST WORK I had after the Depression was at a shell-loading plant in Viola, Kentucky. It is between Paducah and Mayfield. They were large shells: anti-aircraft, incendiaries, and tracers. We painted red on the tips of the tracers. My mother, my sister, and myself worked there. Each of us worked a different shift because we had little ones at home. We made the fabulous sum of thirty-two dollars a week. To us it was just an absolute miracle. Before that, we made nothing.

You won't believe how incredibly ignorant I was. I knew vaguely that a war had started, but I had no idea what it meant. . . . We were just moving around, working wherever we could find work. I was eighteen. My husband was nineteen. We were living day to day. When you are involved in stayin' alive, you don't think about big things like a war. It didn't occur to us that we were making these shells to kill people. It never entered my head.

There were no women foremen where we worked. We were just a bunch of hillbilly women laughin' and talkin.' It was like a social. Now we'd have money to buy shoes and a dress and pay rent and get some food on the table. We were just happy to have work.

I worked in building number 11. I pulled a lot of gadgets on a machine. The shell slid under and powder went into it. Another lever you pulled tamped it down. Then it moved on a conveyer belt to another building where the detonator was dropped in. You did this over and over.

Tetryl was one of the ingredients and it turned us orange. Just as orange as an orange. Our hair was streaked orange. Our hands, our face, our neck just turned orange, even our eyeballs. We never questioned. None of us ever asked, What is this? Is this harmful? We simply didn't think about it. That was just one of the conditions of the job. The only thing we worried about was other women thinking we had dyed our hair. Back then it was a disgrace if you dyed your hair. We worried what people would say.

We used to laugh about it on the bus. It eventually wore off. But I seem to remember some of the women had breathing problems. The shells were painted a dark gray. When the paint didn't come out smooth, we had to take rags wet with some kind of remover and wash that paint off. The fumes from these rags—it was like breathing cleaning fluid. It burned the nose and throat. Oh, it was difficult to breathe. I remember that.

Nothing ever blew up, but I remember the building where they dropped in the detonator. These detonators are little black things about the size of a thumb. This terrible thunderstorm came and all the lights went out. Somebody knocked a box of detonators off on the floor. Here we were in the pitch dark. Somebody was screaming, "Don't move, anybody!" They were afraid you'd step on the detonator. We were down on our hands and knees crawling out of that building in the storm. [Laughs.] We were in slow motion. If we'd stepped on one . . .

Mamma was what they call terminated—fired. Mamma's mother took sick and died and Mamma asked for time off and they told her no. Mamma said, "Well, I'm gonna be with my mamma. If I have to give up my job, I will just have to." So they terminated Mamma. That's when I started gettin' nasty. I didn't take as much baloney and pushing around as I had taken. I told 'em I was gonna quit, and they told me if I quit they would blacklist me wherever I would go. They had my fingerprints and all that. I guess it was just bluff, because I did get other work.

I think of how little we knew of human rights, union rights. We knew Daddy had been a hell-raiser in the mine workers' union, but at that point it hadn't rubbed off on any of us women. Coca-Cola and Dr. Pepper were allowed in every building, but not a drop of water. You could only get a drink of water if you went to the cafeteria, which was about two city blocks away. Of course you couldn't leave your machine long enough to go get a drink. I drank Coke and Dr. Pepper and I hated 'em. I hate 'em today. We had to buy it of course. We couldn't leave to go to the bathroom, 'cause it was way the heck over there. . .

We were awarded the navy E for excellence. We were just so proud of that E. It was like we were a big family, and we hugged and kissed each other. They had the navy band out there celebrating us. We were so proud of ourselves. . . .

My world was really very small. When we came from Oklahoma to Paducah, that was like a journey to the center of the earth. It was during the Depression and you did good having bus fare to get across town. The war just widened my world. Especially after I came up to Michigan.

My grandfather went up to Jackson, Michigan, after he retired from the railroad. He wrote back and told us we could make twice as much in the war plants in Jackson. We did. We made ninety dollars a week. We did some kind of testing for airplane radios.

Ohh, I met all those wonderful Polacks. They were the first people I'd ever known that were any different from me. A whole new world just opened up. I learned to drink beer like crazy with 'em. They were all very union-conscious. I learned a lot of things that I didn't even know existed.

We were very patriotic and we understood that the Nazis were someone who would have to be stopped. We didn't know about concentration camps. I don't think anybody I knew did. With the Japanese, that was a whole different thing. We were just ready to wipe them out. They sure as heck didn't look like us. They were yellow little creatures that smiled when they bombed our boys. I remember someone in Paducah got up this idea of burning everything they had that was Japanese. I had this little ceramic cat and I said, "I don't care, I am not burning it." They had this big bonfire and people came and brought what they had that was made in Japan. Threw it on the bonfire. I hid my cat. It's on the shelf in my bathroom right now. . . .

I believe the war was the beginning of my seeing things. You just can't stay uninvolved and not knowing when such a momentous thing is happening. It's just little things that start happening and you put one piece with another. Suddenly, a puzzle begins to take shape.

My husband was a paratrooper in the war, in the 101st Airborne Division. He made twenty-six drops in France, North Africa, and Germany. I look back at the war with sadness. I wasn't smart enough to think too deeply then. We had a lotta good times and we had money and we had food on the table and the rent was paid. Which had never happened to us before. But when I look back and think of him. . . .

Until the war he never drank. He never even smoked. When he came back he was an absolute drunkard. And he used to have the most awful nightmares. He'd get up in the middle of the night and start screaming. I'd just sit for hours and hold him while he just shook. We'd go to the movies, and if they'd have films with a lot of shooting in it, he'd just start to shake and have to get up and leave. He started slapping me around and slapped the kids around. He became a brute.

One of the things that bothered him most was his memory of this town he was in. He saw something move by a building and he shot. It was a woman. He never got over that. It seems so obvious to say—wars brutalize people. It brutalized him.

The war gave a lot of people jobs. It led them to expect more than they had before. People's expectations, financially, spiritually, were raised. There was such a beautiful dream. We were gonna reach the end of the rainbow. When the war ended, the rainbow vanished. Almost immediately we went into Korea. There was no peace, which we were promised.

I remember a woman saying on the bus that she hoped the war didn't end until she got her refrigerator paid for. An old man hit her over the head with an umbrella. He said, "How dare you!"

Ohh, the beautiful celebrations when the war ended. They were selling cigarettes in Paducah. Up until that hour, you couldn't a bought a pack of cigarettes for love or money. Kirchoff's Bakery was giving away free loaves of bread. Everybody was downtown in the pouring rain and we were dancing. We took off our shoes and put 'em in our purse. We were so happy.

The night my husband came home, we went out with a gang of friends and got drunk. All of us had a tattoo put on. I had a tattoo put up my leg where it wouldn't show. A heart with an arrow through it: Bill and Peggy. When I went to the hospital to have my baby—I got pregnant almost as soon as he came home— I was ashamed of the tattoo. So I put two Band-Aids across it. So the nurse just pulls 'em off, looks at the tattoo, and she says, "Oh, that's exactly in the same spot I got mine." She pulled her uniform up and showed me her tattoo. . . .

[T]he war turned me against religion. I was raised in the fundamentalist faith. I was taught that I was nothing. My feeling is if God created me, if God sent his only begotten son to give his life for me, then I am something. My mother died thinking she was nothing. I don't know how chaplains can call themselves men of God and prepare boys to go into battle. If the Bible says, Thou shalt not kill, it doesn't say, Except in time of war. They'll send a man to the electric chair who in a temper killed somebody. But they pin medals on our men. The more people they kill, the more medals they pin on 'em.

I was just so glad when it was over, because I wanted my husband home. I didn't understand any of the implications except that the killing was over and that's a pretty good thing to think about whether you're political or not. The killing be over forever.

"THERE WAS PREJUDICE AGAINST
CONSCIENTIOUS OBJECTORS"
WILMA AND WILLIAM LUDLOW

While most Americans supported the war and eagerly worked in war-related industries, a small but significant number registered principled opposition. About twenty-five thousand men chose to serve in the military in noncombatant positions and were classified by the Selective Service System as conscientious cooperatives. Another six thousand refused to perform any type of service and went to prison for their beliefs. And about twelve thousand men entered the Civilian Public Service (CPS) to perform alternative service in a civilian capacity. Encompassing both blue-collar workers and middle-class professionals, they performed a variety of duties, from working as aides in mental hospitals to volunteering as smoke jumpers in forest fires or as human subjects in medical and scientific experiments.* *They lived in specially constructed camps across the country and endured much hostility from Americans who supported the war.*

The wives of CPS objectors faced special problems, especially those who did not share their husbands' pacifist beliefs and were dismayed at their refusal to serve in the military. These women were more vulnerable to public discrimination than were their husbands, who often lived apart and secluded at the camps. Female teachers were sometimes fired when their school boards learned about their husbands, and others were turned away when they applied for a teaching position. In the following interview, Wilma and William Ludlow describe their harrowing experience of working as attendants in a mental hospital in Williamsburg, Virginia. William Ludlow entered the CPS in February 1944, and Wilma, who shared his pacifist principles, also worked at the hospital to be near him. She describes her harrowing work experience and the frustration of trying to find a place to live after she left the hospital—with little success because she was the wife of a conscientious objector.

SOURCE: Heather T. Frazer, and John O'Sullivan, eds. *"We Have Just Begun to Not Fight":* *An Oral History of Conscientious Objectors in Civilian Public Service During World War II* (New York: Twayne, 1996), pp. 186–193. Twayne Publishers, reprinted by permission of the Gale Group.

---

* Heather T. Frazer, and John O'Sullivan, eds. *"We Have Just Begun to Not Fight": An Oral History of Conscientious Objectors in Civilian Public Service During World War II* (New York: Twayne, 1996), p. xiii.

When did you enter CPS?

WILLIAM: 1944. I had already had an interview in Baltimore with my draft board and had no problems getting my conscientious objector status.

How did your family feel about your going into CPS?

My father was a very strong supporter of the war, but he accepted my position. He was retired at that time, and he used to write to servicemen and was very active in war-connected things.

You were assigned to Big Flats. What were you doing there?

WILLIAM: Chopping down trees in snows about two feet deep. Then summer came. I wasn't interested in weeding, so I got on the kitchen crew. Wilma got a good job with the Child and Family Services in Elmira, and she had an apartment there.

What made you decide to apply for a transfer?

WILLIAM: Well, Big Flats, you know, is supposed to be an induction camp, and the camp director was putting pressure on me to go somewhere.

WILMA: You first applied for the jaundice experiment, [but] I raised Cain.

WILLIAM: So then I applied for Williamsburg and was accepted there. I was at Big Flats about a year altogether. At Williamsburg we could only have a room together if she worked at the hospital.

What was your job?

WILMA: Attendant. When I resigned, it left 15 attendants, night and day, for 1,200 patients in the women's section.

WILLIAM: The entire men's section staff consisted of conscientious objectors at Williamsburg. See, you're right next to Newport News and all the big army installations there, and everybody could get good jobs and good pay.

Tell me about work at the hospital.

WILMA: It hit me very hard, because I knew absolutely nothing about mental illness. I knew there was such a thing, that's all I knew. And I think it would have been very difficult to tell the difference between me and the patients. Our room was on the top floor, and it had been condemned as unfit for patients, bars still on the windows, wooden construction. There was a ward on the first floor, and you worked a 12-hour shift. Oh, a whole lot of dramatic things happened at that hospital.

Tell me about some of them.

WILMA: Well, the conscientious objectors who arrived before us were locked on the wards with the patients and without a key for 12-hour shifts.

WILLIAM: They would let them out to have a couple of meals.

WILMA: But the hours changed, so that instead of having a 12-hour shift, you had a break, what was it, an hour in the afternoon?

WILLIAM: The superintendent bettered the hours a little bit. First, when you went there, you worked seven to seven, or the night shift seven to seven, and every other Sunday you got a half-day off.

WILMA: But you spent that half-day off thinking what you were going to do the next day.

Incredible. It must have been almost a case of being shell-shocked when you first began to work. What kinds of things were going on?

WILMA: Well, I had tremendous guilt feelings over—well, my childhood fantasies were of St. Francis kissing the leper sores and all that kind of stuff. I hadn't made it at all. My image of myself working with the mentally ill—I would calm their raging spirits—didn't do anything but make mine raging. And so I had tremendous feeling of guilt about that. Later I applied to the government employment agency, and they sent me out as a case worker to Norris-town State Hospital, and I worked there for close to 20 years expiating my guilt.

Do you feel that the level of patient care improved significantly at Williamsburg because of CPS participation?

WILMA: There's no doubt about that, the attitude of the conscientious objector was so different.

How long did you work at Williamsburg?

WILMA: Three months. I had a job waiting for me with the Department of Public Welfare in Newport News, if I could find a place outside of the hospital to live.

Were you successful?

WILMA: That was one nightmare because of all of the big army installations with all of the wives there too, and there was prejudice against conscientious objectors in Williamsburg, and there were no rooms. And when I finally did find a room, I stayed on at the hospital for a couple of weeks because the woman who was supposed to come back on the ward, her husband was going overseas and she wanted two weeks off to be with him. All right, I thought, I stuck it out this long, I can take two more weeks of it. I think I was in a haze. By that time, I was working on a tuberculosis ward all by myself.

WILLIAM: I remember you used to go over and see the doctor, and he gave you pep pills to be able to stay on the wards and tranquilizers to go to sleep afterwards.

And what were you paid, do you recall?

WILMA: I don't know, but I was paid more than he was.

WILLIAM: She was getting the going wage, which was then very, very low.

WILMA: Fifty-eight dollars [per month], or something like that. Anyway, when I finally did find a room and moved out, it was in a house that this woman rented, and I had to room with her. I was kicked out of there when the landlord found out she'd rented a room to the wife of a conscientious objector. I lost my room, and I was out of the hospital, and I remember one total nightmarish day when it was very hot, going from house to house ringing doorbells saying, "Do you have anyplace where I could stay and live? You know, anyplace, maybe just a cot in the cellar." Towards the end of the afternoon, I hit a house that belonged to a Professor Phelan of William and Mary College. He opened the door and started to say no, and his wife came to see who was there. She said, "You look dreadful, you poor thing, what's the matter? Come and sit down." So they got me a little glass of wine, and I sat down. It was a room with books in it and comfortable chairs, so I burst into tears. So they said, "We're going away on vacation tomorrow, and we have a dog. Will you take care of the dog? You can have our house."

And then their next-door neighbor was Dina Willing of William and Mary College, and she was there to be sure I didn't do anything I shouldn't. And she came after church one day and said, "I used to be a conscientious objector in the First World War, and I got thinking about you, and I thought 'Well, I'm going away,' and you can have my house." And so I moved to her house, but she was a little short thing, and I'm not, and she had her house furnished to scale. There was hardly anything to sleep in, or sit in, or anything else, it was all built to her scale. I finally found an old guest house, and we moved in there, and it got to be known as "AWOL Camp," because we were the hangout for whatever. And I had a job near Newport News....

What were some of the psychological effects, either for you or for people you knew, of working in a mental hospital?

WILMA: A good many of the CO wives simply couldn't take it. I would say that even though I did take it, I couldn't.

WILLIAM: Those who couldn't take it went home to stay with their families. . . .

What was the most difficult aspect for you, Wilma?

WILMA: Working at the state hospital at Williamsburg with so little preparation and very little support, because most of the wives were having an even worse time or had cleared out. I stayed even though I couldn't take it. I don't know why I always have to prove that I can take something when I can't. I get a headache for that reason.

Did you see changes in Wilma, particularly during the Williamsburg period?

WILLIAM: Oh, she went through a terrible time really. I would say that Wilma is always a person who rises up in a crisis and resolves it. That's right, when things get tough, why, you're really right there.

What was the most satisfying aspect of CPS for both of you?

WILLIAM: Well, I think detached service in Puerto Rico, because I got back into my professional career right away, and in the same line that I had been doing before, which was where the new things were happening. And when Rex Tugwell went to the University of Chicago to found a planning school, I went up there to teach and get my Ph.D.

What was the most satisfying aspect for you, Wilma?

WILMA: I think a sense of community, particularly in Elmira, but it went straight through, to a degree. I think there would have been more of a sense of community in Williamsburg if more of the wives had stayed.

WILLIAM: I'd say that CPS was a great experience, and I wouldn't have missed it for anything.

WILMA: Well, also it led to my finally becoming a psychiatric social worker, which I found very satisfying.

So it changed your life in that respect. Looking back now, do you have any doubts about your decision to enter CPS?

WILLIAM: No, not about the decision. I think this came from Evan Thomas [peace leader and brother of Norman Thomas] some years ago, that if you become a conscientious objector because you think it may change things, you are then being practical. You can't be a conscientious objector and think you are going to change views necessarily; you are a conscientious objector because you can't do anything else. And look, pacifism's got no answer to the war situation or the war system, or the military-industrial government and now university complexes, because the top people in the universities are the people who are always going off to Washington to consult, and there is federal money coming into the universities.

WILMA: In other words, he used to believe that someday they'd give a war and nobody would come. If we didn't go, we'd be starting a trend. Oh, I think in a sense we sort of did, we stopped a war, the Vietnamese war, and even my son, who I think was going through a delayed adolescent rebellion.

He was a paratrooper in Vietnam?

Yes. I remember he went to Drew University, dropped out, and said he was going to sit around here and wait until they drafted him. He said, "If I do go into the military, I know perfectly well I can never walk in this house again," and I said, "What nonsense, of course you can." Well, he went through the whole damn thing and came out with views about the same as ours, I'd say.

"PLEASE COME BACK TO ME SOON"
LETTERS FROM THE HOME FRONT

During the war American women wrote millions of letters to husbands, sons, brothers, and uncles and nephews stationed in military bases around the country and in Europe and the Pacific theater. The U.S. government and other agencies urged the public to write letters to boost the morale of the soldiers; Americans were exhorted to write not only to their loved ones but also to soldiers they didn't know. Magazine articles, public service announcements, and other boosters for letter writing cautioned correspondents to keep their missives to the soldiers cheerful and upbeat and to refrain from conveying any news that would weaken the soldiers' morale. Government censors also provided rules for what information correspondents could not divulge, such as the name or location of factories and facilities engaged in war work, detailed information about the weather and its potentially harmful impact—for example, storms that disabled power plants or towns that were isolated by storm-related destruction—or the country where their soldier correspondents were stationed.

Despite these many rules, women still managed to write long, newsy, and very poignant letters to their men in the military. Their letters speak of the pride as well as the frustrations and anxieties of running a home in their husbands' absences, the pleasures and challenges of their own wartime employment, and especially their profound love and concern for their beloved ones away at war. And women never stopped writing. By 1943, only two years after the United States formally entered the war, twenty million pieces of mail, including newspapers and packages (which had to adhere to size and weight standards) were being sent overseas. Reported Time magazine: "Mail is so important to troops that a shipment is included on every ship and available plane leaving the U.S."†*

Following is a sample of letters that reflect the range of American women's wartime concerns.

SOURCE: Judy Barrett Litoff and David Smith, eds., *Since You Went Away: World War II Letters from American Women on the Homefront* (New York: Oxford University Press, 1991). Used by permission of Oxford University Press, Inc.

---

* Doris Weatherford, American Women and World War II (New York: Facts on File, 1990), p. 281.

† "Mail Call," Time June 7, 1943, p. 61.

Natalie Mirenda, a second-generation Italian American from New York City, and Frank Maddalena, were married on June 23, 1940. They had two children: a son, Frankie Jr., born in December 1941, in the same month that the Japanese attacked Pearl Harbor, and a daughter, Maria, born a year later. In February 1944, twenty-nine-year-old Frank was drafted. After spending six months in basic training in Florida, he was sent overseas and was killed in battle on November 22, 1944. Natalie Maddalena's letters to her husband express the challenges of being a single parent and of struggling to budget the family's expenses on Frank's wartime pay. After Frank was sent to Europe, her letters speak of her aching longing for him and her growing self-doubt and pessimism. She wrote the last letter included here only days before he was killed in battle.

New York, April 16, 1944

My darling,

This is another Sunday gone by without you. The day has been so long and it rained until late this afternoon. . . .

Honey, from the way things look, I don't think that there can be a very quick finish to this awful war (I hope I'm wrong) cause even if it lasts another week that week will be an eternity just as long as we're not together.

I'll close now as I want to go to bed. Good night, darling and pleasant dreams. I love you.

    Always, Natalie

New York, May 8, 1944

Dearest,

. . . So you hit the jackpot. This crazy mail. . . . I know it's hard to appreciate three letters in one day as going without mail so long must be heartbreaking. And especially since you had such a lousy week too. . . .

Frankie is really a rascal and there are times when I'd like to wring his neck. Like today, I had him in the park and he climbed all over the benches, jumped up and down and yelled like Tarzan, and I'm all worn out from keeping after him. Maria's not so bad as I wouldn't mind anyway because she's such a little doll. . . .

This morning I said, "Frankie, be quiet. I'm reading Daddy's letter." He stuck his little nose under mine and said, "Daddy come home now, finish work." But with such feeling. He's so anxious for you. I persuaded him that you couldn't come yet so he said, "O.K., mommy," just like a little man. . . .

I guess I'll get those pictures this week from you. . . . So darling, till you're all mine forever and a day.

I'll always love you, Natalie

New York, July 27, 1944

Dearest One,

Today I got your letter of Monday. The children just got up from their naps, but I couldn't take them out as we are having a thunderstorm, but good. The heavens just opened and forgot to close. At first baby was frightened, but she saw Frankie imitate and laugh at the thunder and she changed her tears to laughter.

I'm glad you enjoyed my two letters. You asked if I got along on the money that I get. Well the truth of the matter is that I've started to use our savings. I've already had to take $100. Up until now, I had so much in the house that you bought before you went away, plus what you left and you've sent home, I was able to manage for awhile. But now I have to go to the bankroll. When that's gone, well, we won't eat, that's all. . . .

Both the children are on the floor and raising a racket. The call of the wild, I call it. . . .

Gee, honey, if you could only hold me forever, your happiness would be shared by me. I miss you and love you so very much.

I'll close now with a million kisses just for you.

Always, Mommy

P.S. How's the heat? Still bothering you?

After Frank was sent to Europe, Natalie's letters took on a new sense of urgency.

New York, Oct. 11, 1944

My dearest one,

What can you be thinking now? I mean my not writing so often. It's just that I'm so disgusted with this life that I'm beginning to lose courage and faith.

Ten years ago, I was such a happy carefree person, daring and so full of the joy of living. And yet today, I'm so burdened with responsibilities that I fear my shoulders can't carry them all. I could and would want to if I had you here with me to help me.

The kids are fine and today I took Frankie with me and put a deposit on a coat for him. It's a very nice one, brown background with a salt and pepper tweed. He really looks adorable in it. . . .

I'll close for now, and I'll love you always.

Natalie

New York, Oct. 17, 1944

My darling,

Today I got your letter of the 9th in which you said you had missed writing for a few days. . . . Oh God, I think I'll go nuts. I see you everywhere—in the chair, behind me, in the shadows of the rooms. Everyplace I go you are always with me and in the back of my mind. I seem to have a continuous headache because I'm so worried about you. It doesn't look like this war is coming to an end. I've stopped listening to the radio and reading the papers as I only eat my heart out knowing that it will keep you away from me all the more. I see that a 1st Army infantry censor is reading the mail. I hope that I'm not jumping to conclusions but I guess that means you'll be with the 1st Army.

Frankie is fine and tonight asked Pop where you were. He's a lot like you and tries not to show how he feels. That must be the reason he hasn't been asking for you very much. Maria is cutting more teeth and is a little cranky and has lost her appetite for awhile. It's always something!!

I love you my dear, so very much and I just can't see life for me with anyone else but you.

Always, Natalie

New York, Nov. 19, 1944

Dearest One,

Today was endless as I've had no mail from you since Monday. Frank, my dearest, what is happening to us? We were going to grow old together. Enjoy and raise our children. The thought that you may be at this very moment fighting is maddening. I suppose that you are with the 1st Army as most of the letters have been censored by a 1st Army censor. I read in the papers that there is a lot of snow and sleet in northern France. Oh, Frank, take care of yourself. You know you catch cold easily. Take care of yourself also as we need you home so much. . . .

Mom had a letter from my uncle in Rome. He says that the Italian people are all sick from hunger and also that they are in rags. He wanted to know if we had anyone in Italy. I wish I might have told him that you were there. Then I'd be sure that you'd be safe for awhile. . . .

I love you my dear and pray that God keeps you well and safe.

Always, Natalie

Catherine De Mers, who lived in rural South Dakota during World War II, wrote regularly to her stepson, Donald De Mers, an army corporal stationed in the South Pacific. Her letters were chatty and were filled with news from home, such as the crops she and Donald's father were planting and the improvements they were making to the house, And, as this letter shows, she expresses her abiding love and concern for her stepson.

Elk Point, Nov. [?], 1941

Dear Don:

Am so sorry to hear that you're leaving this good old U.S.A. I've been thinking of you so much I forget what I'm doing. I'd give my life to keep you from going if it could be arranged, because I lived thru the other war and I really know what it's all about. I only hope that you won't have to really get into it—just patrolling will be very tame wherever you go. I hope this letter isn't censored because where ever you are, I want you to let us know in code whether things are too bad by saying, "Well, Mom" for poor food or not enough to eat and "Well, Pop" for poor conditions. Now please don't forget this, cause I really want to know and I'll have prayers said for you.

Did you get your candy o.k.? If I thought I would have time I would send you some other stuff, but I'm afraid it would arrive too late. If you can sneak a letter to us out of camp so we'll know where you're going, do so, because we are really worried about you. . . .

This is all for now. God Bless you, Don, and be careful where ever you go and do not pick up diseases because if you go to a warm climate—disease is much worse and I know you've been a model son whether you're my blood or not and I want you always to remain that way. Your self respect means more to me than you'll ever know. Oceans of love and good luck.

Mother

Sonoko Iwata's letters expressed another form of separation that occurred between husbands and wives during the war: the forced relocation of 120,000 Japanese Americans from their communities along the West Coast to camps situated in isolated areas of the United States. (See also the selection by Uchiko Yoshida on pp. 47–51.) Sonoko Iwata and her husband, Shigezo, who was born in Japan, had been married five years when the FBI classified Shigezo as an "enemy alien"—though he was married to a native-born American citizen—and removed him from the family's home in Thermal, California, to a camp in New Mexico. His wife and three young children remained in Thermal until they, too, were relocated to a camp near Poston, Arizona. Sonoko's letters to her husband provide a graphic account of the impact of his absence upon her and their children, the anxiety and uncertainty preceding their own removal, and the wretched conditions of the camp to which they were removed. The letters are all the more remarkable for the scrutiny they underwent by government censors. Many were stamped with these words from a War Department censor stamp: "Detained Alien, Enemy Mail, Examined."

Thermal, May 4, 1942

Dear Shigezo san:

In the papers, they say that all Japanese in the military zones will be evacuated by May 20. So, even if we should be among the last group, we have less than three weeks to go. It makes us all feel so rushed. . . .

This house where we live right now will be entrusted to Mr. Pfost to be rented to someone. I will take an inventory of the things we leave here like the office furniture, refrigerator, range, and chairs and tables and the like and a copy of it and important association papers will be placed in a safe deposit box which Bob will rent. Whatever could be sold, we'll try to sell. At first, the empty building next to us was going to be used as warehouse, but the Federal Reserve Bank owns a garage in Coachilla [California] and it is said, whatever one needs to store, can be stored there. . . .

Yours, Sonoko

Poston, May 28, 1942

Dear Shigezo san:

It's been almost ten days since we've come here and thanks to the efforts of those responsible, many improvements have been brought about, making it much easier for us to adjust ourselves to our new surroundings.

There are three separate settlements which are three miles apart and capable of housing 20,000 people. We are in the northern settlement which has facilities for 10,000. I don't know how many blocks there are here but I know there are more than fifty and each block has a little over 200 residents. We from Indio and Thermal and Palm Springs are more or less grouped together here in Block 42. In every block there is a Dining Hall, Recreation Hall, Block Office, Laundry, and Men and Women's restrooms. So, you see, each block is like one community and it's up to those of us who comprise the community to make it better, through cooperative efforts.

First two days when our block kitchen was not yet ready to serve food, we went over to our neighboring block which is across a wide field. We had to stand in line under the hot sun and when inside we had to again stand in line with our plates and cutlery. Honestly, it made me think of what might be in a cheap restaurant. It was like survival of the fittest, too, as small babies and grown ups had the same chance. On top of all that, there would be just sauerkraut and wienies and rice. Miki couldn't very well eat them and then I couldn't be sure that I could get milk. So, things were pretty awful for a few days. Now that our own block kitchen is working, conditions are much better. There isn't much standing in line and the atmosphere is more like that of a dormitory and more often than not, we have good food. . . .

Love, Sonoko

Poston, June 28, 1942

Dear Shigezo san:

Today being Sunday, there's something in the air that is quiet and peaceful...
I've just given Miki her bath, Masahiro and Misao are playing outside

with Dickie Yano and Jackie Kitagawa; some of the young people are play-ing cards and many of the mothers are resting outside in the shade.

In my first letter to you from this place, I remember telling you that this place was barren and without any trees but upon closer inspection we did find a few along the stream that runs just outside of our block, and those few trees certainly look beautiful. The stream, or perhaps it's large enough to be called a river, runs so slowly and is so muddy that you could hardly tell it is flowing. Even though small, it's deep and the banks are steep so that we mothers with young children have to be careful. No one has fallen in yet. . . .

The heat is quite intense but now that June is almost all over, we'll have only two more months to endure. The other day in the house the thermome-ter registered 114 degrees and was in the neighborhood of 110 degrees for sev-eral days, but now it is a little better. No one in the block has been any worse for it. It was actually cold this morning and we all had to have sweaters or jack-ets for breakfast. Personally, I think the sudden cold after the heat will hit us hard, and we will have to be prepared with plenty of warm clothing.

Today, our neighbors gave us some melons which were brought in from the valley. It certainly was a treat. Like others, I'm saving the seeds for future use. . . .

You wrote interment camp on your letter. I think interment has to do with death and burial. You have your dictionary with you, haven't you?

Until tomorrow,

Yours with much love, Sonoko

Poston, March 5, 1943

Dear Shigezo san:

There is a bowl of fresh wild flowers in our room today. Children and I went across the little stream to the empty field for a walk and found these yellow daisy-like flowers growing in a strip near the water. Their leaves are dainty—like cosmos leaves.

You know, I was thinking today that time marches on and if I'm to keep up, we should bury the past and always look toward what's coming.

Our photograph albums were all confiscated and since I had taken the trouble to mount almost all of the pictures, there's not a single family pic-ture left—except for our wedding picture. . . . I wrote to the F.B.I. asking for the albums and other things like my notebook with defense Savings Stamp Book and Baby Account Book, but they said they didn't take the things into their possession. I felt so bad about it and wanted to ask just who could tell me where the confiscated things are, but upon second thought decide that perhaps such a sentiment is something of the past that I should bury. Then again, I think that perhaps if I persist I could locate those things valuable only to you and me.

By new military order, Poston has become part of free zone. Even if we were free to go out from this camp, the nearest town is Parker, about 19 miles away, and even that is about like the town of Coachilla.

Many are willing to relocate themselves outside but are without means. This will be given consideration, it is hoped.

Love, Sonoko

During World War II, General Douglas MacArthur was commanding officer of American forces in the Pacific. When he arrived in Australia in March 1942, he set up a special unit in his headquarters to respond to the thousands of letters that he received. Among these were scores of letters from friends and relatives of United States military personnel who were missing in action, had been taken prisoner, or were otherwise unable to communicate with their families and friends. MacArthur and his staff answered the letters with empathy and with as much information as they could provide. The following letter by Doris Castelli of New York City is one such heart-wrenching example of the desperate search for information about the fate of a loved one.

Bronx, New York, Early Summer, 1944

Dear General MacArthur:

I am a mother left alone with a broken heart. My son Angelo Castelli fell in action with your troops at Hollandia on April 23. I was not notified of his death by the government. Oh! General MacArthur, doesn't a mother count at all? He was married Dec. 23, 1943 and I did not know it. His wife had him as a married man for 24 hours. He was called back to serve on Dec. 25 Christmas Day and that was the last I saw of him. His wife notified me bluntly over the telephone. His allotment to me stopped in Jan. I did not think it strange because sometimes those things happen. Please General he was a good boy, wasn't he? Did he die a hard death General? Oh! Please won't you drop me a line and tell me if he suffered long or not. My mind is so uneasy. I want just a few words of my boy General if in kindness you will do this for me. General MacArthur was his idol. May the grace of God be with you in your every step.

Sincerely, (Mrs.) Doris Castelli

Marjorie Gaunt and her husband, Rowland, who grew up together in the same neighborhood in Cranston, Rhode Island, had been married only three months when Lieutenant Gaunt, a pilot, was sent to England in November 1943. Three months later he was killed while flying a mission over the North Sea off the coast of Denmark. Marjorie received a telegram from the War Department in early March disclosing that her husband was missing in action. Clinging to the slender hope that he was still alive, she wrote numerous letters to the War Department, the American Red Cross, and even the Danish Underground in hopes of learning his whereabouts. Not until October 1945 did the War Department officially notify her that he had been declared dead. Meanwhile, on November 8, 1944, she wrote this long, loving letter to him in tribute as she slowly come to the painful realization that he would not be returning to her.

Cranston, Nov. 8, 1944

My dear husband:

No couple ever had a harder start in marriage than we did, darling, and yet no couple ever had a more beautiful start. I love you so desperately and I've longed for you so these many months that you have been lost in the wide, wide, world. I know in my heart that you are safe and that God is caring for you, but it has been so very hard to live with this terrible uncertainty.

I'm so proud of you. To me you are everything fine and clean and beautiful in the world, and without you everything fine and clean and beautiful seems to have vanished. I keep thinking about the injustice in the world. You, who are so good and kind, you, the kind of person the world needs, why must it be you who has to suffer, when so many, many boys who do not seem to amount to anything, live on for themselves alone.

Wherever you are, I know you must feel my love for you. My love has grown stronger each day and it is just bursting for expression. I've told you many times how much I love you, and I am so thankful for that now. I'm thankful too, because I feel that we did share a beautiful love; it was so beautiful perhaps that is why the memory of it aches in my heart. I have felt that our short time together as man and wife was perfection in every way. I think you feel as I do, and I'm so glad because the promise of it must sustain you wherever you are. Please, darling, think on those things, keep your eyes uplifted and trust in God. I've prayed continually for His protection over you and His guidance during these long trying months. I pray for Him to give you patience and to bless you and make you strong. Oh, that I might bear it for you. I would gladly die that you might come back to those that love you and live gloriously to serve humanity and God. It is so very hard to understand. My mind is constantly in turmoil—why, why, why, going round and round and round. People say I'm brave and a brick, and all sorts of things, but I'm not. I'm hating and fighting every moment that you are lost. I do go on working and reading and talking, but honestly I don't know how or why I do it. The way I feel, time stopped for me last March when that hateful telegram arrived. I just can't believe it is November and almost a year since last I saw you. Oh, sorrowful year, that took away my love and cast him on the mercy of unseeing men. Darling, I know what you are going through is hell, just as I am in hell, but darling if only we can have the faith and strength to endure it, paradise must be on the other side. I love you so. . . .

We are not truly separated from one another, for spiritually we are very close, but how my heart aches for the physical things—just the touch of your hand, the rough fabric of your coat, and the smoothness of your clean white shirt, but those are minor things compared to how I long for your arms and your lips and your blessed eyes. Oh, darling, please come back to me soon and may God keep you much as you were when you left. Please, dear, don't grow bitter and cynical. God help you keep that joyous youth, that vibrant energy, that clean mind and courageous spirit that you bore when you left. May God bring you proudly back to my arms, and soon, please God.

Be strong, my darling. May God give you courage, patience and strength that will carry you triumphantly through your ordeals to lasting peace, gentleness and love.

Here is my hand and my love, darling. Hold to it tightly as I will yours and surely ours will be a glorious victory.

I love you, Marge

During World War II, American women not only worked in industry and other traditionally male fields, they also joined the armed forces. Over three hundred and fifty thousand women served with the Women's Army Corps (WAC), the Women's Reserves of the Navy (WAVE), the Marine Corps Women's Reserves (MCWR), the Coast Guard Women's Reserves (SPAR), the Army Nurse Corps (ANC), and the Navy Nurse Corps (NNC). Married women could join the WACs, but women with children under fourteen were excluded. Similarly, the WAVEs and MCWR turned away women with children under eighteen, and black women were excluded from the WAVES until October 1944.[*]*

Most military women served in traditionally female jobs as hospital nurses— though some performed their duties right on the battlefield during combat—and as typists, clerks, switchboard operators, and administrators. Black women were usually segregated to all-black units and were assigned to even less skilled work.

Women aviators managed to defy sex-role norms by flying transport missions. In 1939 air force officials refused to allow women to fly noncombatant missions, but by 1943 the need for more pilots to free men up for combat duty prompted military officials to recruit women, and the Woman Airforce Service Pilots (WASP) was born. The WASPs logged over 60 million miles ferrying planes throughout the United States and Canada. They piloted transport planes, B-29 bombers, and fighter craft. They flew simulated strafing tests and radar-jamming and search-light-tracking missions, and towed targets while gunners in training practiced fir-ing live bullets at the targets.

In the following interview, Jacqueline Cochran, director of the WASP, describes how female pilots were willing to test planes that male pilots considered too dan-gerous to fly.

SOURCE: Reminiscences of Jacqueline Cochran, on pages 34–44 in the Columbia University Oral History Research Office Collection.

Q: During the Second World War you did a great deal to get women pilots used properly, to get them recognized?

COCHRAN: Actually, I got called to General Arnold's office late in 1940 and

---

[*] Nancy Cott, ed. No Small Courage (New York: Oxford University Press, 2000), p. 476.

found Air Marshal Harris, Chief of the British Mission, there. Arnold said they needed pilots desperately for ferrying airplanes to England and other places and asked me if I could be of any help. I said I would be happy to volunteer and fly some of them over for them if they wanted me to and my services were immediately accepted.

I got to Canada and found there a large group of American men. Many of them were fine pilots but many of them were what I call riff-raff, getting enormous amounts of money tax free for this particular job. Some of them threatened to quit if they let "that woman fly" but I said: "Let them bluff— they won't quit." And of course they didn't. It was a difficult task, dangerous and with a high mortality rate. Planes and pilots just disappeared en route. You never heard of them again.

Q: You got shot at on the trip?

COCHRAN: Yes, I got shot at over the North Atlantic. Others did too. You couldn't see out. It was overcast and you couldn't tell whether the shots came from our forces or from the enemy. Apparently they were just trigger happy.

In England, they asked me if I could recruit a group of American women. If they could fly as well as they thought I could, they wanted them. I came back then and recruited forty women. Fifteen of the forty were turned down in Canada for lack of efficiency. All twenty-five filled their contracts and some stayed until the war was over. Only one of the twenty-five girls was killed. They were all used in ferrying work. I ferried for eleven months.

We landed planes like the Hurricane and the Spitfire in fields where today I wouldn't put my Lodestar if I could avoid it. When planes were damaged in combat the boys often put them down on the first field. We would then take the damaged aircraft and fly to a depot. Again—when a mission was being organized, Ferry Pilots would assemble the planes. We would fly perhaps five different types in a single day, to a certain field. After the planes were returned to the field, when the mission was over, we would disperse them and put them on satellite fields—two or three planes to a field.

In September 1942 Cochran secured General Arnold's permission to train women pilots as part of the U.S. Army Air Force.

COCHRAN: We started out our first training program. The girls proved to be simply remarkable. There were only two disciplinary cases out of two thousand girls. When the time came and they were ready to be part of the Air

Force, I went to see General Arnold and said: "The girls are ready to do you proud and the country proud as a part of your Air Force. I have only one complaint, however—the attrition is rather high through marriage; seems that maybe it is part of the wartime hysteria of people getting married."

I got a call one day to come into General Arnold's office. I was down in Fort Worth. I stayed down there for about nine months in the early period to be close to the Training Command program. So I came up from Texas to see him.

He said, "What do you know about the B-26?"

I said, "I don't know a thing except scuttlebut—that it won't substitute for an airplane. The wings are too small, etc."

Arnold said, "I want you to go out and fly it and tell me what you think about it."

I said, "I can cure your men of walking off the program." They were, you know, and they were saying that they couldn't fly the plane. They were willing to be killed in a war but they wouldn't fly this plane.

Arnold asked me how and I said, "Just put some girl pilots on."

Arnold said, "But what if you kill some of them?"

And I said, "Suppose I do—there is no difference if a woman is killed or a man if the program has to go forward—and this one has to go forward!"

Anyway, I went out and flew the plane and didn't see anything so difficult about it. I knew if you lost an engine on the takeoff, chances were you weren't going to get away with it. Then it was like flying a single engine plane and you had to accept the fact that it was not two motored. If you had a pretty short field to get into, it was pretty hard to do it—you had to accept that it had a high landing speed and keep to a field that could accommodate it.

I went out and flew [the B-26] and came back and said that there was nothing wrong with it. "They are a bunch of sissies. I am really mad about it. Let's put on the girls."

We subsequently had 150 girls flying the B-26. I mean the A model—the difficult ones for the most part, because they did finally enlarge the wing area to give better landing characteristics. The girls were towing targets while live bullets were being shot at the targets from B-24s. They did seventy thousand operational hours of this tow work [and] there was only one minor accident and not a single fatality.

They also did radio control work which was under [security "wraps"]. One girl would fly the airplane and another girl would sit beside her and, by remote control, fly another without anybody in it. She would control the other airplane over the target line where men on the ground with A/C guns would shoot the plane down. It was an exceedingly difficult operation and hazardous, but we never had a fatality on that. We did have seven girls killed by sabotage.

The girls ferried, of course, but did no overseas work at all. I was the only woman to ferry any airplane of any nationality over the ocean during the war . . . another first!

During the Depression and World War II, First Lady Eleanor Roosevelt played an important role in helping to shape legislation and other government policies that benefited African Americans, women, and the poor and unemployed. Her travels around the country on behalf of FDR, who was crippled from polio and unable to travel easily, and her radio appearances and press conferences—to which she invited only female journalists—brought her unparalleled public attention and influence. She used her position as first lady to draw attention to social ills and to marshall support for programs and legislation to combat these problems.

Yet another way that Roosevelt reached out to Americans was through her syndicated newspaper column, "My Day." From 1936 to 1945 Roosevelt wrote a regular column in which she chatted with the American people as if she were talking to a friend. In fact, the column was an outgrowth of letters she wrote to Lorena Hickock, a reporter and dear friend, describing her daily activities. Hickock urged Roosevelt to transform the letters into a column, and United Feature Syndicate agreed to run the column in newspapers around the country. After spending three weeks writing practice columns, Roosevelt sent off her first column for syndication on December 30, 1935. From then on, she wrote a five-hundred-word column six days a week, stopping only for four days when her husband died on April 12, 1945. She wrote the column late at night, during mealtimes, or on her travels, and often knitted while dictating her words to an assistant. She dealt with everything from homey personal anecdotes to pressing world events and, during the twin national crises of depression and world war, urged Americans to remain calm and hopeful and do their share to help the nation. Many columns focused specifically on women's contributions and strengths. Roosevelt championed female equality and eventually supported the Equal Rights Amendment (ERA). In the following four "My Day" columns, she urges readers to recognize American women's wartime accomplishments and advocates more military responsibilities for them, greater participation in postwar peace preparations, and more equatable treatment in securing civil service positions.

SOURCE: Rochelle Chadakoff, ed., *Eleanor Roosevelt's "My Day": Her Acclaimed Column, 1936–1945* (New York: Pharos, 1989), pp. 270–75, 311–12, 381–82.

Washington, December 10, 1942—I have just received from the Prime Minister of the Republic of Poland, who is visiting in this country, a message transmitted from a secret radio station in Poland: "We send you in the name of the Polish women sincere thanks for the imposing protest which you organized on the 30th of July against the German atrocities on the Polish women. We are enduring awful times here in Poland. We still deplore the loss of our dead in September 1939 and already the shadow of thousands tormented to death in concentration camps in Ravensbruck, and other places hover around us.

"But beyond the pain that stabs us, beyond the despair and longing after the dead, we are dominated by the consciousness that the struggle which we are carrying on will decide the existence of freedom, and no one can remain out of it. We Polish women have, therefore, all joined the ranks of subterranean struggling Poland, and together with our husbands, fathers, brothers and sons we will fight to the end with them. We are prepared either to win or perish. God grant that the sacrifices are the smallest and the sufferings of assaulted nations be reduced to naught."

What courage there is in a message of this kind! Listening to the messages sent from here last July would have cost anyone discovered his life. Sending the reply to London was most dangerous and ten efforts were made before it was finally transmitted. These women, who are keeping alive their faith in freedom in spite of such daily horrors as we can hardly conceive of here, are going to have a right to representation when the machinery for peace is built in the future. I am sure that Russian, Chinese and British women have earned and will demand that same right.

In the last peace conference women had no such voice. In the coming one, women will have a right to a voice and they should be sure to prepare in advance so that their influence will be of the greatest value. Women are idealists and I think they had better study these questions and come to their own conclusions. If they do, I am sure they will find that only cooperation and world understanding and concern for each other is going to keep peace through the years. I hope the women of the United States will awaken to the full sense of the influence which they can wield if they accept the responsibility which all power implies.

Washington, January 2, 1943—Last night we gathered at midnight in the President's study and drank the usual toasts. The first one was to the United States, then we added one to the United Nations before we drank our customary toast to absent members of our family and friends.

I think that the second toast is a very significant one, because it means that we really are conscious of this bond between the United Nations. To us it is a permanent bond, one that must keep us together in war and in peace and gradually extend so that it eventually draws all the nations into a circle of friendship.

At the beginning of this new year, I want to say one word to the women of the country, with whom I feel a very special bond. We have the same anxieties and the same sense of frustration very often, because we feel we cannot do enough in the great war effort. I have a very great pride in the spirit of the women of this country.

Wherever they are needed, they always meet the full demands made on them, whether these requirements are in the home, in the factory or in any other field of endeavor. None of us can ever be satisfied with ourselves, but we can be proud of the aggregate training which the women of the country are making. I feel that this contribution is growing day by day and will be recognized more fully as this year develops.

Washington, October 15, 1943—The film which we saw last night was the story of the British Women's Military Auxiliary Services, and it was one of the most thrilling stories I have seen on the screen.

By and large, I am not sure the men of the United States are encouraging their wives and daughters to go into our auxiliary military services. I am not even sure our women are convinced they are needed in these services. They may wonder whether they really would free a man to do a job which they cannot do.

I realize, of course, that our WACs, WAVEs, Marines and Spars are not being trained for as great a variety of activities as the British women are. That makes the service less interesting. In addition, they probably resent the restrictions put upon them as to the places where they are to be allowed to work.

If I were young enough, I would rather be a nurse in the Army or Navy, for they are allowed to share more nearly the men's existence. They know that there will be no attitude on the part of the boys which says "Oh yes, you have come in to wear a uniform, but you don't really mean ever to do a job which will inconvenience you or change the ease we men are expected to provide for our women."

Life in the armed services is hard and uncomfortable, but I think women can stand up under that type of living just as well as men. It made me unhappy last night to see what the British women are doing and then to remember certain speeches I have read by gentlemen who oppose women's full participation in the auxiliary military services, when there is so much they could do.

Why should British, Australian and New Zealand women render services to and with our men and we be barred?

Washington, February 23, 1945—Every now and then I am reminded that even though the need for being a feminist is gradually disappearing in this country, we haven't quite reached the millennium.

A woman who went down to testify before one of the Congressional committees the other day wrote me an interesting fact on the manpower situation. It appears that the Civil Service Commission has a number of women who could be filling higher positions in the government if the requisitions from government agencies did not usually specify "men only." Perhaps this is another hurdle which we must jump in this period when women are really needed to replace men. We must accept qualified women for positions which in the past have been offered to men, even through civil service.

It looks to me also as though some special consideration should be given to women with husbands in military service, particularly to those whose husbands are missing. It is, of course, not necessary to give them any special preference—they should be capable of doing the jobs which they hold. But they need the jobs very badly, and where they could be appointed without lowering the standards of the Civil Service for those jobs, it seems they might be given some extra consideration.

It is interesting to find so often the little ways in which women are discriminated against, but with the passage of the years one does find a great improvement. One must not let this improvement, however, lull one to complete oblivion, for when the war is over there will be new situations to meet and they must be met with open minds and with fairness to both men and women.

"I LEARNED THINGS I DIDN'T EVEN KNOW
HAPPENED IN THE WORLD"
SUSAN LAUGHLIN

Susan Laughlin went to work in 1942 when her husband lost his job. She began as the lowest paid clerk on the payroll at Lockheed and, through ingenuity and empathy, carved out for herself a highly influential job as a women's counselor. Some companies were more sensitive than others to the unique needs of their new female employees; some provided on-site child-care centers or prepared meals that workers could purchase and take home. But in general, companies offered little concrete help to working mothers. However, the major defense plants did develop a comprehensive program of women counselors to help female workers adjust to their new work assignments and to provide referrals to helpful community services. Lockheed set up a counseling department to deal with the needs and concerns of both male and female employees and promoted Laughlin to the position of company counselor because of her adroit interpersonal skills. Male employees and supervisors mostly spurned her assistance, and she soon found herself focusing more on issues pertaining to women, especially as more women joined the company. From ensuring that the restrooms were adequate to helping women cope with family responsibilities or with husbands who opposed their working, Laughlin dealt with a range of issues, and a large part of her job was advocating for women workers. She even spoke before audiences hostile to working women in an effort to defuse their opposition. Laughlin faced the same opposition from her own husband and coped with many of the same kinds of problems that plagued her female employees. Her account offers many insights into the challenges confronting a major company and its female employees as both prepared for the entree of women into a previously male-dominated industry.

SOURCE: Sherna Berger Gluck, ed., *Rosie the Riveter Revisited* (Boston: Twayne) 1987, pp. 245–52. Reprinted by permission of Sherna Berger Gluck.

I WENT TO Lockheed in July of '42 as the lowest paid clerk, fifty-one cents an hour. I was placed in the medical unit. Everybody had to have a physical before they actually were hired, so I did see every-one who came, men and women. I was thirty and older than most of the people going to work, and I made up my mind I would speak to each person and let them know that I recognized them as a person. I would frequently call them by name, and I would say something personal: "Your hair is nice" or "I like your blouse." So those people kept coming back and saying, "What'll I do?" "Do you know what I should do about this?" It would be company related or it could be "Do you have any idea where I can get a baby-sitter?"

The company began to be aware that this was something that perhaps they should listen to. So they moved me around the corner into a department where the job was not quite as crucial, so I had more time to talk to these people.

There was a man by the name of Jenkins who was the personnel manager, and he talked to a number of women who apparently had been applying for this kind of a job. He called me in and talked to me at great length about what I was doing and how I felt about it. I didn't have anything in my mind at all, except just to do whatever I could. One lady, a psychologist who had written a book with her husband, came out to apply for that position. Mr. Jenkins called me in, too, and he liked my answers better than hers. I remember he stopped and said, "Do you have any children?" She said, "No." And he said, "Well, that's what I find is a problem. Many psychologists write books on children and yet they have not really experienced it."

It was right after that that he assigned me to this job. He said, "I want you to go into the factory and counsel." I did not know what I wanted to do, and the men did not want any part of me; they didn't want my help. So I decided I had to contact every supervisor: "Well, this is what I'm supposed to do. If I can help you, fine; if I can't, fine. I don't want to bug you, but I am here and if there's anything you need, you can call me."

I remember one of the men who wanted nothing to do with me, about the second week that I was on the job, called and said, "Would you please come down here?" A girl had come in in a bare midriff, and all the men were hitting themselves with hammers. Then, he realized that I could be of some help. So I talked to the girl.

They used us more when we ceased to be a threat. What we'd try to do is say to the man, "This is the problem in your department, and how do you think we should handle it?" Or "She seems to need a little more instruction." Then he would say, "Well, I'll take care of it," and he was grateful to know that it was a problem. If you let them solve it, then there wasn't much of a problem.

When I first went into the factory, they thought I was going to be a threat to their authority. When they discovered that that was the farthest thing from my mind, they felt comfortable with me. Like one man said, "You're not a woman, you're just a worker." . . .

They told me to check the restrooms in the plant and see if they were adequate. My husband kidded me. I didn't like that very much and I didn't want to do that very much. But, well, if they want them counted, I'll count them! I came back and wrote a sort of disgusted memo: "We have so many and we have so many women, and we have this and that, and we need this and this." It wasn't my nature to be that way, but I was angry. I gave it to the supervisor of that department, and about a week later it came back from Mr. Gross, the president: "Order everything she says."

Then they wanted me to do every job in production. I think they figured that if I could do it, anybody could do it. And so they tried the different weights of the rivet gun, and all the rest of it. If I could hold it and do it, then they felt comfortable putting a woman on it. Some days I would be down there on a job a full day. I would have like to have stayed longer on each job. Then I would have had a better idea of the job and how tired you got. But I knew what they were doing and what they had to cope with to do it.

In the beginning, I remember one time I was so upset I was going to quit. They were building airplanes in the open and it was pouring rain. The girls' hands would get so cold that they would have to come in the restrooms to warm them. I was so angry. I went down to Mr. Chappellet, the vice president of Lockheed. You didn't darken those executive halls very often, but Elsie Muller, his secretary, said, "Well, go right in." I wasn't quite prepared for that. But I told him that I had intended to give my resignation that day, but before I left I wanted him to know a few things.

At that time I was working for John Fowle, who really thought that all the women belonged in the kitchen. He liked me and we got along all right, but he didn't like women working. He didn't want to do one thing that would help and that just could not go on. I told Mr. Chappellet that and I told him about these women working out there. I went on and on. When I finished, he said, "Well, Susan, I hope you don't quit. I will tell you what we're doing." They had the plans and they were trying. But here were the airplanes; here were the people working on the airplanes; here was the rain coming down; here was the structure coming up.

Just as soon as they had enough women working at one of the other plants, I would go there to see if they were set up, if the facilities were adequate. I would talk to the supervisors and see how much help they needed. Then, as soon as they had enough women that they needed the help of a counselor, we would get somebody up there. Sometimes we would even work with the matrons. They would become conscious of problems through the restrooms. People would go in and maybe they would be in tears or something. The matron might ask the counselor to come to the restroom, and you'd go and talk to her or take her back to your office. Or if she was sick, you got the nurse.

I know that I had to work all three shifts occasionally. I would appear on the midnight shift and on the swing shift. We found that an awful lot of women whose husbands were gone liked that swing shift because the hours when they would most miss their husbands, they were occupied. That was very interesting to me. We recommended it finally to girls who were pretty unstrung. . . .

If a person was absent over a certain number of days, then it really looked like a problem. I remember down at Plant 7 I think it was, this one girl only would work Monday, Tuesday, and Wednesday. She would never work Thursday, Friday, and Saturday. And they couldn't figure out why. And so I went down and talked to her. I think that was before there was a counselor assigned down there. She said, "Well, I had made all the money I wanted that week." She had been used to working day work, where she got just so much and she would only work so many days. So she just did the same thing in the plant, not realizing that she had to carry a full-time job.

And some people just didn't eat well. They would just have colds all the time and would not be well. The nurse would let us know or we would get that through an attendance report. We would start to inquire why they were out. We'd ask them what they were eating. You'd find women cooking for their children and not wanting to eat. So we gave lectures on that and had people in to talk about nutrition, vitamins.

Occasionally, we would have somebody who would come in and discuss family problems. We had people ask how to handle your husband, how to handle your money. Do you put it in one account or keep your own? Those kind of questions. Not so much because a problem existed, but more planning so that a problem would not occur. I had a built-in answer, because I had it myself. As with many of the problems, they were my problems. That's why I could empathize with them. When you say, "This is what I tried to do," people will listen to you.

I WAS THERE when the first Negro was hired at Lockheed. We didn't know what to expect. And we got it! A lot of people objected. And I said, "Well, that person has had the same physical examination that you had and he has a right to the same restroom." Some of the workers were requesting that they be assigned to a different restroom. I said, "No way, why should they be?"

One of the counselors suggested that we speak to Negroes and whites separately, explaining how to get along with each other and what the function of the counselor was. My feeling was that this talk should be given to all the groups of workers, not separating blacks and whites. It wasn't necessary. The only concern that I had was at first when the Negroes came in because we had to assimilate them. But going down there, after that, I don't recall a problem. We just didn't accept a problem. And once you met it immediately without any problem, they pretty well accepted it, like when the women came in.

I LEARNED THINGS I didn't even know happened in the world. Like one time I had to go into a restroom. The FBI had word of a certain woman who was recruiting for the camps, for the girls to go up and sleep with the men. I had to catch her at it. And I did. And I had to catch a couple of lesbians that were at work, and things I didn't even know about, really. And then another time, the FBI came in and they wanted me to talk to this girl who had married, I think, ten men and was just collecting their allotment checks. You name it, I did it. . . .

There were abortions, there was just everything—you name it. And they came to us because they thought we wouldn't discuss it, and we tried to keep that trust pretty sacred. I had a woman call me, if you would believe it, about ten years ago. That's thirty years after. She said, "Are you the Susan Laughlin that used to work at Lockheed?" And I said, "Yes." And she said, "Well, I found this name in the book, and I just wanted to thank you for what you had done for me."

She told me this big long tale. The Christmas party was a big thing then in many offices. She had gone to the party, had gotten drunk, and had become pregnant—didn't know who did it. We referred her to some medical people. We were never allowed to give a single referral, but we could give several and then whatever they selected was their problem. That woman got an abortion—and it was before you did that. I think it saved her marriage and she was thanking me for that. She was so grateful that there was somebody.

But, you know, this kind of counseling is the kind you go to a hairdresser and you crab all your problems, because you know they don't know anybody that you know and it doesn't matter. It was just somebody to talk to, and then if they needed any help, you could give it to them. It's something that everybody needs, and always has, and always has found somewhere. But this was in an accelerated period—offering it right where it was needed.

All we dealt with was the problem. We didn't attempt to analyze it, find out why it happened. All we wanted was that worker on the job. Whatever it took to keep them there, we were going to do. And we did. There's no question about it, it was a necessary and an effective program. We said at the end of the war that in five years we probably learned and did and progressed what normally would take at least twenty years to do. . . .

"THE WAR MARKED ME"
BETTY BASYE HUTCHINSON

Betty Basye Hutchinson grew up in Oroville, California, about eighty miles above Sacramento. She was a freshman at Fresno State College when the Japanese attacked Pearl Harbor. Like so many other American women, she felt impelled to "help our boys" and decided to become a nurse. Because of the large number of regular nurses who left their civilian posts to join the military, her training period was shortened and she assumed nursing duties sooner than she would have during peace time. Her account of working on an orthopedic ward among severely wounded and disfigured soldiers is riveting, and she discloses yet another ugly facet of war—the prejudice against the wounded and disabled.

SOURCE: Studs Terkel, ed., *"The Good War": An Oral History of World War II* (New York: New Press, 1984). Reprinted by permission of the New Press. (800) 233–4830.

I WAS IN the class of '41, the last high school class. You see! By that winter Leslie Bidwell would be dead at Pearl Harbor. My class would be dying.

Oroville was a little mining town eighty miles above Sacramento. My step-father was a tenant farmer and owned just a little bit of land. He had just got electricity three years before. We lived in the kitchen because that's where it was warm. My stepfather kept things to himself. He would read the papers, but he never shared. My mother was busy feeding all her kids. I was the first one of nine children to graduate from high school.

I was dancing at Fresno State, at a big ball, when I first realized Pearl Harbor had happened. It was a whole week later. I was a hayseed Basye.

Immediately, I was going to become a nurse. That was the fastest thing I could do to help our boys. Here I was only one semester at Fresno State, and by February 5, I was out at the hospital as a registered nurse.

It was expensive for me. You had to pay something like twenty dollars a month to live at the nurses' home. I didn't have any money. Fortunately, the Cadet Nurse Corps came into existence. The government paid for us to become nurses. That really saved me.

I remember February 5, '42. Our superintendent called us all together. Two little Japanese girls, sitting in front, who had come into class like me—why in the world are we saying goodbye to them? I couldn't understand what had happened. They were gone and I never, never saw them again. It must have been okay if President Roosevelt said it was okay. But I knew those girls should have been nurses.

I wanted to really have something to do with the war. It meant my kid brother on a tanker in the Mediterranean, delivering oil to Africa, to Italy. It meant losing several more Oroville schoolmates. It meant my boyfriend, whom I'd been engaged to ever since we left high school. He'd joined the marines and was gone. It meant just an end to all that life I had known just a few months before. . . .

All the regular nurses began to drop out and join the army. Many of my instructors left. We were down to just a skeleton crew at the county hospital. In Fresno. The student nurses were running the whole hospital.

You were supposed to stay in for three years as a student nurse, but the army took us out six months early. We went down to our first military assignment at Hoff General Hospital in Santa Barbara. We were given uniforms with a nice little cocky beret. It was basic training really, because most of us were gonna go into the service. About six months later, we went back to Fresno to graduate, get our pins, and say goodbye. The day President Roosevelt died, I was an official army nurse. I felt even more committed to go ahead.

I was on an orthopedic ward. Quite a few wounded paratroopers. I remember rubbing the backs of these people who had casts from head to foot. You could hardly find their backs through all these bandages and pulleys. It's not like plastic surgery where the really deformed people are. I was struck by the horror of it, but it wasn't as bad as what was to come.

Now I go to Dibble General Hospital in Menlo Park. In six weeks, we became so skilled in plastic surgery that they wouldn't let us go. Six-week wonders. It was coming to the end of the war and now they needed plastic surgery. Blind young men. Eyes gone, legs gone. Parts of the face. Burns—you'd land with a fire bomb and be up in flames. It was a burn-and-blind center.

I spent a year and a half in the plastic-surgery dressing room. All day long you would change these dressings. When you were through with those who were mobile, who would come by wheelchair or crutches, you would take this little cart loaded with canisters of wet saline bandages. Go up and down the wards to those fellas who couldn't get out of bed. It was almost like a surgical procedure. They didn't anesthetize the boys and it was terribly painful. We had to keep the skin wet with these moist saline packs. We would wind yards and yards of this wet pack around these people. That's what war really is.

I'll never forget my first day on duty. First Lieutenant Molly Birch introduced me to the whole floor of patients: "This is Lieutenant Basye." They'd say, What? Hayseed? Oh, Basie. Oh Countess. So I got the name Countess.

I was so overwhelmed by the time I got to the third bed: this whole side of a face being gone. I wouldn't know how to focus on the eye that peeked through these bandages. Should I pretend I didn't notice it? Shall we talk about it? Molly led me down to the next bed: The Nose, she called him. He had lost his nose. Later on, I got used to it, all this kidding about their condition. He would pretend to laugh. He would say, "Ah yes, I'm getting my nose." He didn't have any eyebrows, a complete white mass of scars. The pedicle was hanging off his neck. He had no ears—they had been burned off. They were going to be reconstructed. But the nose was the important thing. Everyone nicknamed him The Nose. He didn't mind—well, I don't know that. Molly was right. She was giving them a chance to talk about what happened. At the time, I couldn't stand it.

As soon as we got back to the nurse's station behind glass, I went to the bathroom and threw up. Then she knew. She didn't introduce me to the patients who were in the private room that day, 'cause they were far the worst. They couldn't get up and couldn't joke so much. The next day she took me to them, one at a time. I was beginning to anesthetize myself.

I remember this one lieutenant. Just a mass of white bandages, with a little slit where I knew his eyes were. This one hand reaching out and saying, "Hi, Red." There were many, many, many more with stumps, you couldn't tell if there was a foot there or not, an eye, an arm, the multiple wounds. It wasn't just the one little thing I was used to in nurse's training. This is what got to me.

Oh, there were breakups. The wife of The Nose was going to divorce him. What can we do to make her understand? That was the talk all over. The doctor wanted her to understand it'll take time, he'll get his face back. But they broke up. She couldn't stand it. That was pretty common.

Sitting at the bedside of this young flyer who went down over Leyte. He got his own fire bomb. Next to his bed is a picture of this handsome pilot beside his P-38. He wants to be sure I see it: "Hi, Red, look. This is me." He was never gonna leave that bed until he got his face back. That handsome photograph he insisted be there, so that's the person you'll see.

He was very hard to manage because he would scream when they changed his dressing. He was insistent that he never was gonna leave that room until they brought him back to where he was before. The staff couldn't quite figure this out. Why isn't he quiet? Why can't he be brave when they're changing his dressing? What does he think we are, miracle makers? This mystique builds up that Bill can't handle it as well as the others. Be brave, be brave.

I can't say I ever really became used to it. But I became more effective as a nurse and adopted a kind of jocularity. I began to be able to tell jokes, banter back and forth. When I'd come in pushing the cart, there'd always be hooting and yelling: Hey, Red, Hayseed, Countess, come in, I got a cookie for you. There was a lot of alluding to sexuality. One said to me, "Why do you always walk that way?" I didn't know how I walked, but I had a walk. I said, "I don't know." And they all howled.

Having pretty young nurses around was very important to them. You were not supposed to date enlisted men, but you could date officers. I escorted Bill, the pilot, for the first outing out of his room. I talked him into escorting me to the officers' club. He still had a bandage on his one eye, terrible scars, one side of his face gone, and these pedicles of flesh. You look absolutely grotesque and you know. We had a drink at the club. He looked around and saw other cases there. So he began to get used to it.

One of the nurses in charge fell in love with an enlisted man. She carried on a very quiet love affair with him. We never alluded to it. After about a year, they were married. It was always a secret in those days. It was discouraged. I've always had the theory that they made us officers to keep the army nurses for the officers. We were just technicians. I was just a twenty-two-year-old kid who knew how to do bedpans. Why was I an officer? I feel it was a way to keep us away from the hordes and keep us for the officers. Oh, there was a terrible class feeling.

The doctors were the givers of gifts to these men. They were gods on a pedestal. The elusive, mobile god, who moves in and out and doesn't stay there very long, under a terrible amount of pressure. The nurses were counsel when marriages broke up. The doctors were busy someplace else.

V-J Day occurred while I was still at the hospital. Oh, wow! Just total chaos. Our superintendent of nurses led a conga line up and down the hospital, serpentine, up past every bed. This took hours, because it was ward after ward. Everybody joined in. Absolute bedlam.

The hospital closed and they sent the patients out to other places. Plastic surgery was going to go on for years on these people. I went down to Pasadena. This is '46. We took over the whole hotel, one of the big, nice old hotels right there on the gorge. All my friends were still there, undergoing surgery. Especially Bill. I would walk him in downtown Pasadena—I'll never forget this. Half his face completely gone, right?

Downtown Pasadena after the war was a very elite community. Nicely dressed women, absolutely staring, just standing there staring. He was aware of this terrible stare. People just looking right at you and wondering: What is this? I was going to cuss her out, but I moved him away. It's like the war hadn't come to Pasadena until we came there.

Oh, it had a big impact on the community. In the Pasadena paper came some letters to the editor: Why can't they be kept on their own grounds and off the streets? The furor, the awful indignation: the end of the war and we're still here. The patients themselves showed me these letters: Isn't it better for them if they're kept off the streets? What awful things for us to have to look at. The patients kidded about that. Wow, we're in Pasadena.

This was my slow introduction to peacetime, through the eyes of that woman when she looked at my friend Bill. It's only the glamour of war that appeals to people. They don't know real war. Well, those wars are gone forever. We've got a nuclear bomb and we'll destroy ourselves and everybody else.

I swallowed all this for years and never talked about it. 'Cause I got busy after the war, getting married and having my four children. That's what you were supposed to do. And getting your house in suburbia. You couldn't get anybody to really talk about the war. Oh, the men would say, When I was in Leyte—buddy-buddy talk. Well, their buddies got killed, too. They never talked of the horrors.

My husband had been in the South Pacific. You could never get the father of my four children to talk about the war. It was like we put blinders on the past. When we won, we believed it. It was the end. That's the way we lived in suburbia, raising our children, not telling them about war. I don't think it was just me. It was everybody. You wouldn't fill your children full of these horror stories, would you?

When I think of the kind of person I was, a little hayseed from Oroville, with all this altruism in me and all this patriotism that sent me into the war! Oh, the war marked me, but I put it behind me. I didn't do much except march against Vietnam. And my oldest son, I'm happy to say, was a conscientious objector.

It's just this terrible anger I have. What is this story I want to tell? I even wrote short stories for myself. I started an autobiography, and always the war came up. This disappointment. We did it for what? Korea? Vietnam? We're still at war. Looking back, it didn't work. . . .

CHAPTER 2

THE UNQUIET DECADE: DOMESTICITY, WORK, AND SOCIAL ACTIVISM IN POSTWAR AMERICA

Descriptions of the 1950s usually evoke images of a home in suburbia, backyard barbecues, and young mothers immersed in household chores and PTA meetings. For most middle-class white American women, that was true. But the decade also produced some remarkably singular and courageous women who stood against the political and cultural tide of American life. And beneath the staid, sober facade of postwar domesticity and prosperity lurked cracks and fissures that would erupt in a resurgent and vibrant women's movement in the decades to come.

In 1955 presidential candidate Adlai Stevenson addressed the graduating class of Smith College and exhorted them to embrace their future domestic roles with pride: "Women in the home [can] have an important political influence on man and boy. . . . I think there is much you can do about our crisis in the humble role of housewife." Everywhere white middle-class women looked, the signs pointed toward home, toward that "humble" domestic role. Television situation comedies such as *Leave It to Beaver, Father Knows Best,* and *The Donna Reed Show* portrayed the domestic bliss of family life. Newspapers and magazines bombarded women with advice on housekeeping, raising children, and keeping marriages fresh and happy. Colleges offered courses in subjects pertaining to home and the family; Mills College in Northern California offered a course in "Voluntarism" and a major in marriage. Even the University of Chicago, one of the most stringently academic institutions in the country, offered a course on "Parenthood in a Free Nation."[1] It did seem as if white women across the nation were, as Adlai Stevenson had prophesied, writing laundry lists instead of poetry. Looking back from the vantage point of thirty years, a 1951 Radcliffe graduate and the wife of a college dean observed, "We married what we wanted to *be*. If we wanted to be a lawyer or a doctor we married one."[2]

Although women attended college in record numbers, very few became doctors or lawyers themselves. In 1950, according to a survey conducted by the Human Resources Council, 70 percent of professional women were still ghettoized in traditional female fields: teaching, nursing, and library work.[3] Another study showed that twice as many young women in an all-white sample attended college as did their mothers but were less likely to graduate. In fact, only 37 percent of female college students completed their degrees, and the percentage of women who went on for postgraduate degrees was lower in the 1950s than in the 1920s and 1930s.[4] Those who dropped out did so not because they found academia too demanding but because they had a better chance of finding a husband and setting up housekeeping than pursuing a career after graduating. For white middle-class women, college was the ticket to affluent domesticity—by meeting their future husbands on campus. Because of gender discrimination, few college-educated women had the opportunity to develop careers in fields outside of teaching, nursing, or secretarial work. Many women preferred to drop out and marry than to settle for work that did not satisfy them.

In contrast, black women stayed in college. Like their mothers and grandmothers before them, they expected to work and they knew that a college degree was the pathway to a better job. Although fewer black women than white women were able to attend college, more than 90 percent of black women who went to college graduated and found work in traditional female fields.[5] By 1950 the percentage of black women in professional fields (5.2 percent) had surpassed that of black men (2.6 percent), and black women comprised 58 percent of all black professionals. In contrast, white professional women represented only 35 percent of all white professionals.[6]

But white women, like black women, continued to work after the war. Although women's wages dropped after the war—from an average weekly pay of $50 to $37—and wartime women had to relinquish better-paying jobs in industry to returning veterans, most women who had worked during the war held on to their jobs or were rehired in other occupations. By 1947 more women worked than before the war, and also more wives worked. From 1940 to 1960 the number of employed mothers skyrocketed 400 percent, from 1.5 million to 6.6 million, and 39 percent of women with children between the ages of six to seventeen held jobs.[7] But most working women—black and white—held jobs, not careers. White women worked mainly as secretaries, clerks, saleswomen, and waitresses in the "pink-collar ghetto," while black women still worked primarily as domestic servants in private homes or as service workers in institutions and industry. A few white women managed to climb the corporate ladder to the top. Dorothy Shaver, who started out as a salesperson of handmade dolls, became president of Lord and Taylor, the well-known department store, in 1945, at a salary of $110,000. Similarly, in 1958 in Philadelphia, Mildren Custin became president of Bonwit Teller. The cosmetic industry, another traditional magnet for female achievement, saw the rise to corporate leadership of Hazel Bishop, Helena Rubenstein, Elizabeth Arden, Estee Lauder, and Germaine Monteil as new and more cosmetic products bombarded the market to keep women feminine and attractive by the standards of the decade. Nevertheless, these women were the exception.

Many middle-class women regarded their work as an opportunity to enhance their family's standard of living—to purchase more consumer items for their families or send their children to camp. As their families flocked to the new suburban developments that sprang up all over the country after the war, white women found more opportunities to spend paychecks on household gadgets and appliances. A feature in *Look* magazine noted in 1956, "No longer a psychological immigrant to man's world, she works . . . less toward a big career than as a way of filling a hope chest or buying a new home freezer. She gracefully concedes the top job rungs to men."[8]

For white Americans—ethnic minorities were generally discouraged from purchasing homes in the suburbs—the new suburban development, with its rabbit warren of standardized, mass-produced homes designed to accommodate growing families, became the symbol of postwar prosperity. Most homes were one- or two-story, with open floor plans where children could play safely and in view, roomy kitchens that opened onto family rooms, and kitchen windows facing backyards so that mothers could watch their children while doing household chores. The house was the center of family life and leisure. Barbecues and swing sets adorned most uniformly bounded backyards, while the ubiquitous TV set held a place of honor in the family room. For homemakers who were not employed outside of the home, shopping for groceries and household goods, chauffering children to and from various after-school activities such as music lessons or boy or girl scouts, and doing household chores occupied their entire day. Employed or not, women were responsible for the care of their homes and families. The suburban ideal of an oasis of family togetherness and peace collided with women's feelings of entrapment, isolation, and a Sisyphean round of chores and child care.

Black women lived in very different circumstances after World War II. In the North, as whites moved out of the city into the suburbs, blacks took over urban apartment complexes. Black women also did full-time domestic work—but as a servant in someone else's home. By 1950, 60 percent of all employed black women worked as domestic servants in private homes or as service work-

ers in office buildings, restaurants, and hotels.[9] Among the remaining 40 percent, many worked as farm laborers down South, where many blacks remained
despite continuing migrations up North. They toiled much like their ancestors
had—as sharecroppers for a white farmer, working long hours under a broil-
ing sun and living in crude houses.

Wherever they lived, employed black women did not have the luxury of
spending their earnings on the extra little amenities for their families; because
black men generally earned less than half of what white men earned, black women's wages were vital for the family's survival. Yet while white leaders and the
media praised the full-time mother and looked dimly upon women who
worked, black community leaders and the popular black media held up working black women as modern-day Harriet Tubmans and Sojourner Truths, who,
in the words of *Ebony* magazine, "never accepted the myth that women belong
to a weaker sex."[10] Black professional women such as doctors and teachers garnered the respect, not the opprobium, of their communities.

Whether they worked outside of the home or were full-time homemakers,
the ultimate goal for most women was marriage and motherhood. In the postwar years married couples wanted large families. One study of middle-class
white couples in the mid-1950s revealed that 39 percent wanted at least four children.[11] In 1947 Ferdinand Lundberg and Marynia F. Farnham, two Freudian
psychologists, published *The Modern Woman: The Lost Sex*, a book about women's psychology, which became a bestseller. They claimed that female sexuality was inherently passive, "a willingness to accept dependence without fear or
resentment, with a deep inwardness and readiness for the final goal of sexual
life—impregnation." Women who refused to accept their biological destiny as
mothers, according to Lundberg and Farnham, were "sick, unhappy, neurotic,
wholly or partly incapable of deaing with life . . . the miserable, half-satisfied, the
frustrated, the angered."

With such clinical and cultural emphasis on motherhood, it seems odd that
the birth control movement gained more rather than less support during the
1950s. After birth control became legal in the 1930s, more birth control clinics
arose across the nation. In 1942 Margaret Sanger's organization, the Birth Control Federation of America, changed its name to the Planned Parenthood Federation of America. This name change reflected the changing goals of the organization—from crusading to give women the right to control their own
reproduction to enhancing family life by giving women the means to space out
their childbearing and enjoy sex with their husbands without the fear of pregnancy. Throughout the 1950s an array of birth control devices became widely

available, from condoms, diaphragms, jellies, and foams to intrauterine devices (IUDs). Abortion, however, remained illegal, unless a physician determined that continuing a pregnancy would jeopardize a woman's health or life. Women who wanted to end a pregnancy for other reasons had to resort to back-alley abortionists and risked infection and medical complications. Yet during the 1940s and 1950s, women sought an estimated 250,000 to 1 million illegal abortions each year—and about 40 percent of pregnant women died from these procedures.

In 1960 an oral contraceptive—the Pill—was made available, thus enabling young women to use birth control without the knowledge or involvement of their partners. But birth control was not intended to be used by unmarried women to prevent pregnancy or by married women who did not want children. Rather, it was meant to be another technological innovation—like household appliances—to enhance family life. Nor did the birthrate plummet because of the widespread use of birth control. Between 1947 and 1964—the span of time marking the birth of the baby boom generation—the birthrate skyrocketed as women married and started bearing children at younger ages. In 1945, 83 out of every 1,000 white women and 106 out of every 1,000 non-white women bore children. By 1955, those numbers had risen to 113 and 155, respectively.[12]

Several historians have discerned a link between this emphasis on family and domesticity and a conservative political climate. In *Homeward Bound*, Elaine May linked the suppression of communism in Cold War politics to the containment of women within the family. In an unsafe world, "the family seemed to offer a psychological fortress," writes May—a fortress in which women were expected to create a domestic haven.[13]

A pervasive fear of communism also hindered political activism. The "Red scare" reached near hysterical proportions in the early 1950s when Senator Joseph McCarthy of Wisconsin conducted a veritable witch hunt against communist infiltration in American politics and life. From 1950 to 1954 McCarthy conducted hearings in which suspected communist sympathizers were hauled before his committee and subjected to a near inquisition about their political allegiances. McCarthy's reckless and vicious attacks destroyed the reputations and careers of hundreds of people. In June 1953 Ethel and Julius Rosenberg, accused of spying and selling atomic secrets to the Russians, were executed, despite international appeals for clemency. And throughout the 1950s and early 1960s American schoolchildren were drilled in the procedures of how to escape a nuclear bomb, while many of their families built and equipped bomb shelters in their own backyards to survive nuclear attack. The fear of communism—and the fear of being labeled a communist—helped to stifle political dissent.

Yet, despite the political conservatism and emphasis on home and family, the postwar era actually witnessed some profound social and cultural up-heavals. Many extraordinarily courageous men and women struggled to keep the spirit of dissent alive and to fight for social and political justice. Indeed, some activists, like their predecessors earlier in the century, drew on a renewed conception of maternalist politics; their role and their concerns as wives and mothers obligated them to promote social change that safeguarded their families. This was the very motivation for the establishment of Women Strike for Peace, as Dagmar Wilson recounts in her oral history in this chapter.

In the African American community, black women took the lead in fighting for racial justice. Among such courageous freedom fighters were Rosa Parks, Elizabeth Eckford, and Fannie Lou Hamer, whose accounts are included in this chapter. In December 1955 Parks's refusal to give up her seat on a bus to a white man helped launch the civil rights movement. Two years later Elizabeth Eckford was one of nine black students who helped to integrate a high school in Little Rock, Arkansas, in the wake of the U.S. Supreme Court's decision *Brown v. Board of Education of Topeka, Kansas*, which ruled segregated schools to be unconstitutional. Eckford's harassment by a vicious white mob is recounted in "It Was the Longest Block I Ever Walked in My Life," on pp. 129–32. And Fannie Lou Hamer's testimony before the credentials committee of the Democratic National Committee about the brutal beating she received because of her voter-registration work among blacks shocked the nation and aroused public support for civil rights. Her speech is reprinted on pp. 153–56.

Many other black women supported the movement in less dramatic but equally important ways by providing meals and lodging for civil rights activists. And even a few courageous white women joined the movement as foot soldiers for freedom. The account of Nannie Washburn on pp. 164–70 illustrates the depth of courage and conviction that women marshalled—and the price they paid—to support this movement for social and political justice. Lillian Smith, a novelist and magazine publisher, denounced segregation in *Killers of the Dream*, first published in 1949. Five years later, she published *Now Is the Time*, a manifesto setting out the ways in which people must work for an integrated society. Her words aroused the fury of racists who set fire to her house, hoping to silence her. But Smith would not give in and continued to voice her vision of equality and respect for human differences. She was a friend of the Reverend Martin Luther King Jr. and for many years served on the executive board of the

Congress of Racial Equality (CORE) until that organization no longer supported nonviolence. Her letter to the *New York Times*, which she penned in
1948, a year before she published *Killers of the Dream*, is a searing indictment of
southern liberals who failed to speak out more forcefully against segregation.

Mexican American women also pursued social and political activism within their communities. Undeterred by the conservative social and political climate of the Cold War, they plunged into community improvement projects
throughout the late 1940s and 1950s. Most Mexican American organizations
welcomed both women and men. These included the American G.I. Forum,
founded in Texas by returning Mexican American veterans; the Unity Leagues,
a network of Mexican American groups in California; and the Community Service Organization (CSO). Mexican American women participated in all of
these groups, but they made the greatest impact in the CSO. Although men
served as chapter presidents and women remained in the secondary roles of
recording and corresponding secretaries, women were the backbone of the
CSO. They did the hands-on work of organizing CSO state and national conventions; went door-to-door to register new voters so that Mexican Americans
would have a larger voice in political matters affecting their communities;
launched petition drives within their barrios to demand streetlights, sidewalks,
and other public facilities; and conducted first-aid classes and free vaccination
and hearing tests for the children in their barrios. They also aided striking
workers by joining picket lines and organizing food drives for the strikers. In
Los Angeles and Visalia, California, CSO women helped to prevent Mexican
Americans from being deported by taking their cases before the U.S. Immigration Service.

Like other female activists, CSO women found the inspiration for their activism in their roles as wives, mothers, and neighbors. In the CSO they integrated traditional female skills—cooking, neighborly relations, teaching, clerical
work, and cooking—and women's concerns—neighborhood improvement, education, and health—into the heart of the CSO agenda. Their civic activism,
along with that of their menfolk, set the stage for more visible social activism in
the Mexican American communities of the 1960s.

If white women's political activism was not quite as dramatic, it was nevertheless alive and varied in the postwar era. A number of white women courageously stood up to McCarthyism, including Senator Margaret Chase Smith,
who publicly urged the nation to resist "fear, ignorance, bigotry, and smear,"
and playwright Lillian Hellman, who, when called before the House Un-American Activities Committee in 1952—another virulently anticommunist con-

gressional committee established to investigate subversive activities—refused to name other writers and artists who might have had communist affiliations, declaring, "I cannot and will not cut my conscience to fit this year's fashions." As a result, Hellman was blacklisted and had no work or income for several years. Actresses such as Judy Holliday, Katharine Hepburn, and Lauren Bacall also refused to cooperate with the committee.

Women who were not forced to put their consciences on the line exhibited their political and civic concerns in less dramatic ways by joining a variety of organizations. Among these was the League of Women Voters. Between 1950 and 1958 the league's membership increased by 44 percent, with 1,050 local leagues and 128,000 members.[14] Nonpartisan and moderate in political outlook, the league offered women the opportunity to be politically engaged at a time when both major political parties were indifferent to women's involvement. League members set up study groups to educate themselves on foreign policy and conservation. Women also influenced public policy and life by doing volunteer work in their own communities. In cities, towns, and suburbs across the nation, women joined church groups, PTAs, and local charities and led scout troops. For some middle-class suburban women, volunteer work was as much a part of their daily lives as housework. Although these volunteer activities seldom gave women real political power to shape public policy, women were the "community builders," in the words of historian Sara Evans, much like they were in the frontier towns of an earlier day, "providing the organizational energy behind new churches, schools, park systems, and libraries."[15]

Despite the conservative political climate, women's peace activities continued throughout the 1950s. Women Strike for Peace was an organization that relied on grassroots suburban middle-class support for a radical ideal. On November 1, 1961, fifty thousand American homemakers walked out of their homes and jobs to protest the proliferation of nuclear arms. While several of the leaders had long been active in the peace movement, the mass of strikers were young wives and mothers—full-time homemakers who, like earlier generations of female reformers, were determined to create safe living conditions for their young. In her oral history Dagmar Wilson describes the grassroots nature of this organization, which was made up mostly of young homemakers who were not professional peace activists. During the year following their massive march, Women Strike for Peace organized local groups in sixty communities around the country. Their actions foreshadowed the reemergence of women as activists on behalf of their own rights and concerns. Although Women

Strike for Peace was not a self-consciously feminist organization, it demonstrated what the tactics of solidarity and protest could accomplish and set the stage for the emergence of a powerful and pervasive women's movement in the following years.

Marine biologist Rachel Carson exposed another kind of threat to American life—the misuse of natural resources. Long before the present-day environmental movement, she warned people about the dangers of toxic chemicals and the need to protect the nation's environment and wildlife. A biologist at the United States Fish and Wildlife Service, she published three books that established her as a pioneer environmentalist, the most influential of which was *Silent Spring*, an exposé of toxic chemicals in the environment. With a poet's gift for language, she exposed the dangers of DDT, an insecticide, on bird and plant life and described the potentially disastrous global impact of other toxic chemicals on the natural world. Carson urged readers to stop the indiscriminate plundering of the environment by unchecked industrial and technological growth. *Silent Spring* prompted the creation of a presidential panel to study the effects of pesticides on the environment, and the commission's findings corroborated Carson's conclusions.

FROM ROSIE THE RIVETER to June Cleaver, American women in the 1940s and 1950s were glorified in the public eye as patriotic workers and loving mothers. When the nation needed their muscle, they donned a uniform or pair of overalls and served their country in time of war. And when the crisis was over, they were expected to return home and raise a new generation of loyal, patriotic Americans. The war had opened up new employment opportunities for women and inspired some government agencies and corporations to seek solutions for enabling women to work and carry out their domestic duties. But with peace came an urgent desire to return to a normal state of things, which meant a breadwinning husband and a bread-baking wife. Yet the reality of the postwar era was far more complex. Too many women had tasted the freedom and satisfaction that a paycheck brought, and they chose to remain in the work force even in jobs that offered little career mobility. But for white women, the demands of gender asserted themselves, and just as they had justified their wartime work as a patriotic duty, they now justified their peacetime work as a way to help their families enjoy a better standard of living. For black women, however, there was nothing to justify: they worked because they had to, to supplement their husbands' meager earnings in an economy that did not welcome African Americans.

Amidst the decade's paeans to home and family, American women continued to push back barriers to equal participation in all aspects of American life. Black women continued to be the backbone of their communities' efforts to improve their lives, and in the new mass movement for civil rights in the 1950s they were heroic. Through their volunteer work, white women found opportunites, albeit limited, to create a spirit of community in the isolation and anonymity of the new suburbs. And against the backdrop of postwar complacence and Cold War conservatism, some American women, individually and collectively, kept the spirit of dissent alive, pricking the nation's conscience on issues of race, global peace, workplace equality, and environmental destruction. Beneath the surface somnolence of the 1950s churned new currents of social and cultural upheaval. The next few years would be mighty interesting indeed.

NOTES

1. Eugenia Kaledin, *American Women in the 1950s: Mothers and More* (Boston: Twayne, 1984), p. 53.
2. Quoted in Rona Jaffe, "A Real-Life Class Reunion," *Ladies Home Journal* (June 1980), p. 142.
3. Kaledin, *Mothers and More*, p. 50.
4. Ibid., p. 36.
5. Elaine Tyler May, "Pushing the Limits," in Nancy Cott, ed., *No Small Courage: A History of Women in the United States* (New York: Oxford University Press, 2000), p. 497.
6. Paula Giddings, *When and Where I Enter: The Impact of Black Women on Race and Sex in America* (New York: Bantam, 1984), p. 245.
7. Kaledin, *Mothers and More*, p. 65.
8. Laura Bergquist, "A New Look at the American Woman," *Look*, October 16, 1956, p. 3.
9. May, "Pushing the Limits," p. 494.
10. Quoted in ibid., p. 504.
11. Ibid., p. 513.
12. U.S. Bureau of the Census, Statistical Abstract of the United States, 1960. 81st ed. Washington, D.C.: U.S. Government Printing Office, 1960, table 57, p. 56.
13. Elaine Tyler May, *Homeward Bound: American Families in the Cold War Era* (New York: Basic Books, 1988), p. 11.
14. Kaledin, *Mothers and More*, p. 33.
15. Sara Evans, *Born for Liberty: A History of Women in America* (New York: Free, 1989), p. 247.

MODERN WOMAN: THE LOST SEX
MARYNIA FARNHAM AND FERDINAND LUNDBERG

*The rush to restore women to full-time domesticity had no greater advo-
cates than Marynia Farnham, a female psychoanalyst, and Ferdinand Lundberg,
a male sociologist, who published* Modern Woman: The Lost Sex, *a best-selling
treatise on the discontents of postwar women, in 1947. In their book, heavily lard-
ed with psychoanalytic theory, they attempted to explore the causes of what they
perceived to be women's confusion and despair in present-day American culture—
which they identified as women's rejection of their essentially domestic role and
their desire to compete with men in the public arenas of business and politics.
While paying lip service to the social and political reforms inspired by twentieth-
century feminism, they denounced feminists for being aggressive, maladjusted, and
unable to accept women's "fundamental role as wife and mother." And they
claimed that American women's discontent and desire to pursue "masculine"
strivings also had unfortunate consequences for their husbands: "Instead of supporting and encouraging his manliness and wishes for domination and power, she
may thus impose upon him feelings of insufficiency and weakness."*

*To reinvigorate women's domestic role—and society's approval of this role—
Farnham and Lundberg called for widespread psychoanalysis, public education to
reaffirm women's traditional work, government subsidies to mothers, taxes on bach-
elors, the employment of more married women instead of "spinsters" to teach public school, and the education of girls in "feminine" rather than "masculine" subjects.*

The following excerpt from Modern Woman: The Lost Sex *offers a vigorous
repudiation of wartime female wage earners and the independence, personal fulfillment, and financial rewards they derived from their work. Instead, Farnham
and Lundberg issue a conservative clarion call to restore women to a wholly domestic role.*

SOURCE: Marynia Farnham and Ferdinand Lundberg, *Modern Woman: The Lost Sex*
(New York: Harper and Brothers, 1947), pp. 228–9, 234–41. Reprinted by permission of
HarperCollins Publishers, Inc.

THE GIRL in struggling to become an adult woman must rely upon some pattern or model from which she can derive a design for femininity. She is provided with one in her mother and she will have to believe for a long time that
her mother's nature, temperament and attitudes are ideals toward which she

must strive as a woman. Not until much later in her life will she be free to discover other ideals and models. Thus it is her mother's grasp on femininity on which the little girl chiefly depends.

Here is the real crux of the situation, because the mother's feelings for herself as a woman and acceptance of her feminine role dictate her attitudes toward children and husband. If the girl has the good fortune to have a mother who finds complete satisfaction, without conflict or anxiety, in living out her role as wife and mother, it is unlikely that she will experience serious difficulties. If, however, the mother is beset by distaste for her role, strives for accomplishment outside her home and can only grudgingly give attention to her children, has regrets for whatever reason at being a woman, then, no matter how much or little of it she betrays, the child cannot escape the confused impression that the mother is without love, is not a satisfactory model.

Such a woman is not only an unsatisfactory model for her daughter, but gives her no sure grasp on the solid satisfactions inherent in feminine development. She may produce a still more dangerous impression on the small girl, in that she will inject into her attitudes her own covert strivings toward masculinity. . . .

We come now to the fact that the mother, under conditions of modern social change, is very often deeply disturbed. Although not a feminist or a courtesan type, necessarily, she is herself afflicted very often at a deep level with penis-envy, which plays itself out in various ways with respect to her children. She is disturbed, discontented, complaining, unreasonably demanding, aggressive and shows it directly or indirectly. The damage she does, to boys as well as girls, is great. . . .

It is becoming unquestionably more and more common for the woman to attempt to combine both home and child care and an outside activity, which is either work or career. Increasing numbers train for professional careers. When these two spheres are combined it is inevitable that one or the other will become of secondary concern and, this being the case, it is certain that the home will take that position. This is true, if only for the practical reason that no one can find and hold remunerative employment where the job itself doesn't take precedence over all other concerns. All sorts of agencies and instrumentalities have therefore been established to make possible the playing of this dual role. These are all in the direction of substitutes for the attention of the mother in the home and they vary from ordinary, untrained domestic service through the more highly trained grades of such service, to the public and private agencies now designed for the care, supervision and emotional untanglement of the children. The day nursery and its more elegant counterpart, the nursery school, are outstanding as the major agencies which make it possible for women to relinquish the care of children still in their infancy.

All these services and facilities produce what appears on the surface to be a smoothly functioning arrangement and one that provides children with obviously highly trained, expert and efficient care as well as with superior training in early skills and techniques and in adaptation to social relations. This surface, however, covers a situation that is by no means so smoothly functioning nor so satisfying either to the child or the woman. She must of necessity be deeply in conflict and only partially satisfied in either direction. Her work develops aggressiveness, which is essentially a denial of her femininity, an enhancement of her girlhood-induced masculine tendencies. It is not that work is essentially masculine or feminine, but that the pursuit of a career (which is work plus prestige goal) is essentially masculine because exploitative. The statement may cause enormous protest but it remains a fact.

Work that entices women out of their homes and provides them with prestige only at the price of feminine relinquishment, involves a response to masculine strivings. The more importance outside work assumes, the more are the masculine components of the woman's nature enhanced and encouraged. In her home and in her relationship to her children, it is imperative that these strivings be at a minimum and that her femininity be available both for her own satisfaction and for the satisfaction of her children and husband. She is, therefore, in the dangerous position of having to live one part of her life on the masculine level, another on the feminine. It is hardly astonishing that few can do so with success. One of these tendencies must of necessity achieve dominance over the other. The plain fact is that increasingly we are observing the masculinization of women and with it enormously dangerous consequences to the home, the children (if any) dependent on it, and to the ability of the woman, as well as her husband, to obtain sexual gratification.

The effect of this "masculinization" on women is becoming more apparent daily. Their new exertions are making demands on them for qualities wholly opposed to the experience of feminine satisfaction. As the rivals of men, women must, and insensibly do, develop the characteristics of aggression, dominance, independence and power. These are qualities which insure success as co-equals in the world of business, industry and the professions. The distortion of character under pressure of modern attitudes and upbringing is driving women steadily deeper into personal conflict soluble only by psychotherapy. For their need to achieve and accomplish doesn't lessen, in any way, their deeper need to find satisfactions profoundly feminine. Much as they consciously seek those gratifications of love, sensual release and even motherhood, they are becoming progressively less able unconsciously to accept or achieve them.

First of their demands is for sexual gratification, a problem we discuss at some length in Chapter XI. This is the core of the goal—sexual, orgastic equality with men. These women have intellectualized and rationalized their sexual lives, determining that they will have for themselves the experiences and, therefore, the satisfactions that men have. So far as the experiences are concerned, they can carry out their intentions, but where the gratifications are concerned they meet with abysmal, tragic failure. Sexual gratification is not an experience to be obtained through the simple performance of the sexual act. To a very great extent the unconscious exertions of these women to obtain absolute parity with men have resulted in crippling them precisely for this much desired objective. . . .

The dominant direction of feminine training and development today is directly opposed to . . . those traits necessary to the attainment of sexual pleasure: receptivity and passiveness, a willingness to accept dependence without fear or resentment, with a deep inwardness and readiness for the final goal of sexual life—impregnation. It doesn't admit of wishes to control or master, to rival or dominate. The woman who is to find true gratification must love and accept her own womanhood as she loves and accepts her husband's manhood. Women's rivalry with men today, and the need to "equal" their accomplishments, engenders all too often anger and resentfulness toward men. Men, challenged, frequently respond in kind. So it is that women envy and feel hostile to men for just the attributes which women themselves require for "success" in the world. The woman's unconscious wish herself to possess the organ upon which she must thus depend militates greatly against her ability to accept its vast power to satisfy her when proffered to her in love.

Many women can find no solution to their dilemma and are defeated in attempts at adaptation. These constitute the array of the sick, unhappy, neurotic, wholly or partly incapable of dealing with life. In a veritable army of women, the tensions and anxieties make their way to the surface in physical guise. They have always been known and dimly recognized for what they are—the miserable, the half-satisfied, the frustrated, the angered. Unable to cope with the disappointments that they have met in their emotional lives, they become ill. Their illnesses take varied forms, attack any part of the body and are often disabling. Where formerly the connection was only suspected and assumed between these multifarious physical disorders and disturbing feeling states, we are now coming to the point of really understanding their sources in the child-based emotional disorders that give rise to them. Whether it be "sick headaches," pains of indeterminate nature in the back and limbs, gastric disorders, constipation, hypertension, or the enormous collections of disorders of the reproductive system, it is all one and all arises from an inability to master unconscious feelings constantly aroused by disappointment and frustration. . . .

It is not only the masculine woman who has met with an unhappy fate in the present situation. There are still many women who succeed in achieving adult life with largely unimpaired feminine strivings, for which home, a husband's love and children are to them the entirely adequate answers. It is their misfortune that they must enter a society in which such attitudes are little appreciated and are attended by many concrete, external penalties. Such women cannot fail to be affected by finding that their traditional activities are held in low esteem and that the woman who voluntarily undertakes them is often deprecated by her more aggressive contemporaries. She may come to believe that her situation is difficult, entailing serious deprivations, as against the more glamorous and exciting life other women seemingly enjoy. She may be set away from the main stream of life, very much in a backwater and fearful lest she lose her ability and talents through disuse and lack of stimulation. She may become sorry for herself and somewhat angered by her situation, gradually developing feelings of discontent and pressure. As her children grow older and require less of her immediate attention, the feelings of loss increase. . . .

So it is that society today makes it difficult for a woman to avoid the path leading to discontent and frustration and resultant hostility and destructiveness. Such destructiveness is, unfortunately, not confined in its effects to the woman alone. It reaches into all her relationships and all her functions. As a wife she is not only often ungratified but ungratifying and has, as we have noted, a profoundly disturbing effect upon her husband. Not only does he find himself without the satisfactions of a home directed and cared for by a woman happy in providing affection and devotion, but he is often confronted by circumstances of even more serious import for his own emotional integrity. His wife may be his covert rival, striving to match him in every aspect of their joint undertaking. Instead of supporting and encouraging his manliness and wishes for domination and power, she may thus impose upon him feelings of insufficiency and weakness. Still worse is the effect upon his sexual satisfactions. Where the woman is unable to admit and accept dependence upon her husband as the source of gratification and must carry her rivalry even into the act of love, she will seriously damage his sexual capacity. To be unable to gratify in the sexual act is for a man an intensely humiliating experience; here it is that mastery and domination, the central capacity of the man's sexual nature, must meet acceptance or fail. So it is that by their own character disturbances these women succeed ultimately in depriving themselves of the devotion and power of their husbands and become the instruments of bringing about their own psychic catastrophe.

But no matter how great a woman's masculine strivings, her basic needs make themselves felt and she finds herself facing her fundamental role as wife and mother with a divided mind. Deprived of a rich and creative home in which to find self-expression, she tries desperately to find a compromise. On the one hand she must retain her sources of real instinctual gratification and on the other, find ways of satisfying her need for prestige and esteem. Thus she stands, Janus-faced, drawn in two directions at once, often incapable of ultimate choice and inevitably penalized whatever direction she chooses.

"TO RESCUE US WRETCHED SLAVES"
ADLAI STEVENSON

The following commencement address by Adlai Stevenson, governor of Illinois and two-time Democratic presidential candidate, to the graduating class of Smith College in June 1955 reflects the ambivalence and confusion about women's roles in postwar America. If women were expected to devote themselves to marriage and motherhood, then why give them a rigorous academic education such as that offered at Smith College? Stevenson, one of the most eloquent public speakers in American history, offered a response that was at once patronizing and poetic, urgent and meditative.

While weighing in on the side of full-time domesticity for these young college graduates from an elite women's college, he urged his young listeners to instill in their future husbands and children the democratic values of tolerance, mutual respect, love of freedom, and open-minded inquiry. Stevenson's exhortations to the Smith graduates to "rescue us wretched slaves of specialization and group thinking from further . . . contraction of mind and spirit" recalled the ideas of Catharine Beecher and other early-nineteenth-century purveyors of "Republican motherhood": the notion that women needed to be educated to raise virtuous citizens—specifically male citizens—who would practice the democratic principles of liberty and good government. Like that earlier generation of thinkers and reformers, Stevenson believed that women, as mothers, had the most important role of all—to "educate and form the new generation."

SOURCE: Stevenson, Adlai E. Commencement Address, Smith College, June 6, 1955. Smith College Archives, Northampton, Mass., pp. 4–7. By permission of the Estate of Adlai E. Stevenson.

YOU MAY BE HITCHED to one of these creatures we call "Western man" and I think part of your job is to keep him Western, to keep him truly purposeful, to keep him whole. In short—while I have had very little experience as a wife and mother—I think one of the biggest jobs for many of you will be to frustrate the crushing and corrupting effects of specialization, to integrate means and ends, to develop that balanced tension of mind and spirit which can be properly called "integrity."

This assignment for you, as wives and mothers, has great advantages. In the first place, it is home work—you can do it in the living room with a baby in your lap, or in the kitchen with a can opener in your hands. If you're really clever, maybe you can even practice your saving arts on that unsuspecting man while he's watching television! And, secondly, it is important work worthy of you, whoever you are, or your education, whatever it is—even Smith College because we will defeat totalitarian, authoritarian ideas only by better ideas; we will frustrate the evils of vocational specialization only by the virtues of intellectual generalization. Since Western rationalism and Eastern spiritualism met in Athens and that mighty creative fire broke out, collectivism in various forms has collided with individualism time and again. This 20th Century collision, this "crisis" we are forever talking about, will be won at last not on the battlefield but in the head and heart.

If the Colosseum at Rome is, as some say, the symbol of the Roman failure to integrate mind and spirit, or means and ends, the hydrogen bomb, we might say, is the symbol of our own very similar self-betrayal. And one may hope that Hiroshima, like Rome's bloody arena, may be remembered at some distant day as a scene symbolizing a new beginning for mankind.

So you see, I have some rather large notions about you young ladies and what you have to do to rescue us wretched slaves of specialization and group thinking from further shrinkage and contraction of mind and spirit. But you will have to be alert or you may get caught yourself—even in the kitchen or the nursery—by the steady pressures with which you will be surrounded. . . .

Now, as I have said, women, especially educated women such as you, have a unique opportunity to influence us, man and boy, and to play a direct part in the unfolding drama of our free society. But, I am told that nowadays the young wife or mother is short of time for the subtle arts, that things are not what they used to be; that once immersed in the very pressing and particular problems of domesticity, many women feel frustrated and far apart from the great issues and stirring debates for which their education has given them understanding and relish. Once they read Baudelaire. Now it is the Consumers' Guide. Once they wrote poetry. Now it's the laundry list. Once they discussed art and philosophy until late in the night. Now they are so tired they fall asleep as soon as the dishes are finished. There is, often, a sense of contraction, of closing horizons and lost opportunities. They had hoped to play their part in the crisis of the age. But what they do is wash the diapers.

Now, I hope I have not painted too depressing a view of your future, for the fact is that Western marriage and motherhood are yet another instance of the emergence of individual freedom in our Western society. . . .

The point is that whether we talk of Africa, Islam or Asia, women "never had it so good" as you do. And in spite of the difficulties of domesticity you have a way to participate actively in the crisis in addition to keeping yourself and those about you straight on the difference between means and end, mind and spirit, reason and emotion—not to mention keeping your man straight on the differences between Botticelli and Chianti.

In brief if one of the chief needs in these restless times is for a new quality of mind and heart, who is nearer to the care of this need, the cultivation of this quality, than parents, especially mothers, who educate and form the new generation?

So, add to all of your concerns for Western man, your very special responsibility for Western children. In a family based upon the mutual respect, tolerance and understanding affection, the new generation of children—the citizens of tomorrow—stand their best chance of growing up to recognize the fundamental principle of free society—the uniqueness and value and wholeness of each individual human being. For this recognition requires discipline and training. The first instinct of all our untutored egos is to smash and grab, to treat the boy next door as a means not an end when you pinch his air rifle, or deny the uniqueness of your small sister's personality when you punch her in the stomach and snatch her lollypop.

Perhaps this is merely to say that the basis of any tolerable society—from the small society of the family up to the great society of the State—depends upon its members learning to love. By that I do not mean sentimentality or possessive emotion. I mean the steady recognition of others' uniqueness and a sustained intention to seek their good. In this, freedom and charity go hand in hand and they both have to be learned. Where better than in the home? And by whom better than the parents, especially the mother.

In short, far from the vocation of marriage and motherhood leading you away from the great issues of our day, it brings you back to their very center and places upon you an infinitely deeper and more intimate responsibility than that borne by the majority of those who hit the headlines and make the news and live in such a turmoil of great issues that they end by being totally unable to distinguish which issues are really great.

Yet you may say that these functions of the home could have been as well fulfilled without your years of study, performed perhaps better by instinct and untroubled by those hints of broader horizons and more immortal longings which it is the purpose of a college education to instill.

Well, there are two things to say to that. The first, of course, is that in modern America the home is not the boundary of a woman's life. There are outside activities aplenty. But even more important is the fact, surely, that what you have learned here can fit you as nothing else can for the primary task of making homes and whole human beings in whom the rational values of freedom, tolerance, charity and free inquiry can take root. You have learned discrimination. You have the tolerance which comes from the realization of man's infinite variety. Because you have learned from history the pathos and mutability of human affairs, you have a sense of pity. From literature you have learned the abiding values of the human heart and the discipline and sacrifice from which those values will flower in your own hearts and in the life of your families.

There can be no waste of any education that gives you these things. But you can waste them, or you can use them. I hope you'll use them. I hope you'll not be content to wring your hands, feed your family and just echo all the group, the tribal ritual refrains. I hope you'll keep everlastingly at the job of seeing life steady and seeing it whole.

"I KNEW I WASN'T GOING TO MAKE IT . . .
TO THE 'COLORED LADIES' TOILET"
MELBA PATTILO BEALS

Melba Pattilo Beals is most well known for being one of nine African American student volunteers to help integrate Central High School in Little Rock, Arkansas, after the Supreme Court's ruling in 1954 in the landmark Brown v. Board of Education of Topeka, Kansas. *That ruling declared segregated schools to be unconstitutional because they deprived black children of equal protection under the laws. In her autobiography,* Warriors Don't Cry, *Beals has described the brutal treatment she endured by white students and parents who opposed integrating Central High. (See also the excerpt in this chapter from Daisy Bates's memoir of that momentous but heart-breaking period in American race relations,* The Shadow of Little Rock.)*

In this selection from her autobiography, however, Beals poignantly recounts the daily indignities that blacks across the Jim Crow South faced, as well as the quiet strength and dignity with which her grandmother defused a potentially explosive confrontation with the police. During the civil rights movement black women marched, organized boycotts, and provided food and lodging for other civil rights workers. But they were also frontline warriors in the day-to-day struggle to protect their families from the harsh realities of segregation, marshalling reserves of strength, ingenuity, and astonishing patience, as this excerpt reveals. In freedom as in slavery, African American women skillfully developed ways to resist the daily humiliations and threats on the safety of their families and themselves.

SOURCE: Melba Pattilo Beals, *Warriors Don't Cry: A Searing Memoir of the Battle to Integrate Little Rock's Central High* (New York: Pocket Books, 1994), pp. 18–21. Reprinted with the permission of Simon & Schuster, copyright © 1944, 1955 by Melba Patillo Beals.

I WAS AS IMPATIENT for change as I was with the location of the rest rooms marked "Colored." As a child it seemed they were always located miles away from wherever I was when I felt the urge to go. When we shopped in the downtown stores, the rest rooms were usually located at the end of a dark hallway, or at the bottom of a dingy stairwell. It never failed that either I dampened my pants trying to get there in time or, worse yet, got a horrible ache in my side trying to hold my water until I got home.

An experience I endured on a December morning would forever affect any decision I made to go "potty" in a public place. We were Christmas shopping when I felt the twinge of emergency. I convinced Mother and Grandmother that I knew the way to the rest room by myself. I was moving as fast as I could when suddenly I knew I wasn't going to make it all the way down those stairs and across the warehouse walkway to the "Colored Ladies" toilet.

So I pushed open the door marked "White Ladies" and, taking a deep breath, I crossed the threshold. It was just as bright and pretty as I had imagined it to be. At first I could only hear voices nearby, but when I stepped through a second doorway, I saw several white ladies chatting and fussing with their makeup. Across the room, other white ladies sat on a couch reading the newspaper. Suddenly realizing I was there, two of them looked up at me in astonishment. Unless I was the maid, they said, I was in the wrong place. But it was clear I was too young to be the maid. While they shouted at me to "get out," my throbbing bladder consumed my attention as I frantically headed for the unoccupied stall.

They kept shouting, "Good Lord, do something." I was doing something by that time, seated comfortably on the toilet, listening to the hysteria building outside my locked stall. One woman even knelt down to peep beneath the door to make certain I didn't put my bottom on the toilet seat. She ordered me not to pee.

At first there was so much carrying-on outside my stall that I was afraid to come out. But I wanted to see all the special things about the white ladies' rest room, so I had no choice. A chorus of "Nigger" and other nasty words billowed around me as I washed my hands. One woman waved her finger in my face, warning me that her friend had gone after the police and they would teach me a thing or two. Hearing the word "police" terrified me. Daddy and Mother Lois were afraid of the police. The ladies were hurrying out through the door saying they were going to tell the manager that they would never shop in that store again.

Just then I heard a familiar voice: "Melba Joy Pattillo, just what are you doing in there." It was Grandma India calling out to me. She stepped inside the room. I was so happy to see her that I rushed to give her a hug. Her embrace made me feel safe, but the fear in her voice brought back my fear. My curiosity had gotten us into a real mess, she said. The police and a whole bunch of white folks were outside waiting for me. Grandma pushed me away and wiped my tears. And even as she straightened the bow on my braid, those voices were shouting at us through the door.

"I'm demanding you'all get out here right now. I'm with the Little Rock Police. Don't make us come in after you."

Grandma straightened her shoulders, assuming the posture of a queen as she reached down to take my hand, and instructed me to stand tall. As we walked through the door, I tilted my chin upward to match her chin as she looked the two policemen right in the eye. She spoke to them in a calm, clear voice, explaining that I was not good at reading signs. Then she apologized for any inconvenience I had caused. Her voice didn't sound frightened, but I could feel her hand shaking and the perspiration in her palm.

Suddenly, one of the officers moved close and blocked our way, saying we had to come upstairs for a serious talk. Grandma didn't flinch as he moved too close to her. Instead, she smiled down at me and squeezed my hand. But as he beckoned her to move ahead, I knew we were in more trouble than we'd ever been in before. When she asked where he was taking us, he told her to shut up and do as we were told. Some of the crowd moved with us. When we passed close to Mother Lois, she and Grandma talked to each other with their eyes. I started to speak, but Grandma pinched my arm.

Once inside the upstairs room with the straight-back wooden chairs, long table, and cardboard boxes, both officers lit cigarettes. One of them said we must be part of a communist group from up North, trying to integrate Little Rock's bathrooms. Grandma's voice only cracked once as over and over again she insisted that I had made a mistake. She called them "sir" and "mister" as she protested that we were good Little Rock citizens grateful for the use of our own bathrooms. She said she remembered the time when we couldn't even enter the front door of the store and she was humbly grateful for that privilege.

Finally, after an hour, the older policemen said he'd let us go, calling us harmless niggers gone astray. But he warned if we were ever again caught being curious about what belonged to white folks, we'd be behind bars wearing stripes, or even worse, wearing ropes around our necks.

As we climbed into the car, Grandmother India warned me that curiosity killed the cat and it was going to be my undoing. As punishment for my bad deed, she made me read the Twenty-Third Psalm every day for a month. I also had to look up "patience" in the dictionary and write down the definition. . . .

"THINGS CANNOT GO ON AS THEY ARE IN DIXIE"
LILLIAN SMITH

Lillian Smith was among a handful of white southerners who vehemently denounced racial segregation and prejudice in the South. Born into an affluent white family that supported segregation, she spent her early years happily playing with black friends until her parents taught her to regard them as social inferiors. After briefly attending college, she worked as a principal of a rural school in Georgia and taught music at a Methodist-sponsored school in China, where she first became aware of the corrosive impact of racial and class bigotry.

In 1936 she and her lifelong partner, Paula Snelling, founded a little magazine called Pseudopodia. *Later they changed the name to* South Today. *It was the first white southern magazine to publish the work of black writers and scholars, and it also featured the work of aspiring women writers. While editing the magazine, Smith reflected upon the social and moral damage wrought by segregation and, deeply troubled by what she observed, she crusaded against bigotry in all of her writings, fiction as well as nonfiction.*

In 1949 she published Killers of the Dream, *an extended meditation on the evils of segregation. This became her most famous book and earned her the enduring enmity of the white South. But no level of hostility—including two fires set by arsonists to silence her—could prevent her from continuing to advocate integration and equality.*

In the following letter, published in the New York Times *on April 4, 1948, Smith castigates southern liberals for maintaining a cowardly silence about segregation and other violations against African Americans. She perspicaciously compares the totalitarianism of Russian culture to the suppression of opposing voices in the South and shrewdly reminds readers that only a firm, principled liberal opposition can stem reactionary thought by both right- and left-wing factions. Later Smith noted that the publication of this letter "infuriated Georgia and much of the South" and "tipped off a real battle" against her even before the publication of* Killers of the Dream. *The letter is a courageous call for civil rights by a southern white woman many years before the civil rights movement captured national attention and support.*

SOURCE: Margaret Rose Gladney, ed., *"How Am I To Be Heard?" Letters of Lillian Smith*, pp. 119–22. Copyright © 1993 by the University of North Carolina Press. Used by permission of the publisher.

March 22, 1948

To The Editors of The New York Times:

As a Southern woman, I am deeply shocked that our liberals are putting up no real fight for human rights in the South. It is, of course, the same battle we are losing all over the world. Each day more ground is lost. In Czecho-slovakia—now in Italy we may soon be hearing the same old story. Caution, vacillation, no real program, no strong affirmations of human freedom—these are poor weapons to use against real enemies.

For weeks the front pages of our newspapers have been full of demagog-ic race fear, Yankee hate, affirmations of the "great belief" of White Su-premacy, while Southern liberalism maintains its old grim silence. Not one Southerner has taken a strong stand in a Southern newspaper against segre-gation; not one has affirmed the proud fact that we Southerners are also Americans; not one has said that human rights today are not only the na-tion's but the whole world's business, and its first business. Even those of us who want to speak out are not permitted to. I cannot be heard in Georgia even in the letter columns. If there are honorable exceptions to this solid si-lence, I do not know them.

It is hard to understand such timidity at a time like this, unless we re-member that Georgia, U.S.A., still has a lot in common with Georgia, U.S.S.R. Totalitarianism is an old thing to us down home. We know what it feels like. The unquestioned authority of White Supremacy, the tight polit-ical set-up of one party, nourished on poverty and ignorance, solidified the South into a totalitarian regime under which we were living when commu-nism was still Russian cellar talk and Hitler had not even been born.

To keep us that way, our political demagogues used and still use the same tricks Stalin uses today: an external enemy to hate (the damyankee), an internal enemy to fear (the Negro), an iron curtain which was first forged out of the reluctance of the democratic few to take an open stand against such powerful forces. During those bitter decades liberalism was driven completely underground. Caution was a necessity, temporizing was virtue. This was the only way men could work for human rights under a system that exacted such heavy penalties from its "deviationists" as did Southern tradition.

Thus it came about that men took pride in thinking democratic thoughts and as much pride in never voicing them or putting them into acts. To speak out in those bitter years was truly the dangerous act of a fool (though a great fool); to speak out today is a mildly dangerous act of great wisdom. But it is hard for Southern liberals to believe it. Caution has become a cherished habit; conscience has been split off so long from words and acts that it is not easy to fill up the chasm between them. Into that chasm flow the energy of Southern liberalism and its integrity. We just don't love human freedom enough to take real risks for it.

It is incredible that demagogic oratory could hypnotize not only the poor and ignorant but our liberals into believing that the only way we can work out problems of racial segregation is to set up an even worse regional segregation which, like Russian denial of freedom of speech, book-banning, national isolationism, is so dangerous a withdrawal from the realities of the world we live in. . . .

We must remember that demagogues fatten on the poor man's vote and his loneliness, that they use the psychotic to do their dirty work, but they exist because we liberals let them exist. It is our caution, our lack of energy, our moral impotence and our awful if unconscious snobbery, that make demagoguery unafraid of liberalism.

Look at them today in the South: fanning hate, giving the green light to violence by their almost traitorous incitements against their own national government, while the liberals stand by silently. Silence is a poor way of changing people. It is a poor way of making people fall in love with an idea.

In parts of our South, our people have never heard talk of human rights and the dignity of man; they do not even dream that there are fellow-Southerners who would question segregation. But they hear, in every county, almost every day, on radio and in newspaper, the doctrines of yankeebaiting and White Supremacy; and they hear their "wisest" liberals repeating the old lesson "Whatever is done has to be done by us alone and has to be done under the segregation system." This is the "education" our people are receiving; this is exactly what the demagogues mean too when they say Southerners must change by education, not legislation.

Only the liberals, South and North, can counteract these doctrines. A concerted effort made by newspaper, radio and pulpit, could break the back of demagoguery in a year simply by giving Southerners something else to believe and making them fall in love with their new beliefs. Our long-range rural programs must be put in effect, of course, but it will take ten years to change our Tobacco Roads, even with hard work. We don't have ten years now. Things cannot go on as they are in Dixie. The Communists know it and they are not waiting for liberals to think it over—just as they are not waiting in other parts of the world. It is a tragic fact, but true, that people long used to one authority find it easy to accept another. The Solid South founded on the authority of White Supremacy, held firm by one party and a hatred of "those enemies outside," might not find it too hard to accept the authority and one-party system of the Solid Soviets. . . .

Margaret Chase Smith, Republican senator from Maine, was the first woman to be elected to the United States Senate. After her husband, a congressman from Maine, passed away unexpectedly, a special election enabled her to complete his term in the House of Representatives, and she went on to be elected to three additional terms. In 1948 she ran for the Senate and served in that governing body until 1972. During Smith's long tenure in the Senate, she witnessed everything from the "Red scare" of the early 1950s to the antiwar protests of the late sixties. On June 1, 1950, she became the first Republican in the Senate to publicly chastize Senator Joseph McCarthy for his campaign of fear and intimidation against alleged communist sympathizers. Starting in 1950, McCarthy gained national notoriety when he charged that communists had infiltrated the State Department and the U.S. Army. Without producing any evidence to substantiate his charges, he intensified an already spreading anticommunist hysteria in the nation and managed to suppress any opposition to his bullying tactics—until Smith courageously spoke out. In the following edited record of her remarks, Smith is clearly aware of the importance of her position as the Senate's only female member. Her speech is an eloquent call to her colleagues to uphold the essential American ideals of freedom of speech, thought, and protest without fear of retribution.

In 1972, after being defeated in her final reelection bid, Smith observed, "I hate to leave the Senate when there is no indication another qualified woman is coming in. . . . If I leave and there's a long lapse, the next woman will have to rebuild entirely." *

SOURCE: In the public domain.

Mr. President, I would like to speak briefly and simply about a serious national condition. It is a national feeling of fear and frustration that could result in national suicide and the end of everything that we Americans hold dear. It is a condition that comes from the lack of effective leadership either in the legislative branch or the executive branch of our government. . . .

---

* Quoted in Kathryn Cullen-Dupont, *The Encyclopedia of Women's History in America* (New York: Facts on File, 1997), p. 198.

Mr. President, I speak as a Republican. I speak as a woman. I speak as a United States senator. I speak as an American.

The United States Senate has long enjoyed worldwide respect as the greatest deliberative body in the world. But recently that deliberative character has too often been debased to the level of a forum of hate and character assassination sheltered by the shield of congressional immunity.

It is ironical that we senators can in debate in the Senate, directly or indirectly, by any form of words, impute to any American who is not a senator any conduct or motive unworthy or unbecoming an American—and without that non-senator American having any legal redress against us—yet if we say the same thing in the Senate about our colleagues, we can be stopped on the grounds of being out of order. . . .

I think that it is high time for the United States Senate and its members to do some real soul searching and to weigh our consciences as to the manner in which we are performing our duty to the people of America and the manner in which we are using or abusing our individual powers and privileges. I think that it is high time that we remembered that we have sworn to uphold and defend the Constitution. I think that it is high time that we remembered that the Constitution, as amended, speaks not only of the freedom of speech but also of trial by jury instead of trial by accusation. Whether it be a criminal prosecution in court or a character prosecution in the Senate, there is little practical distinction when the life of a person has been ruined.

Those of us who shout the loudest about Americanism in making character assassinations are all too frequently those who, by our own words and acts, ignore some of the basic principles of Americanism: the right to criticize, the right to hold unpopular beliefs, the right to protest, the right of independent thought. The exercise of these rights should not cost one single American citizen his reputation or his right to a livelihood, nor should he be in danger of losing his reputation or livelihood merely because he happens to know someone who holds unpopular beliefs. Who of us does not? Otherwise none of us could call our souls our own. Otherwise thought control would have set in.

The American people are sick and tired of being afraid to speak their minds lest they be politically smeared as communists or fascists by their opponents. Freedom of speech is not what it used to be in America. It has been so abused by some that it is not exercised by others.

The American people are sick and tired of seeing innocent people smeared and guilty people whitewashed. But there have been enough proved cases— such as the Amerasia case, the Hiss case, the Coplon case, the Gold case—to cause nationwide distrust and strong suspicion that there may be something to the unproved, sensational accusations.

As a Republican, I say to my colleagues on this side of the aisle that the Republican Party faces a challenge today that is not unlike the challenge which it faced back in Lincoln's day. The Republican Party so successfully met that challenge that it emerged from the Civil War as the champion of a united nation, in addition to being a party which unrelentingly fought loose spending and loose programs.

Today our country is being psychologically divided by the confusion and the suspicions that are bred in the United States Senate to spread like cancerous tentacles of "know nothing, suspect everything" attitudes. Today we have a Democratic administration that has developed a mania for loose spending and loose programs. History is repeating itself, and the Republican Party again has the opportunity to emerge as the champion of unity and prudence.

The record of the present Democratic administration has provided us with sufficient campaign issues without the necessity of resorting to political smears. America is rapidly losing its position as leader of the world simply because the Democratic administration has pitifully failed to provide effective leadership. . . .

The nation sorely needs a Republican victory. But I do not want to see the Republican Party ride to political victory on the Four Horsemen of Calumny—Fear, Ignorance, Bigotry, and Smear. I doubt if the Republican Party could do so, simply because I do not believe the American people will uphold any political party that puts political exploitation above the national interest. Surely we Republicans are not that desperate for victory. I do not want to see the Republican Party win that way. While it might be a fleeting victory for the Republican Party, it would be a more lasting defeat for the American people. Surely it would ultimately be suicide for the Republican Party and the two-party system that has protected our American liberties from the dictatorship of a one-party system.

As members of the minority party, we do not have the primary authority to formulate the policy of our government. But we do have the responsibility of rendering constructive criticism, of clarifying issues, of allaying fears by acting as responsible citizens. As a woman, I wonder how the mothers, wives, sisters, and daughters feel about the way in which members of their families have been politically mangled in Senate debate—and I use the word *debate* advisedly. As a United States senator, I am not proud of the way in which the Senate has been made a publicity platform for irresponsible sensationalism. I am not proud of the reckless abandon in which unproved charges have been hurled from this side of the aisle. I am not proud of the obviously staged, undignified countercharges which have been attempted in retaliation from the other side of the aisle. . . .

As an American, I am shocked at the way Republicans and Democrats alike are playing directly into the communist design of "confuse, divide, and conquer." As an American, I do not want a Democratic administration white-wash or cover-up any more than I want a Republican smear or witch hunt.

As an American, I condemn a Republican fascist just as much as I condemn a Democrat communist. I condemn a Democrat fascist just as much as I condemn a Republican communist. They are equally dangerous to you and me and to our country. As an American, I want to see our nation recapture the strength and unity it once had when we fought the enemy instead of ourselves.

"I DIDN'T THINK I SHOULD HAVE TO GIVE IT UP"
ROSA PARKS

Often hailed as "the mother of the freedom movement," Rosa Parks re-
fused to give up her seat on a crowded bus in Montgomery, Alabama, to a white
man—and sparked a historic movement among African Americans for social and
political equality.

Contrary to public mythology, Parks did not give up her seat on the bus simply
because she was tired after a hard work day; long active in civil rights groups, she
wanted to challenge the Jim Crow laws that segregated blacks in public trans-
portation and facilities. Having grown up in rural Alabama, she had a deep
awareness of racial injustice. She was one of the first women to join the Mont-
gomery chapter of the National Association for the Advancement of Colored Peo-
ple (NAACP) and was a member of the Montgomery Voters League, a group that
helped blacks register to vote.

In the following excerpt, Parks recalls the sequence of events surrounding her
historic act of December 1, 1955. Within days Montgomery's black community re-
sponded just as she had hoped it would—by organizing a mass boycott against the
Montgomery transit system. Boycotters walked, hitched rides, or carpooled to
avoid riding on segregated city buses. The bus boycott lasted more than a year, and
on December 20, 1956, 381 days after it had started, the Supreme Court ordered city
officials to integrate Montgomery's buses.

After this victory, blacks in Montgomery and across the South organized a
movement to dismantle segregation in all public facilities, including schools and li-
braries, and in the voting booth, where most blacks had been denied the constitu-
tional right to vote. Parks, like other civil rights workers, endured malicious taunts
and threats on her life because of her civil rights work. Her courage and resistance
were all the more remarkable in an era of few public acts of defiance against law
and custom. She was a true pioneer who helped lead the civil rights movement to
a new era of nonviolent resistance.

SOURCE: Howell Raines, ed., *My Soul Is Rested: Movement Days in the Deep South Remem-*
bered (New York: G. P. Putnam, 1977), pp. 40–42. Used by permission of G. P. Putnam's
Sons, a division of Penguin Putnam Inc.

I HAD LEFT MY WORK at the men's alteration shop, a tailor shop in the Montgomery Fair department store, and as I left work, I crossed the street to a drugstore to pick up a few items instead of trying to go directly to the bus stop. And

when I had finished this, I came across the street and looked for a Cleveland Avenue bus that apparently had some seats on it. At that time it was a little hard to get a seat on the bus. But when I did get to the entrance to the bus, I got in line with a number of other people who were getting on the same bus.

As I got up on the bus and walked to the seat I saw there was only one vacancy that was just back of where it was considered the white section. So this was the seat that I took, next to the aisle, and a man was sitting next to me. Across the aisle there were two women, and there were a few seats at this point in the very front of the bus that was called the white section. I went on to one stop and I didn't particularly notice who was getting on the bus, didn't particularly notice the other people getting on. And on the third stop there were some people getting on, and at this point all of the front seats were taken. Now in the beginning, at the very first stop I had got on the bus, the back of the bus was filled up with people standing in the aisle and I don't know why this one vacancy that I took was left, because there were quite a few people already standing toward the back of the bus. The third stop is when all the front seats were taken, and this one man was standing and when the driver looked around and saw he was standing, he asked the four of us, the man in the seat with me and the two women across the aisle, to let him have those front seats.

At his first request, didn't any of us move. Then he spoke again and said. "You'd better make it light on yourselves and let me have those seats." At this point, of course, the passenger who would have taken the seat hadn't said anything. In fact, he never did speak to my knowledge. When the three people, the man who was in the seat with me and the two women, stood up and moved into the aisle, I remained where I was. When the driver saw that I was still sitting there, he asked if I was going to stand up. I told him, no, I wasn't. He said, "Well, if you don't stand up, I'm going to have you arrested." I told him to go on and have me arrested.

He got off the bus and came back shortly. A few minutes later, two policemen got on the bus, and they approached me and asked if the driver had asked me to stand up, and I said yes, and they wanted to know why I didn't. I told them I didn't think I should have to stand up. After I had paid my fare and occupied a seat, I didn't think I should have to give it up. They placed me under arrest then and had me to get in the police car, and I was taken to jail and booked on suspicion, I believe. The questions were asked, the usual questions they ask a prisoner or somebody that's under arrest. They had to determine whether or not the driver wanted to press charges or swear out a warrant, which he did. Then they took me to jail and I was placed in a cell. In a little while I was taken from the cell, and my picture was made and fingerprints taken. I went back to the cell then, and a few minutes later I was called back again, and when this happened I found out that Mr. E. D. Nixon[*] and Attorney and Mrs. Clifford Durr[†] had come to make bond for me.

In the meantime before this, of course . . . I was given permission to make a telephone call after my picture was taken and fingerprints taken. I called my home and spoke to my mother on the telephone and told her what had happened, that I was in jail. She was quite upset and asked me had the police beaten me. I told her, no, I hadn't been physically injured, but, I was being held in jail, and I wanted my husband to come and get me out. . . . He didn't have a car at that time, so he had to get someone to bring him down. At the time when he got down, Mr. Nixon and the Durrs had just made bond for me, so we all met at the jail and we went home.

---

[*] E. D. Nixon was a leader of the Montgomery and Alabama chapters of the NAACP. He regarded segregated buses as one of the most egregious forms of racial injustice and was eager to challenge municipal bus ordinances in the courts.

[†] Clifford and Virginia Durr were a white couple from Alabama who were active in the civil rights movement.

"IT WAS THE LONGEST BLOCK I EVER WALKED IN MY WHOLE LIFE"
ELIZABETH ECKFORD

In 1954, in the wake of Brown v. Board of Education of Topeka, Kansas, *the landmark Supreme Court ruling that deemed segregated schools unconstitutional, the school board of Little Rock, Arkansas, was the first in the South to announce that it would comply with the Court's ruling to integrate its schools. Over the next three years the school board worked with the city's black leadership to design a voluntary desegregation plan. Daisy Bates, editor-in-chief of the black newspaper the* Arkansas State Press *and president of the Arkansas NAACP, played a key role in promoting integration in the schools. Her home became the headquarters and also a refuge for the nine African American students who volunteered to go to Central High, the previously all-white high school. Among those students was Elizabeth Eckford.*

Initially, the governor of Arkansas, Orval Faubus, called out the Arkansas National Guard to prevent the nine students from entering Central High. But President Dwight D. Eisenhower sent in federal troops to escort the students into school and protect them from violence. All of the students confronted nasty opposition from white students, parents, and others. They faced jeers, taunts, and physical assault at the hands of white students, but young Elizabeth Eckford's attempts to enter Central High elicited a particularly vicious response from unruly mobs. Nor did she get any help from the state's National Guardsmen, who actually raised their bayonets to prevent her from entering the school. This dramatic account of her nightmarish experiences demonstrates the sacrifices and hardships that young black women and men endured in seeking justice and equality in the segregated South.

SOURCE: Daisy Bates, *The Long Shadow of Little Rock* (New York: David McKay, 1966), pp. 406–9. Reprinted by permission of the University of Arkansas Press. Copyright 1986 by Daisy Bates.

ELIZABETH, whose dignity and control in the face of jeering mobsters had been filmed by television cameras and recorded in pictures flashed to newspapers over the world, had overnight become a national heroine. During the next few days newspaper reporters besieged her home, wanting to talk to her. The first day that her parents agreed she might come out of seclusion, she came to my house where the reporters awaited her. Elizabeth was very quiet, speaking only when spoken to. I took her to my bedroom to talk before I let the reporters see her. I asked how she felt now. Suddenly all her pent-up emotion flared.

"Why am I here?" she said, turning blazing eyes on me. "Why are you so interested in my welfare now? You didn't care enough to notify me of the change of plans—"

I walked over and reached out to her. Before she turned her back on me, I saw tears gathering in her eyes. My heart was breaking for this young girl who stood there trying to stifle her sobs. How could I explain that frantic early morning when at three o'clock my mind had gone on strike?

In the ensuing weeks Elizabeth took part in all the activities of the time— press conferences, attendance at court, studying with professors at nearby Philander Smith College. She was present, that is, but never really a part of things. The hurt had been too deep.

On the two nights she stayed at my home I was awakened by the screams in her sleep, as she relieved in her dreams the terrifying mob scenes at Central. The only times Elizabeth showed real excitement were when Thurgood Marshall met the children and explained the meaning of what had happened in court. As he talked, she would listen raptly, a faint smile on her face. It was obvious he was her hero.

Little by little Elizabeth came out of her shell. Up to now she had never talked about what happened to her at Central. Once when we were alone in the downstairs recreation room of my house, I asked her simply, "Elizabeth, do you think you can talk about it now?"

She remained quiet for a long time. Then she began to speak.

"You remember the day we were to go in, we met Superintendent Blossom at the school board office. He told us what the mob might say and do but he never told us we wouldn't have any protection. He told our parents not to come because he wouldn't be able to protect the children if they did.

"That night I was so excited I couldn't sleep. The next morning I was about the first one up. While I was pressing my black and white dress—I had made it to wear on the first day of school—my little brother turned on the TV set. They started telling about a large crowd gathered at the school. The man on TV said he wondered if we were going to show up that morning. Mother called from the kitchen, where she was fixing breakfast, 'Turn that TV off!' She was so upset and worried. I wanted to comfort her, so I said, 'Mother, don't worry.'

"Dad was walking back and forth, from room to room, with a sad expression. He was chewing on his pipe and he had a cigar in his hand, but he didn't light either one. It would have been funny, only he was so nervous.

"Before I left home Mother called us into the living-room. She said we should have a word of prayer. Then I caught the bus and got off a block from the school. I saw a large crowd of people standing across the street from the soldiers guarding Central. As I walked on, the crowd suddenly got very quiet. Superintendent Blossom had told us to enter by the front door. I looked at all the people and thought, 'Maybe I will be safer if I walk down the block to the front entrance behind the guards.'

"At the corner I tried to pass through the long line of guards around the school so as to enter the grounds behind them. One of the guards pointed across the street. So I pointed in the same direction and asked whether he meant for me to cross the street and walk down. He nodded 'yes.' So, I walked across the street conscious of the crowd that stood there, but they moved away from me.

"For a moment all I could hear was the shuffling of their feet. Then someone shouted, 'Here she comes, get ready!' I moved away from the crowd on the sidewalk and into the street. If the mob came at me I could then cross back over so the guards could protect me.

"The crowd moved in closer and then began to follow me, calling me names. I still wasn't afraid. Just a little bit nervous. Then my knees started to shake all of a sudden and I wondered whether I could make it to the center entrance a block away. It was the longest block I ever walked in my whole life.

"Even so, I still wasn't too scared because all the time I kept thinking that the guards would protect me.

"When I got right in front of the school, I went up to a guard again. But this time he just looked straight ahead and didn't move to let me pass him. I didn't know what to do. Then I looked and saw that the path leading to the front entrance was a little further ahead. So I walked until I was right in front of the path to the front door.

"I stood looking at the school—it looked so big! Just then the guards let some white students go through.

"The crowd was quiet. I guess they were waiting to see what was going to happen. When I was able to steady my knees, I walked up to the guard who had let the white students in. He too didn't move. When I tried to squeeze past him, he raised his bayonet and then the other guards closed in and they raised their bayonets.

"They glared at me with a mean look and I was very frightened and didn't know what to do. I turned around and the crowd came toward me.

"They moved closer and closer. Somebody started yelling, 'Lynch her! Lynch her!'

"I tried to see a friendly face somewhere in the mob—someone who maybe would help. I looked into the face of an old woman and it seemed a kind face, but when I looked at her again, she spat on me.

"They came closer, shouting, 'No nigger bitch is going to get in our school. Get out of here!'

"I turned back to the guards but their faces told me I wouldn't get help from them. Then I looked down the block and saw a bench at the bus stop. I thought, 'If I can only get there I will be safe.' I don't know why the bench seemed a safe place to me, but I started walking toward it. I tried to close my mind to what they were shouting, and kept saying to myself, 'If I can only make it to the bench I will be safe.'

"When I finally got there, I don't think I could have gone another step. I sat down and the mob crowded up and began shouting all over again. Someone hollered, 'Drag her over to this tree! Let's take care of the nigger.' Just then a white man sat down beside me, put his arm around me and patted my shoulder. He raised my chin and said, 'Don't let them see you cry.'

"Then, a white lady—she was very nice—she came over to me on the bench. She spoke to me but I don't remember now what she said. She put me on the bus and sat next to me. She asked me my name and tried to talk to me but I don't think I answered. I can't remember much about the bus ride, but the next thing I remember I was standing in front of the School for the Blind, where Mother works.

"I thought, 'Maybe she isn't here. But she has to be here!' So I ran upstairs, and I think some teachers tried to talk to me, but I kept running until I reached Mother's classroom.

"Mother was standing at the window with her head bowed, but she must have sensed I was there because she turned around. She looked as if she had been crying, and I wanted to tell her I was all right. But I couldn't speak. She put her arms around me and I cried."

Following is an excerpt of the Help Wanted section of the Atlanta Journal-Constitution *for January 2, 1960. Note that the ads are categorized by gender and, at the end, by race. This was not unusual for many newspapers, especially those published in the South. Even major northern newspapers such as the* New York Times *separated job listings by gender until the late 1960s. Also note how the jobs listed for men include more skilled positions that paid higher salaries and benefits than the job listings for women or for both black women and men. Here is a telling capsule view of employment expectations and opportunities, or the lack thereof, across the lines of gender and race in the prelude to the civil rights and women's movement.*

SOURCE: © 2002 *The Atlanta Journal-Constitution.* Reprinted with permission from the *Atlanta Journal-Constitution.*

EMPLOYMENT

HELP WANTED MALE

APPRENTICE

Young man wanted for outside serviceman trainee. No experience necessary. Must have good automobile. $75 per week with car allowance, plus gas, oil and expenses. Apply after 10 a.m. to Mr. Whitman, 85 Alabama Street, SW.

ARE YOU A

Securities Salesman?

Are you licensed? Will YOU WORK? If so, a new Georgia corporation is looking for YOU. This is not a usual securities salesman ad where YOU will be looking for another job in a matter of a few months. This is a LIFETIME CONNECTION FOR YOU with opportunity for DISTRICT MANAGER'S COMPENSATION WHEN MERITED. YOUR ANNUAL EARNINGS can be well into the FIVE FIGURE BRACKET IF YOU work. It's up to YOU. We have the securities. Do YOU have the ability? If so, telephone JA 4-6674 or CE 7-0535 for appointment and interview.

BAKERY ROUTE MEN

WE can use 2 men, married, age 22 to 40. High school graduate preferred. This is route sales work, 6-day week. Good pay, no lay-offs. Apply Highland Bakery, 655 Highland Ave., NE.

DISTRICT MANAGER

MAJOR Rubber Company will employ a well-experienced, well-qualified man for District assignment in Atlanta, Georgia. Knowledge of tire marketing in the Georgia, South Carolina and Alabama area helpful but not essential. A clean, successful past record a requirement. Excellent income, bonus, and expenses available. All replies will be treated strictly confidential. Write to C. P. Geddie, 1822 Rosemont St., Mesquite, Texas.

MECHANIC for heavy duty earth-moving equipment. Sober and reliable. References required. Phone Sherwood 2-3691, Macon, Ga., between 8:30 a.m. and 4 p.m. for appointment.

MACHINIST AND ELECTRICIAN

MUST be able to set up and run lathe shaper and milling machines. Prefer those with tool and die experience. Electrician familiar with all phases of plant maintenance. Permanent job. Good pay. Apply Swico, 3707 E. Ponce de Leon Ave.

SALESMAN

NATIONAL manufacturer of Venetian blinds, awnings and woven aluminum window treatment, desires salesman to contact manufacturers in South Carolina, Georgia, Florida Territory, well established. Liberal drawing account against commissions. Must have car. Experience in this field helpful but not essential. Write R. Y. 69, Journal-Constitution, giving resume of background.

TV SERVICEMAN

PERMANENT position, paid vacation, hospitalization, major medical and insurance, profit-sharing plan. Good opportunity for the right man. Apply Friedman's Jewelers, 37 Peachtree.

HELP WANTED FEMALE

GIRLS

With College Training

If you have graduated or do not plan to return to college contact Miss Adams. RETAIL CREDIT CO. Permanent positions of interesting and varied nature. Good opportunities available, many employee benefits. 1600 Peachtree.

HOSPITAL POSITIONS

NURSES' AIDES

18 to 45, 10th grade education, good health. Will train.

CLERK-TYPISTS

20 to 45, high school graduate, medical experience preferred but not necessary.

FOOD SUPERVISORS

24–45, high school graduates. Will train.

PBX OPERATOR

25 to 50, experience necessary.
APPLY Personnel, Georgia Baptist Hospital, 8:30 to 12 weekday mornings. Do not phone.

PUBLISHING firm in Buckhead area needs young lady experienced in light bookkeeping and office routine. Good typing required. 5-day week. Phone CE3-5461, 9 till 5.

STENO-CLERK to replace one retiring person at age 45. Prefer mature lady. Must be able to get along with other employees. Reply in own handwriting, giving age, salary expected, and employment references for past 10 years. 112 Journal-Const.

SALESLADIES

NEEDED (6) for immediate employment. Apply Ben Franklin 5 and 10 Store. 3697 Campbeliton Rd., SW.

TEACHERS WANTED—The Cobb County school system needs a girl physical education teacher, a high school English teacher, and a Glee Club director. Contact W. P. Sprayberry, Marietta 8-1596.

WAITRESSES

EXPERIENCED. Apply in person. Jake's Fine Foods. Rear Trailways Bus Station.

COL. EMPLOYMENT

HELP WANTED MALE, COLORED

MINT Car Wash. 1834 P'dmt, 308 T'wood, 536 P. de L., 2280 P'ree Rd.

FIRST-CLASS broiler and roast cook wanted. Salary open. Apply Atlanta Athletic Club, 166 Carnegie Way, N.W. JA 2-7430.

HELP WANTED FEMALE, COLORED

MAID

MAID to live in, housework and child care. Must have health card and reference. $30 week. BL 5-5690.

EXPERIENCED women's specialty store, marking and pressing. Starting salary $22.50. Apply in person. Norman's 3224 Peachtree Rd.

CHRISTIAN maid, experienced, high school education, day work, Tuesday and Friday, $5.50 day. BL 5-1262.

SALAD GIRL

EXPERIENCED person under 35, dependable, excellent pay. Apply The Pickrick, 891 Hemphill Ave., Northwest.

EXPERIENCED wool presser on the West side, for Marietta, Ga. Transportation furnished. Apply 3956 Buford Hwy. One Hour Martinizing.

"WE SAW WOMEN AS A VEHICLE FOR
A NEW PEACE ACTION"
DAGMAR WILSON

Dagmar Wilson is one of the founding "mothers" of Women Strike for Peace (WSP), a loosely knit organization of women around the nation who, in the early 1960s, marched, picketed, and lobbied the U.S. government to end nuclear-weapons testing and work for nuclear disarmament and world peace. Wilson, who had been outraged by the arrest of the British philosopher Bertrand Russell for taking part in antinuclear bomb demonstrations, contacted several friends about ways to promote peace, and in September 1961 their efforts and ideas crystallized into a movement.

This nascent movement took to the streets on November 1, 1961, when fifty thousand women in sixty cities around the country marched for world peace and against the resumption of nuclear testing by the U.S. government. From there the movement expanded into a comprehensive effort to outlaw the tools of war. Members lobbied Congress, picketed stores that sold war toys, demonstrated in front of the White House, circulated petitions for peace, educated themselves on the dangers of nuclear fallout, and distributed leaflets and conducted press campaigns to publicize their goals. They also dispatched representatives to international conferences on disarmament and appealed directly to President John F. Kennedy and Soviet premier, Nikita Krushchev.

Wilson, the daughter of a foreign correspondent and a children's book illustrator, regarded Women Strike for Peace as a grassroots organization and herself as an "ordinary housewife. I symbolize something."

In the following interview she characterizes WSP not as a branch of the women's liberation movement but as a "peace movement activated by women" and notes the materialist roots of the organization—the motivation to act based on its members' concerns for their children's welfare. The women of WSP put a new and dramatic spin on Adlai Stevenson's exhortations to the Smith College class of 1955 to use their spirit and energy to promote democratic values and safeguard their families' welfare in a postwar world fraught with conflict and danger.

SOURCE: Judith Porter Adams, ed., *Peacework: Oral Histories of American Women Peace Activists* (Boston: Twayne, 1991), pp. 194–99. Macmillan Reference USA, reprinted by permissions of the Gale Group.

THIRTY YEARS AGO I was responsible for an action that resulted in a national peace movement which is still going strong, Women Strike for Peace. I'm not really a "political" person, although I was brought up as a pacifist. As a child growing up in the years following the "war to end wars"—World War I—I believed that nations would work out their conflicts rather than fight. Other wonderful things were happening too. Women had been liberated—my mother was a voter. I went to a progressive school for boys and girls, which in Europe, where I grew up, was not common. Socialism seemed like a wonderful experiment. I really believed that the world was moving forward in many areas, all favorable to mankind.

However, after World War II, I realized that there was something happening that was beyond politics and that affected all human beings. I felt that the question of survival on earth was not a matter of politics, nor a matter of power between governments, but was a matter of deeper concerns common to all humanity.

Many things moved me to become active step by step, but the last straw was the arrest of Bertrand Russell in 1961 in London's Trafalgar Square. He sat down with others to block traffic as a protest. He let it be known that having tried through normal channels to alert the world to the extreme danger that we were in, pitting ourselves against each other with these destructive new weapons, he felt it necessary to make a gesture. I was impressed by that. One night soon after his arrest, I was talking about his protest to some English friends who were visiting my husband and me here in the United States. They were turning me off with jokes and making cynical wisecracks. They were intelligent people distinguished in their professions, and I was distressed by their response. This was also the time of the Berlin Wall. The media had said it might mean war, and of course, war would mean nuclear war. Our administration was telling us to build fallout shelters to protect our families. I felt indignant, more than indignant. I felt insulted as a human being that responsible people, governments, were asking us to do anything so stupid, as ineffectual as this, instead of coming to grips with the problems that were causing the tensions we were facing. My husband, who knew me well enough to realize that I was getting quite tense, said, "Well, women are very good at getting their way when they make up their minds to do something."

That phrase stayed with me. The next day I called a friend at the Committee for a Sane Nuclear Policy in Washington, D.C., to ask if SANE was going to respond to the Committee of 100 in support of Russell's actions. I said, "I feel like chartering a plane and filling it with women to picket the jail." This guy said, "Well, that's an idea for your women's movement." I said, "Women's movement? What do you mean?" I hadn't mentioned anything of that kind; I hadn't even thought about it. Anyway, he gave me an idea.

I stayed by the phone and thought, and thought, and thought. I said to my-self, "Well, what about a women's movement?" I picked up the telephone and started calling all my women friends from my phone book and Christmas card list. I wanted to see what they thought. I have always been very telephone-shy, so this was an unusual thing for me to do. It turned out that everybody that I spoke with had been worrying about this problem. We women thought that the fallout shelter idea was an inane, insane, and an unsuitable response to the world situation and spelled disaster. The response I got was really quite enlightening. Each woman had it in the front of her mind, including a lot of women who were really not politically active.

I soon gathered together in my own living room a small group of women out of those whom I had called. Three days later we met at my house. Six days later, at a big meeting planned by SANE, we announced an "action." This marked the formation of Women Strike for Peace.

What we planned was a one-day event. The women would go on strike and leave the men "holding the baby." We said: "Now what do you think would happen if all the women went on strike?" The whole country would stand still. We thought it was a good way to demonstrate our own power and show that women were an essential part of our social structure and had a right to be heard. Six weeks from that day, there were demonstrations in sixty cities in the United States.

We were not part of the women's liberation movement. Ours was a peace movement activated by women. And there is a difference. We were women working for the good of humanity. One woman in our early group who was a very good writer wrote a statement of purpose that was powerful. One of the strengths of the movement was that it was cliché free. We were not political activists who were used to the old phrases. We were speaking much more out of our everyday experiences, but we were educated and literate. This was our statement:

We represent a resolute stand of women in the United States against the unprecedented threat to life from nuclear holocaust. We're women of all races, creeds, and political persuasions who are dedicated to the achievement of general and complete disarmament under effective international control. We cherish the right and accept the responsibility of the individual in a democratic society to act and influence the course of government. We demand of governments that nuclear weapons tests be banned forever, that the arms race end, and that the world abolish all weapons of destruction under United Nations safeguards. We urge immediate planning at local, state and national levels for a peacetime economy with freedom and justice for all. We urge our government to anticipate world tensions and conflicts through constructive nonmilitary actions and through the United Nations. We join with women throughout the world to challenge the right of any nation or group of nations to hold the power of life or death over the world.

That really sums up my personal beliefs; I couldn't have stated it as well.

We saw women as a vehicle for a new peace action. There were already many peace groups and individuals, but the situation was still grave. These groups had become part of the peace establishment, and we didn't think they were as effective as they once were. We were able to do things that couldn't have happened in an already existing organization. I hoped that WSP would go on as long as it was effective, but I believed that in time it would be replaced by something else.

We had learned that nuclear testing was having hazardous effects on our environment, specifically on the open fields on which cows were grazing. This was contaminating the milk supply with strontium 90. This touched us very closely. We found out that strontium 90 was replacing calcium in children's bones. When we heard voices from Capitol Hill saying, "Well, well, it's too bad; this is just one of the hazards of the nuclear age," we really began to wonder about the sanity of our nation's leaders. Women Strike for Peace was an idea whose time had come. I was the lightning conductor; it just happened to be me. The time had come when either the people of the Earth would live together or die together.

In January of WSP's second year the New York women decided to come to the White House to stage a demonstration. They filled the longest train that had ever left Pennsylvania Station in the history of the railway, all with women. That day President Kennedy was scheduled for a press conference, and we thought no one would pay any attention to our demonstration. There was an enormous rain storm that soaked all the women who were coming off the train, ruining their hats—we always made a "respectable" appearance with hats and gloves. They walked through the rain to the White House and became soaked to the skin. At the president's press conference a well-known journalist representing the *New York Post* asked, "Do you think that demonstrations at this time have any influence on you and on the public and on the direction which we take in policy?" The president replied by saying that he had seen the large numbers of women out there in the rain and that we could understand that he

agreed with our message and that our message had been received. We got wonderful publicity out of that, since the press conference was televised and broadcast nationally.

Soon after we began with one-day actions all over the country. We had permanent relationships with the sixty cities that had demonstrated on the first
day. We had established a phone "tree" so that we could organize actions
quickly. Eventually we realized that we had to have regular meetings and we
had to have a national office, and so a national movement grew from our simple beginning with a one-day action. But we never had elected representatives;
we preferred a movement rather than an organization. We continued to make
decisions by consensus. So many people had been penalized in the past for left-
wing activities. Our structure—or lack of it—meant that it would be very, very
hard for anyone to be held accountable for the whole movement.

We soon had a program researching the effects of strontium 90. We took
groups of people to government offices where we found everybody very willing to give us the facts. They were not reassuring. However, getting the word
out was difficult. We took the press with us wherever we could. The publications that we issued were used in universities. We were respected; we weren't
just a hysterical mob of women. People recognized that we had brains, and we
were sensible.

We organized a delegation of one hundred women—fifty from the United
States and fifty from European countries, including the Soviet Union—to visit
the 1962 eighteen-nation disarmament conference in Geneva. We lobbied all
the delegations and wanted to address the plenary session. We were informed
that instead of addressing the plenary session, we could meet with the Soviet
and United States cochairs. A young woman—she was a Quaker—volunteered
to organize us for the meeting. I learned the power of Quaker silence from her.
We marched through a light rain to where the sessions were held in the suburbs of Geneva. The rain seemed to be a good omen for us; we'd always succeeded in the rain. We walked in silence, which was quite a tour de force for us
chatterboxes. We waited for an hour and forty-five minutes in total silence. Finally the Soviet and American cochairmen, Valaerian Zorin and Arthur Dean,
came in with their translators, secretaries, and a few press. The important thing
was that they walked into a room that was totally silent; the silence was palpa-
ble. Then I got up and spoke, which I did feeling rather like a schoolmistress.
We wanted them to know that we held them responsible for the future of the
human race and we thought it was time they got on with the business of ending the nuclear arms race. We presented them with mountains of petitions. The

press coverage in Europe of our action was excellent. That was our first really international venture.

WSP played a critical role in the 1963 Partial Test Ban Treaty's passage, but our greatest triumph was our confrontation with the House Un-American Activities Committee. They pounced on us in 1962 by subpoenaing nine WSP women. We were advised by others who had a go-around with the Committee that we "should not make a big fuss." But one of our women said, "No, this is not the way we're going to do it. If they're subpoenaing Dagmar Wilson, we should all volunteer to testify." Now that was an absolutely brilliant idea. We sent telegrams through our network saying, "Volunteer to testify. Come if you can. Hospitality offered. Bring your baby." Hundreds of women volunteered to testify. This was a new twist—most people were tempted to run a mile when the Committee pointed its magic wand at them.

I was the last one to be subpoenaed. It was a great relief to me, to be able to have my say. I had the benefit of two days of hearings before my turn came. By that time I felt quite comfortable. My testimony was summed up best by someone who said that I treated the attorney for the Committee just as though he were a rather tiresome dinner partner.

Our WSP meetings were very informal, with no protocol; we ran them like we ran our carpools. Well, that was extremely baffling to these political gentlemen. And at one point one said, "I don't understand how you get anything done at all." I answered, "Well, it puzzles us sometimes too."

The Committee was trying to find out if there was Communist influence in the peace movement. WSP was concerned about war and peace; we didn't think the world was worth blowing up over political differences. We could see ourselves marching arm in arm with Soviet mothers for the sake of our children, so we were not intimidated by the Committee's strategies. I was asked at the end of my testimony whether we would examine our books to see if we had Communist women in our midst, and I said, "Certainly not"—we would not do anything of the kind. "In fact," I said, "unless the whole human race joins us in our quest for peace, God help us."

One of the funny things about our "inquisition" before the Committee was that we were asked, in a sinister tone, if we had a mimeograph machine. It's true that we were mimeographing materials to distribute among ourselves. You know, someone's baby was always around, and we kidded ourselves that the print might appear on a child's diaper. Anybody turning a baby over might find a description of where our next meeting was going to be. So much for the sinister implication of a mimeograph machine. . . .

"THE UNION WASN'T FOR US BLACKS"
FLORENCE RICE

Florence Rice, a long-time resident of Harlem, New York, and a leading activist in tenant and consumer organizations, appeared before the House Committee on Labor, Education, and Welfare in 1962 to give the following testimony about discrimination in the International Ladies Garment Workers Union (ILGWU), the major union of women garment workers. More married women, including women with children, worked in the 1950s, but female workers were mostly ghettoized in clerical and blue-collar "service" jobs, such as health care aides, technicians, beauticians, waitresses, and office cleaners. And, as Rice points out, large numbers of women worked in the garment industry. One of the first unions to organize women, the ILGWU had traditionally been an impressive force for change on behalf of its members, demanding and getting better working conditions and higher wages for women garment workers.

But, as Rice, who was active in the ILGWU during the late 1950s, recounts, the union, like so many other institutions in American society, blatantly discriminated against black female workers by pitting black workers against white and Puerto Rican workers and giving white workers, regardless of their skills, the better-paying jobs. Here is a fascinating but disheartening glimpse into the way that unions undermined gender solidarity by exploiting ethnic divisions among workers.

SOURCE: Testimony by Florence Rice at hearings held in 1962 by the House Committee on Labor, Education, and Welfare. U.S. Congress.

I KNOW the Bronx slave market. We used to stand there and people would come and give you any kind of work. At that time it was at 174th street and Sedgwick Avenue. We used to go up there for domestic work. You were competing against each other, because you went out there and you was looking for a dollar a day.

Many times you got a dollar and a half. I always remember my domestic days. Some of the women, when they didn't want to pay, they'd accuse you of stealing. I remember a couple of times the woman said that I had stole something, which I know I hadn't—I just walked out and left that money. It was like intimidation. In those days a white woman says something about a black person, that was it. And what you were subjected to if you'd go in domestic work, the men—I encountered it one time. This man picked me up and said his wife was ill and then when I got there his wife wasn't there and he wanted to have an affair. It seems like I just had enough sense not to let myself get involved with anything like that and I started crying and he didn't force me and I was able to get out. When maids would get together, they'd talk of it. Some of them was very attractive and good-looking. They always had to fight off the woman's husband.

I got out of domestic and went into the laundry. In fact, it was quite interesting. I got my first laundry job on the slave market. This man came to recruit. If you got there early enough they were recruiting for the laundry. They'd pick you up for a day's work or they'd just pick you up for regular work. I think I got regular work from that time on. I went to work in the Bonn Laundry, which is at 175th street. It was better than domestic work, certainly. You were getting twelve dollars and whatever the change was at that time. This was in '36, I think. I was in the laundry before the unions were organizing there. Twelve dollars—oh God, you had to be there at seven and I know you didn't get off at five. I think you got off at six and you were forced to work Saturdays. I wasn't in there too long before the unions came about. The Laundry Workers Union. It was like the salvation. It certainly got better after the union came in. We got better wages, worked a certain amount of hours.

During the war I worked for Wright Aeronautical. They claim that people can't be trained, that you've got to go through seven, eight weeks of training, when during the war we trained in two weeks. I was an internal grinder. You grind with a great big machine and use a micrometer. And we knew how to use a micrometer and we read blueprints and we read the outline. I think I was making anywhere eighty-five, ninety-five dollars a week, which was utopia. I don't think I belonged to the union. There was a lot of black people in the plant. One of the things, there was no black personnel that I can remember. Our heads was white.

At the end of the war we were turned out in the street. The factory didn't close at that time. The factory continued on. They laid us off. This is no more than I think mostly all of us expected.

I had made up my mind that I wasn't going back into the laundry. I didn't go back to the employment service. What the employment agencies did to the blacks was always direct you back into all the servitude jobs. They never tried to encourage you to get something better. And I had a daughter, but I was just determined I wasn't going to the laundry. At that time in the black community the factory was much better than the laundry, like the laundry was better than domestic work.

It was the same with welfare. I always remember when I went to apply for welfare one time, and the woman said, well she needed someone to clean up her house—the welfare investigator, the intake woman, when they sent me to the investigator. She wanted me to do domestic work, and because I refused to do domestic work, I didn't get welfare at that time.

At that time you found lots of black women coming into the garment area. In the cheap shops you found all black women, black and Puerto Rican. A friend of mine heard of a job that was available in her shop. I never saw the kind of a machine I was supposed to work on, and I lied and I said that I knew that machine. She showed me how, she taught me that machine. She said, "All you have to do is sit down and run the machine, if anything happens I'll come up and thread it."

I worked on leggings as a piece worker in Feldman's shop. It was Local 105, International Ladies Garment Workers Union (ILGWU). It was an integrated local. One of the things, they took care of the whites, you didn't have to worry about that. In other words, the white women, white Jewish women, they did always get the work there. Yet I must say with Feldman, he was a pretty fair guy. You would automatically assume this. He was a pretty good boss compared to many of the other bosses. When I say he was fair, I remember that he wanted me to work two machines. When you finished one you got on another machine, and I refused to do it. And I brought the complaint to the union, and the union man came in there, and was very nasty to me, and told me if I didn't want to do it he would get someone else. Well, the union wasn't for us blacks, that's one of the things you recognize. What happened, instead of the union fighting for me, what I did, I got up, put on my clothes, and left. And Feldman, he came to the door and said, "Florence, you and I can talk this out." He said, "I'll tell you what I'll do. I'll guarantee you a salary, that you'll never make less than that." And we worked it out. But as far as the union, the union never stood up for us.

I was a chairlady for five years, I think, from the bottom of '57 up until '61. When I went in the union, I found myself thinking that the union was the greatest thing. I even believe in unions now. I could never say I'm against them—I'm just against the way that the unions have discriminated against minority people.

I had some illusions at first. Then all of a sudden you begin to recognize that all this that glitters is not gold. Underneath the whole damn thing it's ugliness, because you begin to see, whites are in control. You're not in control yourself. Many of the black workers never felt that the union really represented them. What you always found out was that the union man would say something in front of your face and he would go back to the boss and it would be completely different. So the union members began to learn that it was always a sweetheart arrangement with the manufacturer.

For a time I was what you'd call a "good nigger." Because when you are making like I was anywhere from $135 to $145 a week, then you have reached your utopia, and you were so very happy to be making that that whatever the boss did you never could see it. I was a zipper setter, and zipper setters was paid very well. And I came in the shop first. That was at Melino's. I was a zipper setter, and there was a black guy knew the job was going to be open, the place was opening, and he told me that it was a good job and he wanted to see me with it. But while I was there, there was another white girl came in, she came in as a sample maker. But when work was short, well, she would get all the work. In other words, they kept her working. And generally it was the black girls who did not, and this is I think recognized. Because what you begin to see is that there was discrimination rampant in the ILGWU. I called the union a country club, because there is no black people in the leadership at all. None at all. The union men told me one day they had gotten a colored fellow to come to a meeting, and he sat up and slept. So there was no use bringing in colored fellows—that was the idea. But what was the most interesting thing, they never brought in people who wouldn't sleep. They never brought in an aggressive person, they always liked somebody who was docile. And they found out that I was very resentful; and I was always making trouble, to which they would say, "Well, you're making a good salary." So the idea in the garment area is, "If you're making a good salary, then you be happy and you keep your mouth shut."

I always remember a girl named Maddy. And Maddy had been there almost as long as I was, she came in after I did. And poor Maddy worked for $40 a week for so long, and yet they brought in white girls right off the street and them girls rose to $80 just like that. They'd bring Italian girls from overseas, they'd train them, they would work, but not the black girls.

I felt very guilty of making good money, and I knew that Maddy wasn't making but $40, and other girls weren't making but a bit of money, until I really begin to act like I was them. I would be fighting to bring up their wage scale and trying to get their pay raised. And when you would do that, you found a business agent would tell you one thing but then he'd go back to the boss and tell another thing. It's done very subtly, and you begin to know. And then afterwards everyone begins to dislike you and you're the enemy. They would tell you that I was a troublemaker.

A group of people I later joined, they were white, Jewish, and they were called the rank and file. But to humiliate them at a union meeting they'd call them Communists. So naturally I was known as a Communist. That was a way of putting you down. I generally continued working with them.

One of the things about the union, especially in piece work, they could always see that you never got that work again. They could cut you down. Many people were afraid to really venture out. The way it works is like this: The boss calls to tell you to come in to work. But what he did, he would call in all the white help first. Then we found out this was a pattern. I would say that all the white girls was making exceptionally good pay. Regardless. It was seen that they made good pay. White folks was always supposed to make more money than black folks. It was done in mostly all the shops. It takes a while to recognize that it is discrimination.

Blacks and Puerto Ricans, I would say, are treated the same way, but what they do, they use a Black against a Puerto Rican and a Puerto Rican against a Black. Because if you have a shop where there's all Blacks in it, who are making good money, then they'll bring in a Puerto Rican at a cheaper price. Then the Puerto Ricans will bring in their people, and theyll all come in at a cheaper wage, so the boss steps down the salary scale. It's divide and conquer.

I brought it to the attention of some of the other black chairladies, didn't they realize they were being discriminated against, and could we do something about it together, and one of the ladies said, well, she had children and she could not get involved, she would rather have a little bit than none at all. To organize working people, that's the hardest work of all, because you must remember they have to make a living. Working women do not have the time to organize. They can't allow themselves to get involved in discussions. Because their first duty is to their family. Most of them were married women with children and families—and so therefore it gave them little time. Of course you did have the lucky women, the single women, but those women were really after good homes and good cars, things like that, so they weren't that aggressive. The black workers had a feeling that if you fought the union you automatically lost your job. You found out, that you eventually would be just knocked off, the next year they wouldn't call you back or they'd find a way of eliminating your work. They always found a way of hitting you financially. It was done on me.

At Malena, that was another company, I was the first to be laid off. I had been the first hired, but when work came in I was never the first to get called. Our work always started up early in the season, so you had sample work, but up until that year June I had not been called. My daughter was graduating. I couldn't get no welfare help, I wasn't called in to work. As a result of it, that morning I got up and I played this number 617. This is the way my daughter got her graduation dress, playing that number that day. One hundred thirty-five dollars.

At Malena is where they started giving me very bad work, and half the time they wouldn't call me in, and it just took a toll on my income. I was slowly pushed out. My God, from a hundred and some dollars a week, I had dropped down to sixty, sixty-five. There was never no work for me. So I couldn't stay there. Then I started going elsewhere, I started going into non-union shops. If I went for a job and I'd say, "I'm Florence Rice," which I didn't try to hide, even if they wanted somebody, then they didn't need anybody. I was blacklisted, that's what I was, blackballed. I would say the union did it, it's very easy to do. You never have no kind of proof. Those of us who know what the whole thing is all about, know its quietly done.

The union was running my life and the whites were in control of black people and we could never be able to do anything as long as it was set up like it is now. I see hopes for unions as long as they practice true democracy. The fact is, the democracy that they talk about has never been practiced in this country in anything. And as long as this continues on you're always going to have the frustrations that's in this country now. The unions as they are, they're just a dictatorial power that has power over people's lives.

"A GRIM SPECTER HAS CREPT UPON US
RACHEL CARSON

Like the members of Women Strike for Peace, Rachel Carson, a zoologist by training, aroused people to another environmental hazard: the impact of pesticides on the environment. Born in Springdale, Pennsylvania, Carson graduated from Pennsylvania College for Women (later Chatham College) and went on to get a master's degree in zoology from Johns Hopkins University. In 1935 she joined the United States Bureau of Fisheries in Washington, D.C., as a junior biologist. She was one of the first two women hired by the bureau for a professional-level position. In her spare time, she pursued another interest, writing, and wrote feature articles about fisheries. Over the next fifteen years, she rose steadily up the ranks to biologist and chief editor of publications at the United States Fish and Wildlife Service. She also wrote three books that established her as a pioneer environmentalist, including Silent Spring, *which first exposed the dangers of the insecticide DDT on bird and plant life and described the potentially disastrous global impact of other toxic chemicals on the natural world. With a poet's gift for language and a crusader's urgency for reform, she exhorted readers to stop the indiscriminate plundering of the environment by unchecked industrial and technological growth.*

Silent Spring *prompted the creation of a presidential panel to study the effects of pesticides on the environment; the commission's findings corroborated Carson's own. Almost a decade before the beginning of the environmental movement, Carson used her gift of language to make readers aware of the beauty, mystery, and fragility of the natural world. Following are excerpts from the book's poetic opening and first chapter.*

SOURCE: Rachel Carson, *Silent Spring* (Boston: Houghton Mifflin, 1962) pp. 1–3, 5–8. Copyright © 1962 by Rachel L. Carson. Copyright © renewed 1990 by Roger Christie. Reprinted by permission of Houghton Mifflin Company. All rights reserved.

1. A FABLE FOR TOMORROW

There was once a town in the heart of America where all life seemed to live in harmony with its surroundings. The town lay in the midst of a checkerboard of prosperous farms, with fields of grain and hillsides of orchards where, in spring, white clouds of bloom drifted above the green fields. In autumn, oak and maple and birch set up a blaze of color that flamed and flickered across a backdrop of pines. Then foxes barked in the hills and deer silently crossed the fields, half hidden in the mists of the fall mornings.

Along the roads, laurel, viburnum and alder, great ferns and wildflowers delighted the traveler's eye through much of the year. Even in winter the roadsides were places of beauty, where countless birds came to feed on the berries and on the seed heads of the dried weeds rising above the snow. The countryside was, in fact, famous for the abundance and variety of its bird life, and when the flood of migrants was pouring through in spring and fall people traveled from great distances to observe them. Others came to fish the streams, which flowed clear and cold out of the hills and contained shady pools where trout lay. So it had been from the days many years ago when the first settlers raised their houses, sank their wells, and built their barns.

Then a strange blight crept over the area and everything began to change. Some evil spell had settled on the community: mysterious maladies swept the flocks of chickens; the cattle and sheep sickened and died. Everywhere was a shadow of death. The farmers spoke of much illness among their families. In the town the doctors had become more and more puzzled by new kinds of sickness appearing among their patients. There had been several sudden and unexplained deaths, not only among adults but even among children, who would be stricken suddenly while at play and die within a few hours.

There was a strange stillness. The birds, for example—where had they gone? Many people spoke of them, puzzled and disturbed. The feeding stations in the backyards were deserted. The few birds seen anywhere were moribund; they trembled violently and could not fly. It was a spring without voices. On the mornings that had once throbbed with the dawn chorus of robins, catbirds, doves, jays, wrens, and scores of other bird voices there was now no sound; only silence lay over the fields and woods and marsh.

On the farms the hens brooded, but no chicks hatched. The farmers complained that they were unable to raise any pigs—the litters were small and the young survived only a few days. The apple trees were coming into bloom but no bees droned among the blossoms, so there was no pollination and there would be no fruit.

The roadsides, once so attractive, were now lined with browned and withered vegetation as though swept by fire. These, too, were silent, deserted by all living things. Even the streams were now lifeless. Anglers no longer visited them, for all the fish had died.

In the gutters under the eaves and between the shingles of the roofs, a white granular powder still showed a few patches; some weeks before it had fallen like snow upon the roofs and the lawns, the fields and streams.

No witchcraft, no enemy action had silenced the rebirth of new life in this stricken world. The people had done it themselves.

THIS TOWN does not actually exist, but it might easily have a thousand counterparts in America or elsewhere in the world. I know of no community that has experienced all the misfortunes I describe. Yet every one of these disasters has actually happened somewhere, and many real communities have already suffered a substantial number of them. A grim specter has crept upon us almost unnoticed, and this imagined tragedy may easily become a stark reality we all shall know.

What has already silenced the voices of spring in countless towns in America? This book is an attempt to explain.

2. THE OBLIGATION TO ENDURE

The history of life on earth has been a history of interaction between living things and their surroundings. To a large extent, the physical form and the habits of the earth's vegetation and its animal life have been molded by the environment. Considering the whole span of earthly time, the opposite effect, in which life actually modifies its surroundings, has been relatively slight. Only within the moment of time represented by the present century has one species—man—acquired significant power to alter the nature of his world.

During the past quarter century this power has not only increased to one of disturbing magnitude but it has changed in character. The most alarming of all man's assaults upon the environment is the contamination of air, earth, rivers, and sea with dangerous and even lethal materials. This pollution is for the most part irrecoverable; the chain of evil it initiates not only in the world that must support life but in living tissues is for the most part irreversible. In this now universal contamination of the environment, chemicals are the sinister and little-recognized partners of radiation in changing the very nature of the world—the very nature of its life. Strontium 90, released through nuclear explosions into the air, comes to earth in rain or drifts down as fallout, lodges in soil, enters into the grass or corn or wheat grown there, and in time takes up its abode in the bones of a human being, there to remain until his death. Similarly, chemicals sprayed on croplands or forests or gardens lie long in soil, entering into living organisms, passing from one to another in a chain of poisoning and death. Or they pass mysteriously by underground streams until they emerge and, through the alchemy of air and sunlight, combine into new forms that kill vegetation, sicken cattle, and work unknown harm on those who drink from once pure wells. As Albert Schweitzer has said, "Man can hardly even recognize the devils of his own creation." . . .

These sprays, dusts, and aerosols are now applied almost universally to farms, gardens, forests, and homes—nonselective chemicals that have the power to kill every insect, the "good" and the "bad," to still the song of birds and the leaping of fish in the streams, to coat the leaves with a deadly film, and to linger on in soil—all this though the intended target may be only a few weeds or insects. Can anyone believe it is possible to lay down such a barrage of poisons on the surface of the earth without making it unfit for all life? They should not be called "insecticides," but "biocides."

The whole process of spraying seems caught up in an endless spiral. Since DDT was released for civilian use, a process of escalation has been going on in which ever more toxic materials must be found. This has happened because insects, in a triumphant vindication of Darwin's principle of the survival of the fittest, have evolved super races immune to the particular insecticide used, hence a deadlier one has always to be developed—and then a deadlier one than that. It has happened also because, for reasons to be described later, destructive insects often undergo a "flareback," or resurgence, after spraying, in numbers greater than before. Thus the chemical war is never won, and all life is caught in its violent crossfire.

Along with the possibility of the extinction of mankind by nuclear war, the central problem of our age has therefore become the contamination of man's total environment with such substances of incredible potential for harm—substances that accumulate in the tissues of plants and animals and even penetrate the germ cells to shatter or alter the very material of heredity upon which the shape of the future depends. . . .

Fannie Lou Hamer rose up from poverty to work for social justice for African Americans and all poor people. She was the twentieth child of sharecropping parents and at age six began the tedious, backbreaking work of picking cotton. Altogether, she had about six years of formal schooling pieced together during periods when her labor was not needed in the fields. Gradually she worked her way up to timekeeper at the plantation where she picked cotton, a less arduous but still low-paying job.

In 1962 Hamer joined the staff of the Southern Christian Leadership Conference (SCLC), the civil rights organization established by the Reverend Martin Luther King Jr., and volunteered to challenge voting laws that discriminated against blacks. Not surprisingly, she lost her job and had to flee town. After participating in a civil rights workshop in Charleston, South Carolina, she joined a busload of other blacks trying to integrate segregated bus terminals. They were arrested and jailed in Winona, Mississippi, where she suffered a beating that left her permanently injured.

More committed than ever to ending segregation, Hamer joined other civil rights organizations, and in 1964 she was chosen vice-chairwoman of the newly organized Mississippi Freedom Democratic Party (MFDP), which attempted to challenge the all-white state Democratic party and elect an integrated slate of delegates to the Democratic National Convention in Atlantic City, New Jersey, in 1964. Although the MFDP completed all of the required steps to be credentialed, while the white delegation did not, the MFDP was offered only two seats as delegates-at-large, which, the MFDP, despite the prodding of mainstream civil rights leaders including King, rejected.

During the debate over seating the MFDP, Fannie Lou Hamer testified on national television before the Credentials Committee at the convention. Her riveting account of the abuse she suffered at the hands of local police while returning from a voter-registration workshop in South Carolina helped to arouse public outrage and sympathy for the civil rights movement. Like Rosa Parks, she exemplified the courage and vital contributions of black "mamas" in the civil rights movement.

SOURCE: "Everybody Knows About Mississippi, God Damn," from *This Little Light of Mine: The Life of Fannie Lou Hamer* by Kay Mills, pp. 119–21. Copyright © 1993 by Kay Mills. Used by permission of Dutton, a division of Penguin Putnam Inc.

MR. CHAIRMAN, and the Credentials Committee, my name is Mrs. Fannie Lou Hamer, and I live at 626 East Lafayette Street, Ruleville, Mississippi, Sunflower County, the home of Senator James O. Eastland, and Senator Stennis.

It was the 31st of August in 1962 that eighteen of us traveled twenty-six miles to the county courthouse in Indianola to try to register to try to become first-class citizens. We was met in Indianola by Mississippi men, highway patrol-mens, and they only allowed two of us in to take the literacy test at the time. After we had taken this test and started back to Ruleville, we was held up by the City Police and the State Highway Patrolmen and carried back to Indianola, where the bus driver was charged that day with driving a bus the wrong color.

After we paid the fine among us, we continued on to Ruleville, and Reverend Jeff Sunny carried me four miles in the rural area where I had worked as a timekeeper and sharecropper for eighteen years. I was met there by my children, who told me the plantation owner was angry because I had gone down to try to register. After they told me, my husband came, and said the plantation owner was raising cane because I had tried to register, and before he quit talking the plantation owner came, and said. "Fannie Lou, do you know—did Pap tell you what I said?"

I said, "Yes, sir."

He said, "I mean that," he said. "If you don't go down and withdraw your registration, you will have to leave," said, "Then if you go down and withdraw," he said. "You will—you might have to go because we are not ready for that in Mississippi."

And I addressed him and told him and said, "I didn't try to register for you. I tried to register for myself." I had to leave that same night.

On the 10th of September, 1962, sixteen bullets was fired into the home of Mr. and Mrs. Robert Tucker for me. That same night two girls were shot in Ruleville, Mississippi. Also Mr. Joe McDonald's house was shot in.

And in June, the 9th, 1963, I had attended a voter-registration workshop, was returning back to Mississippi. Ten of us was traveling by the Continental Trailway bus. When we got to Winona, Mississippi, which is Montgomery County, four of the people got off to use the washroom, and two of the people—to use the restaurant—two of the people wanted to use the washroom. The four people that had gone in to use the restaurant was ordered out. During this time I was on the bus. But when I looked through the window and saw they had rushed out, I got off of the bus to see what had happened, and one of the ladies said, "It was a state highway patrolman and a chief of police ordered us out."

I got back on the bus and one of the persons had used the washroom got back on the bus, too. As soon as I was seated on the bus, I saw when they began to get the four people in a highway patrolman's car. I stepped off the bus to see what was happening and somebody screamed from the car that the four workers was in and said, "Get that one there," and when I went to get in the car, when the man told me I was under arrest, he kicked me.

I was carried to the county jail, and put in the booking room. They left some of the people in the booking room and began to place us in cells. I was placed in a cell with a young woman called Miss Euvester Simpson. After I was placed in the cell I began to hear sounds of licks and screams. I could hear the sounds of licks and horrible screams, and I could hear somebody say, "Can you say, yes sir, nigger? Can you say yes, sir?"

And they would say other horrible names. She would say, "Yes, I can say yes, sir."

"So say it."

She says, "I don't know you well enough."

They beat her, I don't know how long, and after a while she began to pray, and asked God to have mercy on those people.

And it wasn't too long before three white men came to my cell. One of these men was a State Highway Patrolman and he asked me where I was from, and I told him Ruleville. He said, "We are going to check this." And they left my cell and it wasn't too long before they came back. He said, "You are from Ruleville all right," and he used a curse word, and he said, "We are going to make you wish you was dead."

I was carried out of that cell into another cell where they had two Negro prisoners. The State Highway Patrolman ordered the first Negro to take the blackjack. The first Negro prisoner ordered me, by orders from the State Highway Patrolman for me, to lay down on a buck bed on my face, and I laid on my face. The first Negro began to beat, and I was beat by the first Negro until he was exhausted, and I was holding my hands behind me at that time on my left side because I suffered from polio when I was six years old. After the first Negro had beat until he was exhausted, the State Highway Patrolman ordered the second Negro to take the blackjack.

The second Negro began to beat and I began to work my feet, and the State Highway Patrolman ordered the first Negro who had beat to set on my feet to keep me from working my feet. I began to scream and one white man got up and began to beat me in my head and tell me to hush. One white man—my dress had worked up high, he walked over and pulled my dress down—and he pulled my dress back, back up.

I was in jail when Medgar Evers was murdered. . . .

All of this is on account we want to register, to become first-class citizens, and if the Freedom Democratic Party is not seated now, I question America, is this America, the land of the free and the home of the brave where we have to sleep with our telephones off the hooks because our lives be threatened daily because we want to live as decent human beings, in America?

Thank you.

"HAVING A BABY INSIDE ME IS THE ONLY TIME I'M REALLY ALIVE"
ANONYMOUS

This young black woman living in a Boston welfare project in the early 1960s probably never read Modern Woman: The Lost Sex *and never tried to pattern herself after such ideal TV mothers as Barbara Cleaver (*Leave It to Beaver*) or Donna Reed (*The Donna Reed Show*). Instead, she finds her own very personal and poignant reasons for embracing motherhood.*

SOURCE: Robert Coles, *Children of Crisis*, pp. 368–9. Copyright © 1964, 1965, 1966, 1967 by Robert Coles. By permission of Little, Brown and Company, (Inc).

THEY CAME telling us not to have children, and not to have children, and sweep up, and all that. There isn't anything they don't want to do to you, or tell you to do. They tell you you're bad, and worse than others, and you're lazy, and you don't know how to get along like others do. Well, for so long they told us we couldn't ever go near anyone else, I suppose we should be grateful for being told we're not going to get near enough if we don't behave in the right way—which is the sermon I get all the time now.

Then they say we should look different, and eat different—use more of the protein. I tell them about the prices, but they reply about "planning"—planning, planning, that's all they tell you. The worst of it is that they try to get you to plan your kids, by the year; except they mean by the ten-year plan, one every ten years. The truth is, they don't want you to have any, if they could help it.

To me, having a baby inside me is the only time I'm really alive. I know I can make something, do something, no matter what color my skin is, and what names people call me. When the baby gets born I see him, and he's full of life, or she is; and I think to myself that it doesn't make any difference what happens later, at least now we've got a chance, or the baby does. You can see the little one grow and get larger and start doing things, and you feel there must be some hope, some chance that things will get better; because there it is, right before you, a real, live, growing baby. The children and their father feel it, too, just like I do. They feel the baby is a good sign, or at least he's *some* sign. If we didn't have that, what would be the difference from death? Even without children my life would still be bad—they're not going to give us what *they* have, the birth control people. They just want us to be a poor version of them, only without our children and our faith in God and our tasty fried food, or anything.

They'll tell you we are "neglectful"; we don't take proper care of the children. But that's a lie, because we do, until we can't any longer, because the time has come for the street to claim them, to take them away and teach them what a poor nigger's life is like. I don't care what anyone says: I take the best care of my children. I scream the ten commandments at them every day, until one by one they learn them by heart—and believe me they don't forget them. (You can ask my minister if I'm not telling the truth.) It's when they leave for school, and start seeing the streets and everything, that's when there's the change; and by the time they're ten or so, it's all I can do to say anything, because I don't even believe my own words, to be honest. I tell them, please to be good; but I know it's no use, not when they can't get a fair break, and there are the sheriffs down South and up here the policemen, ready to kick you for so much as breathing your feelings. So I turn my eyes on the little children, and keep on praying that one of them will grow up at the right second, when the schoolteachers have time to say hello and give him the lessons he needs, and when they get rid of the building here and let us have a place you can breathe in and not get bitten all the time, and when the men can find work—because *they* can't have children, and so they have to drink or get on drugs to find some happy moments, and some hope about things.

"BEFORE I KNEW IT, I WAS CAUGHT UP"
ADRIENNE MANN

Founded in 1867, Howard University in Washington, D.C., had been the traditional pathway to middle-class professional success for African Americans. Graduates of Howard went on to become at least half of the nation's black physicians, dentists, pharmacists, and engineers.* For many students and faculty, this adherence to the prevailing values of white middle-class America came at the expense of an unfettered expression of black culture and identity. Earlier generations of Howard students had worked toward integrating the U.S. Army during the 1940s and public bus transportation in the 1950s. But in the thick of the civil rights movement, some Howard students felt that the university was too insular and out of step with the tempo of the times. In the following excerpt, Adrienne Mann, a Howard freshman in 1964, describes the transformative power of participating in her first protest march and the exhilaration of being exposed to Stokely Carmichael's militant response to the mainstream civil rights movement.

SOURCE: Henry Hampton and Steve Fayer, ed., *Voices of Freedom* (New York: Bantam, 1990), pp. 429–31. Copyright © 1990 by Blackside, Inc. Used by permission of Bantam Books, a division of Random House, Inc.

WHEN I FIRST CAME to Howard in 1964, I came there expecting a black environment. I came out of a white high school and white town; we were in a minority. I was coming to Howard because I wanted black people, black teachers, and positive role models and all of this. When I got there, first of all, I knew I was out of place because my roommates had to have an extra closet brought into the dormitory room. People were going to class in high heels. It was just a totally bourgeois environment, unlike the one I'd come from. I really had never known any middle-class black people except for a doctor and a teacher. So I felt out of place. I felt alone. I didn't have any good friends for about a year and I thought I had made a mistake.

I came looking for black history courses, black literature, black music. It was a kind of void in my life I wanted filled. Black studies is what it was called. Sterling Brown was there, which was very exciting because he was a poet I had admired for a long time, and Arthur Davis. I was expecting to study black literature

---

* Henry Hampton, ed., *Voices of Freedom* (New York: Bantam Books, 1990), p. 425.

with Sterling Brown, and what I found was he told us that he could not teach black literature, that it did not fit into the curriculum and it was not offered. There was only one course and that was "Negro History" and you had to be a history major or an upperclassman to take that. And you couldn't fit it in your schedule. After you got finished with all the humanities and the Western Civ. type of courses, you couldn't fit that one course in. It was very hard to get in.

There was no music. You couldn't play jazz in the Fine Arts Building. All you heard when you passed the Fine Arts Building was opera—all day long, opera, opera, opera. And so-called classical music, National Symphony, and this kind of thing. So I was very disappointed and, well, I think they said they were making it the black Harvard or something like that. And it was just not what I wanted.

There were two things that got me involved politically and helped me move out of where I was to somewhat more consciousness. One of them was when one of the students was expelled from school because she had stayed out overnight, violated the curfew regulations. And for this she was not only put out of the dorm, but they put her out of the college altogether. And Jay Greene, who was a law student, he started supporting her and taking up her case. And he would come out at lunchtime in front of the law school and there would be rallies. So I started coming to the rallies. I was working on the newspaper as a reporter my freshman year and we were covering the story. And the editor of the newspaper was interested in it. I think he was friends with Jay. So I started following this case and Jay was saying that we had no rights as students, that she should at least have a hearing, that it wasn't right for her to be put out of school with no hearing. And that was the first time that really I began to think that, well, maybe there were others who didn't like the situation and there were other people concerned and they were willing to do something.

The next thing that happened was second semester, I believe it was, when the Selma campaign took place, and we were in freshman assembly, which was a mandatory gathering all freshmen had to go to on Tuesdays. I think it was like one o'clock. I had to sit there for an hour and listen to, quote, culture. And this particular day they announced that there was a march down at the White House to protest Reverend Reeb's murder in Selma, and if we wanted to go, the student government had rented a bus and we could get out of freshman assembly. Honestly, I just wanted to get out of freshman assembly. I was tiring of sitting there, and some of the other students were going that I knew, so I went along. And when we got down to the White House, first started out picketing, I didn't know much about what was happening, but then across the street the

Nazi counterdemonstrators and the Klansmen and other people started counterdemonstrations, and the soldiers moved in. It got very tense, and a couple of my friends said they were going to sneak in the White House and stay there. They were later arrested, I think, and sent to prison. And they kept saying, "Well, let's stay." I said, "My feet hurt. I want to go." And they kept saying, "Oh no. We got to stay." And before I knew it, I was caught up. I was listening. I think I stayed there 'til about two in the morning. And it made sense to me. The civil rights movement never made any sense to me until then, and then it really did. And I said, "Wow."

I heard Stokely Carmichael in the summer of 1966 when I was at Harvard University for the summer school. When he started talking, it was as if I were talking—he was speaking for me, things that I had been feeling and thinking about, he was articulating them so well, especially about the attitude that we should have as black people toward ourselves and the country, and how we shouldn't be begging and pleading for our rights. But we ought to get together and organize and take what rightfully belonged to us. And I liked that. I didn't like the passive kind of beggar mentality that I thought we were into in the civil rights movement. The speech changed me, because when I realized that what I had been feeling and thinking was not just personal, it wasn't just me—somebody else, in fact someone of prominence and stature, felt the same way and could articulate it—I really felt encouraged.

"I WAS THERE TO HELP THEM"
MARY DORA JONES AND NANNIE WASHBURN

Some of the most heroic participants in the civil rights movement were the unsung, anonymous women and men who marched or tried to register to vote. They did not lead marches, develop strategy, or give eloquent speeches. But they gave their time, energy, and lives to the movement in a multitude of ways. Following are the recollections of two very different women: Mary Dora Jones, a black woman from Marks, Mississippi, who housed voter-registration volunteers in her home when other residents were too fearful to take them, and Nannie Washburn, a white working-class woman from Douglasville, Georgia, who joined Dr. Martin Luther King's march from Selma to Montgomery in March 1965. Both women supported the movement in different but equally important ways. Washburn's account of being incarcerated in a mental institution because of her participation in the march is especially harrowing, a bitter reminder that for this passionately aroused woman who trammeled Jim Crow culture there could be no protection under the mantle of southern stereotypes of genteel white womanhood.

SOURCE: Howell Raines. *My Soul Is Rested: Movement Days in the Deep South Remembered* (New York: Putnam's, 1977) pp. 279–81, 402–9. Used by permission of G. P. Putnam's Sons, a division of Penguin Putnam Inc.

MARY DORA JONES

I had about seven blacks and four whites in my house, wouldn't nobody else take'em.

In Marks?

Right . . . they really move. They comes in, they mean business. They didn't mind dyin', and as I see they really mean business, I just love that for 'em, because they was there to help us. And since they was there to help us, I was there to help them.

Did that cause you any problems in the community . . . opening your home up?

Oh, really, because they talkin' 'bout burnin' my house down . . . Some of the black folks got the news that they were gonna burn it down. . . . My neighbors was afraid of gettin' killed. People standin' behind buildin's, peepin' out behind the buildin's, to see what's goin' on. So I just told 'em, "Dyin' is all right. Ain't but one thing 'bout dyin'

That's make sho' you right, 'cause you gon' die anyway." . . . If they had burnt it down, it was just a house burned down. . . .

That's the attitude that changed the South.

So that's the way I thought about it. So those kids, some of 'em from California, some of 'em from Iowa, some of 'em from Cincinnati, they worked, and they sho' had them white people up there shook up.

. . . youngsters that came in, particularly the white ones from outside the South, did they have a hard time adjusting . . .?

They had a hard time adjustin' because most all of the blacks up there didn't want to see 'em comin' . . . said they ain't lettin' no damn civil rights come. "If they come up here to my house, I'm gon' shoot 'em."

See, this is what the black folks were sayin', and those kids had went to the preachers' houses, they had done went to the deacons' houses, they had done went to the teachers' houses, all tryin' to get in. Some of 'em come in around five o'clock that evenin', landed in my house. I give 'em my house. "My house is yo' house." I was workin' for a man, he was workin' at the Post Office, and he and his wife was beggin' me everyday, "Don't fool with them Communists."

The white people?

That's what they was tellin' me, those kids was Communists. I said, "Well, I tell you what. I don't think they no more Communist than right here where I am, because if they Communists, then you Communists. They cain't hurt me no mo' than I already been hurt." Anything that helped the peoples, then I'm right there. So I didn't stop, although I got him scared to fire me. He would have fired me, but I got him scared to fire me. . . .

This was your white boss?

This was my white boss I was working for. His wife was sick, and every day she would talk to me about those people, askin' me where they lived. I said, "Well, they ain't livin' at yo' house. Why you want to know where they live?" So she said, "They ain't livin' with you?" And I said, "Well, I'm payin' the last note on that house," just like that. And I never did tell her.

Finally one day she brought me home, and it was a car sittin' there in my driveway, and two white men was in there, and there were some sittin' on the porch. She put me out and she went on back. When I went to work the next morning, she say, "Mary, was them, ah, civil rights peoples at yo' house?" I said, "Now when you turned around and stopped and they were sittin' there, you oughta been askin' 'em what they was. They'da told you."

And I never did tell 'em anything. So it went on some, she said, "Ain't but one thing I hate about it, this intermarriage." And I said, "Well, ain't no need in worryin' about that, because if you wanna worry about that, you oughta been talkin' to your granddaddy. . . ."

NANNIE WASHBURN

I called Dr. Abernathy and he wasn't at home. . . . She answered the phone, his wife, and I asked her was there anything she could do or we could do to help. And she said, "Yes, honey, you just don't know how it is down there and you go down there and you'll learn a lot." Says, "You'll never believe it."

My daughter was alistenin' in, and she was aworryin' herself to death about it, because of that bridge . . . So she got the car ready and tuned up. . . . So my blind son, Joe, and Nellie, my youngest daughter, and I went to Selma. . . .

How long did it take you to get there?
It was about ten o'clock that night, and we started out fairly early, but everybody put us off, sent us another route after we got into Alabama. They'd say, "Oh, that's eighty miles from here," and all that kind of stuff. . . . When we arrived, we got registered at the church, Selma church,* and then the food proposition come up. They had Jim Crow food in the kitchen.

How was that?
Well, . . . my daughter, son, and I refused to eat the Jim Crow food because there wasn't anybody in the kitchen accokin' except black women that was older than . . . as old as I was and I was sixty-five. . . . I went to Rev. Hollis† and asked him. I said, "I'm not gonna eat . . . we not gonna eat ya Jim Crow food." And he says, "Why?" I said, ". . . My daughter has droved us, my son

---

* Brown Chapel.
† A black minister directing activities at the church.

and I, down here, and I didn't think I'd come to a Jim Crow kitchen." And he said, "You just a guest." I said, "No, I'm not. I just one of 'em." And he said then, "I don't know nothin' we could do about it." I says, "Well, don't you think the black women's been in the kitchen too long cookin' for the white people?" And he commenced studyin', and he said, "They only thing I can do is to let yo'r daughter go in the kitchen. I wouldn't let you." You know, I was sixty-five. . . .

You accused them of having a Jim Crow kitchen in a black church?

Yeah. They didn't have no white people in there cookin', and if I'm a white and comin' in there to eat the food, wouldn't you call it Jim Crow . . .?

By way of a compromise, her daughter became a cook and she became "hostess" in the dining room there in the basement of Brown's Chapel. " . . . but they didn't know what I was a doin.'"

I was a vanguard, but they didn't know it. . . . I know George Wallace. I knew what he was. He was a Klannish sagergationist. So I knew he'd pay any price if he wanted it bad enough to send in somebody in there, Klan or some drunk person come in there and get to fightin', maybe get to shootin.' . . . And I took care of all the dangers. You know what a vanguard is?

No.

Well, it's a detective for the workin'-class people. When I go any place, I keep my eyes open, courts or anywhere . . . watch the people, see that they don't hurt nobody. See that they don't have no weapons to hurt anybody with. . . .

See, I couldn't vote for years 'cause I didn't have a dollar. Used to be I worked on that poll tax years ago. And so I kept my eye open in the office and in the whole church and in the kitchen, too, to protect the workin' class people, 'cause, we didn't know what might happen . . . they did shoot in at winders.

And it was two weeks before we marched, and they's a lot went on. I know one day we was fixin' to go to City Hall and march to get them to let 'em vote, and we lined up. 'Course, the National Guards was out there, the National Guards. And this man I was standin' by was a big, heavyset black man, and my blind son, and they knocked that big, heavyset man, weighed about two or three hundred pounds, 'bout two hundred and fifty anyhow. Well, when they hit him, you see, when he was agoin' over the line where they told him not to, well, it knocked my blind son and I both down. We was amarchin.' Nellie, my daughter, was in the kitchen acookin.' . . .

Did you make the march?

I certainly did make it in good spirits, except my feet. I never did give up. My feet was in bad shape when I got there at Montgomery, had to have 'em treated. I walked the fifty miles . . . and my blind son walked the fifty miles. He was in the Jet [magazine] several different times. Then they was a man, Leatheree,* he was a big ballplayer, one-legged. marched it, too. But Joe made it, but it was ro-o-ough trip. You know, Klan was aburnin' crosses and everything like that, even if the airplines was aflyin' over, helicopters or whatever they was.

Why did you feel it was important for y'all to march with these physical ailments that you had?

I didn't feel like I had any. 'Course, my feet hurt a little. I didn't feel like I had any physical ailments. I was only class conscious of my duty. That's what I walked for. I walked for freedom, because I knew I'd never be free in white skin as long as the black people was in chains with black skin. See, a white person can't be free . . . poor people, they cain't be free, until the black people's free. Now, I'm not speaking just those two nationalities: I'm aspeakin' about the 'Canos and havin' the Indians on the reservations after takin' their land away from them. I'm angry about that. I'm very angry about 'em chaining the black people and bringin' 'em over here to be chattel slaves. I think it was a awful thing. Against their will. And then black markin' them when they didn't want no more over here, and chainin' five hundred, and sinkin' 'em in the ocean or sea. His tory'll tell the truth on what the white man's done and I'm ashamed. And I cain't be free in white skin until they free. . . .

You mentioned you met Mrs. Liuzzo. . . .

I certainly did . . . and my daughter and her was 'sposed to be together that night. Anyhow, it didn't happen. She got another assignment some way or 'nother that changed it. . . .

I requested Mrs. Liuzzo, I said, "Mrs. Liuzzo, I'm a lot older'n you and I've had a lot of experience with Jim Crow . . . I wanna give you a little *my*

---

* Jim Leatherer.

kinda advice." I said, "Don't you git in no car with no black man. If you do, they'd a lot ruther kill you'n a black man, 'cause I've done been through experience of it." And she just shook her head. . . .

She went on anyhow with transportin' people, and my daughter had her car, and she was 'sposed to do the same thing. But my daughter, some other assignment come up that she had to do or use it some way.

But we went on . . . you want me to finish that up? We went on to Montgomery, Alabama. We walked. We slept in cow pastures, unbelievable conditions. But we had the actors and actresses . . . I cain't call all their names. . . .

I would criticize that march: it was too fast. They walked the people to git the march over in, I think, about five days. But I don't think that the marchers shoulda had to walk that fast. Now, that's one of my criticisms.

When we got to Montgomery, of course, they didn't let 'em on the capitol steps, but they was pretty close, and they had a lotta people, and they all had the big meeting, and then we caught a bus to come back. And when we caught a bus to come back, the ambulance that was agoin' to pick up Mrs. Liuzzo passed our bus, but we didn't know what it was. But we learnt later. And we went back to Selma.

I didn't run off quick as the march was over. I stayed around there. . . . You see, I'm an LPN, licensed nurse, and they picked me to be on the Medical Committee for Human Rights.* They had a lotta trouble in Demopolis, Alabama, and wait'll you hear this. The doctors said would I go to Demopolis, that they was adoin' so much meanness to the people down there, and I said, "Sure, I'll go," and my daughter said, "I will, too," and my son, too.*

The demonstrations in Demopolis were rough. Her son was arrested. She set up a makeshift infirmary in a church, treating victims of tear gas and billy clubs. The police cordoned off the building in an effort to stop the marches.

But then I stayed in the church, and we slept in there with the black men. We slept on the benches. I've never been respected as highly by white men as we were those black men. Now, they was young ones, from about nineteen to on up. They was one in there forty. He lived in Alabama, but he was

---

* The Medical Committee for Human Rights, composed mainly of Eastern physicians and medical students, provided everything from first aid to on-the-spot psychiatric counseling for civil rights workers. It was especially active in those areas of Alabama and Mississippi where workers found it difficult to secure reliable treatment at community hospitals.

very educated. I would call him . . . I don't know whether he's still a Communist, but he had been one. Anyhow, we had to sleep with the lights out, in the dark; 'cause they shot in. They'd shoot in or one time they throwed a dead snake there, six foot long, rattlesnake. So that was a warnin.' . . .

Now this man, this young man, he . . . they respected us to the highest, and Nellie and I was all that was in there. You see, I'm far-sighted and when I'd haveta go to the bathroom, they would . . . this young man would take me down the steps. And he'd had a little flashlight and he'd take me, where I wouldn't be in any danger of fallin.' And then he'd come on back upstairs. And they treated me just like a mother. My sons. And I loved 'em.

So, that just wouldn't do for the white man. They couldn't take it no longer, and so one day I was cleanin.' Early one mornin' I was cleanin' . . . havin' everything nice and clean for the first aid . . . the fountain at the little hall when you go out of the church. And one of those big guys grabbed me . . . the sheriff. And he liked to have pinched my arm off, and he drug me out in a car, and he hauled me then to jail, put me in jail, and they was several black men in there, preachers and so on. And I stayed there until they transferred me to another jail . . . The judge sent a doctor down there. We was right in front of the courthouse, and I was aspeakin' of the conditions and so on.

You were shouting out the jail window?

Yeah, I was ahollerin' out the jail window, and they couldn't take it. . . . I went in that second jail on my birthday, the third of May and this doctor come down and picked me, tryin' to talk to me about the background of my family and so on. So wasn't but just a short time til they sent two of the polices down there, and the sheriff come up there and told me to come downstairs. . . . I said, "I don't have my shoes on, let them come up here." It was just a little bitty jail . . . I mean cell. Smallest one I've ever seen. . . . He said, "No, come on." I went downstairs. These two cops, one of them said, "Goddamnit, get them shoes on." Slammed the handcuffs on me, and I didn't know what was agoin' on you know."

Did you ever find out what charge they had you on?

I didn't have no lawyer . . . they didn't defend me. I mean, I asked 'em what they was gonna do. They said it wasn't "none of my damn business." And I couldn't get no information, or they didn't tell me what. Then when we started out, they says, "We're takin' you to the mental institution where you belong, you bitch, you."

And I went on with 'em and everywhere they said, "You oughta throw ya hands up and pet them niggers." Niggers, niggers, that's all they talked about, niggers. So I had a little incident happened to me. See they got my pocketbook . . . I didn't have a cigarette and I just said to 'em I said; "Would you loan me a cigarette?" I says, "I got money to buy 'em, but I just don't have 'em. They took my pocketbook." And he said "You goddamn bitch, you, I'd throw you in the river." Says, "I wouldn't give you nothin.'" I just kept quiet, and every time I passed a station a place where they was black people, I always helt my hand up. They was handcuffed . . . and they taken me to Tuscaloosa mental institution. And oooooh, if they didn't use . . . they cursed me from the time we started, 'fore we started, until we got there. We passed through Scottsboro, Alabama, and I remembered so well aworkin' so hard—we did here in Atlanta—for the "Scottsboro Boys."[*] In fact, all over the country. . . .

And we worked so hard for the "Scottsboro Boys," I'd always longed to pass through that town, so I did, but it was the wrong direction.

How long did they keep you in Tuscaloosa?

They kept me twenty-one days. . . . That's the most ridiculousest thing in the world. You know, capitalism is the most rottenest thing on earth. Any country or any society that would give you tranquilizers and that's the way they keep all the people down in Milledgeville.[†] They keep 'em down all over the country. Now I've done been there, I know. And those people's eyes is like rattlesnake eyes, they hate you so bad . . . you see, they knowed I was in Dr. King's march, and they cussed me all the time.

Did they claim you were mentally ill?

Uh-huh, they sure did. I got the papers here. . . . So they commenced to lock me in a cell the first night, to see that I wasn't gonna kill nobody. And then from then on, they didn't lock me, they put me in the ward. And oh, how they hated me. Especially a couple of the matrons. The head matron, oh, how she hated me. You could see the hate in her face. You can tell a per-

---

* Editor's note: Nine black youths convicted on trumped-up rape charges in a 1931 trial at Scottsboro, a small town in north Alabama. Eventually the convictions were reversed. An organization affiliated with the Communist party provided defense lawyers and worked to focus national attention on the case.

† Location of the state mental hospital in Georgia.

sonality of a person when they hate you so bad. So I stayed there, and the doctor was a Indian doctor, and he wanted to examine me, and I said, "I don't need no examination, I'm not sick." I says, "I've got money to have as good a doctor as anybody needs, and I don't want yo' treatment. I don't want yo' examination. I am not sick."

And he said yeah; and he made 'em carry me anyhow, and he examined me. And I shamed him about how the white man, how they had mistreated the Indians and took all their land and put them on the concentration camps. So he—he wasn't no good.

Was this an American Indian doctor?

Uh-mm, down at Tuscaloosa. I got after him one day. He was apassin', and I said, "Dr. So-and-so, I wanta tell you, I don't see how you could hardly hold yo' head up, the way they've done yo' race of people, the white man, takin' their land, stealin' their land, and takin' it away from 'em, and murderin' 'em and puttin' 'em on the reservation." I said, "I don't see how you could be a doctor for a place like this."

But I stayed there twenty-one days and they wanted to give me shock treatment. Well I'm a out-of-the-state person, and there're certain laws on that, so my daughter in there, my sightless daughter, she got her husband . . . I wouldn't give no name whatever here in Atlanta. But finally I give her name, and her husband called down there and said, "You got the wrong woman." Said, "She's not mentally sick."

"THE NEWEST GLAMOUR GIRL OF OUR TIMES"
HELEN GURLEY BROWN

Helen Gurley Brown was the doyenne of women's fashion magazines throughout the 1960s and 1970s. In 1965 she became the editor-in-chief of Cosmopolitan *and transformed it into the self-proclaimed mouthpiece of the young, chic, urban working woman on the fast track to self-fulfillment and success. In her magazine Brown promoted a provocative mix of stereotypes and untraditional images of women's lives. She vigorously advocated women's sexual freedom and, through* Cosmopolitan *and her quasi-autobiographical book,* Sex and the Single Girl, *which sold 150,000 copies within its first year of publication, urged women to enjoy and also use their sexuality to promote their ambitions. But as the following excerpt from* Sex and the Single Girl *makes clear, she never questions traditional notions that women's first priority is to be alluring to men. Brown's single girl is independent, protects her self-interests, and zealously pursues pleasure and freedom, but hers is a pleasure and freedom bought by the favor of men and never challenges the fundamental social and political inequality of women in American society.*

SOURCE: Helen Gurley Brown, *Sex and the Single Girl* (New York: Bernard Geis Associates, 1962), pp. 3–10. Reprinted by permission of Helen Gurley Brown.

WOMEN ALONE? OH COME NOW!

I married for the first time at thirty-seven. I got the man I wanted. It *could* be construed as something of a miracle considering how old I was and how eligible *he* was.

David is a motion picture producer, forty-four, brainy, charming and sexy. He was sought after by many a Hollywood starlet as well as some less flamboyant but more deadly types. And I got him! We have two Mercedes-Benzes, one hundred acres of virgin forest near San Francisco, a Mediterranean house overlooking the Pacific, a full-time maid and a good life.

I am not beautiful, or even pretty. I once had the world's worst case of acne. I am not bosomy or brilliant. I grew up in a small town. I didn't go to college. My family was, and is, desperately poor and I have always helped support them. I'm an introvert and I am sometimes mean and cranky.

But *I* don't think it's a miracle that I married my husband. I think I deserved him! For seventeen years I worked hard to become the kind of woman who might interest him. And when he finally walked into my life I was just worldly enough, relaxed enough, financially secure enough (for I also worked hard at my job) and adorned with enough glitter to attract him. He wouldn't have looked at me when I was twenty, and I wouldn't have known what to do with *him*.

There is a tidal wave of misinformation these days about how many more marriageable women there are than men (that part is true enough) and how tough is the plight of the single woman—spinster, widow, divorcee.

I think a single woman's biggest problem is coping with the people who are trying to marry her off! She is so driven by herself and her well-meaning but addlepated friends to become married that her whole existence seems to be an apology for *not* being married. Finding *him* is all she can think about or talk about when (a) she may not be psychologically ready for marriage; (b) there is no available husband for every girl at the time she wants one; and (c) her years as a single woman can be too rewarding to rush out of.

Although many's the time I was sure I would die alone in my spinster's bed, I could never bring myself to marry just to get married. If I had, I would have missed a great deal of misery along the way, no doubt, but also a great deal of fun.

I think marriage is insurance for the *worst* years of your life. During your best years you don't need a husband. You do need a man of course every step of the way, and they are often cheaper emotionally and a lot more fun by the dozen.

I believe that as many women over thirty marry out of fear of being alone someday—not necessarily now but *some* day—as for love of or compatibility with a particular man. The plan seems to be to get someone while the getting's good and by the time you lose your looks he'll be too securely glued to you to get away.

Isn't it silly? A man can leave a woman at fifty (though it may cost him some dough) as surely as you can leave dishes in the sink. He can leave any time *before* then too, and so may you leave *him* when you find your football hero developing into the town drunk. Then you have it all to do over again as if you hadn't gobbled him up in girlish haste.

How much saner and sweeter to marry when you have both jelled. And how much safer to marry with part of the play out of his system *and yours*. It takes guts. It can be lonely out there out of step with the rest of the folks. And you may *not* find somebody later. But since you're not finding somebody *sooner* as things stand, wouldn't it be better to stop driving . . . to stop fretting . . . to start recognizing what you have *now*?

As for marrying to have children, you can have babies until you're forty or older. And if you happen to die before *they* are forty, at least you haven't lingered into their middle age to be a doddering old bore. You also avoid those tiresome years as an unpaid baby sitter.

Frankly, the magazines and their marriage statistics give me a royal pain.

There is a more important truth that magazines never deal with, that single women are too brainwashed to figure out, that married women know but won't admit, that married men *and* single men endorse in a body, and that is that the single woman, far from being a creature to be pitied and patronized, is emerging as the newest glamour girl of our times.

She is engaging because she lives by her wits. She supports herself. She has had to sharpen her personality and mental resources to a glitter in order to survive in a competitive world and the sharpening looks good. Economically she is a dream. She is not a parasite, a dependent, a scrounger, a sponger or a bum. She is a giver, not a taker, a winner and not a loser.

Why else is she attractive? Because she isn't married, that's why! She is free to be The Girl in a man's life or at least his vision of The Girl, whether he is married or single himself.

When a man thinks of a married woman, no matter how lovely she is, he must inevitably picture her greeting her husband at the door with a martini or warmer welcome, fixing little children's lunches or scrubbing them down because they've fallen into a mudhole. She is somebody else's wife and somebody else's mother.

When a man thinks of a single woman, he pictures her alone in her apartment, smooth legs sheathed in pink silk Capri pants, lying tantalizingly among dozens of satin cushions, trying to read but not very successfully, for *he* is in that room—filling her thoughts, her dreams, her life. . . .

SEX—WHAT OF IT?

Theoretically a "nice" single woman has no sex life. What nonsense! She has a better sex life than most of her married friends. She need never be bored with one man per lifetime. Her choice of partners is endless and they seek *her*. They never come to her bed duty-bound. Her married friends refer to her pursuers as wolves, but actually many of them turn out to be lambs—to be shorn and worn by her.

Sex of course is more than the act of coitus. It begins with the delicious feeling of attraction between two people. It may never go further, but sex it is. And a single woman may promote the attraction, bask in the sensation, drink it like wine and pour it over her like blossoms, with never a guilty twinge. She can promise with a look, a touch, a letter or a kiss—and she doesn't have to deliver. She can be maddeningly hypocritical and, after arousing desire, insist that it be shut off by stating she wants to be chaste for the man she marries. Her pursuer may strangle her with his necktie, but he can't *argue* with her. A flirtatious married woman is expected to Go Through With Things.

Since for a female getting there is at *least* half the fun, a single woman has reason to prize the luxury of taking long, gossamer, attenuated, pulsating trips before finally arriving in bed. A married woman and her husband have precious little time and energy for romance after they've put the house, animals and children to bed. A married woman with her lover is on an even tighter schedule.

During and after an affair, a single woman suffers emotional stress. Do you think a married woman can bring one off more blissfully free of strain? (One of my close friends, married, committed suicide over a feckless lover. Another is currently in a state of fingernail-biting hysteria.) And I would rather be the other woman than the woman who watches a man *stray* from her.

Yet, while indulging her libido, which she has plenty of if she is young and healthy, it is still possible for the single woman to be a lady, to be highly respected and even envied if she is successful in her work.

I did it. So have many of my friends. . . .

Brains are an asset but it doesn't take brainy brains like a nuclear physicist's. Whatever it is that keeps you from saying anything unkind and keeps you asking bright questions even when you don't quite understand the answers will do nicely. A lively interest in people and things (even if you aren't *that* interested) is why bosses trust you with new assignments, why men talk to you at parties . . . and sometimes ask you on to dinner.

Fashion is your powerful ally. Let the "secure" married girls eschew shortening their skirts (or lengthening them) and wear their classic cashmeres and tweeds until everybody could throw up. You be the girl other girls look at to see what America has copied from Paris.

Roommates are for sorority girls. You need an apartment alone even if it's over a garage.

Your figure can't harbor an ounce of baby fat. It never looked good on anybody but babies.

You must cook well. It will serve you faithfully.

You must have a job that interests you, at which you work hard.

I say "must" about all these things as though you were under orders. You don't have to do anything. I'm just telling you what worked for me.

CHAPTER 3

MAKING THE WORLD ANEW:
DIFFERENT PATHS TO SEXUAL EQUALITY

On August 26, 1970, fifty thousand women marched down Fifth Avenue in New York City demanding equal rights and a stronger political voice. They were also commemorating the fiftieth anniversary of the passage of the 19th Amendment to the U.S. Constitution—the amendment that granted women the right to vote. Yet fifty years after the ratification of the 19th Amendment, American women still chafed under social and political restrictions and stereotypes about their lives. At Bryant Park behind the New York Public Library, they gathered to hear Betty Friedan, who, with the publication of *The Feminine Mystique*, had helped spark the decade of activism leading up to this march. Standing before a sea of faces, Friedan, a Jew, declared, "Down through the generations in history, my ancestors prayed, 'I thank Thee, Lord, I was not created a woman,' and from this day forward I trust that women all over the world will be able to say, 'I thank Thee, Lord, I *was* created a woman.'"[1]

In this simple but eloquent statement, Friedan, one of the midwives of the reemergence of feminism, captured the spirit of the day, and also the times: throughout the decade women not only fought for their rights and freedoms, they also celebrated their womanhood. The rebirth of feminism in the 1960s and 1970s was fraught with fissures and conflicts as American women moved from a celebration of sisterhood based purely on gender to the politics of difference. But the spirit that characterized the feminist struggles of this period was one of pride, even joy, in being a woman. Women reaffirmed their gender identity in the plethora of alternative feminist institutions and organizations they created.

A complex web of events and social conditions gave rise to the reemergence of feminism. In 1963 Friedan published *The Feminine Mystique*, a collective portrait of the white middle-class women of 1950s domesticity. In this best-selling book—it sold three million copies within a matter of months—Friedan set out "the problem that has no name"—the entrapment and despair felt by educated suburban middle-class women who tried to reconcile themselves to lives of full-time domesticity while craving involvement in the world beyond their homes. Friedan, a journalist by training, advocated meaningful work for women outside the home. Her book struck a nerve, and she was inundated by mail from readers describing their frustration and despair.

The same year that Friedan's book came out, a presidential commission on the status of women, appointed by President John F. Kennedy and chaired by former first lady Eleanor Roosevelt, issued a report detailing economic and legal discrimination in all aspects of women's lives. In response the Kennedy Administration issued a presidential order requiring that all career civil service positions be filled on merit only, without regard to sex. The Administration and Congress also passed the Equal Pay Act in 1963, which stipulated equal pay for equal work performed by women and men. With this act, the federal government took a historic step to abolish discrimination against female employees in the private sector.

The following year witnessed another historic first: passage of Title VII of the Civil Rights Act, which prohibited discrimination in employment on the basis of race, creed, national origin, and sex. With passage of the Civil Rights Act came the creation of the Equal Employment Opportunity Commission (EEOC) to arbitrate cases of racial and sexual discrimination. But the EEOC did not take seriously its responsibility to outlaw sexual discrimination and even approved of the practice of separate want ads for male and female employment positions.

In 1966, at the third National Conference of State Commissions on the Status of Women, several delegates, including Friedan, expressed concern at women's lack of political power to enforce Title VII and other antidiscrimination laws, and planned to introduce a resolution. When they learned that the conference would not even allow a resolution or any other action, they decided the time had come to organize an advocacy group on behalf of women—and the National Organization for Women (NOW) was born. Its goal was clear: "To take action to bring women into full participation in the mainstream of American society now, assuming all the privileges and responsibilities thereof in truly equal partnership with men." Initially NOW was committed to recruiting both women and men who shared a belief in women's equality. It catered to the needs of and largely recruited middle-class and mostly white professional women, although Pauli Murray and Aileen Hernandez, two African American women, were founding members. Like the original Seneca Falls Declaration of

Rights and Sentiments, drafted in 1848 by Elizabeth Cady Stanton, Lucretia Mott, and three other women, and, later, the goals of the National American Woman Suffrage Association (NAWSA), NOW strove to achieve for women the republican ideals of equality and individual rights within American society without advocating fundamental social or economic change. Almost as soon as it was created, however, NOW members feverishly debated this question: should NOW's agenda be limited to improving women's employment and educational opportunities or should it embrace the larger goals of confronting and eliminating sexism and all forms of inequality throughout American society? While expressing concern about professional opportunities, many younger women and women of color were also confronting other barriers to full equality, and NOW's limited focus on individual rights and career advancement did not fully address their needs.

Another source of feminist activism was rooted in the idealism and radical hopes of the civil rights movement and the New Left student movement; indeed, from these two social and political movements came the most creative and transformative ideas for achieving sexual equality. Both movements—one focused on achieving an end to racial discrimination and to promoting harmony between blacks and whites and the other committed to combating hatred and exploitation throughout American society—were dedicated to achieving the ideals of fraternity, equality, and community. But for women in both movements, these goals remained abstractions because of the condescending, second-class treatment they endured from male activists.

At a staff retreat of the Student Nonviolent Coordinating Committee (SNCC), the major student-led civil rights organization, SNCC women presented a position paper anonymously drafted by Casey Hayden, Mary King, and Mary Varela, three white female members. The message of the paper was unmistakable. In clear, reasoned, and persuasive language, they denounced men's arrogance toward women in SNCC and the lack of leadership roles available to women. "[The] assumption of male superiority [among SNCC men] is widespread and deep-rooted and as crippling to women as the assumptions of white supremacy are to the Negro." Regardless of the hard work that women performed for SNCC, they had little voice or power within the organization. "This is no more a man's world than it is a white world," the paper concluded, and it was time for the men in SNCC to realize that.[2]

In 1965 King and Hayden refined their position in another paper, "Sex and Caste: A Kind of Memo." This time they directly linked the situation of women and blacks, claiming that both were "caught up in a common law caste system."

They urged women to organize on their own behalf: "Perhaps we can start to talk to each other more openly than in the past and create a community of support for each other so we can deal with ourselves and others with integrity and therefore keep working."[3] What they suggested was the forerunner of a consciousness-raising group—a collective way to explore the issues and concerns they shared as women in order to work together for sexual equality. The civil rights movement had imbued King, Hayden, and other women in SNCC with a vision of freedom, equality, and community, which they used to challenge men's hegemony within the movement as well as within American society. This early demand for gender equality, inspired by frontline work for racial equality, was yet another gear that set into motion the women's liberation movement. The memo was addressed to black women in SNCC, but, in reality, it expressed the isolation and second-class membership that white women felt in SNCC. Black women would gradually find a different way to feminism.

Similarly women began to rethink their deferential position in the student movement. The Students for a Democratic Society (SDS) was one of several national campus organizations whose members came primarily from middle- to upper-middle-class families. Some were the children of the suburban mothers who had spent their days chauffeuring them from Scouts to music lessons and other after-school activities, while others could point to a legacy of political activism from parents who had participated in radical political causes. They had come of age in the shadow of McCarthyism, in a world clearly demarcated by good and evil. They espoused the values of freedom, equality, love, and hope, and at first they directed their efforts not to changing their own lives but to transforming the institutions around them—from the university to the military to Wall Street. At a convention in Port Huron, Michigan, in 1962, they articulated their goals in what came to be known as the Port Huron Statement: "We seek the establishment of a democracy of individual participation. . . . Human relations should involve fraternity and honesty."[4] They focused on issues beyond the scope of their personal lives, such as civil rights, nuclear testing, and the pernicious actions of the House Un-American Activities Committee. In these early years of SDS activism, leadership lay with the men, despite the SDS's lip service to egalitarianism and participatory democracy. Unlike SNCC, which carried out direct actions such as sit-ins, voter registration drives, and protests to achieve their goals, SDS relied on ideas, rather than action, to effect social change. Members conducted occasional pickets and marches, but they devoted as much time and energy to developing an ideological critique of American society, and most of this intellectual activity fell to men.

In 1963 SDS strategy began to evolve from theorizing solutions about social ills to dealing directly with those problems. When the United Auto Workers (UAW) gave SDS a five-thousand-dollar grant to set up a new program—Economic Research and Action Projects (ERAP)—SDS moved off the campus and into the ghetto, and women, like the women in SNCC, pursued frontline social activism. Both SDS men and women moved into impoverished urban neighborhoods and went door-to-door talking to residents, figuring out what the problems were, and devising collective strategies to resolve them. SDS women helped organize welfare mothers into their own organizations to fight for free lunch programs for their children, better playgrounds and streetlights, and safer living conditions. Like SNCC women, they exposed themselves to dangerous conditions and also found strong female role models among welfare women who were determined to fight for their rights.

As the SDS moved into the forefront of combating American involvement in the war in Vietnam, women once again felt marginalized; they could not carry out the dramatic gesture of burning their draft cards or going to jail instead of into the military. Women were expected to fill an auxiliary role. "Girls Say Yes to Guys Who Say No!" was a popular slogan of the movement. Although women participated in draft resistance projects, such as writing and distributing leaflets and counseling draft resistors, they still felt subservient and insignificant.

The growing antiwar movement helped to usher in a new movement: the counterculture. Many of the new student converts to SDS also embraced the values of this sister movement, including a rejection of the "uptight" emphasis on money and acquisitiveness in capitalist society, a celebration of sexual freedom outside of monogamy, and, in general, a desire to live more freely and in pursuit of personal fulfillment. For many women the theory of free love translated into the practice of sex with anyone at any time—or risk being labeled "uptight," a cardinal countercultural sin. Women in the New Left often felt like sexual commodities for the men who were supposed to be their comrades.

As early as 1964 some SDS women raised the contradiction of women's subservient role in an organization ostensibly committed to human equality and liberation. In SDS groups across the country, women began to raise the "woman question" in the pages of SDS publications and at meetings. But they mostly met a wall of indifference from male members, and by 1967 they were ready to work on their own behalf. Using their organizing skills and the networks of activist women from around the nation, they set up small discussion groups—modeled after the early SNCC meetings and SDS gatherings—which they called consciousness-raising groups. They had adapted the values of

SNCC, the SDS, and the counterculture—an emphasis on fraternity and equality, a commitment to direct action to effect social change, a belief in their right to achieve their full human potential—to their situation as women. The analogy was not lost on them. Kathie Amatniek, who had been a member of both SNCC and SDS, said of her women's group, "Well, when those meetings began, I felt like it was almost being back in the South. . . . I was very conscious that this was a grassroots movement again, and, you know, that these were real people, really seriously going to do something about their lives . . . that could affect people in a mass way."[5]

The first meetings were exciting, intense, and profoundly revelatory of the depth of unhappiness and oppression they had felt in relation to men. Dana Densmore's recollection of her early involvement in the women's liberation movement (starting on p. 207) describes the near-conversion experience she and other women felt as they now worked on behalf of their own freedom. Adapting practices used in the civil rights movement and the New Left, women explored in their groups the political implications of their personal experience. They began to realize that their individual experiences were neither unique nor insignificant but instead emblematic of women's cramped lives in American society. Thus was born the notion "The personal is political"—all personal experience had political underpinnings; the way women were raised and how they related to their parents, their brothers, their teachers, and their bosses and spouses reflected ingrained values and ideas about women's role in American society. These gatherings were empowering and liberating, because women felt supported by their peers. Consciousness-raising soon moved from political cells to city apartment complexes, suburban neighborhoods, and even corporate cafeterias as women gathered together to explore the political implications of their lives. See pp. 242–57 for a transcript of one such consciousness-raising session.

By 1968 the fledgling women's movement had moved out of private meeting places and into the street. At the 1968 Miss America pageant, activists crowned a live sheep, threw the symbols of female subjugation—girdles, bras, curlers, issues of the *Ladies Home Journal*—into a "freedom trashcan," and auctioned off an effigy: "Gentlemen, I offer you the 1969 model. She's better every year. She walks. She talks. She smiles on cue. And she does housework."[6] Other activists crashed bridal fairs, sat in at male-only bars, or "hexed" Wall Street.

These guerilla theater tactics reflected the improvisational aspects of the new movement. Like a spark igniting dry timber, the movement spread with astonishing speed, intensity, and spontaneity. Unlike their older sisters in NOW, the radical younger women of the women's liberation movement did not only seek legal and political equality within the framework of capitalist society, they demanded fundamental personal and political change in all aspects of life. The psychic sloughing off of modes of behavior that had kept women passive and deferential was as important as dismantling political and economic barriers to women's equality. With spirit and vitality, the radical members of the women's movement celebrated womanhood and strove to unleash their full potential as women.

By 1970 the term "women's lib" was used by everyone, supporters as well as detractors of the movement. The mainstream media—newspapers, magazines, prime-time television—carried stories about the movement and about cases of sexual discrimination. When two hundred women occupied the offices of the *Ladies Home Journal,* demanding a higher weekly wage, day-care facilities, a more ethnically diverse staff, and the replacement of a male editor with a senior all-female staff, the *Journal* agreed to give them an eight-page supplement in its August 1970 issue. Women who found NOW's legalistic approach to social and political change too tame joined such radical separatist groups as Redstockings or WITCH (Women's International Terrorist Conspiracy from Hell). The Redstockings Manifesto (reprinted on pp. 216–218) sets forth the separatist ideas and strategies of this radical New York–based group. Perhaps the heterogeneity of the early days of the movement was best represented by a Women's Strike for Equality, called by NOW. On August 26, 1970, thousands of women across the nation marched. Moderate and radical, they gave the movement new visibility and brought more women into its fold.

The early 1970s saw the fruits of these first efforts through real political and legislative victories for women's equality. By 1972 the organizations that supported the Equal Rights Amendment (ERA) spanned the spectrum from the League of Women Voters to the United Auto Workers. The YWCA, the American Association of University Women (AAUW), Common Cause, and Business and Professional Women also supported a constitutional amendment to guarantee sexual equality. That same year Congress finally approved the ERA, and by the end of the year twenty-two of the needed thirty-five states had also approved it. Also in 1972 Congress passed Title IX of the Higher Education Act, which forbade sexual discrimination in any educational program or activity that received federal funds. This legislation helped pave the way for the growth of women's organized high school and college athletics.

Nineteen seventy-two was also a banner year for women in politics. In 1971 Bella Abzug, a flamboyant and newly elected congresswoman from New York; Shirley Chisholm, an African American congresswoman also from New York;

and Betty Friedan founded the National Women's Political Caucus (NWPC), a bipartisan organization dedicated to expanding women's voices and visibility in the political arena. Their efforts quickly paid off. At both the Democratic and Republican presidential conventions that summer, the number of female delegates more than doubled from the conventions held four years earlier. Both political parties, which had previously ignored women's issues, adopted most of the NWPC agenda, including endorsement of the ERA, antidiscrimination legislation, and measures for tax and wage equity for women.

In 1973 American women achieved a stunning victory for reproductive freedom when the Supreme Court handed down *Roe v. Wade*, which legalized abortion within the first two trimesters (six months) of a pregnancy. Although that victory set in motion counterefforts by religious and conservative political groups to ban abortion, American women, for the first time, had access to legal, medically supervised abortions without the need for a doctor's approval.

During the 1970s the women's movement entered a vibrant, creative phase. As significant as were the political victories, so, too, were the cultural changes that feminism summoned forth. Like women in every generation before who had organized on behalf of themselves, feminists of the 1970s, from college students to grandmothers, learned the power of collective action and of building separate institutions. Women wasted no time setting up rape crisis centers, battered women's shelters, women's health clinics, and women's coffee houses, bookstores, and publishing houses.

Even the popular media reflected these cultural changes. Traditional women's magazines such as *Ladies Home Journal*, *McCall's*, and *Redbook* began featuring articles about the new feminist movement, though the editorial content of these magazines still mostly reinforced traditional views of women as homemakers, wives, and mothers. In 1971 Gloria Steinem and several other feminist activists published a supplement to *New York Magazine* entitled *Ms.* Steinem and her colleagues envisioned *Ms.* as the voice of the women's movement, committed to spreading the feminist message through its features and advertising. The first issue sold 250,000 copies, and by the following year *Ms.* had become a monthly periodical independent of *New York*. *Ms.* adroitly appealed to a general audience, composed of women gradually making their way into the feminist movement, as well as to those already converted. Its contributors included prominent writers, thinkers, and activists such as Alice Walker, Catharine Stimpson, and Letty Cottin Pogrebin. But the magazine also featured letters and articles by less illustrious women who wrote about their feminist awakenings. Just as *Ladies Home Journal* had been a prime source of information and inspiration for an earlier generation of American women, *Ms.* became the compass for feminist awakening for a new generation.

In Boston a women's health collective wrote a book to help women become more knowledgeable about their bodies and choices for health care. The book sold 200,000 copies in a newsprint edition from a nonprofit press and then came out in a commercial edition in 1973 as *Our Bodies, Ourselves*, an excerpt of which appears on pp. 277-83. It has been reissued several times in revised editions and has even spawned an edition for older women, entitled *Ourselves Growing Older* (1987).

On the job and at the office, women organized. While professional women such as lawyers, doctors, editors, and professors organized within their fields, clerical and working-class women also found strength in numbers. In 1974 clerical workers in Boston and Chicago organized Nine-to-Five and Women Employed, respectively. They enlisted Title VII and affirmative action guidelines to confront discriminatory hiring practices and engaged in attention-catching spectacles by celebrating Secretaries' Day with slogans such as "Raises Not Roses" and awards to the stingiest boss of the year. In Chicago in 1977 fifty secretaries from the downtown Loop organized a protest on behalf of a legal secretary who had refused to make coffee for her bosses. They presented a mock lesson in how to make coffee, ending with step 5: "Turn switch to on. This is the most difficult step, but with practice, even an attorney can master it."

Women in the labor movement also organized. In 1974 they created the Coalition of Labor Union Women (CLUW). Although the organization remained closely aligned with organized labor and resisted taking independent action, it brought together women from different unions and made them a force to reckon with inside the labor movement. On pp. 295–303, Dorothy Bolden, who organized the National Domestic Workers in the early 1970s, describes the tangible achievements and sense of empowerment that the organization accomplished for its members.

The tidal wave of feminist thinking swept through the institutions of higher learning, religion, and medicine as well. By 1979, 23 percent of medical school graduates and 28.5 percent of law school graduates were women, compared to 8.4 percent and 5.4 percent respectively in 1970.[7] New medical specialties in women's health emerged, and new theories in psychology and approaches to counseling were developed; most of these new psychologies rejected traditional Freudian orthodoxies and incorporated new theories about the impact of gender socialization on women's emotional makeup. In the academy two new disciplines emerged: women's studies and women's history. As women reclaimed their lives, they also strove to reclaim their history. Coupled with an eagerness to give voice to the lives of ordinary people—an ideal that came out of the political activism of their student protest years—a new generation of feminist scholars set about unearthing women's lives in the past. Initially they focused on well-known women, whose papers were more accessible, but as their theories and methods became more sophisticated, an enormous body of scholarship on women across the cultural and economic spectrum emerged. See pp. 231–39 for an essay by Gerda Lerner, a pioneering feminist historian, who articulated many of the new methodologies used by other scholars. In history, literature, anthropology, sociology, psychology, linguistics, theater, even the hard sciences, scholarship about women was integrated into the curriculum, and feminist scholars established a plethora of cross-disciplinary organizations and journals to handle this ever-growing scholarship. From the start conferences such as the Berkshire Conference on the History of Women, founded in 1972, and the National Women's Studies Association Annual Meeting, beginning in 1977, had an underlying activist spirit, because their members were on a mission to overturn assumptions and orthodoxies about women's lives and to examine anew their disciplines from the perspective of female experience. They set out to create new paradigms and entirely new areas of inquiry, such as sexuality and reproduction.

Religious institutions, which have historically been reluctant to draw women into leadership roles, were also influenced by feminist thinking. In 1972 the Reform movement in Judaism ordained its first female rabbi, Sally Priesand. The Conservative movement followed in 1985 by ordaining Amy Eilberg, and the Orthodox movement has yet to admit women into the rabbinate. In 1976 Episcopalian women achieved the right to be ordained as priests, a right earlier granted to Presbyterian women. Catholic women are still fighting for the right to serve as priests, but, as Terri Berthiaume Hawthorne points out in her oral history on pp. 258–61, they have found ways to incorporate feminist rites and rituals in their observance. Indeed, some of the most creative feminist thinking has come from feminist efforts to revise theological orthodoxies. In her writings Mary Daly has boldly and playfully invented new words to proclaim a distinct female spirituality and to explore female images of the divine, making use of spiraling, dazzling images to evoke her notion of a female god. Starting in the late 1970s Jewish feminist theorists began to look anew at women's roles in scripture and in Jewish practice. Although traditional Judaism does not give women a defined religious role within the synagogue, Jewish feminists have reinterpreted Jewish ideas and practices to incorporate feminist ideas. Feminist seders and haggadahs, for example, such as the one featured on pp. 304–7, celebrate the Jewish women of the Bible who helped lead their people out of bondage and draw parallels between the Israelites' triumphant delivery out of slavery and women's own journey toward liberation and equality.

By the mid-1970s, the women's movement encompassed—uneasily—a range of outlooks, from the moderate views of Betty Friedan, who was interested primarily in achieving legal and economic equality for women within the parameters of capitalist American society, to Marxist and socialist feminists who called for a restructuring of America's economic institutions to achieve equality for women, to radical feminists who placed the problem squarely on patriarchal values and advocated creating separate feminist communities with alternative value systems.

Many lesbian women found a comfortable home in the radical feminist camp. They argued that lesbianism represented the fullest expression of female autonomy. While facing rebuff by some moderate feminist leaders who were homophobic or feared the loss of public support if the movement became too closely associated with lesbianism, lesbian women of the early 1970s felt increasingly emboldened to "come out," organize as a group to combat discrimination, and celebrate their sexuality and women-centered values.

Black and working-class women expressed a different kind of ambivalence about the women's movement. They felt that the movement, which they mostly equated with NOW, did not address their needs, such as the necessity to reform the social and workplace conditions that resulted in women's lack of power and economic hardships. Black women believed that the struggle to combat racism within American society was as important as the struggle to end sexism; in fact, they claimed, the two goals must go hand-in-hand. They accused white feminists of denying their own prejudice and of neglecting black women's vital contributions to achieving sexual equality throughout American history. And they believed that the struggles they faced as black women—the double edge of oppression—were far more severe than that of privileged white women seeking to gain admission into a white capitalist patriarchal power structure.

Yet, despite their reservations about the methods and goals of the movement, black women clearly found their way to organized feminism. In 1973 the National Black Feminist Organization (NBFO) was created, which set out to achieve political, social, and economic equality specifically for black women. The following year the Combahee River Collective, one of several black lesbian groups, was organized in New York City. Dedicated to combating not only sexism but also heterosexism, racism, and class exploitation, they enlarged their feminist vision to demand freedom, respect, and equality for all oppressed people. See pp. 316–22 for their founding statement. Black feminists identified specific issues that needed urgent attention. For example, while black women had made significant strides in getting more education and increasing their earnings, they still earned the lowest median income of all social groups, as did their families. The number of families below the poverty level headed by black women was at an alarming rise. A 1972 Louis Harris–Virginia Slims poll revealed that 62 percent of black women supported "efforts to strengthen or change women's status in society," compared to only 45 percent of white women. Even more astonishing, 67 percent of black women expressed "sympathy with efforts of women's liberation groups," compared to 35 percent of white women.[8]

While these battles over ideology, strategies, and goals were being played out on campuses and in academic or otherwise obscure journals, American women around the nation offered their own reactions to the women's movement. In November 1977, in Houston, Texas, twenty thousand women, men, and children came together at the National Women's Conference, a government-sponsored gathering, to focus on problems and issues of concern to women. The conference delegates represented a microcosm of America, with delegates from around the country and from a range of ethnic and economic backgrounds. The declaration that came out of the conference, reprinted on pp. 313–15, offered a wide-ranging agenda of change for women's lives.

This diversity enabled the movement to remain elastic and flourishing despite the many internal conflicts, for the movement *had* transformed the lives of millions of American women. The *idea* of equal opportunity for women, of enabling women to choose any number of life paths besides that of marriage and motherhood caught on and was roundly embraced. Such mainstream organizations as the YWCA and Girl Scouts and religious groups such as United Methodist Women and the National Council of Jewish Women became increasingly attuned to, and supported, issues of concern to women. Public schools began to integrate their shop and cooking classes. In 1975 Harvard accepted its first female students—no longer would women undergraduates be forced to attend Radcliffe if they wanted a Harvard education—and other previously all-male colleges such as Amherst and Princeton followed suit. From 1961 to 1973, the first decade of the women's movement, the percentage of female college graduates rose from 35 percent to 45 percent. Women received 9 percent of the nation's medical degrees in 1973, up from 5 percent in 1961; 8 percent of law degrees compared to 2.6 percent in 1961; and 18 percent of Ph.Ds, up from 10 percent in 1961.[9]

Women made gains in the workplace as well. The percentage of married women in the work force had been steadily rising, but throughout the 1960s and 1970s more women entered previously all-male occupations. After protracted negotiations between NOW and the EEOC, AT&T agreed to hire women as line workers on telephone poles and place men as operators. Other companies quickly implemented similar plans to integrate the work force. By 1980 women made up nearly 50 percent of all bus drivers, up from 3 percent in 1950. Minority women, in particular, found better job prospects; increasingly they left agricultural and domestic-service jobs for better-paying white-collar and service occupations. From 1965 to 1978 the percentage of black women who worked in white-collar positions nearly doubled.[10]

But the movement still suffered from a major image problem: although many women, and men, expressed their support for women's economic and political equality, they were far more wary of calling themselves feminist because of the frightening extremist policies and images this term conjured up. A roundtable of letters by young high school women published by *Ms.* magazine (see pp. 284–94) expressed the conflicts and ambivalence they felt in identifying themselves as feminists.

No one exploited these fears more skillfully than Phyllis Schlafly and the anti-ERA movement. The ensuing debate touched the very heart of ongoing public perceptions of the meaning of gender and the proper role of women in American society. An Equal Rights Amendment banning gender-based discrimination had languished in Congress for several decades. Earlier opponents, including some feminists of the 1920s and 1930s, had feared it would erode protective workplace legislation for working women—legislation they had fought so hard to attain. By the late 1960s feminists were less concerned about that and more concerned about finding a way to guarantee that women would receive equal treatment under the law as individuals rather than as a sex-defined group. They believed that the ERA would achieve this. Section 1 of the ERA stated simply: "Equality of rights under the law shall not be denied or abridged by the United States or by any State on account of sex."

Greater media attention to women's liberation in the early 1970s generated welcome publicity for the movement as well as a backlash by several new organizations of women who opposed what they believed to be the goals of the movement: an end to marriage and the nuclear family and to "feminine" women and "masculine" men. Declaring themselves "Women Who Want to Be Women," "Females Opposed to Equality," and "Happiness of Womanhood," they rallied behind the politically adroit Phyllis Schlafly. Schlafly, who had worked as a financial analyst in a bank and was active in Republican politics, waged a ferocious campaign against the ERA and the women's movement, which she described as "a bunch of bitter women seeking a constitutional cure for their personal problems." Characterizing feminists as "unkempt" and as "the lesbians, the radicals, the socialists," she developed a powerful grassroots following, which shared her opposition to the ERA. Schlafly argued that an equal rights amendment was unnecessary because existing legislation already protected women's rights. But at heart she believed that a woman's true place was in the home as wife and mother and that the ERA would destroy that role. She and other right-wing opponents also declared that the ERA would decriminalize rape, sanction homosexuality, abolish separate men's and women's public restrooms, and make abortion easily available on demand—all scenarios they passionately opposed. Schlafly viewed *Ms.* magazine as the power behind the pro-ERA forces and lashed out at its readers and editors as "anti-family, anti-children, and proabortion. . . . Women's lib is a total assault on the role of the American woman as wife and mother, and on the family as the basic unit of society. . . . They are promoting Federal 'day-care centers' for babies instead of homes. They are promoting abortions instead of families."[11] An excerpt from her book *The Power of the Positive Woman*, which sets out her conservative agenda, appears on pp. 322–25.

Supporters of the ERA were hard-pressed to argue rationally against the doomsday scenarios deftly fashioned by Schlafly and other right-wing activists. Schlafly had struck a chord in women who were satisfied with their roles as homemakers and who felt the women's movement, with its emphasis on careers and on personal rights and fulfillment, did not speak to their lives. Wrote one Oklahoma woman to her state legislator: "I want to remain a woman. I want to remain on a pedestal, I want to remain a homemaker."[11] In large measure because of Schlafly's efforts, the ERA died a slow, withering death. By January 1973, when she embarked on her campaign, both the House and the Senate had passed the amendment and twenty-eight states had ratified it. Supporters were confident that they could get the necessary three-fourths of the states to ratify it. By 1974 five more states had ratified it, but Nebraska and Tennessee had rescinded their prior ratification, and by 1978 it had become clear that the original seven-year period would expire without the necessary approval. NOW made ratification of the ERA its primary goal, but it was too late. Anti-ERA forces had managed to stir up public fears about the power of the ERA to throw society into chaos by obliterating the traditional division of gender roles and duties. In

1983 the House of Representatives reintroduced the ERA, but it has yet to win congressional approval.

By the end of the 1970s the women's movement was embattled. Internal conflicts and assault from right-wing opponents on the outside had forced activists to rethink many of their strategies and goals. They would soon need all the energy and resources available to counteract a Republican juggernaut against many of the issues for which they had fought so hard: government programs to help women in the workplace, reproductive rights, social welfare programs, antidiscrimination laws. But, however they viewed organized feminism, American women were putting many of its precepts into practice by going to college and pursuing careers, choosing to delay marriage and childbirth, enjoying greater sexual freedom—in short, taking control and responsibility for their lives and reshaping ideas about gender to accommodate their new visions of freedom.

NOTES

1. Quoted in Joyce Antler, *The Journey Home: How Jewish Women Shaped Modern America* (New York: Schocken Books, 1997), p. 257.
2. Quoted in Sara Evans, *Personal Politics: The Roots of Women's Liberation in the Civil Rights Movement and the New Left* (New York: Knopf, 1979), p. 60.
3. Quoted in ibid., pp. 83, 87, 100.
4. Quoted in ibid., p. 113.
5. Quoted in ibid., p. 203.
6. Quoted in Sara Evans, *Born for Liberty: A History of Women in America* (New York: Free, 1989), p. 283.
7. Winifred Wandersee, *On the Move: American Women in the 1970s* (Boston: Twayne, 1988), p. 120.
8. Paula Giddings, *When and Where I Enter: The Impact of Black Women on Race and Sex in America* (New York: Bantam, 1984), p. 345.
9. Rosalind Rosenberg, *Divided Lives: American Women in the Twentieth Century* (New York: Hill and Wang, 1992), p. 218.
10. Ibid., pp. 236–37.
11. Phyllis Schlafly Report 5, February 1972; quoted in Jane J. Mansbridge, *Why We Lost the ERA* (Chicago: University of Chicago Press, 1986), p. 104.
12. Quoted in the *New York Times*, 21 March 1979, p. 24.

"I FELT THE WORLD WAS PASSING ME BY"
HERMA L. SNIDER

From 1960 to 1961 Redbook *magazine ran a series of articles entitled "Why Young Mothers Feel Trapped." In these articles, which appeared periodically throughout 1960, young mothers described how cramped their lives felt. Perhaps reflecting the editorial viewpoint of the magazine's editors who selected the articles, the only solutions proposed by the writers were to accept their lives as they were, find more efficient ways to handle housework and child-rearing, or, like Herma Snider, find work that would get them out of the house. None of the writers questioned the traditional gender roles they were following or the social and cultural values that had defined those roles. Although she chafed at her life of homemaking and child rearing, Snider clearly believed that only men, and not women, could choose what kind of life they wanted and that women were destined for domesticity. And though she found a way to combine homemaking and paid work, it is clear that her job is a stopgap solution to her restlessness, not a vocation that brings fulfillment, as Betty Friedan advocates in the selection from* The Feminist Mystique, *which follows this document.*

SOURCE: Herma L. Snider, "I Stopped Feeling Sorry for Myself," *Redbook* 115, no. 5 (December 1960): 32–3, 104.

I GREW UP on a farm in Michigan, surrounded by 11 brothers and sisters and countless other relatives and friends. My world was full of people and companionship and talk. Ten years after my marriage it was a very different world. Cemented to my house by three young children, there were days in which I saw no adult human being except the milkman as he made his deliveries and spoke to none from the time my husband left in the morning until he returned at night.

My husband is a young pharmacist in his mid-30s. He is gifted in his work, dedicated to his ideals and a good husband and father. . . .

I pride myself upon being a woman of average intelligence and understanding. During my high-school and college days I had dreams of a career in journalism. . . . But after my marriage these dreams were abandoned.

At first I rather enjoyed the routine of cooking and cleaning. Inclined to be a perfectionist in anything I undertook, I was proud of my ability to keep my floors gleaming and my closets in good order. Then my three children arrived in rapid succession and I found myself riding on a whirling merry-go-round,

vainly attempting to keep a level head in a topsy-turvy world filled with baby
bottles, sterilizers, diapers, formulas, vaporizers, aspirins and vitamin pills.
With my morale sagging even lower than my tired stomach muscles I managed
to cook, bake, iron, scrub, shop, clean and wash: I flopped into bed at night like
a wilting lettuce leaf, only to be rudely awakened at all hours by the urgent wail
of a hungry baby.

How I survived those hectic years, I do not know. . . . The only consolation
I could give myself each night was the knowledge that my children were one
day older. I looked forward to the day when they would be toilet-trained, to the
day when they would be in school, to the mythical, wonderful, ever-approach-
ing, never-arriving day when I would have "a little time to myself."

The culmination of all this discontent came when my husband accepted an
offer of a position in Nevada, far from our friends and family and everything I
had ever known or loved. Actually I did not protest too much about this move,
for I felt that it might be my salvation. Perhaps in a new home, in new surroundings, with new friends and a new background, I would develop a fresh
outlook on life. I recognize this now as wishful thinking. . . .

I quickly found myself in the same old rut, existing on cigarettes and
cleanser fumes, up to my elbows in dishwater, up to my armpits in the inces-
sant demands of home and community. . . .

I developed a host of ailments: headaches, nausea, dishpan hands, matron-
ly bulge (despite a loss of appetite) and housemaid's knee. I screeched at my
children in a voice that rivaled a hog caller at the peak of condition, swilled
three pots of coffee a day and nagged my husband incessantly.

Meanwhile, the mind that I thought I had camphored away refused to stay
put. It yearned for a chance to flex its muscles on something besides the grocery bills and the perpetual "why?" of three small boys. . . .

I yearned for a full, satisfying life and I felt that the world was passing me by.
Each night as I tucked my sons into bed, I thanked God that they would grow
up to be *men*, that they would be able to teach, write, heal, advise, travel or do
anything else they chose. Not for them the endless tasks of clearing up, picking
up, cleaning up, cheering up, washing up, hanging up, sewing up, mopping up
and all the other ups and downs of household work which I found so difficult
to accept.

At last I became the phantom of the doctor's office with my weekly list of
ailments. The doctor examined me thoroughly and finally informed me that I
was suffering from "nerves."

"My God," I said bluntly, "I could have told you that. Even my nerves have nerves."

"I have a prescription for you," he told me after he had listened to my impressive array of symptoms. "I want you to go out and get yourself a job."

I was appalled. How could I work? I had a big house to care for, three children to rear and a weekly laundry that attained the height of Pike's Peak. Besides, my husband had a good position and an adequate salary. I had never thought it right for a woman to hold a job when it was unnecessary. Not only that but I was unprepared, unskilled. I could set a mean dinner table, but I had forgotten how to type, I couldn't figure percentages and the multiplication table was beyond my abilities. . . .

[But] I had reached the point where a glass of spilled milk could send me into a rage. . . . Quietly, desperately, I walked outside the world of skinned knees and macaroni casseroles and found myself a job as a cashier in a local hotel.

It wasn't easy. I made mistakes, but luckily I had found a patient employer who smiled at my fears and helped me gain confidence in my ability. Daily I struggled with my feeling of guilt at leaving my children with a baby sitter for a few hours each day. I imagined all sorts of disasters overtaking them while I was away. I drove home from work and I had to muster courage to turn into the drive, so frightened had I become of what I would find when I arrived. I worried about my husband too. Suppose he wasn't eating enough? Suppose he became tired of me and turned to another woman? Suppose? . . .

I was a tired, inefficient, unorganized woman who could not possibly handle two jobs. I hired a girl to help with the cleaning, sent the laundry out, and then discovered that my expenses overpowered my meager salary. Talking it over with my husband and with my employer solved the problem. I began to work three days of the week. In this way I could work with a clear conscience and still have time for my housework and my family.

My cashier's job is not the glamorous career I once dreamed of. And I know that it can be said that my solution is not a solution at all, merely an escape. But it seems to me that when the demands of children and household threaten to suffocate you, an escape *is* a solution, although perhaps just a temporary one. . . .

A part-time job whereby I swap some of the drudgery and confinement of housework for the refreshing free air of the adult world may be only an escape, but for me it is also a solution.

If I can spend a few hours away from the children, I can enjoy them and allow them to enjoy me for the rest of the day.

If I can find time to write this, then I don't resent the pile of ironing. . . .

The ultimate solution, if there is one, will have to come later, when the children are a little older, when I understand better exactly what it is that I want, or perhaps when I learn to accept some of the things that I have been battering my head against. But for the time being I know that as long as I am not confined to the premises, my house is a home instead of the place I once dubbed my "chintz prison."

"THE PROBLEM THAT HAS NO NAME"
BETTY FRIEDAN

Like a tremor warning of an earthquake, The Feminine Mystique, *published in 1963, appeared just as the social and economic fault lines of American society were shifting. In the book, a ten-year follow-up study of Smith College graduates, Betty Friedan documented a pervasive unhappiness among American middle-class women, which she called "the problem that has no name." She defined this problem as a restlessness and dissatisfaction with full-time homemaking, especially among women who had attended elite colleges and had envisioned broader lives for themselves. Friedan condemned the automatic coupling of women with domesticity, both in the mass media and in the reality of American life, and deplored the attitude of religious leaders, psychologists, and other influential public figures who equated a woman's desire to achieve professional success beyond the home with psychological disorder.*

The book, laced with testimonials by frustrated and unhappy homemakers who felt no sense of worth because they had not carved a life outside of their homes and families, became an instant best-seller and was widely serialized in the major women's magazines. Friedan's solutions now seem limited and elitist; she urged women to return to school or take on demanding, professional occupations without questioning why women alone should shoulder the tasks of housework and child care or how low-income women could seek the professional fulfillment she extolled. But in its day The Feminine Mystique *helped to sow discontent and prompt women to question social norms and expectations—the essential precursor to social change. In the following excerpt, Friedan describes the problem that has no name and offers her solutions.*

SOURCE: Betty Friedan, *The Feminine Mystique* (1963; reissued New York: Norton, 1997), pp. 15–21, 32, 342–48, 368, 374–75. Copyright © 1983, 1974, 1973, 1963 by Betty Friedan. Used by permission of W. W. Norton & Company, Inc.

THE PROBLEM lay buried, unspoken, for many years in the minds of American women. It was a strange stirring, a sense of dissatisfaction, a yearning that women suffered in the middle of the twentieth century in the United States. Each suburban wife struggled with it alone. As she made the beds, shopped for groceries, matched slipcover material, ate peanut butter sandwiches with her children, chauffeured Cub Scouts and Brownies, lay beside her husband at night—she was afraid to ask even of herself the silent question—"Is this all?"

For over fifteen years there was no word of this yearning in the millions of words written about women, for women, in all the columns, books and articles by experts telling women their role was to seek fulfillment as wives and mothers. Over and over women heard in voices of tradition and of Freudian sophistication that they could desire no greater destiny than to glory in their own femininity. Experts told them how to catch a man and keep him, how to breast-feed children and handle their toilet training, how to cope with sibling rivalry and adolescent rebellion; how to buy a dishwasher, bake bread, cook gourmet snails, and build a swimming pool with their own hands; how to dress, look, and act more feminine and make marriage more exciting; how to keep their husbands from dying young and their sons from growing into delinquents. They were taught to pity the neurotic, unfeminine, unhappy women who wanted to be poets or physicists or presidents. They learned that truly feminine women do not want careers, higher education, political rights—the independence and the opportunities that the old-fashioned feminists fought for. Some women, in their forties and fifties, still remembered painfully giving up those dreams, but most of the younger women no longer even thought about them. A thousand expert voices applauded their femininity, their adjustment, their new maturity. All they had to do was devote their lives from earliest girlhood to finding a husband and bearing children. . . .

If a woman had a problem in the 1950's and 1960's, she knew that something must be wrong with her marriage, or with herself. Other women were satisfied with their lives, she thought. What kind of a woman was she if she did not feel this mysterious fulfillment waxing the kitchen floor? She was so ashamed to admit her dissatisfaction that she never knew how many other women shared it. If she tried to tell her husband, he didn't understand what she was talking about. She did not really understand it herself. For over fifteen years women in America found it harder to talk about this problem than about sex. Even the psychoanalysts had no name for it. When a woman went to a psychiatrist for help, as many women did, she would say, "I'm so ashamed," or "I must be hopelessly neurotic." "I don't know what's wrong with women today," a suburban psychiatrist said uneasily. "I only know something is wrong because most of my patients happen to be women. And their problem isn't sexual." Most women with this problem did not go to see a psychoanalyst, however. "There's nothing wrong really," they kept telling themselves. "There isn't any problem."

But on an April morning in 1959, I heard a mother of four, having coffee with four other mothers in a suburban development fifteen miles from New

York, say in a tone of quiet desperation, "the problem." And the others knew, without words, that she was not talking about a problem with her husband, or her children, or her home. Suddenly they realized they all shared the same problem, the problem that has no name. They began, hesitantly, to talk about it. Later, after they had picked up their children at nursery school and taken them home to nap, two of the women cried, in sheer relief, just to know they were not alone.

GRADUALLY I came to realize that the problem that has no name was shared by countless women in America. As a magazine writer I often interviewed women about problems with their children, or their marriages, or their houses, or their communities. But after a while I began to recognize the telltale signs of this other problem. I saw the same signs in suburban ranch houses and split-levels on Long Island and in New Jersey and Westchester County; in colonial houses in a small Massachusetts town; on patios in Memphis; in suburban and city apartments; in living rooms in the Midwest. Sometimes I sensed the problem, not as a reporter, but as a suburban housewife, for during this time I was also bringing up my own three children in Rockland County, New York. I heard echoes of the problem in college dormitories and semiprivate maternity wards, at PTA meetings and luncheons of the League of Women Voters, at suburban cocktail parties, in station wagons waiting for trains, and in snatches of conversation overheard at Schrafft's. The groping words I heard from other women, on quiet afternoons when children were at school or on quiet evenings when husbands worked late, I think I understood first as a woman long before I understood their larger social and psychological implications.

Just what was this problem that has no name? What were the words women used when they tried to express it? Sometimes a women would say "I feel empty somehow . . . incomplete." Or she would say, "I feel as if I don't exist." Sometimes she blotted out the feeling with a tranquilizer. Sometimes she thought the problem was with her husband, or her children, or that what she really needed was to redecorate her house, or move to a better neighborhood, or have an affair, or another baby. Sometimes, she went to a doctor with symptoms she could hardly describe: "A tired feeling . . . I get so angry with the children it scares me . . . I feel like crying without any reason." (A Cleveland doctor called it "the housewife's syndrome.") A number of women told me about great bleeding blisters that break out on their hands and arms. "I call it the housewife's blight," said a family doctor in Pennsylvania. "I see it so often lately in these young women with four, five and six children who bury

MAKING THE WORLD ANEW

themselves in their dishpans. But it isn't caused by detergent and it isn't cured by cortisone." . . .

If I am right, the problem that has no name stirring in the minds of so many American women today is not a matter of loss of femininity or too much education, or the demands of domesticity. It is far more important than anyone recognizes. It is the key to these other new and old problems which have been torturing women and their husbands and children, and puzzling their doctors and educators for years. It may well be the key to our future as a nation and a culture. We can no longer ignore that voice within women that says: "I want something more than my husband and my children and my home." . . .

It would be quite wrong for me to offer any woman easy how-to answers to this problem. There are no easy answers, in America today; it is difficult, painful, and takes perhaps a long time for each woman to find her own answer. First, she must unequivocally say "no" to the housewife image. This does not mean, of course, that she must divorce her husband, abandon her children, give up her home. She does not have to choose between marriage and career; that was the mistaken choice of the feminine mystique. In actual fact, it is not as difficult as the feminine mystique implies, to combine marriage and motherhood and even the kind of lifelong personal purpose that once was called "career." It merely takes a new life plan—in terms of one's whole life as a woman.

The first step in that plan is to see housework for what it is—not a career, but something that must be done as quickly and efficiently as possible. Once a woman stops trying to make cooking, cleaning, washing, ironing, "something more," she can say "no, I don't want a stove with rounded corners, I don't want four different kinds of soap." She can say "no" to those mass day dreams of the women's magazines and television, "no" to the depth researchers and manipulators who are trying to run her life. Then, she can use the vacuum cleaner and the dishwasher and all the automatic appliances, and even the instant mashed potatoes for what they are truly worth—to save time that can be used in more creative ways.

The second step, and perhaps the most difficult for the products of sex-directed education, is to see marriage as it really is, brushing aside the veil of over-glorification imposed by the feminine mystique. Many women I talked to felt strangely discontented with their husbands, continually irritated with their children, when they saw marriage and motherhood as the final fulfillment of their lives. But when they began to use their various abilities with a purpose of their own in society, they not only spoke of a new feeling of "aliveness" or "completeness" in themselves, but of a new, though hard to define, difference in the way they felt about their husbands and children. Many echoed this woman's words:

> The funny thing is, I enjoy my children more now that I've made room for myself. Before, when I was putting my whole self into the children, it was as if I was always looking for something through them. I couldn't just enjoy them as I do now, as though they were a sunset, something outside me, separate. Before, I felt so tied down by them, I'd try to get away in my mind. Maybe a woman has to be *by herself* to be really *with* her children. . . .

The only way for a woman, as for a man, to find herself, to know herself as a person, is by creative work of her own. There is no other way. But a job, any job, is not the answer—in fact, it can be part of the trap. Women who do not look for jobs equal to their actual capacity, who do not let themselves develop the lifetime interests and goals which require serious education and training, who take a job at twenty or forty to "help out at home" or just to kill extra time, are walking, almost as surely as the ones who stay inside the housewife trap, to a nonexistent future. . . .

Ironically, the only kind of work which permits an able woman to realize her abilities fully, to achieve identity in society in a life plan that can encompass marriage and motherhood, is the kind that was forbidden by the feminine mystique; the lifelong commitment to an art or science, to politics or profession. Such a commitment is not tied to a specific job or locality. It permits year-to-year variation—a full-time paid job in one community, part-time in another, exercise of the professional skill in serious volunteer work or a period of study during pregnancy or early motherhood when a full-time job is not feasible. It is a continuous thread, kept alive by work and study and contacts in the field in any part of the country.

The women I found who had made and kept alive such long-term commitments did not suffer the problem that has no name. Nor did they live in the housewife image. But music or art or politics offered no magic solution for the women who did not or could not, commit themselves seriously. The "arts" seem, at first glance, to be the ideal answer for a woman. They can, after all, be practiced in the home. They do not necessarily imply that dreaded professionalism, they are suitably feminine, and seem to offer endless room for personal growth and identity, with no need to compete in society for pay. But I have noticed that when women do not take up painting or ceramics seriously enough to become professionals—to be paid for their work, or for teaching it to others, and to be recognized as a peer by other professionals—sooner or later, they cease dabbling; the Sunday painting, the idle ceramics do not bring that needed sense of self when they are of no value to anyone else. The amateur or dilettante whose own work is not good enough for anyone to want to pay to hear or see or read does not gain real status by it in society, or real personal identity. These are reserved for those who have made the effort, acquired the knowledge and expertise to become professionals. . . .

It is essential, above all, for educators themselves to say "no" to the feminine mystique and face the fact that the only point in educating women is to educate them to the limit of their ability. Women do not need courses in "marriage and the family" to marry and raise families; they do not need courses in homemaking to make homes. But they must study science—to discover in science; study the thought of the past—to create new thought; study society—to pioneer in society. Educators must also give up these "one thing at a time" compromises. That separate layering of "education," "sex," "marriage," "motherhood," "interests for the last third of life," will not solve the role crisis. Women must be educated to a new integration of roles. The more they are encouraged to make that new life plan—integrating a serious, lifelong commitment to society with marriage and motherhood—the less conflicts and unnecessary frustrations they will feel as wives and mothers, and the less their daughters will make mistaken choices for lack of a full image of woman's identity. . . .

It also is time to stop giving lip service to the idea that there are no battles left to be fought for women in America, that women's rights have already been won. It is ridiculous to tell girls to keep quiet when they enter a new field, or an old one, so the men will not notice they are there. In almost every professional field, in business and in the arts and sciences, women are still treated as second-class citizens. It would be a great service to tell girls who plan to work in society to expect this subtle, uncomfortable discrimination—tell them not to be quiet, and hope it will go away, but fight it. A girl should not expect special privileges because of her sex, but neither should she "adjust" to prejudice and discrimination.

She must learn to compete then, not as a woman, but as a human being. Not until a great many women move out of the fringes into the mainstream will society itself provide the arrangements for their new life plan. But every girl who manages to stick it out through law school or medical school, who finishes her M.A. or Ph.D. and goes on to use it, helps others move on. Every woman who fights the remaining barriers to full equality which are masked by the feminine mystique makes it easier for the next woman. . . .

When enough women make life plans geared to their real abilities, and speak out for maternity leaves or even maternity sabbaticals, professionally run nurseries, and the other changes in the rules that may be necessary, they will not have to sacrifice the right to honorable competition and contribution anymore than they will have to sacrifice marriage and motherhood. It is wrong to keep spelling out unnecessary choices that make women unconsciously resist either commitment or motherhood—and that hold back recognition of the needed social changes. It is not a question of women having their cake and eating it, too. A woman is handicapped by her sex, and handicaps society, either by slavishly copying the pattern of man's advance in the professions, or by refusing to compete with man at all. But with the vision to make a new life plan of her own, she can fulfill a commitment to profession and politics, and to marriage and motherhood with equal seriousness.

The Civil Rights Act of 1964 was a comprehensive and enormously important law. Divided into eleven major sections, or titles, it outlawed various forms of discrimination against women and minorities. Title I, for example, strengthened voting rights for minorities; Title III provided for the desegregation of public facilities; Title V established a Commission on Civil Rights. Title VII enumerated a long list of discriminatory practices no longer available to employers and labor unions, required the federal government to create an "affirmative" program of equal employment opportunity for all job applicants and employees, and created an Equal Employment Opportunity Commission (EEOC) to monitor compliance with the law.

For women, Title VII was especially significant because it outlawed discrimination on the basis of gender as well as race. Sex was added to the categories "race, color, religion and national origin" by Congressman Howard Smith, a conservative Democrat from Virginia, who fiercely opposed civil rights legislation but, oddly enough, supported the Equal Rights Amendment (ERA). He introduced his motion at the prodding of Republican supporters of the National Women's Party, who had been lobbying for the ERA and who wanted to equate sexual discrimination with racial discrimination. The debate on Smith's motion was filled with misogyny; Smith joked that his amendment would protect the "right" of every woman to a husband. But the amendment passed, ironically enough, because of the support of conservative congressmen who wanted to weaken the impact of civil rights legislation with legal protections for white women.

The Equal Employment Opportunity Commission, which began work in 1965, expected that most of its complaints would come from African Americans. The commissioners were surprised to discover that 25 percent of the complaints they received during the first year were filed by women. As they dealt with these complaints, both the EEOC and the courts were forced to refine their perceptions of female job categories and sexual discrimination. During the following decade most states drafted their own version of Title VII, establishing laws that prohibited gender discrimination on the job. Although conservative presidential administrations, such as the Reagan and George H. Bush administrations, have tried to weaken the monitoring powers of the EEOC, Title VII remains a beacon of protection for equal rights under the law.

SOURCE: Title VII, government legislation

SEC. 703.(A) It shall be an unlawful employment practice for an employer—

(1) to fail or refuse to hire or to discharge any individual, or otherwise to discriminate against any individual with respect to his compensation, terms, conditions, or privileges of employment, because of such individual's race, color, religion, sex, or national origin; or
(2) to limit, segregate, or classify his employees in any way which would deprive or tend to deprive any individual of employment opportunities or otherwise adversely affect his status as an employee, because of such individual's race, color, religion, sex, or national origin.

(b) It shall be an unlawful employment practice for an employment agency to fail or refuse to refer for employment, or otherwise to discriminate against, any individual because of his race, color, religion, sex, or national origin, or to classify or refer for employment any individual on the basis of his race, color, religion, sex, or national origin.

(c) It shall be an unlawful employment practice for a labor organization—

(1) to exclude or to expel from its membership, or otherwise to discriminate against, any individual because of his race, color, religion, sex, or national origin;
(2) to limit, segregate, or classify its membership, or to classify or fail or refuse to refer for employment any individual, in any way which would deprive or tend to deprive any individual of employment opportunities, or would limit such employment opportunities or otherwise adversely affect his status as an employee or as an applicant for employment, because of such individual's race, color, religion, sex, or national origin; or
(3) to cause or attempt to cause an employer to discriminate against an individual in violation of this section. . . .

(e) Notwithstanding any other provision of this title, (1) it shall not be an unlawful employment practice for an employer to hire and employ employees, for an employment agency to classify, or refer for employment any individual, for a labor organization to classify its membership or to classify or refer for employment any individual, or for an employer, labor organization, or joint labor-management committee controlling apprenticeship or other training or retraining programs to admit or employ any individual in any such program, on the basis of his religion, sex, or national origin in those certain instances where religion, sex, or national origin is a bona fide occupational qualification reasonably necessary to normal operation of that particular business or enterprise. . . .

Sec. 705.(a) There is hereby created a Commission to be known as the Equal Employment Opportunity Commission, which shall be composed of five members, not more than three of whom shall be members of the same political party, who shall be appointed by the President by and with the advice and consent of the Senate. . . .

(g) The Commission shall have power—

(1) to cooperate with and, with their consent, utilize regional, State, local, and other agencies, both public and private, and individuals; . . .

(3) to furnish to persons subject to this title such technical assistance as they may request to further their compliance with this title or an order issued thereunder;

(4) upon the request of (i) any employer, whose employees or some of them, or (ii) any labor organization, whose members or some of them, refuse or threaten to refuse to cooperate in effectuating the provisions of this title, to assist in such effectuation by conciliation or such other remedial action as is provided by this title;

(5) to make such technical studies as are appropriate to effectuate the purposes and policies of this title and to make the results of such studies available to the public;

(6) to refer matters to the Attorney General with recommendations for intervention in a civil action brought by an aggrieved party under section 706, or for the institution of a civil action by the Attorney General under section 707, and to advise, consult, and assist the Attorney General on such matters. . . .

"THE TIME HAS COME FOR A NEW MOVEMENT TOWARD TRUE EQUALITY"
NATIONAL ORGANIZATION FOR WOMEN (NOW)

The National Organization for Women (NOW) was founded in 1966 by Betty Friedan, author of The Feminist Mystique, *and other women delegates to the third National Conference of State Commissions on the Status of Women. When they learned that the conference organizers would not allow resolutions or action of any kind to abolish discrimination against women, specifically employment discrimination, they decided that women needed an advocacy organization of their own. Indeed, even the Equal Economic Opportunity Commission (EEOC) refused to enforce the sex discrimination provision of Title VII of the Civil Rights Act of 1964. As she later recalled, Friedan and several other delegates "cornered a large table at the [conference] luncheon, so that we could start organizing before we had to rush for planes." Each woman chipped in five dollars, Friedan scrawled the word* NOW *on a paper napkin, and a new women's rights organization—soon to become the most visible and powerful feminist organization—was born.*

NOW focused on the plight of professional women who sought to alleviate the burden of domestic responsibilities and aspired to professional achievement. NOW's solutions were legalistic; the organization strove to change laws that discriminated against women, pressured the EEOC to issue sex-discrimination guidelines, and was an early supporter of the Equal Rights Amendment. Despite internal feuding, NOW achieved important legislative victories. But in its zeal to increase women's presence in the workplace, it alienated working-class women and women of color, who, forced to work to supplement meager family earnings, shared none of NOW's romantic notions about the "liberating" quality of paid labor; indeed, many of them would have preferred to stay home with their children. NOW strove to achieve equal rights and responsibilities for women within the present structure of American society without questioning the need or desire to change that structure. Nor did it reach beyond legalistic solutions to promote a new vision of womanhood and female solidarity. Compare the emphasis in NOW's Statement of Purpose on changing laws and policies to achieve equality to the defiant challenge in the Redstockings Manifesto (pp. 216–18) to overthrow male supremacy and forge a new conception of female liberation.

SOURCE: Reprinted by permission of NOW

WE, MEN AND WOMEN who hereby constitute ourselves as the National Organization for Women, believe that the time has come for a new movement toward true equality for all women in America, and toward a fully equal partnership of the sexes, as part of the world-wide revolution of human rights now taking place within and beyond our national borders.

The purpose of NOW is to take action to bring women into full participation in the mainstream of American society now, exercising all the privileges and responsibilities thereof in truly equal partnership with men.

We believe the time has come to move beyond the abstract argument, discussion and symposia over the status and special nature of women, which has raged in America in recent years; the time has come to confront, with concrete action, the conditions that now prevent women from enjoying the equality of opportunity and freedom of choice which is their right as individual Americans, and as human beings.

NOW is dedicated to the proposition that women first and foremost are human beings, who, like all other people in our society, must have the chance to develop their fullest human potential. We believe that women can achieve such equality only by accepting to the full the challenges and responsibilities they share with all other people in our society, as part of the decision-making mainstream of American political, economic and social life.

We organize to initiate or support action, nationally or in any part of this nation, by individuals or organizations, to break through the silken curtain or prejudice and discrimination against women in government, industry, the professions, the churches, the political parties, the judiciary, the labor unions; in education, science, medicine, law, religion and every other field of importance in American society. . . .

There is no civil rights movement to speak for women, as there has been for Negroes and other victims of discrimination. The National Organization for Women must therefore begin to speak.

WE BELIEVE that the power of American law, and the protection guaranteed by the U.S. Constitution to the civil rights of all individuals, must be effectively applied and enforced to isolate and remove patterns of sex discrimination, to ensure equality of opportunity in employment and education, and equality of civil and political rights and responsibilities on behalf of women, as well as for Negroes and other deprived groups.

We realize that women's problems are linked to many broader questions of social justice, their solution will require concerted action by many groups. Therefore, convinced that human rights for all are indivisible, we expect to give active support to the common cause of equal rights for all those who suffer discrimination and deprivation, and we call upon together organizations committed to such goals to support our efforts toward equality for women.

WE DO NOT ACCEPT the token appointment of a few women to high-level positions in government and industry as a substitute for a serious continuing effort to recruit and advance women according to their individual abilities. To this end, we urge American government and industry to mobilize the same resources of ingenuity and command with which they have solved problems of far greater difficulty than those now impeding the progress of women. . . .

WE REJECT the current assumptions that a man must carry the sole burden of supporting himself, his wife, and a family, and that a woman is automatically entitled to lifelong support by a man upon her marriage; or that marriage, home and family are primarily a woman's world and responsibility—hers, to dominate, his to support. We believe that a true partnership between the sexes demands a different concept of marriage, an equitable sharing of the responsibilities of home and children, and of the economic burdens of their support. We believe that proper recognition should be given to the economic and social value of homemaking and child care. To these ends, we will seek to open a reexamination of laws and mores governing marriage and divorce, for we believe that the current state of "half-equality" between the sexes discriminates against both men and women, and is the cause of much unnecessary hostility between the sexes.

WE BELIEVE that women must now exercise their political rights and responsibilities as American citizens. They must refuse to be segregated on the basis of sex into separate-and-not-equal ladies' auxiliaries in the political parties, and they must demand representation according to their numbers in the regularly constituted structure, participating fully in the selection of candidates and political decision-making, and running for office themselves.

IN THE INTERESTS OF THE HUMAN DIGNITY OF WOMEN, we will protest and endeavor to change the false image of women now prevalent in the mass media, and in the texts, ceremonies, laws and practices of our social institutions. Such images perpetuate contempt for women by society and by women for themselves. We are similarly opposed to all policies and practices—in church, state, college, factory or office—which, in the guise of protectiveness, not only deny opportunities but also foster in women self-denigration, dependence, and evasion of responsibility, undermine their confidence in their own abilities and foster contempt for women. . . .

"1968, A YEAR OF EXHILARATION"
DANA DENSMORE

Like mother, like daughter, Dana Densmore joined the women's move-
ment after her mother, Donna Allen, a founder of Women Strike for Peace (see pp.
137–42), called her one day and intoned two "magic words": women's liberation.
Densmore soon switched her allegiance from the antiwar to the women's move-
ment. From 1968 to 1974 she was active in the Boston area movement and served
as founding editor and, later, publisher of the radical feminist journal No More
Fun & Games. She also led many feminist study groups and workshops, and in
general devoted her energies to women's liberation.

Densmore lays bare both the exhilaration and sense of danger inherent in or-
ganizing the women's movement—the exhilaration that women were going to
usher in not only a new world of equality with men but of self-respect and self-love
among women. No longer would men dictate women's conduct and choices in life.
But, as Densmore dramatically describes, there was also danger in thwarting men's
sense of superiority and privilege in gender relations. Densmore chronicles the
roller-coaster journey of creating a new movement: the thrill of sharing new ideas
with other women even when those women were not ready to discard old patterns
of behavior, the almost theatrical (and sometimes dangerous) strategies used to
promote new ideas or protest sexist views of women, the sheer intellectual pleasure
of creating new theories of female liberation, and the supremely satisfying goal of
living by her own values and standards rather than by someone else's. Densmore
emphasizes the importance of achieving psychological liberation as much if not
more than achieving tangible social or economic rights. For her, as for other femi-
nists who found NOW's agenda too limiting, true liberation began from within,
with each woman choosing, in her words, to "live authentically."

SOURCE: Rachel DuPlessis and Ann Snitow, eds., *The Feminist Memoir Project: Voices from Women's Liberation* (New York: Three Rivers Press/Crown, 1998), pp. 271–84, 289. Copyright © 1998 by Ann Snitow. Used by permission of Crown Publishers, a division of Random House, Inc.

IN JANUARY 1968, I got a phone call from my mother, Donna Allen. "Women's liberation!" she pronounced in a tone of incantation. The resonance
and ring with which she invested the words conveyed her sense that the
words themselves, sacred and momentous, constituted in their utterance the
missing piece of a puzzle. Each word and all it signified, connected, and im-

plied—for each word a great rich world of context—was electrically alive to both of us.

We knew "women," being women ourselves, and coming from a long line of independent-minded, woman-valuing women. We also knew the disrespect women met in the world, as a gender, and we had watched as many fine, intelligent women's brilliant and heroic efforts came to very little. We knew "liberation," the central value and key verbal formula in many of the progressive causes in which we had always been activists. "Liberation" represented a heady, psychologically and ideologically clean process of thought and commitment. Injustice, perceived and analyzed, was met with a self-sacrificing determination to right the wrongs. It felt "clean," wholesome, and unsullied, because the impulses were relatively unfettered by the inhibitions and the trade-offs necessary in mainstream politics which make one feel compromised and bought off. To those who spoke of "liberation," matters were simple: If it was wrong, it must be changed. What more was there to say? The clean energy that welled up when conscience was clear and committed seemed equal to any adversity.

Two rich words, each with important values to us—but we had never heard them uttered together. The implications were dizzying. Suddenly the progressive causes we had always worked for were revealed as having been other people's causes. Was it possible that we could finally be turning to the most radical cause of all?

"It has begun!" The words were galvanizing, chilling; the implications were massive, dangerous, and revolutionary; their seriousness precluded euphoria. I knew that the liberation of women was not going to be easily won, nor won through any moderate means. I knew that once I had embarked on this path, there would be no stopping short. Reality shifted, and I felt myself to be in a new world.

My mother, Donna Allen, a national antiwar activist and a founder of Women Strike for Peace, had been in New York at a meeting to plan a peace demonstration, and, from fellow activist Bernardine Dohrn, had heard rumblings of women's discontent in SDS and other organizations in the movements for social justice. Some women were asking whether it was ideologically defensible to fight for the liberation of every single class and category other than women, while accepting female subservience.

"Liberation for *us!*" my mother said in her phone call. "It has begun! Women are organizing, and we're going to turn the men's world upside down, throw the bums out, and run things as they should be run!" In her enthusiasm she skipped over the hard part, but I wasn't fooled. I knew that the disaffection of a few women was only a small start in a very big job. . . .

At the time of the phone call, I had been very active in the draft resistance movement, counseling conscientious objectors, men who opposed the Vietnam War, and the undecided, who were confused or questioning. I helped them to understand their options and to sort through the ins and outs of the law and the procedures and practice of draft boards and the Selective Service. With others, I supported the men refusing induction through "The Resistance": a loose support group of and for men who had already refused or were about to refuse induction, and the women who were keeping a world of meaningfulness and love around the men who were setting their lives in turmoil.

Yet the weekly dinner meetings of The Resistance were exercises in self-laceration for the women. It went without saying that we cooked and cleaned up while the men bonded, strategized, and postured. They were laying their balls on the line, and we were . . . what? The girls enjoined to say yes to the boys who said no? Of course, in reality we were more than that. We would not personally be going to jail, but our lives were equally disrupted. We were preparing to go to Canada or Sweden with husbands who chose exile, preparing to postpone children or to raise those we already had without the support of husbands who chose jail. But for "the boys" we were nonentities. Though of equal intelligence and thoughtfulness, and equal commitment, we had no legitimacy as part of the struggle. Should a woman have the temerity to voice a thought in the course of one of the conversations, there was a silence in which the men looked embarrassedly away from her before picking up just where they had been.

After Donna's two magic words—"women's liberation"—I went to no more Resistance dinners. . . .

I began following up leads to women's liberation and, by the beginning of May 1968, was corresponding with Joreen [Jo Freeman], editor of a newsletter published in Chicago entitled *Voice of the Women's Liberation Movement*. I was now part of an actual movement, although I needed the right catalyst to launch me into activism. I had done the basic thinking; my consciousness was already raised. Now I needed comrades who were ready for revolution; I didn't want to sit around with housewives concerned about getting more help with child care from their husbands or with New Left women wanting to persuade their male cohorts to be more respectful. The magnitude of the problem obviously required a much more radical and activist approach. But would I find any such comrades? . . .

It was a terrifying and dangerous time. We felt that we were laying our lives on the line in a way the boys of The Resistance weren't even contemplating. We saw the violence and hatred that demands of personhood and dignity for women brought out in men who until then appeared normal. These were many women's "nice men." They were the apparently dignified conservatives, the open-minded liberals, the justice-hungry leftists, the apolitical hippies. These men gave us every indication that they would choose open warfare, to the death, rather than yield any privilege, including the psychological privilege of feeling superior. We felt we were girding for an apocalypse in male-female relations. It was startling—and deeply disturbing—how frequently men responded to our direct but courteous remonstrances about sometimes small issues of behavior with the verbal and body language of physical violence. . . .

In one action, we picketed the Playboy Club, at night, in an unpopulated and desolate part of town, trying to hand leaflets to men or to their wives and dates. Now, I had encountered danger and the threat of violence before. I had been charged by New York City police on horseback wielding clubs to break up a peace demonstration. I had faced angry rednecks threatening me in a very personal way with rape, mutilation, and lynching in a civil rights sit-in in the South. And one night during the Cuban missile crisis, my sister Martha and I were picketing the White House as part of an around-the-clock vigil for peace; at 2 A.M. we found ourselves alone, two teenage girls with our peace signs facing off against Nazi Party members who took ugly issue with our stance. But looking back, I think I may have felt most vulnerable facing the well-dressed patrons of the Playboy Club and the hatred aroused by our challenging the systematic objectification of women through sex.

In another political event at a local movie house, we sponsored a showing of *The Queens*, about a transvestite beauty pageant. The film portrayed men making themselves into women who were so convincing that one forgot that they were men. This evinced, we thought, better than any arguments in a leaflet, that womanly appearance and feminine mannerisms were purely convention. Around this time or a little later, our first black woman member had joined the group: Marianne, a feisty character who had been laughing raucously at our showing of *The Queens*. Somewhere else we had connected with our first out-and-militant lesbian member, Gail, a poet. In addition, Roxanne had acquired an apartment-mate, Maureen, whom she recruited into the group. She had also found Marilyn, high-strung and intellectual, who was to stay with us into Cell 16. Betsy and Stella and Ellen from the original group were still with us. . . .

In August 1968, there was a meeting in Maryland of women mostly from New Left movements to talk about women's liberation. Roxanne and I drove down from Boston, bearing our revolutionary ideas. These women wanted to talk about improving their treatment from their leftist male comrades and about their wish for more respect from their lovers. However, Roxanne was not one to try to meet people on their own level; on the contrary, she considered shock tactics to be the most salutary. Whether intending to shock or whether naively expecting this to be enthusiastically received, she insisted on reading aloud to them from the *Scum Manifesto*. To make matters worse, we talked about celibacy as a revolutionary tactic. The other women were horrified by us. They thought Valerie was clearly crazy (as her incarceration in a mental institution only confirmed). And they weren't a bit impressed by our political analysis on that: as Roxanne and I interpreted the ideology of patriarchy, when a man shoots someone, he is either justified or a criminal, but when a woman shoots someone, well, she must be crazy, since women don't do such things. Such a woman gets shut up in a mental institution where they can keep her drugged to mute her. And even if Valerie *were* crazy, we proposed that she was still worthy of our support as one probably driven to illness by the same pressures we were facing, and also valuable as theoretician and symbol.

More surprising than their reaction to Valerie were their stories of abusive relationships with men. Why stay? They're all that way, was the response; besides, we need sex. Why? Uncomprehending looks. They seemed to think that we were hopelessly out of touch with reality: how could one talk to people so unaware of basic psychology and physiology? These women had not missed the message of the so-called sexual revolution: to wit, that a woman who doesn't make sure she "gets plenty" (from men, of course) will "dry up inside," as one woman there anxiously characterized it. We responded to their stories of abusive male-female relationships with the suggestion—rather mild, so it seemed to us—that women aren't going to be able to respect themselves so long as they stay in such relationships. We suggested that women did not, in fact, need sex. What we needed was autonomy. . . .

Although we were disappointed not to find women more in tune with our own views, we came home feeling enlightened about the nature of the work to be done and energized by the clear direction. I saw that it wasn't going to be enough to say a couple of magic words; we needed to explain why we saw what we did. We decided to start a theoretical journal.

We called the journal *No More Fun & Games: A Journal of Female Liberation*. The main title was meant to show our uncompromising intentions. We were not promising men that the liberation of women was going to be to their advantage; on the contrary, we were going to end the game playing they found so appealing. The subtitle asserted our name for the movement: "female" rather than "women's" liberation. In addition it was "a" journal, not "the" journal, thus inviting others to publish other journals, each contributing the particular perspective of their group to weave a rich tapestry of female liberation theory. Roxanne had wrangled a typesetting machine from IBM—under pretenses that didn't bear looking into. We had it for the weekend only, so we worked all day and far into the night, each woman in our group typesetting her own articles. We were a strange manic crew, still "scum" as Valerie would have had us, but now, as our numbers increased, our bonds were looser. Ideologically, we were surfing on the same exhilarating wave, tolerant of differences of style and perspective, coherent in the importance of the primary goals, feeling fully committed to the cause. But we would no longer have trusted one another with our lives as the tighter group had rather rashly been prepared to do earlier in the summer.

The journal, which came out in late August 1968, contained no address at which we could be contacted; we sold it on the street for a dollar a copy (pretty much exactly what it cost to print, as I recall). The issue was also undated. Looking back as editor and publisher of some of the later of the six issues, it seems strange that it never occurred to us to date the first issue, but it accurately reflected our state of mind then. We didn't foresee an orderly future that would in turn become history and require documentation. Instead, we saw ourselves on the verge of a great upheaval. Perhaps it was like the anticipation of the end of the world for early Christians.

The journal reflected our diversity, a dizzying mix of styles reflecting our group and the each-woman-speaks-her-mind editorial philosophy. The issue featured practical what-to-do analyses of ways we were tricked into supporting our own oppression. There were views on left movement politics, essays with an academic tone, militant diatribes, Marxist-influenced analysis, poetry, drawings, and collages. The cover drawing, done by my sister Indra, was a naked woman whose massive curls of hair completely enclosed and imprisoned her. In fact, our first prospective printer had refused to take the job, claiming that the cover was pornographic, but perhaps he was really more confused and offended by it being brought to him by women. Or perhaps he'd had a peek at the contents.

I wrote quite a few pieces for this journal. Essays on sexuality and celibacy inspired by our conference in Maryland. A couple of ambitious analyses of how women's current condition came to be, how that condition was enforced, how women reacted to it, and what needed to be done; some of that analysis was noticeably influenced by Simone de Beauvoir's classic *The Second Sex*, which I had been reading. A short bit addressing the draft resisters and the irritating slogan "Girls say yes to boys who say no" left me with a sense of closure on my experience with The Resistance.

The journal was exciting. It said things that hadn't yet been said, things no one else was saying, things that needed to be said, things that had the shock of truth. Our message, as it emerged in gradually more coherent form in later journals, was to women, not men. It was women that we intended to change. We didn't flatter ourselves that we had anything we could say to men that would have any weight in balance with the privileges that the subordination of women conferred. (Oh, probably Roxanne thought some bullying of men couldn't hurt, but she only tossed her harangues out as a public service, for their own good, as it were; she didn't imagine that our liberation would come from them.)

We meant to empower women to reject enslavement on its many levels. We threatened men not with violence but with the refusal to play the games through which women built up men and misrepresented themselves, through which men manipulated women and rewarded them for inauthenticity. It was my focus in particular to expose the games, in as much telling detail as possible, so that women could see them for what they are and not be taken in.

The matter of a name for our group had been given some thought. We had toyed from the beginning with the name Women Against Society, and had even told importunate representatives of the media (who seemed unable to focus on the issues until they could get our label) that we were "tentatively" using that name. But we resisted the idea of having any name; it seemed limiting and invited pigeonholing and marginalization. We wanted to act in the name of liberation for women in the broadest and most radical sense. But we were certain and explicit about one thing regarding names, and had talked about this from our first meetings. We wanted the *movement* to be characterized as "female" liberation, not "women's" liberation, as it had begun to be called in the first stirrings by the women of the student peace and civil rights movements. To us, "woman" was a constructed and conventional role, created by men for their convenience and satisfaction. With the term "female" we went to the root of the matter, clearing away all the false accretions and making room for whatever was true in our natures to show itself. The term "feminism" had a respectable past history, but it was too close to the prescriptive term "feminine" to sit comfortably with us. . . .

In November there was to be another, larger conference for women in Chicago. . . . The conference was huge (so it seemed at the time) and exhilarating. The general impression was one of tremendous richness. Women came from all around the country. Women from the thick of the civil rights struggle in the South. Women with particular contributions, like Anne Koedt (who seemed very much in tune with my approach), with her forthright article "The Myth of the Vaginal Orgasm." The Red-stocking women from New York offered the "pro-woman line," proposing that anything women do is right and good and that it's just a matter of looking at any female action from a women's perspective to see its intelligence and value. This was refreshing, and often revealed more truth than the conventional view, which could be called the "anti-woman line": that anything women do is trivial or base. Much of the analysis of the conference, however, suggested that men were being unfair and that they should have this pointed out to them so that they would change, thus solving the problem. As I saw it, men knew perfectly well that they were being unfair to women, and chose their behavior because it was to their advantage. Thus men wouldn't voluntarily change. We had to change. And declaring everything women did to be good wasn't going to create change if it justified and honored things we were doing that locked us into the system of subservience and oppression. . . .

Of the female liberation groups, we in our Boston group seemed the most wholeheartedly ready to overturn and to sacrifice everything: the old coherence and whatever conveniences or privileges it might be offering us, all our systems of getting along in the man's world, our very lives. Of course, as it turned out over the next twenty years, it was not necessary to sacrifice our lives, and it did not come to armed revolution. We had been misled by men's vicious response to our suggestions for change. In fact, it turned out that men were a great deal more dependent on women than they let on, and, as long as we had the ability to leave them, we had a trump card. When enough women were willing to say they didn't need men, willing to walk out and make it stick, men began to change. Of course, the men tried every trick of manipulation and bullying, used economic pressure and played on our sense of responsibility to our children. And of course there was violence: then and still now, many women who leave men are murdered by them, and sometimes their children are murdered as well. But enough succeeded in leaving that men learned that certain behavior was not in their interests, and things began gradually to improve.

Didn't this come from women following the very strategy we recommended, whether or not they knew it was ours? We proposed women respecting themselves, valuing their lives, and insisting on being treated fairly if they are going to give of themselves, whether in the workplace or marriage or anywhere else. I still think our uncompromising approach was right. One has to be willing to face it all, to say that one's dignity and self-respect are more important than keeping a man or a job, more important perhaps even than life, if it comes to a need to take some risk. . . .

The groundwork for all that was to come of our part of the women's movement had been laid in 1968, a year of exhilaration, terror, and upheaval such as everyone should have in her life, but perhaps not more than once.

"WOMEN ARE AN OPPRESSED CLASS"
REDSTOCKINGS MANIFESTO

Redstockings was a radical feminist organization founded in 1969 in New York City by Shulamith Firestone, Kathie Sarachild, and Ellen Willis. The name was a playful twist on the word "bluestockings," a term of derision that opponents of the early twentieth-century movement used to mock suffragists; by calling their organization Redstockings, its founders intended to honor their feminist forebears while emphasizing the red, or revolutionary nature, of their group.

Like other radical feminist groups, Redstockings engaged in street theater, organized speakouts on abortion and other issues once considered taboo, and contributed such now-classic concepts as "the personal is political." The original Redstockings disbanded in 1971, but in its brief lifetime it injected energy, controversy, and sport to the emerging second wave of feminism.

The following manifesto, issued in New York City on July 7, 1969, as a mimeographed flier designed for distribution at women's liberation events, squarely places the root cause of women's oppression not only on economic and political inequality but on "male supremacy," which, according to Redstockings, is the source of all forms of inequality. Regardless of their class or ethnic background, declares the Redstockings perspective, women are united as a class in opposition to male supremacy. How does this definition of oppression and the solutions proposed differ from NOW's Statement of Purpose on pp. 204–6?

SOURCE: Redstockings Women's Liberation Archives for Action Distribution Project. P.O. Box 2625, Gainesville, Fla. 32602-2625. Reprinted by permission.

1

After centuries of individual and preliminary political struggle, women are uniting to achieve their final liberation from male supremacy. Redstockings is dedicated to building this unity and winning our freedom.

2

Women are an oppressed class. Our oppression is total, affecting every facet of our lives. We are exploited as sex objects, breeders, domestic servants, and cheap labor. We are considered inferior beings, whose only purpose is to enhance men's lives. Our humanity is denied. Our prescribed behavior is enforced by the threat of physical violence.

Because we have lived so intimately with our oppressors, in isolation from each other, we have been kept from seeing our personal suffering as a political condition. This creates the illusion that a woman's relationship with her man is a matter of interplay between two unique personalities, and can be worked out individually. In reality, every such relationship is a *class* relationship, and the conflicts between individual men and women are *political* conflicts that can only be solved collectively.

3

We identify the agents of our oppression as men. Male supremacy is the oldest, most basic form of domination. All other forms of exploitation and oppression (racism, capitalism, imperialism, etc.) are extensions of male supremacy: men dominate women, a few men dominate the rest. All power structures throughout history have been male-dominated and male-oriented. Men have controlled all political, economic and cultural institutions and backed up this control with physical force. They have used their power to keep women in an inferior position. *All men* receive economic, sexual, and psychological benefits from male supremacy. *All men* have oppressed women.

4

Attempts have been made to shift the burden of responsibility from men to institutions or to women themselves. We condemn these arguments as evasions. Institutions alone do not oppress; they are merely tools of the oppressor. To blame institutions implies that men and women are equally victimized, obscures the fact that men benefit from the subordination of women, and gives men the excuse that they are forced to be oppressors. On the contrary, any man is free to renounce his superior position provided that he is willing to be treated like a woman by other men.

We also reject the idea that women consent to or are to blame for their own oppression. Women's submission is not the result of brainwashing, stupidity, or mental illness but of continual, daily pressure from men. We do not need to change ourselves, but to change men.

The most slanderous evasion of all is that women can oppress men. The basis for this illusion is the isolation of individual relationships from their political context and the tendency of men to see any legitimate challenge to their privileges as persecution.

5

We regard our personal experience, and our feelings about that experience, as the basis for an analysis of our common situation. We cannot rely on existing ideologies as they are all products of male supremacist culture. We question every generalization and accept none that are not confirmed by our experience.

Our chief task at present is to develop female class consciousness through sharing experience and publicly exposing the sexist foundation of all our institutions. Consciousness-raising is not "therapy," which implies the existence of individual solutions and falsely assumes that the male-female relationship is purely personal, but the only method by which we can ensure that our program for liberation is based on the concrete realities of our lives.

The first requirement for raising class consciousness is honesty, in private and in public, with ourselves and other women.

6

We identify with all women. We define our best interest as that of the poorest, most brutally exploited woman.

We repudiate all economic, racial, educational or status privileges that divide us from other women. We are determined to recognize and eliminate any prejudices we may hold against other women.

We are committed to achieving internal democracy. We will do whatever is necessary to ensure that every woman in our movement has an equal chance to participate, assume responsibility, and develop her political potential.

We call on all our sisters to unite with us in struggle.

We call on all men to give up their male privileges and support women's liberation in the interest of our humanity and their own.

In fighting for our liberation we will always take the side of women against their oppressors. We will not ask what is "revolutionary" or "reformist," only what is good for women.

The time for individual skirmishes has passed. This time we are going all the way.

—July 7, 1969, Redstockings, New York

"YOUR TIME IS NOW, MY SISTERS"
SHIRLEY CHISHOLM

*Shirley Chisholm, a diminutive woman with crackling energy and pres-
ence, accomplished two firsts: she was the first African American woman to be
elected to Congress (in 1968), and she was the first black to seek the endorsement
of a major political party—the Democratic party—as candidate for U.S. president. Born in Brooklyn, New York, she spent her early years in Barbados, where
she received a rigorous education. After graduating from Brooklyn College with a
major in psychology, she embarked on a master's degree in early childhood education at Columbia University but soon heard the siren call of politics. In 1964 she
became a New York State assemblywoman and four years later won the first of six
terms in the U.S. House of Representatives. She served until 1982, focusing on
achieving minimum-wage increases and federal funding for day-care centers—
issues that benefited women and low-income constituents.*

*Although Chisholm did not capture the party's presidential nomination at the
1972 Democratic National Convention, her short-lived campaign broke new
ground in the struggle to make the political arena more inclusive and diverse. As
she explained later, "What I hope most is there will be others who will feel themselves as capable of running for high political office as any wealthy, good-looking
white male."*

*In the following speech, delivered at a congressional hearing on women's em-
ployment, Chisholm discusses the twin evils of sexism and racism but pinpoints the
more entrenched economic and political roots of women's second-class citizenship.
She exhorts women to combat sexism wherever they confront it—at home, in their
workplaces, in their religious institutions, and in their interpersonal relationships.
But, ultimately, for her, the solution lies in welcoming more women into politics.
She thus exemplifies an early strand of liberal feminism.*

SOURCE: Speech delivered at the Conference on Women's Employment. Hearings before
the Special Subcommittee on Education of the Committee on Education and Labor, House
of Representatives, 91st Congress, 2d session (Washington, D.C.: Government Printing Office, 1970): pp. 909–15.

. . . I AM, as it is obvious, both black and a woman. And that is a good vantage
point from which to view at least two elements of what is becoming a social
revolution: the American black revolution and the women's liberation movement. But it is also a horrible disadvantage. It is a disadvantage because Amer-

ica as a nation is both racist and anti-feminist. Racism and anti-feminism are two of the prime traditions of this country. For any individual, breaking with social tradition is a giant step—a giant step because there are no social traditions which do not have corresponding social sanctions—the sole purpose of which are to protect the sanctity of those traditions.

That's when we ask the question, "Do women dare?" We're not asking whether women are capable of a break with tradition so much as we're asking whether they are capable of bearing the sanctions that will be placed upon them. . . .

Each—black male and black female, white male and white female—must escape first from their own intolerable trap before they can be fully effective in helping others to free themselves. Therein lies one of the major reasons that there are not more involved in the women's liberation movement. Women cannot, for the most part, operate independently of men because they often do not have sufficient economic freedom.

In 1966, the median earnings of women who worked full time for the whole year was less than the median income for males who worked full time for the whole year. In fact, white women workers made less than black male workers, and of course, black women workers made the least of all. Whether it is intentional or not, women are paid less than men for the same work, no matter what their chosen field of work. Whether it is intentional or not, employment for women is regulated more in terms of the jobs that are available to them. This is almost as true for white women as it is for black women. Whether it is intentional or not, when it becomes time for a high school girl to think about preparing for her career, her counselors, whether they be male or female, will think first of her so-called natural career—housewife and mother—and begin to program her for a field with which children and marriage will not unduly interfere.

That's exactly the same as the situation of the young black students who the racist counselor advises to prepare for service-oriented occupations, because he does not even think of them entering the professions. And the response of the average young female is precisely the same as the response of the average young black or Puerto Rican—tacit agreement—because the odds seem to be stacked against them.

This is not happening as much as it once did to young minority group people. It is not happening because they have been radicalized, and the country is becoming sensitized to its racist attitudes. Women must learn a lesson from that experience. They must rebel! . . .

The law cannot do it for us. *We must do it for ourselves.* Women in this country must become revolutionaries. We must refuse to accept the old, the traditional roles and stereotypes. . . . We must replace the old, negative thoughts about our femininity with positive thoughts and positive action affirming it, and more. But we must also remember that we will be breaking with tradition, and so we must prepare ourselves educationally, economically, and psychologically in order that we will be able to accept and bear with the sanctions that society will immediately impose upon us.

I'm a politician. . . . I have been in politics for 20 years, and in that time I have learned a few things about the role of women in power. And the major thing that I have learned is that women are the backbone of America's political organizations. They are the letter writers, the envelope stuffers, the telephone answerers; they're the campaign workers and the organizers. Perhaps it is in America, more than any other country, that the inherent proof of the old bromide, "The power behind the throne is a woman" is most readily apparent.

Let me remind you once again of the relatively few women standard bearers on the American political scene. There are only 10 United States Representatives; one Senator; no cabinet members who are women; no women on the Supreme Court and only a small percentage of lady judges at the federal court level who might be candidates.

It is true that at the state level the picture is somewhat brighter, just as it is true that the North presents a service that is somewhat more appealing to the black American when compared to the South. But even though in 1967 there were 318 women who were in the state legislatures, the percentage is not good when compared with the fact that in almost all 50 states, there are more women of voting age than there are men and that in each state, the number of women of voting age is increasing at a greater rate than the number of men. Nor is it an encouraging figure when compared with the fact that in 1966 there were not 318 women in the state legislatures, as now, but there were 328, which shows that there has been a decline. . . .

I have pointed out time and time again that the harshest discrimination that I have encountered in the political arena is anti-feminism, both from males and brain-washed, Uncle Tom females. When I first announced that I was running for the United States Congress, both males and females advised me, as they had when I ran for the New York State legislature, to go back to teaching—a woman's vocation—and leave the politics to the men.

And one of the major reasons that I will not leave the American scene—that is, voluntarily—is because the number of women in politics is declining. There are at least 2,000,000 more women than men of voting age, but the fact is that while we get out the vote, we also do not get out to vote. In 1964, for example, 72% of registered males voted, while only 67% of the registered females voted. We seem to want to become a political minority by choice. I believe that women have a special contribution to make to help bring order out of chaos in our nation today because they have special qualities of leadership which are greatly needed today. And these qualities are the patience, tolerance, and perseverance which have developed in many women because of suppression. And if we can add to these qualities a reservoir of information about the techniques of community action, we can indeed become effective harbingers for change.

Women must participate more in the legislative process, because even of the contributions that I have just mentioned, the single greatest contribution that women could bring to American politics would be a spirit of moral fervor, which is sorely needed in this nation today. But unfortunately, women's participation in politics is declining, as I have noted. . . .

Your time is now, my sisters. . . . New goals and new priorities, not only for this country, but for all of mankind must be set. Formal education will not help us do that. We must therefore depend upon informal learning. We can do that by confronting people with their humanity and their own inhumanity—confronting them wherever we meet them: in the church, in the classroom, on the floor of the Congress and the state legislatures, in the bars, and on the streets. We must reject not only the stereotypes that others hold of us, but also the stereotypes that we hold of ourselves.

In a speech made a few weeks ago to an audience that was predominately white and all female, I suggested the following, if they wanted to create change. You must start in your own homes, your own schools, and your own churches. I don't want you to go home and talk about integrated schools, churches, or marriages if the kind of integration you're talking about is black and white. I want you to go home and work for, fight for, the integration of male and female—human and human. . . .

"WHAT IS LIBERATION?"
EDITORIAL IN *WOMEN: A JOURNAL OF LIBERATION*

Among the feminist strands of thought that contributed new visions of women's lives was socialist feminism. Socialist feminists grafted the ideas of socialism—a belief in a society based on mutual support, collective decision making, shared resources, fulfilling work, and an end to the profit mode, which leads to greed and competition—to a feminist critique of patriarchal structures, both in the nuclear family and the workplace and in American society as a whole. Many socialist feminists call for communal alternatives to the nuclear family, such as collective households where two or more families live together and all labor and decision making is shared equally. In addition, they advocate a restructuring of the workplace to give workers control over the terms, processes, and results of the work.

In the following unsigned editorial from Women: A Journal of Liberation, *published in 1970, the vision of women's liberation is firmly embedded in a critique of capitalism, which, according to the authors, produces alienation from work, other people, and the natural world. The goals of women's liberation—access to abortion and birth control, child-care services, a better education, and more meaningful work—cannot be achieved in a capitalist society. How does this vision of women's liberation differ from the goals expressed in NOW's Statement of Purpose?*

SOURCE: *Women: A Journal of Liberation* 1, no. 2 (Winter 1970).

THE WORDS which movements use to describe themselves often suggest the terms of their struggle. In the early part of this century and before, women described themselves as "suffragettes" or "abolitionists"—the very words showed the limitation of their struggle: to gain the vote or to end slavery. These limited goals were not enough to achieve full equality for women or for black people. It is significant that the common phrase which describes the present women's movement is the word, "liberation." This word implies a deep consciousness of the significance of our struggle: Women are asking for nothing less than the total transformation of the world.

Before discussing the meaning of liberation, it is necessary to explore three basic concepts: (1) the material conditions for liberation, (2) the problem of alienation, and (3) the method of dialectic thought.

THE MATERIAL CONDITIONS FOR LIBERATION

When we discuss liberation, we are not talking about an abstract "idea"; we are talking about a potential that is firmly rooted in reality. We are talking about actual possibilities. The possibility for liberation exists because the material conditions of the world have evolved enough that our oppression and secondary status are no longer necessary. By "material conditions" we mean technology, scientific discoveries, industrialization, and the economic system which defines the way human beings relate to each other. For example, the full liberation of women was not possible until humanity evolved to the stage where reproduction could be controlled. The oppression of women began in primitive times when the biological nature of women severely limited their mobility. Now that women have a choice about reproduction in advanced industrial countries, one of the crucial fetters to our liberation has been removed.

We are not blaming women's oppression *only* on material conditions. Something more than technology or reproduction must explain the kind of myths and attitudes which have devalued women. For example, many religions perpetuate abusive concepts: the myth that Eve caused the fall of man, or that the Orthodox Jew in a morning prayer thanks God that he was not born a woman.

ALIENATION

In a capitalist society alienation has three forms. People are alienated from their work because they do not receive the full benefits produced by their labor. People are alienated from each other because they must compete for survival and success. The alienation between the sexes is a key aspect of this social alienation in which people see themselves as isolated units and women are viewed as objects of pleasure. Humans cannot feel a genuine comfort in the world in which they are forced to conceive of others as competitors and of the opposite sex as dominant or inferior. Finally, there is an alienation from nature. Instead of using the resources of nature for the benefit of all people, they are ravaged for the benefit of a few.

DIALECTIC THOUGHT

Contradiction exists in the process of development of all things. In the process of development there exists a conflict of opposites. For example, in personality development we are both being and becoming. At the moment of conception we begin to die as well as grow. This formulation comes not from a deductive assumption, but it follows from a scientific observation of nature and human behavior. All processes involve change or motion, and change occurs through the interaction of contradictions. Dialectic thought, another mode of thinking, helps us understand the realities of change. Change occurs because a given concept is challenged by its opposite until a synthesis occurs which is unlike either conflicting idea. History has progressed because humans have acquired new knowledge and technology which contradicts earlier formulations and the struggle between the old and the new result in different understandings of the world.

With these three concepts in mind, it is possible to discuss liberation.

LIBERATION: A LINGUISTIC DEFINITION

The linguistic function of the word "liberation" carries within it the dynamics of struggle. The word means "to set free," and thus implies that we must know both the oppressed and the liberated state. Within the word is the understanding that one is struggling *against* some oppression in order *to do* something else. When applied to women's oppression, liberation is the struggle *against* the limitations of our reproductive function which minimizes our personal potential, against the concepts which make us solely responsible for raising children, against the rigid social mores which limit our contribution to the world. But the word also suggests that we want liberation in order *to define* new social relationships, in order *to find* meaningful work, in order *to discover* new self concepts.

LIBERATION: AN EVOLVING PROCESS

Liberation is an evolving concept which proceeds in stages: (1) survival, (2) greater comforts and civil liberties, and (3) non-alienation (happiness). Before the Industrial Revolution most people spent most of their lives struggling for survival. Since the Industrial Revolution certain classes of people have reaped the benefits of technology. Middle class and upper class people live comfortable lives and have guarantees of civil liberties from their governments. Clearly, masses of people, even in the modern world, still subsist at the survival level. But the important point is that because of the existence of technology, these people can perceive the contradiction between their own impoverished conditions and the affluent, highly industrialized world around them. The implications are that people do not necessarily proceed from stage to stage. Once the possibility for liberation exists in the material conditions for some people, it becomes possible for all. At this stage in history, people are beginning to perceive the possibilities of living in a world in which people are no longer alienated from their work, from each other and from nature. The women's liberation movement is adding a crucial dimension to the vision of the non-alienated state.

LIBERATION: A WIDENING OF CHOICES

Liberation means choice among alternatives, something which has consistently been denied women. Women have been conditioned to accept passive roles in which all major decisions are made by nature or by men. The major choice in a woman's life is who her husband will be, and he then will determine all future choices. In another way, marriage can be seen as a way of avoiding the difficult and serious human choice of establishing an identity and purpose in life. To achieve liberation, each person must discover herself as an individual with significance in her own right. A woman cannot fulfill herself through her children or through her husband; she must do it alone. Identity comes only through making choices and liberation is the process of obtaining ever-wider choices for people.

LIBERATION: HAPPINESS

We do not mean the glib, syrupy concept of happiness which suggests that we will be happy if we buy this car or that deodorant, or if we find someone to marry. Happiness is more than the end emotion of gratified desire. That conception of happiness serves the outmoded capitalist system. It is our belief that true happiness is living in a non-alienated world. We are not fully capable at this stage of history to conceive of all the dynamics of happiness, but we do know that if a person is suffering, there is a cause. And if all the causes of unnecessary suffering could be removed—like the isolation of the individual, the inequality of the sexes, meaningless work—we could begin to comprehend what the potential life state of mankind could be.

DIALECTICS OF STRUGGLE

Our definitions of liberation reveal to us the evolutionary nature of human progress and provide us with a vision of the future. The issues taken up in this volume of the magazine—abortion, birth control, childcare, education, self-defense, and work are the problems which oppress women in the second stage of human history. We believe: 1) that these problems cannot be solved until basic economic relationships are altered in society, and 2) that women's liberation involves the solution of these problems and the end to human alienation. As we see it, the women's liberation movement is the key in the struggle for more advanced social relationships.

When we look at the material potential (technology, etc.) for life in this century, we can only be awed at the great benefits all humans could receive. All people could at least be clothed, fed, and housed decently. In spite of this great possibility and hope, we discover that the treasures of the earth, and the labors of workers are being exploited by an outmoded economic system which benefits a few. Capitalism, or the present ordering of human relationships, does not allow for the full realization of human potential. We must think of profit being used for all the people. We must begin to conceive of human relationships in cooperative rather than competitive ways.

On the face of it, abortion, child care, education, etc. appear to be reforms. Can the present system meet these demands? If we consider the problem of abortion, it is clear that even if the laws are liberalized, the problem of cost remains. Unless abortions are free, the poor woman who needs one will not be helped. Until hospitals, doctors, and the medical system are free from the profit motive, these reforms are meaningless. Child care, as we envision it, could not be provided by this system unless priorities are reordered to place children's growth and mothers' freedom as of primary importance. This would require providing large portions of manpower and funds for this purpose, which this society is unable to do without destroying the profit motive. Any attempt to reform the schools, where young girls are conditioned to passive roles and low-paying jobs, would encounter the needs of the system for women to serve their husbands and the society as a whole.

It is clear that the present system is not equipped to handle the full demands for abortion, childcare and education. The conclusion we reach is that women must work against all of these specific oppressions, but in a special way. We must realize that although specific problems can be eased, we must be aware that the full solution for all people is not possible under capitalism.

"I GAVE EVERY OUNCE OF TIME AND ENERGY . . .
TO LET PEOPLE KNOW HOW GHASTLY THE WAR WAS"
LUCY WHITAKER HAESSLER

Like a Greek chorus, public opposition to American involvement in Viet-
nam ran steadily through the 1960s and early 1970s. Women were at the forefront of
protest and efforts to stop the carnage. Among them was Lucy Whitaker Haessler,
who began a lifetime of social activism as a child when she joined her mother in
marches, leafleting, and other activities on behalf of women's suffrage. Later on she
promoted child care for working mothers and was a union organizer and activist in
the civil rights and peace movements. During the height of the Vietnam War, she
drove draft resisters to Canada. From her efforts to meet with Vietnamese women
peace leaders to the two years she spent ferrying draft resisters to Canada, Haessler,
like the members of Women Strike for Peace (see pp. 137–42), viewed the war and the
peace movement as a prime issue of concern for women and proudly credits Amer-
ican women with playing a significant role in ending U.S. involvement in the war.

SOURCE: Judith Adams Porter, *Peacework: Oral Histories of Women Peace Activists* (Boston: Twayne, 1991), pp. 144–46. Macmillan Reference USA, reprinted by permission of the
Gale Group.

THE ERA of which I am most proud and the time I look back on with the most
poignant memories was the Vietnam era because I gave every ounce of time
and energy and money and love that I could possibly muster to let people know
how ghastly the war was. We are still paying the bills for that time; we're paying them not only in money and budget deficits, but we're paying them in ruined lives and broken homes and crime, drug addiction, alcoholism, all of
which have increased since Vietnam.

I did very practical things. I spoke at meetings. I helped organize the student
movement on the campus at Wayne State University in Detroit where I was living. I went—and took people with me—to every one of the major demonstrations in Washington from 1965 to 1971. The first time I went, there were just a
handful of us on the flight from Detroit to Washington. The next time I
booked fifty seats and filled them. By the time we went to the last demonstration, which was called the Spring Offensive, in April 1971, I had chartered two
planes. My husband almost had a heart attack when I signed a contract for five
thousand dollars' worth of airline tickets on two different airlines. But I sold
every seat. It was wonderful. And I think we can take some credit in the women's movement for finally ending the war.

I went to Moscow in 1963. It was at that meeting that the French women wept with us and held our hands and said, "We know what you're going to go through in Vietnam. We went through it. And it's going to be worse for you." And it was worse for us. Much worse. At that conference we met with Vietnamese women leaders of the peace movement, all from the Vietnamese Women's Union. They were from both the north and the south of Vietnam, which they, of course, regarded as one country. There must have been six or eight women. They came with great difficulty, and they were uneasy about going back to Vietnam. They knew their reentry would be difficult. They had details as to the use of defoliants. How many acres of land had been cleared for airplane strips. How much weaponry was coming into the country. How many advisors were there. They talked about their struggle; their attempts to have elections that were promised under the Geneva accords in 1954, which were never held, and which the United States kept from being held. They talked about what they were going through. What was happening to their families, their land. There was only one issue, and that was that it was their country and they wanted everyone to get out so they could run it themselves.

Later on in the Vietnam War—living in Detroit, we were right on the border of Canada—I was one of a handful of women who ferried draft resisters over to Canada. I never got caught. In the early years of the war, men simply went over to Canada and stayed there. There were organizations that took care of them and got them jobs. Then unemployment began to be a factor in Canada, and they had to—rather reluctantly, I think—have some restrictions. To get into Canada, you had to come in as a landed immigrant, which was quite a complicated procedure. In order for the men who were already in Canada to qualify as landed immigrants, they had to be brought out secretly and then reenter with funds and a job.

I would get a call in the late afternoon or around dinner time which simply said. "We have somebody who needs a ride." I would go over to Windsor, Canada, through the tunnel. I would make a note of which entrance I used because there were two or three gates that you could go through, and I couldn't use the same gate again that night. I'd drive to a house near the other end of the tunnel, and there I'd pick up a man whose name I never knew. I would be given an envelope, which I'd lock in the glove compartment of my car. It would have his papers and some money. I was very careful to wear a hat and gloves and rather conventional, unobtrusive dress.

Then I would drive this young man back to the United States. We often talked; they would tell me a little bit about themselves and they would ask me about myself. I would come back into Detroit over the Ambassador Bridge. I was asked at the immigration window, "Are you an American citizen?" and I would say, "Yes." They would say, "How long were you in Canada?" and I would say, "Oh, I was just over for the evening. My friend and I were just over for the evening," or, "This is my nephew" or "cousin."

Then I would drive back to the tunnel and go through a different gate. At the other end of the tunnel was the immigration office. I would walk into the office and say. "This young man wishes to apply for landed immigrant status." By then I would have given him the papers and the three hundred dollars that was in my glove compartment. Then I would wait, sometimes twenty minutes, sometimes two or three hours, just sitting there in my car, waiting for this young man to come out. If he was refused, I had to take him back to the United States. If he got his immigrant status, I took him back to the house where I picked him up.

I didn't know the names of these young men. They didn't know my name. They didn't even know my first name. The safe house had to be moved several times. I must have done it twenty or thirty times over a period of a couple of years. They were very careful not to have you come too regularly. I don't know how many other women there were—I think they were mostly women.

I loved doing it for this reason: every one of those young men was a decent guy. I thought how awful it was to be taking fine young men like this with principles and skills—men who want to be teachers and doctors and health workers—and send them to another country. A lot of them never came back. I felt a very great sadness that young men had to leave their families, their lives, their jobs, their futures as Americans, and go to another country because they opposed the war.

When President Carter initiated draft registration we were down on the post office steps with placards and information about draft counseling. There were some people there saying, "Don't register." We didn't do that, but we talked to them about alternatives. We showed them a sample of the card they would have to fill out. Down at the bottom of the card was a place for you to mark if you wanted a military recruiter to come and call on you. We had tiny stickers that fit in that space that said, "I am registering under protest."

You wouldn't believe some of the men who came and talked to us on the post office steps. It was heartbreaking. Many were veterans; they would come up and thank us for what we were doing and say, "I was over there. I don't want my son to go. I don't want my brother to go. I don't want the kid down the block to go. I don't ever want anybody to have to go to war."

"NEW APPROACHES TO THE STUDY OF
WOMEN IN AMERICAN HISTORY"
GERDA LERNER

The women's movement had a profound impact on a range of academic disciplines, from science and sociology to linguistics and history. Starting in the nineteenth century, foresighted scholars and historians tried to reverse the dearth of research on American women. The first comprehensive study of American women's political and historical experience was none other than Elizabeth Cady Stanton and Susan B. Anthony's monumental three-volume History of Woman Suffrage, *which was published from 1881 to 1886. Three more volumes were published by their successors from 1902 to 1922. Subsequent studies by professionally trained historians further contributed to the scholarship on American women.*

But starting in the 1970s a new generation of feminist historians, inspired by their participation in the antiwar and civil rights movements and by the scholarly goals and methodology of social history, embarked on a historic project of retelling history from the point of view of women's experiences and created a new academic field of historical inquiry: women's history. Young as the field is, its practitioners have produced an astonishing body of rich, mostly first-rate scholarship on all aspects of women's lives, from sexuality and reproduction to housework, factory work, and social reform—areas of inquiry that traditional historians did not perceive to have scholarly merit.

Following is an early essay by Gerda Lerner, a pioneering feminist historian. Her exhortations to view women from the multiple lenses of gender, race, and class and to assess the ways in which women wrested power and visibility in a patriarchal society continue to guide historical inquiry today.

SOURCE: Reprinted by permission from *Journal of Social History* IV, no. 4 (Fall 1969): 333–56; copyright © 1971 by Peter N. Stearns.

THE STRIKING FACT about the historiography of women is the general neglect of the subject by historians. As long as historians held to the traditional view that only the transmission and exercise of power were worthy of their interest, women were of necessity ignored. There was little room in political, diplomatic, and military history for American women, who were, longer than any other single group in the population, outside the power structure. At best their relationship to power was implicit and peripheral and could easily be passed over as insignificant. With the rise of social history and increasing concern with groups out of power, women received some attention, but interest was focused mainly on their position in the family and on their social status. The number of women featured in textbooks of American history remains astonishingly small to this day, as does the number of biographies and monographs on women by professional historians.

The literature concerning the role of women in American history is topically narrow, predominantly descriptive, and generally devoid of interpretation. Except for the feminist viewpoint, there seems to be no underlying conceptual framework.

Feminist writers, not trained historians, were the first to undertake a systematic approach to the problem of women's role in American life and history. This took the forms of feminist tracts, theoretical approaches, and compilations of woman's "contributions." The early compilers attacked the subject with a missionary zeal designed, above all, to right wrong. Their tendency was to praise anything women had done as a "contribution" and to include any women who had gained the slightest public attention in their numerous lists. Still, much positive work was done in simply recounting the history of the woman's rights movement and some of its forerunners and in discussing some of the women whose pioneering struggles opened opportunities to others. Feminist writers were hampered by a twofold bias. First, they shared the middle-class, nativist, moralistic approach of the Progressives and tended to censure out of existence anyone who did not fit into this pattern. Thus we find that women like Frances Wright and Ernestine Rose received little attention because they were considered too radical. "Premature feminists" such as the Grimké sisters, Maria Weston Chapman, and Lydia Maria Child are barely mentioned. The second bias of the feminists lies in their belief that the history of women is important only as representing the history of an oppressed group and its struggle against its oppressors.

This latter concept underlies the somewhat heroic, collectively authored *History of Woman Suffrage*. This work, probably because it represents an easily available though disorganized collection of primary sources, has had a pervasive influence on later historians. Following the lead and interpretation of the feminists, professional historians have been preoccupied with the woman's rights movement in its legal and political aspects. Modern historians, too, think that what is important to know about women is how they got the ballot.

The only serious challenge to this conceptual framework was offered by Mary Beard in the form of a vigorous though often fuzzy polemic against the feminists. What is important about women, said Mary Beard, is not that they were an oppressed group—she denied that they ever were—but that they have made a continuous and impressive contribution to society throughout all of history. It is a contribution, however, which does not fit into the value system generally accepted by historians when they make decisions as to who is or is not important to history. Mary Beard undertook in several of her books to trace the positive achievements of women, their social role, and their contributions to community life. Her concepts are most successfully reflected in *The Rise of American Civilization*, which she wrote with her husband Charles Beard. In it the position of women is treated throughout in an integrated way with great attention to the economic contributions made by women. But the Beards' approach to the subject of women had little influence on the historical profession. Perhaps this was due to the fact that in the 1930s and 1940s both the general public and historians became somewhat disenchanted with the woman's rights movement.

The winning of suffrage had made only a slight change in the actual status of women, and other factors—technological and economic changes, access to higher education, changing sexual mores—now loomed a great deal larger. The impact of Freudianism and psychology had made reformers in general somewhat suspect. Feminism was not infrequently treated with the same humorous condescension as that other successful failure: temperance.

Women have received serious attention from economic historians. There is a good deal of excellent literature dealing with the problem of women workers. Women as contributors to the economy from colonial times on, the laws affecting them, their wages and working conditions, and their struggle for protective legislation have been fully described. Although female labor leaders have not generally been given much attention, their activities are on record. Excellent collections of material pertaining to women at Radcliffe and Smith College are available but remain insufficiently explored.

Modern historians of the reform movements have done much to restore a sane balance to female achievement in reform; yet one still finds excluded from notice certain women who would have been included as a matter of course had they been men. Sophie Loeb, Grace Dodge, and Mary Anderson could be cited as examples.

The historical literature on the family in America is quite scanty, but there seems to be a revival of interest in the subject. Several interesting monographs have begun to deal with the family role of women in its various aspects. This approach is promising and will, one hopes, be pursued by other historians.

A new conceptual framework for dealing with the subject of women in American history is needed. The feminist frame of reference has become archaic and fairly useless. The twentieth-century revolution in technology, morality, education, and employment patterns has brought enormous changes in the status and role of American women; these changes demand a historical perspective and understanding. The emergence of a recent "new feminism" is a social phenomenon requiring interpretation. Most important, women themselves are as entitled as minority group members are to having "their" history fully recorded.

Yet the subject is complex. It is difficult to conceptualize women as a group, since they are dispersed throughout the population. Except for special-interest organizations, they do not combine. The subject is full of paradoxes which elude precise definitions and defy synthesis.

Women at various times and places were a majority of the population, yet their status was that of an oppressed minority, deprived of the rights men enjoyed. Women have for centuries been excluded from positions of power, both political and economic, yet as members of families, as daughters and wives, they often were closer to actual power than many a man. If women were among the most exploited of workers, they were also among the exploiters. If some women were dissatisfied with their limited opportunities, most women were adjusted to their position in society and resisted efforts at changing it. Women generally played a conservative role as individuals and in their communities, the role of conserving tradition, law, order, and the status quo. Yet women in their organizations were frequently allied with the most radical and even revolutionary causes and entered alliances with the very groups threatening the status quo.

If women themselves acted paradoxically, so did society in formulating its values for women. The rationale for women's peculiar position in society has always been that their function as mothers is essential to the survival of the group and that the home is the essential nucleus of society as we know it. Yet the millions of housewives and homemakers have throughout our history been deprived of the one tangible reward our society ranks highest: an income of their own. Neither custom, law, nor changes of technology, education, or politics have touched this sacred tradition. The unpaid housewife-and-mother has affected attitudes toward the women who perform homemaking services for strangers. Traditionally women in the service trades have been the lowest paid among all workers. Nor has this pattern been restricted to the unskilled groups. When women have entered an occupation in large numbers, this occupation has come to be regarded as low status and has been rewarded by low pay. Examples for this are readily found in the teaching and nursing fields. Even intellectual work has been treated with the same double standard. Creative fields in which women excel—poetry, the short story—have been those carrying the lowest rewards in money and esteem. Only in the performing arts has individual female talent had the same opportunity as male talent. Yet a cursory glance at the composition of any major symphony orchestra even today will reveal that in this field, too, opportunities for women have been restricted.

In dealing with the subject of women, studies frequently use other distinctive groups in our society as models for comparison. Women's position has variously been likened to that of the slaves, oppressed ethnic or racial minorities, or economically deprived groups. But these comparisons quickly prove inadequate. The slave comparison obviously was a rhetorical device rather than a factual statement even at the time when Harriet Martineau first made it. While the law denied women equal citizenship and for certain purposes classed them with "Indians and imbeciles," it never denied them physical freedom nor did it regard them as "chattel personnel." In fact, even within the slavery system, women were oppressed differently from men. The "minority group model" is also unsatisfactory. All members of a minority group which suffers discrimination share, with a very few exceptions, in the low-status position of the entire group. But women may be the wives of cabinet members, the daughters of congressmen, the sisters of business leaders, and yet, seen simply as persons, they may be disfranchised and suffer from economic and educational discrimination. On the other hand, a lower-class woman may advance to a position of economic or social power simply by marriage, a route which is generally not open to members of racial minority groups. In one particular respect the minority group comparison is illuminating: like Negroes, women suffer from "high visibility"; they remain more readily identifiable for their group characteristics than for their personal attainments.

Modern psychology, which has offered various conflicting theories about the role and place of women, has further complicated the task of the historian. A social historian who wishes to study a particular ethnic or religious minority can study its location and economy, its culture, leadership, adjustment to American society, and contributions. The question of psychology would only arise in dealing with personal biographies. But the historian of women is at once faced with the necessity of making psychological judgments. Is it not a basic fact that the psychology as well as the physiology of women is different from that of men? Therefore they must of necessity have different expectations, needs, demands, and roles. If so, is the difference in "rights" not simply natural, a reflection of reality? The problems become more vexing when dealing with individual women. The biographer feels obliged first of all to concern himself with his subject's sexual role. Was she married? A mother? If she was not, this indicates that whatever she achieved was the result of sexual frustration. If she was married, one is under an obligation to explain that she did not neglect her children or perhaps that she did. And always there is the crucial question: "What was her relationship to her father?" This is not intended to disparage the efforts of those biographers who wish to enlist the aid of modern psychology for their work. But it should be pointed out that a great deal of excellent history about men has been written without the author's feeling compelled to discuss his subject's sex life or relationship to his mother in explaining his historical significance. In dealing with women, biographers are impeded by the necessity of dealing first with sex, then with the person. This is an approach which must be examined in each case for its applicability: where it is useful, it should be retained; where it is not, it should be discarded without apology.

In order to broaden the study of women in American history, it is not really necessary to suggest new sources. Primary research material is readily available, not only in the several manuscript collections devoted to the subject, but in the usual primary sources for social historians: local historical records, letters, diaries, the organizational records of women's clubs, religious and charitable organizations, labor unions in fields employing women workers. There are numerous magazines especially written for women which provide good source material. Archives of Congress and of state governments contain petitions and statements made at hearings which can yield valuable information about the activities and interests of women. Many of these readily available sources remain neglected.

A fresh approach to known material and to available sources could provide valuable new insights. The following suggestions might make a useful beginning.

First, the subject "Women" is too vast and diffuse to serve as a valid point of departure. Women are members of families, citizens of different regions, economic producers, just as men are, but their emphasis on these various roles is different. The economic role of men predominates in their lives, but women shift readily from one role to another at different periods in their lives. It is in this that their function is different from men and it is this which must form the basis for any conceptual framework. In modern society the only statement about women in general which can be made with validity concerns their political status. Therefore the subject should be subsumed under several categories and any inquiry, description, and generalization should be limited to a narrower field. It is useful to deal with the *status* of women at any given time—to distinguish among their economic status, family status, and political-legal status. There must also be a consideration of class position, as has been usefully proven in recent studies of the feminist movement.

Second, we should look at different aspects of women's role in American history. We must certainly be concerned with the woman's rights movement, but only as part of the total story. Historians must painstakingly restore the actual record of women's contributions at any given period in history. It is interesting that the history of women before the advent of the feminist movement has been more fully recorded and in a more balanced way than it has afterward, so that the story of colonial women can be quite fully traced through secondary literature. But when we deal with the period after 1800, it often proves difficult to establish even descriptive facts. During the early national period, women organized elaborate welfare and relief systems which they staffed and administered. This story should be part of the history of the period; it is not now. Women were the teachers in most of the nation's public schools during the nineteenth century; this is worth recording and exploring. Women made a significant contribution to the growth and development of frontier communities. These are but a few of the many areas in which more research and uncovering of factual information are needed.

Third, we might well discard the "oppressed group model" when discussing women's role in the political life of the nation. Instead, we might start with the fact that one generalization about women which holds up is that they were, longer than any other group in the nation, deprived of political and economic power. Did this mean they actually wielded no power or did they wield power in different forms? My research has led me to believe that they wielded considerable power and in the middle of the nineteenth century even political power. They found a way to make their power felt through organizations, through pressure tactics, through petitioning, and through various other means; these later became models for other mass movements for reform.

Fourth, another important fact is that women are a group who for a considerable period of history were deprived of equal access to education. While they were not illiterate, their education was limited, usually to below the high school level. This was true of the majority of women until the end of the nineteenth century. It might be very useful to investigate what impact this had on female behavior and more specifically, women's performance as a group in terms of outstanding achievement. To put it another way, how many generations of educated women are necessary to produce a significant number of outstanding women academicians? How many generations of college-trained women are necessary before women in sizable numbers make contributions in the sciences? When do women begin to move from the small-scale, home-centered creative forms, the fiction, poetry, and article-writing, to the larger-scale work within the framework of cultural institutions? Is the proverbial dearth of female philosophers really a result of some innate distinctiveness of female mental function or rather the product of centuries of environmental and institutional deprivation? This type of inquiry lends itself to a comparative cross-cultural approach. A comparison between the educational deprivation of women and that suffered by certain minority groups might lead us to a demonstrable correlation between educational deprivation and a gap of several generations before adequate and competitive performance is possible. This could explain a great deal about some of our problems with minority groups, public schooling, and academic achievement.

Fifth, it would be most worthwhile to distinguish the ideas society held at any given moment in regard to woman's proper "place" from what was actually woman's status at that time. The two do not necessarily overlap. On the contrary, there seems to be a considerable gap between the popular myth and reality. Social historians might legitimately be concerned with the significance of this gap, how to account for it, and whether it fits any distinguishable pattern. It would also be important to understand the function of ideas about women in the general ordering of society. Was the fact that colonial women were idealized as thrifty housewives and able helpmeets a cause or effect of the labor shortage in the colonies? Are the idealized suburban housewife, the fashion-conscious teenager, the sex-symbol model, causes or effects of our consumer-oriented society? And what effect does the societally held concept of woman's role have on the development of female talent, on woman's contribution to the society?

Finally, we come back to the initial problem of how to judge the contribution of women. Are women noteworthy when their achievement falls exactly in a category of achievement set up for men? Obviously not, for this is how they have been kept out of the history books up to now. Are women noteworthy then, as the feminists tended to think, if they do anything at all? Not likely. The fact remains that women are different from men and that their role in society and history is different from that of men. Different, but equal in importance. Obviously their achievements must also be measured on a different scale. To define and devise such a scale is difficult until the gaps in our historical knowledge about the actual contributions of women have been filled. This work remains to be done.

But we already know enough about the subject to conclude that the role women played at different times in our history has been changing. The patterns and significance of these changes, the continuities and discontinuities, the expectations and strivings of the pioneers, and the realities of the social scene—all these await study and new interpretations. One would hope at once for a wider framework and a narrower focus—a discarding of old categories and a painstaking search of known sources for unknown meanings. It is an endeavor that should enlist the best talents of the profession and, hopefully and at long last, not primarily female talent.

The women's movement unleashed a wave of cultural expression and creativity dedicated to celebrating women's lives and promoting new images of women. From feminist publishing houses to women's coffee houses, women devised new ways to reclaim their history and express their creative concerns. Music was no exception. Songwriters such as Holly Near, Peggy Seeger, Malvina Reynolds, and others created songs that expressed new hopes and possibilities for women's lives, celebrated feminist heroines of the past, and condemned the many forms of discrimination against women throughout history.

"Talking Want Ad" is a satirical send-up of the traditional helpmate role that women have long been expected to play. It turns images of the docile, devoted housewife inside out and presents a radical message in the style of traditional talking blues.

SOURCE: by Janet Smith, copyright © 1973 Bella Roma Music, ASCAP.

JANET SMITH is a professional musician, singer, and songwriter. She has been performing and teaching since high school and ran a folk club in Rome in the late sixties. She has her own music company and has spent many years unearthing and recording traditional women's early songs from a variety of cultures.

> Well, I'm lookin' for a man to wash my clothes, and iron my shirts and
> blow my nose, an' sweep the floor and wax the kitchen, while I sit playin'
>   my guitar
> and bitchin'—Mud all over my boots, feet up on the table . . . . . just
>   doin' my thing.

2

> Well I'm lookin' for a guy who'll cook my meals
> An' wash my dishes and take the peels
> Off my bananas with a grin
> And ask me how my workday's been . . .
> Terrible as always . . . playin' the guitar is such a struggle!

3

Well I'm lookin' for a guy with curly hair
And great big muscles and a nice derriere
Who'll get up nights and feed the baby
An' bring my coffee when I'm ready . . .
I gotta feel good in the morning . . .
That's when I make my best music.

4

So if you feel you'd like to apply
Why just send a photo or drop on by,
An' you can shine my shoes today
An' if you're lucky I'll let you stay
And cook supper . . . and after you've finished the dishes . . .
I might even let you stay and listen to me play the guitar!

"CONSCIOUSNESS:
THAT'S EXACTLY WHY WE'RE HERE"
VIVIAN GORNICK

Consciousness-raising, as Vivian Gornick acutely observes, was a phe-nomenon unique to the second wave of feminism. While nineteenth- and early-twentieth-century feminists forged new ideas and strategies to win political and economic equality for women, radical feminists of the 1960s and 1970s used the technique of consciousness-raising to root out deeply embedded social, cultural, and psychological assumptions about women's lives. In small groups across the country, drawn from women who worked together, lived near each other, belonged to the same religious or social organizations, or were otherwise connected in some fashion, women explored the daily experiences of their lives, from housework and child-rearing to sex and workplace politics, to understand the common assump-tions and patterns that marked their lives as women—and to develop the strength, courage, and political vocabulary to change those patterns.

Consciousness-raising was oftentimes a three-step process. In the first stage, each member of the group relates her experiences and feelings while the other members listen and encourage her to delve further. The members then try to place experiences into a larger pattern in order to understand the social and political roots of these shared experiences. Finally, the members of the group look for solu-tions or try to link their analyses of their experiences to other theories of social in-justice. As Gornick astutely observes, consciousness-raising became the ultimate grassroots tool for change and empowerment, inspiring new resolve in each mem-ber to reject male-defined norms and values and create new, egalitarian forms of female community.

In this transcript from a consciousness-raising group in New York City in 1970, composed of women who were not politically identified either with the antiwar movement or the burgeoning feminist movement, the members use the dynamics of self-revelation, group support, and cultural analysis of personal experience to understand how they conduct their work lives.

SOURCE: Vivian Gornick, "Consciousness," *New York Times Magazine*, 10 January 1971, pp. 72–82.

EARLY IN THE EVENING, on a crisp autumn night, a young woman in an apart-ment in the Gramercy Park section of Manhattan signed a letter, put it in an en-velope, turned out the light over her desk, got her coat out of the hall closet, ran down two flights of stairs hailed a taxi and headed west directly across the city. At the same time, on the Upper West Side, another woman, slightly older than the first, bent over a sleeping child, kissed his forehead, said goodnight to the babysitter, rode down 12 flights in an elevator, walked up to Broadway and disappeared into the downtown subway. Across town, on the Upper East Side, another woman tossed back a head of stylishly fixed hair, pulled on a beautiful pair of suede boots and left her tiny apartment, also heading down and across town. On the Lower East Side, in a fourth-floor tenement apartment, a woman five or six years younger than all the others combed out a tangled mop of black hair, clomped down the stairs in her Swedish clogs and started trudging west on St. Marks Place. In a number of other places all over Manhattan other women were also leaving their houses. When the last one finally walked into the Greenwich Village living room they were all headed for, there were 10 women in the room.

These women ranged in age from the late 20's to the middle 30's; in appearance, from attractive to very beautiful; in education, from bachelor's degrees to master's degrees; in martial status, from single to married to divorced to imminently separated; two were mothers. Their names were Veronica, Lucie, Diana, Marie, Laura, Jen, Sheila, Dolores, Marilyn and Claire. Their occupations, respectively, were assistant television producer, graduate student, housewife, copywriter, journalist, unemployed actress, legal secretary, unemployed college dropout, school-teacher and computer programmer.

They were not movement women; neither were they committed feminists; nor were they marked by an especial sense of social development or by personal neurosis. They were simply a rather ordinary group of women who were drawn out of some unresolved, barely articulated need to form a "woman's group." They were in their third month of meetings; they were now at Marie's house (next week they would meet at Laura's, and after that at Jen's, and so on down the line); the subject for discussion tonight was "Work."

The room was large, softly lit, comfortably furnished. After 10 or 15 minutes of laughing, chatting, note and book exchanging, the women arranged themselves in a circle, some on chairs, others on the floor. In the center of the circle was a low coffee table covered with a coffeepot, cups, sugar, milk, plates of cheese and bread, cookies and fruit. Marie suggested they begin, and turning to the woman on her right, who happened to be Dolores, asked if she would be the first.

DOLORES (*THE UNEMPLOYED COLLEGE DROPOUT*):
I guess that's okay . . . I'd just as soon be the first . . . mainly because I hate

to be the last. When I'm last, all I think about is, soon it will be *my* turn. (*She looked up nervously.*) You've no idea how I *hate* talking in public. (*There was a long pause; silence in the circle.*) . . . Work! God, what can I say? The whole question has always been absolute hell for me . . . A lot of you have said your fathers ignored you when you were growing up and paid attention only to your brothers. Well, in my house it was just the opposite. I have two sisters, and my father always told me I was the smartest of all, that I was smarter than he was, and that I could do anything I wanted to do . . . but somehow, I don't really know *why*, everything I turned to came to nothing. After six years in analysis I still don't know *why*. (*She looked off into space for a moment and her eyes seemed to lose the train of her thought. Then she shook herself and went on.*) I've always drifted . . . just drifted. My parents never forced me to work. I needn't work even now. I had every opportunity to find out what I really wanted to do. But . . . nothing I did satisfied me, and I would just stop. . . . Or turn away. . . . Or go on a trip. I worked for a big company for a while. . . . Then my parents went to Paris and I just went with them. . . . I came back . . . went to school . . . was a researcher at Time-Life . . . drifted . . . got married . . . divorced . . . drifted. (*Her voice grew more halting.*) I feel my life is such a *waste*. I'd like to write, I really would; I feel I'd be a good writer, but I don't know. I just can't get going. . . . My father is so disappointed in me. He keeps hoping I'll really do something. Soon. (*She shrugged her shoulders but her face was very quiet and pale, and her pain expressive. She happened to be one of the most beautiful woman in the room.*)

DIANA (*THE HOUSEWIFE*):
What do you think you will do?

DOLORES (*IN A DEFIANT BURST*):
Try to get married!

JEN (*THE UNEMPLOYED ACTRESS*) AND MARIE (*THE COPY WRITER*):
Oh, no!

CLAIRE (*THE COMPUTER PROGRAMMER*):
After all that! Haven't you learned yet? What on earth is marriage going to do for you? Who on earth could you marry? Feeling about yourself as you do? Who could save you from yourself? Because that's what you want.

MARILYN (*THE SCHOOL TEACHER*):
That's right. It sounds like "It's just all too much to think out so I might as well get married."

LUCIE (*THE GRADUATE STUDENT*):

Getting married like that is bound to be a disaster.

JEN:

And when you get married like that it's always to some creep you've convinced yourself is wonderful. So understanding. (*Dolores grew very red and very quiet through all this.*)

SHEILA (*THE LEGAL SECRETARY*):

Stop jumping on her like that! I know *just* how she feels. . . . I was *really* raised to be a wife and a mother, and yet my father wanted me to do something with my education after he sent me to one of the best girls' schools in the East. Well, I didn't get married when I got out of school like half the girls I graduated with, and now seven years later I'm *still* not married. (*She stopped talking abruptly and looked off into the space in the center of the circle, her attention wandering as though she'd suddenly lost her way.*) I don't know how to describe it exactly, but I know just how Dolores feels about drifting. I've always worked, and yet something was always sort of confused inside me. I never really knew which way I wanted to go on a job: up, down, sideways . . . I always thought it would be the most marvelous thing in the world to work for a really brilliant and important man. I never have. But I've worked for some good men and I've learned a lot from them. But (*her dark head came up two or three inches and she looked hesitantly around*) I don't know about the rest of you, but I've always wound up being propositioned by my bosses. It's a funny thing. As soon as I'd being doing really well, learning fast and taking on some genuine responsibility, like it would begin to excite them, and they'd make their move. When I refused, almost invariably they'd begin to *browbeat* me. I mean, they'd make my life miserable! And, of course, I'd retreat. . . . I'd get small and scared and take everything they were dishing out . . . and then I'd move on. I don't know, maybe something in my behavior was really asking for it, I honestly don't know anymore. . . .

MARIE:

There's a good chance you *were* asking for it. I work with a lot of men and I don't get propositioned every other day. I am so absolutely straight no one *dares*. . . . They all think I am a dike.

SHEILA (*PLAINTIVELY*):

Why is it like that, though? Why are men like that? Is it something they have more of, this sexual need for ego gratification? Are they made differently from us?

JEN (*PLACING HER COFFEE CUP ON THE FLOOR BESIDE HER*):

No! You've just never learned to stand up for yourself! And goddammit, they know it, and they play on it. Look, you all know I've been an actress for years. Well, once, when I was pretty new in the business, I was playing opposite this guy. He used to feel me up on the stage. All the *time*. I was scared. I didn't know what to do. I'd say to the stage manager: That guy is feeling me up. The stage manager would look at me like I was crazy, and shrug his shoulders. Like: What can *I* do? Well, once I finally thought: I can't stand this. And I bit him. Yes, I bit the bastard, I bit his, tongue while he was kissing me.

A CHORUS OF VOICES:

You *bit* him????

JEN (WITH GREAT DIGNITY):

Yes, dammit, I bit him. And afterward he said to me, "Why the hell did you do that?" And I said, "You know goddam well why I did that." And do you know? He respected me after that. (*She laughed.*) Didn't *like* me very much. But he respected me. (*She looked distracted for a moment.*) . . . I guess that *is* pretty funny. I mean, biting someone's tongue during a love scene.

VERONICA (*THE ASSISTANT TV PRODUCER*):

Yeah. Very funny.

LAURA (*THE JOURNALIST*):

Listen, I've been thinking about something Sheila said. That as soon as she began to get really good at her job her boss would make a pass—and that would pretty much signal the end, right? She'd refuse, he'd become an S.O.B., and she'd eventually leave. It's almost as if sex were being used to cut her down, or back, or in some way stop her from rising. An *instinct* he, the boss, has—to sleep with her when he feels her becoming really independent.

LUCIE (*EXCITEDLY*):

I'll buy that! Look, it's like Samson and Delilah in reverse. *She* knew that sex would give her the opportunity to destroy his strength. Women are famous for wanting to sleep with men in order to enslave them, right? That's the great myth, right? He's all spirit and mind, she's all emotion and biological instinct. She uses this instinct with *cunning* to even out the score, to get some power, to bring him down—through sex. But, look at it another way. What are these guys always saying to us? What are they always saying about women's liberation?—"All she needs is a good—." They say that *hopefully*. *Prayerfully*. They know. We all know what all that "All she needs is a good—" stuff is all about.

CLAIRE:

This is ridiculous. Use your heads. Isn't a guy kind of super if he wants to sleep with a woman who's becoming independent?

MARIE:

Yes, but not in business. There's something wrong every time, whenever sex is operating in business. It's always like a secret weapon, something you hit your opponent below the belt with.

DIANA:

God, you're all crazy! Sex is *fun*. Wherever it exists. It's warm and nice and it makes people feel good.

DOLORES:

That's a favorite pipe dream of yours, isn't it?

SHEILA:

It certainly doesn't seem like very much fun to me when I watch some secretary coming on to one of the lawyers when she wants a raise, then I see the expression on her face as she turns away.

MARIE:

God, that sounds like my mother when she wants something from my father!

VERONICA (*FEEBLY*):

You people are beginning to make me feel *awful!* (*Everyone's head snapped in her direction.*)

MARIE:

Why?

VERONICA:

The way you're talking about using sex at work. As if it were so horrible. Well, I've *always* used a kind of sexy funniness to get what I want at work. What's wrong with that?

LUCIE:

What do you do?

VERONICA:

Well, if someone is being very stuffy and serious about business, I'll say something funny—I guess in a sexy way—to break up the atmosphere which sometimes gets so heavy. You know what I mean? Men can be so pretentious in business! And then, usually, I get what I want—while I'm being funny and cute, and they're laughing.

DIANA (*HEATEDLY*):

Look, don't you see what you're doing?

VERONICA (*TESTILY*):

No, I don't. What am I doing?

DIANA (*HER HANDS MOVING AGITATEDLY THROUGH THE AIR BEFORE HER*):

If there's some serious business going on you come in and say: Nothing to be afraid of, folks. Just frivolous, feminine little me. I'll tell a joke, wink my eye, do a little dance, and we'll all pretend nothing's really happening here.

VERONICA:

My God, I never thought of it like that.

LAURA:

It's like those apes. They did a study of apes in which they discovered that apes chatter and laugh and smile a lot to ward off aggression.

MARILYN:

Just like women! Christ, aren't they always saying to us: *Smile!* Who tells a man to smile? And how often do you smile for no damned reason, right? It's so *natural* to start smiling as soon as you start talking to a man, isn't it?

LUCIE:

That's right! You're right! You know—God, it's amazing!—I began to think about this just the other day. I was walking down Fifth Avenue and a man in the doorway of a store said to me, "Whatsamatta, honey? Things can't be *that* bad." And I was startled because I wasn't feeling depressed or anything, and I couldn't figure out why he was saying that. So I looked, real fast, in the glass to see what my face looked like. And it didn't look like anything. It was just a face at rest. I had just an ordinary, sort of thoughtful expression on my face. And he thought I was *depressed*. And, I couldn't help it, I said to myself: "Would he have said that to you if you were a man?" And I answered myself immediately: "No!"

DIANA:

That's it. That's really what they want. To keep us barefoot, pregnant, and *smiling*. Always sort of begging, you know? Just a little supplicating—at all times. And they get anxious if you stop smiling. Not because you're depressed. Because you're *thinking!*

DOLORES:

Oh, come on now. Surely, there are lots of men who have very similar kinds of manners? What about all the life-of-the-party types? All those clowns and regular guys?

CLAIRE:

Yes, what about them? You *never* take those guys seriously. You never think of the men of real power, the guys with serious intentions and real strength, acting that way, do you? And those are the ones with real responsibility. The others are the ones women laugh about in private, the ones who become our confidantes, not our lovers, the ones who are *just like ourselves.*

SHEILA (*QUIETLY*):

You're right.

LUCIE:

And it's true, it really does undercut your seriousness, all that smiling.

SHEILA (*LOOKING SUDDENLY SAD AND VERY INTENT*):

And underscore your weakness.

DOLORES:

Yes, exactly. We smile because we feel at a loss, because we feel vulnerable. We don't quite know how to accomplish what we want to accomplish or how to navigate through life, so we act *feminine.* That's really what this is all about, isn't it? To be masculine is to take action, to be feminine is to smile. Be coy and cute and sexy—and maybe you'll become the big man's assistant. God, it's all so sad . . .

VERONICA (*LOOKING A BIT DAZED*):

I never thought of any of it like this. But it's true, I guess, all of it. You know (*and now her words came in a rush and her voice grew stronger*), I've always been afraid of my job, I've always felt I was there by *accident,* and that any minute they were gonna find me out. Any minute, they'd know I was a fraud. I had the chance to become a producer recently, and I fudged it. I didn't realize for two weeks afterward that I'd done it deliberately, that I don't *want* to move up, that I'm afraid of the responsibility, that I'd rather stay where I am, making my little jokes and not drawing attention to myself . . . (*Veronica's voice faded away, but her face seemed full of struggle, and for a long moment no one spoke.*)

MARILYN (*HER LEGS PULLED UP UNDER HER ON THE COUCH, RUNNING HER HAND DISTRACTEDLY THROUGH HER SHORT BLOND HAIR*):

Lord, does *that* sound familiar. Do I know that feeling of being there by accident, any minute here comes the ax. I've never felt that anything I got— any honor, any prize, any decent job—was really legitimately mine. I always felt it was luck, that I happened to be in the right place at the right time and that I was able to put up a good front and people just didn't *know* . . . but if I stuck around long enough they would . . . So, I guess I've drifted a lot, too. Being married, I took advantage of it. I remember when my husband was urging me to work, telling me I was a talented girl and that I shouldn't just be sitting around the house taking care of the baby. I wanted so to be persuaded by him, but I just couldn't do it. Every night I'd say: Tomorrow's the day and every morning I'd get up feeling like my head was full of molasses, so sluggish I couldn't *move*. By the time I'd finally get out of that damn bed it was too late to get a baby-sitter or too late to get a job interview or too late to do anything, really. (*She turned toward Diana.*) You're a housewife, Diana. You must know what I mean. (*Diana nodded ruefully.*) I began concentrating on my sex life with my husband, which had never been any too good, and was now getting really bad. It's hard to explain. We'd always been very affectionate with one another, and we still were. But I began to *crave* . . . passion. (*She smiled, almost apologetically.*) What else can I call it? There was no passion between us, practically no intercourse. I began to *demand* it. My husband reacted very badly, accused me of—oh God, the most awful things! Then I had an affair. The sex was great, the man was very tender with me for a long while. I felt *revived*. But then, a funny thing happened. I became almost hypnotized by the sex. I couldn't get enough, I couldn't stop thinking about it, it seemed to consume me; and yet, I became as sluggish now with sexual desire as I had been when I couldn't get up to go look for a job. Sometimes, I felt so sluggish I could hardly prepare myself to go meet my lover. And then . . . (*She stopped talking and looked down at the floor. Her forehead creased, her brows drew together, she seemed pierced suddenly by memory. Everyone remained quiet for a long moment.*)

DIANA (*VERY GENTLY*):

And then?

MARILYN (*ALMOST SHAKING HERSELF AWAKE*):

And then the man told my husband of our affair.

JEN:

Oh, Christ!

MARILYN:

My husband went wild . . . (*her voice trailed off and again everyone remained silent, this time until she spoke again.*) He left me. We've been separated a year and a half now. So then I *had* to go to work. And I have, I have. But it remains a difficult, difficult thing. I do the most ordinary kind of work, afraid to strike out, afraid to try anything that involves real risk. It's almost as if there's some *training* necessary for taking risks, and I just don't have it . . . and my husband leaving me, and forcing me out to work, somehow didn't magically give me whatever it takes to get that training.

LAURA (*HARSHLY*):

Maybe it's too late.

DIANA:

Well, that's a helluva thought. (*She crossed her legs and stared at the floor. Everyone looked toward her, but she said no more. Jen stretched, Claire bit into a cookie, Lucie poured coffee and everyone rearranged themselves in their seats.*)

MARIE (*AFTER A LONG PAUSE*):

It's your turn, Diana.

DIANA (*TURNING IN HER CHAIR AND RUNNING THIN HANDS NERVOUSLY THROUGH HER CURLY RED HAIR*):

It's been hard for me to concentrate on the subject. I went to see my mother in the hospital this afternoon, and I haven't been able to stop thinking about her all day long.

JEN:

Is she very sick?

DIANA:

Well, yes, I think so. She underwent a serious operation yesterday—three hours on the operating table. For a while there it was touch and go. But today she seemed much better and I spoke to her. I stood by her bed and she took my hand and she said to me: "You need an enormous strength of will to live through this. Most people need only one reason to do it. I have three: you, your father and your grandmother. And suddenly I felt furious. I felt *furious* with her. God, she's always been so strong, the strongest person I know, and I've loved her for it. All of a sudden I felt tricked. I felt like saying to her: "Why don't you live for yourself?" I felt like saying: "I can't take this burden on me! What are you doing to me?" And now suddenly, I'm here, being asked to talk about work, and I have nothing to say. I haven't a goddamn thing to say! What do I do? After all, what do I *do?* Half my life is passed in a fantasy of desire that's focused on leaving my husband and finding some marvelous job ... At least, my mother worked *hard* all her life. She raised me when my real father walked out on her, she put me through school, she staked me to my first apartment, she never said no to me for anything. And when I got married she felt she'd accomplished *everything*. That was the end of the rainbow. ...

DOLORES (*TIMIDLY*):

What's so terrible, really, your mother saying she lived for all of you? God, that used to be considered a moral virtue. I'm sure lots of men feel the same way, that they live for their families. Most men *hate* their work ...

MARILYN:

My husband used to say that all the time, that he lived only for me and the baby, that that was everything to him.

LUCIE:

How did you feel about that? What did you think of him when he said it?

MARILYN (*FLUSHING*):

It used to make me feel peculiar. As though something wasn't quite right with him.

LUCIE (*TO DIANA*):

Did you think something wasn't *quite* right, when your mother said what she said?

DIANA (*THINKING BACK*):

No. It wasn't that something wasn't quite right. It seemed "right," if you know what I mean, for her to be saying that, but terribly wrong suddenly.

LUCIE:

That's odd, isn't it? When a man says he lives for his family it sounds positively unnatural to me. When a woman says it, it sounds so "right." So expected.

LAURA:

Exactly. What's pathology in a man seems normal in a woman.

CLAIRE:

It comes back, in a sense, to a woman always looking for her identity in her family and a man never, or rarely, really doing that.

MARIE:

God, this business of identity! Of wanting it from my work, and not looking for it in what my husband does . . .

JEN:

Tell me, do men ever look for their identities in their wives' work?

VERONICA:

Yes, and then we call them Mr. Streisand. (*Everybody breaks up, and suddenly cookies and fruit are—being devoured. Everyone stretches and one or two women walk around the room. After 15 minutes . . .*)

MARIE (*PEELING AN ORANGE, SITTING YOGI-FASHION ON THE FLOOR*):

I first went to work for a small publicity firm. They taught me to be a copy-writer, and I loved it from the start. I never had any trouble with the people in that firm. It was like one big happy family there. We all worked well with each other and everyone knew a bit about everybody else's work. When the place folded and they let me go I was so depressed, and so lost. For the longest time I couldn't even go out looking for a job. I had no sense of how to go about it. I had no real sense of myself as having a transferable skill, somehow. I didn't seem to know how to deal with Madison Avenue. I realized then that I'd somehow never taken that job as a period of preparation for independence in the world. It was like a continuation of my family. As long as I was being taken care of I functioned, but when I was really on my own I folded up. I just didn't know how to operate . . . And I still don't, really. It's never been the same. I've never had a job in which I felt I was really operating responsibly since that time.

SHEILA:

Do you think maybe you're just waiting around to get married?

MARIE:

No, I don't. I know I really want to work, no matter what. I know that I want some sense of myself that's not related to a husband, or to anyone but myself, for that matter . . . But I feel so lost, I just don't know where it's all at, really. (*Five or six heads nodded sympathetically.*)

CLAIRE:

I don't feel like any of you. Not a single one.

DOLORES:

What do you mean?

CLAIRE:

Let me tell you something. I have two sisters and a brother. My father was a passionately competitive man. He loved sports and he taught us all how to play, and he treated us all exactly as though we were his equals at it. I mean, he competed with us exactly as though we were 25 when we were 8. Everything: sailing, checkers, baseball, there was nothing he wouldn't compete in. When I was a kid I saw him send a line drive ball right into my sister's stomach, for God's sake. Sounds terrible, right? We loved it. All of us. And we thrive on it. For me, work is like everything else. *Competitive.* I get in there, do the best I can, compete ferociously against man, woman or machine. And I use whatever I have in the way of equipment: sex, brains, endurance. You name it, I use it. And if I lose I lose, and if I win I win. It's just doing it as well as I can that counts. And if I come up against discrimination as a woman. I just reinforce my attack. But the name of the game is competition. (*Everyone stared at her, openmouthed, and suddenly everyone was talking at once; over each other's voices; at each other; to themselves; laughing; interrupting; generally exploding.*)

LAURA (*DRYLY*):

The American dream. Right before our eyes.

DIANA (*TEARFULLY*):

Good God, Claire, that sounds awful!

LUCIE (*AMAZED*):

That's the kind of thing that's killing our men. In a sense, it's really why we're here.

SHEILA (*MAD*):

Oh, that love of competition!

MARIE (*ASTONISHED*):

The whole idea of just being is completely lost in all this.

JEN (*OUTRAGED*):

And to act *sexy* in order to compete! You degrade every woman alive!

VERONICA (*INTERESTED*):

In other words, Claire, you imply that if they give you what you want they get you?

DIANA (*WISTFULLY*):

That notion of competition is everything we hate most in men, isn't it? It's responsible for the most brutalizing version of masculinity. We're in here trying to be men, right? Do we want to be men at their worst?

LUCIE (*ANGRILY*):

For God's sake! We're in here trying to be ourselves. Whatever that turns out to be.

MARILYN (*WITH SUDDEN AUTHORITY*):

I think you're wrong, all of you. You don't understand what Claire's really saying. (*Everyone stopped talking and looked at Marilyn.*) What Claire is really telling you is that her father taught her not how to win but how to lose. He didn't teach her to ride roughshod over other people. He taught her how to get up and walk away intact when other people rode roughshod over her. And he so loved the idea of teaching *that* to his children that he ignored the fact that she and her sisters were girls, and he taught it to them, anyway. (*Everyone took a moment to digest this.*)

LAURA:

I think Marilyn has a very good point there. That's exactly what Claire has inside her. She's the strongest person in this room, and we've all known it for a long time. She has the most integrated and most *separate* sense of herself of anyone I know. And I can see now that that probably has developed from her competitiveness. It's almost as though it provided the proper relation to other people, rather than no relation.

SHEILA:

Well, if that's true then her father performed a minor miracle.

JEN:

You're not kidding. Knowing where you stand in relation to other people, what you're supposed to be doing, not because of what other people want of you but because of what you want for yourself . . . *knowing* what you want for yourself . . . that's everything, isn't it?

LAURA:

I think so. When I think of work, that's really what I think of most. And when I think of *me* and work, I swear I feel like Ulysses after 10 years at sea. I, unlike the rest of you, do not feel I am where I am because of luck or accident or through the natural striving caused by a healthy competitiveness. I feel I am like a half-maddened bull who keeps turning and turning and turning, trying to get the hell out of this maze he finds himself in . . . I spent 10 years not knowing what the hell I wanted to do with myself. So I kept getting married and having children. I've had three children and as many husbands. All nice men, all good to me, all meaningless to me. (*She stopped short, and seemed to be groping for words . . .*) I wanted to do something. Something that was real, and serious, and would involve me in a struggle with myself. Every time I got married it was like applying Mercurochrome to a festering wound. I swear sometimes I think the thing I resent most is that women have always gotten married as a way out of the struggle. It's the thing we're encouraged to do, it's the thing we rush into with such *relief*, it's the thing we come absolutely to *hate*. Because marriage itself, for most women, is so full of self-hatred. A continual unconscious reminder of all our weakness, of the heavy price to be paid for taking the easy way out. Men talk about the power of a woman in the home . . . That power has come to seem such a lopsided and malevolent thing to me. What kind of nonsense is that, anyway, to divide up the *influences* on children's lives in that bizarre way? The mother takes care of the *emotional* life of a child? The vital requirement for nourishment? Out of what special resources does *she* do that? What the hell principle of growth is operating in *her*? What gives a woman who never tests herself against structured work the wisdom or the self-discipline to oversee a child's emotional development? The whole thing is crazy. Just crazy. And it nearly drove me crazy . . . What can I say? For 10 years I felt as though I were continually vomiting up my life. . . . And now I work. I work hard and I work with great relish. I want to have a family, *too*. Love. Home.

Husband. Father for the children. Of course, I do. God, the loneliness! The longing for connection! But work first. And family second. (*Her face split wide open in a big grin*). Just like a man.

LUCIE:

I guess I sort of feel like Laura. Only I'm not sure. I'm not sure of anything. I'm in school now. Or rather "again." Thirty years old and I'm a graduate student again, starting out almost from scratch . . . The thing is I could never take what I was doing seriously. That is, not as seriously as my brother, or any of the boys I went to school with, did. Everything seemed too long, or too hard, or too something. Underneath it all, I felt sort of *embarrassed* to study seriously. It was as if I was really feeling: "That's something the *grownups* do. It's not something for *me* to do." I asked my brother about this feeling once, and he said most men felt the same way about themselves, only they fake it better than women do. I thought about that one a long time, and I kept trying to say myself: What the hell, it's the same for them as it is for us. But . . . (*she looked swiftly around the circle*) it's not! Dammit, it's *not*. After all, style is content, right? And ours are worlds away . . .

VERONICA:

Literally.

LUCIE:

I don't know . . . I still don't know. It's a problem that nags and nags and nags at me. So often I wish some guy would just come along and I'd disappear into marriage. It's like this secret wish that I can just withdraw from it all, and then from my safe position look on and comment and laugh and say yes and no and encourage and generally play at being the judging mother, the "wise" lady of the household . . . But then I know within six months I'd be miserable! I'd be climbing the walls and feeling guilty . . .

MARILYN:

Guilty! Guilty, guilty. Will we ever have a session in which the word guilty is not mentioned once? (*Outside, the bells in a nearby church tower struck midnight.*)

DIANA:

Let's wrap it up okay?

VERONICA (*REACHING FOR HER BAG*):

Where shall we meet next week?

MARIE:

Wait a minute. Aren't we going to sum up? (*Everyone stopped in mid-leaving, and sank wearily back into her seat.*)

LUCIE:

Well, one thing became very clear to me. Everyone of us in some way have struggled with the idea of getting married in order to be relieved of the battle of finding and staying with good work.

DIANA:

And every one of us who's actually done it has made a mess of it!

JEN:

And everyone who *hasn't* has made a mess of it.

VERONICA:

But, look. The only one of us who's really worked well—with direction and purpose—is Claire. And we all jumped on her! (*Every one was started by this observation and no one spoke for a long moment.*)

MARILYN (*BITTERLY*):

We can't do it, we can't admire anyone who *does* do it, and we can't let it alone . . .

JEN (*SOFTLY*):

That's not quite true. After all, we were able to see finally that there was virtue in Claire's position. And we are here, aren't we?

MARIE:

That's right. Don't be so down. We're not 10 years old, are we? We're caught in a mess, damned if we do and damned if we don't. All right. That's exactly why we're here. To break the bind. (*On this note everyone took heart, brightened up and trooped out into the darkened Manhattan streets. Proud enough of being ready to battle.*)

By the early 1970s women began to incorporate feminist ideas in their re-
ligious worship. Just as the process of consciousness-raising inspired new personal
connections and larger social solutions, and just as feminist historians began cre-
ating a rich body of scholarship on women, small, grassroots women's spiritual
groups embarked on an exciting odyssey of reexamining traditional religious
ideas, exploring ancient goddess rites and myths, and incorporating these ideas
and rituals into their religious observance. The following oral history by Terri
Berthiaume Hawthorne, a wife, mother, and observant Catholic who lived near
Minneapolis, chronicles the exciting process of discovery and renewal that feminist
ideas have brought to religious observance. As Hawthorne and the other members
of her women's church group delved into personal issues during the early 1970s,
they became more aware of the patriarchal values of the Catholic church and be-
gan to explore other spiritual pathways that reflected their experiences as women.
Gradually they incorporated goddess worship and wicca, or witchcraft, into their
observance. Hawthorne views her group and other grassroots women's spirituali-
ty groups as a new form of consciousness-raising, a place where women can draw
on their diverse spiritual backgrounds to create new rituals that express their pow-
er and pride as women.

SOURCE: Bonnie Watkins and Nina Rothchild, eds., *In the Company of Women: Voices from the Women's Movement* (St. Paul: Minnesota Historical Society, 1996), pp. 292–96. Used with permission.

DURING THOSE EARLY YEARS in the 1960s, my church was one of the few places that was interested in me. I was in a sort of cocoon out in the suburbs. I didn't have a car, so I really was isolated. Like many women, I found a great deal of help in the church. They would provide free child care, and there were seminars, and there were ideas that were intellectually stimulating. They want-ed my services to teach religious education. There were book groups and dis-cussion groups—it was a "home place" for me.

In 1972, our women's group at St. Thomas started this six-week series called, "Women: Who Are We?" The group still meets, although now it's only a birth-day group. In the beginning, we were looking for a place, I think a personal place, for us to talk about ourselves and about ideas and about our lives. In this group, our kids went to school together, we had joint baby-sitting, we went to lunches together. We helped each other when we had new babies. Our lives were intertwined in many, many different ways.

Our group differed from the traditional altar societies. We were the study group, the self-focused ones, doing personal-growth things—and social actions on women's issues. Later we were known as the real liberal far-out feminists. Then, some of the other women got afraid to join us. . . .

At about the same time, I became interested in the Equal Rights Amendment, and my group decided to investigate that. So I started calling my church and asking questions. I knew my church was not in favor of it, but I couldn't figure out why. I went to the legislative hearings, and then I called the diocese to see if they could give me some literature, or some information on why this was a problem. And they told me, basically, "Drop it." They said there was no literature and it was enough that the bishops were saying it was not appropriate. I was supposed to just believe them.

At this point, probably with the media and the focus on women's issues and on women's rights, I began to be aware that the church that had provided me a home was also the place that taught the sexist codes. The church passed them from generation to generation, and did it mostly through women. Women are responsible for teaching those codes to both boys and girls. There was that incongruity between the "home place" for women and the place where the sexist messages were passed.

A few years later, we started doing innovative women's rituals. Our women's group at St. Thomas wanted to bring the sense of community and warmth and camaraderie we were feeling together into our spiritual place. A ritual is not much different from a birthday party or a Halloween party, that kind of thing. I think most people have a lot more creativity than they know. Ritual is really a lot about art. You have prayer, but then you put it into art forms. You can use music and dance and visual images.

It all coincided with the "home" masses and the other things that were happening in the early '70s, with the opening up in the Catholic Church. The effects of Vatican II were really being felt, and our priest was very open and creative in this worship. We would find poems and prayers and write songs, and then he would add wonderful little things to what we were doing. He would let us have almost complete control.

We were having a wonderful time and, because we were all mothers, we started doing things like Mother's Day masses at the church. Then when our kids were fussing about going to church and so on, we started having a series of children's masses. In one of those we did a "velveteen rabbit" mass. We had this little home mass in the summer, with all our kids in shorts, and with real rabbits there, and had this wonderful, wonderful service.

Our women's rituals were . . . in the beginning, we were just combing the scriptures for things that were relevant to women. Positive images. And then we would maybe put an Adrienne Rich poem into the mass instead of the traditional reading. Like on Mother's Day, we might pick honoring of women, but we wouldn't do just the sentimentalized version. We might pick a poem that talked about how hard it was, and how you were sometimes frustrated and angry at your children.

Women in my art circle found the Goddess in '75. I ended up studying creation-goddess myths from all over the world. I mean, this information is pretty commonly known today, even among people who aren't doing a lot of spirituality. But back then it was all brand-new. There might be one woman artist's name in an art book but no pictures. So we'd have to take this tiny fragment, and track it back in multiple ways. It wouldn't be in the textbooks, but if we went back to the archaeological finds, then it would be just everywhere.

Most of the early Goddess scholarship was done by art historians not by regular historians. That's not accidental, because the texts, the words, the interpretations are from a male perspective. But the images alone allow multiple interpretations. I studied creation myths, another friend would be doing Egyptian goddesses, another one would be doing African, and somebody else would be . . . we were all pooling this stuff. It was collective in a way that was really unusual, and very exciting.

We started to do more earth-based traditions somewhere out of this growing Goddess awareness. We started, well, passing babies in a circle and blessing them, and a lot of things that were old ways of doing home-based rituals. We began to celebrate the earth—to ritualize our beliefs about ecology and ecofeminism. At some point, some of us found that there was a European history of earth-based traditions called witchcraft or wicca. Some people began actively researching and reclaiming that. It's very closely connected to Native American spirituality. Wicca can mean willingness to bend or it can mean wise woman. . . .

ONE OF THE EXCITING THINGS that's happening now is that I get asked to go out all the time and do these one-time evening presentations. And there are *hundreds* of little grassroots women's spirituality groups, all over the city, and all over the country. This is where women are getting together, becoming more earth-based. Spirituality has always been—has always asked—the same questions as science. Where do we come from? And how do we get here? What are we? And what are we about? Looking at beliefs from many cultures and times challenges the "one right way" of monotheism.

These small groups are happening all over, in surprising places. Most of the groups are between 10 and 20 people. I think they've replaced the consciousness-raising groups, but there hasn't been much written about them. I had a small group at my house the other night—a cross-section, some of them are homemakers and witches and some of them are Catholic nuns and Protestant ministers. A wide spectrum of people—and most of them have background in ritual. . . .

Because I'm around feminists so much, I'm often struck that—when I move into non-feminist worlds, I'm struck by how differently I see the world. I'm struck by how often we're taught to see the world from a male perspective, and how radical it is to see the world from a woman's perspective. I think the people who are involved in both spirituality and politics have run up against a wall, the patriarchal wall, that has forced them to either open their eyes or to go way backwards.

Now when I go back to the Catholic Church, the male God-language is just so overwhelming to me. Feminists started by objecting to not being part of "all men," and by the time that changed, we were objecting to all-male God-language. Now we object to hierarchical terms, like "Lord" and "King." Once you start seeing in a new way, everything begins to change. And the more you think about it, the deeper it goes.

Margaret Wright, a community activist in the early 1970s and a member of Women Against Repression, a black women's liberation group, wrote this piece in 1970. Fed up with being exploited by black men—both in the civil rights movement and in personal relationships—who wanted to duplicate the male-dominant position of white men, and with discrimination in the workplace, she proclaims the right to find and celebrate her own unique identity as a black woman. That identity, according to her, eschews exploitation of any form. Wright also addresses uncomfortable truths about black men's perceptions of white women as status symbols. Hers is a clear-eyed view that identifies hypocrisy among black men and white feminists, thus forcing black women to create their own alliances and seek their own personal and collective solidarity.

SOURCE: Quoted from Mary Reinholz, "Storming the All Electric Dollhouse," *West Magazine, Los Angeles Times*, June 7, 1970. Copyright © 2003 Tribune Media Services.

BLACK WOMEN have been doubly oppressed. On the job, we're low women on the totem pole. White women have their problems. They're interviewed for secretarial instead of the executive thing. But we're interviewed for mopping floors and stuff like that. Sometimes we have to take what's left over in Miss Ann's refrigerator. This is all exploitation. And when we get home from work, the old man is wondering why his greens aren't cooked on time.

We're also exploited in the Movement. We run errands, lick stamps, mail letters and do the door-to-door. But when it comes to the speaker's platform, it's all men up there blowing their souls, you dig?

Some white man wrote this book about the black matriarchy, saying that black women ran the community. Which is bull. We don't run no community. We went out and worked because they wouldn't give our men jobs. This is where some of us are different from the white women's liberation movement. We don't think work liberates you. We've been doing it so damned long.

The black man used to admire the black women for all they'd endured to keep the race going. Now the black man is saying he wants a family structure like the white man's. He's got to be head of the family and women have to be submissive and all that nonsense. Hell, the white woman is already oppressed in that setup.

Black man have been brainwashed into believing they've been emasculated. I tell them they're nuts. They've never been emasculated. Emasculated men don't revolt. And if they were so emasculated, these blondes wouldn't be running after them. Black women aren't oppressing them. We're helping them get their liberation. It's the white man who's oppressing, not us. All we ever did was scrub floors so they could get their little selves together!

It used to be that only older women felt like this. But now the younger sisters, and the ones in college, are beginning to feel the same way. They see a brother walking around campus with a blonde on his arm just after he's left the BSU blowing black is beautiful. So it tees them off. Also, black women feel they have to move to the front now, because they're doing our men in. Whenever effective male leaders come up, they either get their brains blown out, or they're thrown in jail.

In black women's liberation we don't want to be equal with men, just like in black liberation we're not fighting to be equal with the white man. We're fighting for the right to be different and not be punished for it. Equal means sameness. I don't want to be equal with the white community because I don't think it's very groovy. And why do I want to be equal with something that ain't groovy?

Men are chauvinistic. I don't want to be chauvinistic. Some women run over people in the business world, doing the same thing as men. I don't want to compete on no damned exploitative level. I don't want to exploit nobody. I don't want to be on no firing line, killing people. I want the right to be black and me.

"I AM ANGRY FOR MY SISTERS"
A LETTER TO *MS.* MAGAZINE

Founded in 1972 by Gloria Steinem, Ms. became the major mass-circula-tion organ of the mainstream feminist movement. In its early years, it reported on the whole terrain of women's lives, from national and international news of concern to women to fiction and poetry by female writers to the new academic field of wo-men's history. It elicited strong opinions, both pro and con, about feminism, includ-ing this letter from a reader in California in July 1973. She expresses a reaction shared by so many women as they reexamined their lives through a feminist perspective—anger at the subordinate, socially constructed images and roles that women had learned to uphold. For this writer and thousands of other women, anger was an es-sential step from a sense of victimization to personal and political empowerment.

SOURCE: *Letters to Ms., 1972–1987* (New York: Henry Holt, 1987), p. 209.

I AM A WOMAN who, almost all my life, believed without question what I was told—women aren't as smart as men, women aren't happy being suc-cessful, to get ahead you should be pretty, witty, and secretly wise. I conse-quently floundered around in secretarial jobs for years, involving myself in work that was never challenging to me intellectually, work that never lit a spark in me. I tried to find meaning through the men in my life—fortu-nately for me I *was* pretty and witty. But I never wanted to marry, and when-ever I looked forward to the rest of my life, I felt lost, because the thought of being autonomous by doing work I hated far, far into the future, made me panic.

Then I discovered the movement, both through a consciousness-raising group and through a heavy amount of reading. I realized that I wasn't the only woman who felt inferior, stupid, restless, underutilized, unused, intel-lectually underfed. That realization turned to anger, anger turned slowly to action, and action, eventually, forced me to change my life around. At the age of twenty-five, I started college on a full-time basis and finished my first semester with a four-point average and a small scholarship.

But I am still an angry woman. I am not angry for myself, for all the under-utilized years, because things have turned out well for me in the end at a rela-tively young age. But I am angry for my sisters. I am angry for Ann, who has a master's degree and a brilliant mind—she has been made to think that men really *do* know more, and I have watched her flounder in debates with those men who are intellectually inferior to her. I am angry for Lucille, an artist, highly sensitive, who, rather than trying to find herself in her art, is trying to find it in her man—she's tried to commit suicide once so far. I am angry for Roberta, who drinks too much because she hates who she is. I am angry for Cathy, whose grandfather tried to rape her when she was seven; for Lydia, who is sixty and doing work she has been doing well for forty years; for Carol, who is sad about her lack of beauty; for Jan, who keeps looking for new men in the bars every Friday night; for Darlene, who is not afraid to love her six cats but is afraid to love anything human. I could go on. Almost every women I know suffers with her hidden or not-so-hidden scars. The joy I feel at having finally gotten a handle on myself dissipates, quite suddenly, when I take a half glance around me.

We have made a start, but it is discouraging to realize how very far there is to go. Discouragement = anger = action. We can only move forward.

"A NEW REVOLUTION WITHIN
A REVOLUTION HAS BEGUN"
JENNIE V. CHAVEZ

*In the early 1970s Mexican American women, like African American wo-
men, began to speak out about sexism within their respective cultures. But they still
kept their distance from the mainstream women's movement. They were uncomfortable with what they viewed as white feminists' emphasis on individual fulfillment over communal ties and obligations. While confirming their allegiance to
their communities of color, both African American and Mexican American women
nonetheless sought ways to promote sisterhood within their respective cultures.*

*In 1970 Jennie Chavez, who had been a student at the University of New Mex-
ico in the late 1960s, organized La Chicana women's group on the campus to combat discrimination against Mexican American women both in the larger white society and within the Mexican American community. Writing in* Mademoiselle *in
1972, she attempts to forge a new feminist alliance among Mexican American women, one that proclaims their emergence as proud, strong women who will combine marriage and a vocation while creating with Mexican American men new
communities of respect and equality.*

SOURCE: Jennie V. Chavez, *Mademoiselle*, April 1972; pp. 82, 150–52. Reprinted by permission of Lennie V. Chavez.

AS THE WOMEN'S LIBERATION MOVEMENT is becoming stronger, there is another women's movement that is effecting change in the American revolution
of the 1970s—the Mexican-American women, las Chicanas, las mujeres.

In contrast to some of the white women of the liberation movement, who
appear to encourage an isolationist method of acquiring equality, Mexican-
American women want unity with their men. Here I am not negating the validity of white women's lib (as I am in support of the majority of its ideas) but
am writing rather of how, as Chicanas, we are relating to the entire movement.

As Chicanas, discriminated against not only by the white dominant society,
but also by our own men who have been adhering to the misinterpreted tradition of machismo, we cannot isolate ourselves from them for a simple (or complex) reason. We must rely on each other to fight the injustices of the society
which is oppressing our entire ethnic group.

On May 28–30, 1971, the first national Mujeres Por La Raza Conference was
held in Houston, Texas. Its being held in the "heart of Texas" struck me as be-

ing a gigantic step forward in the entire Chicano movement, as tejanos have always been considered the Mexican's main antagonists. Five hundred Latin women from states as far away as Washington, New York, Michigan and, of course, California attended.

Just six months prior to this conference I was being called a white woman for organizing a Las Chicanas group on the University of New Mexico campus. I was not only ostracized by men but by women. Some felt I would be dividing the existing Chicano group on campus (the United Mexican-American Students, UMAS), some were simply afraid of displeasing the men, some felt that I was wrong and my ideas "white" and still others felt that their contribution to La Causa of El Movimiento was in giving the men moral support from the kitchen.

It took two months of heartbreak on both sides for the organization to be recognized as valid. A handful of women supported it. These women were physically as well as intellectually beautiful, breaking the media stereotype of the women's libber. Ninety percent wore makeup, bras, didn't use four-letter words every other sentence and were aware of their sex roles. I was one of the ten percent who frequently did the opposite, thus causing suspicion even amongst those women who saw the need for a Chicana organization. One mistake which caused tension and suspicion was the fact that I dressed and spoke differently from the average college Chicana. I was more into the white revolutionary rhetoric and the "hippie" lifestyle. I see now that one of the newest themes of the entire social movement, in the labor movement, in the ethnic movement, is the use of tolerance on both sides.

Previously, as one of the first members of UMAS when it got started in 1969 on the UNM [University of New Mexico] campus, I was given special attention, being fairly attractive and flirtatious. But as soon as I started expounding my own ideas the men who ran the organization would either ignore my statement or make a wisecrack about it and continue their own discussion. This continued for two years until I finally broke away because of being unable to handle the situation. I turned to student government. There I was considered a radical racist Mexican militant, yet with the Chicano radicals I was considered a sellout. I was caught in the middle, wanting to help but with neither side allowing me. . . .

Now, however, because a few women were willing to stand strong against some of the macho men who ridiculed them, called them white and avoided them socially, [Las Chicanas] has become one of the strongest and best-known in the state. Prior to the Houston conference, Las Chicanas was being used as the work club by the other male-run Chicano organizations in the city of Albuquerque. Every time they needed maids or cooks, they'd dial-a-Chicana. Every time there was a cultural event they would call the Chicana Glee Club to sing a few songs. For three months Las Chicanas was looked upon as a joke by most of the UMAS men and some of the other Chicano organizations. Needless to say, I became very frustrated with my brainchild and left it for two months. I would not and could not set myself up as a leader as I felt I would only cause more hard feelings, so I felt the women to choose their own and straighten out the new ideas in their heads.

It has taken what I consider a long time for them to realize and to speak out about the double oppression of the Mexican-American woman. But I think that after the Houston Conference they have more confidence (certainly I regained it) in speaking up for our recognition.

Chicanas, traditionally, have been tortilla-makers, baby-producers, to be touched but not heard. As the social revolution for all people's freedoms has progressed, so Chicanas have caught the essence of freedom in the air. The change occurred slowly. Mexican-American women have been reluctant to speak up, afraid they might show up the men in front of the white man—afraid that they may think our men not men.

Now, however, the Chicana is becoming as well-educated and as aware of oppression, if not more so, as the Mexican-American male. The women are now ready to activate themselves. They can no longer remain quiet and a new revolution within a revolution has begun. . . .

Women, as women's lib advocates know, are capable of great physical endurance and so it has been with women of our ethnic group. In order to someday obtain those middle-class goods (which in my eyes oppress more people than they liberate from "drudgery") our women have not only been working at slave jobs for the white society as housemaids, hotel maids and laundry workers, but have tended also to the wants of a husband and many children—many children because contraceptives have been contrary to the ethnic idea of La Familia (with all its socio-political-economic implications).

The new breed of Chicanas are changing their puritanical mode of dress, entering the professions of law, business, medicine and engineering. They are no longer afraid to show their intellect, their capabilities and their potential. More and more they oppose the Catholic Church, to which a large majority of our ethnic group belongs, challenging its sexual taboos as well as the idea that all Catholic mothers must be baby-producing factories and that contraceptives are a sin.

Out of the workshop on "Sex and La Chicana" came the following resolutions:

(1) that Chicanas should develop a more healthy attitude toward sex and get rid of all the misconceptions about its "evil," thus allowing ourselves to be

as aggressive as men; (2) that we object to the use of sex as a means of exploiting women and for commercial purposes; (3) that no religious institution should have the authority to sanction what is moral or immoral between a man and a woman.

As the new breed of Mexican-American women we have been, and probably will continue to be, ridiculed by our men for attempting the acrobatics of equity. We may well be ostracized by La Familia for being vendidos, sellouts to the "white ideas" of late marriage, postponing or not wanting children and desiring a vocation other than tortilla-rolling, but I believe that this new breed of bronze womanhood, as all women today, will be a vanguard for world change.

Speaking for myself, I feel that Chicana women are capable of doing both and bearing children to retain the good characteristics of La Familia. We have so long endured the sufferings imposed on us by dominant white society, and the psychological and physical suppression of the men's reactions caused by their inability to cope with that oppression, that I now firmly believe that we Mexican-American women are stronger and better prepared to accept the challenge of a liberation-within-a-liberation movement. We will have our babies when we want and also follow a responsible vocation.

My understanding of the white women in the liberation movement is that they have no other choice but to isolate themselves from what is recognizably bad—white male chauvinist bourgeois imperialists, and the other thousand revolutionary cliches. These women have no one to turn to but themselves (which may be a reason for the Gay caucuses in the women's movement.) Naturally, there are also liberated men in both the Chicano and the white groups who respect and treat women as equals, but they are so few that at this point I still have to generalize. Fortunately, Mexican-American women can work for liberation with our men and make them understand, more easily than one could a white man, the oppression women feel, because they themselves have been oppressed by the same society.

Mexican-American men, as other men of oppressed groups, have been very reluctant to give up their machismo because it has been a last retention of power in a society which dehumanizes and mechanizes them. But now they are comprehending the meaning of carnalismo (brotherhood) in the feminine gender as well.

The reincarnation of Adelitas and Valentinas throughout the Southwest leaves the men no choice but to listen to the heroines of the past revived—lest we all perish together in our struggle to change a racist society.

"THE WOMAN IS THE VICTIM"
SARAH WEDDINGTON

Sarah Weddington, a twenty-five-year-old lawyer, made history when she argued the landmark Roe v. Wade *case before the United States Supreme Court. That Court found her arguments so persuasive that it ruled seven to two in favor of upholding a woman's fundamental right to a safe, legal abortion. (See the following document, which presents excerpts of the Court's decision.) Weddington represented a poor, single, twenty-one-year-old woman in Dallas, Texas, named Norma McCorvey—identified in the trial as "Jane Roe"—who could not obtain a legal abortion in Texas because of a law dating back to 1854 that banned abortions. The case ultimately made its way to the U.S. Supreme Court, where, on December 13, 1971, Weddington stood before the nine justices and argued that the Constitution guaranteed a "right to privacy," including the most private and fundamental right of all—to decide whether to continue or end a pregnancy. In clear, concrete, and persuasive language, Weddington laid out before the Court the profound social, emotional, and economic impact of pregnancy upon a woman's life and the necessity of giving her the power to control the terms of this life-changing event.*

SOURCE: U.S. Supreme Court Case 410 U.S. 113

MR. CHIEF JUSTICE, and may it please the Court: . . .

In Texas, the woman is the victim. The state cannot deny the effect that this law has on the women of Texas. Certainly there are problems regarding even the use of contraception. Abortion now, for a woman, is safer than childbirth. In the absence of abortions—or, legal, medically safe abortions—women often resort to the illegal abortions, which certainly carry risks of death, all the side effects such as severe infections, permanent sterility, all the complications that result. And, in fact, if the woman is unable to get either a legal abortion or an illegal abortion in our state, she can do a self-abortion, which is certainly, perhaps, by far the most dangerous. And that is no crime.

Texas, for example, it appears to us, would not allow any relief at all, even in situations where the mother would suffer perhaps serious physical and mental harm. There is certainly a great question about it. If the pregnancy would result in the birth of a deformed or defective child, she has no relief. Regardless of the circumstances of conception, whether it was because of rape, incest, whether she is extremely immature, she has no relief.

I think it's without question that pregnancy to a woman can completely disrupt her life. Whether she's unmarried, whether she's pursuing an education, whether she's pursuing a career, whether she has family problems—all of the problems of personal and family life for a woman are bound up in the problem of abortion.

For example in our state there are many schools where a woman is forced to quit if she becomes pregnant. In the City of Austin that is true. A woman, if she becomes pregnant, and if in high school, must drop out of the regular education process. And that's true of some colleges in our state. In the matter of employment, she often is forced to quit at an early point in her pregnancy. She has no provision for maternity leave. She has—she cannot get unemployment compensation under our laws, because the laws hold that she is not eligible for employment, being pregnant, and therefore is eligible for no unemployment compensation. At the same time, she can get no welfare to help her at a time when she has no unemployment compensation and she's not eligible for any help in getting a job to provide for herself.

There is no duty for employers to rehire women if they must drop out to carry a pregnancy to term. And, of course, this is especially hard on the many women in Texas who are heads of their own households and must provide for their already existing children. And, obviously, the responsibility of raising a child is a most serious one, and at times an emotional investment that must be made cannot be denied.

So a pregnancy to a woman is perhaps one of the most determinative aspects of her life. It disrupts her body. It disrupts her education. It disrupts her employment. And it often disrupts her entire family life. And we feel that, because of the impact on the woman, this certainly—in as far as there are any rights which are fundamental—is a matter which is of such fundamental and basic concern to the woman involved that she should be allowed to make the choice as to whether to continue or to terminate her pregnancy.

I think the question is equally serious for the physicians of our state. They are seeking to practice medicine in what they consider the highest methods of practice. We have affidavits in the back of our brief from each of the heads of public—of heads of obstetrics and gynecology departments from each of our public medical schools in Texas. And each of them points out that they were willing and interested to immediately begin to formulate methods of providing care and services for women who are pregnant and do not desire to continue the pregnancy. They were stopped cold in their efforts, even with the declaratory judgment, because of the DA's position that they would continue to prosecute. . . .

[Concerning the constitutionality of the case], in the lower court, as I'm sure you're aware, the court held that the right to determine whether or not to continue a pregnancy rested upon the Ninth Amendment—which, of course, reserves those rights not specifically enumerated to the government to the people. I think it is important to note, in a law review article recently submitted to the Court and distributed among counsel by Professor Cyril Means Jr. entitled "The Phoenix of Abortional Freedom," that at the time the Constitution was adopted there was no common-law prohibition against abortions, that they were available to the women of this country. . . .

[And] insomuch as members of the Court have said that the Ninth Amendment applies to rights reserved to the people, and those which were most important—and certainly this is—that the Ninth Amendment is the appropriate place insofar as the Court has said that life, liberty, and the pursuit of happiness involve the most fundamental things of people; that this matter is one of those most fundamental matters. I think, in as far as the Court has said there is a penumbra that exists to encompass the entire purpose of the Constitution, I think one of the purposes of the Constitution was to guarantee to individuals the right to determine the course of their own lives. . . .

Abortion was a legal procedure in the United States until the mid-nineteenth century. By 1900 no state allowed abortion, because physicians deemed it to be an unsafe medical procedure and because of social and cultural proscriptions against giving women control over their reproduction. Until 1973, when Roe v. Wade *legalized abortion, it is estimated that between 200,000 to 1,200,000 illegal abortions were performed each year, resulting in about 200 deaths every year.**

    But in 1970 four states—Alaska, Hawaii, New York, and Washington—legalized abortion. Most states, however, continued to prohibit abortion except when the mother's life was at risk. In 1969 Norma McCorvey, a single pregnant woman, brought a class-action suit on behalf of herself and all pregnant women against the Texas district attorney, charging that Texas's 1859 antiabortion law, which allowed abortions only for the purposes of saving a woman's life, was unconstitutional. Her lawyers, Linda Coffee and Sarah Weddington, based their argument in part on the Fourteenth Amendment's due process clause, which guarantees to all citizens equal protection under the law and also requires that laws be clearly written.

    But, eager to prove that women had an inviolable right to make their own decisions about pregnancy, Coffee and Weddington also relied heavily on the Ninth Amendment, which courts had long interpreted as granting to the states any rights that the Constitution did not explicitly reserve for the federal government. A 1965 ruling by Supreme Court Justice William O. Douglas in Griswold v. Connecticut, *a case involving the right to use birth control, stated that the* people, *not the* states, *possessed all rights not specifically enumerated in the Constitution, including the right to privacy. Coffee and Weddington argued that this right to privacy protected a woman's right to make decisions about her own body, including the decision to end a pregnancy. The case made its way through the Texas court system before reaching the U.S. Supreme Court, which ruled in a seven to two decision that state laws could not restrict a woman's access to safe, legal abortion during the first trimester, or first three months of pregnancy. During the second trimester, the Court ruled, a state may regulate abortion only to protect a woman's health, and during the final trimester states may prohibit abortions unless the pregnancy endangers the mother's health. Justice Harry Blackmun wrote the majority opinion,*

---

* James C. Mohr. *Abortion in America: The Origins and Evolution of National Policy, 1800–1900* (New York: Oxford University Press, 1978), pp. 229–30.

expressing at the outset the Court's awareness that it was delving into an enor-
mously complex and volatile issue. There have been numerous judicial and leg-
islative attempts to weaken or even overturn Roe v. Wade, *but to date it still re-*
mains the law of the land. It is a landmark court case that gave women control of
their reproduction without having to resort to illegal and medically unsound
methods of ending an unwanted pregnancy.

SOURCE: U.S. Supreme Court Case 410 U.S. 113

MR. JUSTICE HARRY A. BLACKMUN Delivered the Opinion of the Court:

We forthwith acknowledge our awareness of the sensitive and emotional nature of the abortion controversy, of the vigorous opposing views, even among
physicians, and of the deep and seemingly absolute convictions that the subject
inspires. One's philosophy, one's experiences, one's exposure to the raw edges
of human existence, one's religious training, one's attitudes toward life and
family and their values, and the moral standards one establishes and seeks to
observe, are all likely to influence and to color one's thinking and conclusions
about abortion.

In addition, population growth, pollution, poverty, and racial overtones
tend to complicate and not to simplify the problem.

Our task, of course, is to resolve the issue by constitutional measurement,
free of emotion and of predilection. We seek earnestly to do this. . . .

The principal thrust of the appellant's attack on the Texas statutes is that
they improperly invade a right, said to be possessed by the pregnant woman, to
choose to terminate her pregnancy. Appellant would discover this right in the
concept of personal "liberty" embodied in the Fourteenth Amendment's Due
Process Clause; or in personal, marital, familial and sexual privacy said to be
protected by the Bill of Rights . . . or among those rights reserved to the people
by the Ninth Amendment. . . .

It perhaps is not generally appreciated that the restrictive criminal abortion laws in effect in a majority of States today are of relatively recent vintage.
Those laws, generally proscribing abortion or its attempt at any time during
pregnancy except when necessary to preserve the pregnant woman's life, are
not of ancient or even of common-law origin. Instead, they derive from
statutory changes effected, for the most part, in the latter half of the nineteenth century. . . . At common law, at the time of the adoption of our Constitution, and throughout the major portion of the nineteenth century . . . a

woman enjoyed a substantially broader right to terminate a pregnancy than she does in most states today. . . .

When most criminal abortion laws were first enacted, the procedure was a hazardous one for the woman. This was particularly true prior to the development of antisepsis. . . . Abortion mortality was high. . . . Modern medical techniques have altered this situation. Appellants . . . refer to medical data indicating that abortion in early pregnancy, that is, prior to the end of the first trimester, although not without its risk, is now relatively safe. Mortality rates for women undergoing early abortions, where the procedure is legal, appear to be as low as or lower than the rates for normal childbirth. Consequently, any interest of the State in protecting the woman from an inherently hazardous procedure . . . has largely disappeared. . . . The State has a legitimate interest in seeing to it that abortion, like any other medical procedure, is performed under circumstances that insure maximum safety for the patient. . . .

The Constitution does not explicitly mention any right of privacy. In a line of decisions, however . . . the Court has recognized that a right of personal privacy, or a guarantee of certain areas or zones of privacy, does exist under the Constitution. . . . This right . . . whether it be founded in the Fourteenth Amendment's concept of personal liberty . . . or . . . in the Ninth Amendment's reservation of rights to the people, is broad enough to encompass a woman's decision whether or not to terminate her pregnancy. . . . We . . . conclude that the right of personal privacy includes the abortion decision, but that this right is not unqualified and must be considered against important state interests in regulation. . . .

. . . the State does have a important and legitimate interest in preserving and protecting the health of the pregnant woman . . . and . . . it has still *another* important and legitimate interest in protecting the potentiality of human life. These interests are separate and distinct. Each grows in substantiality as the woman approaches term, and, at a point during pregnancy, each becomes "compelling."

With respect to the State's important and legitimate interest in the health of the mother, the "compelling" point, in the light of present medical knowledge, is at approximately the end of the first trimester. This is so because of the now-established medical fact . . . that until the end of the first trimester mortality in abortion may be less than mortality in normal childbirth. It follows that . . . for the period of pregnancy prior to this "compelling" point, the attending physician, in consultation with his patient, is free to determine, without regulation by the State, that in his medical judgment, the patient's pregnancy should be terminated.

. . . For the state subsequent to approximately the end of the first trimester, the State, in promoting its interest in the health of the mother, may, if it chooses, regulate the abortion procedure in ways that are reasonably related to maternal health.

For the state subsequent to viability, the State in promoting its interest in the potentiality of human life may, if it chooses, regulate, and even proscribe, abortion except where it is necessary, in appropriate medical judgment, for the preservation of the life or health of the mother.

Our conclusion . . . is . . . that the Texas abortion statutes, as a unit, must fall. . . .

OUR BODIES, OURSELVES
BOSTON WOMEN'S HEALTH BOOK COLLECTIVE

Along with seeking gender equality in the home, the workplace, and the political arena, the women's movement ushered in fresh new ideas for addressing women's health care beyond the traditional male-dominated medical establishment. Rape crisis centers, battered women's shelters, and women's health collectives were all part of a network of education, care, and support services designed by women to take control of their physical and emotional needs. An important event in this ongoing endeavor was the publication of Our Bodies, Ourselves, *a volume of medical information written and published by women. First published in 1970—and, several editions later, still in print and selling strong—the book was an outgrowth of a 1969 women's health workshop at the Boston Women's Conference at Emmanuel College in Boston, Massachusetts. After the workshop ended, some of the participants continued to meet and research women's health issues. They compiled their findings in mimeographed pamphlets and circulated them, thus creating a truly grassroots network of information on women's health. As more women requested this information, the authors paid to have an edition printed and bound by the New England Free Press, then went to Simon and Schuster, a commercial publisher, to produce an edition for wider circulation.*

This edition, published in 1973, offered vital information on birth control, pregnancy, menopause, breast and ovarian cancer, and other diseases of the reproductive organs. It also described the safe, medically sound techniques used in abortion and offered down-to-earth information on sexuality, nutrition, sports, and exercise. It included chapters on achieving emotional balance, making the choice to marry or stay single, and learning how to navigate the American health care system, with sections entitled "The Power and Role of Male Doctors" and "The Profit Motive in Health Care." The book sold several million copies, and its authors incorporated themselves, in their words, as a nonprofit organization "devoted to education about women and health."

In the following selection, which is from the preface and the section on childbearing, the authors emphasize their desire to make medical facts accessible in clear, honest, empathetic language and also to describe their own experiences and emotional reactions to their health-care needs. They view their book as a tool to help women make informed choices about their medical needs and take control over their own health and well-being—a power that, in the past, belonged mostly to male physicians. The authors further hope that female readers will be inspired to take control over other aspects of their lives and work for needed changes in the

*delivery of health care. An innovative mixture of how-to and self-help manual, po-
litical manifesto, and inspiration literature,* Our Bodies, Ourselves *exemplifies
the feminist view of the early 1970s, in which personal issues, such as health, are
also collective and political concerns.*

SOURCE: Boston Women's Health Book Collective, *Our Bodies, Ourselves* (New York: Simon and Schuster, 1973), pp. 11–13, 248–49. Copyright © 1971, 1973, 1976 by The Boston Women's Health Book Collective. Reprinted with the permission of Simon & Schuster.

YOU MAY WANT to know who we are. We are white, our ages range from twenty-four to forty, most of us are from middle-class backgrounds and have had at
least some college education, and some of us have professional degrees. Some
of us are married, some of us are separated, and some of us are single. Some of
us have children of our own, some of us like spending time with children, and
others of us are not sure we want to be with children. In short, we are both a
very ordinary and a very special group, as women are everywhere. We are white
middle-class women, and as such can describe only what life has been for us.
But we do realize that poor women and non-white women have suffered far
more from the kinds of misinformation and mistreatment that we are describing in this book. In some ways, learning about our womanhood from the inside out has allowed us to cross over the socially created barriers of race, color,
income, and class, and to feel a sense of identity with all women in the experience of being female. . . .

Many, many other women have worked with us on the book. A group of gay
women got together specifically to do the chapter on lesbianism. Other papers
were done still differently. For instance, along with some friends the mother of
one woman in the group volunteered to work on menopause with some of us
who have not gone through that experience ourselves. Other women contributed thoughts, feelings and comments as they passed through town or
passed through our kitchens or workrooms. There are still other voices from
letters, phone conversations, a variety of discussions, etc., that are included in
the chapters as excerpts of personal experiences. Many women have spoken for
themselves in this book, though we in the collective do not agree with all that
has been written. Some of us are even uncomfortable with part of the material. We have included it anyway, because we give more weight to accepting that
we differ than to our uneasiness. We have been asked why this is exclusively a
book about women, why we have restricted our course to women. Our answer
is that we are women and, as women, do not consider ourselves experts on men

(as men through the centuries have presumed to be experts on us). We are not implying that we think most twentieth-century men are much less alienated from their bodies than women are. But we know it is up to men to explore that for themselves, to come together and share their sense of themselves as we have done. We would like to read a book about men and their bodies.

We are offering a book that can be used in many different ways—individually, in a group, for a course. Our book contains real material about our bodies and ourselves that isn't available elsewhere, and we have tried to present it in a new way—an honest, humane, and powerful way of thinking about ourselves and our lives. We want to share the knowledge and power that comes with this way of thinking and we want to share the feelings we have for each other—supportive and loving feelings that show we can indeed help one another grow.

From the very beginning of working together, first on the course that led to this book and then on the book itself, we have felt exhilarated and energized by our new knowledge. Finding out about our bodies and our bodies' needs, starting to take control over that area of our lives, has released for us an energy that has overflowed into our work, our friendships, our relationships with men and women, for some of us our marriages and our parenthood. In trying to figure out why this has had such a life-changing effect on us, we have come up with several important ways in which this kind of body education has been liberating for us and may be a starting point for the liberation of many other women.

First, we learned what we learned equally from professional sources—textbooks, medical journals, doctors, nurses—and from our own experiences. The facts were important, and we did careful research to get the information we had not had in the past. As we brought the facts to one another we learned a good deal, but in sharing our personal experiences relating to those facts we learned still more. Once we had learned what the "experts" had to tell us, we found that we still had a lot to teach and to learn from one another. For instance, many of us had "learned" about the menstrual cycle in science or biology classes—we had perhaps even memorized the names of the menstrual hormones and what they did. But most of us did not remember much of what we had learned. This time when we read in a text that the onset of menstruation is a normal and universal occurrence in young girls from ages ten to eighteen, we started to talk about our first menstrual periods. We found that, for many of us, beginning to menstruate had not felt normal at all, but scary, embarrassing, mysterious. We realized that what we had been told about menstruation and what we had not been told, even the tone of voice it had been told in—all had had an effect on our feelings about being female. Similarly, the information from enlightened texts describing masturbation as a normal, common sexual activity did not really become our own until we began to pull up from inside ourselves and share what we have never before expressed—the confusion and shame we had been made to feel, and often still felt, about touching our bodies in a sexual way.

Learning about our bodies in this way really turned us on. This is an exciting kind of learning, where information and feelings are allowed to interact. It has made the difference between rote memorization and relevant learning, between fragmented pieces of a puzzle and the integrated picture, between abstractions and real knowledge. We discovered that you don't learn very much when you are just a passive recipient of information. We found that each individual's response to information is valid and useful, and that by sharing our responses we can develop a base on which to be critical of what the experts tell us. Whatever we need to learn now, in whatever area of our life, we know more how to go about it.

A second important result of this kind of learning has been that we are better prepared to evaluate the institutions that are supposed to meet our health needs—the hospitals, clinics, doctors, medical schools, nursing schools, public health departments, Medicaid bureaucracies, and so on. For some of us it was the first time we had looked critically, and with strength, at the existing institutions serving us. The experience of learning just how little control we had over our lives and bodies, the coming together out of isolation to learn from each other in order to define what we needed, and the experience of supporting one another in demanding the changes that grew out of our developing critique—all were crucial and formative political experiences for us. We have felt our potential power as a force for political and social change.

The learning we have done while working on *Our Bodies, Ourselves* has been such a good basis for growth in other areas of life for still another reason. For women throughout the centuries, ignorance about our bodies has had one major consequence—pregnancy. Until very recently pregnancies were all but inevitable, biology *was* our destiny—that is, because our bodies are designed to get pregnant and give birth and lactate, that is what all or most of us did. The courageous and dedicated work of people like Margaret Sanger started in the early twentieth century to spread and make available birth control methods that women could use, thereby freeing us from the traditional lifetime of pregnancies. But the societal expectation that a woman above all else will have babies does not die easily. When we first started talking to each other about this we found that that old expectation had nudged most of us into a fairly rigid role of wife-and-motherhood from the moment we were born female. Even in

1969, when we first started the work that led to this book, we found that many of us were still getting pregnant when we didn't want to. It was not until we researched carefully and learned more about our reproductive systems, about birth-control methods and abortion, about laws governing birth-control and abortion, not until we put all this information together with what it meant to us to be female, did we begin to feel that we could truly set out to control whether and when we would have babies.

This knowledge has freed us to a certain extent from the constant, energy-draining anxiety about becoming pregnant. It has made our pregnancies better, because they no longer happen to us; we actively choose them and enthusiastically participate in them. It has made our parenthood better, because it is our choice rather than our destiny. This knowledge has freed us from playing the role of mother if it is not a role that fits us. It has given us a sense of a larger life space to work in, an invigorating and challenging sense of time and room to discover the energies and talents that are in us, to do the work we want to do. And one of the things we most want to do is to help make this freedom of choice, this life space, available to every woman. That is why people in the women's movement have been so active in fighting against the inhumane legal restrictions, the imperfections of available contraceptives, the poor sex education, the highly priced and poorly administered health care that keeps too many women from having this crucial control over their bodies.

There is a fourth reason why knowledge about our bodies has generated so much new energy. For us, body education is core education. Our bodies are the physical bases from which we move out into the world; ignorance, uncertainty—even, at worst, shame—about our physical selves create in us an alienation from ourselves that keeps us from being the whole people that we could be. Picture a woman trying to do work and to enter into equal and satisfying relationships with other people—when she feels physically weak because she has never tried to be strong; when she drains her energy trying to change her face, her figure, her hair, her smells, to match some ideal norm set by magazines, movies, and TV; when she feels confused and ashamed of the menstrual blood that every month appears from some dark place in her body; when her internal body processes are a mystery to her and surface only to cause her trouble (an unplanned pregnancy, or cervical cancer); when she does not understand nor enjoy sex and concentrates her sexual drives into aimless romantic fantasies, perverting and misusing a potential energy because she has been brought up to deny it. Learning to understand, accept, and be responsible for our physical selves, we are freed of some of these preoccupations and can start to use our untapped energies. Our image of ourselves is on a firmer base, we can be better friends and better lovers, better *people*, more self-confident, more autonomous, stronger, and more whole.

CHILDBEARING

We want to understand our childbearing experience. We literally have been kept in the dark about what we can expect physically and emotionally when we conceive and give birth to our children.

We have needs that are not being met. One great need we have is to experience our childbearing year as a continuum. This continuum begins with conception and our decision to carry our child to term. It includes pregnancy, labor, and delivery, the period immediately after our child is born and the postpartum period. (Adjustments may last up to a year or more after birth.) We have a great need for knowledgeable medical care, which begins early in pregnancy and sometimes continues for several months after our child is born. And we need personal support, one or more people to be with us and support us throughout the whole cycle.

The present medical system doesn't provide for these needs. Pretending to help us, it tends to interfere with natural processes. For instance, doctors and hospitals have set what to us are artificial boundaries. Each period of childbearing is handled by a different set of "experts." During our pregnancy we see one private doctor or a series of doctors or nurses in a clinic. We might deliver our baby with someone we know or with someone we've never seen before. After the birth we're cared for by a new set of attendants and nurses, while our baby will have his or her own doctor. When we come home we don't have a doctor anymore, and we care for ourselves or depend on family or friends. So an experience that could be a unified one is all broken up. We begin to rely on one person or set of people, then we are shunted to another set.

In this country we are denied control over our own very personal childbearing experience. Childbirth, which could be as much a part of our everyday lives as pregnancy and child care, is removed to an unfamiliar place for sick people. There we are separated at a crucial time from family and friends. We and our present children suffer from this sudden removal; to our children it's a mysterious absence. In the hospital we are depersonalized; usually our clothes and personal effects, down to glasses and hairpins, are taken away. We lose our identity. We are expected to be passive and acquiescent and to make no trouble. (Passivity is considered a sign of maturity.) We are expected to depend not on ourselves but on doctors. Most often for the doctor's convenience, we are given drugs to "ease" our labor. (We have let ourselves be convinced by doctors who have never experienced labor and by our unprepared frightened forebears that our labor will be too painful to bear.) After our baby is born s/he is taken away for an hour, for a day, or longer. We pay a lot of money for our hospital space, sometimes more than we can afford.

Our obstetricians are trained mainly to deal with complications of childbirth. "Well," we say, "you never know. Something might happen. We need our doctor." We are afraid on many levels. We have been taught to have very little confidence in ourselves, our bodies, in other women's experience. In fact, 95 percent of our deliveries are normal. Most of us could very easily give birth with the experience and help of a trained midwife, either in a hospital, a special maternity house, or at home among family and friends. However, emergency equipment must be present or ready.

We want to improve maternity care for ourselves and all women by calling into question the present care we receive. This care interferes with the rhythm of our lives. It turns us into objects. We want to be able to choose where and how we have our babies. We want adequate flexible medical institutions that correspond to our needs. . . .

"WHAT IT'S LIKE TO BE ME"
A ROUND TABLE OF PERSPECTIVES
BY YOUNG *MS.* READERS

Like their elders, young high school and college-age feminists endured the derision and scorn of families and friends who did not share their views. Some young women were fortunate enough to find support among teachers and schoolmates, while others downplayed their allegiance to the movement for fear of being labeled "women's libbers." In the following round-up of letters from across the country by younger Ms. readers, sparked by an earlier letter published in the magazine, high school women from across the country describe their frustrations, fears, and strategies for expressing their feminist allegiances in the face of parental scorn and peer pressure. Voicing the usual fears of young people who are trying to define their own values and identities while still seeking acceptance from others, these young women are also struggling with deeply ingrained definitions of gender—a desire to please and look attractive for men, a tendency to restrict themselves to traditional female activities, and a fear of seeming too intelligent—that run counter to their beliefs in gender equality and self-determination. These letters are remarkable not only for their authors' honesty and ability to articulate their thoughts but for their courage and determination to adhere to their beliefs in the face of so many social pressures.

SOURCE: *Ms.* magazine 2, no. 12 (June 1974), pp. 75–80, 82–83. Reprinted by permission of *Ms.* magazine, © 2001.

WHAT IT'S LIKE TO BE ME:
YOUNG WOMEN SPEAK FOR THEMSELVES

IN JANUARY, 1974, *Ms.* published a letter from a 16-year-old feminist, who wrote about her support for the women's movement. She also wrote of her fear that, because she had been labeled a "crazy women's libber," she would not be accepted as a person. Her letter struck a responsive chord in young *Ms.* readers who were experiencing similar conflicts, many of which were unique to their age group. Most young women are dependent on their parents for emotional and financial support, on their peers for affirmation of their lifestyle, and on their school to prepare them for the "real world." Yet many feel that they are not taken seriously by parents, teachers, and friends, who often tell them that being a feminist is "just a stage they are going through." The accompanying feelings of isolation and self-doubt contradict their new-found pride and joy in being female.

Several young women have written about the strength they have received from a friend, a sympathetic parent or teacher, or a consciousness-raising group. One energetic group of high school women, "women on the move" . . . has offered to serve as a clearing-house for *Ms.* readers. The organization is especially eager to share its ideas and activities. Anyone interested may write to Lisa Lucheta or Candace Boyer, "Women on the Move," Redwood high school, Larkspur, California 94939.

As with every aspect of growth and liberation, there are no easy answers. But *Ms.* hopes that this forum will open an ongoing dialogue of exploration, sharing, and support among young women themselves and with their older—and younger—sisters.

IF MY DATE HAD ON BLUE JEANS, I'D STILL HAVE TO WEAR A DRESS

One big problem I have is how to dress on dates. If my date turns up in blue jeans and a sweat shirt, I still have to put on a dress because girls should look feminine and ladylike at all times. Just once I would like to be able to wear jeans to a ball game.

I am always being told that all the "little extras" boys give us—opening doors, and helping us on with our coats—are worth so much more than our equality. Reasoning like that from either sex is unbelievable.

There are boys who take the news that I'm a feminist quite well—if I break it *very* slowly. Most of them, however, think the word is poison. I'll never understand why.

CAN YOU BE BEAUTIFUL AND FOR WOMEN'S LIB?

When I graduated from junior high school in June of 1971, I optimistically anticipated high school as a challenge, an opportunity to find myself and to grow. The realization of my goals was made exceedingly difficult because of two uncontrollable factors—my sex and my appearance. You see, I happen to be "good looking," and my looks left me friendless with the members of my own sex

As I unhappily evaluated my reception at school, I realized that it was not the Real Me that they were reacting to but merely my appearance. The idea that I was the stereotyped blonde was something that people just couldn't divorce from me. Whenever I got the highest grade on a math test, kids would accuse:

"Yeah, no wonder you've been wearing all those short skirts to school!" If I had a problem in a technically oriented class, the teacher would say: "Well—blondes, what can you expect?"

After two and a half years at high school, I came to realize that it was I and not the fat girl who was most discriminated against. Both the educators and the kids understood her insecurity, anxieties, and loneliness. My unhappiness was met with incredulity and malice, but never sympathy. "She's a snob," they said.

I shocked people when I defended my "radical" beliefs. When I told them that I was for Women's Liberation, they laughed. Even my "best friend" called me a hypocrite behind my back. "How can you be beautiful and be for Women's Lib?" It's a paradox in itself, everyone contended. "Women's Libbers" are big, strong uglies who couldn't get a man if they tried.

I'm hoping that things will be better at college. However, recently a friend and I went to visit the college where I've been accepted for next fall. After we'd arrived, my friend explained to a student there that I had been accepted—"early decision." The guy looked at me, winked, and replied: "Oh, I get it; the interviewer was a man!"

I'll never stop fighting, but I'm beginning to lose hope.

I'M NOT ANTI-MALE; I'M PRO-FEMALE

I am writing to let you know that I am proud to be a black feminist teenager and would like to let all black women who have suffered or are suffering in society from being black and female in a country that is both racist and sexist that they are not alone. I am a member of the National Black Feminist Organization (NBFO), which believes in political, economic, and social equality of the sexes. I think a feminist is one who believes that society should provide the opportunity for women to develop as human beings and that choices should be provided according to interests and talents, not *solely* according to a person's sex. I am not anti-male, but I am pro-female. Keep on keeping on.

I'D LIKE TO ASK A BOY TO A MOVIE

I am a senior in high school and I have trouble speaking out and acting as I feel I should—I find myself saying and doing things that, deep down, contradict my basic beliefs. I would like to have the courage to ask a boy to a movie, or to go for a bike ride, because inside I know there is no reason on earth not to, but society and my upbringing make me suppress any act of this kind. (God forbid

I should be aggressive!) I would like to behave like a normal human being instead of a giggling idiot when I'm around boys, but sometimes I find myself playing this game without even realizing it, until it's too late. I would like to pay my way on a date, but never have the nerve to speak up and tell this to the guy I'm with—I become the traditionally passive female. I find myself wanting to look pretty, to be outgoing, to be all the things that boys supposedly look for in girls, while at the same time I feel angry at society for programming such bullshit into me. My only hope is that someday soon my anger will overcome my fear and I will be able to speak and act in accordance with *my* beliefs, not society's rules.

SNIDE REMARKS FROM OTHER FEMALES

I learned of discrimination against females early, at age 10, when I wanted to take advantage of my school district's free music-teaching program by learning to play drums. I was informed that drum-playing was a male pastime, certainly not fitting for any little lady! Instead I was given the violin (which I angrily gave up on, two weeks later).

Now 15, I am painfully aware that I am supposedly on this earth to please males, do housework, be popular, have many dates, and finally to have children. Unfortunately, I don't fit that mold. I dress in clothes that are practical and comfortable. I refuse to be flirty or coy, or fake helplessness in order to gain the attention of a male. I refuse to be pretentious or superficial for the sake of "friendship," since I realize that friendship based on superficiality is itself only superficial. I admit that I smile seldom and have few friends, but I believe I am much happier and more comfortable than many of the girls I see in school, who dress and make themselves up to attract male attention. I pity these girls for their pettiness and sharp competitiveness—which is probably not their fault. But I resent the many snide remarks and superior stares which I receive from other females. For some reason it is they who feel threatened by my ideas! Males either laugh at my ideas or take them seriously.

I have always loved horses, and I work after school and on weekends at a stable. I have ridden for five years, and I plan to teach, train, ride, and raise horses professionally. My parents and my boss (a woman) encourage me. I plan to go to college to learn basic veterinary skills, animal husbandry, and stable management.

I am 16, "brainy" (as it is called when someone goes to school to learn), and I do not have a boyfriend. Neither does my friend Jane. It never used to bother us before, because we did have each other. However, as time progresses and we get older, our other "friends" begin to get into society where most teenagers fall into their traditional roles and stereotypes. So now the two of us are left alone. It is starting to hurt us very much because we have been scorned, mocked, laughed at, and labeled "outcast." This helps to knock down our self-confidence, self-respect, and sometimes even our friendship.

After reading that letter in the January issue from the 16-year-old woman. I immediately called my friend and read her the letter so she could hear the similarity of the writer's life to ours. Both of us had no idea that there were any other 16-year-old women who felt as we did. Often, though, we thought there *must* be others experiencing the same feelings we did. When we read the letter we were so excited, happy, thankful, and overwhelmed, that we were spurred to write this letter. I am writing this so fast because words and emotions just keep flowing into my mind and I want to get them all down. That letter has strengthened us to stand firm in our beliefs in the Women's Movement and to help us realize that nothing is wrong with us. If only we knew other students in the same boat, we could support each other, share experiences, and grow together.

MY FAITH RESIDES IN WOMANKIND

I am a junior in high school. While talking to some male friends this year about what a good thing the Women's Movement is, I picked up the sorry nickname, "Women's Libber." What a curse. It wasn't long until I wished I had never opened my mouth. It got to the point where boys opening doors for me would say "Oh, yeah! You're one of them!" and walk through the door, letting it close in my face!

Well, it's going to be a long time until all people can face and love each other as equals, but it is that day that I live for! My faith resides in Womankind and always will. After all, if you can't believe in yourself, who can you believe in?

I SEE NO REAL CHANGE IN PEOPLE

I am writing this letter in a moment of extreme anger. I am a 16-year-old high school senior with the misfortune of having to walk to and from school and many of the other places I go. This, in itself, would not be bad, as I enjoy walking. However, my city has a *huge* collection of rude, inconsiderate, sexist, usually middle-aged, men who take it upon themselves to comment about me and other females they pass on the street. I do not find whistling, or staring, or honking car horns complimentary.

Maybe I live in the wrong area, but I see no real change in the attitudes of many people since the beginning of the present Women's Movement. This discourages and saddens me. I sincerely hope you *have* seen a marked change.

EMERGENCY, SEND BRAS AND A RAZOR!

I am a junior high schooler, and I come from a family with liberal ideas. Upon reaching camp, I realized that every girl over the age of 10 wore a bra. I quickly put on the one bra I had (which I packed for one see-through white shirt), and shaved my legs with a friend's razor. I sent a letter home, writing *Emergency: send bras and razor*. For the two weeks it took the package to arrive, I wore the same bra every day. Once I tried to discuss the idea of not wearing a bra, and was told anyone who does not wear a bra is a "whore."

When I got back to school I was informed that anyone who wore a bra was a turtle (why a turtle?).

A FRIEND SAYS FEMINISM IS A PERSONAL THING, LIKE ALCOHOLISM

The main thing that I think faces feminists of my age (16) is that we're not taken seriously. People say we'll grow out of it ("She's going through one of her stages"), or we've been brainwashed ("It's those books she's been reading—putting all kinds of ideas in the poor girl's head"). No one seems to think that we've actually come to be feminists of our own accord. A friend in her early forties seems to think that my feminism is my own personal problem, like alcoholism, and has nothing to do with. The World Out There! She said that my problem was that I loathed men! Then there's the type with the look on her or his face that tells you that they don't give a damn what this 16-year-old punk thinks she's saying. So after a while you keep your crazy "maniac" ideas to yourself and hope that doubts don't break your spirit completely!

When the Supreme Court first made its ruling on abortion, hysteria prevailed here in Puerto Rico. There were protest marches led by priests, and the funny thing was that almost only men were marching! It was against Puerto Rican culture, they lamented, the *yanquis* were intruding on them again. The sad thing is that they've swallowed up all the "bad" *yanqui* influence, while rejecting a progressive move like this!

MY PHYSICAL CHANGES WEREN'T AS DIFFICULT AS MY MENTAL CHANGES

Adolescence can be the most trying time of a person's life. I found that adjusting to my physical changes wasn't nearly as difficult or as painful as adjusting to my mental changes. My emotions would say: *be sweet and appealing so people will like you.* My intellect would say: *that's false, be how you feel and are.* Most of the time my emotions won, and I was miserable because of the guilt.

My consciousness-raising group showed me that many other women played the games I did, and were just as miserable about it as I was. I was not alone— that was the most important thing to me. Once I discovered I was not alone, my life was like dominoes: I developed self-confidence, then self-love, which in turn made me less narcissistic (as I was more at peace with myself and not constantly wondering where I stood with others), which helped me to be more compassionate with others. Even though I revert to a lot of the shit games of last year, at least now I realize it and catch myself when I do it.

I HOLD MY HEAD UP

I'm 15, and when I first made my views regarding the Movement known in class discussions two years ago, not only did boys disagree with my ideas, but many girls also felt embarrassed that one of their sex was actually competing against males. Many times I would play down my involvement with the Movement, only to be confronted by my conscience later. I was gradually losing self-respect because I felt I was forfeiting personal dignity for group acceptance.

Disgusted at myself for what I considered a sellout to the system, I began to look people in the eye and hold my head up when I spoke of Women's Liberation. When people sensed the pride I felt in being part of the Movement, they listened with more respect.

WOMEN'S LIBERATION IS AN ELECTIVE

I am vice-president of the student council in my junior high school in Pennsylvania. This is a supposedly modern school district that advocates most of the new concepts in education. Although the girls' sports program is insufficient (only a field hockey and a basketball team, compared to three football, two soccer, two basketball, and two baseball teams, a track and a wrestling team for boys), and the shop and home economics classes are still segregated, we are trying. One good thing is that Women's Liberation is offered as an elective in the social studies curriculum, and many teachers and students support the Movement.

However, a big blow came when we were discussing, at a council meeting, what to do about refreshments for an upcoming dance. Someone suggested all the girls make cookies. I asked, "What about the boys?" My adviser (both advisers are men) replied, "Yeah, if the boys want to bring in cookies, they can get their mothers to make some." Click!

I WOULD NEVER ASK A GUY ON A DATE

I discuss Women's Liberation with the guys I know at school and am now treated as an equal. Yet, liberation hasn't fully changed me. I'm 16 and still love the dating game. Regardless of equality, I still expect the guy to be polite—opening doors, and so on. I would never ask a guy on a date but do not feel "naughty" suggesting what I'd like to do. Once in a while, my friend and I have Women's Liberation parties for our boyfriends. We have fondue, candlelight, and fireside romance, and the guys do the cooking. We enjoy the meals and so do they.

I know a lot about cars and my passion is spending hours working on my car, but this doesn't make me less of a woman.

I EXPERIENCED THE CLICK AND EVERYTHING

I am an 18-year-old college student and about a year and a half ago I *became* a feminist—I mean, experienced the click and everything. At first I was extremely devoted to the Movement. I became enraged at other women who seemed content and didn't sense injustice or, if they did, didn't really care to do anything about it. I would frequently mutter to myself, "*She's* not my sister," upon seeing a woman willingly submit to blatant discrimination.

But I slowly began to realize that I wasn't accomplishing my purpose by being so defensive and so eager to refute others' statements. Instead of helping to promote the equality of my sex, I was completely turning people off and becoming known as "one of those Women's Libbers." Hence I have been slowly "mellowing." I now remain silent and smile wanly when someone (usually a man) says something that turns my stomach. I realize that silence and apparent condonation are not correct tactics in achieving equality either, but I don't know how to demonstrate my feelings without appearing to be the stereotype of a bra-burner, or some other well known but false impression of the liberated woman.

YOUNG BLACKS FEEL THAT THE BLACK WOMAN
IS ALREADY LIBERATED

I am a 17-year-old black feminist. This means that I'm not only being op-pressed as a woman, but also as an Afro-American. I've always made my beliefs known because I'm proud of myself as a person. It has cost me a couple of boyfriends who couldn't understand why I had to believe in such stuff. I've also lost women friends who thought about nothing except catching a man to sup-port them for life.

The young blacks around me are aware of the Movement but they don't take it seriously. They feel that, because the black woman has been viewed as the dominant force of the black race, she is already liberated.

I am serious about writing and I want to be a *successful* journalist. I would re-ally like to share a poem of mine with other teenage (especially black) feminists.

LIVIN

> We are born into this world crying
> And we leave it dying
> But between the two times we must live
> Love
> Hate
> Endure
> Experience happiness
> Experience fear
> Experience sadness
> Be loved
> Be needed
> Be confident
> And accept, yet be proud of being a Black Woman

I am both a feminist *and* a high school student (I'm 17), and believe me, the two do not easily coincide. I have to, more or less, stick it out alone. I *do* have sev-eral friends (mostly females) who agree with my beliefs, but that's all they do— sit back and agree. Thank God, I also have two dear male friends who have been a real comfort to me, and have contributed greatly to the consciousness-raising of others.

I am also quite religious and there are very few things I enjoy more than per-forming services of good. It looks as though I may be joining the Daughters of

Charity of St. Vincent de Paul after graduation. They are the largest community in the world and they help and teach all kinds of people: from unwed mothers to prisoners, lepers, and so on. The community offers practically every type of occupation. The Daughters of Charity are not recognized as religious, per se, in the Catholic Church because the women take yearly vows rather than permanent vows.

My goal is to educate people, particularly children, that they are "Free To Be . . . You and Me"; and at the same time, become closer to my God. Although most of my friends and relatives would consider me more of a radical feminist than a devout Catholic (which is indeed true), my dream is to unite both my feminist and religious beliefs into a worthwhile and satisfying occupation of service to others. I *know* it can be done.

THE SITUATION AT HOME IS UNBEARABLE

I am 14 years old. Not too many other girls my age, if any, admit to being for Women's Liberation. I am the target for jokes, teasing, and malicious comments from my family. They're always reminding me not to be too loud-mouthed or pushy and to remember that a boy likes a girl best when she lets *him* be the intelligent one. This all causes numerous problems, and the situation at home is unbearable to me. I have an older brother, and while I do all the house-hold chores he watches TV, and pals around with my dad. My dad has openly admitted his preference for him. "He's my son," he says

WHEN I NOTICED DISCRIMINATION, I WAS ELATED

I became aware of feminism and the Women's Liberation Movement in high school. We formed a group and became a recognized school club. When I began to notice subtle discriminations by teachers and "deferential" treatment by the boys in my class, which lowered my self-esteem as a student and person— I was elated! Of course there was pain in the realization, but suddenly so much incoherent hurt and anger became focused and articulated. From the women in the group, I gained a lot of strength and courage which I needed to take myself and my career aspirations seriously. Together, we built a protective shield for each other, reinforcing our hopes, and reassuring one another that we were not "tomboys," or "crazy Women's Libbers." I got a sense of power from the growth of the Movement, and I felt everything was possible.

However, as I grow older I find myself dealing with realities, not ideological conflicts. The pressures to choose a career or a mate have become greater. It is hard to be a woman. It is even harder to be a woman who is assuming new roles and questioning old expectations. Each one of us does battle with our up-bringing, the opinions of our parents and peers, and, most difficult of all, our own grave self-doubts.

We are beautiful in our conviction, our sisterhood, and our struggle. Each of us must remember that we are not alone. We can seek and find each other. Only if we are true to ourselves, our aspirations and dreams, can our lives have meaning.

Born in a small African American section of Atlanta, Georgia, Dorothy Bolden spent her life working in service jobs, including in a laundry, as a cleaner for Greyhound buses, and as a private domestic. She was once jailed for walking out on an employer who had been abusive to her. She first became politically active when the school board planned to relocate her daughter's eighth-grade class to a condemned school building. Bolden organized a protest among other parents, and they pressured the school superintendent to have a new school built. Although it took six years to get that school, during which Bolden's daughter and her classmates attended classes in the condemned building, the superintendent finally made good on his promise—in large part because Bolden went down to the school board every week to keep the pressure on.

Bolden was also active in the civil rights movement, but in 1965 she turned her attention to the plight of other domestics, whose meager earnings barely helped to support their families. When local community and civil rights leaders wouldn't help her, the Urban League, a national organization that promotes job training and better housing and education for blacks, came to her assistance. As Bolden recalls in the following oral history, it was a short step from gathering information about domestics' wages and job conditions to becoming president of the newly formed National Domestic Workers. As president, she organized domestics to ask for higher wages and eventually helped place domestic workers in suitable positions in Atlanta and developed training programs.

Bolden views herself as an advocate for African American and low-income women. As such, she takes issue with what she perceives to be the white, middle-class focus of the mainstream women's movement of the 1970s. Here is an illuminating glimpse into a woman who sympathized with the movement's goal of equal wages for equal work and shared the strategy of empowering women through collective organizing, but whose opposition to abortion and to what she perceived to be the movement's disdain for marriage and motherhood put her at odds with its priorities.

SOURCE: Extracted from "National Domestic Workers, Inc." by Dorothy Bolden, with the permission of Simon & Schuster Adult Publishing Group from Nancy Seifer, ed., *Nobody Speaks for Me* (New York: Simon & Schuster, 1976), pp. 158–67, 170–72. Copyright © 1976 by Nancy Seifer.

WHEN I CAME OUT of the Civil Rights Movement, I came out in a big force. My children can tell you, even though they were very small. But I've been my own woman all my life. I had to be, because my mama and daddy were separated and I didn't want to see my mama's head locked in her shoulders. So my little bit helped her a great deal and that made her strong.

I had thought about organizing us in 1960. We just needed more money to survive. But what got me going was when they wanted to send the children across town to an integrated school. That was in 1965 when I was demonstrating against the Board of Education. I knew that maids weren't making anything for anyone to talk about sending their children across town. We couldn't afford to pay twenty cents round-trip for the bus. And you couldn't afford to give your child forty-five cents for lunch. So why send your children out and then have to thumb a ride back and not have lunch money and a part of the time didn't have school shoes?

You're talking about poor children and you're talking about women who are the head of the household. We hadn't gotten farther than about seven dollars a day then. That wasn't any money, but it was some money to us. It was better than not making anything at all. So I was thinking about these poor women taking on more responsibility and earning so little. If you had three or four children . . . I had five in school, but I was lucky.

I just could barely afford to send mine downtown, twenty cents round-trip. And I gave mine sandwiches. They didn't get no hot lunch. I was just lucky my husband had a job, so they had fresh milk and cookies. And my mother only had one daughter, so my children were her children and she kept them supplied with goodies like apples and oranges, and cold drinks for when they'd come home from school.

She was the same way about me. And she was proud of what I was doing, so she helped me a great deal. She never turned me down on anything. If I spent my last dime doing something and I didn't have the grocery money, she said, "Come on, let's go shopping." And she would give me good advice. Before she died, we talked about the maids. And she said, "If you believe in it, go to it. I'll help you however I can." She was my sister, my mother, my dearest friend.

Also what made me strong was my husband. I had a finance supporter who took care of my children, so I didn't have to worry about where the rent money was coming from or where the food money was coming from and that's got lots to do with it. If they all needed something, I'd buy a batch of socks this payday, and underwear the next payday, and that way they all had enough until school opened up the next year. But it was geared to where Mama was helping and Daddy was doing the supporting. And this was the most important thing.

Well, when they started with this cross-town thing, I said, "Now this is wrong. Somebody needs to organize us." So I started in 1965, before my mother died, and I called several community leaders and our Civil Rights Movement leaders. I talked a long time with them, and they said they just couldn't do it. It was just too much.

Then after a while the Urban League* heard about what I was trying to do, and they called a meeting at the YMCA. We got down there and there was all types of people there, black and white. I listened to them throw things around which I knew were so far wrong. So one of the ladies said, "Stand up, Mrs. Bolden, and tell it straight to the people." So I got up and told them that they actually didn't know what they were talking about. They were giving some off-the-wall stuff. They never worked as maids, never knew how our own labor field really was. And I told them, "You don't even know the price we even want or how much money we'd start trying to get."

So then this John Stenson at the Urban League, he said, "Mrs. Bolden, why don't you go out and bring us back something you think we can deal with." So from then on, I started going around just about every night talking about the domestic. Sometimes I'd be gone till two o'clock in the morning talking with these women.

After that first meeting with the Urban League when they sent me out, we met again at the Y. Then I had to go out of town for two weeks and before I left, I wrote down, "$15 plus carfare a day." Then they started to meet, and I didn't want to come back because I knew that if I'd been at these meetings, they were going to pick me to be the president. I thought I'd give another woman a chance to do something. I wanted to sit back and be a part of it, but I didn't want the responsibility. I knew you were going to have to give up something if you were going to be a full-time representative, and this is what we really needed.

Well, I got back and they called me and they said, "They're waiting on you this afternoon." So I said, "Well, I'll be down there later." I let them get into their meeting. They had a temporary president then, and when I walked in somebody said, "We nominate Mrs. Bolden to be our founding president." Then a lady got up and seconded the motion and I told them to take a vote on it, and they elected me that night overwhelmingly. So that put me in the driver's

---

* National Urban League, founded in 1910, one of the most affluent and effective civil rights organizations, with ninety-five local offices around the country. With an emphasis on economic progress for blacks, it operates job training and job-development programs and works in fields of housing and education as well.

seat and I've been here ever since. I had to give up my job then, in the last of '68. Then the OEO [Office of Economic Opportunity] here gave me office space with a telephone and a secretary.

So we went on in '68 struggling and I set the price at fifteen dollars plus car-fare and up, per day. I began passing out the leaflets every morning downtown here. Sometimes it'd be freezing out here, but I'd stay out there. Then after we set the price, you had to teach those women how to ask for it. If you were mak-ing ten dollars a day, you had to learn how to communicate with the lady and tell her about the cost of living. If she didn't want to pay it, you'd just have to find a new job that's willing to.

But I didn't want anybody to protest. We women didn't believe in it, espe-cially in this field. Because if thirty thousand women get without a job, and that's how many maids there are in Atlanta, where else have we got to go to? So we couldn't go out demonstrating, and we weren't ramrodding anything down anybody's throat. Just if we weren't getting paid, we just walk off the job. So this is the way the fifteen dollars came around. . . .

The women named all of this the way they wanted it, so it's National Do-mestic Workers, Inc., but we're not really national. I didn't want to accept that because you get bogged down in paperwork and you never do anything con-crete for the people you're developing for. You have to worry about your chap-ters, and then you have to worry about dues, and then they call you over here and there because they have a problem and the area's so large that it wouldn't show what I was really organizing these women for—to upgrade them. I wouldn't be here long enough to develop a new career for them. I think this was more important than me having to go across country. . . .

At the beginning, I knew some harsh words were going to be said by the maids and the employers. A lot of the maids were afraid to join. They were skeptical because they knew what unions had done in the past, and at first "union" was part of the name. I don't think we realized how much "union" frightens people. They think you're coming in to stampede and bargain and harass and talk about striking and this kind of thing. Some time during a maid's life, they have probably switched for a time and worked at a laundry or something, and they just didn't want to be bothered with a union. They start collecting money from you, and then "I don't want nobody communicating with my employer except me."

Then I had telephone calls coming in from employers calling me a bitch. Or they'd say, "The bitch wasn't worth that type of salary." I didn't bang the phone up and I didn't get angry. I always had kind words that would erase their little ugly words, so we would hit it off pretty good after that. I'd listen to them, and when they'd get through I'd tell them, "Now you be willing to listen to me."

It was a constant thing, all day long and half of the night. I had to stay away from home much more than I had anticipated. But it wasn't too hard for my children to adjust, because they were brought into this life that way. I remember when we first started demonstrating about civil rights. My husband would gather all the young around and they'd have the television on when I'd come in, and we'd all cuddle around it. I was usually there during the daytime. If I had to work, I'd come home at five, I'd fix dinner and he would bathe the children, and then I'd usually go to a meeting. . . .

I guess the most encouraging time for me was when the women began to call for me to place them in jobs. That really got going in about '70. I give them jobs free of charge. I don't charge anybody anything, the employer or the employee. I can't, because I'm a nonprofit organization. I'd have to buy the license, then I'd have to contribute so much out of each dollar I received, and I just wouldn't want to go through that. This way I help people in the community, and we help the employers and employees by helping them find each other. And it seems we get all the advertising we need because I'm on television and radio so much, and in the papers.

It was also very encouraging when maids began to meet me on the streets and tell me, "We're so proud of you. We're so happy to have someone like you to really speak for us." I'd speak for senior citizens too. And then I started to do counseling. I was concerned about all areas of the maids' lives, not just one area. If somebody was having problems with her husband, they'd come and talk it over with me. Then some of the employers tell me some of the problems they have. So I have all types of social problems that people call on me for, and I like to be able to help people.

I have over two thousand members now. We have over thirty thousand maids in Atlanta, but I would never try to take those type of people in. We still have meetings, but I don't have them like I used to. It's dangerous now to have women out at night and they work in the daytime. But I have an executive board that meets once a month. I tell them what we're doing, how we're progressing. They want to know if we're developing things for the maids, and I let them know about the studies and proposals and things.

You have to be a developer here. You can't just elaborate on fifteen dollars a day plus carfare and up to twenty dollars, for seven years. It's a constant thing. You must know how to change it as the years pass on. The philosophy and the mold must change, You can't continue doing what you did ten years ago, or even five years ago. And I didn't organize just on money. I organized to upgrade the field, to make the field more professional.

The first program I did was for the State of Georgia in 1971. That was a homemakers' skills training program, how to train inner city housekeepers. I let Economic Opportunity of Atlanta administrate the funds for me. That's a community action program with funds from the federal government. They had the machinery already set up for the payroll checks, and I didn't want to ever have it said that I misappropriated some money. I had thirteen women working with me and that program really proved some points.

Now the Equal Opportunity is administering another grant for a study on domestics that I completed this year. We found out how the maids felt about getting some type of training and if they would participate in the training program with the employers. See, I knew I had to go to them to ask them because they don't care what *you* want, they might not want it. You have to go to them so they could have a say in it. I got Atlanta University to put all the data and the findings together for me with a computer, and then I circulated it and I carried it to Washington. . . .

Now I'm writing a manual for the maids. It's to give them and the employers a kind of guide for communications between them. A lot of times, people don't have understanding of this field. It has been so overlooked and overshadowed. I'm trying to give them a guide on what it's really all about, and how the relationship should be established in it—how they should work together, being two women, and that kind of thing.

I don't get any salary. The only money I get is if we have some projects going. I've been here seven years and I've been running out like this, but I always come out on top. It's just who I know and how I get around. . . .

I'm still struggling for black women. They've been the burden bearer of all segments of blacks and I think they need the opportunity to demonstrate their skills, their abilities, and their knowledge. We have some professional women that have had the opportunity to be branched out, but not that many.

In the past seven years there's been a great deal of change. These women used to be embarrassed about saying they were maids. You had to take such hardships that you didn't want nobody to know you were. Now it's different. You can't tell a maid from a secretary anymore. In the past, if a black woman was a maid you could tell by the way she dressed. Now they don't carry the shopping bags as much, they go neater, and they look more lively and intelligent. They're making between fifteen and twenty dollars, up to twenty-two dollars a day. And the heart of the Deep South like this never paid that kind of salary before.

There's so much I still want to accomplish for them. I want to leave an institution for them to be able to go through, so when they have problems or sickness, they can have someone that really can help see that things are properly taken care of. I'm expecting to leave a foundation here, an institution that will give them pride. The AFL-CIO started like this, struggling. I don't expect we'll become a union, but we'll be a strong organization, beneficial to both races. This is what I'm working for. . . .

Once I was a speaker at the Tarrytown Conference Center in New York. I think it was the National Women's Political Caucus or something like that. But it really bothered me to see that they don't include low-income women. Maybe one or two black women, but no poor women. You can't talk about women's rights until we include all women. When you deny one woman of her rights, you deny all. I'm getting tired of going to those meetings, because there's none of us participating.

They're still trying to put their amendment to the constitution, but they're not going to be able to do it until they include us. Some of these states know this, that you don't have all women up front supporting that amendment. They are talking about women's rights, but which women?

I would tell them this: "We're not on your agenda. We're not in your by-laws. We're just scrubwomen and you're not even considering motivating us." Some of them don't even want to pay us. They talk about rights, but they are violating my rights. They got to talking that they better do their own housework. I said, "Well, how are you going to do it when you don't know it? You need me just as much as I need you. So there's no use to lying and saying that we don't. We need each other."

You take a force of thirty thousand women that never asked the federal government, "What have you done for me, and I'm a working woman?" Thirty thousand domestics right here in Atlanta, and they are feeding into the economy. They're putting their little bit of money back. They are not on welfare. They are not asking for a handout. "I'm struggling and what have you done for me? What type of training have you developed for me? What have you offered me?" These are women who work every day. Working class women. They're poor but they're working class and now they're classed as a work force.

"You don't see me. You never have seen me because I'm off at seven o'clock in the morning, I'm catching a bus and I'm not off until black dark, and you're gone home and I'm probably serving you your dinner. What kind of help are you offering me?" That's the kind of thing we need to ask. We've been here since slavery, before any other class of labor. Before we had cars here or even a steel plant, we were here and we were working.

We built this country on our sweat. We wonder when they're ever going to say, "Let's grant these women some training." You've got your education, but you don't have what you need to have at home. You have to use the education you got outside of your home. I come into your home every day. And what are you offering me?

There isn't any movement ever going to be as powerful as the Civil Rights Movement. Women haven't been denied their God-given rights. I've been free to do what I want to do. It's because a woman looked up to the man. But also, civil rights had love. With the women, they're fighting over each other. The minute you go in there you can feel it. We've got to have love and they don't have it in there.

They call me and they ask me what I feel on abortion. I say, "No, I'm bitterly against it." I love an infant when he is born. If I hear him cry, it goes all over me. And I don't care if he's white or black. Whether it's that or something else, they're always squabbling with one another. And then this whole professional thing. We get too professional, always dealing with this here paper. We can't ever correct nothing when we professionalize it right here on this paper. Common sense ought to be in print too, but we don't do that.

In years to come, women may defeat themselves. So overanxious. I'm proud that women began to get up and let them know that we can shape this world into a form together, but some of them are trying to be men. If God wanted you to have everything that a man has, he would have given it to you.

A woman is a helpmaker. She's not to get up and dominate man. I can't see things like pushing a man out of a job, or say you have a man who's president of an organization and you think you should have a woman. If she is president, she's going to get the ambition the same as he gets. She could make as big a mess as he can make. And we weren't put here to take over.

I look at a man and I am his helpmaker. But I don't put him up on no pedestal either. My husband waits on me as much as I wait on him. I've been a free woman all my life. I've been making my own decisions, but I respect yours and I'll go half-way with yours. But a man is your protection. When he walks up to accept you from your mother and your father, he asks for you, doesn't he? Then he takes on the full responsibility that he's taken from Daddy. So why do you think that he's taking your rights?

When I look at the Women's Movement, there's so many little things in there I dislike. But it's not for me to tell them, it's for them to learn it. It makes sense to some extent, but they carry it a little too far sometimes. All people exaggerate sometimes. I like to see progress and I like to see a woman making a decent salary. If she's doing a man's job in an office or any other place, I feel she needs to be equally paid. Everybody ought to be equally paid on this earth for what they're sweating for. But not just to prove a point that a man is pouring cement so I want to pour cement too.

This is why men are not respecting us anymore. The womanhood has lost something. It has lost its beautiful effectiveness out of it, because women are trying to be like men. "I don't want to have babies. I don't want to have this and I don't want to do this." They have lost the effect. And womanhood is the most beautiful thing in the world.

Many Jewish women were strong supporters or activists in the women's movement; indeed, two of the movement's guiding spirits, Betty Friedan and Gloria Steinem, came from Jewish backgrounds. Like women of other faiths, Jewish feminists tried to synthesize their religious identity with their feminist consciousness. They began to challenge the patriarchal practices and assumptions of Judaism, such as the prescript that only men could say kaddish, the practice of not counting women as part of a minyan, the number of Jews needed to conduct religious services. Jewish feminists also sought to uncover the lives and experiences of Jewish women in the past and reclaimed often long-neglected rituals such as the mikveh, an immersion after the monthly menses. One uniquely creative way of celebrating Jewish sisterhood was by conducting a Jewish women's seder, using a Haggadah—the book containing the Passover story and ritual—rewritten from a feminist point of view. Because Passover celebrates the liberation of Jews from the oppression of slavery, it is a holiday that encourages participants to reflect on the meaning of freedom and equality and the ongoing struggle against all forms of oppression. Like their foremothers, Jewish women today must grapple with new forms of struggle and oppression as they seek equality within their religious communities and the larger secular world. The following Haggadah, compiled in the early 1970s by Aviva Cantor Zuckoff, a writer and political activist in New York City, for a seder conducted by members of her Jewish consciousness-raising group, reflects the participants' desire to celebrate their solidarity as women, pay tribute to the struggles and contributions of their Jewish foremothers to the survival of Judaism, and rededicate themselves to the creation of a strong and vital community of Jewish women.

SOURCE: Aviva Cantor Zuckoff, "A Jewish Women's Haggadah," excerpted from *Sistercelebrations*, edited by Arlene Swidler. Reprinted courtesy of Cantor (Zuckoff), Aviva. Copyright © 1974 by Fortress Press. "A Jewish Women's Haggadah" was dedicated to Nadia Borochov.

Haverot, shalom.

We have gathered here tonight to celebrate Pesah, the festival of the liberation of the Jewish people. Pesah is the night when all the families of Israel gather to celebrate and to strengthen their ties—to each other and to all Jews. We too are a family, a growing family. We too have ties we hope to strengthen. For while we are not related by blood, we are related by something perhaps even stronger: sisterhood.

Then follows the blessing on the wine, the dipping of the greens in salt water, the breaking of the middle matzah, the Four Questions, and the core of the Seder—the telling of the story of the Jews' struggle for liberation from slavery in Egypt. As the first cup of wine—dedicated to the first uprising of the Jews against oppression and the first liberation—is lifted, the following is said:

As we hold this cup of wine, we remember our sisters in the land of Egypt who fearlessly stood up to the Pharaoh.

Our legends tell us that Pharaoh, in the time-honored pattern of oppressors, tried to get Jews to collaborate in murdering their own people. He summoned the top two Jewish midwives, Shifra and Puah—some legends say one of them was Yocheved, who was also Moshe's mother—and commanded them to kill newborn Jewish males at birth and to report the birth of Jewish females so that they could be raised to become prostitutes. Pharaoh tried at first to win over the midwives by making sexual advances to them. When they repulsed these, he threatened them with death by fire. The midwives did not carry out Pharaoh's command. Instead of murdering the male infants, they took special care of them. If a mother was poor, they went around to the other women, collecting food for her and her child. When Pharaoh asked the midwives to account for all the living children, they made up the excuse that Jewish women gave birth so fast that they did not summon midwives in time.

Like our Jewish sisters through the ages, those in Egypt were strong and courageous in the face of oppression. Our sages recognized this when they said: "The Jews were liberated from Egypt because of the righteousness of the women."

The parable of the four sons is here retold as "The Four Daughters," in language reflecting our struggle to find ourselves as Jewish women. The nature of oppression is also defined and the Holocaust described in "Go and Learn":

Go and learn how the enemies of the Jews have tried so many times and in so many places to destroy us. We survived because of our spiritual resistance and our inner strength. Throughout the ages Jewish women have provided much of this strength, courage, and loyalty. During very desperate times, Jewish women were allowed to show their strength openly. Yocheved, Miriam, Deborah, Yael, Judith, Esther—who was called a "redeemer"—how few are the names of the heroic Jewish women which have come down to us! How many more were there whose names we will never know?

We speak of rebellion as the only way to overthrow oppression. The Ten Plagues are mentioned one by one. Then we raise and dedicate the second cup of wine to the ghetto fighters.

We drink this second of four cups of wine to honor the glorious memory of the Jewish fighters in the ghettos, concentration camps, and forests of Nazi Europe. They fought and died with honor and avenged the murder of our people. Their courage and hope in the face of unutterable brutality and despair inspires us.

As we hold this cup of wine, we remember our glorious and brave sisters who fought so courageously against the Nazi monsters. We remember Hannah Senesh and Haviva Reik, who parachuted behind enemy lines in Hungary and Slovakia to organize resistance and rescue Jews. We remember Vladka Meed, and Chaika and Frumka Plotnitski, who served as couriers and smuggled arms for the ghetto fighters. We remember Rosa Robota who organized the smuggling of dynamite to blow up a crematorium in Auschwitz. Chaika Grossman, Gusta Drenger, Zivia Lubetkin, Gisi Fleischman, Tosia Altman, Zofia Yamaika, Niuta Teitelboim—these are but a few of the names we know. Their willingness to sacrifice their lives for their people shines through the words of Hannah Senesh, written shortly before her execution (Nov. 7, 1944):

> Blessed is the match that is consumed
> in kindling the flame
> Blessed is the flame that burns
> in the secret fastness of the heart
> Blessed is the heart strong enough to
> stop beating in dignity
> Blessed is the match that is consumed
> in kindling the flame.

We sing the traditional Dayeynu, eat matzah *and the bitter herbs and discuss their symbolism, and then talk of liberation and the importance of the Jewish homeland. . . .*

The third cup of wine is blessed.

We drink the third cup of wine to honor the Jews of our own time who fought and died to establish Israel.

As we lift this cup of wine, we also bring to mind our many sisters in Israel who started the "first wave" of feminism there. We remember the *halutzot*, the women pioneers who won their struggle to work in the fields and as laborers in the cities—as equals in the upbuilding of Israel.

We remember our sisters Manya Schochat, Sarah Malchin, Yael Gordon, Techia Lieberson, Hannah Meisel, and so many others, who set up women's collectives and women's agricultural training farms and organized the working women's movement in Eretz Yisrael. We remember two of these organizers, Sarah Chisick and Dvora Drachler, who fell in the defense of Tel-Hai with Yosef Trumpeldor. We remember our many sisters who fought in the underground and in the army during the War of Independence. . . .

> *We talk of what Jewish identity means and how assimilation is self-oppression. We bless and then drink the fourth and last cup of wine.*
> We drink this fourth and last cup of wine on this Seder night to honor our Jewish sisters who are struggling to find new and beautiful ways to say "I am a Jew."
> We honor all our sisters in the small but growing Jewish feminist movement, here, all over North America, in Europe and Israel; our mothers and our grandmothers whom we have so often misunderstood and fought with; our daughters and granddaughters.
> We are liberating ourselves from the assimilationist dream-turned nightmare and moving toward creating Jewish life-styles, rediscovering our history and our traditions, our heritage and our values, and building on them and from them. It is possible that in struggling to free ourselves, we shall at one and the same time be instrumental in the struggle to liberate the Jewish people as well. That, too, is our goal.
> *Now we speak of what we've been waiting for—the food! We eat, sing, share the afikoman, say Grace After Meals, and sing the traditional Had Gadya—"One Goatling." After singing "Next Year in Jerusalem," we conclude:*
> We have talked on this Pesah night about our liberation from oppression and thus we conclude the formal part of the Seder. Just as we have been privileged to join with our sisters in holding this Seder, so may we be privileged to join with them in struggling for our liberation as Jewish women. May we carry out our self-liberation soon, joyously returning to our heritage and our homeland and our people—to be redeemed and to participate in the redemption of the Jewish people.

Next Year in Jerusalem!

As other documents in this chapter demonstrate, a central goal of the women's movement was to challenge women to think about their lives in new ways, to examine facets of their daily life experiences to understand the sources of their inequality and to seek ways to create personal and collective change. In the following document, Michelle Russell, a freelance journalist when she wrote this piece in the mid-1970s, recounts her experiences teaching a black studies class for inner-city women in Detroit, Michigan. Russell illustrates two basic precepts of feminist thinking: first, that ordinary women, and men, are makers of history; and second, that daily life experiences, such as her students' efforts merely to get to class, have political implications. Russell skillfully shows that raising consciousness—the precursor for any political change—must begin with women understanding and giving new meaning to their own life experiences.

SOURCE: Michelle Russell, "Black-Eyed Blues Connections: Teaching Black Women," in Gloria T. Hull et al., ed., *But Some of Us Are Brave: Black Women's Studies* (New York: The Feminist Press, 1984), pp. 196–207.

POLITICAL EDUCATION for Black women in America begins with the memory of four hundred years of enslavement, diaspora, forced labor, beatings, bombings, lynchings, and rape. It takes on inspirational dimensions when we begin cataloguing the heroic individuals and organizations in our history who have battled against these atrocities and triumphed over them. It becomes practical when we are confronted with the problems of how to organize food cooperatives for women on food-stamp budgets or how to prove one's fitness as a mother in court. It becomes radical when, as teachers, we develop a methodology that places daily life at the center of history and enables Black women to struggle for survival with the knowledge that they are making history.

One setting where such connections can be made is the classroom. In the absence of any land—or turf—that we actually control, the classroom serves as a temporary space where we can evoke and evaluate our collective memory of what is done to us and what we do in turn.

In Detroit, I am at the Downtown YWCA. Rooms on the upper floors are used by Wayne County Community College as learning centers. It is 10 A.M. and I am convening an introductory Black studies class for women on Community and Identity. The twenty-two women who appear are all on their way from somewhere to something. This is a breather in their day. They range in age from nineteen to fifty-five. They all have been pregnant more than once and have made various decisions about abortion, adoption, monogamy, custody, and sterilization. Some are great-grandmothers. A few have their children along. They are a cross-section of hundreds of Black women I have known and learned from in the past fifteen years, inside the movement and outside of it.

We have an hour together. The course is a survey. The first topic of conversation—among themselves and with me—is what they went through just to make it in the door, on time. That, in itself, becomes a lesson.

We start where they are. We exchange stories of children's clothes ripped or lost, of having to go to school with sons and explain why Che* is always late and how he got that funny name, anyway, to teachers who shouldn't have to ask and don't really care. They tell of waiting for men to come home from the night shift so they can get the money or car necessary to get downtown, or power failures in the neighborhood, or administrative red tape at the college, or compulsory overtime on their own jobs, or the length of food stamp lines, or just being tired and needing sleep. Some of the stories are funny, some sad; some elicit outrage and praise from the group. It's a familiar and comfortable ritual in Black culture. It's called testifying.

The role of the teacher? Making the process conscious, the content significant. Want to know, yourself, how the problems in the stories got resolved. Learn what daily survival wisdom these women have. Care. Don't let it stop at commiseration. Try to help them generalize from the specifics. Raise issues of who and what they continually have to bump up against on the life-road they've planned for themselves. Make lists on the board. Keep the scale human. Who are the people that get in the way? The social worker, the small-claims court officer, husbands, the teacher, cops, kids on the block. Ask: what forces do they represent? Get as much consensus as possible before moving on. Note that there is most argument and disagreement on "husbands" and "kids on the block." Define a task for the next meeting. To sharpen their thinking on husbands and kids, have them make three lists. All the positive and negative things they can think of about men, children, and families. Anticipate in advance that they probably won't have the time or will to write out full lists. But they will think about the question and be ready to respond in class.

---

* *Editor's note:* Probably a name derived from Che Guevara, 1928–1967, a Latin American guerilla leader who helped Fidel Castro take power in Cuba and served in his first regime. Guevara became a hero to New Left radicals in the 1960s.

Stop short of giving advice. Build confidence in their own ability to make it through whatever morass to be there at 10 A.M. the next day. Make showing up for class a triumph in itself. Because it is.

Try to make the class meeting a daily activity. Every day during the week. Like a language, new ways of seeing and thinking must be reinforced, even if only for half an hour. Otherwise the continuity is lost. The perpetual bombardment of other pressures upsets the rhythm of your movement together. No matter how much time you take with them or who they are, the following methodological principles are critical:

Take one subject at a time—but treat it with interdisciplinary depth and scope. In a variety of ways the women in class have been speeding. Literally, they may either be on medication, be suffering from chronic hypertension, or be skittish from some street encounter. Encourage them to slow down. This does not mean drift—they experience that too much already. Have at least three directions in mind for every class session, but let their mood and uppermost concerns determine your choice. . . .

Encourage storytelling. The oldest form of building historical consciousness in community is storytelling. The transfer of knowledge, skill, and value from one generation to the next, the deliberate accumulation of a people's collective memory, has particular significance in diaspora culture. Robbed of all other continuities, prohibited free expression, denied a written history for centuries by white America, Black people have been driven to rely on oral recitation for our sense of the past. Today, however, that tradition is under severe attack. Urban migrations, apartment living, mass media dependency, and the break-up of generational units within the family have corroded our ability to renew community through oral forms. History becomes "what's in books." Authority depends on academic credentials after one's name or the dollar amount of one's paycheck: the distance one has traveled, rather than the roots one has sunk. . . .

Piecing together our identity and community under these circumstances requires developing each other's powers of memory and concentration. . . . Formalize the process. Begin with blood lines. Share your own family history and have class members do the same. Curiosity will provoke diligence, and the abstractions of "identity" and "community" will give way before the faces of ancestry. . . .

Give political value to daily life. Take aspects of what they already celebrate and enrich its meaning so that they see their spontaneous tastes in a larger way than before. This means they will see themselves with new significance. . . . No life-area is too trivial for political analysis. Note that a number of Black women, myself included, have begun choosing long dresses for daily wear. In one class session, discussion begins with the remark that they're more "comfortable" in this mode. What does comfort consist of? For those who are heavy, it means anything not physically constricting. For working mothers, comfort means "easy to iron." For the budget-conscious, "easy to make." For some of the young women in class, comfort is attached to the added respect this mode of dress elicits from brothers they pass on the street. For a Muslim grandmother, cleanliness and modesty are signified. For her daughter, also in the Nation, Africa is being invoked. The general principle which emerges is that this particular form of cover allows us greater freedom of expression and movement. . . .

Go beyond what is represented in class. Recall all the ways, historically, that Black women in America have used physical disguise for political purposes. Begin with Ellen Craft, escaping from a Georgia plantation to Boston in 1848, passing as a white man. Talk about the contradictory impact of miscegenation on their thinking and action. Then connect this to class members' public demeanor: the variations they choose and the purposes at work. What uniforms do they consciously adopt? Focus on motive as well as image; make intent as important as affect, a way to judge results. . . .

Take the blues. Study it as a coded language of resistance. In response to questions from class members about whether feminism has ever had anything to do with Black women, play Ma Rainey* singing, "I won't be your dog no more." Remind them of our constant complaints about being treated as a "meal-ticket woman," our frustration at baking powder men losing their risables and of going hungry for days. . . .

Bring the idiomatic articulation of Black women's feminism up to date by sharing stories of the first time we all *heard* what Aretha [Franklin]† was asking us to *think* about, instead of just dancing to it. Let Esther Phillips‡ speak on how she's *justified* and find out if class members feel the same way. . . .

Use everything. Especially, use the physical space of the classroom to illustrate the effects of environment on consciousness. The size and design of the desks, for example. They are wooden, with one-sided, stationary writing arms attached. The embodiment of a poor school. Small. Unyielding. Thirty years old. Most of the Black women are ample-bodied. When the desks were new

---

* Stage name for Gertrude Pridgett (1886–1939), an influential pioneer blues singer.

† *Editor's note:* Born in 1942, Franklin, a versatile gospel and rhythm and blues singer, is known as the "Queen of Soul."

‡ *Editor's note:* Phillips (1935–1984) was a well-known rhythm and blues singer.

and built for twelve-year-old, seventh-grade bodies, some class members may have sat in them for the first time. Now, sitting there for one hour—not to mention trying to concentrate and work—is a contortionist's miracle, or a stoic's. It feels like getting left back. . . .

Have a dream. The conclusion to be drawn from any study of our history in America is that the balance of power is not on our side, while the burden of justice is. This can be an overwhelming insight, particularly in times of economic stagnation, physical deterioration, and organizational confusion. Therefore, it is important to balance any discussion of the material circumstances of Black women's lives with some attention to the realm of their dreams. . . . In dreams, we seek the place in the sun that society denies us. And here, as in everything, a continuum of consciousness will be represented. . . .

As teachers, we should be able to explore all these things and more without resorting to conventional ideological labels. This is the basic, introductory course. Once the experiential base of the class-in-itself is richly felt and understood, theoretical threads can be woven between W. E. B. DuBois,* Zora Neale Hurston,† and Frantz Fanon.‡

Then bridges can be built connecting the lives of ghettoized women of every color and nationality. In the third series of courses, great individuals can be put in historical perspective; organized movements can be studied. In the fourth stage, movements, themselves, may arise. Political possibilities for action then flow from an understanding conditioned by life on the block, but not bound by it. . . . But the first step, and the most fundamental, should be the goal of the first course: recognizing our*selves* in history.

---

* *Editor's note:* African American historian and civil rights activist, DuBois (1886–1963) spearheaded an African nationalist movement to resettle American blacks in Africa, believing they would never achieve equality in countries with a white majority.

† *Editor's note:* Hurston (1891–1960) was an African American author and anthropologist who turned her observations and studies of African-American folklore into classic novels about black rural culture.

‡ *Editor's note:* Born on the island of Martinique, Fanon (1925–1961), a psychiatrist by training, fought in the Algerian Civil War against French control of Algeria and wrote two seminal works on anticolonial revolutionary theory.

"WE ARE HERE TO MOVE HISTORY FORWARD"
DECLARATION OF AMERICAN WOMEN, 1977

The National Women's Conference, held in Houston, Texas, from November 18–21, 1977, offered several historical firsts: it was the first time that Congress and the president of the United States had authorized, sponsored, and financed a national gathering of women to focus on problems and issues of concern to women. It was the first time that women chosen from every state and territory in the nation had gathered together to voice their common concerns. And it was also the first time that women from such a variety of ethnic, economic, religious, and geographic backgrounds had come together in one place. Thirty-five percent of the delegates were nonwhite; nearly one in five came from a low-income background; and sizable numbers of Catholic and Jewish women, as well as Protestant women, were in attendance. Women from completely different ethnic backgrounds and opposing political camps came together in astonishingly honest and substantive dialogue.

Twenty thousand women, men, and children gathered in Houston for three days of panels, presentations, and policy discussions. The conference was mandated by Public Law 94–167 and was sponsored by several congresswomen, including Bella Abzug of New York and Patsy Mink of Hawaii. That law directed a national commission previously established by President Gerald Ford to convene a National Women's Conference.

The main work of the conference was to vote on a proposed National Plan of Action, a twenty-six-plank program that had already been formulated during the previous year. All twenty-six planks were debated and voted on in Houston. Perhaps the most important plank was the ERA, which passed overwhelmingly. Among the demands included in the rest of the planks were equal opportunities for women in business and the professions, politics, the arts, and education; extension of social security benefits to homemakers and programs to help homemakers get back into the work force; assistance to battered women, older and disabled women, and women of color; more attention to women's health-care needs and guaranteed access to safe, legal abortions; pregnancy disability benefits for employed women; civil rights for lesbians; comprehensive child-care facilities; and welfare reform. The following declaration illustrates the breadth of voices, issues, and visions that came together at this momentous gathering.

SOURCE: National Women's Conference, mandated by Public Law 94–167.

We are here to move history forward.

We are women from every State and Territory in the Nation.

We are women of different ages, beliefs and lifestyles.

We are women of many economic, social, political, racial, ethnic, cultural, educational and religious backgrounds.

We are married, single, widowed and divorced.

We are mothers and daughters.

We are sisters.

We speak in varied accents and languages but we share the common language and experience of American women who throughout our Nation's life have been denied the opportunities, rights, privileges and responsibilities accorded to men.

For the first time in the more than 200 years of our democracy, we are gathered in a National Women's Conference, charged under Federal law to assess the status of women in our country, to measure the progress we have made, to identify the barriers that prevent us from participating fully and equally in all aspects of national life, and to make recommendations to the President and to the Congress for means by which such barriers can be removed.

We recognize the positive changes that have occurred in the lives of women since the founding of our nation. In more than a century of struggle from Seneca Falls 1848 to Houston 1977, we have progressed from being non-persons and slaves whose work and achievements were unrecognized, whose needs were ignored, and whose rights were suppressed to being citizens with freedoms and aspirations of which our ancestors could only dream.

We can vote and own property. We work in the home, in our communities and in every occupation. We are 40 percent of the labor force. We are in the arts, sciences, professions and politics. We raise children, govern States, head businesses and institutions, climb mountains, explore the ocean depths and reach toward the moon.

Our lives no longer end with the childbearing years. Our lifespan has increased to more than 75 years. We have become a majority of the population, 51.3 percent, and by the 21st century, we shall be an even larger majority.

But despite some gains made in the past 200 years, our dream of equality is still withheld from us and millions of women still face a daily reality of discrimination, limited opportunities and economic hardship.

Man-made barriers, laws, social customs and prejudices continue to keep a majority of women in an inferior position without full control of our lives and bodies.

From infancy throughout life, in personal and public relationships, in the family, in the schools, in every occupation and profession, too often we find our individuality, our capabilities, our earning powers diminished by discriminatory practices and autmoded ideas of what a woman is, what a woman can do, and what a woman must be.

Increasingly, we are victims of crimes of violence in a culture that degrades us as sex objects and promotes pornography for profit.

We are poorer than men. And those of us who are minority women—blacks, Hispanic Americans, Native Americans, and Asian Americans—must overcome the double burden of discrimination based on race and sex.

We lack effective political and economic power. We have only minor and insignificant roles in making, interpreting and enforcing our laws, in running our political parties, businesses, unions, schools and institutions, in directing the media, in governing our country, in deciding issues of war or peace.

We do not seek special privileges, but we demand as a human right a full voice and role for women in determining the density of our world, our nation, our families and our individual lives.

We seek these rights for all women, whether or not they choose as individuals to use them.

We are part of a worldwide movement of women who believe that only by bringing women into full partnership with men and respecting our rights as half the human race can we hope to achieve a world in which the whole human race—men, women and children—can live in peace and security.

Based on the views of women who have met in every State and Territory in the past year, the National Plan of Action is presented to the President and the Congress as our recommendations for implementing Public Law 94–167.

We are entitled to and expect serious attention to our proposals.

We demand immediate and continuing action on our National Plan by Federal, State, public, and private institutions so that by 1985, the end of the International Decade for Women proclaimed by the United Nations, everything possible under the law will have been done to provide American women with full equality.

The rest will be up to the hearts, minds and moral consciences of men and women and what they do to make our society truly democratic and open to all.

We pledge ourselves with all the strength of our dedication to this struggle "to form a more perfect Union."

"BLACK WOMEN ARE INHERENTLY VALUABLE"
COMBAHEE RIVER COLLECTIVE

Although black feminists and white middle-class feminists were both committed to achieving gender equality, they disagreed on the strategies for doing so. While white feminists idealized paid work as the pathway to independence and self-realization, many black women, who still suffered from employment discrimination, regarded work as an unpleasant reality of life and wanted to have the choice of not working outside the home in order to spend more time with their families. White feminists were adamantly in favor of legalized abortion, but black women feared that abortion, as well as sterilization, could become a tool of population control aimed at the black community. Nor were black women so willing to target men, especially black men, as the enemy; they viewed black men as partners in the struggle against racism.

As a result, black women did not flock to join the organized women's rights movement of the late 1960s and early 1970s. But, as writer Toni Cade (Bambara) observed in 1970, within the black community women were creating informal "work-study groups, discussion clubs, cooperative nurseries, cooperative businesses, consumer education groups, women's workshops on the campuses, women's caucuses within existing organizations, Afro-American women's magazines."*

In 1973 black feminists on both the East and West Coast formed feminist organizations. Although these groups did not survive beyond the end of the decade, the energy and ideas they generated brought new spirit and a more sophisticated level of dialogue to the movement as a whole. Among the most compelling documents produced by black feminists is the Combahee River Collective Statement, drafted by the group of the same name in 1974. Founded that year in Boston, the Combahee River Collective took its name from a guerrilla action planned and led by Harriet Tubman during the Civil War. Tubman, a runaway slave, led Union soldiers on a successful raid up the Combahee River in South Carolina, resulting in the capture of Confederate supplies and armaments and the liberation of more than 750 slaves. Composed by three members of the Collective—Barbara Smith, Beverly Smith, and Demita Frazier—the Combahee River Collective Statement adroitly identifies and pledges to work against the multiple and interconnected sources of oppression in black women's lives: from racial and sexual discrimination to homophobic and classist social policies and attitudes. As such, the solutions that

---

* Toni Cade, ed., *The Black Woman* (New York: Signet, 1970), p. 9.

the statement proposes are equally multifaceted and interconnected. The authors assert that black women's liberation can be achieved only in the context of combating inequality and injustice for all people of color.

SOURCE: Barbara Smith, ed., *Home Girls: A Black Feminist Anthology* (Latham, N.Y.: Kitchen Table/Women of Color Press, 1983), pp. 272–282. Copyright © 1978 by MR Press. Reprinted by permission of Monthly Review Foundation.

WE ARE A COLLECTIVE of Black feminists who have been meeting together since 1974. During that time we have been involved in the process of defining and clarifying our politics, while at the same time doing political work within our own group and in coalition with other progressive organizations and movements. The most general statement of our politics at the present time would be that we are actively committed to struggling against racial, sexual, heterosexual, and class oppression, and see as our particular task the development of integrated analysis and practice based upon the fact that the major systems of oppression are interlocking. The synthesis of these oppressions creates the conditions of our lives. As Black women we see Black feminism as the logical political movement to combat the manifold and simultaneous oppressions that all women of color face. . . .

1. THE GENESIS OF CONTEMPORARY BLACK FEMINISM

Before looking at the recent development of Black feminism, we would like to affirm that we find our origins in the historical reality of Afro-American women's continuous life-and-death struggle for survival and liberation. Black women's extremely negative relationship to the American political system (a system of white male rule) has always been determined by our membership in two oppressed racial and sexual castes. As Angela Davis points out in "Reflections on the Black Woman's Role in the Community of Slaves," Black women have always embodied, if only in their physical manifestation, an adversary stance to white male rule and have actively resisted its inroads upon them and their communities in both dramatic and subtle ways. There have always been Black women activists—some known, like Sojourner Truth, Harriet Tubman, Frances E. W. Harper, Ida B. Wells Barnett, and Mary Church Terrell, and thousands upon thousands unknown—who have had a shared awareness of how their sexual identity combined with their racial identity to make their whole life situation and the focus of their political struggles unique. Contemporary Black feminism is the outgrowth of countless generations of personal sacrifice, militancy, and work by our mothers and sisters.

A Black feminist presence has evolved most obviously in connection with the second wave of the American women's movement beginning in the late 1960s. Black, other Third World, and working women have been involved in the feminist movement from its start, but both outside reactionary forces and racism and elitism within the movement itself have served to obscure our participation. In 1973, Black feminists, primarily located in New York, felt the necessity of forming a separate Black feminist group. This became the National Black Feminist Organization (NBFO).

Black feminist politics also have an obvious connection to movements for Black liberation, particularly those of the 1960s and 1970s. Many of us were active in those movements (Civil Rights, Black nationalism, the Black Panthers), and all of our lives were greatly affected and changed by their ideologies, their goals, and the tactics used to achieve their goals. It was our experience and disillusionment within these liberation movements, as well as experience on the periphery of the white male left, that led to the need to develop a politics that was anti-racist, unlike those of white women, and anti-sexist, unlike those of Black and white men.

There is also undeniably a personal genesis for Black feminism, that is, the political realization that comes from the seemingly personal experiences of individual Black women's lives. Black feminists and many more Black women who do not define themselves as feminists have all experienced sexual oppression as a constant factor in our day-to-day existence. As children we realized that we were different from boys and that we were treated differently. For example, we were told in the same breath to be quiet both for the sake of being "ladylike" and to make us less objectionable in the eyes of white people. As we grew older we became aware of the threat of physical and sexual abuse by men. However, we had no way of conceptualizing what was so apparent to us, what we *knew* was really happening. . . .

A combined anti-racist and anti-sexist position drew us together initially, and as we developed politically we addressed ourselves to heterosexism and economic oppression under capitalism.

2. WHAT WE BELIEVE

Above all else, our politics initially sprang from the shared belief that Black women are inherently valuable, that our liberation is a necessity not as an adjunct to somebody else's but because of our need as human persons for autonomy. This may seem so obvious as to sound simplistic, but it is apparent that no other ostensibly progressive movement has ever considered our specific oppression as a priority or worked seriously for the ending of that oppression. Merely naming the pejorative stereotypes attributed to Black women (e.g., mammy, matriarch, Sapphire, whore, bulldagger), let alone cataloguing the cruel, often murderous, treatment we receive, indicates how little value has been placed upon our lives during four centuries of bondage in the Western hemisphere. We realize that the only people who care enough about us to work consistently for our liberation are us. Our politics evolve from a healthy love for ourselves, our sisters and our community, which allows us to continue our struggle and work.

This focusing upon our own oppression is embodied in the concept of identity politics. We believe that the most profound and potentially most radical politics come directly out of our own identity, as opposed to working to end somebody else's oppression. In the case of Black women this is a particularly repugnant, dangerous, threatening, and therefore revolutionary concept because it is obvious from looking at all the political movements that have preceded us that anyone is more worthy of liberation than ourselves. We reject pedestals, queenhood, and walking ten paces behind. To be recognized as human, levelly human, is enough.

We believe that sexual politics under patriarchy is as pervasive in Black women's lives as are the politics of class and race. We also often find it difficult to separate race from class from sex oppression because in our lives they are most often experienced simultaneously. We know that there is such a thing as racial-sexual oppression which is neither solely racial nor solely sexual, e.g., the history of rape of Black women by white men as a weapon of political repression.

Although we are feminists and Lesbians, we feel solidarity with progressive Black men and do not advocate the fractionalization that white women who are separatists demand. Our situation as Black people necessitates that we have solidarity around the fact of race, which white women of course do not need to have with white men, unless it is their negative solidarity as racial oppressors. We struggle together with Black men against racism, while we also struggle with Black men about sexism.

We realize that the liberation of all oppressed peoples necessitates the destruction of the political-economic systems of capitalism and imperialism as well as patriarchy. We are socialists because we believe that work must be organized for the collective benefit of those who do the work and create the products, and not for the profit of the bosses. Material resources must be equally distributed among those who create these resources. We are not convinced, however, that a socialist revolution that is not also a feminist and anti-racist revolution will guarantee our liberation. We have arrived at the necessity for developing an understanding of class relationships that takes into account the specific class position of Black women who are generally marginal in the labor force, while at this particular time some of us are temporarily viewed as doubly desirable tokens at white-collar and professional levels. We need to articulate the real class situation of persons who are not merely raceless, sexless workers, but for whom racial and sexual oppression are significant determinants in their working/economic lives. Although we are in essential agreement with Marx's theory as it applied to the very specific economic relationships he analyzed, we know that his analysis must be extended further in order for us to understand our specific economic situation as Black women. . . .

As we have already stated, we reject the stance of Lesbian separatism because it is not a viable political analysis or strategy for us. It leaves out far too much and far too many people, particularly Black men, women, and children. We have a great deal of criticism and loathing for what men have been socialized to be in this society: what they support, how they act, and how they oppress. But we do not have the misguided notion that it is their maleness, per se—i.e., their biological maleness—that makes them what they are. As Black women we find any type of biological determinism a particularly dangerous and reactionary basis upon which to build a politic. We must also question whether Lesbian separatism is an adequate and progressive political analysis and strategy, even for those who practice it, since it so completely denies any but the sexual sources of women's oppression, negating the facts of class and race. . . .

4. BLACK FEMINIST ISSUES AND PROJECTS

During our time together we have identified and worked on many issues of particular relevance to Black women. The inclusiveness of our politics makes us concerned with any situation that impinges upon the lives of women, Third World and working people. We are of course particularly committed to working on those struggles in which race, sex, and class are simultaneous factors in oppression. We might, for example, become involved in workplace organizing at a factory that employs Third World women or picket a hospital that is cutting back on already inadequate health care to a Third World community, or set up a rape crisis center in a Black neighborhood. Organizing around welfare and daycare concerns might also be a focus. The work to be done and the countless issues that this work represents merely reflect the pervasiveness of our oppression.

Issues and projects that collective members have actually worked on are sterilization abuse, abortion rights, battered women, rape, and health care. We have also done many workshops and educationals on Black feminism on college campuses, at women's conferences, and most recently for high school women.

One issue that is of major concern to us and that we have begun to publicly address is racism in the white women's movement. As Black feminists we are made constantly and painfully aware of how little effort white women have made to understand and combat their racism, which requires among other things that they have a more than superficial comprehension of race, color, and Black history and culture. Eliminating racism in the white women's movement is by definition work for white women to do, but we will continue to speak to and demand accountability on this issue.

In the practice of our politics we do not believe that the end always justifies the means. Many reactionary and destructive acts have been done in the name of achieving "correct" political goals. As feminists we do not want to mess over people in the name of politics. We believe in collective process and a nonhierarchical distribution of power within our own group and in our vision of a revolutionary society. We are committed to a continual examition of our politics as they develop through criticism and self-criticism as an essential aspect of our practice. . . .

As Black feminists and Lesbians we know that we have a very definite revolutionary task to perform and we are ready for the lifetime of work and struggle before us.

"THE POSITIVE WOMAN KNOWS WHO SHE IS"
PHYLLIS SCHLAFLY

Phyllis Schlafly has made a career out of urging women to stay home as wives and mothers while struggling to make her way in the male-dominated realms of business and politics. Born in 1924, she attended Washington University in St. Louis, Missouri, supporting herself by working nights in a lab testing explosives. After attaining a fellowship to Radcliffe College, she earned a master's degree in government, and from 1945 to 1949 she worked as a financial analyst in a bank and became involved in Republican politics.

In 1949 she married, and bore six children over the following decade. During the 1950s she ran for Congress twice, losing both races, and became a fervent supporter of the Republican party. She also coauthored five books on strategic defense policy.

But in 1972, with the resurgence of the women's movement, Schlafly embarked on a new—and highly visible—career as a leading and vocal opponent of feminism. She has characterized feminists as a "bunch of bitter women seeking a constitutional cure for their personal problems." She developed a powerful grassroots following among both women and men who shared her opposition to the ERA, and in the early 1980s her "Stop ERA" campaign helped to derail passage of a Constitutional amendment guaranteeing equal rights under the law for women.

In the following selection from the The Power of the Positive Woman, *published in 1977, Schlafly argues that what she perceives to be uniquely female attributes, such as women's "innate maternal instinct" and their "practical approach" to problem solving, are divinely given and therefore unchangeable. She rails at feminists for denying that women have an essentially maternal role and for creating a negative, adversarial relationship with men. Positive women, claims Schlafly, are happy and optimistic and contribute to their social order by celebrating their differences from men; in contrast, feminists are shrill and angry and undermine women's special attributes. Like Marynia Farnham and Ferdinand Lundberg, authors of* The Modern Woman: The Lost Sex, *Schlafly takes an essentially conservative view of gender roles, one that does not allow for change over time: men and women have different roles in life to play based on inborn differences in their physical and emotional makeup, and to alter those roles is to defy the fixed order of the universe. Such a world view does not allow women and men to experiment with new forms of social relations and new structures of family and community life.*

SOURCE: Phyllis Schlafly, *The Power of the Positive Woman* (New Rochelle, N.Y.: Arlington House, 1977), pp. 11–19. Used by permission of Arlington House, a division of Random House, Inc.

THE FIRST REQUIREMENT for the acquisition of power by the Positive Woman is to understand the differences between men and women. Your outlook on life, your faith, your behavior, your potential for fulfillment, all are determined by the parameters of your original premise. The Positive Woman starts with the assumption that the world is her oyster. She rejoices in the creative capability within her body and the power potential of her mind and spirit. She understands that men and women are different, and that those very differences provide the key to her success as a person and fulfillment as a woman.

The women's liberationist, on the other hand, is imprisoned by society's negative view of herself and of her place in the world around her. This view of women was most succinctly expressed in an advertisement designed by the principal women's liberationist organization, the National Organization for Women (NOW), and run in many magazines and newspapers and as spot announcements on many television stations. The advertisement showed a darling curlyheaded girl with the caption: "This healthy, normal baby has a handicap. She was born female."

This is the self-articulated dog-in-the-manger, chip-on-the-shoulder, fundamental dogma of the women's liberation movement. Someone—it is not clear who, perhaps God, perhaps the "Establishment," perhaps a conspiracy of male chauvinist pigs—dealt women a foul blow by making them female. It becomes necessary, therefore, for women to agitate and demonstrate and hurl demands on society in order to wrest from an oppressive male-dominated social structure the status that has been wrongfully denied to women through the centuries.

By its very nature, therefore, the women's liberation movement precipitates a series of conflict situations—in the legislatures, in the courts, in the schools, in industry—with man targeted as the enemy. Confrontation replaces cooperation as the watchword of all relationships. Women and men become adversaries instead of partners.

The second dogma of the women's liberationists is that, of all the injustices perpetrated upon women through the centuries, the most oppressive is the cruel fact that women have babies and men do not. Within the confines of the women's liberationist ideology, therefore, the abolition of this overriding inequality of women becomes the primary goal. This goal must be achieved at any and all costs—to the woman herself, to the baby, to the family, and to society. Women must be made equal to men in their ability *not* to become pregnant and *not* to be expected to care for babies they may bring into the world.

This is why women's liberationists are compulsively involved in the drive to make abortion and child-care centers for all women, regardless of religion or income, both socially acceptable and government-financed. Former Congresswoman Bella Abzug has defined the goal: "to enforce the constitutional right of females to terminate pregnancies that they do not wish to continue."

On some college campuses, I have been assured that other methods of reproduction will be developed. But most of us must deal with the real world rather than with the imagination of dreamers.

Another feature of the woman's natural role is the obvious fact that women can breast-feed babies and men cannot. This functional role was not imposed by conspiratorial males seeking to burden women with confining chores, but must be recognized as part of the plan of the Divine Architect for the survival of the human race through the centuries and in the countries that know no pasteurization of milk or sterilization of bottles.

The Positive Woman looks upon her femaleness and her fertility as part of her purpose, her potential, and her power. She rejoices that she has a capability for creativity that men can never have.

The third basic dogma of the women's liberation movement is that there is no difference between male and female except the sex organs, and that all those physical, cognitive, and emotional differences you *think* are there, are merely the result of centuries of restraints imposed by a male-dominated society and sex-stereotyped schooling. The role imposed on women is, by definition, inferior, according to the women's liberationists. . . .

The Positive Woman remembers the essential validity of the old prayer: "Lord, give me the strength to change what I can change, the serenity to accept what I cannot change, and the wisdom to discern the difference." The women's liberationists are expending their time and energies erecting a make-believe world in which they hypothesize that *if* schooling were gender-free, and *if* the same money were spent on male and female sports programs, and *if* women were permitted to compete on equal terms, *then* they would prove themselves to be physically equal. Meanwhile, the Positive Woman has put the ineradicable physical differences into her mental computer, programmed her plan of action, and is already on the way to personal achievement. . . .

The Positive Woman recognizes the fact that, when it comes to sex, women are simply not the equal of men. The sexual drive of men is much stronger than that of women. That is how the human race was designed in order that it might perpetuate itself. The other side of the coin is that it is easier for women to control their sexual appetites. A Positive Woman cannot defeat a man in a wrestling or boxing match, but she can motivate him, inspire him, encourage him, teach him, restrain him, reward him, and have power over him that he can never achieve over her with all his muscle. How or whether a Positive

Woman uses her power is determined solely by the way she alone defines her goals and develops her skills.

The differences between men and women are also emotional and psychological. Without woman's innate maternal instinct, the human race would have died out centuries ago. There is nothing so helpless in all earthly life as the newborn infant. It will die within hours if not cared for. Even in the most primitive, uneducated societies, women have always cared for their newborn babies. They didn't need any schooling to teach them how. They didn't need any welfare workers to tell them it is their social obligation. Even in societies to whom such concepts as "ought," "social responsibility," and "compassion for the helpless" were unknown, mothers cared for their new babies.

Why? Because caring for a baby serves the natural maternal need of a woman. Although not nearly so total as the baby's need, the woman's need is nonetheless real.

The overriding psychological need of a woman is to love something alive. A baby fulfills this need in the lives of most women. If a baby is not available to fill that need, women search for a baby-substitute. This is the reason why women have traditionally gone into teaching and nursing careers. They are doing what comes naturally to the female psyche. The schoolchild or the patient of any age provides an outlet for a woman to express her natural maternal need. . . .

Finally, women are different from men in dealing with the fundamentals of life itself. Men are philosophers, women are practical, and 'twas ever thus. Men may philosophize about how life began and where we are heading; women are concerned about feeding the kids today. No woman would ever, as Karl Marx did, spend years reading political philosophy in the British Museum while her child starved to death. Women don't take naturally to a search for the intangible and the abstract. The Positive Woman knows who she is and where she is going, and she will reach her goal because the longest journey starts with a very practical first step.

"DEAR MARY CATHERINE"
A COLLECTION OF LETTERS BY
RURAL KENTUCKY WOMEN

By 1980 women who would never call themselves feminists or formally identify with the women's movement were nonetheless beginning to reexamine their lives, their marriages, and the choices—or lack thereof—they had made in life. And they were expressing a restlessness and dissatisfaction with marriages that had gone sour or had never been satisfying from the start. These letters by women in rural Kentucky to "Dear Mary Catherine," an advice show on a local television station, reveal a nascent anger and sadness at unfulfilling marriages or at husbands who have betrayed them. Although these women have few resources to draw on, such as money, education, or family support, their letters are not only a poignant cry for help but an indication that these women are no longer willing to quietly endure lives of despair and hopelessness.

SOURCE: From *Speaking for Ourselves: Women of the South*, by Institute for Southern Studies, edited by Maxine Alexander, copyright © 1984 by Institute for Southern Studies, pp. 166–69. Used by permission of Pantheon Books, a division of Random House, Inc.

Dear Mary Catherine,

I'm twenty-eight years old and I have six children. I'm Fat. I've tryed to diet every way I know how my husband gets worried about me being Fat but seem's to never give me any constalations of helping me or taking me out to make me feel better—lot's of time's I don't even feel like living. Everything seems to be a mess. Please tell me something to do. I'll be listening tuesday morning don't tell my name on TV. Just call me

overweight & sad

Dear Mary Catherine,

I think your program is very helpful for women who don't know what to do when something bad is happening to them. Whenever my husband says he'd like to make love to me I feel sick and when he touches me I think I'll actually throw up. I have to stop myself from shuddering by thinking about something. I daren't have the light on in case it shows. He doesn't hold an erection for very long and he always wants me to help and he doesn't even have an emission now except rarely and I feel hateful. His apologies set my teeth on edge. I wait to be alone to masterbate to a climax. When I think about our children and our good times I feel a remembered love. But he hasn't been attractive to me sexually for years. I've thought of leaving him but I can't hurt his pride and the family would never forgive.

Help me please.

Dear Mary Catherine,

I'm a wife and mother of four children been married twenty years. We went to a picnic one Sunday afternoon, we came home and out of the blue he says he is going to leave, he packs his clothes and leaves. He'll tell us the reason sometimes. He works away from home a lot so I guess there is another woman. But he won't admit it. He comes in and out all the time. We see him almost everyday. We don't want for anything; he pays the bills and keeps us in money. We don't even have to ask for it. I'd say we see him more now than we did when he lived with us. He's been gone five months now. What I want to know is do you think he will ever return. Or should I just give up?

Dear Mary Catherine,

I am forty-two years of age; have been married twelve years; and have two children, a girl eight and a boy six. We have had an ideal marriage except for finances; however, both of us work and we enjoy the simple things of life and stretch our combined checks from one payday to the next.

Yesterday I became ill at work and returned home about 10:30 to find my husband in *my* bed with a mentally retarded girl who is twenty or twenty-one years of age. My love, respect, and admiration for my husband died on the spot. I want out. The only trouble is the joint bank account has a total of $8.73. I have no mother, father, brother, or sister to whom I can go. My friends are casual acquaintances with their own problems. What can a forty-two-year-old woman with two children do under the circumstances. Please help me.

Sincerely,

lonesome toots

P.S. Don't suggest seeing a psychiatrist or psychologist please. There is no money. Don't suggest going back to school as I have two children and no money. I was never very good at school anyway.

Personal

Dear Mary Catherine,

I have a very personal problem that I would like a personal answer to.

I have been married for nearly eight years and have a daughter five years old. I love them both dearly, more than I think is humanly possible. Two years ago I went to work on a part-time basis and really enjoy my job. I work five hours a day.

This is my problem. There is this man I do not work with directly but see several times a day. He is a very dear friend. My husband had met him and likes him. The problem is the man has told me that he would like more than friendship and all I have to do is say the word. He does not pressure me, but he has told me that if I ever need him he'll be there. I would like to keep him as a friend, but I am afraid, also, that if the right mood hits me at the wrong time this relationship is going to go farther than friendship. He is a person that is very easy to talk to and is really an understanding person. I think that is why he is so appealing to me. He understands me, I think, more than my husband does. I'm not falling in love with him, but I am very attracted to him and I feel very guilty about it. He is fifteen years my senior but he is not old, if you know what I mean.

My husband and I went together for about two years before we were married, and I did not have any other relations with men other than my husband before we were married, but have always wondered what it would have been like to have had other lovers. . . .

Am I alone in the way I feel? Am I crazy to wonder about myself and this guilty feeling I have? Please help me understand myself if you can. Write me soon, if possible, at this address.

Dear Mary Catherine,

I thought I would write to you, I got your address when I was over there. I just loved to hear John ever morning on town and country. But I had to come back over here on the 27th, because I was layed off, and my rent was High, I couldn't pay it. But I sure Hated to leve my apt. But now this old man is sick, and I am very funny, I hate to move off. But if things don't change, and he won't even speak to me or ask me how I feel, but soon as I get breakfast on the table, comes in eats, walks back in, gets in his chair, sits there until lunch is on the table, but I am lonely and depressed, all I have to talk to is my little dogs. And my cousins are gone now they both died with cancer. One was buried at Lex. Ky. Cemetry, and one here at Dayton.

I guess you think I am nuts or crazy, but I can't have *no love* here *or peace* and no happiest, so I want you to write me a letter and give me a little advice. I am coming back to Lexington in July. Send me your phone number I will call you one morning. But tell me something I can't stand for to be mistreated.

Dear Mary Catherine,

I am a fifty-three-year-old woman mother wife and Grandmaw. I am young-looking for my age but I have lived and had children without *Love*. I still am. My children were borned thru desire not love. All I know is work and clean houses for money as my Husband no longer desires me as a woman or wife. I have done everything I know like having talks discussions my feelings but he doesn't care, only for my chores. But to seek another person would be disgracing my children and grandchildren but I am depressed. I am lonely I keep my house clean cook wash and do for other people. I got to church but I never have love not even a kiss or goodbye. I have a fifteen-year-old boy still at home but my Happies are writting Songs.

CHAPTER 4

RETRENCHMENT: GAINS AND LOSSES
DURING THE REAGAN/BUSH ERA

On a clear June morning in 1982, Sally Ride, an astrophysicist at NASA, boarded the space shuttle *Challenger* and rocketed to history as the first American woman in space. Though she denied joining the space program out of such history-making motivations, her participation in that shuttle mission was an important symbolic event—yet one more barrier dismantled to full female equality within American society. In the 1980s American women, especially young, professional women, were reaping the benefits of the previous decade's struggles by the women's movement. They had found more opportunities in the labor force, were exerting greater choice over when or whether to marry and bear children, and were continuing to enjoy greater sexual freedom.

Despite the influence of a growing radical right movement, with its conservative agenda for women's lives, American women did make significant educational and professional gains during the Reagan/Bush years of 1980 to 1992. By the early 1990s one in five doctors and one in five lawyers were women—compared to one in twenty and one in one hundred, respectively, in 1900—and the percentage of women achieving a college degree rose to 22 percent from a much smaller percentage at the turn of the century.[1] By 1991, 2,339,000 women in America had personal incomes of about fifty thousand dollars a year. Although black women and women of color continued to have a poverty rate of almost twice that of white women, according to U.S. census data, the top levels of the job market revealed rapid progress for all American women during the 1980s. By 1992, 7 percent of Hispanic women, 7.4 percent of black women, and 11.9 percent of white women were executives or managers. Membership in the National Association of Black Women Attorneys rose from less than one thousand in 1972 to seventeen thousand in 1993. There were over six hundred women's business organizations in the nation, ranging from women in film to women in construction, along with hundreds of professional and academic women's groups.[2] Clearly, in the latter part of the twentieth century, American women had learned the power of collective strength.

Yet for every advance there were setbacks. While women's job opportunities and income rose dramatically, their *overall* economic well-being—measured by income and leisure time—did not, compared with that of men. In two-income families, women still shouldered most of the domestic and child-rearing responsibilities, and the continuing rise in the number of divorced women with children increased women's financial responsibility for their families.

But, as historian Sara Evans has noted, the "real battle" was over the *meaning* of those changes, both for individuals and for society.[3] The election of Ronald Reagan as president in 1980 brought new challenges to the political and economic progress that American women had been making—especially to low-income women and women of color. In the first four years of the Reagan Administration, nearly 2 million female-headed families and 5 million more women dropped below the poverty line because of budget cuts engineered by the so-called Reagan Revolution. Reaganomics, as it came to be called, hoped to restimulate sluggish economic growth and reduce inflation by cutting taxes—and, as a result, some of the government programs funded by those taxes—to encourage the flow of capital through investment. According to Reagan's advisors, by freeing capital through tax cuts that favored the wealthy, the benefits of economic growth would "trickle down" to the rest of society. In reality, however, Reagan's economic policies, which clearly benefited the wealthy, helped to widen a growing gap between rich and poor and had a devastating impact on women and children. One-third of the Reagan budget cuts came out of programs that helped this constituency—food stamps, unemployment insurance, aid to dependent children, educational and vocational programs for women on welfare—even though all of these programs together constituted only about 10 percent of the federal budget.[4] Reagan claimed that such programs had promoted "indolence, promiscuity, casual attitudes toward marriage and divorce, and maternal indifference to child-rearing responsibilities."[5] Excerpts from the Republican platform dealing with welfare reform and from a report outlining the bleak impact of Reaganomics on American women over a three-year period are included in this chapter.

Despite the social and sexual freedoms they enjoyed, American women also faced a growing assault on those freedoms. Reagan came into office crusading for a return to traditional values. The components of this crusade included an emphasis on the traditional nuclear family as the core unit of society; a zealous campaign, heartily endorsed by a powerful coalition of fundamentalist religious groups, to outlaw abortion by overturning *Roe v. Wade* and restrict legal access to contraception; and a near indifference to enforcing affirmative action policies that benefited women and minorities. The Moral Majority, a particularly powerful organization of fundamentalist Christians, founded by televangelist Jerry Falwell in 1979, spearheaded a conservative campaign to ban abortion, homosexual rights, and school busing for integration. Its members supported conservative candidates such as Reagan, advocated mandatory prayer in public schools, and targeted feminism as an enemy of the traditional values they espoused—values that squarely put men at the head of the family and conservative religious ideas as the arbiter of public policy. Along with Phyllis Schlafly's Stop-ERA organization, the Moral Majority opposed the Equal Rights Amendment—which stated in part, "Equality of rights under the law shall not be denied or abridged by the United States or any State on account of sex"—and helped prevent its ratification to the U.S. Constitution. The amendment failed to muster the required number of states for ratification just three days short of the deadline of June 30, 1982. For Schlafly, Falwell, and other opponents of equal rights, Constitutional protection of women's equality spelled the demise of the traditional American family as they viewed it and of the American way of life. Falwell's conservative vision of family life is excerpted in this chapter from his book *Listen, America!*.

The implications of female equality and the tensions inherent in differing perceptions of women as workers and women as nurturers reverberated throughout the Reagan/Bush era and preoccupied thinkers across the ideological spectrum. Even Pope John Paul II entered the fray by issuing an apostolic letter on "the Woman's Part." Although the pope upheld a traditional view of women's role as that of wife and mother, he also affirmed their "essential equality" with men. An edited version of the pope's letter is presented in this chapter.

If, as it became increasingly clear, women were to constitute a growing sector of the labor force, how could they reconcile the demands of the workplace with the responsibilities of marriage and motherhood? Feminist writers and thinkers themselves grappled with this question and seemed to tailor their answers to accord with the Mom-and-apple-pie ethos of the Reagan Administration. Yet, on a more profound level, they were struggling to redefine gender roles in order to meet emerging challenges from the religious right to women's quest for autonomy. In 1981, Betty Friedan published *The Second Stage* (see "The Problem That Has No Name" in chapter 3), an appeal to the women's movement to address the issues most germane to women's lives, notably how to balance paid work outside the home with family responsibilities. In *The Feminine Mystique* (1963) Friedan had viewed the home and family life as the locus of women's malaise; now she urged women—and men—to make family life a priority and the arena in which both parents shared domestic responsibilities. She also urged the creation of new social policies, such as a period of paid leave from work for either parent in order to attend to family needs. And her exhortation to feminist activists to stop promoting a "feminist mystique" of antagonism toward men and instead cooperate with them to find new family-friendly solutions drew the most ire from colleagues who felt she was betraying the movement. Friedan also brought criticism upon herself for chastizing women who, to her way of thinking, embraced male values and priorities such as competition and aggressiveness and failed to "affirm the differences between men and women" and celebrate the "female sensitivities to life."[6]

Some have accused Betty Friedan of walking right into the " 'pro-family semantics trap' of the New Right" or of reinforcing traditional views of women's attributes. While Friedan perhaps packaged her ideas to appeal to those who most denigrated the women's movement—notably right-wing Reagan supporters—by urging women not to give up their "feminine tasks and frills" or to stop baking cookies, she astutely recognized that the movement was out of step with the concerns of many women's lives: how to reconcile their desire or need for paid work with their obligations as wives and mothers. Friedan further realized that concrete social change would come about not only by legislating new laws but also by reconstructing gender roles to give both women and men more opportunity to be parents as well as workers, and to create models of cooperative and egalitarian home life for their children.

Friedan's desire to celebrate women's distinctively "feminine" traits reflected a growing trend by popular and academic thinkers in the 1980s to identify and extol a special female "nature." Whether this nature was biologically based or culturally derived was the subject of endless debate, but what concerned the purveyors of these ideas was how to harness this "feminine caring" for the good of society. In a late-twentieth-century spin on the Progressive-era vision of municipal motherhood, psychologists such as Carol Gilligan, whose book *In a Different Voice* (see "An Ethic of Care" in this chapter) became one of the most widely quoted and influential feminist works of the 1980s, argued that women made moral decisions not based on the abstract principles allegedly used by men, as some leading male psychologists posited, but rather on an ethic of caring and concern for the particular individuals involved. Although Gilligan did not judge women's ethical approach to be superior to men's—just different—

and was quick to claim that such differences were not biologically based but culturally constructed, her findings—based on classroom observation of a small sample of schoolchildren—inspired feminists and others to embrace her study as an example of women's uniquely female capacity for caring and kindness—and of the necessity to avail all of society of this nurturant magic.

While Friedan and others hoped to "domesticate" the women's movement, such groups as the Homemakers' Equal Rights Association (HERA) sought to promote the equal rights of full-time homemakers by supporting the Equal Rights Amendment and advocating legislation that granted homemakers the same economic protections that paid workers enjoyed, including social security. The members of HERA creatively used the political tool of the Equal Rights Amendment to elevate a traditional domestic role for women who chose to stay home, thereby endowing that role with new political potency. The charter of their principles appears in this chapter.

Felice Schwartz, president of Catalyst, a nonprofit research and advocacy group for women, inadvertently provoked a roiling debate over the personal and professional costs of trying to have it all—career and family—when she proposed two career paths for women: the "career primary" path for women who were willing to sacrifice personal time and needs to advance in their careers, and the "family and career path"—which critics derisively termed the "mommy track"—for women who were willing to work fewer hours and sacrifice some career advancement to devote more time to family needs. Although Schwartz viewed these two paths as fluid and impermeable, with female employees able to move from one path to the other according to the cycle of priorities in their lives, her critics charged that the "mommy track" would lead to a career dead end. An excerpt from Schwartz's article appears in this chapter.

As more mothers, especially mothers of young children, joined the workforce, journalists, sociologists, and others wondered how those mothers handled domestic demands with workplace responsibilities. Arlie Hochschild, a professor of sociology at the University of California at Berkeley, studied the domestic arrangements of two-income families from a range of professional and economic levels and discovered that women still bore the brunt of domestic responsibilities—the "second shift," as Hochschild termed it. She concluded that working mothers were the "primary victims" of a "speed-up of work and family life."[7] Other investigators were more sanguine about the dilemma of the working mother. In "The Myth of the Miserable Working Woman," a research psychologist and a journalist teamed up to survey the existing research literature and interview working mothers from around the country. They found that working mothers experienced greater self-confidence and a stronger sense of well-being by doing work they enjoyed. Both documents appear in this chapter. See also the two interviews by Frances Wells Burck for different perspectives on how women experienced motherhood in the 1980s.

First Lady Barbara Bush unwittingly became a lightning rod in the debate over gender, family, and work. The choice of Barbara Bush as commencement speaker for the 1990 graduating class of Wellesley drew the wrath of seniors who felt that she was not a worthy example of the kind of career-oriented woman they wished to emulate; she had dropped out of Smith College to marry, raise a family, and promote her husband's aspirations for a political career. Other students supported Bush's choice and honored her as an exemplar of all the unheralded women who chose to serve their families. In her address Bush urged her audience to pursue professional careers but not to forget what counts the most—the "cherished human connections" of family and friends. Her address appears in this chapter.

Although college-educated women made gains in the professions during the 1980s, their sisters in the clerical and service sectors lagged behind. Many women continued to work in occupations that have traditionally been female and that offer little opportunity for upward mobility or wage increases. Though the labor market became less segregated by race after the 1960s, it remained distinctly sex segregated, with women shunted into the least skilled and lowest-paying occupations, such as bank teller, bookkeeper, cashier, data-entry clerk, secretary, typist, telephone operator, waitress, nursing aide, domestic, and garment worker. For these workers there was little discussion about balancing domesticity with work; rather, their concern was about stretching meager incomes. The concept of equal pay for equal work, or comparable worth, introduced during World War II, reappeared in policy debates and union negotiations during the mid-1970s. In 1980 Eleanor Holmes Norton, chairperson of the Equal Economic Opportunity Commission (EEOC), declared comparable worth to be the "issue of the eighties." Despite the Reagan Administration's opposition to comparable worth, by 1987 more than forty states and seventeen hundred local governments had begun to implement a policy of comparable worth to raise wages in female-dominated occupations.[8] "You Just Want to Do a Little Better," in this chapter, details the work of 9 to 5, an organization that lobbies for better wages and working conditions for service and administrative workers such as cafeteria workers and secretaries. Along with other organizations, unions, and workplace advocates, 9 to 5 drew public attention to the continuing gap between women's and men's wages despite the legal tools of affirmative action and the growing support for equal pay for equal work.

In the political realm, the Reagan/Bush administrations also delivered setbacks to the struggles for workplace equity, reproductive freedom, and social welfare programs that benefited women, and set in motion a pattern of differences in the voting preferences of women and men. The "gender gap"—the difference between women's and men's voting preferences—appeared for the first time in 1980 when more women than men supported the Democrats by a distinct, albeit small, margin of 5 to 7 percent. Exit polls revealed that a majority of men (55 percent) supported Reagan, while a minority of women (47 percent) did. The split along gender lines was greater than in any previous election, and the number of women office holders grew at the state and local levels; the number of congresswomen and female senators remained stagnant however. Although Geraldine Ferraro made history when she accepted the Democratic nomination for vice president in 1984 (see her acceptance speech in this chapter), and women contributed a record $4 million to her campaign, her presence on the ticket could not prevent President Reagan and Vice-President George H. Bush from winning a second term.

By the end of the 1980s Reagan had appointed over half of the federal judges in the country, and his appointment of three new Supreme Court judges, including the first female jurist on the High Court, Sandra Day O'Connor, ensured that the Court had a conservative majority. This majority, which remained in place under the Bush Administration, had a significant impact in reversing or narrowing affirmative action and sexual harassment decisions favorable to women and minorities and, in particular, whittling away a woman's right to a safe, legal abortion. In 1989 the Court upheld a Missouri law that forbade any institution receiving state funds from performing abortions, even if those funds were not used for abortions. This case, *Webster v. Reproductive Health Services*, sparked a growing number of legislative battles around the country to pass increasingly more restrictive antiabortion statues. Three years later the Court upheld even more restrictive state measures in *Planned Parenthood v. Casey*. Excerpts from both decisions are reproduced in this chapter. Although *Roe v. Wade* survived attempts by the Reagan/Bush administrations to overturn it, the conservative majority of the U.S. Supreme Court, along with the strong-arm tactics of a growing grassroots antiabortion movement, made access to safe, legal abortions more difficult for American women.

It was perhaps poetic justice that Bush's efforts to place another highly conservative judge on the Supreme Court helped to galvanize women's political reawakening and contributed in no small measure to Bush's defeat in the presidential election of 1992 and to a striking increase in the number of women in public office. In the fall of 1991 the country was riveted by the unprecedented televised Senate Judiciary Committee hearings on Bush's nomination of Judge Clarence Thomas to the high court. Thomas, an African American federal judge and former director of the Equal Economic Opportunity Commission (EEOC), was nominated to replace Justice Thurgood Marshall, the first African American Supreme Court justice and a towering champion of civil rights. In political outlook and judicial philosophy, Thomas was the antithesis of Marshall; he opposed affirmative action, took a dim view of legalized abortion, and was a strict constructionist on Constitutional questions. Despite the reservations of many lawyers, judges, and members of Congress about Thomas's credentials, the president and his advisors expected the confirmation process to proceed smoothly.

But allegations by Anita Hill, also African American and a former staffer at the EEOC under Thomas, that he had made sexually provocative comments to her and had badgered her for dates, created a major stumbling block and turned the nomination process into a televised spectacle. Hill's abrasive grilling by the all-male Senate Judiciary Committee was a wake-up call for American women who were outraged both by the committee's insensitive treatment of her and by their realization of how pervasive sexual harassment is in the workplace. (An excerpt from Hill's testimony before the committee appears in this chapter.) Women voted their outrage in the 1992 presidential election by helping to defeat Bush's bid for reelection and by contributing millions of dollars to the campaigns of female candidates for local, state, and federal office. At the Democratic National Convention, nine Republican women, fed up with the conservative antiabortion stance of Bush and the Republican party, dramatically declared their defection from the party and their intention to vote for Governor Bill Clinton of Arkansas, the Democratic nominee. A number of factors, most important of which was a weak economy, led to George Bush's defeat, but the conservative social policies of the Reagan/Bush years, which came to a dramatic climax in the hearings for Clarence Thomas's nomination to the Supreme Court, clearly contributed to his downfall.

From the "mommy track" and the "second stage" to comparable worth and Anita Hill, American women during the 1980s and 1990s—the years bracketed by two politically conservative presidential administrations opposed to the seismic gender shifts already taking place in American society—grappled with the complex changes generated by the women's movement. They struggled with trying to create a delicate balance between work and family, to preserve hard-won reproductive freedoms, to find ways to stay afloat economically while social programs that many relied upon were severely cut, and to find new ways to interact with men socially and in the workplace as old assumptions about male-female relationships and gender roles rapidly changed. Was motherhood "just another life-style choice" as Vice President Dan Quayle put it in a sermon on family values or was it the "gentle life" as Kate Grimes Weingarten, a new mother, calmly observed in her interview with Frances Wells Burck? Or was it, in the brave words of Patricia Godley, an inner-city mother, the battle to recover from a crippling drug addiction while attempting to save one son from the maw of prison, which had destroyed her other son? Against a backdrop of reactionary forces hoping to turn the tide away from enlarged social and sexual freedoms for all Americans, and women in particular, even those women who supported the conservative social and political agenda of the Reagan/Bush administrations asserted their deeply held views of gender and of citizenship.

NOTES

1. Rosalind Rosenberg, *Divided Lives: American Women in the Twentieth Century* (New York: Hill and Wang, 1992), pp. 245–46.
2. Naomi Wolf, *Fire with Fire: The New Female Power and How It Will Change the 21st Century* (Random House: New York: 1993), p. 307.
3. Sara Evans, *Born for Liberty* (New York: Free, 1987), p. 307.
4. Susan Faludi, *Backlash: The Undeclared War Against American Women* (New York: Crown, 1991), p. xvii.
5. Quoted in Rosenberg, *Divided Lives*, p. 232.
6. Quoted in Betty Friedan, *The Second Stage* (New York: Summit, 1991), p. 362.
7. Arlie Hochschild, *The Second Shift: Working Parents and the Revolution at Home* (New York: Viking, 1989), pp. 8–9.
8. Evans, *Born for Liberty*, p. 310.

"WE SUPPORT EQUAL RIGHTS AND
EQUAL OPPORTUNITIES FOR WOMEN"
1980 REPUBLICAN PARTY PLATFORM

Ronald Reagan's election to the presidency in 1980 issued in a revolution—some would say a backlash—in cultural values and, in particular, in the social and economic status of many women. Reagan campaigned on a theme of getting the nation back on track after what he and his campaign strategists perceived to be the incompetent and aimless leadership of President Jimmy Carter. He also campaigned on a platform of deep tax cuts to rally a weak economy, more defense spending to restore America's stature around the world, and less government regulation of business. The platform also made clear the party's essentially conservative agenda by supporting a Constitutional ban on abortion, cuts in welfare programs that would severely harm impoverished women and children, repeal of statutory restrictions on guns, greater use of the death penalty, and efforts to permit nondenominational voluntary prayer in public schools.

For the first time since 1940, missing from the Republican platform was a statement of support for ratification of the Equal Rights Amendment (ERA) to the Constitution. Reagan opposed the ERA, and in an effort to make the platform consistent with his views, Republican strategists decided that the platform should not take a stand on this issue. Although the platform expressed support for equal rights for women, this failure to support the ERA, coupled with the party's opposition to abortion, suggested that the coming Republican administration would not look kindly upon women's rights. As Mary Dent Crisp, the Republican National Committee co-chairperson who was forced to resign shortly before the convention, put it, the party was "about to bury the rights of over 100 million American women under a heap of platitudes."* Following are excerpts from the platform dealing with welfare, women's rights, child care, and abortion.

SOURCE: 1980 Republican Platform, Republican National Committee.

THE REPUBLICAN PARTY convenes, presents this platform, and selects its nominees at a time of crisis. America is adrift. Our country moves agonizingly, aimlessly, almost helplessly into one of the most dangerous and disorderly periods in history.

At home, our economy careens, whiplashed from one extreme to another.

---

* Quoted in Historic Documents of 1980, copyright © 1981 by Congressional Quarterly, Inc.

Earlier this year, inflation skyrocketed to its highest levels in more than a century; weeks later, the economy plummeted, suffering its steepest slide on record. Prices escalate at more than 10 percent a year. More than eight million people seek employment. Manufacturing plants lie idle across the country. The hopes and aspirations of our people are being smothered.

Overseas, conditions already perilous, deteriorate. The Soviet Union for the first time is acquiring the means to obliterate or cripple our land-based missile system and blackmail us into submission. Marxist tyrannies spread more rapidly through the Third World and Latin America. Our alliances are frayed in Europe and elsewhere. Our energy supplies become even more dependent on uncertain foreign suppliers. In the ultimate humiliation, militant terrorists in Iran continue to toy with the lives of Americans.

These events are not isolated, or unrelated. They are signposts. They mark a continuing downward spiral in economic vitality and international influence. Should the trend continue, the 1980s promise to be our most dangerous years since World War II. History could record, if we let the drift go on, that the American experiment, so marvelously successful for 200 years, came strangely, needlessly, tragically to a dismal end early in our third century. . . .

It doesn't have to be this way; it doesn't have to stay this way. We, the Republican Party, hold ourselves forth as the Party best able to arrest and reverse the decline. We offer new ideas and candidates, from the top of our ticket to the bottom, who can bring to local and national leadership firm, steady hands and confidence and eagerness. We have unparalleled unity within our own ranks, especially between our Presidential nominee and our Congressional membership. Most important, we go forth to the people with ideas and programs for the future that are as powerful and compelling as they are fresh. Together, we offer a new beginning for America. . . .

IMPROVING THE WELFARE SYSTEM

The measure of a country's compassion is how it treats the least fortunate. In every society there will be some who cannot work, often through no fault of their own.

Yet current federal government efforts to help them have become counterproductive, perpetuating and aggravating the very conditions of dependence they seek to relieve. The Democratic Congress has produced a jumble of degrading, dehumanizing, wasteful, overlapping, and inefficient programs that invite waste and fraud but inadequately assist the needy poor.

Poverty is defined not by income statistics alone, but by an individual's true situation and prospects. For two generations, especially since the mid-1960s, the Democrats have deliberately perpetuated a status of federally subsidized poverty and manipulated dependency for millions of Americans. This is especially so for blacks and Hispanics, many of whom remain pawns of the bureaucracy, trapped outside the social and economic mainstream of American life.

For those on welfare, our nation's tax policies provide a penalty for getting a job. This is especially so for those whose new income from a job is either equal to, or marginally greater than, the amount received on welfare. In these cases, due to taxes, the individual's earned income is actually less than welfare benefits. This is the "poverty trap" which will continue to hold millions of Americans as long as they continue to be punished for working.

The Carter Administration and the Democratic Party continue to foster that dependency. Our nation's welfare problems will not be solved merely by providing increased benefits. Public service jobs are not a substitute for employable skills, nor can increases in the food stamp program by themselves provide for individual dignity. By fostering dependency and discouraging self-reliance, the Democratic Party has created a welfare constituency dependent on its continual subsidies.

The Carter Administration has proposed, and its allies in the House of Representatives actually voted for, legislation to nationalize welfare, which would have cost additional billions and made millions more dependent upon public assistance. The Democrats have presided over—and must take the blame for—the most monstrous expansion and abuse of the food stamp program to date. They have been either unable or unwilling to attack the welfare fraud that diverts resources away from the truly poor. They have sacrificed the needy to the greedy, and sent the welfare bills to the taxpayers.

We categorically reject the notion of a guaranteed annual income, no matter how it may be disguised, which would destroy the fiber of our economy and doom the poor to perpetual dependence.

As a party we commit ourselves to a welfare policy that is truly reflective of our people's true sense of compassion and charity as well as an appreciation of every individual's need for dignity and self-respect. We pledge a system that will:

Provide adequate living standards for the truly needy;

End welfare fraud by removing ineligibles from the welfare rolls, tightening food stamp eligibility requirements, and ending aid to illegal aliens and the voluntarily unemployed;

Strengthen work incentives, particularly directed at the productive involvement of able-bodied persons in useful community work projects;

Provide educational and vocational incentives to allow recipients to become self-supporting; and

Better coordinate federal efforts with local and state social welfare agencies and strengthen local and state administrative functions.

We oppose federalizing the welfare system; local levels of government are most aware of the needs in their communities. We support a block grant program that will help return control of welfare programs to the states. Decisions about who gets welfare, and how much, can be better made on the local level.

Those features of the present law, particularly the food stamp program, that draw into assistance programs people who are capable of paying for their own needs should be corrected. The humanitarian purpose of such programs must not be corrupted by eligibility loopholes. Food stamp program reforms proposed by Republicans in Congress would accomplish the twin goals of directing resources to those most in need and streamlining administration.

WOMEN'S RIGHTS

We acknowledge the legitimate efforts of those who support or oppose ratification of the Equal Rights Amendment.

We reaffirm our Party's historic commitment to equal rights and equality for women.

We support equal rights and equal opportunities for women, without taking away traditional rights of women such as exemption from the military draft. We support the enforcement of all equal opportunity laws and urge the elimination of discrimination against women. We oppose any move which would give the federal government more power over families.

Ratification of the Equal Rights Amendment is now in the hands of state legislatures, and the issues of the time extension and rescission are in the courts. The states have a constitutional right to accept or reject a constitutional amendment without federal interference or pressure. At the direction of the White House, federal departments launched pressure against states which refused to ratify ERA. Regardless of one's position on ERA, we demand that this practice cease.

At this time, women of America comprise 53 percent of the population and over 42 percent of the work force. By 1990, we anticipate that 51 percent of the population will be women, and there will be approximately 57 million in the work force. Therefore, the following urgent problems must be resolved:

Total integration of the work force (not separate but equal) is necessary to bring women equality in pay;

Girls and young women must be given improved early career counseling and job training to widen the opportunities for them in the world of work;

Women's worth in the society and in the jobs they hold, at home or in the workplace, must be reevaluated to improve the conditions of women workers concentrated in low-status, low-paying jobs;

Equal opportunity for credit and other assistance must be assured to women in small businesses; . . .

CHILD CARE

One of the most critical problems in our nation today is that of inadequate child care for the working mother. As champions of the free enterprise system, of the individual, and of the idea that the best solutions to most problems rest at the community level, Republicans must find ways to meet this, the working woman's need. The scope of this problem is fully realized only when it is understood that many female heads of households are at the poverty level and that they have a very large percentage of the nation's children.

The important secret about old age in America today is that it is primarily a woman's issue, and those over 65 are the fastest growing segment of the population. With current population trends, by the year 2020, 15.5 percent of our population will be over 65; by 2035, women in this age group will outnumber men by 13 million.

In 1980, 42 percent of women between 55 and 64 are in the work force. Half of the six million elderly women who live alone have incomes of $3,700 or less, and black women in that category have a median income of $2,600. How do they survive with the present rate of inflation? The lower salaries they earned as working women are now reflected in lower retirement benefits, if they have any at all. The Social Security system is still biased against women, and non-existent pension plans combine with that to produce a bereft elderly woman. The Republican Party must not and will not let this continue.

We reaffirm our belief in the traditional role and values of the family in our society. The damage being done today to the family takes its greatest toll on the woman. Whether it be through divorce, widowhood, economic problems, or the suffering of children, the impact is greatest on women. The importance of support for the mother and homemaker in maintaining the values of this country cannot be over-emphasized.

In other sections of this platform, we call for greater equity in the tax treatment of working spouses. We deplore this marriage tax which penalizes married two-worker families. We call for a reduction in the estate tax burden, which creates hardships for widows and minor children. We also pledge to address any remaining inequities in the treatment of women under the Social Security system.

Women know better than anyone the decline in the quality of life that is occurring in America today. The peril to the United States and especially to women must be stressed. Women understand domestic, consumer, and economic issues more deeply because they usually manage the households and have the responsibility for them. With this responsibility must also come greater opportunity for achievement and total equality toward solution of problems. . . .

ABORTION

There can be no doubt that the question of abortion, despite the complex nature of its various issues, is ultimately concerned with equality of rights under the law. While we recognize differing views on this question among Americans in general—and in our own Party—we affirm our support of a constitutional amendment to restore protection of the right to life for unborn children. We also support the Congressional efforts to restrict the use of taxpayers' dollars for abortion.

We protest the Supreme Court's intrusion into the family structure through its denial of the parent's obligation and right to guide their minor children. . . .

"YOU JUST WANT TO DO A LITTLE BETTER"
WENDY ROBINSON BROWER

9 to 5 is an organization of women office workers dedicated to improving the working lives and conditions of administrative support staff—mostly women—in American businesses. Founded in 1973 as the Working Women Organizing Project, and known from 1978 to 1982 as Working Women, National Association of Office Workers, 9 to 5 seeks to banish sexual harassment and discrimination based on race, sex, and pregnancy from the workplace. It also lobbies for higher wages for clerical workers and for regulations protecting employees, especially pregnant employees, from overexposure to video display terminals. In addition, it sponsors a summer school for wage-earning women and a "job survival hotline."

In 1980 Wendy Robinson Brower organized Minnesota Working Women, which became an affiliate of 9 to 5. At the time, she was working for an employment and training program for low-income people. There she had a front-row view of the staggering wage discrepancies between male and female workers. Following are her recollections of the goals and activities of her organization and of the dreadful on-the-job treatment of many of its members and supporters. Robinson notes that, unlike herself, many women in the organization did not regard themselves as feminists or as participants in a social movement. For them, Working Women was simply a means to make their working lives more bearable.

SOURCE: Bonnie Watkins and Nina Rothchild, eds., *In the Company of Women: Voices from the Women's Movement* (St. Paul: Minnesota Historical Society, 1996), pp. 110–14. Used with permission.

ONE OF THE JOBS I almost took, back in 1978, was as a classified-ad person at the St. Paul newspaper. I thought, "I'll get to work for a newspaper, it's a step in the door." Well, it was a roomful of women, about 20 of them, lined up in rows with the supervisor on a riser behind them, behind glass. And this was for a $4.30-an-hour job. That's the way the workplace is organized. You've got these women running around out of control, you've got to keep them penned in, you've got to watch them every minute.

Instead of that, I got a clerical job at the University of Minnesota, in the vice president's office. That was when the inequities of what men and women are paid for the work they are doing became most apparent to me. In the basement of my building there were job postings every week: your clerical, your technical, your professional, your academic, and then you had maintenance or janitorial.

At that time there was a secretarial shortage. And there were lots of qualifications to be a secretary. Grammar and spelling, post-secondary education, three to five years experience, type 60 words a minute—all those things. My job paid about $800 a month. And right across on the other side of the job board, they were looking for janitors. It only required an eighth grade education, and it paid $200 a month more. For starters.

Then I went to work at an art museum. I was secretary to the executive director, and this man treated me like absolute garbage. He thought of me more as his slave, I think, than as a human being with any feelings or contributions other than jumping at his every demand.

I ended up typing about 90 words a minute when I worked there, because there was so much to be done. But it was the kind of job where I would get to work, I would hear him come in, and immediately my stomach would start to churn. It was so stressful, I had to leave.

I went to work for an employment and training program. We were working with really disadvantaged low-income people. And I'm not kidding you, we had some men that were getting trained and employed, and they'd start working at about $9 an hour. These guys had just been incarcerated for 10 years, they'd battered their wives, or they'd been on the lam, and we could get them fairly high-paid jobs.

Then we'd get women who were single moms, and they'd been to technical school or something, and they had all these skills, and we couldn't get them placed at anything higher than $4.50 an hour. I thought, something's wrong with this system.

In that job, I had the opportunity to go to a lot of conferences. At one of them, someone was there from Working Women, from the national office, and that's when I learned about that organization. She was talking about how women are treated differently, the pay, all this stuff. And I thought, "You're right, this is it, this is the answer. You're speaking the language of all the things I'm feeling." So I wanted to get something like that started here.

In 1980, we organized a little group to meet one Saturday morning at the downtown YWCA. I had put a little announcement in the *Skyway News* inviting people to a meeting. About 30 people showed up. There were actually people who wanted to do something!

Soon after that, a prominent feminist sent us a check. I just started to cry when I opened up the envelope, I couldn't believe anybody was doing this. That really helped get us from day one to day two. I quit my job and started as the Working Women organizer. The Y gave us a little cubicle. Then the national organization gave us a little money. The Christian Sharing Fund gave us a little money. We never had a lot of money, we were always on a shoestring.

We had a lot of fun in that organization. When Governor Perpich was elected in 1982, we set up a meeting with him about issues affecting women in the workplace. Pay equity was first on the agenda. We dressed up one of our members as a white-out* bottle and we wrote on there, "White out low pay." At first, nobody wanted to be the white-out bottle, but we said, "Listen, nobody will know who you are." We used a cardboard ice cream container to make the cap, with just eye holes to see out.

So I remember being in the grand reception area with the big polished table, sitting there with the governor, and there was this white-out bottle. The governor really supported pay equity, but he didn't get it about the white-out. I'm sure he didn't have a clue what white-out was. And the white-out bottle couldn't sit down—we kind of failed to think about everything, there she was in this cardboard tube that didn't bend.

Another thing we did that was fun, that got a lot of media attention, was our annual Boss Award. We were getting applications from people about the crummiest thing they had to do for their boss, and we got amazing things. One woman wrote to us about her boss making her put out her hand so he could flick his cigarette ashes into it. We didn't even mention that one, because it was so atrocious.

There were women that were expected to clean up the bathrooms. One woman submitted a nomination, she was working for a law office. Her boss would come into the office on Mondays and make her go to the nearby laundromat with his clothes. She had to do his laundry. We called it the "Jockey" award.

But the best one was this executive who was having a romance. When he traveled out of the country, he would have his secretary call up his girlfriend and repeat all these love messages over the phone. The secretary found this totally obnoxious. She had gone through all the proper channels at work about getting him to stop. She talked to him directly on numerous occasions, told him she didn't like it, but he wouldn't do anything.

So she came to us. When the day arrives, here we are with these TV cameras rolling. We give him this award, and he doesn't realize this is a putdown until we're halfway through.

---

* "Wite-out" is a brand of typewriter correction fluid.

On National Secretary's Day, we would try to draw attention to our situation. We were always in competition with the Professional Secretaries International. They wanted to make sure people knew that *we* were the rank and file, and *they* were "executive assistants." We had a lot of things in common, but there were definitely two schools of thought here. We were the rabble-rousers. But they secretly, in their hearts, loved what we were doing.

For one Secretaries' Day, I analyzed the wages at Minneapolis City Hall. The city's head of affirmative action gave me all the information. I showed graphically the wage rates and the occupational segregation, all that horrible stuff.

The numbers were really dismal. Less than 2 percent of the females working for the city made over $30,000 a year. Dismal. And about 75 percent of the males were earning that amount of money. The men were making all the bucks. It didn't matter if they were sweeping the streets or doing management, they got themselves into high-paid positions. And the women, of course, were all clustered in the low-paid positions.

After that, the city told the affirmative-action director he couldn't ever give that kind of information to anybody, ever again.

We raised that whole issue of comparable worth/pay equity. When we started, people had no idea what we were talking about. "Are they nuts?" The other thing we were really ahead of our time on: we were talking about worker safety, the tight-building syndrome, the effects of computer terminals.

In fact we had a bill at the state legislature. Was it 1982? Just a little bill to give work breaks for people who worked at computer terminals all day. Oh, my gosh! The manufacturers' association, IBM, everybody sent out the big guns. We got a few votes in the senate employment committee, but we didn't get any votes in the house employment committee. Not a one. I was flattered that the big guns came out, though.

We were just ahead of our time, there's no question about it. The word "ergonomic" is not so foreign to people now, they understand about chairs and positions and shields on the screens and tilting them. The computers themselves are better, they're more flexible than they used to be in the old days.

A lot of people thought we were organizing a union, but that wasn't the case. In fact, the women dealt with so much unfairness and sexism during the day that the last thing some wanted to do was to become part of another institution where sexism was just as rampant. And they couldn't fathom paying union dues on top of the rotten wages they were already getting.

But to other members, unions made great sense. I ran into one of our former members the other day. She's a union organizer for clerical workers at the university now.

We never got much support from unions, except for the Coalition of Labor Union Women. The male-dominated unions saw us as a threat. Someone who was working at the AFL-CIO called me up one time, shortly after we started. I was working in this little cubicle all by myself. The AFL-CIO person just screamed at me, because we had the gall to put out a flyer without the union bug. Well, I didn't know what a union bug was, and the labor for the flyer was donated.

A lot of the Working Women members did not identify as feminists. For clerical workers who were not making much money, maybe had a couple of kids at home, had to pay the rent or the mortgage, maybe the husband isn't too well off either . . . you don't see yourself as part of a social movement. You see yourself as struggling to survive. You just want to do a little better.

It wasn't until I got involved with establishing Working Women that I started to understand feminism myself. Sometime in there I said to myself, "I guess I *am* one!"

"GOOD HUSBANDS ARE GOOD LEADERS"
JERRY FALWELL

Ronald Reagan came to office in 1980 with significant help from the Moral Majority, a political action group composed of conservative, fundamentalist Christians. Founded in 1979 by tele-evangelist Jerry Falwell, the group lent financial and political support to conservative candidates and lobbied for prayer in the public schools, the teaching of creationism, and the defeat of the Equal Rights Amendment (ERA). The Moral Majority also opposed the legalization of abortion and any legislation to prevent discrimination against gay and lesbian Americans. It dissolved in 1989.

Like Phyllis Schlafly (see "The Positive Woman" in chapter 3), Falwell made a career out of lobbying against the ERA and legalized abortion, and promulgated a highly traditional view of the family, with the husband and father as leader of his own family flock. Falwell's strongly denominational view of social and family issues, as evinced in the following document, greatly helped to influence public policy in the Reagan Administration.

SOURCE: Jerry Falwell, *Listen, America!* (Garden City, N.Y.: Doubleday, 1980), pp. 121–23, 128–30. Copyright © 1980 by Jerry Falwell. Used by permission of Doubleday, a division of Random House, Inc.

THERE ARE ONLY three institutions God ordained in the Bible: government, the church, and the family. The family is the God-ordained institution of the marriage of one man and one woman together for a lifetime with their biological or adopted children. The family is the fundamental building block and the basic unit of our society, and its continued health is a prerequisite for a healthy and prosperous nation. No nation has ever been stronger than the families within her. America's families are her strength and they symbolize the miracle of America.

Families in search of freedom to educate their children according to religious principles originally settled this land. Families in search of religious freedom, determined to work and enjoy the fruits of their labor, tamed this wild continent and built the highest living standard in the world. Families educating their children in moral principles have carried on the traditions of this free republic. Historically the greatness of America can be measured in the greatness of her families. But in the past twenty years a tremendous change has taken place.

There is a vicious assault upon the American family. More television programs depict homes of divorced or of single parents than depict the traditional family. Nearly every major family-theme TV program openly justifies divorce, homosexuality, and adultery. Some sociologists believe that the family unit, as we know it, could disappear by the year 2000. Increased divorce and remarriage have broken family loyalty, unity, and communications. We find increased insecurity in children who are the victims of divorced parents. Many of these children harden themselves to the possibility of genuine love, for fear that they will be hurt again. Their insulated lives make them poor future candidates for marriage, and many young people have no desire to marry whatsoever. But I believe that most Americans remain deeply committed to the idea of the family as a sacred institution. A minority of people in this country is trying to destroy what is most important to the majority, and the sad fact is that the majority is allowing it to happen. Americans must arise and accept the challenge of preserving our cherished family heritage.

I quote again from the Washington *Post* poll of December 16, 1979, "Americans' Hopes and Fears About the Future": "To be alone—those are dreadful words to most Americans, expressed repeatedly in this era supposedly dedicated to self." I recently read that one of our leading political commentators said that loneliness will be a major political issue in the 1980s. God said in the Book of Genesis that it was not good that man should be alone. God made men and women with the need for fellowship and the desire for a family life.

The home was the first institution established by God. God's program cannot be improved. In the Book of Genesis in the Bible we find these words: "And the LORD God caused a deep sleep to fall upon Adam, and he slept: And he took one of his ribs, and closed up the flesh instead thereof; And the rib, which the LORD God had taken from man, made he a woman, and brought her unto the man. And Adam said, This is now bone of my bones, and flesh of my flesh: She shall be called Woman, because she was taken out of Man. Therefore shall a man leave his father and his mother, and shall cleave unto his wife: And they shall be one flesh. And they were both naked, the man and his wife, and were not ashamed." (Gn. 2:21–25) Nothing is more right than a man and a woman joined together in holy wedlock. As a family, they are in submission to the Lordship of Jesus Christ—the most heavenly thing on earth.

A commentator from one of the major networks once asked me, "What right do you Baptists have to promote your ideas about the family being the acceptable style for all of humanity?" I replied that it was not Baptists who started the family; it was God Almighty, and He is not a Baptist. God made a helpmeet for man. The family is that husband-wife relationship that God established in the Garden of Eden, later producing children. God gave Adam authority and dominion over the creation and told him to multiply and replenish the earth. The family is that basic unit that God established, not only to populate but also to control and contain the earth. The happiest people on the face of this earth are those who are part of great homes and families where they are loved, protected, and shielded. When I have been out having a long, hard day, often in a hostile environment, it is great to walk into my home, to close the front door, and to know that inside the home there are a wife and children who love me. Home is a haven to which I run from the troubles of this world, a place of security and warmth, where each member has the knowledge of belonging. Most of the people who are leading the antifamily efforts in America are failures in the family business because they have not committed their lives to Jesus Christ and so do not know His perfect plan for their lives.

The single most important influence on the life of a child is his family.

The strength and stability of families determine the vitality and moral life of society. Too many men and women, trying to protect their own sinfulness and selfishness, are for the desires of self-gratification destroying the very foundation of the family, as we know it.

In the war against the family today, we find an arsenal of weapons. The first weapon is the cult of the playboy, the attitude that has permeated our society in these last twenty years. This playboy philosophy tells men that they do not have to be committed to their wife and to their children, but that they should be some kind of a "cool, free swinger." Sexual promiscuity has become the life style of America. . . .

The answer to stable families with children who grow up to be great leaders in our society and who themselves have stable homes will not come from [. . .] more part-time work for fathers and mothers, or parental leaves of absence, or thirty-hour weeks, or parental co-operatives and other forms of sharing childraising responsibilities. It will come only as men and women in America get in a right relationship to God and His principles for the home. Statistics show that couples who profess a born-again relationship have much happier, healthier marriages. In a January 22, 1979, *U.S. News & World Report* interview with Dr. Robert B. Taylor, specialist in family medicine, entitled, "Behind the Surge in Broken Marriages," Dr. Taylor says: "We find that couples who are actively religious tend to have more stable marriages. Worshiping together and attending church activities help develop strong couple bonds that are very hard to break." The Bible gives men and women God's plan.

Scripture declares that God has called the father to be the spiritual leader in his family. The husband is not to be the dictator of the family, but the spiritual leader. There is a great difference between a dictator and a leader. People follow dictators because they are forced to do so. They follow leaders because they want to. Good husbands who are godly men are good leaders. Their wives and children want to follow them and be under their protection. The husband is to be the decisionmaker and the one who motivates his family with love. The Bible says that husbands are to love their wives even as Christ also loved the church and gave Himself for it. A man is to be a servant to his family while at the same time being a leader. A husband and father is first of all to be a provider for his family. He is to take care of their physical needs and do this honestly by working and earning an income to meet those needs. Then he is to be a protector. He is to protect them not only from physical harm but from spiritual harm as well. He is to protect them from television programs and from magazines that would hurt them. Child abuse involves much more than physical abuse. We have little children today who are growing up in homes where mothers and fathers literally hate each other. Those children are living in a constant perpetual hate war that is destroying them. A father has a God-given responsibility to lead his family in their worship of God. A father is to be a godly example to his wife and children; he must be consistently living a good life style before his family. He is to pray with his family and read to them from the Word of God. A man cannot do these things if he does not know Jesus Christ as his Lord and Savior. The Bible says, "But as many as received him, to them gave he power to become the sons of God, even to them that believe on his name." (Jn. 1:12) The love of God is available to every man, and God has made an offer to us and asked us to receive the gift of salvation. Until men are in right relationship with God, there is no hope for righting our families of our nation. Because we have weak men we have weak homes, and children from these homes will probably grow up to become weak parents leading even weaker homes.

Dr. Harold M. Voth, M.D., senior psychiatrist and psychoanalyst at the Menninger Foundation, Topeka, Kansas, has said, "The correct development of a child requires the commitment of mature parents who understand either consciously or intuitively that children do not grow up like Topsy. Good mothering from birth on provides the psychological core upon which all subsequent development takes place. Mothering is probably the most important function on earth. This is a full-time, demanding task. It requires a high order of gentleness, commitment, steadiness, capacity to give, and many other qualities. A woman needs a good man by her side so she will not be distracted and depleted, thus making it possible for her to provide rich humanness to her babies and children. Her needs must be met by the man, and above all she must be made secure. A good man brings out the best in a woman, who can then do her best for the children. Similarly, a good woman brings out the best in a man, who can then do his best for his wife and children. Children bring out the best in their parents. All together they make a family, a place where people of great strength are shaped, who in turn make strong societies. Our nation was built by such people." . . .

In the mid-1970s an informal group of Illinois women organized House-wives for ERA to counteract the idea that housewives were opposed to the Equal Rights Amendment (ERA). In 1979 the organization changed its name to the Homemakers' Equal Rights Association (HERA) to improve the homemaker's legal, economic, and social status by passage of the ERA and other measures. By 1981 there were chapters of HERA in twenty states. The organization sponsored workshops, seminars, and a speakers' bureau on behalf of the ERA and published a quarterly newsletter.

The organization's initials, HERA, happen to be the name of the Greek goddess of home and hearth, a symbolism that HERA's members roundly embraced. Following are the bylaws of the organization. Note the emphasis on the equal value of the homemaker's work to the wage earner's work outside of the home, and the assertion that the ERA will help improve the homemaker's legal standing and strengthen family life. HERA creatively grafts feminist strategies—an awareness of the social and legal handicaps that women have traditionally faced in marriage and support for the ERA to correct those handicaps—to promote traditional gender roles for women.

SOURCE: HERA charter reproduced in Anne Bowen Follis, *I'm Not a Women's Libber, But: Other Confessions of a Christian Feminist* (Nashville, Tenn.: Abingdon Press, 1981), pp. 127–28. Used by permission.

ARTICLE I

Name and Symbol

The name of this organization shall be The Homemakers' Equal Rights Association, hereinafter to be abbreviated to HERA. The symbol of the organization shall be the pink rose.

ARTICLE II

Beliefs of HERA

Section A. We believe that the homemaker makes a valuable contribution to our society.

Section B. We believe that the institution of the family is vital to our society, and that the nurturing and care of the homemaker is important to keeping the family unit healthy.

Section C. We believe that the principle underlying the law in many states which regards the wife as the property of her husband places the homemaker in an unfair, precarious position under the law, and is destructive to the family unit.

Section D. We believe that laws should recognize the homemaker's non-monetary contribution to the family welfare as being of equal value to that of the wage earner, and that the married woman should be recognized by law to be a full and equal partner to her husband.

ARTICLE III

Goals of HERA

Section A. Because the Equal Rights Amendment will establish that the married woman is a partner in the family enterprise; because it will remove a married woman from the legal mercy of her husband, and assure her of equal justice under the law; and because it will serve to raise the legal status of the homemaker and strengthen the family unit: Our primary goal shall be ratification of the Equal Rights Amendment.

1. In this regard we are committed to establishing a membership of individuals who favor ratification of the Equal Rights Amendment and support our goals in order to demonstrate to lawmakers and the general public that homemakers do want and need the Equal Rights Amendment.

2. In unratified states to actively work toward ratification through lobbying and educational efforts, and to support efforts to elect candidates who support the Equal Rights Amendment.

3. In ratified states to actively participate in lobbying and education efforts to protect ratification; to keep public interest in the amendment alive; and to support the efforts of unratified states.

Section B. To promote full and equal partnership under the law for homemakers.

Section C. To promote recognition, in government, in business, and in all areas of society, of the importance of work done in the home.

"WE ARE GATHERING BECAUSE
LIFE ON THE PRECIPICE IS INTOLERABLE"
WOMEN'S PENTAGON ACTION

In 1981 President Ronald Reagan took office promising a massive buildup of American military might. His Star Wars program, an antiballistic missile defense system, cost tens of millions of dollars and was financed in part by deep cuts in social welfare programs. On November 16, 1980, shortly after Reagan's election, about two thousand women gathered at the Pentagon to protest the proliferation of arms, especially nuclear arms. The march was originally conceived at an ecofeminist conference. Ecofeminists apply feminist principles to concern for the environment. For them, patriarchal forms of power are the root cause of women's oppression and also of war and other forms of violence, including the destruction of natural resources. The activists emphasize what they perceive to be the unity of women's experiences and concerns, and they eschew any hierarchical forms of political protest. Instead, their form of protest is a direct-action group endeavor with no keynote speakers or leaders.

Following are excerpts from the statement that came out of the Pentagon gathering. Subsequent protests took place at the Pentagon and in New York City, and the Women's Pentagon Action also spawned women's peace camps at military bases around the world, from England and Italy to Japan and elsewhere. Like Women Strike for Peace (see "We Saw Women as a Vehicle for Peace" in chapter 2), the participants in the Women's Pentagon Action express their outrage as women—mothers, wives, sisters, and daughters—at the cycle of destruction engulfing the planet. The statement also expresses their feminist vision of a world order free of the ills generated by what they perceive to be the violence and exploitation of a privileged male elite.

SOURCE: Women's Pentagon Action. Copyright 2000 Crime and Social Justice Associates. Reprinted in *Social Justice* 27 (winter 2000) and by courtesy of Margo Okazawa-Rey.

WE ARE GATHERING at the Pentagon on November 16 because we fear for our lives. We fear for the life of this planet, our Earth, and the life of the children who are our human future.

We are mostly women who come from the northeastern region of our United States. We are city women who know the wreckage and fear of city streets; we are country women who grieve the loss of the small farm and have lived on the poisoned earth. We are young and older, we are married, single, lesbian. We live in different kinds of households: in groups, families, alone, or as single parents.

We work at a variety of jobs. We are students, teachers, factory workers, office workers, lawyers, farmers, doctors, builders, waitresses, weavers, poets, engineers, home workers, electricians, artists, and blacksmiths. We are all daughters and sisters.

We have come here to mourn and rage and defy the Pentagon because it is the workplace of the imperial power that threatens us all. Every day while we work, study, and love, the colonels and generals who are planning our annihilation walk calmly in and out of the doors of its five sides. They have accumulated over 30,000 nuclear bombs, at the rate of three to six bombs every day. They are determined to produce the billion-dollar MX missile. They are creating a technology called Stealth—the invisible, unperceivable arsenal. They have revised the cruel old killer, nerve gas. They have proclaimed Directive 59, which asks for "small nuclear wars, prolonged but limited." The Soviet Union has worked hard to keep up with U.S. initiatives. We can destroy each other's cities, towns, schools, and children many times over. The United States has sent "advisors," money, and arms to El Salvador and Guatemala to enable those juntas to massacre their own people.

The very same men, the same legislative committees that offer trillions of dollars to the Pentagon have brutally cut day care, children's lunches, and battered women's shelters. The same men have concocted the Family Protection Act, which will mandate the strictly patriarchal family and thrust federal authority into our home life. They have prevented passage of the Equal Rights Amendment's simple statement and supported the Human Life Amendment, which will deprive all women of choice and many women of life itself.

We are in the hands of men whose power and wealth have separated them from the reality of daily life and from the imagination. We are right to be afraid.

At the same time, our cities are in ruins, bankrupt; they suffer the devastation of war. Hospitals are closed, our schools deprived of books and teachers. Our Black and Latino youth are without decent work. They will be forced, drafted to become the cannon fodder for the very power that oppresses them. Whatever help the poor receive is cut or withdrawn to feed the Pentagon, which needs about $500,000,000 a day for its murderous health. It extracted $157 billion dollars last year from our own tax money, $1,800 from a family of four. . . .

We women are gathering because life on the precipice is intolerable. We want to know what anger in these men, what fear, which can only be satisfied by destruction, what coldness of heart and ambition drives their days. We want to know because we do not want that dominance, which is exploitative and murderous in international relations, and so dangerous to women and children at home—and we do not want that sickness transferred by the violent society through the fathers to the sons. . . .

We want enough good food, decent housing, communities with clean air and water, and good care for our children while we work. We want work that is useful to a sensible society. There is a modest technology to minimize drudgery and restore joy to labor. We are determined to use skills and knowledge from which we have been excluded—like plumbing or engineering or physics or composing. We intend to form women's groups or unions that will demand safe workplaces that are free of sexual harassment, and equal pay for work of comparable value. We respect the work women have done in caring for the young, their own and others, in maintaining a physical and spiritual shelter against the greedy and militaristic society. In our old age we expect our experience, our skills, to be honored and used.

We want health care that respects and understands our bodies. Physically challenged sisters must have access to gatherings, actions, happy events, and work. For this, ramps must be added to stairs and we must become readers, signers, and supporting arms. So close, so many, why have we allowed ourselves not to know them?

We want an education for children that tells the true story of our women's lives, which describes the earth as our home to be cherished, to be fed as well as harvested.

We want to be free from violence in our streets and in our houses. One in every three of us will be raped in her lifetime. The pervasive social power of the masculine ideal and the greed of the pornographer have come together to steal our freedom, so that whole neighborhoods and the life of the evening and night have been taken from us. For too many women, the dark country road and the city alley have concealed the rapist. We want the night returned: the light of the moon, special in the cycle of our female lives, the stars, and the gaiety of the city streets.

We want the right to have or not to have children—we do not want gangs of politicians and medical men to say we must be sterilized for the country's good. We know that this technique is the racists' method for controlling populations. Nor do we want to be prevented from having an abortion when we need one. We think this freedom should be available to poor women as it always has been to the rich. We want to be free to love whomever we choose.

We will live with women or with men or we will live alone. We will not allow the oppression of lesbians. One sex or one sexual preference must not dominate another. . . .

We want to see the pathology of racism ended in our time. It has been the imperial arrogance of white male power that has separated us from the suffering and wisdom of our sisters in Asia, Africa, South America, and in our own country. Many North American women look down on the minority nearest them: the Black, the Hispanic, the Jew, the Native American, the Asian, and the immigrant. Racism has offered them privilege and convenience; they often fail to see that they themselves have bent to the unnatural authority and violence of men in government, at work, at home. Privilege does not increase knowledge or spirit or understanding. There can be no peace while one race dominates another, one people, one nation, or where one sex despises another. . . .

We want an end to the arms race. No more bombs. No more amazing inventions for death. . . .

We know there is a healthy, sensible, loving way to live and we intend to live that way in our neighborhoods and on our farms in these United States, and among our sisters and brothers in all the countries of the world.

"LIBERATION . . . ISN'T FINISHED"
BETTY FRIEDAN

Having sparked the resurgence of feminism with The Feminist Mystique *(see "The Problem That Has No Name" in chapter 3), Betty Friedan began to rethink some of the assumptions that shaped the thesis of that seminal book and helped to guide the movement in its early years—notably that meaningful paid work outside the home is the only antidote to the malaise of full-time domesticity. In 1981 she published* The Second Stage, *both an inquiry into where the movement had gone awry in not addressing women's concerns about balancing family life with paid employment and a blueprint for charting a new course. In the second stage, proclaims Friedan, women must regard men as their partners, not as their nemesis, in seeking ways to manage family responsibilities and workplace demands. Friedan claims that family concerns must now be at the center of feminist discourse. That is, feminists must acknowledge women's desire to be parents as well as professionals. As she did in* The Feminine Mystique, *Friedan primarily addresses an educated middle-class readership and offers little understanding of the very real problems of working-class men and women who cannot choose to work part time and who do not have access to quality, affordable child care. Nevertheless, like her first book,* The Second Stage *was a daring, bold, and thought-provoking meditation on women's, and men's, lives in the late twentieth century.*

SOURCE: Betty Friedan, *The Second Stage* (New York: Summit Books, 1981), pp. 15–41. Copyright © 1981, 1986, 1991, 1998 by Betty Friedan. Reprinted by permission of Curtis Brown, Ltd.

IN THE FIRST STAGE, our aim was full participation, power and voice in the mainstream, inside the party, the political process, the professions, the business world. Do women change, inevitably discard the radiant, inviolate, idealized feminist dream, once they get inside and begin to share that power, and do they then operate on the same terms as men? Can women, will women even try to, change the terms?

What are the limits and the true potential of women's power? I believe that the women's movement, in the political sense, is both less and more powerful than we realize. I believe that the personal is both more and less political than our own rhetoric ever implied. I believe that we have to break through our own *feminist* mystique now to come to terms with the new reality of our personal and political experience, and to move into the second stage. . . .

The second stage cannot be seen in terms of women alone, our separate person-hood or equality with men.

The second stage involves coming to new terms with the family—new terms with love and with work.

The second stage may not even be a women's movement. Men may be at the cutting edge of the second stage.

The second stage has to transcend the battle for equal power in institutions. The second stage will restructure institutions and transform the nature of power itself.

The second stage may even now be evolving, out of or even aside from what we have thought of as our battle. . . .

THE YOUNGER WOMEN have the most questions:

"How can I have it all? Do I *really* have to choose?"

"How can I have the career I want, and the kind of marriage I want, and be a good Mother?"

"How can I get him to share more responsibility at home? Why do I always have to be the one with the children, making the decisions at home?"

"I can't count on marriage for my security—look what happened to my mother—but can I get all my security from my career?"

"Can I make it in a man's world, doing it the man's way? What other way is there? But what is it doing to me? Do I want to be like men?"

"What do I have to give up? What are the tradeoffs?"

"Will the jobs open to me now still be there if I stop to have children?"

"Does it really work, that business of 'quality, not quantity' of time with the children? How much is enough?"

"How can I fill my loneliness, except with a man?"

"Do men really want an equal woman?"

"Why are men today so gray and lifeless, compared to women? How can I find a man I can really look up to?"

"How can I play the sex kitten now? Can I ever find a man who will let me be myself?"

"If I put off having a baby till I'm thirty-eight, and can call my own shots on the job, will I ever have kids?"

"How can I juggle it all?"

"How can I put it all together?"

"Can I risk losing myself in marriage?" . . .

This is the jumping-off point to the second stage, I believe: these conflicts and fears and compelling needs women feel about the choice to have children now and about success in the careers they now seek. . . .

There is no going back. The women's movement was necessary. But the liberation that began with the women's movement isn't finished. The equality we fought for isn't livable, isn't workable, isn't comfortable in the terms that structured our battle. The first stage, the women's movement, was fought within, and against, and defined by that old structure of unequal, polarized male and female sex roles. But to continue reacting against that structure is still to be defined and limited by its terms. What's needed now is to transcend those terms, transform the structure itself. . . .

How do we surmount the reaction that threatens to destroy the gains we thought we had already won in the first stage of the women's movement? How do we surmount our own reaction, which shadows our feminism and our femininity (we blush even to use that word now)? How do we transcend the polarization between women and women and between women and men, to achieve the new human wholeness that is the promise of feminism, and get on with solving the concrete, practical, everyday problems of living, working and loving as equal persons? This is the personal and political business of the second stage.

"THE BEST-KEPT SECRET ABOUT MEN"
ELLEN KREIDMAN

In 1981 Ellen Kreidman, a Southern California homemaker and motivational speaker, rented a small office, furnished it classroom style, and began offering courses on how to improve flagging marriages. She called her course "Light His Fire" and soon expanded it into a six-week workshop on self-esteem and self-improvement as well as on strategies to enhance married life. Several years later, to complement her women's classes, she began teaching men how to "Light Her Fire." She then wrote a book for women who could not attend her program and also for graduates who wanted a "refresher course." While the book offers some sound strategies for achieving personal and professional goals and for creating better lines of communication between partners, many of the suggestions and "practice exercises" that Kreidman offers rely on manipulative flattery and stereotypes of male-female behavior. Nevertheless, the book went on to become a national best-seller, resulted in a highly successful paperback edition and book-and-cassette set, which sold over sixty thousand copies, and continues to generate avid popular support.

SOURCE: Ellen Kreidman, *Light His Fire: How to Keep Your Man Passionately and Hopelessly in Love with You* (New York: Villard Books, 1989) pp. 59–69. Copyright © 1989 by Ellen Kreidman. Used by permission of Random House, Inc.

A WOMAN WHO KNOWS that inside every man, no matter how old, how successful, or how powerful, there is a little boy who wants to be loved and to feel as if he's special is a woman who knows a powerful secret. A man wants to know that he matters to you more than anyone else in the world. He wants to matter to you more than your parents, more than your children, more than your friends, and more than your job.

If he could verbalize it, a man would say, "Tell me why I make a difference. Tell me why I matter to you. Tell me over and over again. Don't tell me just once. Tell me every day of my life. Keep complimenting me and recognize my strengths. I want to be your knight in shining armor. I want to be your hero."...

When you let a man know you value an ability or strength that he doesn't even know he possesses, he wants to prove you right. . . .

Instead of being critical, start to notice your mate's positive traits. Notice what is wonderful and good about him. Find at least one thing to compliment him on every day, no matter how small. Even something as simple as telling him you love his smile, or that every time he walks into the room he makes it brighter, besides making him feel good and look forward to coming home, will make him want to please you.

Most of our men come from environments with varying degrees of positive reinforcement. A man who grew up with very few compliments will need double the dose, and anyone who brags, boasts, or stretches the truth needs three times the praise that an ordinary person does. Remember this rule:

The more I like myself, the less I have to impress or convince you how great I am. The less I like myself, the more I have to convince people how wonderful I am. The degree to which I either like or dislike myself has a great deal to do with how much or how little praise I received as a child.

If your mate was deprived of praise as a child, be prepared to give him *all* that he's been missing. I mean, I want you to "pour it on" so thick that anyone else would think you'd gone mad! What you'll find is that it is not too thick and it's not too much. It is never, ever "too much" to appreciate, praise, and compliment another human being. . . .

COMPLIMENT HIM FOR THE THINGS HE DOES:

- If he washes the car—
- Tell him how much you appreciate the pride he takes in keeping the car clean.
- If he fixes the car—
- Tell him how lucky you are to have someone with so much mechanical ability.
- If he fixes things around the house—
- Sing, "It's so nice to have a man around the house."
- If he exercises—
- Tell him how wonderful it is to have a man who is in great shape and takes pride in his body.
- If he's taking classes—
- Tell him you love his quest for knowledge.
- If he's on any volunteer committees—
- Tell him how wonderful he is to give his time to causes.
- If he plays with the children—
- Tell him how lucky the children are to have a father like him.
- If he plays with the dog—
- Tell him how terrific it is to have a strong man who also has a tender side.
- If he earns a great deal of money—
- Tell him you never dreamed you'd have the lifestyle he has provided for you.

COMPLIMENT HIM ON THE THINGS HE SAYS

- If he's funny—
- Tell him you love his sense of humor and how great it makes you feel.
- If he's complimentary—
- Tell him how lucky you are to have a man who notices.
- If he's always dreaming—
- Tell him you love him because he is goal-oriented and thinking of the future.
- If he solves a problem—
- Tell him how much his logic improves the quality of your life.
- If he's very verbal—
- Tell him he's the "life of the party," how much you love to listen to him, and how he always makes people feel at ease.
- If he's nonverbal—
- Tell him what a good listener he is, and what a calming influence he has on you. . . .

BE AN ACTRESS

What if you tend to be a negative person and you're saying, "I can't possibly do this, it's just *not me*"? Well then, don't be you. Be someone else! Make believe you're a positive person who easily notices everything wonderful about your man. . . .

. . . Become a woman who is indispensable to your man and his self-image, and you will be a woman to whom a man feels deeply committed.

Action Assignment #2

Take out another index card and write on it:

Make sure that once a day
I give my love a compliment.
Compliment what he does,
What he says, or what he stands for.
Tell him how much he matters to me.

On the same card, make a list of some of the famous characters who have been especially masculine. Find opportunities to compare your mate to these characters, saying something like, "Oh, honey, you're as strong as the Incredible Hulk," after he does something that requires masculine strength.

Other examples are:

1) Tarzan
2) King Kong
3) Rocky
4) Rambo
5) Superman
6) Casanova
7) Adonis
8) Latin lover (if it applies. On second thought, even if it doesn't apply!)

"AN ETHIC OF CARE"
CAROL GILLIGAN

In the early 1980s psychologist Carol Gilligan challenged accepted views of women's psychological development and sparked a debate that reached beyond academia over the social implications of women's ways of forming ethical judgments. Basing her views on observations of children puzzling over ethical dilemmas, Gilligan, in her groundbreaking study, In a Different Voice, *argued that the accepted criteria for assessing ethical standards—in which women's wish to please or assist others is regarded as inferior to men's alleged ability to apply abstract principles—do not take into account or, at best, dismiss women's ways of forming moral judgments. In her observations of children, Gilligan noted that girls were more inclined to assess the impact of a course of action on the people involved or recognize altruistic motives, even when the action taken was morally questionable, while the boys relied on self-defined notions of right and wrong. Consequently, claimed Gilligan, women's ways of formulating ethical standards were different from men's—"relational" rather than abstract—and took into account the needs and situation of the people involved.*

Gilligan claimed that the differences between women's and men's ethical approaches were culturally constructed, not rooted in biological or genetic makeup, and that women's ethical standards were as valid as men's. Many feminists seized upon her findings as evidence that women brought a unique ethic of caring into their thoughts and actions and that this ethic was needed at every level of public life. Some critics, however, charged that Gilligan used a small sample to make sweeping generalizations and that her ideas helped set feminism back by casting women as essentially maternal figures. In the popular media, as well as in academic circles, Gilligan's views aroused controversy and debate over these very issues and added a new vocabulary to public discourse.

SOURCE: Reprinted by permission of the publisher from "Images of Relationship" in Carol Gilligan, *In a Different Voice: Psychological Theory and Women's Development* (Cambridge: Harvard University Press, 1982), pp. 24–32. Copyright © 1982, 1993 by Carol Gilligan.

IN 1914, with his essay "On Narcissism," Freud swallows his distaste at the thought of "abandoning observation for barren theoretical controversy" and extends his map of the psychological domain. Tracing the development of the capacity to love, which he equates with maturity and psychic health, he locates its origins in the contrast between love for the mother and love for the self. But in thus dividing the world of love into narcissism and "object" relationships, he finds that while men's development becomes clearer, women's becomes increasingly opaque. The problem arises because the contrast between mother and self yields two different images of relationships. Relying on the imagery of men's lives in charting the course of human growth, Freud is unable to trace in women the development of relationships, morality, or a clear sense of self. This difficulty in fitting the logic of his theory to women's experience leads him in the end to set women apart, marking their relationships, like their sexual life, as "a 'dark continent' for psychology."

Thus the problem of interpretation that shadows the understanding of women's development arises from the differences observed in their experience of relationships. To Freud, though living surrounded by women and otherwise seeing so much and so well, women's relationships seemed increasingly mysterious, difficult to discern, and hard to describe. While this mystery indicates how theory can blind observation, it also suggests that development in women is masked by a particular conception of human relationships. Since the imagery of relationships shapes the narrative of human development, the inclusion of women, by changing that imagery, implies a change in the entire account.

The shift in imagery that creates the problem in interpreting women's development is elucidated by the moral judgments of two eleven-year-old children, a boy and a girl, who see, in the same dilemma, two very different moral problems. While current theory brightly illuminates the line and the logic of the boy's thought, it casts scant light on that of the girl. The choice of a girl whose moral judgments elude existing categories of developmental assessment is meant to highlight the issue of interpretation rather than to exemplify sex differences per se. Adding a new line of interpretation, based on the imagery of the girl's thought, makes it possible not only to see development where previously development was not discerned but also to consider differences in the understanding of relationships without scaling these differences from better to worse.

The two children were in the same sixth-grade class at school and were participants in the rights and responsibilities study, designed to explore different conceptions of morality and self. The sample selected for this study was chosen to focus the variables of gender and age while maximizing developmental potential by holding constant, at a high level, the factors of intelligence, education, and social class that have been associated with moral development, at least as measured by existing scales. The two children in question, Amy and Jake, were both bright and articulate and, at least in their eleven-year-old aspirations, resisted easy categories of sex-role stereotyping, since Amy aspired to become a scientist while Jake preferred English to math. Yet their moral judgments seem initially to confirm familiar notions about differences between the sexes, suggesting that the edge girls have on moral development during the early school years gives way at puberty with the ascendance of formal logical thought in boys.

The dilemma that these eleven-year-olds were asked to resolve was one in the series devised by [Laurence] Kohlberg to measure moral development in adolescence by presenting a conflict between moral norms and exploring the logic of its resolution. In this particular dilemma, a man named Heinz considers whether or not to steal a drug which he cannot afford to buy in order to save the life of his wife. In the standard format of Kohlberg's interviewing procedure, the description of the dilemma itself—Heinz's predicament, the wife's disease, the druggist's refusal to lower his price—is followed by the question. "Should Heinz steal the drug?" The reasons for and against stealing are then explored through a series of questions that vary and extend the parameters of the dilemma in a way designed to reveal the underlying structure of moral thought.

Jake, at eleven, is clear from the outset that Heinz should steal the drug. Constructing the dilemma, as Kohlberg did, as a conflict between the values of property and life, he discerns the logical priority of life and uses that logic to justify his choice:

For one thing a human life is worth more than money, and if the druggist only makes $1,000, he is still going to live, but if Heinz doesn't steal the drug, his wife is going to die. (*Why is life worth more than money?*) Because the druggist can get a thousand dollars later from rich people with cancer, but Heinz can't get his wife again. (*Why not?*) Because people are all different and so you couldn't get Heinz's wife again.

Asked whether Heinz should steal the drug if he does not love his wife. Jake replies that he should, saying that not only is there "a difference between hating and killing," but also, if Heinz were caught, "the judge would probably think it was the right thing to do." Asked about the fact that, in stealing, Heinz would be breaking the law, he says that "the laws have mistakes, and you can't go writing up a law for everything that you can imagine."

Thus, while taking the law into account and recognizing its function in maintaining social order (the judge, Jake says, "should give Heinz the lightest possible sentence"), he also sees the law as man-made and therefore subject to error and change. Yet his judgment that Heinz should steal the drug, like his view of the law as having mistakes, rests on the assumption of agreement, a societal consensus around moral values that allows one to know and expect others to recognize what is "the right thing to do."

Fascinated by the power of logic, this eleven-year-old boy locates truth in math, which, he says, is "the only thing that is totally logical." Considering the moral dilemma to be "sort of like a math problem with humans," he sets it up as an equation and proceeds to work out the solution. Since his solution is rationally derived, he assumes that anyone following reason would arrive at the same conclusion and thus that a judge would also consider stealing to be the right thing for Heinz to do. Yet he is also aware of the limits of logic. Asked whether there is a right answer to moral problems. Jake replies that "there can only be right and wrong in judgment," since the parameters of action are variable and complex. Illustrating how actions undertaken with the best of intentions can eventuate in the most disastrous of consequences, he says, "like if you give an old lady your seat on the trolley, if you are in a trolley crash and that seat goes through the window, it might be that reason that the old lady dies."

Theories of developmental psychology illuminate well the position of this child, standing at the juncture of childhood and adolescence, at what Piaget describes as the pinnacle of childhood intelligence, and beginning through thought to discover a wider universe of possibility. The moment of preadolescence is caught by the conjunction of formal operational thought with a description of self still anchored in the factual parameters of his childhood world—his age, his town, his father's occupation, the substance of his likes, dislikes, and beliefs. Yet as his self-description radiates the self-confidence of a child who has arrived, in Erikson's terms, at a favorable balance of industry over inferiority—competent, sure of himself, and knowing well the rules of the game—so his emergent capacity for formal thought, his ability to think about thinking and to reason things out in a logical way, frees him from dependence on authority and allows him to find solutions to problems by himself.

This emergent autonomy follows the trajectory that Kohlberg's six stages of moral development trace, a three-level progression from an egocentric understanding of fairness based on individual need (stages one and two), to a conception of fairness anchored in the shared conventions of societal agreement (stages three and four), and finally to a principled understanding of fairness that rests on the free-standing logic of equality and reciprocity (stages five and six). While this boy's judgments at eleven are scored as conventional on Kohlberg's scale, a mixture of stages three and four, his ability to bring deductive logic to bear on the solution of moral dilemmas, to differentiate morality from law, and to see how laws can be considered to have mistakes points toward the principled conception of justice that Kohlberg equates with moral maturity.

In contrast, Amy's response to the dilemma conveys a very different impression, an image of development stunted by a failure of logic, an inability to think for herself. Asked if Heinz should steal the drug, she replies in a way that seems evasive and unsure:

> Well, I don't think so. I think there might be other ways besides stealing it, like if he could borrow the money or make a loan or something, but he really shouldn't steal the drug—but his wife shouldn't die either.

Asked why he should not steal the drug, she considers neither property nor law but rather the effect that theft could have on the relationship between Heinz and his wife:

> If he stole the drug, he might save his wife then, but if he did, he might have to go to jail, and then his wife might get sicker again, and he couldn't get more of the drug, and it might not be good. So, they should really just talk it out and find some other way to make the money.

Seeing in the dilemma not a math problem with humans but a narrative of relationships that extends over time, Amy envisions the wife's continuing need for her husband and the husband's continuing concern for his wife and seeks to respond to the druggist's need in a way that would sustain rather than sever connection. Just as she ties the wife's survival to the preservation of relationships, so she considers the value of the wife's life in a context of relationships, saying that it would be wrong to let her die because, "if she died, it hurts a lot of people and it hurts her." Since Amy's moral judgment is grounded in the belief that, "if somebody has something that would keep somebody alive, then it's not right not to give it to them," she considers the problem in the dilemma to arise not from the druggist's assertion of rights but from his failure of response.

As the interviewer proceeds with the series of questions that follow from Kohlberg's construction of the dilemma, Amy's answers remain essentially unchanged, the various probes serving neither to elucidate nor to modify her initial response. Whether or not Heinz loves his wife, he still shouldn't steal or let her die; if it were a stranger dying instead, Amy says that "if the stranger didn't have anybody near or anyone she knew," then Heinz should try to save her life, but he should not steal the drug. But as the interviewer conveys through the repetition of questions that the answers she gave were not heard or not right. Amy's confidence begins to diminish, and her replies become more constrained and unsure. Asked again why Heinz should not steal the drug, she simply repeats, "Because it's not right," Asked again to explain why, she states again that theft would not be a good solution, adding lamely, "if he took it, he might not know how to give it to his wife, and so his wife might still die." Failing to see the dilemma as a self-contained problem in moral logic, she does not discern the internal structure of its resolution; as she constructs the problem differently herself, Kohlberg's conception completely evades her.

Instead, seeing a world comprised of relationships rather than of people standing alone, a world that coheres through human connection rather than through systems of rules, she finds the puzzle in the dilemma to lie in the failure of the druggist to respond to the wife. Saying that "it is not right for someone to die when their life could be saved," she assumes that if the druggist were to see the consequences of his refusal to lower his price, he would realize that "he should just give it to the wife and then have the husband pay back the money later." Thus she considers the solution to the dilemma to lie in making the wife's condition more salient to the druggist or, that failing, in appealing to others who are in a position to help.

Just as Jake is confident the judge would agree that stealing is the right thing for Heinz to do so Amy is confident that, "if Heinz and the druggest had talked it out long enough, they could reach something besides stealing." As he considers the law to "have mistakes," so she sees this drama as a mistake, believing that "the world should just share things more and then people wouldn't have to steal." Both children thus recognize the need for agreement but see it as mediated in different ways—he impersonally through systems of logic and law, she personally through communication in relationship. Just as he relies on the conventions of logic to deduce the solution to this dilemma, assuming these conventions to be shared, so she relies on a process of communication, assuming connection and believing that her voice will be heard. Yet while his assumptions about agreement are confirmed by the convergence in logic between his answers and the questions posed, her assumptions are belied by the failure of communication, the interviewer's inability to understand her response.

Although the frustration of the interview with Amy is apparent in the repetition of questions and its ultimate circularity, the problem of interpretation is focused by the assessment of her response. When considered in the light of

Kohlberg's definition of the stages and sequence of moral development, her moral judgments appear to be a full stage lower in maturity than those of the boy. Scored as a mixture of stages two and three, her responses seem to reveal a feeling of powerlessness in the world, an inability to think systematically about the concepts of morality or law, a reluctance to challenge authority or to examine the logic of received moral truths, a failure even to conceive of acting directly to save a life or to consider that such action, if taken, could possibly have an effect. As her reliance on relationships seems to reveal a continuing dependence and vulnerability, so her belief in communication as the mode through which to resolve moral dilemmas appears naive and cognitively immature.

Yet Amy's description of herself conveys a markedly different impression. Once again, the hallmarks of the preadolescent child depict a child secure in her sense of herself, confident in the substance of her beliefs, and sure of her ability to do something of value in the world. Describing herself at eleven as "growing and changing," she says that she "sees some things differently now, just because I know myself really well now, and I know a lot more about the world." Yet the world she knows is a different world from that refracted by Kohlberg's construction of Heinz's dilemma. Her world is a world of relationships and psychological truths where an awareness of the connection between people gives rise to a recognition of responsibility for one another, a perception of the need for response. Seen in this light, her understanding of morality as arising from the recognition of relationship, her belief in communication as the mode of conflict resolution, and her conviction that the solution to the dilemma will follow from its compelling representation seem far from naive or cognitively immature. Instead, Amy's judgments contain the insights central to an ethic of care, just as Jake's judgments reflect the logic of the justice approach. Her incipient awareness of the "method of truth," the central tenet of nonviolent conflict resolution, and her belief in the restorative activity of care, lead her to see the actors in the dilemma arrayed not as opponents in a contest of rights but as members of a network of relationships on whose continuation they all depend. Consequently her solution to the dilemma lies in activating the network by communication, securing the inclusion of the wife by strengthening rather than serving connections.

But the different logic of Amy's response calls attention to the interpretation of the interview itself. Conceived as an interrogation, it appears instead as a dialogue, which takes on moral dimensions of its own, pertaining to the interviewer's uses of power and to the manifestations of respect. With this shift in the conception of the interview, it immediately becomes clear that the interviewer's problem in understanding Amy's response stems from the fact that Amy is answering a different question from the one the interviewer thought had been posed. Amy is considering not *whether* Heinz should act in this situation ("*should* Heinz steal the drug?") but rather *how* Heinz should act in response to his awareness of his wife's need ("Should Heinz *steal* the drug?"). The interviewer takes the mode of action for granted, presuming it to be a matter of fact: Amy assumes the necessity for action and considers what form it should take. In the interviewer's failure to imagine a response not dreamt of in Kohlberg's moral philosophy lies the failure to hear Amy's question and to see the logic in her response, to discern that what appears, from one perspective, to be an evasion of the dilemma signifies in other terms a recognition of the problem and a search for a more adequate solution.

Thus in Heinz's dilemma these two children see two very different moral problems—Jake a conflict between life and property that can be resolved by logical deduction. Amy a fracture of human relationship that must be mended with its own thread. Asking different questions that arise from different conceptions of the moral domain, the children arrive at answers that fundamentally diverge, and the arrangement of these answers as successive stages on a scale of increasing moral maturity calibrated by the logic of the boy's response misses the different truth revealed in the judgment of the girl. To the question, "What does he see that she does not?" Kohlberg's theory provides a ready response, manifest in the scoring of Jake's judgments a full stage higher than Amy's in moral maturity; to the question, "What does she see that he does not?" Kohlberg's theory has nothing to say. Since most of her responses fall through the sieve of Kohlberg's scoring system, her responses appear from his perspective to lie outside the moral domain.

Yet just as Jake reveals a sophisticated understanding of the logic of justification, so Amy is equally sophisticated in her understanding of the nature of choice. Recognizing that "if both the roads went in totally separate ways, if you pick one, you'll never know what would happen if you went the other way," she explains that "that's the chance you have to take, and like I said, it's just really a guess." To illustrate her point "in a simple way," she describes her choice to spend the summer at camp:

I will never know what would have happened if I had stayed here, and if something goes wrong at camp, I'll never know if I stayed here if it would have been better. There's really no way around it because there's no way you can do both at once, so you've got to decide, but you'll never know.

In this way, these two eleven-year-old children, both highly intelligent and perceptive about life, though in different ways, display different modes of moral understanding, different ways of thinking about conflict and choice. In resolving Heinz's dilemma, Jake relies on theft to avoid confrontation and turns to the law to mediate the dispute. Transposing a hierarchy of power into a hierarchy of values, he defuses a potentially explosive conflict between people by casting it as an impersonal conflict of claims. In this way, he abstracts the moral problem from the interpersonal situation, finding in the logic of fairness an objective way to decide who will win the dispute. But this hierarchical ordering, with its imagery of winning and losing and the potential for violence which it contains, gives way in Amy's construction of the dilemma to a network of connection, a web of relationships that is sustained by a process of communication. With this shift, the moral problem changes from one of unfair domination, the imposition of property over life, to one of unnecessary exclusion, the failure of the druggist to respond to the wife.

By the end of President Ronald Reagan's first administration, the severe impact of his economic policies on women, and especially women of color, was well documented. For several years running, the Coalition on Women and the Budget, an ad hoc group of eighty organizations, tracked the impact of the Reagan Administration's budget on women. Their summary report for 1984, excerpted below, shows some stunning setbacks for American women in the areas of welfare, job training and education, public housing, energy subsidies, and assistance to older women who are dependent on Medicare and Medicaid. The report concludes that women, and in particular women of color and older women living alone, have borne the major hardship of sacrifice, because monies once allocated to social programs on which they depend were shifted to finance increased military spending and because a tax cut that disproportionately benefited wealthier Americans reduced money available to fund social welfare programs. The report also notes a 4 percent increase in the number of Americans living below the poverty line, many of whom were women and children. The report clearly illustrates the meaning of the catchphrase the "feminization of poverty," which was coined during the Reagan years.

SOURCE: Coalition on Women and the Budget, *Inequality of Sacrifice* (1984), National Women's Law Center, pp. 1–5. Reprinted courtesy of Natonal Women's Law Center, Washington, D.C.

THIS MARKS the third year that an ad hoc Coalition on Women and the Budget, composed of nearly 80 organizations, has come together to analyze the impact of the Administration's proposed federal budget on women. The cuts proposed for this year, particularly when combined with the cuts of the past three years, are devastating.

WOMEN IN FAMILIES

- AFDC.* Cuts would reduce benefits by $1.2 billion. This comes on top of benefit cuts in AFDC of over $1 billion since 1981.
- Food stamps. Cuts of $375 million, on top of the cuts of almost $5 billion

---

* Aid to Families with Dependent Children.

since 1981 which eliminated 1 million people from coverage, would mean more hungry women and families.

- Women, Infants and Children program. WIC, which provides food supplements and health care to pregnant and nursing women and young children, would be cut 15%, resulting in 450,000 fewer participants.
- Legal services. The legal services program would be eliminated, severely affecting women who constitute 67% of legal services clients.
- Child nutrition. Cuts in the four child nutrition programs would further decrease aid for child nutrition, especially when combined with the cuts of 20% to 35% in these programs since 1981.
- Housing. The bulk of the funding for housing would be through vouchers. Some new subsidized housing would be provided but no new public housing, a particularly important program for women.

GIRLS AND YOUNG WOMEN

- Job training. One million young women under age 22 head families; most work in low-wage jobs. The President would provide them with a gross wage of $90 per week for summer employment, and only level funding for most other youth employment programs.
- Educational programs. The Women's Education Equity Act and Title IV are marked for extinction. Programs currently funded under the Vocational Education Act would be folded into a block grant; nondiscrimination and targeting provisions for women would be eliminated. Further cuts in student financial aid would eliminate one million awards to students.
- Family planning. The family planning program would be replaced with a block grant that would also fund other programs. For teen-agers, each $1 the government invests saves $3 in services; last year 425,000 teen-age pregnancies were averted.
- Juvenile justice. Juvenile justice programs would be either entirely eliminated or held at level funding, affecting the young women who over half of individuals the served by these programs.

WOMEN AND THE WORKFORCE

- Work Incentive Program. WIN, which offers job counseling, training and placement to AFDC recipients, would be eliminated.
- Job Training Partnership Act. Funds would be frozen at last year's levels, but

pilot and demonstration program for persons facing special barriers to employment would be cut 13%.

- Social Security disability. This program would be cut $1 billion by continuing to terminate disabled workers from the program; nearly 1 million women now receive benefits as disabled workers.

OLDER WOMEN

- Medicare. Part B premiums would increase 300% by 1990, from $175 to over $500 per year. Deductibles would increase, and eligibility would be delayed.
- Medicaid. This program for low-income persons would be cut $1 billion by requiring recipients to pay for services, and reducing federal Medicaid payments to the states.
- Housing. Construction of public housing for the elderly and disabled would be cut 30%, at a time when waiting lists of several years are common.
- Low Income Energy Assistance Program. This program, through level fund and a charge in the funding mechanism, could be left with no money to help the 21-million eligible households (40% elderly) with fuel bills.

CHAPTER 1
Overview

President Reagan's proposed budget of $925.5 billion for fiscal year 1985 again demands an inequality of sacrifice from the women of America. This budget continues past Administration policies of unwarranted cuts in social programs on which millions of women depend. For the past three years similar budgets have been submitted to Congress; these budgets overspend militarily in the name of "security," while ignoring threats to the health and security of American citizens, many of whom are sicker, poorer, and hungrier today then they were three years ago because of this imbalance.

According to a Census Bureau study released in February 1984, the share of the U.S. population living below the poverty line has risen sharply over the last several years. (The rise in poverty exists even when in-kind benefits like Medicaid and food stamps are counted as income). Between 1979 and 1982, the number of people living in poverty rose from 26.1 million to 34.4 million persons (from 11.7% to 15% of the population).

Women, especially women of color, are disproportionately represented among these persons, particularly as heads of household with dependent children and as older women living alone. Even when they are employed full-time, women earn less than 60% of what men earn in full-time employment. Throughout their lifetimes . . . women have substantially lower median incomes than men. So women have been forced to rely on social programs as they struggle to secure a decent living for themselves and their families.

The social programs women rely upon have not been able to provide the support women need, however. The Congressional Budget Office estimates that, relative to the laws existing at the beginning of 1981, cuts in income security programs (food stamps, AFDC, child nutrition, low-income energy assistance, unemployment insurance, housing assistance, and the Women, Infants and Children (WIC) program) have totaled approximately $27 billion. Employment programs and retirement/disability programs have been cut about $25 billion each. In all human resources programs, reductions will total over $100 billion over the fiscal year 1982–1985 period. And those reductions were greatest, CBO concludes, for households with income below $10,000.

When President Reagan took office in 1981, he promised to increase the standard of living of all Americans through a combination of tax cuts and federal spending reductions that would, in turn, reduce the federal deficit. His tax cuts have, however, helped the rich at the expense of the poor. And his reductions in federal spending, as our analysis makes clear, have harmed individuals in and near poverty—a disproportionate number of whom are women. Finally, the deficit has not been reduced but has grown substantially, because of the President's refusal to hold military spending level or to raise taxes to obtain greater revenues from those more able to provide them. Deficit projections are already being used as a weighty argument either against increases in spending or, worse, for further decreases in the social programs on which women depend.

The excessive growth of projected deficits since 1980 can be attributed to three factors: increased military spending, huge tax cuts, and higher interest payments on the national debt. The military budget has swelled from $135.9 billion in 1980 to $245.3 billion in 1984, an increase of $109.4 billion. Three years of tax cuts have resulted in a treasury loss of $93 billion in 1984 alone. And interest on the national debt has increased from $52.5 billion in 1980 to $103.2 billion in 1984, a jump of $50.7 billion.

For each dollar cut from low-income programs since 1981, $4.15 has been added to the military budget, while $5.40 has been cut from taxes. Moreover, the Reagan tax changes have resulted in increased taxes for families earning under $15,000 a year, a less than 1% increase in after-tax income for families earning between $20,000 and $40,000 annually, and increases of 1.2% to 7.4% in after-tax income for families in the $50,000 to $250,000 income range. If taxes had been cut 10% less, we would not have had to cut low-income programs by a single penny. Another factor adding to the unfairness of the Reagan tax policy is the declining share of total federal receipts that come from corporate taxes and estate and gift taxes. Under the Reagan tax cut, corporate taxes declined to 5.9% of total receipts in 1983, as compared to 12.5% in 1980. . . .

More and more, women have made the connection between tax policy, military spending and budget deficits. We see just how fiscal and budgetary priorities affect our families and our lives. We recognize the difference between necessary and wasteful military spending, between tax policy that fosters a health economy and tax policy that provides privileged individuals with personal advantage. With this emergence of understanding comes the gender gap. If the gender gap continues to grow in 1984, it should further underscore the need for the Administration and Congress to pay attention to women's issues which include the economy, war and peace, and women's inequality of sacrifice.

Women are as ready to sacrifice for their country as any other Americans. But over the past three years, we have seen that the burden of sacrifice has not been equally shared. The Administration's fiscal year 1985 budget again asks for sacrifice, again from those least able to bear it, and again disproportionately from women. This is unconscionable. A workable budget must be developed that does not ask so much of some and so little of others.

"I PROUDLY ACCEPT YOUR NOMINATION"
GERALDINE FERRARO

On July 19, 1984, Geraldine Ferraro stood before a cheering, flag-waving crowd of delegates at the Democratic National Convention in San Francisco and accepted her party's nomination as the vice-presidential running mate of Walter Mondale—thus becoming the first woman vice-presidential candidate of a major political party.

Born in Newburgh, New York, into a working-class Italian family, Ferraro received her B.A. in English from Marymount College in 1956 and taught elementary school in Queens, New York, while attending Fordham University Law School at night. After receiving her law degree, she worked in private practice for several years and then as an assistant district attorney in Queens. In 1978 she ran for a seat in the U.S. House of Representatives and served three terms before Mondale selected her to be his running mate.

Despite some controversy in the campaign over her husband's questionable business practices, Ferraro proved to be a popular candidate and an effective campaigner. She received $4 million in campaign contributions from women alone. Although the Mondale-Ferraro ticket lost to incumbent President Ronald Reagan and his vice president, George Bush, Ferraro's candidacy put women in the political arena as significant contenders. In her acceptance speech Ferraro declared her support for issues of concern to women, such as reproductive rights, the Equal Rights Amendment, and equal pay for equal work, and she clearly emphasized the historic nature of her candidacy. Throughout the rest of her speech and the campaign, however, she did not limit herself only to such issues; instead, she addressed the whole range of issues and positions upheld by the Democratic party, from decrying the growing national debt under the Reagan Administration to supporting a strong national defense. Ferraro made clear that she was a serious, substantive candidate, not merely a political symbol.

SOURCE: In the public domain.

LADIES AND GENTLEMEN of the convention: My name is Geraldine Ferraro. I stand before you to proclaim tonight: America is the land where dreams can come true for all of us. . . .

Tonight, the daughter of a woman whose highest goal was a future for her children talks to our nation's oldest party about a future for us all.

Tonight, the daughter of working Americans tells all Americans that the future is within our reach—if we're willing to reach for it.

Tonight, the daughter of an immigrant from Italy has been chosen to run for [vice] president in the new land my father came to love.

Our faith that we can shape a better future is what the American dream is all about. The promise of our country is that the rules are fair. If you work hard and play by the rules, you can earn your share of America's blessings.

Those are the beliefs I learned from my parents. And those are the values I taught my students as a teacher in the public schools of New York City.

At night, I went to law school. I became an assistant district attorney, and I put my share of criminals behind bars. I believe: If you obey the law, you should be protected. But if you break the law, you should pay for your crime.

When I first ran for Congress, all the political experts said a Democrat could not win in my home district of Queens. But I put my faith in the people and the values that we shared. And together, we proved the political experts wrong. . . .

Americans want to live by the same set of rules. But under this administration, the rules are rigged against too many of our people.

It isn't right that every year, the share of taxes paid by individual citizens is going up, while the share paid by large corporations is getting smaller and smaller. The rules say: Everyone in our society should contribute their fair share.

It isn't right that this year Ronald Reagan will hand the American people a bill for interest on the national debt larger than the entire cost of the federal government under John F. Kennedy.

Our parents left us a growing economy. The rules say: We must not leave our kids a mountain of debt.

It isn't right that a woman should get paid 59 cents on the dollar for the same work as a man. If you play by the rules, you deserve a fair day's pay for a fair day's work.

It isn't right that—that if trends continue—by the year 2000 nearly all of the poor people in America will be women and children. The rules of a decent society say, when you distribute sacrifice in times of austerity, you don't put women and children first. . . .

Change is in the air, just as surely as when John Kennedy beckoned America to a new frontier; when Sally Ride* rocketed into space and when Rev. Jesse Jackson† ran for the office of president of the United States.

---

* The first American woman to fly in space.

† African American civil rights leader.

By choosing a woman to run for our nation's second highest office, you sent a powerful signal to all Americans. There are no doors we cannot unlock. We will place no limits on achievement.

If we can do this, we can do anything.

Tonight, we reclaim our dream. We're going to make the rules of American life work fairly for all Americans again.

To an Administration that would have us debate all over again whether the Voting Rights Act should be renewed and whether segregated schools should be tax exempt, we say, Mr. President: Those debates are over.

On the issue of civil, voting rights and affirmative action for minorities, we must not go backwards. We must—and we will—move forward to open the doors of opportunity.

To those who understand that our country cannot prosper unless we draw on the talents of all Americans, we say: We will pass the Equal Rights Amendment. The issue is not what America can do for women, but what women can do for America.

To the Americans who will lead our country into the 21st century, we say: We will not have a Supreme Court that turns the clock back to the 19th century.

To those concerned about the strength of American family values, as I am, I say: We are going to restore those values—love, caring, partnership—by including, and not excluding, those whose beliefs differ from our own. Because our won faith is strong, we will fight to preserve the freedom of faith for others.

To those working Americans who fear that banks, utilities, and large special interests have a lock on the White House, we say: Join us; let's elect a people's president; and let's have government by and for the American people again. . . .

Let no one doubt, we will defend America's security and the cause of freedom around the world. But we want a president who tells us what America is fighting for, not just what we are fighting against. We want a president who will defend human rights—not just where it is convenient—but wherever freedom is at risk—from Chile to Afghanistan, from Poland to South Africa. . . .

My fellow Americans: We can debate policies and programs. But in the end what separates the two parties in this election campaign is whether we use the gift of life—for others or only ourselves.

Tonight, my husband, John, and our three children are in this hall with me. To my daughters, Donna and Laura, and my son, John Jr., I say: My mother did not break faith with me . . . and I will not break faith with you. To all the children of America, I say: The generation before ours kept faith with us, and like them, we will pass on to you a stronger, more just America.

Thank you.

"IT CREATED A MYTH AMONG WOMEN"

Smart Women, Foolish Choices

This how-to guide from the mid-1980s sold over one million copies and stayed on the New York Times *best-seller list for many months. Addressed to the "smart woman"—that is, the successful professional woman—who can't seem to find the right mate, the book offers some useful insights on the complexities of interpersonal relationships but points an accusing finger at the women's movement for romanticizing career and autonomy at the expense of marriage and motherhood, as well as for creating a "cold war" between women and men. The authors fail to acknowledge that feminist leaders such as Betty Friedan were now seeking ways to integrate family and interpersonal life with women's career aspirations. And, like any popular self-help guide, this one engages in simplistic stereotypes of male and female behavior, such as "waiting for the prince," the "pseudo-liberated male," and "the all-powerful mother." Still, the book struck a chord for readers who believed they could find in print answers to unsatisfying relationships.*

SOURCE: Connell Cowan and Melvyn Kinder, *Smart Women, Foolish Choices* (New York: Clarkson N. Potter, 1985), pp. xv–xvii, 3–7, 10–13. Copyright © 1995 by Connell O'Brien Cowan and Melvyn Kindes. Used by permission of Clarkson Potter/Publishers, as division of Random House, Inc.

WHO IS THE "smart woman" to whom we address this book? She is career-oriented and actively involved in her personal development. She strives for a strong identity as a woman and as a person. She has assumed responsibility for the direction of her life. She is confident and values her self-esteem. She is curious about and involved in the changing nature of male/female relationships. Yet she is likely to feel that her love relationships with men are disappointing, frustrating, and very confusing. She senses her choices may be foolish.

We're optimistic, however. We believe there are a lot of good men out there—giving, caring men who deeply want a lasting relationship. As men, we believe we understand how other men think, feel, and react. We're going to tell you about strategies that work with men. We believe that if we can communicate these "insiders' tips" to you, they can help make your relationships less baffling and frustrating, more fulfilling.

Though we initially were cautious about using the term "foolish" in the title of this book, for fear that it might put people off, we knew it fit what our female patients felt and expressed to us with chagrin as well as puzzlement. We believe there is a paradoxical tendency on the part of women today, especially smart ones, to make even greater "errors" with the opposite sex than they might have done in previous years, and there is a very real reason for this. Today, for most women there is a greater gap between unconscious motivations—that is to say, old programming and conditioning—and new conscious aspirations, beliefs, expectations. There is, in effect, often a clash between the conscious, which has been dramatically influenced by recent social change, and the unconscious, which still may be fueled by those early childhood learnings. It is because of this discrepancy that it is possible for "smart" women to occasionally behave in "foolish" ways.

We further believe that for the mothers of our readers, the central developmental issues were relationship, intimacy, and nurturance. But for those women who matured during the feminist-influenced era, the central issues were personal identity, autonomy, and assertion. Now the issue for most women is the challenging task of reintegrating relationship and intimacy into often very autonomous and career-oriented life-styles. . . .

Diane is 28, single, an ambitious and successful freelance writer. Most men find her attractive, and she is never without a relationship. Yet she always seems to attract men who are independent, self-centered, emotionally closed, and unwilling to make a lasting commitment to her.

Diane decided she would like to find a more open, sensitive, and vulnerable man. She thought she had found what she was longing for in Neil. A 30-year-old architect, he was as open and giving as her previous lovers had been aloof and uncommitted. As they grew closer, Neil confided in her about certain career insecurities. He frequently told Diana he cared for her and needed to feel close to her.

Rather than enjoying his openness, Diane found herself pulling away. Justifying her decision, she exclaimed, "I guess I just got bored." Diane is no longer seeing Neil. Sadly, she is once again in a new relationship—this time with a workaholic attorney—that will leave her unfulfilled.

Carla, 42, is a real estate broker who founded a company that now employs thirty people. From the day at age 23 when she experienced the exhilaration of closing her first million-dollar sale, Carla consciously and enthusiastically chose to put her career before a marriage and family. She had been involved with a number of men over the years, but nothing lasting ever developed. Now she finds herself feeling oddly melancholy in her private moments. When she thinks about her past love affairs, she remembers very few joyful moments. She is currently involved with a European film director who she knows is secretly living with another woman.

Samantha, 27, is a junior associate at a law firm. Eric, one of the partners in the firm, was immediately drawn to her intelligence, ambition, and independence. As they dated, however, Samantha went through a metamorphosis Eric found profoundly puzzling: She became increasingly dependent, possessive, and in need of constant reassurance of his love and commitment. Although Samantha's behavior concerned Eric, they continued to see each other regularly, and their relationship grew.

One evening a couple of months later, as they finished a romantic dinner at her apartment for which she had spent hours cooking his very favorite dishes, Samantha told Eric that she wanted to get married, stop working, and have his baby. Shocked by the suddenness of her announcement, Eric began to gradually withdraw from the relationship, leaving Samantha feeling confused and emotionally devastated.

These women are very different from one another. But they share at least one thing in common—they have all made foolish choices in their romantic lives. By choices, we don't mean simply their selection of romantic partners; we also mean how they choose to act with these men.

How many times have you heard these statements, or perhaps even said them yourself at one time or another?

"I always seem to end up with the wrong men."

"If there's one 'rat' in a room full of nice men, I'll find him."

"All the men I meet are either boring or gay. If I'm lucky enough to meet a man who's interesting, warm, and attentive, sure enough, sooner or later, I find out he's married."

"I know it's never going to go anywhere and I know he's never going to leave his wife, but he has this kind of power over me. He walks all over me, and I just let him."

"My relationships always start out great, but something seems to happen that causes the man to drift away."

As psychologists, we hear these remarks every day. In fact, lately it seems there is a rising tide of utter frustration among women concerning men. We became intrigued because we knew these feelings and dilemmas reflect an almost epidemic attitude of disheartening resignation and pessimism.

But women don't simply "end up" with men who are wrong for them. Relationships that have strong initial promise don't sour as a result of inexplicable forces beyond human comprehension or control. Rather, the women who make these complaints have made foolish choices.

We find, so often, that *the more intelligent and sophisticated the woman, the more self-defeating and foolish her choices and her patterns of behavior with romantic partners.* We believe these foolish choices are triggered and perpetuated, in part, by modern, destructively inaccurate myths women believe about men today. Moreover, women's expectations regarding relationships have been exaggerated by the belief they can "have it all." It is our observation that smart women still look for and hope to find the perfect man—the Prince.

HISTORICAL FORCES AFFECTING WOMEN

In order to understand some of the forces operating on women today, it's important to review the tremendous changes that have occurred between the sexes in recent years.

The beginning of the 1980s signaled the thaw of the cold war between the sexes, a revival in the perceived value of the importance to the human experience of intimate, committed love. This latest swing of the social pendulum has breathed new life into the importance of relationships and family. Men and women are reconnecting with traditional values and integrating new ones. Here are a few of the comments we have been hearing lately from our women clients and friends.

"I'd like to fall in love, get married, and have babies . . . all those things that sounded so cowardly and provincial a couple of years ago."

"I'm confused. I spent five years getting my master's and I'd like to continue to pursue my career. But I'm 34 now and I realize I haven't had a decent relationship with a man in six years. During that time, my company has moved me to four different cities. It's not that I don't like my work but there has got to be something more."

"I feel as if I'm being torn in different directions. Marriage is very appealing to me, but I'm also aware that there are a lot of obligations that go along with it. There is no question in my mind that I want a baby. I couldn't tell you exactly why; it's just this strong emotional thing that grabs me when I see a mother and a child. I feel I have to have one of my own, but I don't want to become one of those women whose kids are the only highlight of her life. I'm also torn about my job. I enjoy being an attorney, but I know that to do it right takes a huge chunk of time. There just is no way I can do all the things I want to do. . . ."

These confusions and strong but divergent forces in women are new. Smart women today want to reembrace many of the truly substantive traditional values without relinquishing the gains of recent years. They are addressing complex questions both within themselves and in their relationships with men. Today they want men in their lives and want to value and feel comfortable with their femininity without compromising equality.

Two decades have passed since the publication of Betty Friedan's *The Feminine Mystique*, which reactivated the long-dormant women's movement in this country. The central thrust of feminism was to free women from the tyranny of sexist education, attitudes, and practices. It sought to create meaningful reform not only in the marketplace but also within the context of marriage and family and, perhaps most important, within women themselves.

But, as the movement has continued to evolve, important changes have occurred, most of them involving a reevaluation of the traditional institutions of marriage and family. An unfortunate consequence of feminism was, in our opinion, that it created a myth among women that the apex of self-realization could be achieved only through autonomy, independence, and career. Finding a mate and having a family were secondary goals. In recent years, many women have discovered that, with few exceptions, work is hard, stressful, and not totally fulfilling over the long haul.

Even as we write this book, the wariness women have felt toward men during the last decade continues to diminish. Yet women are still concerned about becoming overly dependent on men or obsessed with them. And, we might add, these are legitimate concerns. . . .

We believe that a new era is now emerging for both women and men. The prized independence of the autonomous and divorced all too frequently pays off in loneliness, economic woes, and regret. While marriage might carry along with it new forms of obligation, it also promises new forms of freedom and fulfillment. Children can be incredibly taxing and exhausting, but they're magical and rewarding in ways that deepen and complete their parents' lives.

The women's movement gave women a sense of options and a clearer vision of their own worth and potential. It made them aware that their needs were important, that they could and should make important decisions about the quality and structure of their lives. But women today also want to establish love relationships with men. With that in mind, they are abandoning the residues of anger and distrust of men and are establishing relationships on more consciously and more clearly negotiated footings of equality. They are feeling a greater acceptance of their own capacity for love and nurturance, and are experiencing the biological and emotional drives to have children.

More and more, we believe, smart women are discovering that self-fulfillment cannot be realized through career and self-mastery alone. Neither can it be gained through love alone. Self-realization comes from the achievement of both love and mastery.

"IT'S A GENTLE LIFE, SOMETIMES"
FRANCES WELLS BURCK, ED.

In the early 1980s, Frances Wells Burck, a writer with three young daughters, wanted to know if motherhood had changed the lives of other women as much as it had changed hers. She was particularly eager to know, as she wrote in the preface of the book that followed, how a mother "saw herself in her children, what she thought was hard as well as what was satisfying [and] how she maintained her identity beyond motherhood."*

For two years, she criss-crossed the country and interviewed mothers from all walks of life. She was astonished to discover how much her interviewees wanted to talk about their lives and how willing they were to discuss very intimate issues. Following are excerpts from two interviews with very different perspectives on motherhood. Note especially the speakers' differing perceptions on feeling connected with other mothers.

SOURCE: Frances Wells Burck, *Mothers Talking: Sharing the Secret* (New York: St. Martin's Press, 1986), pp. 23–25, 31–35. Reprinted by permission of St. Martin's Press, LLC.

KATE GRIMES WEINGARTEN

When I was about to go on maternity leave, the company wouldn't negotiate about it at all. They didn't want to talk about my taking four months, or five months, or six months. They have very little experience in the matter of women managers going out on maternity leave, and their rigid policy was three months maximum.

I called up the personnel man in September, and I told him I couldn't come back the first of October, but that I would like to come in and talk about it. I had been with the company for eight years, and was also due for a promotion. There are only three times in the year when raises and promotions are given. One of them was last month. The personnel manager called me up the next day and said, "Your promotion has been withdrawn, and we will accept your resignation!" I could not believe that I had invested so much of my life in such people.

I said, "I've tried to deal with you as decently as I can about my time to have a baby, and I wanted to talk to you about the possibilities of coming back in the

---

* Frances Wells Burck, *Mothers Talking: Sharing the Secret* (New York: St. Martin's Press, 1986), p. xiv.

future, but you are just so small of mind, and so ungenerous of spirit." He was a fairly decent guy. The official reason, he said, was that they don't give promotions to people who are on leave. What really happened was they thought I was going to play by their October first rules, but I couldn't, so goodbye.

I was one of the four major investment people in an eight-billion-dollar pension fund, and now I'm just another boob! There was this article in the *Wall Street Journal* recently about pregnant professional women. As I recall, the only people they talked to were those who went right back to work. The implication is if you want to be a professional-type businesswoman, then you're going to have to surrender the fact that you are a mother to the corporate structure.

They give you an office as if you are one of the boys. They try to forget you are a woman and treat you as an equal. Then you get pregnant, and don't come back when the baby is only twelve weeks old, and it is betrayal. One way you get to be one of the boys is not to be perceived as a woman. They don't want someone who could be like one of their wives. The women who are coming up the ladder and getting MBA's are being forced to be a cookie-cutter image of the men they work with. Look at the three-piece suits they wear!

There was a soft-spoken, very demure woman at the company, and they were confused about how to deal with her. She was the kind of person who, when she was on a business trip with the men and the luggage carousel came around, they felt like picking up her suitcase. That is intimidating because on some level these men realized she was like their wives. They wouldn't want their own wives to leave a twelve-week-old baby. They also understand that a woman with a twelve-week-old baby is still recovering from childbirth and is exhausted from getting up all the time, and is tired from nursing the baby, and probably isn't going to be the most productive worker in the world. At some level they understand that. But the other aspect is obviously much stronger. They expect you to play their game by their rules. When I didn't want to do that, they just said, "Screw you."

It would have been nice if they'd said, "You were a valued worker. We would like to talk to you about working it out." Instead, they told me they had overpaid my Social Security, and now that I was quitting I would be getting a bill from them. I felt like saying, "You can shove your Social Security bill where the sun don't shine."

I will eventually go back to work, just as I will eventually wean Danny from my breast—when it seems right for him or for both of us. I want to be with him: not twenty-four hours a day every day, but I don't want to be without him two or three days a week. I just love being with him. It's very hard to realize that caretaking begets love unless you've done it. I never thought—of course who knows what it's like to have a baby until you have one—that I would.

There are some things I find hard. I have no particular structure to my life except what he imposes. I sat at home yesterday. It was so quiet, so very quiet in my house. All the kids were in school. Danny was taking one of his rare daytime naps. I realized that in front of me stretches the fall, the winter, the spring, and finally summer. You know, I wanted this child. I waited a long time to have this child, but there was something about the isolation I felt yesterday that truly scares me. I have to build a whole new life.

On the other hand, there's a gentleness to this life that is unlike anything I've ever experienced. There is a rhythm to it. I love the early morning feeding. It's not quite light. He sucks on me in his sleep. Occasionally I'll hear the geese fly over. It's lovely. And then I'll bring him back into our bed next to Seymour.

Just to have the time to sit in a rocking chair and love this baby, or to spend fifteen minutes playing peekaboo with this baby, or to make pumpkin bread at ten o'clock in the morning . . . I've never had the time. No, that's not true; I've never had the inclination to do anything like that. It's just so totally pleasurable to watch this little guy, to have this little guy. I don't know what, just to be with him, to have him love me, have him need me, to watch him change and laugh.

It's also nice to be able to care for other women with whom I have this in common. I had almost lost touch with my friends who had children. Now I know them in a new and different way. That's part of the gentleness, too, to love other peoples' babies and children.

Even though we were married, Seymour and I have lived our lives separately, in a sense.

LINDA STEIN

My husband, Ken, wanted a big family. He's one of four and liked it. He wanted a child every two years. After the first kid you'd think he would have learned.

It took us a long, long time to have our first. We were under the impression it would take a long time for the second, so we started trying a little bit earlier than we would have normally, and, of course, the first shot out . . . I was just enraged. I was furious. I was sick with the whole thing—physically sick. I had thought it was a safe time; I was just doing it to get him off my back.

I wasn't going to have an abortion just because this baby was inconvenient, so I've gone ahead. But I feel like somebody has put a bag over my head after

I've just started to climb out of the first bag. An extra six months would have made a big difference. Peter would have been toilet trained, and he might have been a little bit less dependent on me.

I'm in my ninth month now, and I still look down sometimes and think, "You're pregnant?" I don't imagine any of the nice things. I really don't ever see myself playing with two children. I know I should be happier about having this baby, but I just see two children crawling into my bed on Saturday morning and jumping on my head. I feel like I've had that already. It's not cute anymore, and it's not what I want. I don't want any more children!

Peter was born early. He was in the hospital for six weeks. They weren't sure how well he was because he was so little. It had been my nightmare: My baby would be born, and it would take them a long time to say he was okay. It was like a prophecy. I didn't even want to know him. I didn't want to touch him. I didn't want to be involved. Ken kept saying, "Well, we have to go and visit the baby. We have to do it."

Every day I would go to the hospital to see him in his little box. Always something new, some new crisis. His head was small. "Can you remember offhand if your husband has a small head?" the doctor wanted to know. I didn't know. The doctor said, "Well, does he wear hats?" I said "No," and so the doctor said, "Maybe it's because he can't find a hat to fit him." I made Ken leave work in the middle of the day. I was frantic to have some jerk measure his head. It turned out he had a large head, which made it worse, because then Peter's head wasn't hereditary.

I was so ashamed that I couldn't love this . . . I mean a chicken is bigger than he was. I didn't want to hold him. I didn't want to touch him. I didn't even want to give him a name. Not that he would not live, but because this was not the way it was supposed to be.

This pregnancy is different: It has been normal. But I'm worried that I don't have any place to hide these negative feelings. I don't have any place to put the fact that I don't want to breast-feed. With Peter I'd say, "Oh, I couldn't do it because he was in the hospital." But it's not my style. I'm not the nurturing type, I guess.

People give you a hard time if you aren't nursing. They say, "Why not? It's much healthier, and what about the bonding? You're not giving your child the love it needs, you know." Peter was also very colicky. They said, "If you breast-feed, no colic." When he got too old for colic, and would still scream from six in the morning until ten at night, we discovered he had a milk allergy. Then, of course, it was, "Breast-fed babies don't have allergies," and "You're telegraphing these negative messages."

You want to be the best at whatever you do. You're not working, so motherhood is like your career, and you'd better be good. Other mothers weren't any help. They made me feel like I had to be supermom. Somehow, everybody else's child either slept through the night or started to roll over or weighed twenty-three pounds before mine did. If I had a problem and asked, "What do you do for it?" and got an answer, I'd go home and try it, and it didn't work. I'd make myself crazy. There's only so much you can do to make a child the way you want. If they get a good kid, these women really are stupid enough to believe it has to do with them!

Now Peter bites. He's a real two-year-old boy, a real motor kid. At our playschool, one of the mothers was complaining, "Today he tried and tried to get the other kids to play train with him." "Well," I said, "why didn't you let them? He wasn't asking them to vandalize the neighborhood! He wanted to play train!" She said, "Because it was arts and crafts time." I said, "You can't expect all two-year-olds to sit still for an hour and do that. You just can't." Someday, the fact that he's active and alive and imaginative might be the thing that is most precious about him.

I have to stick up for my kid, but then I have doubts. Doubt is also where other mothers come into play. "Maybe you ought to do this. Maybe you should try that." Even my own mother sows doubt. We'd take Peter to their house, and he'd get the crazies and beat up on his cousin. She'd call the next day. "Having trouble with Peter? It could be the sugar in his diet. Do you give him much sugar?" "Sure, Mom, Every morning I say, 'Open your mouth,' and I pour it down his throat." Doubt. She tinkles on the piano of doubt. And you know, in this business of motherhood, that doubt is your worst enemy. If you're positive and you're wrong, at least you can forge ahead, but if you're feeling "I'm not sure," you're in trouble.

In the beginning, though, nobody admits their deepest, darkest dreams to another mother. I'd been up all day with a screaming kid. I wanted to put him in an oven like a duck. But nobody else would admit to that anger. I've got to connect with these women. But they don't sympathize with me. You're not friendly for any other reason except that you're a mother, so what else do you talk about but your kids?

Their babies ate, slept for four hours, woke up and ate again. Mine didn't. I felt like a baby-sitter watching a stranger's child, because I couldn't believe this horrendous baby was mine. I used to sit with this baby and think, 'When is his mother coming to relieve me?'

My mother said, "What's your problem, Linda? Why are you letting it make you so crazy? We'll find somebody to take care of the kid. If you're not happy, and the kid is giving you the business, go someplace. Go shopping. Be better to yourself. A happy mother is a good mother." I couldn't do that. Then she would say, "Somebody else can't be with him and change his diaper?"

Finally, we got the formula straight, and he started eating real food. He wasn't unhappy anymore. I found I *wanted* to go into his room at night to make sure he was okay. That was wonderful. Then I would stand for a long time and look at him sleeping and smile all over.

Will that happen with this baby? Where does the time for this baby come in? It seems as if I'm constantly in motion now. I've already let so much go. How can I get any looser? I don't read anymore. We don't see friends. I used to make regular dinners, even though when Peter was tiny, five o'clock was his zaniest hour. I was compulsive about trying to get this meal on the table. There was no pressure from Ken. He'd say, "We'll eat at ten o'clock. Don't worry about it." But I would think, I've got to do this. It's not fair to him. What kind of wife would I be if I served the vegetables out of a pot?

Now, after we've finally eaten and Peter has gone to sleep, I go into the bedroom and flop down like a zombie. Ken sits in the living room, and he's a zombie. I said to him the other night, "Do you think it's bad that we don't talk at all?" He said "I need quiet." I said, "I need quiet, too." "Then it's okay, Linda," he said. But that quiet time is probably going to be when this new baby is up and wanting to boogie! . . .

I suppose I'll get it together some day, and it will be all right. But tell me, where is the time, the energy, the psychic energy going to come from to take care and love and nurture another person? It must come from somewhere. I just can't imagine where unless love is like a muscle. The more you exercise it, the more you have to give. *Please*, tell me.

"SOMETHING MOVED—
SOME POSSIBILITY OF TRUST WAS CREATED"
RACHEL BAGBY

In August 1986 forty women—mostly white and some women of color— gathered at Hampshire College in Amherst, Massachusetts, ostensibly for the purpose of sharing and developing ideas to promote peace activities locally as well as nationally and internationally. But they also came together to break down barriers of class and ethnic differences among them. The gathering was sponsored by the WomanEarth Feminist Peace Institute, an ecofeminist educational organization formed the year before to disseminate ideas and information about peace activities. What ensued, as Rachel Bagby reports in this wonderfully cheeky account, was a lively free-for-all of women expressing deeply felt, even ruthlessly harsh opinions and perspectives about their sisters on both sides of the color divide. And what came out of the gathering was a joyous, eager, grassroots collective commitment to get on with the work of peace and environmental reform.

SOURCE: Rachel Bagby, "A Power of Numbers," in Judith Plant, ed., *Healing the Wounds: The Promise of Ecofeminism* (Philadephia: New Society Publishers, 1989), pp. 91–95. Reprinted by permission of Rachel Ragby.

IMAGINE. A room fulla women and nary a one in the minority or majority, if the measuring question is of-color or not of-color.

That's right. Imagine yourself in a gathering of committed, dynamic, earth-, self-, and other-loving women, where there, amidst many, many differences is parity; color-wise. No one can say"we don't do it that way" because there is no established *we*. Everyone is equally a guest and shaper of the party.

It only happens by design; and by design, only rarely. But when it happens ... *girl* let me tell you! folks walk away a little bit changed. I know because I've been there. Twice. One event reached parity by conscious, painstaking effort, the other, with a deceptive ease. Both gatherings were sponsored by WomanEarth Institute.

A bit of background. WomanEarth is currently hubbed by a volunteer staff of two: Rachel Bagby—Black, attorney, writer, musician, organizer, workshop leader; and Gwyn Kirk—white, teacher, writer, "currently free to follow my interests through the generosity and support of others." *What* we hub is a growing network of women committed to helping each other and the earth thrive.

The women of WomanEarth are activists, grandmothers, carpenters, scholars, artists, scientists, healers . . . Whatever professional/sociopolitical-economic hats we wear, and most of us wear several, we share a commitment to create a world that reflects and nurtures our multi-dimensional and diverse interests. The issues on which WomanEarth focuses are ecology, feminism, spirituality, common differences, and public action.

While not all of us are actively involved in all of these issues—either as scholars or activists or both—some of us are. Whatever our issues, we are unified by the principles/processes underlying our work: challenging the dominant, destructive theories and practices of patriarchy with the wisdom of our analysis and lives; creating/refining intellectual, emotional, political, cultural and life-supporting tools of transformation; and a strong commitment to parity between women of color and white women in all aspects of WomanEarth's organization and activities; a most powerful way to put our lives where our mouths are. . . .

As we bond and build with the various thems of our various us(s), the fragmentary constructs of us/them begin to dissolve. Along the way, we continue to witness the evolving influence of class, economics, language, and emotional/racial history on the process. Thus, WomanEarth is a fertile ground for advancing the theories and practices involved in this woefully neglected (or persistently perplexing) aspect of the women's movement—how white women and women of color can join forces to advance our mutual interests. . . .

Our first gathering in August 1986 at Hampshire College in Amherst, Massachusetts was a unique event. It was the first time any of us had been to a gathering where there was parity between women-of-color and white women, or where women decided to stop the planned program at points to spend time processing issues which separate us.

Not surprising, given our demographics. WomanEarth's first gathering brought women together from all over the world. Other than the fact that most of us were the kind of women people are unable to control and therefore call "uppity," it would be hard to be on the outside looking in and make generalizations about the group. . . .

First, it was invitational; had to be if the goal of parity had a chance of being realized. The announcement reading in part:

This summer, WomanEarth Feminist Peace Institute, an educational Institute formed in 1985 to provide resources and create educational settings where women from all racial and socio-economic backgrounds can meet to broaden their understanding of peace politics, is sponsoring an invitational meeting of women activists and scholars to work on "Reconstituting Feminist Peace Politics." . . .

From our perspective, the established peace movement has an overly narrow focus. Discussion continues to be dominated by technicalities of weapons systems and the conception of peace often limited to disarmament. This movement has not been able to build on the mass mobilizations of 1982/83 and is still overwhelmingly white and middle class.

Story has it that responses to the controlled access to WomanEarth I from some white women active in the peace and ecology movements was fiery. "We don't *do* things that way," some said. Or, "that's a good idea, but, *of course, I'll be able to come no matter what,* right?" The women catching that fire, also white, also active in those movements, were both shocked and equal to the responses. Why this fear and anger in response to an experiment? What are you feeling as you read this paragraph?

And it took many calls, much coaxing from Papusa Molina, a Mexican woman who worked in the WomanEarth office for the the summer, to convince the few women-of-color on *the list* to agree to come to Amherst that summer. Over and over came the questions. Why should we go there? Take a whole week off from work? Will it be worth it? What's the purpose?

Why did we come? Because we believed Molina's assurances. The possibility, the chance that YES! would have a place in the gathering. That we could and would embody the invitational possibility of *truly* working together. I was eager to meet other women-of-color who care about ideas and ways of being that I care about. I was eager to have my mother talk about her efforts to revitalize the North Philadelphia slum I called home; a place touched with her care in the form of community gardens, shared housing for elders and employment development for the young.

The invitation said we would "discuss how militarism affects ecological issues, world hunger, racism, the role of the US in the global economic and political power struggle, the movement of women in other countries for peace and equality, and the role of spirituality in working for peace. We seek to develop a broad-based feminist peace politics, to work together effectively across race and class lines, and to share ideas for imaginative, effective actions we can take locally, regionally, nationally and internationally."

It said nothing about the speak-out, however. We couldn't anticipate the scene of that Wednesday, white women on one side of the room, women-of-color on another. First the women-of-color then the white women answering two questions: What do you absolutely adore about being (Mexican, Black, Native American, Jewish, White Anglo-Saxon . . .)? What is it that you never, ever as long as you live want to hear from women who look like the women on the other side of the room?

With over forty of us speaking out, it took all night. Organically, the need to speak out was acknowledged as tensions rippled through this group of uppity women, women used to speaking our hearts and minds and guts. . . .

Few of us had ever spoken out like we did at the speak-out. I hadn't. Mary Arnold, in introducing the process, said it would be empowering. Mary Arnold, a member of an ongoing multicultural network in Iowa that works on internalized and externalized racism, was right.

We entered the process with an oath of confidentiality. So the only story I can tell without breaking that oath is my own. I was shaken by the suggestion that we divide ourselves along color lines—in this corner, women-of-color . . . I heard a woman to my right say she was glad we were doing with our bodies what was going on in our minds and hearts. I didn't like it. Said so.

Then we celebrated. What is it that I absolutely love about my self? Clothed in a flowing outfit handmade by a friend, I strutted. Said nothing. My 5' 9" cherrywood being spoke for itself, arms outstretched to show off my lines. Then I danced as I sang a celebration of life that brought the house *up*! "And I love alla that," I said. And the fact that I survived Stanford Law School and can still love alla that. And that I have a mutually nurturing relationship with a Black man. And recognize my mother as the wise elder that she is. There is more, much much more.

After we each celebrated our selves, we got up to say what we never, ever, as long as we lived, wanted to hear from a white women. With many colored sisters at my back, facing that crowd of white faces, some familiar, some loved, some simply white. With every cell threatening to go its own way. Fast. (What was *my* fear?) I said, "Don't tell me you understand what it means to be Black just because you've had a Black lover." After we were all done, the white women said what they heard. It was empowering to say to twenty-some white women what I'd never said to any white woman before, but wanted to. It was empowering to know we were heard, as several white women got up to reflect back to us our words and feelings.

It was empowering to hear what the white women there liked about themselves. And rare. Especially so since this was, after all, a "gathering." All too often, my encounters with white women at ecology/peace gatherings have been of a limited variety. Either they are so glad to see me there. Or they are so sorry there aren't more of me there. ("But," I never say, "there is only one of me on this entire planet.") Or they want to know the Black perspective on this or that. Or they want to tell me the trouble they've had convincing people-of-color that issues of ecology and peace are of the utmost importance.

To hear what the white women liked about themselves and what they never, ever, as long as they lived wanted to hear from a woman-of-color ever again—*that* was an education. One comment stuck in my heart and brought tears—that any woman would be denied the joy of learning another's dance because she had "white-skinned privileges . . ."

Something moved. This group of white women facing me became more human, more women with hopes and dreams and fears and pains that I could see and feel. I became more of myself, able to revel in it. Closer to telling folks who looked like folks who have a legacy of hurting folks who look like me to STOP IT. Something moved. Some little corner of consciousness was cleared out. Some possibility of trust, or at least of honesty, was created. Some ability to speak and listen to those we see as "other." All critical qualities and skills to develop as we work to create a world where environmental responsibility is as natural as breathing in a world controlled by folks who look and act like folks who have a legacy of hurting folks and plants and animals and entire ecosystems that share this planet with us.

Imagine. Attending an ecofeminist gathering where there is parity no group being able to call it their thang to be done this way. No one or two bits of color there to be glad about, or wonder why they're there. As many different perspectives as there are people there, and the recognition of the need and eagerness to work at working together.

By design. Imagine how empowering it would be. Create it.

Nina Barrett, a journalist who published two books and numerous articles about child-rearing in the 1980s, loved being the mother of a young son but was honest enough to admit the frustrations, loneliness, and limitations of trying to care for her newborn while picking up the threads of her journalism career. Barrett's account, which is excerpted from her book The Playgroup, *about her experiences as a new mother and those of two friends, is humorous and honest, deftly describing the juggling act that working mothers, a growing phenomenon during the 1980s, must undertake, especially when home and office are under the same roof.*

SOURCE: Nina Barrett, *The Playgroup* (New York: Simon and Schuster, 1994), pp. 147–158.

I SPENT the first two months of Sam's life cross-legged on the bed with a stack of fat pillows piled up on each knee. At any given moment, Sam would be on one or the other stack, latched ferociously onto one or the other breast, his little jaw working relentlessly to squeeze out every last possible drop of the Substance of Life Itself, while I paged just as relentlessly through yet another child-care book or parenting magazine, which I rested on the opposite stack of pillows, searching desperately for the currency that would allow me to redeem the rights to my apparently forfeited Life Story. Every twenty minutes or so I would switch breasts, and then after another twenty minutes I would hoist Sam onto my shoulder and pat pat pat his back until he belched like Falstaff, ejected a stream of the Substance of Life Itself down my back, and began to wail. Then I, too, would begin to wail, hurling the book or magazine across the room in frustration, and I would pull myself to my feet, and begin the long and ultimately fruitless process of trying to calm the baby down.

There was no question in my mind that I was going to return to work as soon as possible. The question was: What did I have to return to? There was nothing, as far as I could tell, that I was on leave *from*, unless it was the basic core of my twenty-six-year-old identity as a competent, in-control, overachieving performer of logical verbal tasks. But if I went back to that, in the gung ho fifty-hour-a-week way that the Superwoman articles suggested I would naturally want to, then wouldn't I simply be on leave from the other, more fragile, newly born shoot of my core identity: the person who wanted to provide my miraculous infant with the moral, emotional, social, and intellectual—as well as physical—Substance of Life Itself; the reservoir in me that had been filling up for all those years purely in order to be drained? . . .

At five o'clock every afternoon, I would allow myself to have a beer (not one minute earlier, or I might start to lose it)—my big treat: to feel pleasantly fuzzy, as the screaming began to escalate and I began to count the minutes until Ellis [her husband] would walk in the door at six (not one minute later, or I would start to lose it). At the sound of his key in the lock, I would run to the front door, throw Sam into his arms, and race into the kitchen to cook dinner. Usually, the changing of the guard seemed to distract Sam into relative calm long enough for me to actually set dinner on the table. Then Ellis would deposit Sam into his baby bouncer, and Ellis and I would sit down at the table and hopefully begin a conversation, and then, within a bite or two, Sam's face would contort into a mask of tragedy and he would begin to howl.

I would slam down my fork and glare at Ellis. "It's been like this all fucking day. I can't stand it anymore. *You* take him for once." And I would stalk out.

Ellis (half an hour later, appearing tentatively in the doorway of the bedroom, where I am lying across the bed, leafing through yet another parenting publication): "I think he's hungry. He keeps sucking at my finger. Why don't you try nursing him?"

Me (half an hour later): "He's nursed. Listen, I've had him all day. You take him. Play with him or something."

(Ellis lies down on the couch, zooms Sam above his head like an airplane. Sam screams louder and spits up onto Ellis's head. Phone rings.)

Ellis: "Neen, it's for me. Can you come get Sam and take him in the other room?"

Me (half an hour later): "Ellis, I've had him *all day*. TAKE HIM!!"

(By nine-thirty or ten, Ellis gets Sam soothed to sleep and places him gently in the bassinet, then we both collapse into bed. At midnight Sam wakes, screaming. I get up and nurse him back to sleep, then lie awake anticipating the next interruption. I am still awake two hours later, when he screams again.) . . .

All right, it is clear: I cannot go on day after day like this. I must return to my "I"—my Paper Self—as soon as possible. I must start writing about something. The byline under every single parenting magazine story reads, "So-and-So is a freelance writer who lives in — with her two small/teenage/grown children." So the logical thing to write about must be this motherhood business. . . .

When an idea for a book began to take shape in the murk of my severely sleep-deprived mind, my answer to the child-care question was to take Sam

two afternoons a week a few blocks away to the apartment of a Chinese graduate student and his wife who answered a classified ad I had placed in the local
newspaper. They had neither experience nor references, but they did have a
daughter six months older than Sam who had also screamed through her entire early infancy, and the wife gravely confided to me that babies who start out
like that in life "are much smarter than those quiet ones." This remark, together with the clear child-centeredness of the small apartment, as well as some
very fragrant and soothing green tea they served me on my first visit, convinced
me to take a chance, even though at five dollars per hour, three hours per afternoon, the total weekly cost of thirty dollars was going to severely strain our
budget. I was going to have to work fast. . . .

As for the housekeeping duties, Sam and I handled those together on our
days off, which, after we moved from Chicago to Westerville in the spring of
1988, were usually organized according to the ebb and flow of activity in the Tot
Lot across the street, which in turn obeyed the ebb and flow of children's bio-
rhythms and the programming schedule of the local PBS affiliate. There was
rarely anyone in the Tot Lot until the second showing of *Sesame Street* ended
at ten, but Sam woke up between six and six-thirty, so he usually got to watch
both showings plus a Raffi tape because he lost interest in the television as soon
as he heard the first notes of "It's a Beautiful Day in the Neighborhood" (and
informed me, the moment he learned to talk, "I doesn't like Rogers").

I would use this time to make coffee, feed myself and Sam, pack Ellis an economical lunch, take a shower, get dressed, clean up the kitchen, make our bed
(there never seemed to be any point in making Sam's), and do whatever vacu-
uming or floor-scrubbing could no longer decently be delayed. At some point
during the morning, usually while I had Comet all over my hands and the second *Sesame Street* was just ending, I would get a phone call from an editor or a
source about some small freelance project I was doing. (I made calls only on
the days when I had baby-sitting, but people called me back only on days when
I didn't.) So then I would attempt to do a quick phone interview, trying to
sound professional while Sam grabbed the phone cord, because he had recently got the impression that we thought it was extremely adorable for him to talk
to people on the phone, or else he would be ominously quiet during the conversation and I would come back out to the living room afterward to find him
sitting sheepishly next to a disaster that had occurred because I had taken off
his diaper just before the phone rang and had not had a chance to replace it.

So then there would be more cleaning up, and chasing Sam around to get
the new diaper and some clothes on him, which would mean dumping out the

baskets of clean laundry that would have been sitting around for several days (after spending several days in the dryer, after spending several days in the washer, because the facilities were in the basement of the building, where I refused to go since women were occasionally raped in the laundry rooms of neighborhood buildings; and Ellis's attitude toward laundry was somewhat casual). Sam would take this as his cue to demonstrate the juggling skills he had been practicing ever since seeing the Ringling Bros. and Barnum & Bailey Circus, which meant I had to make circus music while he stood at the foot of his bed, announced dramatically, "Ladies and gemmun," and hurled an armful of laundry into the air. Eventually he would start to throw the clothes at me and I would throw them at him, until finally one of us glanced out the window and noticed Phoebe or Gabriel in the Tot Lot. Then I would have an hour or two of simultaneous disjointed conversations with various mothers who were constantly being pulled away by children who wanted to be pushed or chased or caught or had gotten into a fight with other children or were climbing on something above a safe altitude. . . .

Then there was making lunch, eating lunch, picking the remnants of lunch off the floor, and putting the child down for a nap. Then there was an hour and a half or so of Time to Myself, of which I typically wasted the first forty-five minutes trying to decide whether to read a book or read the paper or call a friend or transcribe a tape or clean the mold out of the refrigerator or switch the spring clothes to the front of the closet or take a nap or write a letter or write in my journal—because, after all, this was my only, very valuable, irreplaceable Time to Myself and I didn't want to waste it doing the wrong thing.

After Sam woke up, between two and three, we might go back to the Tot Lot or to the beach, or, as winter closed in, to Angie's apartment, or, more frequently, to do errands. But errands were always traumatic for both of us, because going into almost any store entailed confronting a large number of things each of us wanted and wasn't likely to get: for Sam, the endless succession of Teenage Mutant Ninja Turtle cookies, cereals, and snacks displayed throughout the supermarket, the Ghostbuster paraphernalia throughout Toys "R" Us, where we went to buy cheap diapers; for me, the interesting books I wouldn't have time to read, the elegant clothes I had no place to wear, the velvety plush towels that would get stolen from the laundry room—none of which Sam would let me drool over for long, always having an agenda of his own in every store, which was just as well, since we couldn't afford any of it, anyway.

By five o'clock, my head would be buzzing with amputated thoughts and conversation fragments, with yelled, unheeded "nos" and strangled longings, and my back would ache with the strain of innumerable boosts into and out of car seats and swings. Then I would turn on the news, pour myself a glass of red wine, and cook dinner. . . . And while I concocted beef stews or pot roasts or stir fries or homemade spaghetti sauce, Sam would methodically unload all the drawers and cabinets below counter level, strewing cookie pans and rolling pins and egg-beaters across the floor, beating on pots with wooden spoons, clinging to my legs as I moved from sink to stove, commanding me to come play with him. . . .

Ellis would walk through the door sometime around six, and I would be mad at him because he was late and dinner had burned or cooled off, or because he didn't immediately peel Sam off my legs, or just because I had had a long and frustrating day and he had gone to a quiet office where I supposed he was left alone to think in peace. And he would be in a bad mood because he had gotten stuck on the packed El train or because he had walked in to find me mad at him.

And so the civilized dinner conversation at the rickety teak card table would eventually degenerate into an argument over whose turn it was to clean up the kitchen and whose it was to perform the still-daunting task of coaxing Sam into the mood to sleep. And this might in turn lead us into even more dangerous territory: an argument over which of us worked harder, the one who'd spent the day Working, or the one who Hadn't. . . .

"THE WOMAN'S 'PART'"
POPE JOHN PAUL II, APOSTOLIC LETTER ON WOMEN

On September 30, 1988, Pope John Paul issued a theological response to the women's movement. The pope issued the letter, entitled "On the Dignity and Vocation of Women," as a meditation inspired by analyses of relevant biblical passages. Although the letter did not carry the weight of a papal encyclical or claim to espouse infallible truths, it was nonetheless an important expression of the pope's views on contemporary women's roles and would likely influence Catholic religious and lay leaders around the world.

Though the pope upholds and even enshrines traditional views of women's role as that of wife and mother, he does affirm, by analyzing Scripture, the dignity of women and their "essential equality" with men. His is a conservative message couched in moderate, progressive language.

Among American Catholics, the reaction to the pope's letter was mixed. Some applauded him for affirming sexual equality, while others lamented his inability or refusal to acknowledge other life paths for women.

SOURCE: From the Apostolic Letter *Mulieris Dignitatem*. Reprinted courtesy of the Vatican.

IN THE DESCRIPTION found in *Gen* 2:18–25, the woman is created by God "from the rib" of the man and is placed at his side as another "I," as the companion of the man, who is alone in the surrounding world of living creatures and who finds in none of them a "helper" suitable for himself. Called into existence in this way, the woman is immediately recognized by the man as "flesh of his flesh and bone of his bones" (cf *Gen* 2:23) and for this very reason she is called "woman." In biblical language this name indicates her essential identity with regard to man—*'is-'issah*—something which unfortunately modern languages in general are unable to express: "She shall be called woman ('issah) because she was taken out of man ('is): *Gen* 2:23.

The biblical text provides sufficient bases for recognizing the essential equality of man and woman from the point of view of their humanity. From the very beginning, both are persons, unlike other living beings in the world about them. *The woman is another "I" in a common humanity.* . . .

In our times the question of "women's rights" has taken on new significance in the broad context of the rights of the human person. *The biblical and evangelical message* sheds light on this cause, which is the object of much attention today, *by safeguarding the truth about the "unity" of the "two,"* that is to say the truth about that dignity and vocation that result from the specific diversity and personal originality of man and woman. Consequently, even the rightful opposition of women to what is expressed in the biblical words "He shall rule over you" (*Gen* 3:16) must not under any condition lead to the "masculinization" of women. In the name of liberation from male "domination," women must not appropriate to themselves male characteristics contrary to their own feminine "originality." There is a well-founded fear that if they take this path, women will not "reach fulfilment," but instead will *deform and lose what constitutes their essential richness.* It is indeed an enormous richness. In the biblical description, the words of the first man at the sight of the woman who had been created are words of admiration and enchantment, words which fill the whole history of man on earth.

The personal resources of feminity are certainly no less than the resources of masculinity: they are merely different. Hence a woman, as well as a man, must understand her "fulfilment" as a person, her dignity and vocation, on the basis of these resources, according to the richness of the feminity which she received on the day of creation and which she inherits as an expression of the "image and likeness of God" that is specifically hers. *The inheritance of sin* suggested by the words of the Bible—"Your desire shall be for your husband, and he shall rule over you"—*can be conquered* only by following this path. The overcoming of this evil inheritance is, generation after generation, the task of every human being, whether woman or man. For whenever man is responsible for offending a woman's personal dignity and vocation, he acts contrary to his own personal dignity and his own vocation. . . .

MOTHERHOOD-VIRGINITY

Two Dimensions of Women's Vocation

We must now focus our meditation on virginity and motherhood as two particular dimensions of the fulfillment of the female personality. In the light of the Gospel, they acquire their full meaning and value in Mary, who as a Virgin became the Mother of the Son of God. These *two dimensions of the female vocation* were united in her in an exceptional manner, in such a way that one did not exclude the other but wonderfully complemented it. . . .

This *mutual gift of the person in marriage* opens to the gift of a new life, *a new human being,* who is also a person in the likeness of his parents. Motherhood implies from the beginning a special openness to the new person: and this is precisely the woman's "part." In this openness, in conceiving and giving birth to a child, the woman "discovers herself through a sincere gift of self." The gift of interior readiness to accept the child and bring it into the world is linked to the marriage union which—as mentioned earlier—should constitute a special moment in the mutual self-giving both by the woman and the man. . . .

Virginity for the Sake of the Kingdom

In the teaching of Christ, *motherhood is connected with virginity*, but also *distinct from it*. Fundamental to this is Jesus' statement in the conversation on the indissolubility of marriage. Having heard the answer given to the Pharisees, the disciples say to Christ: "If such is the case of a man with his wife, it is not expedient to marry" (*Mt* 19:10). Independently of the meaning which "it is not expedient" had at that time in the mind of the disciples, *Christ* takes their mistaken opinion as a starting point for instructing them *on the value of celibacy*. He distinguishes celibacy which results from natural defects—even though they may have been caused by man—from *"celibacy for the sake of the Kingdom of heaven."* . . . Consequently, *celibacy for the kingdom of heaven* results not only from a free *choice* on the part of man, but also from a special *grace* on the part of God, who calls a particular person to live celibacy. . . . Christ's answer, in itself, has a *value both for men and for women.* . . .

The Gift of the Bride

. . . In every age and in every country we find many "perfect" women (cf. *Prov.* 31:10) who, despite persecution, difficulties and discrimination, have shared in the Church's mission. It suffices to mention: Monica, the mother of Augustine, Macrina, Olga of Kiev, Matilda of Tuscany, Hedwig of Silesia, Jadwiga of Cracow, Elizabeth of Thuringia, Brigitta of Sweden, Joan of Arc, Rose of Lima, Elizabeth Ann Seton and Mary Ward.

The witness and the achievements of Christian women have had a significant impact on the life of the Church as well as of society. Even in the face of serious social discrimination, holy women have acted "freely," strengthened by their union with Christ. Such union and freedom rooted in God explain, for example, the great work of Saint Catherine of Siena in the life of the Church, and the work of Saint Teresa of Jesus in the monastic life.

In our own days too the Church is constantly enriched by the witness of the many women who fulfil their vocation to holiness. Holy women are an incarnation of the feminine ideal; they are also a model for all Christians, a model of the *"sequela Christi,"* an example of how the Bride must respond with love to the love of the Bridegroom.

"THE GREATEST OF THESE IS LOVE"

Awareness of a Mission

A woman's dignity is closely connected with the love which she receives by the very reason of her femininity; it is likewise connected *with the love which she gives in return*. The truth about the person and about love is thus confirmed. . . .

While the dignity of woman witnesses to the love which she receives in order to love in return, the biblical "exemplar" of the Woman also seems to reveal *the true order of love which constitutes woman's own vocation*. Vocation is meant here in its fundamental, and one may say universal significance, a significance which is then actualized and expressed in women's many different "vocations" in the Church and the world. . . .

In our own time, the successes of science and technology make it possible to attain material well-being to a degree hitherto unknown. While this favours some, it pushes others to the edges of society. In this way, unilateral progress can also lead to a gradual *loss of sensitivity for man, that is, for what is essentially human*. In this sense, our time in particular *awaits the manifestation* of that "genius" which belongs to women, and which can ensure sensitivity for human beings in every circumstance: because they are human!—and because "the greatest of these is love" (cf. 1 *Cor* 13:13). . . .

"THE HUGE, HIDDEN EMOTIONAL COST TO WOMEN"
ARLIE HOCHSCHILD

From 1980 to 1988 Arlie Hochschild, a professor of sociology at the University of California at Berkeley, interviewed fifty couples from a variety of economic and professional levels, along with their neighbors and friends and their children's teachers, babysitters, and day-care providers. She also spent time in the couples' homes, observing their meal preparations and evening routines and even accompanied them on family outings. With the number of working mothers—especially mothers of young children—growing, she wanted to find out how working wives and husbands divided up domestic tasks and what adjustments and accommodations each partner made to complete the second shift, as she titled her book—the work of childrearing and housekeeping squeezed in before and after a full day at the office. She discovered that, in general, women juggled "three spheres—job, children, and housework," while men juggled two: job and children.* "All in all," she concluded, "if . . . the two-job family is suffering from a speed up of work and family life, working mothers are its primary victims.**

Hochschild's study was not just a dry academic exercise. It was soon hailed as a landmark study of the pressures and dilemmas faced by American families, and especially by working mothers, at the end of the twentieth century, and garnered considerable popular and academic attention.

Following is an excerpt from an interview with one middle-class couple whom she observed. The interview reveals the texture and tensions of a working woman's life in the latter part of the twentieth century as she struggles to balance paid work and work at home.

SOURCE: "Joey's Problem: Nancy and Evan Holt," from *The Second Shift* by Arlie Hochschild and Ann Machung, copyright © 1989 by Arlie Hochschild. Used by permission of Viking Penguin, a division of Penguin Putnam Inc.

NANCY HOLT arrives home from work, her son, Joey, in one hand and a bag of groceries in the other. As she puts down the groceries and opens the front door, she sees a spill of mail on the hall floor, Joey's half-eaten piece of cinnamon toast on the hall table, and the phone machine's winking red light: a still-life

---

* Arlie Hochschild, The Second Shift: Working Parents and the Revolution at Home (New York: Viking, 1989), pp. 8–9.
** Ibid., p. 9.

reminder of the morning's frantic rush to distribute the family to the world outside. Nancy, for seven years a social worker, is a short, lithe blond woman of thirty who talks and moves rapidly. She scoops the mail onto the hall table and heads for the kitchen, unbuttoning her coat as she goes. Joey sticks close behind her, intently explaining to her how dump trucks dump things. Joey is a fat-cheeked, lively four-year-old who chuckles easily at things that please him.

Having parked their red station wagon, Evan, her husband, comes in and hangs up his coat. He has picked her up at work and they've arrived home together. Apparently unready to face the kitchen commotion but not quite entitled to relax with the newspaper in the living room, he slowly studies the mail. Also thirty, Evan, a ware-house furniture salesman, has thinning pale blond hair, a stocky build, and a tendency to lean on one foot. In his manner there is something both affable and hesitant.

From the beginning, Nancy describes herself as an "ardent feminist," an egalitarian (she wants a similar balance of spheres and equal power). Nancy began her marriage hoping that she and Evan would base their identities in both their parenthood and their careers, but clearly tilted toward parenthood. Evan felt it was fine for Nancy to have a career, if she could handle the family too.

As I observe in their home on this evening, I notice a small ripple on the surface of family waters. From the commotion of the kitchen, Nancy calls, "Evan, will you *please* set the table?" The word *please* is thick with irritation. Scurrying between refrigerator, sink, and oven, with Joey at her feet, Nancy wants Evan to help; she has asked him, but reluctantly. She seems to resent having to ask. (Later she tells me, "I *hate* to ask; why should I ask? It's begging.") Evan looks up from the mail and flashes an irritated glance toward the kitchen, stung, perhaps, to be asked in a way so barren of appreciation and respect. He begins setting out knives and forks, asks if she will need spoons, then answers the doorbell. A neighbor's child. No, Joey can't play right now. The moment of irritation has passed.

Later as I interview Nancy and Evan separately, they describe their family life as unusually happy—except for Joey's "problem." Joey has great difficulty getting to sleep. They start trying to put him to bed at 8:00. Evan tries but Joey rebuffs him; Nancy has better luck. By 8:30 they have him *on* the bed but not *in* it; he crawls and bounds playfully. After 9:00 he still calls out for water or toys, and sneaks out of bed to switch on the light. This continues past 9:30, then 10:00 and 10:30. At about 11:00 Joey complains that his bed is "scary," that he can only go to sleep in his parents' bedroom. Worn down, Nancy accepts this proposition. And it is part of their current arrangement that putting Joey to bed is "Nancy's job." Nancy and Evan can't get into bed until midnight or later, when Evan is tired and Nancy exhausted. She used to enjoy their love-making, Nancy tells me, but now sex seems like "more work." The Holts consider their fatigue and impoverished sex life as results of Joey's Problem.

The official history of Joey's Problem—the interpretation Nancy and Evan give me—begins with Joey's fierce attachment to Nancy, and Nancy's strong attachment to him. On an afternoon walk through Golden Gate Park, Nancy devotes herself to Joey's every move. Now Joey sees a squirrel; Nancy tells me she must remember to bring nuts next time. Now Joey is going up the slide; she notices that his pants are too short—she must take them down tonight. The two enjoy each other. (Off the official record, neighbors and Joey's baby-sitter say that Nancy is a wonderful mother, but privately they add how much she is "also like a single mother.")

For his part, Evan sees little of Joey. He has his evening routine, working with his tools in the basement, and Joey always seems happy to be with Nancy. In fact, Joey shows little interest in Evan, and Evan hesitates to see that as a problem. "Little kids need their moms more than they need their dads," he explains philosophically; "All boys go through an oedipal phase."

Perfectly normal things happen. After a long day, mother, father, and son sit down to dinner. Evan and Nancy get the first chance all day to talk to each other, but both turn anxiously to Joey, expecting his mood to deteriorate. Nancy asks him if he wants celery with peanut butter on it. Joey says yes. "Are you sure that's how you want it?" "Yes." Then the fidgeting begins. "I don't like the strings on my celery." "Celery is made up of strings." "The celery is too big." Nancy grimly slices the celery. A certain tension mounts. Every time one parent begins a conversation with the other, Joey interrupts. "I don't have anything to drink." Nancy gets him juice. And finally, "Feed me." By the end of the meal, no one has obstructed Joey's victory. He has his mother's reluctant attention and his father is reaching for a beer. But talking about it later, they say, "This is normal when you have kids."

Sometimes when Evan knocks on the baby-sitter's door to pick up Joey, the boy looks past his father, searching for a face behind him: "Where's Mommy?" Sometimes he outright refuses to go home with his father. Eventually Joey even swats at his father, once quite hard, on the face for "no reason at all." This makes it hard to keep imagining Joey's relation to Evan as "perfectly normal." Evan and Nancy begin to talk seriously about a "swatting problem."

Evan decides to seek ways to compensate for his emotional distance from Joey. He brings Joey a surprise every week or so—a Tonka truck, a Tootsie Roll.

He turns weekends into father-and-son times. One Saturday, Evan proposes the zoo, and hesitantly, Joey agrees. Father and son have their coats on and are nearing the front door. Suddenly Nancy decides she wants to join them, and as she walks down the steps with Joey in her arms, she explains to Evan, "I want to help things out."

Evan gets few signs of love from Joey and feels helpless to do much about it. "I just don't feel good about me and Joey," he tells me one evening, "that's all I can say." Evan loves Joey. He feels proud of him, this bright, good-looking, happy child. But Evan also seems to feel that being a father is vaguely hurtful and hard to talk about.

The official history of Joey's problem was that Joey felt the "normal" oedipal attachment of a male child to his mother. Joey was having the emotional problems of growing up that any parent can expect. But Evan and Nancy add the point that Joey's problems are exacerbated by Evan's difficulties being an active father, which stem, they feel, from the way Evan's own father, an emotionally remote self-made businessman, had treated him. Evan tells me, "When Joey gets older, we're going to play baseball together and go fishing."

As I recorded this official version of Joey's Problem through interviews and observation, I began to feel doubts about it. For one thing, clues to another interpretation appeared in the simple pattern of footsteps on a typical evening. There was the steady pacing of Nancy, preparing dinner in the kitchen, moving in zigzags from counter to refrigerator to counter to stove. There were the lighter, faster steps of Joey, running in large figure eights through the house, dashing from his Tonka truck to his motorcycle man, reclaiming his sense of belonging in this house, among his things. After dinner, Nancy and Evan mingled footsteps in the kitchen, as they cleaned up. Then Nancy's steps began again: click, click, click, down to the basement for laundry, then thuck, thuck, thuck up the carpeted stairs to the first floor. Then to the bathroom where she runs Joey's bath, then into Joey's room, then back to the bath with Joey. Evan moved less—from the living room chair to Nancy in the kitchen, then back to the living room. He moved to the dining room to eat dinner and to the kitchen to help clean up. After dinner he went down to his hobby shop in the basement to sort out his tools; later he came up for a beer, then went back down. The footsteps suggest what is going on: Nancy was at work on her second shift.

"THE HIGH-PERFORMING CAREER-AND-FAMILY WOMAN CAN BE A MAJOR PLAYER"
FELICE SCHWARTZ

In 1989 Felice Schwartz, the president of Catalyst, a nonprofit research and advocacy organization for professional women in the workforce, published an article entitled "Management Women and the New Facts of Life" in the Harvard Business Review *and unwittingly set off a heated debate over the interpretation of her words. Schwartz argued that women employees proved to be more expensive than their male counterparts because they take maternity leaves or leave the workforce completely to raise families after corporations have invested time and money in their training. To retain what she clearly perceived to be valued female employees, Schwartz proposed that businesses and law firms offer two career tracks for their female employees: "career-primary" and "career-and-family." The latter track would be tailored to employees who want to combine family and career by offering more part-time and flex-time positions. As Schwartz explains, these employees could "trade some career growth and compensation for freedom from the constant pressure to work long hours."*

Critics zeroed in on Schwartz's claim that women were more expensive to employ than men and derisively coined the term "mommy track" to characterize her proposed "career-and-family" track as a one-way detour to a professional dead-end, because companies would be less willing to hire, promote, or respect women who chose this career path.

Schwartz restated her position in a New York Times *op-ed piece and also protested, in an unpublished letter to the* Times, *the phrase "mommy track" as denigrating what she called "committed professionals," primarily women "who are also committed to being integral to their children's lives and, through them, to the future of the firm and the country."**

Nonetheless, the catchphrase stuck and has become a buzz word to describe a less committed female professional who chooses to focus her energies on family life instead of career advancement. Even Betty Friedan, who, eight years earlier in The Second Stage *(see her document in this chapter), had urged women to find ways to balance workplace commitments with family needs, called Schwartz's article a "dangerous retrogression and acquiescence to sex discrimination."*†

---

* Quoted in Felice Schwartz, *Breaking with Tradition* (New York: Warner, 1992), p. 103.

† Quoted in ibid., p. 123.

*In 1990, the year after Schwartz's article first appeared, a Virginia Slims poll found that 70 percent of respondents viewed the notion of a "mommy track" as discriminatory and "just an excuse for paying women less than men."**

SOURCE: Felice Schwartz, "Management Women and the New Facts of Life," *Harvard Business Review* 1 (January/February 1989): 65–76. Reprinted by permission of *Harvard Business Review*. Copyright © 1989 by the Harvard Business School Publishing Corporation; all rights reserved.

THE COST OF EMPLOYING women in management is greater than the cost of employing men. This is a jarring statement, partly because it is true, but mostly because it is something people are reluctant to talk about. A new study by one multinational corporation shows that the rate of turnover in management positions is 2 1/2 times higher among top-performing women than it is among men. A large producer of consumer goods reports that one half of the women who take maternity leave return to their jobs late or not at all. And we know that women also have a greater tendency to plateau or to interrupt their careers in ways that limit their growth and development. But we have become so sensitive to charges of sexism and so afraid of confrontation, even litigation, that we rarely say what we know to be true. Unfortunately, our bottled-up awareness leaks out in misleading metaphors ("glass ceiling" is one notable example), veiled hostility, lowered expectations, distrust, and reluctant adherence to Equal Employment Opportunity requirements.

Career interruptions, plateauing, and turnover are expensive. The money corporations invest in recruitment, training, and development is less likely to produce top executives among women than among men, and the invaluable company experience that developing executives acquire at every level as they move up through management ranks is more often lost.

The studies just mentioned are only the first of many, I'm quite sure. Demographic realities are going to force corporations all across the country to analyze the cost of employing women in managerial positions, and what they will discover is that women cost more.

But here is another startling truth: The greater cost of employing women is not a function of inescapable gender differences. Women *are* different from

---

* Quoted in Kathryn Cullen-Dupont, *The Encyclopedia of Women's History in America* (New York: Facts on File, 1997), p. 136.

men, but what increases their cost to the corporation is principally the clash of their perceptions, attitudes, and behavior with those of men, which is to say, with the policies and practices of male-led corporations.

It is terribly important that employers draw the right conclusions from the studies now being done. The studies will be useless—or worse, harmful—if all they teach us is that women are expensive to employ. What we need to learn is how to reduce that expense, how to stop throwing away the investments we make in talented women, how to become more responsive to the needs of the women that corporations *must* employ if they are to have the best and the brightest of all those now entering the work force.

The gender differences relevant to business fall into two categories: those related to maternity and those related to the differing traditions and expectations of the sexes. Maternity is biological rather than cultural. We can't alter it, but we can dramatically reduce its impact on the workplace and in many cases eliminate its negative effect on employee development. We can accomplish this by addressing the second set of differences, those between male and female socialization. Today, these differences exaggerate the real costs of maternity and can turn a relatively slight disruption in work schedule into a serious business problem and a career derailment for individual women. If we are to overcome the cost differential between male and female employees, we need to address the issues that arise when female socialization meets the male corporate culture and masculine rules of career development—issues of behavior and style, of expectation, of stereotypes and preconceptions, of sexual tension and harassment, of female mentoring, lateral mobility, relocation, compensation, and early identification of top performers.

THE ONE IMMUTABLE, enduring difference between men and women is maternity. Maternity is not simply childbirth but a continuum that begins with an awareness of the ticking of the biological clock, proceeds to the anticipation of motherhood, includes pregnancy, childbirth, physical recuperation, psychological adjustment, and continues on to nursing, bonding, and child rearing. Not all women choose to become mothers, of course, and among those who do, the process varies from case to case depending on the health of the mother and baby, the values of the parents, and the availability, cost, and quality of child care.

In past centuries, the biological fact of maternity shaped the traditional roles of the sexes. Women performed the home-centered functions that related to the bearing and nurturing of children. Men did the work that required great physical strength. Over time, however, family size contracted, the community assumed greater responsibility for the care and education of children, packaged foods and house-hold technology reduced the work load in the home, and technology eliminated much of the need for muscle power at the workplace. Today, in the developed world, the only role still uniquely gender related is childbearing. Yet men and women are still socialized to perform their traditional roles.

Men and women may or may not have some innate psychological disposition toward these traditional roles—men to be aggressive, competitive, self-reliant, risk taking, women to be supportive, nurturing, intuitive, sensitive, communicative—but certainly both men and women are capable of the full range of behavior. Indeed, the male and female roles have already begun to expand and merge. In the decades ahead, as the socialization of boys and girls and the experience and expectations of young men and women grow steadily more androgynous, the differences in workplace behavior will continue to fade. At the moment, however, we are still plagued by disparities in perception and behavior that make the integration of men and women in the workplace unnecessarily difficult and expensive.

Women also bring counterproductive expectations and perceptions to the workplace. Ironically, although the feminist movement was an expression of women's quest for freedom from their home-based lives, most women were remarkably free already. They had many responsibilities, but they were autonomous and could be entrepreneurial in how and when they carried them out. And once their children grew up and left home, they were essentially free to do what they wanted with their lives. Women's traditional role also included freedom from responsibility for the financial support of their families. Many of us were socialized from girlhood to expect our husbands to take care of us, while our brothers were socialized from an equally early age to complete their educations, pursue careers, climb the ladder of success, and provide dependable financial support for their families. To the extent that this tradition of freedom lingers subliminally, women tend to bring to their employment a sense that they can choose to change jobs or careers at will, take time off, or reduce their hours.

Finally, women's traditional role encouraged particular attention to the quality and substance of what they did, specifically to the physical, psychological, and intellectual development of their children. This traditional focus may explain women's continuing tendency to search for more than monetary reward—intrinsic significance, social importance, meaning—in what they do.

This too makes them more likely than men to leave the corporation in search of other values.

One result of these gender differences has been to convince some executives that women are simply not suited to top management. Other executives feel helpless. If they see even a few of their valued female employees fail to return to work from maternity leave on schedule or see one of their most promising women plateau in her career after the birth of a child, they begin to fear there is nothing they can do to infuse women with new energy and enthusiasm and persuade them to stay. At the same time, they know there is nothing they can do to stem the tide of women into management ranks.

Another result is to place every working woman on a continuum that runs from total dedication to career at one end to a balance between career and family at the other. What women discover is that the male corporate culture sees both extremes as unacceptable. Women who want the flexibility to balance their families and their careers are not adequately committed to the organization. Women who perform as aggressively and competitively as men are abrasive and unfeminine. But the fact is, business needs all the talented women it can get. Moreover, as I will explain, the women I call career-primary and those I call career-and-family each have particular value to the corporation.

WOMEN IN THE CORPORATION are about to move from a buyer's to a seller's market. The sudden, startling recognition that 80% of new entrants in the work force over the next decade will be women, minorities, and immigrants has stimulated a mushrooming incentive to "value diversity."

Women are no longer simply an enticing pool of occasional creative talent, a thorn in the side of the EEO officer, or a source of frustration to corporate leaders truly puzzled by the slowness of their upward trickle into executive positions. A real demographic change is taking place. The era of sudden population growth of the 1950s and 1960s is over. The birth rate has dropped about 40%, from a high of 25.3 live births per 1,000 population in 1957, at the peak of the baby boom, to a stable low of a little more than 15 per 1,000 over the last 16 years, and there is no indication of a return to a higher rate. The tidal wave of baby boomers that swelled the recruitment pool to overflowing seems to have been a one-time phenomenon. For 20 years, employers had the pick of a very large crop and were able to choose males almost exclusively for the executive track. But if future population remains fairly stable while the economy continues to expand, and if the new information society simultaneously creates a greater need for creative, educated managers, then the gap between supply and demand will grow dramatically and, with it, the competition for managerial talent.

The decrease in numbers has even greater implications if we look at the traditional source of corporate recruitment for leadership positions—white males from the top 10% of the country's best universities. Over the past decade, the increase in the number of women graduating from leading universities has been much greater than the increase in the total number of graduates, and these women are well represented in the top 10% of their classes.

The trend extends into business and professional programs as well. In the old days, virtually all MBAs were male. I remember addressing a meeting at the Harvard Business School as recently as the mid-1970s and looking out at a sea of exclusively male faces. Today, about 25% of that audience would be women. The pool of male MBAs from which corporations have traditionally drawn their leaders has shrunk significantly.

Of course, this reduction does not have to mean a shortage of talent. The top 10% is at least as smart as it always was—smarter, probably, since it's now drawn from a broader segment of the population. But it now consists increasingly of women. Companies that are determined to recruit the same number of men as before will have to dig much deeper into the male pool, while their competitors will have the opportunity to pick the best people from both the male and female graduates.

UNDER THESE CIRCUMSTANCES, there is no question that the management ranks of business will include increasing numbers of women. There remains, however, the question of how these women will succeed—how long they will stay, how high they will climb, how completely they will fulfill their promise and potential, and what kind of return the corporation will realize on its investment in their training and development.

There is ample business reason for finding ways to make sure that as many of these women as possible will succeed. The first step in this process is to recognize that women are not all alike. Like men, they are individuals with differing talents, priorities, and motivations. For the sake of simplicity, let me focus on the two women I referred to earlier, on what I call the career-primary woman and the career-and-family woman.

Like many men, some women put their careers first. They are ready to make the same trade-offs traditionally made by the men who seek leadership positions. They make a career decision to put in extra hours, to make sacrifices in their personal lives, to make the most of every opportunity for professional development. For women, of course, this decision also requires that they remain single or at least childless or, if they do have children, that they be satisfied to have others raise them. Some 90% of executive men but only 35% of executive women have children by the age of 40. The *automatic* association of all women with babies is clearly unjustified.

The secret to dealing with such women is to recognize them early, accept them, and clear artificial barriers from their path to the top. After all, the best of these women are among the best managerial talent you will ever see. And career-primary women have another important value to the company that men and other women lack. They can act as role models and mentors to younger women who put their careers first. Since upwardly mobile career-primary women still have few role models to motivate and inspire them, a company with women in its top echelon has a significant advantage in the competition for executive talent.

Men at the top of the organization—most of them over 55, with wives who tend to be traditional—often find career women "masculine" and difficult to accept as colleagues. Such men miss the point, which is not that these women are just like men but that they are just like the *best* men in the organization. And there is such a shortage of the best people that gender cannot be allowed to matter. It is clearly counterproductive to disparage in a woman with executive talent the very qualities that are most critical to the business and that might carry a man to the CEO's office.

Clearing a path to the top for career-primary women has four requirements:

1. Identify them early.
2. Give them the same opportunity you give to talented men to grow and develop and contribute to company profitability. Give them client and customer responsibility. Expect them to travel and relocate, to make the same commitment to the company as men aspiring to leadership positions.
3. Accept them as valued members of your management team. Include them in every kind of communication. Listen to them.
4. Recognize that the business environment is more difficult and stressful for them than for their male peers. They are always a minority, often the only woman. The male perception of talented, ambitious women is at best ambivalent, a mixture of admiration, resentment, confusion, competitiveness, attraction, skepticism, anxiety, pride, and animosity. Women can never feel secure about how they should dress and act, whether they should speak out or grin and bear it when they encounter discrimination,

stereotyping, sexual harassment, and paternalism. Social interaction and travel with male colleagues and with male clients can be charged. As they move up, the normal increase in pressure and responsibility is compounded for women because they are women.

Stereotypical language and sexist day-to-day behavior do take their toll on women's career development. Few male executives realize how common it is to call women by their first names while men in the same group are greeted with surnames, how frequently female executives are assumed by men to be secretaries, how often women are excluded from all-male social events where business is being transacted. With notable exceptions, men are still generally more comfortable with other men, and as a result women miss many of the career and business opportunities that arise over lunch, on the golf course, or in the locker room.

THE MAJORITY OF WOMEN, however, are what I call career-and-family women, women who want to pursue serious careers while participating actively in the rearing of children. These women are a precious resource that has yet to be mined. Many of them are talented and creative. Most of them are willing to trade some career growth and compensation for freedom from the constant pressure to work long hours and weekends.

Most companies today are ambivalent at best about the career-and-family women in their management ranks. They would prefer that all employees were willing to give their all to the company. They believe it is in their best interests for all managers to compete for the top positions so the company will have the largest possible pool from which to draw its leaders.

"If you have both talent and motivation," many employers seem to say, "we want to move you up. If you haven't got that motivation, if you want less pressure and greater flexibility, then you can leave and make room for a new generation." These companies lose on two counts. First, they fail to amortize the investment they made in the early training and experience of management women who find themselves committed to family as well as to career. Second, they fail to recognize what these women could do for their middle management.

The ranks of middle managers are filled with people on their way up and people who have stalled. Many of them have simply reached their limits, achieved career growth commensurate with or exceeding their capabilities, and they cause problems because their performance is mediocre but they still want to move ahead. The career-and-family woman is willing to trade off the pressures and demands that go with promotion for the freedom to spend more time with her children. She's very smart, she's talented, she's committed to her career, and she's satisfied to stay at the middle level, at least during the early child-rearing years. Compare her with some of the people you have there now.

Consider a typical example, a woman who decides in college on a business career and enters management at age 22. For nine years, the company invests in her career as she gains experience and skills and steadily improves her performance. But at 31, just as the investment begins to pay off in earnest, she decides to have a baby. Can the company afford to let her go home, take another job, or go into business for herself? The common perception now is yes, the corporation can afford to lose her unless, after six or eight weeks or even three months of disability and maternity leave, she returns to work on a full-time schedule with the same vigor, commitment, and ambition that she showed before.

But what if she doesn't? What if she wants or needs to go on leave for six months or a year or, heaven forbid, five years? In this worst-case scenario, she works full-time from age 22 to 31 and from 36 to 65—a total of 38 years as opposed to the typical male's 43 years. That's not a huge difference. Moreover, my typical example is willing to work part-time while her children are young, if only her employer will give her the opportunity. There are two rewards for companies responsive to this need: higher retention of their best people and greatly improved performance and satisfaction in their middle management.

The high-performing career-and-family woman can be a major player in your company. She can give you a significant business advantage as the competition for able people escalates. Sometimes too, if you can hold on to her, she will switch gears in mid-life and re-enter the competition for the top. The price you must pay to retain these women is threefold: you must plan for and manage maternity, you must provide the flexibility that will allow them to be maximally productive, and you must take an active role in helping to make family supports and high-quality, affordable child care available to all women.

THE KEY TO MANAGING maternity is to recognize the value of high-performing women and the urgent need to retain them and keep them productive. The first step must be a genuine partnership between the woman and her boss. I know this partnership can seem difficult to forge. One of my own senior executives came to me recently to discuss plans for her maternity leave and subsequent return to work. She knew she wanted to come back. I wanted to make certain that she would. Still, we had a somewhat awkward conversation, because I knew that no woman can predict with certainty when she will be able to return to work or under what conditions. Physical problems can lengthen her leave. So can a demanding infant, a difficult family or personal adjustment, or problems with child care.

I still don't know when this valuable executive will be back on the job full-time, and her absence creates some genuine problems for our organization. But I do know that I can't simply replace her years of experience with a new recruit. Since our conversation, I also know that she wants to come back, and that she *will* come back—part-time at first—unless I make it impossible for her by, for example, setting an arbitrary date for her full-time return or resignation. In turn, she knows that the organization wants and needs her and, more to the point, that it will be responsive to her needs in terms of working hours and child-care arrangements.

In having this kind of conversation it's important to ask concrete questions that will help to move the discussion from uncertainty and anxiety to some level of predictability. Questions can touch on everything from family income and energy level to child care arrangements and career commitment. Of course you want your star manager to return to work as soon as possible, but you want her to return permanently and productively. Her downtime on the job is a drain on her energies and a waste of your money.

FOR ALL THE WOMEN who want to combine career and family—the women who want to participate actively in the rearing of their children and who also want to pursue their careers seriously—the key to retention is to provide the flexibility and family supports they need in order to function effectively.

Time spent in the office increases productivity if it is time well spent, but the fact that most women continue to take the primary responsibility for child care is a cause of distraction, diversion, anxiety, and absenteeism—to say nothing of the persistent guilt experienced by all working mothers. A great many women, perhaps most of all women who have always performed at the highest levels, are also frustrated by a sense that while their children are babies they cannot function at their best either at home or at work.

In its simplest form, flexibility is the freedom to take time off—a couple of hours, a day, a week—or to do some work at home and some at the office, an arrangement that communication technology makes increasingly feasible. At the complex end of the spectrum are alternative work schedules that permit the woman to work less than full-time and her employer to reap the benefits of her experience and, with careful planning, the top level of her abilities.

Part-time employment is the single greatest inducement to getting women back on the job expeditiously and the provision women themselves most desire. A part-time return to work enables them to maintain responsibility for critical aspects of their jobs, keeps them in touch with the changes constantly occurring at the workplace and in the job itself, reduces stress and fatigue, often eliminates the need for paid maternity leave by permitting a return to the office as soon as disability leave is over, and, not least, can greatly enhance company loyalty. The part-time solution works particularly well when a work load can be reduced for one individual in a department or when a full-time job can be broken down by skill levels and apportioned to two individuals at different levels of skill and pay.

I believe, however, that shared employment is the most promising and will be the most widespread form of flexible scheduling in the future. It is feasible at every level of the corporation except at the pinnacle, for both the short and the long term. It involves two people taking responsibility for one job.

Two red lights flash on as soon as most executives hear the words "job sharing": continuity and client-customer contact. The answer to the continuity question is to place responsibility entirely on the two individuals sharing the job to discuss everything that transpires—thoroughly, daily, and on their own time. The answer to the problem of client-customer contact is yes, job sharing requires reeducation and a period of adjustment. But as both client and supervisor will quickly come to appreciate, two contacts means that the customer has continuous access to the company's representative, without interruptions for vacation, travel, or sick leave. The two people holding the job can simply cover for each other, and the uninterrupted, full-time coverage they provide together can be a stipulation of their arrangement.

Flexibility is costly in numerous ways. It requires more supervisory time to coordinate and manage, more office space, and somewhat greater benefits costs (though these can be contained with flexible benefits plans, prorated benefits, and, in two-paycheck families, elimination of duplicate benefits). But the advantages of reduced turnover and the greater productivity that results from higher energy levels and greater focus can outweigh the costs.

A few hints:

Provide flexibility selectively. I'm not suggesting private arrangements subject to the suspicion of favoritism but rather a policy that makes flexible work schedules available only to high performers.

Make it clear that in most instances (but not all) the rates of advancement and pay will be appropriately lower for those who take time off or who work part-time than for those who work full-time. Most career-and-family women are entirely willing to make that trade-off.

Discuss costs as well as benefits. Be willing to risk accusations of bias. Insist, for example, that half time is half of whatever time it takes to do the job, not merely half of 35 or 40 hours.

The woman who is eager to get home to her child has a powerful incentive to use her time effectively at the office and to carry with her reading and other work that can be done at home. The talented professional who wants to have it all can be a high performer by carefully ordering her priorities and by focusing on objectives rather than on the legendary 15-hour day. By the time professional women have their first babies—at an average age of 31—they have already had nine years to work long hours at a desk, to travel, and to relocate. In the case of high performers, the need for flexibility coincides with what has gradually become the goal-oriented nature of responsibility.

FAMILY SUPPORTS—in addition to maternity leave and flexibility—include the provision of parental leave for men, support for two-career and single-parent families during relocation, and flexible benefits. But the primary ingredient is child care. The capacity of working mothers to function effectively and without interruption depends on the availability of good, affordable child care. Now that women make up almost half the work force and the growing percentage of managers, the decision to be come involved in the personal lives of employees is no longer a philosophical question but a practical one. To make matters worse, the quality of child care has almost no relation to technology, inventiveness, or profitability but is more or less a pure function of the quality of child care personnel and the ratio of adults to children. These costs are irreducible. Only by joining hands with government and the public sector can corporations hope to create the vast quantity and variety of child care that their employees need.

Until quite recently, the response of corporations to women has been largely symbolic and cosmetic, motivated in large part by the will to avoid litigation and legal penalties. In some cases, companies were also moved by a genuine sense of fairness and a vague discomfort and frustration at the absence of women above the middle of the corporate pyramid. The actions they took were mostly quick, easy, and highly visible—child care information services, a three-month parental leave available to men as well as women, a woman appointed to the board of directors.

When I first began to discuss these issues 26 years ago, I was sometimes able to get an appointment with the assistant to the assistant in personnel, but it was only a courtesy. Over the past decade, I have met with the CEOs of many large corporations, and I've watched them become involved with ideas they had never previously thought much about. Until recently, however, the shelf life of that enhanced awareness was always short. Given pressing, short-term concerns, women were not a front-burner issue. In the past few months, I have seen yet another change. Some CEOs and top management groups now take the initiative. They call and ask us to show them how to shift gears from a responsive to a proactive approach to recruiting, developing, and retaining women.

I think this change is more probably a response to business needs—to concern for the quality of future profits and managerial talent—than to uneasiness about legal requirements, sympathy with the demands of women and minorities, or the desire to do what is right and fair. The nature of such business motivation varies. Some companies want to move women to higher positions as role models for those below them and as beacons for talented young recruits. Some want to achieve a favorable image with employees, customers, clients, and stockholders. These are all legitimate motives. But I think the companies that stand to gain most are motivated as well by a desire to capture competitive advantage in an era when talent and competence will be in increasingly short supply. These companies are now ready to stop being defensive about their experience with women and to ask incisive questions without preconceptions.

Even so, incredibly, I don't know of more than one or two companies that have looked into their own records to study the absolutely critical issue of maternity leave—how many women took it, when and whether they returned, and how this behavior correlated with their rank, tenure, age, and performance. The unique drawback to the employment of women is the physical reality of maternity and the particular socializing influence maternity has had. Yet to make women equal to men in the workplace we have chosen on the whole not to discuss this single most significant difference between them. Unless we do, we cannot evaluate the cost of recruiting, developing, and moving women up.

Now that interest is replacing indifference, there are four steps every company can take to examine its own experience with women:

1. Gather quantitative data on the company's experience with management-level women regarding turnover rates, occurrence of and return from maternity leave, and organizational level attained in relation to tenure and performance.

2. Correlate this data with factors such as age, marital status, and presence and age of children, and attempt to identify and analyze why women respond the way they do.

3. Gather qualitative data on the experience of women in your company and on how women are perceived by both sexes.

4. Conduct a cost-benefit analysis of the return on your investment in high-performing women. Factor in the cost to the company of women's negative reactions to negative experience, as well as the probable cost of corrective measures and policies. If women's value to your company is greater than the cost to recruit, train, and develop them—and of course I believe it will be—then you will want to do everything you can to retain them.

WE HAVE COME a tremendous distance since the days when the prevailing male wisdom saw women as lacking the kind of intelligence that would allow them to succeed in business. For decades, even women themselves have harbored an unspoken belief that they couldn't make it because they couldn't be just like men, and nothing else would do. But now that women have shown themselves the equal of men in every area of organizational activity, now that they have demonstrated that they can be stars in every field of endeavor, now we can all venture to examine the fact that women and men are different.

On balance, employing women is more costly than employing men. Women can acknowledge this fact today because they know that their value to employers exceeds the additional cost and because they know that changing attitudes can reduce the additional cost dramatically. Women in management are no longer an idiosyncrasy of the arts and education. They have always matched men in natural ability. Within a very few years, they will equal men in numbers as well in every area of economic activity.

The demographic motivation to recruit and develop women is compelling. But an older question remains: Is society better for the change? Women's exit from the home and entry into the work force has certainly created problems—an urgent need for good, affordable child care, troubling questions about the kind of parenting children need, the costs and difficulties of diversity in the workplace; the stress and fatigue of combining work and family responsibilities. Wouldn't we all be happier if we could turn back the clock to an age when men were in the workplace and women in the home, when male and female roles were clearly differentiated and complementary?

Nostalgia, anxiety, and discouragement will urge many to say yes, but my answer is emphatically no. Two fundamental benefits that were unattainable in the past are now within our reach. For the individual, freedom of choice—in this case the freedom to choose career, family, or a combination of the two. For the corporation, access to the most gifted individuals in the country. These benefits are neither self-indulgent nor insubstantial. Freedom of choice and self-realization are too deeply American to be cast aside for some wistful vision of the past. And access to our most talented human resources is not a luxury in this age of explosive international competition but rather the barest minimum that prudence and national self-preservation require.

On July 3, 1989, the U.S. Supreme Court upheld a 1986 Missouri law that imposed restrictions on abortion. Although the Court did not go so far as to reverse its 1973 Roe v. Wade decision, which legalized abortion throughout the country (see chapter 3), it let stand significant restrictions in the Missouri law, leading abortion opponents to declare the decision a victory for their side and abortion-rights backers to regard it as a defeat. In a five to four decision, the Court let stand the following restrictions embedded in the law: a preamble that declared that human life begins at conception; a ban on performing abortions at public hospitals or other tax-supported facilities and by any health-care providers paid by public funding; and a requirement that doctors perform tests to determine the viability of the fetus.

The Webster decision was a turning point for two reasons: first, it reflected the increasingly conservative bent of the Court; no longer did a majority of the justices consider abortion to be a fundamental right, as expressed in the Roe decision. Second, it shifted the battleground for abortion from the federal government to the states by giving state courts and legislatures more authority to impose restrictions, such as requiring a waiting period and the permission of a parent or notification of a spouse. In fact, the Court ruled on these very restrictions in Planned Parenthood v. Casey in 1992, excerpts of which are also included in this chapter.

In his dissent, Justice Harry Blackmun, who had written the Court's majority opinion in Roe v. Wade, bitterly dissented. He concluded, "For today, the women of this Nation still retain the liberty to control their destinies. But the signs are evident and very ominous, and a chill wind blows."

SOURCE: *Webster v. Reproductive Health Decision*, No. 88–605

[CHIEF JUSTICE REHNQUIST delivered the opinion of the Court.] This appeal concerns the constitutionality of a Missouri statute regulating the performance of abortions. The United States Court of Appeals for the Eighth Circuit struck down several provisions of the statute on the ground that they violated this Court's decision in *Roe v. Wade* (1973), and cases following it. We noted probable jurisdiction . . . and now reverse.

1

In June 1986, the Governor of Missouri signed into law Missouri Senate Committee Substitute for House Bill No. 1596 (hereinafter Act or statute), which amended existing state law concerning unborn children and abortions. The Act consisted of 20 provisions, 5 of which are now before the Court. The first provision, or preamble, contains "findings" by the state legislature that "[t]he life of each human being begins at conception," and that "unborn children have protectable interests in life, health, and well-being." The Act further requires that all Missouri laws be interpreted to provide unborn children with the same rights enjoyed by other persons, subject to the Federal Constitution and this Court's precedents. Among its other provisions, the Act requires that, prior to performing an abortion on any woman whom a physician has reason to believe is 20 or more weeks pregnant, the physician ascertain whether the fetus is viable by performing "such medical examinations and tests as are necessary to make a finding of the gestational age, weight, and lung maturity of the unborn child." The Act also prohibits the use of public employees and facilities to perform or assist abortions not necessary to save the mother's life, and it prohibits the use of public funds, employees, or facilities for the purpose of "encouraging or counseling" a woman to have an abortion not necessary to save her life.

In July 1986, five health professionals employed by the State and two nonprofit corporations brought this class action in the United States District Court for the Western District of Missouri to challenge the constitutionality of the Missouri statute. Plaintiffs, appellees in this Court, sought declaratory and injunctive relief on the ground that certain statutory provisions violated the First, Fourth, Ninth, and Fourteenth Amendments to the Federal Constitution. They asserted violations of various rights, including the "privacy rights of pregnant women seeking abortions"; the "woman's right to an abortion"; the "righ[t] to privacy in the physician-patient relationship"; the physician's "righ[t] to practice medicine"; the pregnant woman's "right to life due to inherent risks involved in childbirth"; and the woman's right to "receive . . . adequate medical advice and treatment" concerning abortions.

Plaintiffs filed this suit "on their own behalf and on behalf of the entire class consisting of facilities and Missouri licensed physicians or other health-care professionals offering abortion services or pregnancy counseling and on behalf of the entire class of pregnant females seeking abortion services or pregnancy counseling within the State of Missouri." The two nonprofit corporations are Reproductive Health Services, which offers family planning and gynecological services to the public, including abortion services up to 22 weeks "gestational age," and Planned Parenthood of Kansas City, which provides abortion services up to 14 weeks gestational age. The individual plaintiffs are three physicians, one nurse, and a social worker. All are "public employees" at "public facilities" in Missouri, and they are paid for their services with "public funds," as those terms are defined by Mo. Rev. Stat. <st> 188.200 (1986). The individual plaintiffs, within the scope of their public employment, encourage and counsel pregnant women to have nontherapeutic abortions. Two of the physicians perform abortions. . . .

2

Decision of this case requires us to address four sections of the Missouri Act: (a) the preamble; (b) the prohibition on the use of public facilities or employees to perform abortions; (c) the prohibition on public funding of abortion counseling; and (d) the requirement that physicians conduct viability tests prior to performing abortions. We address these *seriatim*.

A

. . . The State contends that the preamble itself is precatory and imposes no substantive restrictions on abortions, and that appellees therefore do not have standing to challenge it. Appellees, on the other hand, insist that the preamble is an operative part of the Act intended to guide the interpretation of other provisions of the Act. They maintain, for example, that the preamble's definition of life may prevent physicians in public hospitals from dispensing certain forms of contraceptives, such as the intrauterine device.

. . . It will be time enough for federal courts to address the meaning of the preamble should it be applied to restrict the activities of appellees in some concrete way. Until then, this Court "is not empowered to decide . . . abstract propositions, or to declare, for the government of future cases, principles or rules of law which cannot affect the result as to the thing in issue in the case before it." . . . We therefore need not pass on the constitutionality of the Act's preamble.

B

. . . [The Court of Appeals] reasoned that the ban on the use of public facilities "could prevent a woman's chosen doctor from performing an abortion because of his unprivileged status at other hospitals or because a private hospital adopted a similar anti-abortion stance." It also thought that "[s]uch a rule could increase the cost of obtaining an abortion and delay the timing of it as well."

We think that this analysis is much like that which we rejected in *Maher* [v. *Roe*, 1977], *Poelker* [v. *Doe*, 1977], and [*Harris* v.] *McRae* [1980]. As in those cases, the State's decision here to use public facilities and staff to encourage childbirth over abortion "places no governmental obstacle in the path of a woman who chooses to terminate her pregnancy" (*McRae*). Just as Congress' refusal to fund abortions in *McRae* left "an indigent woman with at least the same range of choice in deciding whether to obtain a medically necessary abortion as she would have had if Congress had chosen to subsidize no health-care costs at all," Missouri's refusal to allow public employees to perform abortions in public hospitals leaves a pregnant woman with the same choices as if the State had chosen not to operate any public hospitals at all. The challenged provisions only restrict a woman's ability to obtain an abortion to the extent that she chooses to use a physician affiliated with a public hospital. This circumstance is more easily remedied, and thus considerably less burdensome, than indigency, which "may make it difficult—and in some cases, perhaps, impossible—for some women to have abortions" without public funding (*Maher*). Having held that the State's refusal to fund abortions does not violate *Roe v. Wade*, it strains logic to reach a contrary result for the use of public facilities and employees. If the State may "make a value judgment favoring childbirth over abortion and . . . implement that judgment by the allocation of public funds," surely it may do so through the allocation of other public resources, such as hospitals and medical staff. . . .

Maher, *Poelker*, and *McRae* all support the view that the State need not commit any resources to facilitating abortions, even if it can turn a profit by doing so. In *Poelker*, the suit was filed by an indigent who could not afford to pay for an abortion, but the ban on the performance of nontherapeutic abortions in city-owned hospitals applied whether or not the pregnant woman could pay. The Court emphasized that the Mayor's decision to prohibit abortions in city hospitals was "subject to public debate and approval or disapproval at the polls," and that "the Constitution does not forbid a state or city, pursuant to democratic processes, from expressing a preference for normal childbirth as St. Louis has done." Thus we uphold the Act's restrictions on the use of public employees and facilities for the performance or assistance of nontherapeutic abortions.

[Section C omitted]

D

Section 188.029 of the Missouri Act provides:

> "Before a physician performs an abortion on a woman he has reason to believe is carrying an unborn child of twenty or more weeks gestational age, the physician shall first determine if the unborn child is viable by using and exercising that degree of care, skill, and proficiency commonly exercised by the ordinarily skillful, careful, and prudent physician engaged in similar practice under the same or similar conditions. In making this determination of viability, the physician shall perform or cause to be performed such medical examinations and tests as are necessary to make a finding of the gestational age, weight, and lung maturity of the unborn child and shall enter such findings and determination of viability in the medical record of the mother."

. . . The viability-testing provision of the Missouri Act is concerned with promoting the State's interest in potential human life rather than in maternal health. Section 188.029 creates what is essentially a presumption of viability at 20 weeks, which the physician must rebut with tests indicating that the fetus is not viable prior to performing an abortion. It also directs the physician's determination as to viability by specifying consideration, if feasible, of gestational age, fetal weight, and lung capacity. The District Court found that "the medical evidence is uncontradicted that a 20-week fetus is not viable," and that "23 1/2 to 24 weeks gestation is the earliest point in pregnancy where a reasonable possibility of viability exists." But it also found that there may be a 4-week error in estimating gestational age, which supports testing at 20 weeks.

In *Roe v. Wade*, the Court recognized that the State has "important and legitimate" interests in protecting maternal health and in the potentiality of human life. During the second trimester, the State "may, if it chooses, regulate the abortion procedure in ways that are reasonably related to maternal health." After viability, when the State's interest in potential human life was held to become compelling, the State "may, if it chooses, regulate, and even proscribe, abortion except where it is necessary, in appropriate medical judgment, for the preservation of the life or health of the mother." . . .

Stare decisis is a cornerstone of our legal system, but it has less power in constitutional cases, where, save for constitutional amendments, this Court is the only body able to make needed changes. . . . We have not refrained from reconsideration of a prior construction of the Constitution that has proved "unsound in principle and unworkable in practice." . . . We think the *Roe* trimester framework falls into that category.

In the first place, the rigid *Roe* framework is hardly consistent with the notion of a Constitution cast in general terms, as ours is, and usually speaking in general principles, as ours does. The key elements of the *Roe* framework—trimesters and viability—are not found in the text of the Constitution or in any place else one would expect to find a constitutional principle. Since the bounds of the inquiry are essentially indeterminate, the result has been a web of legal rules that have become increasingly intricate, resembling a code of regulations rather than a body of constitutional doctrine. As JUSTICE WHITE has put it, the trimester framework has left this Court to serve as the country's "*ex officio* medical board with powers to approve or disapprove medical and operative practices and standards throughout the United States." . . .

In the second place, we do not see why the State's interest in protecting potential human life should come into existence only at the point of viability, and that there should therefore be a rigid line allowing state regulation after viability but prohibiting it before viability. The dissenters in *Thornburgh*, writing in the context of the *Roe* trimester analysis, would have recognized this fact by positing against the "fundamental right" recognized in *Roe* the State's "compelling interest" in protecting potential human life throughout pregnancy. "[T]he State's interest, if compelling after viability, is equally compelling before viability." . . .

The tests that 188.029 requires the physician to perform are designed to determine viability. The State here has chosen viability as the point at which its interest in potential human life must be safeguarded. See Mo. Rev. Stat. 188.030 (1986) ("No abortion of a viable unborn child shall be performed unless necessary to preserve the life or health of the woman"). It is true that the tests in question increase the expense of abortion, and regulate the discretion of the physician in determining the viability of the fetus. Since the test will undoubtedly show in many cases that the fetus is not viable, the tests will have been performed for what were in fact second-trimester abortions. But we are satisfied that the requirement of these tests permissibly furthers the State's interest in protecting potential human life, and we therefore believe 188.029 to be constitutional. . . .

The dissent also accuses us, *inter alia*, of cowardice and illegitimacy in dealing with "the most politically divisive domestic legal issue of our time." There is no doubt that our holding today will allow some governmental regulation of abortion that would have been prohibited under the language of cases such as

Colautti v. Franklin, and *Akron v. Akron Center for Reproductive Health, Inc.* [1983]. But the goal of constitutional adjudication is surely not to remove inexorably "politically divisive" issues from the ambit of the legislative process, whereby the people through their elected representatives deal with matters of concern to them. The goal of constitutional adjudication is to hold true the balance between that which the Constitution puts beyond the reach of the democratic process and that which it does not. We think we have done that today. The dissent's suggestion, that legislative bodies, in a Nation where more than half of our population is women, will treat our decision today as an invitation to enact abortion regulation reminiscent of the dark ages not only misreads our views but does scant justice to those who serve in such bodies and the people who elect them.

3

Both appellants and the United States as *Amicus Curiae* have urged that we overrule our decision in *Roe v. Wade*. The facts of the present case, however, differ from those at issue in *Roe*. Here, Missouri has determined that viability is the point at which its interest in potential human life must be safeguarded. In *Roe*, on the other hand, the Texas statute criminalized the performance of *all* abortions, except when the mother's life was at stake. . . . This case therefore affords us no occasion to revisit the holding of *Roe*, which was that the Texas statute unconstitutionally infringed the right to an abortion derived from the Due Process Clause, and we leave it undisturbed. To the extent indicated in our opinion, we would modify and narrow *Roe* and succeeding cases.

Because none of the challenged provisions of the Missouri Act properly before us conflict with the Constitution, the judgment of the Court of Appeals is
    Reversed.

Throughout the 1980s and 1990s, antiabortion groups such as Operation Rescue, headed by the charismatic Randall Terry, resorted to increasingly violent and confrontational tactics to try to dissuade women from seeking a legally protected abortion. Planned Parenthood and other clinics that offered medically safe and legal abortions became prime targets of mob violence, arson, and even murder by antiabortion groups determined to shut them down. At a number of clinics around the country, doctors, nurses, even clerks and receptionists who staffed the front rooms were gunned down by violent opponents of abortion. The Operation Rescue demonstration detailed in the following selection is not unlike countless scenes played around the country at clinics and other abortion providers, where women clients had to run a gauntlet of harassment and verbal abuse to obtain a legally safeguarded medical procedure. These demonstrations have managed to drive many abortion providers out of business, with the end result being that women in rural areas and even many mid-sized towns must now drive long distances to obtain a safe, legal abortion. Note how the first speaker for Operation Rescue links the movement to liberation struggles of the past.

SOURCE: Catherine Whitney, *Whose Life?* (New York: William Morrow, 1991), pp. 99–104. Copyright © 1991 by Catherine Whitney. Reprinted by permission of HarperCollins Publishers Inc.

LOS ANGELES, CALIFORNIA, SPRING 1989

Bernard Nathanson stood in front of the packed church and squinted at the crowd of one thousand people through thick, black-rimmed glasses that gave his face an owlish look. He was not an attractive man. His jet black hair didn't fit his aging, heavy face; his suit was out of date and ill-fitting. His eyes behind the thick glasses were without charm or light. He looked grim, even angry. But when Nathanson began to speak, his voice was firm and clear. The room was hushed as the crowd hung on every word of the movement's most famous convert. Dr. Nathanson, once called the Abortion King, now sounded the battle cry for the Operation Rescue squads that were preparing to descend on abortion clinics the following day.

"You are the shock troops of the Lord," he told the crowd. "The soldiers of Spartacus, the colonial freedom fighters, the Underground Railroad." The crowd was on its feet now, stamping and cheering.

Nathanson stepped aside, and a younger, intense-looking man with curly hair stood center stage. He smiled widely as the crowd erupted in cheering and waving. There was fire in his eyes. His thin frame trembled with emotion. When he spoke, his voice had a strength and maturity that belied his age and stature. He was Randall Terry.

"We live in a child-hating culture," he cried. "We send our children off to school as soon as possible. . . . We don't bring them to worship with us. I know there are some women, even here tonight, who are saying, 'But I have four children already. I can't afford more.' But I tell you"—his voice resonated, bouncing off the walls of the room—"my God will provide!" Some of the women in the room were crying; many had their eyes tightly shut as though they were praying.

Terry stopped speaking, and the room grew silent again. His next words were delivered softly, reverently. "Tonight we are going to have a memorial service for Baby Choice." He stood aside as two women descended to the stage; one held a tiny coffin in her hands. Terry told the crowds to follow the ushers, one row at a time, to view the body. The lines began to form, and the men and women in the room, some holding small children by the hands, filed past the white coffin, each person looking down. Some gasped and shut their eyes. Others exclaimed in horror. The fetus in the coffin had been preserved in formaldehyde. It was a terrible sight, curled into itself, its body a strangely marbled black and white, the effects of having been burned in the womb of its mother during abortion. The viewing lasted more than an hour. Many people were crying now. There was a renewed fervor in the air, a revived determination. Baby Choice was the murdered outcome of abortion. The hundreds of people gathered here, these shock troops of the Lord, were preparing now to stage several days of rescue efforts at abortion clinics throughout the area. They were to start early the following morning. A minister stepped forward to deliver a final prayer. He closed his eyes. "Lord, bless your enemies, they know not what they are doing," he crooned, swaying against the microphone. "Stand beside us, your humble servants. Give us strength and courage against the evil forces who would murder your most beloved of creatures, your children. Stand beside us so your light might shine in the darkness of this evil age. In your name we pray . . . amen."

"Amen!" A thousand voices responded in unison.

It was nearly midnight, but Kathy L. was still on the phone. She had been calling people all night, organizing supporters around the area, pro-choicers willing to show up at her women's health clinic the following day and escort clients past the Operation Rescue mobs. This was not the first time Operation Rescue had paid a visit to her clinic. She knew the scene would be ugly.

The clinic had just reopened after an arson attack earlier in the year had caused nearly eighty thousand dollars in damage, and already Operation Rescue had targeted it for a sit-in. This week the "big guns" were in town: Randall Terry himself and Bernard Nathanson, the famous antiabortion doctor. Kathy expected a bitter fight.

Out of fairness she warned all the women scheduled for appointments the next day to expect trouble. Some of them had chosen to stay away. Those who tried to keep their appointments would be in for a shock; it was impossible to prepare anyone for the trauma of several hundred voices raised against her, the shouts of "Don't murder your baby!," or the signs bearing bloody pictures of aborted fetuses. The men and women she had organized to try to escort patients past the protesters wouldn't be able to shield women from the impact.

The media would be there, too, and this presented another dilemma. The women were rightfully concerned about appearing on the evening news for all the world to see.

Sometimes Kathy L. believed it was her rage that kept her going in the face of this impossible uphill battle. She had never been so furious in her life as the day after the arson, when she stood in the burned-out clinic. The equipment was a melted mess; the furniture was charred and molten. The carpets were soaked with water. Her first reaction was a deep feeling of grief and hopelessness. How could anyone do this? But the initial reaction was followed quickly by anger. She could not let this stop her. She called her staff and instructed them to come to work. They would do counseling and give pregnancy tests out of their cars if they had to. She found a friend who lent her a van. The arson slowed down business; but it did not stop the operation, and she was proud of that.

It was long after midnight when Kathy L. finally put down the phone. She had to get some sleep. She needed every last ounce of strength available for the next day's battle.

The sun was just coming up when the cars and buses began to arrive. Kathy L. and her staff were already at the clinic, preparing for the day's work. The twelve staff members would remain inside to treat the women who made it through the army of protesters. Kathy was to station herself in the parking lot and help the escorts get the women inside.

The clinic had two entrances, one in front and one in back near the parking lot. The Operation Rescue troops poured from their vehicles and began to sit on the porch and on the ground surrounding the doorways. They were strangely quiet, not talking or shouting, just peacefully singing Christian songs. Their voices—"Ama-zing grace . . . how sweet the sound"—formed an eerie backdrop to the promise of violence. Several policemen were leaning against their cars across the street, yawning and drinking coffee.

By the time the clinic opened at nine, the front and back yards were covered with hundreds of bodies, tightly squeezed together to form a human barrier. Behind them were hundreds more pro-choice activists, who above the strains of "Amazing Grace," shouted "Operation Rescue, your name's a lie! You don't care if women die!" A police bullhorn blared over the din, "Please remove yourselves. This is private property." The demand was ignored. The demonstrators kept singing. The bullhorn blasted again: "Please remove yourselves immediately or you will be arrested."

Of course, the protesters knew this. It was part of the plan. When the police finally moved in to begin the arrests, they would lie on the ground and become dead weight. It would take three or four officers to carry each protester to the van, with lengthy delays while each group of protesters was transported to the police station. It would be late in the day before enough protesters were removed to allow clear passage into the clinic.

A car drove up and paused hesitantly near the parking lot, which was crowded with protesters from both sides. Immediately a group from Operation Rescue rushed over to plaster pictures of bloody fetuses against the windshield. The young man and woman inside looked frightened. They quickly rolled up their windows. The Operation Rescue "counselors" shouted through the windows, "Don't murder your baby! Please don't kill your baby!"

The woman inside the car was crying. The man shook his head helplessly and finally drove away.

A woman from Operation Rescue screamed with joy, "A baby has been saved!"

The crowd of protesters cried, "Praise the Lord, praise the Lord . . . a baby saved!"

The policemen were carrying out the dead-weight bodies of protesters. As each person was removed, the others scooted together to tighten their ranks.

A young girl arrived with her friend, and Kathy and her aides took their arms and tried to push through the crowds. "It's murder! It's murder!" screamed the rescuers, shoving pictures into the girls' faces.

Pro-choicers surrounded the girls and there was pushing and shoving as the two sides collided. The girls were young, and they looked scared. "Let us through," sobbed one.

"Have your baby!" cried the rescuers.

It was impossible to get through.

One girl tugged at Kathy's sleeve. "I'm sorry, I can't," she said, tears streaming down her cheeks. She and her friend broke away and ran down the street.

"Another life saved!" shouted one of the rescuers, and the protesters on the ground cheered.

It went on and on. The protesters began to sing "The Battle Hymn of the Republic." By noon at least two hundred of them had been carried away by police, but those remaining were like the shifting sands of a sieve. They held together. No one had yet entered the clinic. The police were sweating and looked exhausted from their heavy labors.

Randall Terry perched on a van across the street, calling to the protesters through a bullhorn. "Squeeze together, hold your ranks. Have courage! Be strong! You are doing the Lord's work; you are saving innocent lives." Whenever the singing died down, his voice boomed out, picking up the tune— "Holy, Holy, Holy, Lord God Almighty"—and other voices rose once again.

By midafternoon tempers were flaring. "You have blood on your hands," shouted an Operation Rescue woman to the pro-choice group that was chanting, "Women's bodies, women's choice."

"I pity you!" screamed a young man as he was carried off by police. Reporters and cameramen scrambled on hands and knees to interview protesters and film the action. A line of policemen had secured the back door, and Kathy and her helpers were escorting women along a tightly formed police line. Operation Rescue protesters sobbed and screamed at them as they headed toward the door of the clinic. "Don't murder your baby! Please don't murder your baby!" One of the protesters, an elderly woman, fainted and was carried away by police. Only about fifty protesters remained in front of the clinic. They seemed to be uncertain of what to do.

"Hold your ground . . . be strong," Randall Terry shouted from the safety of his perch across the street.

It was 8:00 P.M. before the action was over. Coffee cups and food wrappers cluttered the grass in front of the clinic. Brochures showing gruesome color photographs of bloody fetuses fluttered in the wind. Wearily Kathy and her staff and supporters began the cleanup. The frustration was thick in the air.

"How long can this go on?" pleaded one of the workers, looking to Kathy for words of hope.

Kathy shook her head. "Seems like forever," she replied.

"I WANT THE CHANCE TO EXCEL"
PATRICIA GODLEY

With the widespread availability of crack, a mixture of baking soda, water, and cocaine, drug use reached epidemic proportions in America during the 1980s, especially in the inner cities. Crack was a relatively inexpensive and highly addictive drug, and it made few age or gender distinctions among its victims; parents and children and men and women alike became addicted, and the crime rate across the country soared as a result. The overall murder rate increased from 7.9 deaths per 100,000 people in 1985 to 9.8 deaths in 1991.[*]

On April 30, 1989, Nightline, an ABC late-night news and talk show, broadcast a town hall meeting in Washington, D.C., about the drug epidemic. Toward the end of the evening, Patricia Godley, a thirty-seven-year-old mother and recovering addict, stood up and spoke extemporaneously about her own searing battle with drugs and the problems of raising a child in the war zone of drug addiction. She also exhorted judges and policy makers to treat addicts like human beings who need help, not punishment. Her extraordinary words follow.

SOURCE: Reprinted by permission of ABC News/*Nightline*.

I'M—I'M A MOTHER, you understand. I heard a lot of things in here said. My son passed two weeks ago when he got killed, but that's okay. That's not even— that's not even the issue, that he's dead. The issue is that I have another one. And if other people have sons, you understand what I'm saying. I heard the man say on the television—this is addressed to you, sir—that parents need to get more involved. Okay, I'm a recovering addict. I'm a recovering convict. I've never been a parent, you understand? Society says that I have to be responsible. I'm trying to be responsible. I'm trying to be a productive member of society. I came from nothing because I thought nothing of myself. Today I see myself as someone, something.

I lost my child, but I have not had a drink or a drug behind his death, because that's not going to bring him back to me. What I do know is that I have another child that I know that needs me desperately. You all take us to jail, you all think I'm going steer straight. Bullshit! Pardon my expression. We learn

---

[*] Cited in Robert Torricelli and Andrew Carroll, eds., *In Our Own Words: Great Speeches of the Twentieth Century* (New York: Kodansha America, 1999), p. 380.

how to survive in the penal system. That's no problem. All we have to do is overlook somebody telling us when to get up and when to go to bed. But all your friends are there with you. How can it be rough?

You sent my son to Oak Hill to teach him a lesson. Judge, that city was a menace to society. No one took the time once to work with him, to evaluate him, to see what the penal system could do to help him be more productive. My son was handicapped. He could not read or write. And it was not his fault. I'm bad, not him. I brought him into this world, suffering. I did not know any better at the time, but that does not fix the wrong that I did. I can't give it back, I can't take it back. But I'm trying today. What can you do to help me to be something I've never been, a parent? I'm trying to assist my child. Can you do that?

I want that sister that said something about her brother to understand that there is a program, although they do close doors on programs every day. They're making the time shorter and shorter. It don't get you in seven days it's not going to get you to take a look at yourself, to see what you need on the inside. It's not the outside, it's the inside that needs help, you understand, that makes me feel like I'm worth fighting for my life. Seven days in the detox, that ain't gonna give me that. That's not going to make me look at me to feel like I'm worth fighting for my life.

Because that's what I'm fighting for today, you understand that? I'm not fighting for your seat. I don't want your damn job. I'm working hard. I pay my bills, goddamn it, I ain't on welfare. You understand what I'm saying? I'm a working taxpayer today. I'm off parole. I walked it down, because I wanted to. You can open up all the jails in the world that you choose to, but if you don't get to the core of the human being that you are incarcerating, nothing is ever going to change, nothing. Make me know that I'm worth fighting for instead of closing the door in my damn face. It took a judge, one judge, A. Franklin Burgess Jr., to see something in me that I didn't see in myself. When you shooting drugs you can't see nothing. You don't care about nothing. How could I care about me?

You got a lot of addicts out there that are suffering. I am recovering today, but you have a lot of them out there, man, that are suffering still, that don't see no hope, that don't see no way out. Do you know that the jail is a relief? They glad when you lock them up! They get three meals, a hot and a cot. They get more than they get out on the street. They need some help. We're learning that their life is worth something more than a piece of rock in a pipe or a piece of junk in a hype, you understand? I got a fourteen-year-old baby that I want to live to see. I swear to God, I do.

But I'm powerless over that part. I'm powerless over that part. You all also told me one thing to remember, that I'll run nothing, that I can't make my child do nothing, and you understand that. I can't put enough locks on my goddamn door to keep him in. If I'm going to work, if I'm going to take care, where do you go when you got people—you got young boys twenty-one years old out there with apartments of their own, seventeen, pay their own rent. Ain't no mother in there. They tell them, "Well, look, if you see my son, please send him home." Ain't nobody in there but kids. Kids dictating to kids.

Some of you all need to come down off them high horses you're up on and deal with it. Because you're watched on TV, you got a lot of clout. Mr. Koppel, you got a lot of clout. You understand? Granted, I ain't mad 'cause you had it. I have no animosity in my heart, because you had the potential to excel. I don't have that. I want the chance to excel. Make me feel like I can do it. That's what our children are asking for. The punk rock, the rapping, all that, that's not what I'm talking about. I'm talking about trying to give a child, the child, while they're young, man. You can take them off them porch out there and teach them that they have the potential to excel because somebody cares. Not just mouth service. The mouth'll say anything, but, hey, you don't lie. Thank you.

"CHERISH YOUR HUMAN CONNECTIONS"
BARBARA BUSH

First Lady Barbara Bush delivered the 1990 commencement address at Wellesley College in Wellesley, Massachusetts. About 150 members of the graduating class objected because she did not represent the committed career woman whom, they claimed, the college strove to produce. Bush had dropped out of Smith College to marry and help further her husband's political career. The protesting seniors circulated a petition against Bush's selection as speaker, which generated even more public support for the already quite popular first lady. Indeed, on commencement day, a new student petition supporting Bush's choice as speaker was unveiled. It declared: "In honoring Barbara Bush as our commencement speaker, we celebrate all the unknown women who have dedicated their lives to the service of others." Some students even wore purple armbands, the class color, to honor those women.

In her gracious commencement speech, Bush made light of the controversy surrounding her selection. Compare her speech to that of Adlai Stevenson's at the 1955 Smith commencement exercises. Bush certainly acknowledged and applauded the career aspirations of the young women whom she addressed, but at heart how different is her view of what women should most aspire to?

SOURCE: In the public domain.

THANK YOU VERY MUCH. Thank you President [Nan] Keohane, Mrs. [Raisa] Gorbachev, trustees, faculty, parents, Julie Porter, Christine Bicknell and, of course, the Class of 1990. I am thrilled to be with you today, and very excited, as I know you must all be, that Mrs. Gorbachev could join us. This is an exciting time in Washington, D.C. But I am so glad to be here. I knew coming to Wellesley would be fun, but I never dreamed it would be this much fun.

More than ten years ago when I was invited here to talk about our experiences in the People's Republic of China, I was struck by both the natural beauty of your campus . . . and the spirit of this place.

Wellesley, you see, is not just a place . . . but an idea . . . an experiment in excellence in which diversity is not just tolerated, but is embraced.

The essence of this spirit was captured in a moving speech about tolerance given last year by the student body president of one of your sister colleges. She related the story by Robert Fulghum about a young pastor who, finding himself in charge of some very energetic children, hits upon a game called "Giants,

Wizards and Dwarfs." "You have to decide now," the pastor instructed the children, "which you are . . . a giant, a wizard or a dwarf?" At that, a small girl tugging at his pants leg, asked, "But where do the mermaids stand?"

The pastor told her there are *no* mermaids, and she says, "Oh yes there are," she said. "I am a mermaid."

Now this little girl knew what she was and she was not about to give up on either her identity *or* the game. She intended to take her place wherever mermaids fit into the scheme of things. Where *do* mermaids stand. . . . All those who are different, those who do not fit the boxes and the pigeon-holes? "Answer that question," wrote Fulghum, "and you can build a school, a nation, or a whole world."

As that very wise young women said . . . "Diversity . . . like anything worth having . . . requires *effort*." Effort to learn about and respect difference, to be compassionate with one another, to cherish our own identity . . . and to accept unconditionally the same in others.

You should all be very proud that this is the Wellesley spirit. Now I know your first choice today was Alice Walker, known for *The Color Purple*. And guess how I know?

Instead you got me—known for . . . the color of my hair! Alice Walker's book has a special resonance here. At Wellesley, each class is known by a special color . . . for four years the Class of '90 has worn the color purple. Today you meet on Severance Green to say goodbye to all of that . . . to begin a new and very personal journey . . . to search for your own true colors.

In the world that awaits you beyond the shores of Lake Waban, no one can say what your true colors will be. But this I do know: You have a first class education from a first class school. And so you need not, probably cannot, live a "paint-by-numbers" life. Decisions are not irrevocable. Choices do come back. As you set off from Wellesley, I hope that many of you will consider making three very special choices.

The first is to believe in something larger than yourself. . . . To get involved in some of the big ideas of your time. I chose literacy because I honestly believe that if more people could read, write and comprehend, we would be that much closer to solving so many of the problems plaguing our society.

Early on I made another choice which I hope you will make as well. Whether you are talking about education, career or service, you are talking about life . . . and life must have joy. It's supposed to be fun!

One of the reasons I made the most important decision of my life . . . to marry George Bush . . . is because he made me laugh. It's true, sometimes we've laughed through our tears . . . but that shared laughter has been one of our strongest bonds. Find the joy in life, because as Ferris Bueller said on his day off . . . "Life moves pretty fast. Ya don't stop and look around once in a while, ya gonna miss it!" . . .

The third choice that must not be missed is to cherish your human connections: your relationships with friends and family. For several years, you've had impressed upon you the importance to your career of dedication and hard work. This is true, but as important as your obligations as a doctor, lawyer or business leader will be, you are a human being first and those human connections—with spouses, with children, with friends—are the most important investments you will ever make.

At the end of your life, you will never regret not having passed one more test, not winning one more verdict or not closing one more deal. You will regret time not spent with a husband, a friend, a child or a parent.

We are in a transitional period right now . . . fascinating and exhilarating times . . . learning to adjust to the changes and the choices we . . . men and women . . . are facing. . . .

Maybe we should adjust faster, maybe slower. But whatever the era . . . whatever the times, one thing will never change: Fathers and mothers, if you have children . . . they must come first. You must read to your children, you must hug your children, you must love your children.

Your success as a family . . . our success as a society . . . depends *not* on what happens at the White House, but on what happens inside your house.

For over 50 years, it was said that the winner of Wellesley's annual hoop race would be the first to get married. Now they say the winner will be the first to become a C.E.O. [chief executive officer]. Both of those stereotypes show too little tolerance for those who want to know where the mermaids stand. So I want to offer you today a new legend: The winner of the hoop race will be the first to realize her dream . . . not society's dream . . . her own personal dream. Who knows? Somewhere out in this audience may even be someone who will one day follow in my footsteps, and preside over the White House as the president's spouse. I wish him well!

The controversy ends here. But our conversation is only beginning. And worthwhile conversation it has been. So as you leave Wellesley today, take with you deep thanks for the courtesy and the honor you have shared with Mrs. Gorbachev and me. Thank you. God bless you. And may your future be worthy of your dreams.

"MEN ARE FROM MARS, WOMEN ARE FROM VENUS"
JOHN GRAY

First published in 1992, Men Are from Mars, Women Are from Venus *became a phenomenally popular self-help guide to male-female relationships and launched its author, John Gray, a couples counselor from Mill Valley, California, on an international career as a modern-day guru of marriage. To date, the book has sold more than ten million copies and has spawned a sequel, workshops and seminars, and a Web site. It continues to be a best-seller in this country and around the world. Echoing other popular self-help books of the early 1990s that emphasized gender differences in the interactions between women and men, Gray uses the metaphor of the planets to help his readers understand that they are "supposed to be different" and that awareness of these differences will help couples communicate better. In the following excerpt from the book, Gray explains what he perceives these differences to be, indulging in some long-held stereotypes about male and female behavior.*

SOURCE: John Gray, *Men Are from Mars, Women Are from Venus* (New York: Harper-Collins, 1992), pp. 9–13. Copyright © 1992 by John Gray. Reprinted by permission of HarperCollins Publishers Inc.

IMAGINE that men are from Mars and women are from Venus. One day long ago the Martians, looking through their telescopes, discovered the Venusians. Just glimpsing the Venusians awakened feelings they had never known. They fell in love and quickly invented space travel and flew to Venus.

The Venusians welcomed the Martians with open arms. They had intuitively known that this day would come. Their hearts opened wide to a love they had never felt before.

The love between the Venusians and Martians was magical. They delighted in being together, doing things together, and sharing together. Though from different worlds, they reveled in their differences. They spent months learning about each other, exploring and appreciating their different needs, preferences, and behavior patterns. For years they lived together in love and harmony.

Then they decided to fly to Earth. In the beginning everything was wonderful and beautiful. But the effects of Earth's atmosphere took hold, and one morning everyone woke up with a peculiar kind of amnesia—*selective amnesia*!

Both the Martians and Venusians forgot that they were from different planets and were supposed to be different. In one morning everything they had learned about their differences was erased from their memory. And since that day men and women have been in conflict.

REMEMBERING OUR DIFFERENCES

Without the awareness that we are supposed to be different, men and women are at odds with each other. We usually become angry or frustrated with the opposite sex because we have forgotten this important truth. We expect the opposite sex to be more like ourselves. We desire them to "want what we want" and "feel the way we feel."

We mistakenly assume that if our partners love us they will react and behave in certain ways-the ways we react and behave when we love someone. This attitude sets us up to be disappointed again and again and prevents us from taking the necessary time to communicate lovingly about our differences.

Men mistakenly expect women to think, communicate, and react the way men do; women mistakenly expect men to feel, communicate, and respond the way women do. We have forgotten that men and women are supposed to be different. As a result our relationships are filled with unnecessary friction and conflict.

Clearly recognizing and respecting these differences dramatically reduce confusion when dealing with the opposite sex. When you remember that men are from Mars and women are from Venus, everything can be explained.

AN OVERVIEW OF OUR DIFFERENCES

Throughout this book I will discuss in great detail our differences. Each chapter will bring you new and crucial, insights. Here are the major differences that we will explore:

In chapter 2 we will explore how men's and women's values are inherently different and try to understand the two biggest mistakes we make in relating to the opposite sex: men mistakenly offer solutions and invalidate feelings while women offer unsolicited advice and direction. Through understanding our Martian/Venusian background it becomes obvious why men and women *unknowingly* make these mistakes. By remembering these differences we can correct our mistakes and immediately respond to each other in more productive ways.

In chapter 3 we'll discover the different ways men and women cope with stress. While Martians tend to pull away and silently think about what's bothering them, Venusians feel an instinctive need to talk about what's bothering them. You will learn new strategies for getting what you want at these conflicting times.

We will explore how to motivate the opposite sex in chapter 4. Men are motivated when they feel needed while women are motivated when they feel cherished. We will discuss the three steps for improving relationships and explore how to overcome our greatest challenges: men need to overcome their resistance to giving love while women must overcome their resistance to receiving it.

In chapter 5 you'll learn how men and women commonly misunderstand each other because they speak different languages. A *Martian/Venusian Phrase Dictionary* is provided to translate commonly misunderstood expressions. You will learn how men and women speak and even stop speaking for entirely different reasons. Women will learn what to do when a man stops talking, and men will learn how to listen better without becoming frustrated.

In chapter 6 you will discover how men and women have different needs for intimacy. A man gets close but then inevitably needs to pull away. Women will learn how to support this pulling-away process so he will spring back to her like a rubber band. Women also will learn the best times for having intimate conversations with a man.

We will explore in chapter 7 how a woman's loving attitudes rise and fall rhythmically in a wave motion. Men will learn how correctly to interpret these sometimes sudden shifts of feeling. Men also will learn to recognize when they are needed the most and how to be skilfully supportive at those times without having to make sacrifices.

In chapter 8 you'll discover how men and women give the kind of love they need and not what the opposite sex needs. Men primarily need a kind of love that is trusting, accepting, and appreciative. Women primarily need a kind of love that is caring, understanding, and respectful. You will discover the six most common ways you may unknowingly be turning off your partner.

In chapter 9 we will explore how to avoid painful arguments. Men will learn that by acting as if they are always right they may invalidate a woman's feelings. Women will learn how they unknowingly send messages of disapproval instead of disagreement, thus igniting a man's defenses. The anatomy of an argument will be explored along with many practical suggestions for establishing supportive communication.

Chapter 10 will show how men and women keep score differently. Men will learn that for Venusians every gift of love scores equally with every other gift, regardless of size. Instead of focusing on one big gift men are reminded that the little expressions of love are just as important; 101 ways to score points with women are listed. Women, however, will learn to redirect their energies into ways that score big with men by giving men what they want.

In chapter 11 you'll learn ways to communicate with each other during difficult times. The different ways men and women hide feelings are discussed along with the importance of sharing feelings. The Love Letter Technique is recommended for expressing negative feelings to your partner, as a way of finding greater love and forgiveness.

You will understand why Venusians have a more difficult time asking for support in chapter 12, as well as why Martians commonly resist requests. You will learn how the phrases "could you" and "can you" turn off men and what to say instead. You will learn the secrets for encouraging a man to give more and discover in various ways the power of being brief, direct, and using the correct wording.

In chapter 13 you'll discover the four seasons of love. This realistic perspective of how love changes and grows will assist you in overcoming the inevitable obstacles that emerge in any relationship. You will learn how your past or your partner's past can affect your relationship in the present and discover other important insights for keeping the magic of love alive.

In each chapter of *Men Are from Mars, Women Are from Venus* you will discover new secrets for creating loving and lasting relationships. Each new discovery will increase your ability to have fulfilling relationships.

GOOD INTENTIONS ARE NOT ENOUGH

Falling in love is always magical. It feels eternal, as if love will last forever. We naïvely believe that somehow we are exempt from the problems our parents had, free from the odds that love will die, assured that it is meant to be and that we are destined to live happily ever after.

But as the magic recedes and daily life takes over, it emerges that men continue to expect women to think and react like men, and women expect men to feel and behave like women. Without a clear awareness of our differences, we do not take the time to understand and respect each other. We become demanding, resentful, judgmental, and intolerant.

With the best and most loving intentions love continues to die. Somehow the problems creep in. The resentments build. Communication breaks down. Mistrust increases. Rejection and repression result. The magic of love is lost.

"I AM NOT GIVEN TO FANTASY"

ANITA HILL

For several days in early October 1991, millions of Americans sat riveted to their television sets watching the Senate Judiciary hearings on the nomination of Judge Clarence Thomas, former chairman of the Equal Employment Opportunity Commission (EEOC), to the United States Supreme Court. What occasioned this unprecedented public fascination with an event normally treated with only passing interest by most Americans were the allegations leveled by law professor Anita Hill, who had been one of Thomas's deputies at the EEOC, that Thomas had sexually harassed her for several years prior to his nomination. She alleged that he had pressured her for dates, described pornographic movies in disturbing detail, bragged about his sexual prowess, and made uncomfortable sexual jokes. Hill, who had been contacted by investigators on the Senate Judiciary Committee, had not wanted her name publicly disclosed but soon found herself on television and radio being grilled by the all-male committee and forced to recount uncomfortable details of her interactions with Thomas.

For his part, Thomas vehemently denied all of her allegations and compared himself to a lynching victim—thereby offending many African Americans who accused him of misappropriating for his own purposes a painful chapter in African American history. Apart from the somewhat lurid sexual contents of the hearings, the conflict between Hill and Thomas, both highly educated and intelligent African American professionals, also captured public attention because of the public airing of conflicts between black women and men.

The harsh grilling of Hill, along with Thomas's confirmation to the highest court in the land, galvanized more women to run for office in 1992 and also contributed to Bill Clinton's strong support among women in the 1992 presidential campaign against incumbent George Bush, who had nominated Thomas to the High Court. Other women made record-breaking contributions to the campaigns of female candidates. The article by Eloise Salholz et al. in the following chapter describes the impact of the Thomas confirmation hearings on the "year of the woman" in politics.

For black women, the confirmation hearings finally exposed the long-simmering issue of sexual harassment within the African American community. One woman compared the hearings to "a hurricane that whipped across the landscape of our lives," yet left "a rainbow in the wake." Following are excerpts from Anita Hill's testimony.*

SOURCE: U.S. Senate, Committee on the Judiciary, *Nomination of Clarence Thomas to Be Associate Justice of the Supreme Court of the United States,* hearing, part 4, October 11, 12, 13, 1991 (Washington, D.C.: Government Printing Office, 1993), pp. 83–4, 96–7.

SEN. SPECTER:

. . . I want to ask you about one statement of Charles Kothe, Dean Kothe, because he knew you and Judge Thomas very well. I want to ask you for your comment on it. There is a similar reference in the Doggett statement which I am not going to ask you about because you haven't read the Doggett statement and you say you do not remember him. Out of fairness I want to give you a chance to read that first, but you do know Dean Kothe and he does know Judge Thomas.

And this is—his concluding statement: "I find the references to the alleged sexual harassment not only unbelievable but preposterous. I am convinced that such are the product of fantasy." Would you care to comment on that?

MS. HILL:

Well I would only say that I am not given to fantasy. This is not something that I would have come forward with, if I were not absolutely sure about what it is I am saying. I weighted this very carefully, I considered it carefully and I made a determination to come forward. I think it is unfortunate that that comment was made by a man who purports to be someone who says he knows me, and I think it is just inaccurate. . . .

SEN. SPECTER:

Well, you have added, during the course of your testimony today, two new witnesses whom you made this complaint to. When you talked to the FBI, there was one witness, and you are testifying today that you are now, "recalling more," that you had "repressed a lot." And the question which I have for you is, how reliable is your testimony in October 1991 on events that occurred 8, 10 years ago, when you are adding new factors, explaining them by saying you have repressed a lot? And in the context of a sexual harassment charge where the Federal law is very firm on a 6-month period of limitation, how sure can you expect this committee to be on the accuracy of your statements?

MS. HILL:

Well, I think if you start to look at each individual problem with the statement, then you're not going to be satisfied that it's true, but I think the state-

---

* Nellie Y. McKay, "Remembering Anita Hill and Clarence Thomas: What Really Happened When One Black Woman Spoke Out," in *Race-ing Justice, Engendering Power*, edited by Toni Morrison (New York: Pantheon, 1992), pp. 269, 277.

ment has to be taken as a whole. There's nothing in the statement, nothing in my background, nothing in my statement, there is no motivation that would show that I would make up something like this. I guess one really does have to understand something about the nature of sexual harassment. It is very difficult for people to come forward with these things, these kinds of things. It wasn't as though I rushed forward with this information.

I can only tell you what happened, to the best of my recollection what occurred and ask you to take that into account. Now, you have to make your own judgments about it from there on, but I do want you to take into account the whole thing.

SEN. SPECTER:

Well, I will proceed with the question of motivation on my next round, because the red light is now on. . . .

SEN. SPECTER:

. . . Professor Hill, I had started to question you about this affidavit. I had desisted in mid sentence because I wanted you to have an opportunity to read it. There was a concern on my part about the document, but I think it has sufficient value, and since you are willing to respond to it, I'm going to discuss it with you briefly.

This is an affidavit provided by a man who knew both you and Judge Thomas, and its relevancy, to the extent that it is relevant, arises on page 2 where Mr. Doggett says the following:

"The last time I saw Professor Anita Hill was at a going away party that her friends held for her at the Sheraton Carlton Hotel on K Street, just before she left for Oral Roberts Law School. During this party, she said that she wanted me to talk in private. When we moved to a corner of the room she said, 'I am very disappointed in you. You really shouldn't lead on women and then let them down.' When she made that statement, I had absolutely no idea what she was talking about. When I asked her what she meant she stated that she had assumed that I was interested in her. She said it was wrong for me not to have dinner with her or to try to get to know her better. She said that my actions hurt her feelings, and I shouldn't lead women on like that. Quite frankly, I was stunned by her statement and I told her that her comments were totally uncalled for and completely unfounded. I reiterated that I had never expressed a romantic interest in her and had done nothing to give her any indication that I might be romantically interested in her in the future. I also stated that the fact that I lived three or four blocks away from her but never came over to her house or invited her to my condominium should have been a clear sign that I had no personal or romantic interest in her. I came away from her going-away party feeling that she was somewhat unstable and that in my case she had fantasied about my being interested in her romantically."

On page 3,

"It was my opinion at the time and it is now my opinion that Ms. Hill's fantasies about sexual interest in her were an indication of the fact that she was having a problem being rejected by men she was attracted to. Her statements and actions in my presence during the time when she alleges that Clarence Thomas harassed her were totally inconsistent with her current descriptions and are, in my opinion, yet another example of her ability to fabricate the idea that someone was interested in her when, in fact, no such interest existed."

My question to you, Professor Hill, is, is Mr. Doggett accurate when he quotes you as saying, "I am very disappointed in you. You really shouldn't lead on women, and then let them down."

MS. HILL:
No, he is not.

SEN. SPECTER:
What, if anything, did he say to you?

MS. HILL:
As I recall, before we broke I told you that I had very limited memory of Mr. Doggett. The event that he is talking about was a party where there were 30 or 40 people. I was talking to a lot of people, they were people who I had known while I was here in Washington, and we might have had some conversation, but this was not the content of that conversation. I have very limited memory of him. I did not at any time have any fantasy about a romance with him.

"YOU HAVE MADE US LADIES AGAIN"
SARAH J. McCARTHY

Not all women were happy with the intense scrutiny accorded sexual ha-rassment in the aftermath of the Anita Hill–Clarence Thomas testimony. (See the previous document.) Sarah J. McCarthy, proprietor of a small restaurant, took is-sue with provisions of a 1991 civil rights bill that punishes small business owners and employees for using offensive language. As McCarthy points out, this "cultural fascism" may boomerang against the very people it is intended to help—women, whom employers might shy away from hiring for fear of potential litigation. Here is a forceful voice raised in opposition to what McCarthy views as political correct-ness run amok.

SOURCE: Sarah J. McCarthy, "Cultural Fascism," *Forbes* 148 (December 9, 1991), p. 116. Reprinted by permission of Forbes Magazine © 2002 Forbes Inc.

ON THE SAME DAY that Ted Kennedy asked forgiveness for his personal "shortcomings," he advocated slapping lottery-size punitive damages on small-business owners who may be guilty of excessive flirting, or whose em-ployees may be guilty of talking dirty. Senator Kennedy expressed regrets that the new civil rights bill caps punitive damages for sexual harassment as high as $300,000 (depending on company size), and he promises to push for in-creases next year. Note that the senators have voted to exempt themselves from punitive damages.

I am the owner of a small restaurant/bar that employs approximately 20 young males whose role models range from Axl Rose to John Belushi. They work hard in a high-stress, fast-paced job in a hot kitchen and at times they are guilty of colorful language. They have also been overheard telling Pee-wee Her-man jokes and listening to obnoxious rock lyrics. They have discussed pornog-raphy and they have flirted with waitresses. One chef/manager has asked out a pretty blonde waitress probably 100 times in three years. She seems to enjoy the game, but always says no. Everyone calls everyone else "Honey"—it's a ritual, a way of softening what sound like barked orders; "I need the medium rare shish kebab *now!*"

"Honey" doesn't mean the same thing here as it does in women's studies de-partments or at the EEOC. The auto body shop down the street has pinups. Perhaps under the vigilant eyes of the feminist political correctness gestapo we can reshape our employees' behavior so they act more like nerds from the Yale women's studies department. The gestapo will not lack for potential informers seeking punitive damages and instant riches.

With the Civil Rights Bill of 1991 we are witnessing the most organized and systematic assault on free speech and privacy since the McCarthy era. The vagueness of the sexual harassment law, combined with our current litigation explosion, is a frightening prospect for small businesses. We are now financially responsible for sexually offensive verbal behavior, even if we don't know it is occurring, under a law that provides no guidelines to define "offensive" and "harassment." This is a cultural fascism unmatched since the Chinese communists outlawed hand-holding, decorative clothing and premarital sex.

This law is detrimental even to the women it professes to help. I am a feminist, but the law has made me fearful of hiring women. If one of our cooks or managers—or my husband or sons—offends someone, it could cost us $100,000 in punitive damages and legal expenses. There will be no insurance fund or stockholders or taxpayers to pick up the tab.

When I was a feminist activist in the Seventies, we knew the dangers of a pedestal—it was said to be as confining as any other small place. As we were revolted and outraged by the woman-hatred in violent pornography, we reminded each other that education, not laws, was the solution to our problems. In Women Against Sexist Violence in Pornography and Media in Pittsburgh, we were well aware of the dangers of encroaching on the First Amendment. Free speech was, perhaps more than anything else, what made our country grow into a land of enlightenment and diversity. The lesbians among us were aware that the same laws used to censor pornography could be used against them if their sexual expressions were deemed offensive.

We admired powerful women writers such as Marge Piercy and poets like Robin Morgan who swooped in from nowhere, writing break-your-chains poems about women swinging from crystal chandeliers like monkey vines and defecating in punch bowls. Are we allowed to talk about these poems in the current American workplace?

The lawyers—the prim women and men who went to the politically correct law schools—believe with sophomoric arrogance that the solution to all the world's problems is tort litigation. We now have eternally complicated questions of sexual politics judged by the shifting standards of the reasonable prude.

To the leadership of the women's movement: You do women a disservice. You ladies—and I use that term intentionally—have trivialized the women's movement. You have made us ladies again. You have not considered the unintended effects of your sexual harrasment law. You are saying that too many things men say and do with each other are too rough-and-tumble for us. Wielding the power of your $300,000 lawsuits, you are frightening managers into hiring men over women. I know that I am so frightened. You have installed a double pane of glass on the glass ceiling with the help of your white knight and protector, Senator Kennedy.

You and your allies tried to lynch Clarence Thomas. You alienate your natural allies. Men and women who wanted to work shoulder to shoulder with you are now looking over their shoulders. You have made women into china dolls that if broken come with a $300,000 price tag. The games, intrigue, nuances and fun of flirting have been made into criminal activity.

We women are not as delicate and powerless as you think. We do not want victim status in the workplace. Don't try to foist it on us.

"Construction of the glass ceiling begins not in the executive suite but in the classroom," declared Alice McKee, president of the AAUW (American Association of University Women) Education Foundation. With that, the AAUW released a report on February 12, 1992, entitled* How Schools Shortchange Girls. *The report, sponsored by the AAUW Education Foundation and based on a study of current research by the Wellesley College Center for Research on Women, highlighted in stunning detail the many ways in which the educational, and specifically classroom, experience of girls was inferior to that of boys. The report concluded that teachers paid less classroom attention to girls than to boys, used a punitive double standard for responding to female students who answered questions without first raising their hands, and paid even less attention to African American girls, even though these students attempted to initiate contact more frequently than did white girls or boys of either race.*

The report also cited a 1989 study that found that, among the ten books most frequently assigned in high school English classes, only one was written by a woman and none by an ethnic author. Equally disturbing, the report also documented the small percentage of girls who were majoring in science and engineering in college and traced an alarming decline in girls' self-confidence as they progressed from childhood to adolescence.

Besides compiling and analyzing research findings of numerous individual studies, the report's major contribution to understanding the obstacles that lay in the way of girls' academic achievement was a comprehensive blueprint for change, including a variety of specific recommendations. Among educators and government officials, the report garnered strong reactions. Many educators praised the scope of the report and promised to make renewed efforts to abolish gender discrimination in the classroom. But Diane Ravitch, assistant secretary for educational research and improvement in the U.S. Department of Education, declared, "I really think the report is a lot of special interest whining" by "some overheated feminists." What is often construed as bias in the classroom, she contended, is

---

* Quoted in *Historic Documents of 1992* (Washington, D.C.: Congressional Quarterly, Inc., 1993), p. 141.

merely the teacher's effort to encourage boys to answer questions when girls "are eager to participate and have their hands up."[*]

SOURCE: From the executive summary of the report *How Schools Shortchange Girls*, American Association of University Women, released 12 February 1992. Reprinted by permission of AAUW Educational Foundation.

THE INVISIBILITY of girls in the current education debate suggests that girls and boys have identical educational experiences in school. Nothing could be further from the truth. Whether one looks at achievement scores, curriculum design, or teacher-student interaction, it is clear that sex and gender make a difference in the nation's public elementary and secondary schools.

The educational system is not meeting girls' needs. Girls and boys enter school roughly equal in measured ability. Twelve years later, girls have fallen behind their male classmates in key areas such as higher-level mathematics and measures of self-esteem. Yet gender equity is still not a part of the national debate on educational reform. . . .

WHAT THE RESEARCH REVEALS

What Happens in the Classroom?

- Girls receive significantly less attention from classroom teachers than do boys.
- African American girls have fewer interactions with teachers than do white girls, despite evidence that they attempt to initiate interactions more frequently.
- Sexual harassment of girls by boys—from innuendo to actual assault—in our nation's schools is increasing.

A large body of research indicates that teachers give more classroom attention and more esteem-building encouragement to boys. In a study conducted by Myra and David Sadker, boys in elementary and middle school called out answers eight times more often than girls. When boys called out, teachers listened. But when girls called out, they were told to "raise your

---

[*] Quoted in ibid., p. 143.

hand if you want to speak." Even when boys do not volunteer, teachers are more likely to encourage them to give an answer or an opinion than they are to encourage girls.

Research reveals a tendency, beginning at the preschool level, for educators to choose classroom activities that appeal to boys' interests and to select presentation formats in which boys excel. The teacher-student interaction patterns in science classes are often particularly biased. Even in math classes, where less-biased patterns are found, psychologist Jacquelynne Eccles reports that select boys in each math class she studied received particular attention to the exclusion of all other students, female and male. . . .

Researchers, including Sandra Damico, Elois Scott, and Linda Grant, report that African American girls have fewer interactions with teachers than do white girls, even though they attempt to initiate interactions more often. Furthermore, when African American girls do as well as white boys in school, teachers often attribute their success to hard work while assuming that the white boys are not working up to their potential.

Girls do not emerge from our schools with the same degree of confidence and self-esteem as boys. The 1990 AAUW poll, *Shortchanging Girls, Shortchanging America*, documents a loss of self-confidence in girls that is twice that for boys as they move from childhood to adolescence. Schools play a crucial role in challenging and changing gender-role expectations that undermine the self-confidence and achievement of girls.

Reports of boys sexually harassing girls in schools are increasing at an alarming rate. When sexual harassment is treated casually, as in "boys will be boys," both girls and boys get a dangerous, damaging message: "girls are not worthy of respect; appropriate behavior for boys includes exerting power over girls."

What Do We Teach Our Students?

- The contributions and experiences of girls and women are still marginalized or ignored in many of the textbooks used in our nation's schools.
- Schools, for the most part, provide inadequate education on sexuality and healthy development despite national concern about teen pregnancy, the AIDS crisis, and the increase of sexually transmitted diseases among adolescents.
- Incest, rape, and other physical violence severely compromise the lives of

girls and women all across the country. These realities are rarely, if ever, discussed in schools. . . .

Studies have shown that multicultural readings produced markedly more favorable attitudes toward nondominant groups than did the traditional reading lists, that academic achievement for all students was linked to use of nonsexist and multicultural materials, and that sex-role stereo-typing was reduced in students whose curriculum portrayed males and females in nonstereotypical roles. Yet during the 1980s, federal support for reform regarding sex and race equity dropped, and a 1989 study showed that of the ten books most frequently assigned in public high school English courses only one was written by a woman and none by members of minority groups. . . .

Perhaps the most evaded of all topics in schools is the issue of gender and power. As girls mature they confront a culture that both idealizes and exploits the sexuality of young women while assigning them roles that are clearly less valued than male roles. If we do not begin to discuss more openly the ways in which ascribed power—whether on the basis of race, sex, class, sexual orientation, or religion—affects individual lives, we cannot truly prepare our students for responsible citizenship.

*How Do Race/Ethnicity and Socioeconomic Status Affect
Achievement in School?*

- Girls from low-income families face particularly severe obstacles. Socioeconomic status, more than any other variable, affects access to school resources and educational outcomes.
- Test scores of low-socioeconomic-status girls are somewhat better than for boys from the same background in the lower grades, but by high school these differences disappear. Among high-socioeconomic-status students, boys generally outperform girls regardless of race/ethnicity.
- Too little information is available on differences among various groups of girls. While African Americans are compared to whites, or boys to girls, relatively few studies or published data examine differences by sex *and* race/ethnicity.

All girls confront barriers to equal participation in school and society. But minority girls, who must confront racism as well as sexism, and girls from low-income families face particularly severe obstacles. These obstacles can include poor schools in dangerous neighborhoods, low teacher expectations, and inadequate nutrition and health care. . . .

How Are Girls Doing in Math and Science?

- Differences between girls and boys in math achievement are small and declining. Yet in high school, girls are still less likely than boys to take the most advanced courses and be in the top-scoring math groups.
- The gender gap in science, however, is *not* decreasing and may, in fact, be increasing.
- Even girls who are highly competent in math and science are much less likely to pursue scientific or technological careers than are their male classmates.

Girls who see math as "something men do" do less well in math than girls who do not hold this view. In their classic study, Elizabeth Fennema and Julia Sherman reported a drop in both girls' math confidence and their achievement in the middle school years. The drop in confidence *preceded* the decline in achievement. . . . Even when girls take math and science courses and do well in them, they do not receive the encouragement they need to pursue scientific careers. A study of high school seniors found that 64 percent of the boys who had taken physics and calculus were planning to major in science and engineering in college, compared to only 18.6 percent of the girls who had taken the same subjects. Support from teachers can make a big difference. Studies report that girls rate teacher support as an important factor in decisions to pursue scientific and technological careers. . . .

Why Do Girls Drop Out and What Are the Consequences?

- Pregnancy is not the only reason girls drop out of school. In fact, less than half the girls who leave school give pregnancy as the reason.
- Dropout rates for Hispanic girls vary considerably by national origin: Puerto Rican and Cuban American girls are more likely to drop out than are boys from the same cultures or other Hispanic girls.
- Childhood poverty is almost inescapable in single-parent families headed by

women without a high school diploma: 77 percent for whites and 87 percent for African Americans.

In a recent study, 37 percent of the female drop-outs compared to only 5 percent of the male drop-outs cited "family-related problems" as the reason they left high school. Traditional gender roles place greater family responsibilities on adolescent girls than on their brothers. Girls are often expected to "help out" with caretaking responsibilities; boys rarely encounter this expectation. . . .

The current education-reform movement cannot succeed if it continues to ignore half of its constituents. We must move girls from the sidelines to the center of education planning. The issues are urgent; our actions must be swift and effective.

The Recommendations

Strengthened reinforcement of Title IX is essential. . . .

Teachers, administrators, and counselors must be prepared and encouraged to bring gender equity and awareness to every aspect of schooling. . . .

The formal school curriculum must include the experiences of women and men from all walks of life. Girls and boys must see women and girls reflected and valued in the materials they study. . . .

Girls must be educated and encouraged to understand that mathematics and the sciences are important and relevant to their lives. Girls must be actively supported in pursuing education and employment in these areas. . . .

Continued attention to gender equity in vocational education programs must be a high priority at every level of educational governance and administration. . . .

Testing and assessment must serve as stepping stones not stop signs. New tests and testing techniques must accurately reflect the abilities of both girls and boys. . . .

Girls and women must play a central role in educational reform. The experiences, strengths, and needs of girls from every race and social class must be considered in order to provide excellence and equity for all our nation's students. . . .

"THE MYTH OF THE MISERABLE WORKING WOMAN"
ROSALIND C. BARNETT AND CARYL RIVERS

Do working homemakers suffer from greater bouts of stress, depression, and other illnesses? In an article studded with an array of surveys and studies, Rosalind C. Barnett, a research psychologist, and Caryl Rivers, a journalist, answered with a resounding no. On the contrary, they reported, working women across the income spectrum experience higher levels of self-confidence and better mental and physical health. And their children also benefit by having mothers who are more satisfied with their own lives and who provide less sex-stereotyped images of women. While paying lip service to the need for quality, affordable child care, the authors gloss over the double burden of paid work and home work that working mothers contend with—the "second shift" that Arlie Hochschild describes in this chapter.

SOURCE: Rosalind C. Barnett and Caryl Rivers, "The Myth of the Miserable Working Woman," *Working Woman* 17, no. 2 (February 1992): 62. Copyright © 1992 by Working Woman, Inc. Reprinted with permission.

IF YOU BELIEVE what you read, working women are in big trouble—stressed out, depressed, sick, risking an early death from heart attacks, and so overcome with problems at home that they make inefficient employees at work.

In fact, just the opposite is true. As a research psychologist whose career has focused on women and a journalist-critic who has studied the behavior of the media, we have extensively surveyed the latest data and research and concluded that the public is being engulfed by a tidal wave of disinformation that has serious consequences for the life and health of every American woman. Since large numbers of women began moving into the work force in the 1970s, scores of studies on their emotional and physical health have painted a very clear picture: Paid employment provides substantial health *benefits* for women. These benefits cut across income and class lines; even women who are working because they have to—not because they want to—share in them.

There is a curious gap, however, between what these studies say and what is generally reported on television, radio, and in newspapers and magazines. The more the research shows work is good for women, the bleaker the media reports seem to become. Whether this bizarre state of affairs is the result of a backlash against women . . . or of well-meaning ignorance, the effect is the same: Both the shape of national policy and the lives of women are at risk. . . .

THE CORONARY THAT WASN'T

In the 19th century it was accepted medical dogma that women should not be educated because the brain and the ovaries could not develop at the same time. Today it's PMS, the wrong math genes or rampaging hormones. Hardly anyone points out the dire predictions that didn't come true.

You may remember the prediction that career women would start having more heart attacks, just like men. But the Framingham Heart Study—a federally funded cardiac project that has been studying 10,000 men and women since 1948—reveals that working women are not having more heart attacks. They're not dying any earlier, either. Not only are women not losing their health advantages; the lifespan gap is actually widening. Only one group of working women suffers more heart attacks than other women: those in low-paying clerical jobs with many demands on them and little control over their work pace, who also have several children and little or no support at home.

As for the recent publicity about women having more problems with heart disease, much of it skims over the important underlying reasons for the increase—namely, that by the time they have a heart attack, women tend to be a good deal older (an average of 67, six years older than the average age for men), and thus frailer, than males who have one. Also, statistics from the National Institutes of Health show that coronary symptoms are treated less aggressively in women—fewer coronary bypasses, for example. In addition, most heart research is done on men, so doctors do not know as much about the causes—and treatment—of heart disease in women. None of these factors have anything to do with work.

But doesn't working put women at greater risk for stress-related illnesses? No. Paid work is actually associated with *reduced* anxiety and depression. . . .

For example:

- A 1989 report by psychologist Ingrid Waldron and sociologist Jerry Jacobs of Temple University on nationwide surveys of 2,392 white and 892 black women, conducted from 1977 to 1982, found that women who held both work and family roles reported better physical and mental health than homemakers.
- According to sociologists Elaine Wethington of Cornell University and Ronald Kessler of the University of Michigan, data from three years (1985 to 1988) of a continuing federally funded study of 745 married women in Detroit "clearly suggests that employment benefits women emotionally."

Women who increase their participation in the labor force report lower levels of psychological distress; those who lessen their commitment to work suffer from higher distress.

- A University of California at Berkeley study published in 1990 followed 140 women for 22 years. At age 43, those who were homemakers had more chronic conditions than the working women and seemed more disillusioned and frustrated. The working mothers were in good health and seemed to be juggling their roles with success.

In sum, paid work offers women heightened self-esteem and enhanced mental and physical health. It's unemployment that's a major risk factor for depression in women.

DOING IT ALL—AND DOING FINE

This isn't true only for affluent women in good jobs; working-class women share the benefits of work, according to psychologists Sandra Scarr and Deborah Phillips of the University of Virginia and Kathleen McCartney of the University of New Hampshire. In reviewing 80 studies on this subject, they reported that working-class women with children say they would not leave work even if they didn't need the money. Work offers not only income but adult companionship, social contact and a connection with the wider world that they cannot get at home. . . .

So what about the second shift we've heard so much about? It certainly exists: in industrialized countries, researchers found, fathers work an average of 50 hours a week on the job and doing household chores: mothers work an average of 80 hours. Wethington and Kessler found that in daily "stress diaries" kept by husbands and wives, the women report more stress than the men do. But they also handle it better. In short, doing it all may be tough, but it doesn't wipe out the health benefits of working.

THE ADVANTAGES FOR FAMILIES

What about the kids? Many working parents feel they want more time with their kids, and they say so. But does maternal employment harm children? In 1989 University of Michigan psychologist Lois Hoffman reviewed 50 years of research and found that the expected negative effects never materialized. Most often, children of employed and unemployed mothers didn't differ on measures of child development. But children of both sexes with working mothers have a less sex-stereotyped view of the world because fathers in two-income families tend to do more child care.

However, when mothers work, the quality of nonparental child care is a legitimate worry. Scarr, Phillips and McCartney say there is "near consensus among developmental psychologists and early-childhood experts that child care per se does not constitute a risk factor in children's lives." What causes problems, they report, is poor-quality care and a troubled family life. The need for good child care in this country has been obvious for some time. . . .

One question we never used to ask is whether having a working mother could be *good* for children. Hoffman, reflecting on the finding that employed women—both blue-collar and professional—register higher life-satisfaction scores than housewives, thinks it can be. She cites studies involving infants and older children, showing that a mother's satisfaction with her employment status relates positively both to "the quality of the mother-child interaction and to various indexes of the child's adjustment and abilities." . . .

Again, this isn't true only for women in high-status jobs. In a 1982 study of sources of stress for children in low-income families, psychologists Cynthia Longfellow and Deborah Belle of the Harvard University School of Education found that employed women were generally less depressed than unemployed women. What's more, their children had fewer behavioral problems.

But the real point about working women and children is that work *isn't* the point at all. There are good mothers and not-so-good mothers, and some work and some don't. When a National Academy of Sciences panel reviewed the previous 50 years of research and dozens of studies in 1982, it found no consistent effects on children from a mother's working. Work is only one of many variables, the panel concluded in *Families That Work*, and not the definitive one.

What is the effect of women's working on their marriages? Having a working wife can increase psychological stress for men, especially older men, who grew up in a world where it was not normal for a wife to work. But men's expectations that they will—and must—be the only provider may be changing. Wethington and Kessler found that a wife's employment could be a significant buffer *against* depression for men born after 1945. Still, the picture of men's psychological well-being is very mixed, and class and expectations clearly play a role. Faludi cites polls showing that young blue-collar men are especially angry at women for invading what they see as their turf as bread winners, even though a woman with such a job could help protect her husband from economic hardship. But in highly educated, dual-career couples, both partners say the wife's career has enhanced the marriage. . . .

THE PERILS OF PART-TIME

Perhaps the most dangerous myth is that the solution to most problems women suffer is for them to drop back—or drop out. What studies actually show is a significant connection between a reduced commitment to work and increased psychological stress. In their Detroit study, Wethington and Kessler noted that women who went from being full-time employees to full-time housewives reported increased symptoms of distress, such as depression and anxiety attacks; the longer a woman worked and the more committed she was to the job, the greater her risk for psychological distress when the stopped.

What about part-time work, that oft-touted solution for weary women? Women who work fewer than 20 hours per week, it turns out, do not get the mental-health work benefit, probably because they "operate under the fiction that they can retain full responsibility for child care and home maintenance," wrote Wethington and Kessler. The result: Some part-timers wind up more stressed-out than women working full-time. Part-time employment also provides less money, fewer or no benefits and, often, less interesting work and a more arduous road to promotion.

That doesn't mean that a woman shouldn't cut down on her work hours or arrange a more flexible schedule. But it does mean she should be careful about jumping on a poorly designed mommy track that may make her a second-class citizen at work.

Many women think that when they have a baby, the best thing for their mental health would be to stay home. Wrong once more. According to Wethington and Kessler, having a baby does not increase psychological distress for working women—*unless* the birth results in their dropping out of the labor force. This doesn't mean that any woman who stays home to care for a child is going to be a wreck. But leaving the work force means opting out of the benefits of being in it, and women should be aware of that. . . .

What the myth of the miserable working woman obscures is the need to focus on how the *quality* of a woman's job affects her health. Media stories warn of the alleged dangers of fast-track jobs. But [we] found that married women in high-prestige jobs were highest in mental well-being; another study of life stress in women reported that married career women with children suffered the least from stress. Meanwhile, few media tears are shed for the women most at risk: those in the word-processing room who have no control at work, low pay and little support at home.

Women don't need help getting out of the work force; they need help staying in it. As long as much of the media continues to capitalize on national ignorance, that help will have to come from somewhere else. (Not that an occasional letter to the editor isn't useful.) Men need to recognize that they are not just occasional helpers but vital to the success of the family unit. The corporate culture has to be reshaped so that it doesn't run totally according to patterns set by the white male workaholic. This will be good for men *and* women. The government can guarantee parental leave and affordable, available child care. (It did so in the '40s, when women were needed in the factories.) Given that Congress couldn't even get a bill guaranteeing *unpaid* family leave passed last year [1991], this may take some doing. But hey, this is an election year.

"RAPE IN AMERICA IS A TRAGEDY OF YOUTH"
FROM *RAPE IN AMERICA: A REPORT TO THE NATION*

On April 23, 1992, a landmark report documenting the incidence of rape among American women was released. The report, Rape in America, *found that women suffer rape in much higher numbers than previously estimated and that only 16 percent of the crimes were reported to the police. Using data from two national studies—the National Women's Study, which polled 4,008 women, and the State of Services for Victims of Rape, which included data collected from 370 agencies that provided crisis assistance to rape victims—the report estimated that the number of rape victims in 1990, 683,000, was more than five times larger than the Justice Department's National Crime Survey figure of 130,000 for that same year. The report also found that many of the women surveyed had been raped before the age of eighteen. Defining rape as an act of sexual penetration without consent and involving the use or threat of violence, the report also documented victims' concerns over friends and families finding out about their assault, the lack of medical care after the assault, and the subsequent high rate of depression and substance abuse among victims.*

Among the report's recommendations for action were passage of legislation to prevent media disclosure of victims' names and addresses; education about rape in primary and secondary schools; better training for medical personnel, including mental health professionals, about appropriate forms of treatment; and public awareness campaigns to correct deeply rooted stereotypes about rape and rape victims.

Intended to be a wake-up call to the growing public crisis of rape, the report concluded, "It is imperative that rape be classified as a major public health issue in the United States. The traumatic consequences of rape . . . affect the long-term physical, mental and emotional health of millions of American women." Beyond the significance of its findings and the large cross-section of women interviewed, the report documented in stark, indisputable language the pervasiveness of rape, especially among young women, and its profound impact on victims' physical and emotional well-being.

SOURCE: From *Rape in America: A Report to the Nation*, prepared by the National Victim Center and the Crime Victims Research and Treatment Center, 1992. Reprinted by permission of the National Center for Victims of Crime.

The National Women's Study is a longitudinal survey of a large national probability sample of 4,008 adult American women (age 18 or older), 2,008 of whom represent a cross section of all adult women and 2,000 of whom are an over-sample of younger women between the ages of 18 and 34. Eighty-five percent of women contacted agreed to participate and completed the initial (Wave One) telephone interview. At the one year follow-up (Wave Two), 81% of *The National Women's Study* participants (n = 3220) were located and re-interviewed. The two year follow-up (Wave Three) is currently in progress, but preliminary data from the first 2,785 women who completed the 45-minute Wave Three interview are included in this Report. In addition to gathering information about forcible rapes that occurred throughout women's lifetimes, *The National Women's Study* also assessed such major mental health problems as depression, Post-traumatic Stress Disorder, suicide attempts, as well as alcohol and drug-related problems and consumption. . . .

THE NATIONAL WOMEN'S STUDY

During Wave One of the study, information was gathered about forcible rape experiences occurring *any time* during a woman's lifetime. Thirteen percent of women surveyed reported having been victims of *at least one completed rape* in their lifetimes. Based on U.S. Census estimates of the number of adult women in America, one out of every eight adult women, or at least *12.1 million American women*, has been the victim of forcible rate sometime in her lifetime.

Many American women were raped more than once. While 56%, or an estimated 6.8 million women experienced only one rape, 39%, or an estimated 4.7 million women were raped more than once, and five percent were unsure as to the number of times they were raped.

Prior to this study, national information about rape was limited to data on reported rapes from the *FBI Uniform Crime Reports* or data from the *Bureau of Justice Statistics, National Crime Survey (NCS)* on reported and non-reported rapes occurring in the past year. However, the *NCS* provides no information about rapes occurring over the lifetime of a victim, and has been recently re-designed due to criticisms that it failed to detect a substantial proportion of rape cases. Therefore, the results of these two new surveys fill a large gap in current knowledge about rape at the national level.

Information from *The National Women's Study* indicates that 0.7% of all women surveyed had experienced a completed forcible rape in the past year. This equates to an estimated *683,000 adult American women who were raped during a twelve-month period.*

The National Women's Study estimate that 683,000 adult American women were raped in a one year period *does not include all rapes that occurred in America that year*. Rapes that occurred to female children and adolescents under the age of 18—which comprised more than six out of ten of all rapes occurring over women's lifetimes—were not included, nor were any rapes of boys or men.

Thus the 683,000 rapes of adult women probably constitute well less than half of all the rapes that were experienced by all Americans of all ages and genders during that one year period.

How do these estimates from *The National Women's Study* compare with those from the *FBI Uniform Crime Reports* and from the *National Crime Survey*? The FBI estimate of the number of attempted or completed forcible rapes that were reported to police in 1990 was 102,560. The *National Crime Survey* estimates include both reported and non-reported rapes that are either attempted or completed. The *NCS* estimate for 1990 is 130,000 attempted or completed rapes of female Americans age 12 or older. *The National Women's Study* estimate was based on completed rapes of adult women (age 18 or older) that occurred between Wave One (conducted in the fall of 1989), and Wave Two (conducted in the fall of 1990). Thus, the time periods were not identical, but were roughly comparable. . . . Although it did not include attempted rapes or rapes of adolescents between the ages of 12 and 18 as did the *NCS*, *The National Women's Study* estimate was still 5.3 times larger than the *NCS* estimate.

In *The National Women's Study*, information was gathered regarding up to three rapes per person: the first rape she ever experienced, the most recent rape, and the "worst" rape if other than the first or most recent. Information was available from Wave One about 714 such *cases* of rape that 507 *victims* of rape had experienced. The survey found that rape in America is a tragedy of youth, with the majority of rape cases occurring during childhood and adolescence. Twenty-nine percent of all forcible rapes occurred when the victim was *less than 11 years old*, while another 32% occurred *between the ages of 11 and 17*. Slightly more than one in five rapes (22%) occurred between the ages of 18 and 24; seven percent occurred between the ages of 25 and 29, with *only six percent* occurring when the victim was older than 29 years old. Three percent of the respondents were not sure or refused to answer.

CHARACTERISTICS OF RAPE

The National Women's Survey clearly dispels the common myth that most women are raped by strangers. To the contrary, only 22% of rape victims were assaulted by someone they had never seen before or did not know well. Nine percent of victims were raped by husbands or ex-husbands; eleven percent by their fathers or step-fathers; ten percent by boyfriends or ex-boyfriends; sixteen percent by other relatives; and twenty-nine percent by other non-relatives, such as friends and neighbors.

Another common misconception about rape is that most victims sustain serious physical injuries. Over two-thirds (70%) of rape victims reported no physical injuries; only 4% sustained serious physical injuries, with 24% receiving minor physical injuries. Of considerable importance is the fact that many victims who did *not* sustain physical injuries nonetheless *feared being seriously injured or killed* during the rape. Almost half of all rape victims (49%) described being fearful of serious injury or death during the rape. . . .

Rape victims were at least somewhat or extremely concerned about the following:

- Her family knowing she had been sexually assaulted (71%);
- People thinking it was her fault or that she was responsible (69%);
- People outside her family knowing she had been sexually assaulted (68%);
- Her name being made public by the news media (50%);
- Becoming pregnant (34%);
- Contracting a sexually transmitted disease not including HIV/AIDS (19%); and
- Contracting HIV/AIDS (10%). . . .

It is clear that rape victims are extremely concerned about people *finding out* and *finding reasons* to blame them for the rape. If the *stigma* of rape was not *still* a very real concern in victims' eyes, perhaps fewer rape victims in America would be concerned about invasion of their privacy and other disclosure issues.

Somewhat surprisingly, concerns about exposure to sexually transmittable diseases and HIV/AIDS were lower than might be expected. However, many victims were raped years ago as children, prior to America's AIDS epidemic.

Victims were asked if they had a medical examination following the assault. In *only 17%* of all rape cases did such an exam occur. Of these, 60% of rape victims who did receive a medical examination had it within 24 hours of the assault. However, in 40% of the cases, the exam occurred more than 24 hours *after* the assault. Victims told their doctors in only two-thirds of rape cases that they had been sexually assaulted; the doctor was never told about the rape in one-third of such cases. . . .

Rape remains the most underreported violent crime in America. *The National Women's Study* found that only 16%, or approximately one out of every six rapes, are ever reported to police. Of reported rapes, one-quarter (25%) were reported to police more than 24 hours *after* the rape occurred. . . .

THE MENTAL HEALTH IMPACT OF RAPE

. . . Almost one-third (31%) of all rape victims developed PTSD [post-traumatic stress disorder] sometime during their lifetimes, and more than one in ten rape victims (11%) still has PTSD at the present time. Rape victims were 6.2 times more likely to develop PTSD than women who had never been victims of crime (31% vs. 5%). Rape victims were also 5.5 times more likely to have current PTSD than their counterparts who had never been victims of crime (11% vs. 2%). . . .

[R]ape victims were *three times more likely than non-victims of crime* to have ever had a major depressive episode (30% vs. 10%), and were 3.5 times more likely to be currently experiencing a major depressive episode (21% vs. 6%).

Some mental health problems are life-threatening in nature. When asked if they ever thought seriously about committing suicide, 33% of the rape victims and 8% of the non-victims of crime stated that they had seriously considered suicide. Thus, rape victims were *4.1 times more likely* than non-crime victims *to have contemplated suicide.* Rape victims were also *13 times more likely* than non-crime victims to have *actually made a suicide* attempt (13% vs. 1%). The fact that 13% of all rape victims had actually attempted suicide confirms the devastating and potentially life-threatening mental health impact of rape.

Finally, there was substantial evidence that rape victims had higher rates of drug and alcohol consumption and a greater likelihood of having drug and alcohol-related problems than non-victims of crime. . . .

Thus, rape is a problem for America's mental health and public health systems as well as for the criminal justice system.

The dramatically higher risk of substance abuse problems among American women who have been raped and develop PTSD suggests that America may need to commit greater resources to the war on rape, as it has to win its war on drugs.

"A WOMAN'S RIGHT TO REPRODUCTIVE CHOICE IS ONE OF THOSE FUNDAMENTAL LIBERTIES"
JUSTICE HARRY BLACKMUN, *PLANNED PARENTHOOD V. CASEY*

In the two decades following the 1973 Supreme Court ruling Roe v. Wade, *which established women's legal right to an abortion, opponents made several attempts to weaken or overturn this historical decision. Among the most serious was* Planned Parenthood of Southern Pennsylvania v. Casey, *which the Court ruled on in 1992. This decision, narrowly decided five to four, reaffirmed* Roe v. Wade, *but three of the justices among the majority—Sandra Day O'Connor, Anthony Kennedy, and David Souter—also upheld restrictive provisions of the Pennsylvania law in question. These provisions included a waiting period of twenty-four hours between a woman's initial visit to a physician or clinic and the actual procedure, which imposed a hardship on women who were forced to travel long distances to obtain an abortion; a requirement that clinics provide women with materials prepared by the state about the development of a fetus and the procedure itself; a requirement that underage girls obtain the permission of one parent or a judge before undergoing an abortion; and a requirement that physicians or clinics keep statistical abortion records for the state. To its credit, the Court struck down provisions of the Pennsylvania law that required women to notify their spouses before obtaining an abortion.*

Following are excerpts from the majority opinion of Justices O'Connor, Kennedy, and Souter; from the minority opinion, which upholds the Pennsylvania law in its entirety; and from Justice Blackmun's defense of Roe v. Wade. *Blackmun wrote the majority opinion for* Roe v. Wade *and was a vigorous defender of women's reproductive freedom.*

SOURCE: Supreme Court decision 112 S. Ct. 2791 (1992)

JUSTICES O'CONNOR, KENNEDY, SOUTER:

Liberty finds no refuge in a jurisprudence of doubt. Yet 19 years after our holding that the Constitution protects a woman's right to terminate her pregnancy in its early states . . . that definition of liberty is still questioned. . . . After considering the fundamental constitutional questions resolved by *Roe*, principles of institutional integrity, and the rule of *stare decisis* [the principle that decisions of previous courts should be let stand unless there is overwhelming reason to change them], we are led to conclude this: the essential holding of *Roe* v. *Wade* should be retained and once again reaffirmed. . . . Constitutional protection of the woman's decision to terminate her pregnancy derives from the Due Process Clause of the Fourteenth Amendment. It declares that no State shall "deprive any person of life, liberty, or property, without due process of law." . . . It is a premise of the Constitution that there is a realm of personal liberty which the government may not enter. We have vindicated this principle before. Marriage is mentioned nowhere in the Bill of Rights and interracial marriage was illegal in most States in the 19th century, but the Court was no doubt correct in finding it to be an aspect of liberty protected against state interference by the substantive component of the Due Process Clause in *Loving* v. *Virginia* 388 U.S. 1 (1967). . . .

Men and women of good conscience can disagree, and we suppose some always shall disagree, about the profound moral and spiritual implications of terminating a pregnancy, even in its earliest stage. Some of us as individuals find abortion offensive to our most basic principles of morality, but that cannot control our decision. Our obligation is to define the liberty of all, not to mandate our own moral code. . . .

Our law affords constitutional protection to personal decisions relating to marriage, procreation, contraception, family relationships, child rearing, and education. . . . These matters, involving the most intimate and personal choices a person may make in a lifetime, choices central to personal dignity and autonomy, are central to the liberty protected by the Fourteenth Amendment. At the heart of liberty is the right to define one's own concept of existence, of meaning, of the universe, and of the mystery of human life. Beliefs about these matters could not define the attributes of personhood were they formed under compulsion of the State. The woman's right to terminate her pregnancy before viability is the most central principle of *Roe* v. *Wade*. It is a rule of law and a component of liberty we cannot renounce.

On the other side of the equation is the interest of the State in the protection of potential life. The *Roe* Court recognized the State's "important and legitimate interest in protecting the potentiality of human life." . . . That portion of the decision in *Roe* has been given too little acknowledgment and implementation by the Court in its subsequent cases. . . . Though the woman has a right to choose to terminate or continue her pregnancy before viability, it does not at all follow that the State is prohibited from taking steps to ensure that this choice is thoughtful and informed. Even in the earliest stages of pregnancy, the State may enact rules and regulations designed to encourage her to know that there are philosophic and social arguments of great weight that can be brought to bear in favor of continuing the pregnancy to full term. . . . We reject the trimester framework, which we do not consider to be part of the essential holding of *Roe*. . . . Measures aimed at ensuring that a woman's choice contemplates the consequences for the fetus do not necessarily interfere with the right recognized in *Roe* . . . not every law which makes a right more difficult to exercise is, ipso facto, an infringement of that right. . . .

. . . We . . . see no reason why the State may not require doctors to inform a woman seeking an abortion of the availability of materials relating to the consequences to the fetus. . . . Whether the mandatory 24-hour waiting period is . . . invalid because in practice it is a substantial obstacle to a woman's choice to terminate her pregnancy is a closer question. [We do not agree with the District Court] that the waiting period constitutes an undue burden. . . . [From Part D: We have already established the precedent, and] we reaffirm today, that a State may require a minor seeking an abortion to obtain the consent of a parent or guardian, provided that there is an adequate judicial bypass procedure. . . .

. . . Pennsylvania's abortion law provides, except in cases of medical emergency, that no physician shall perform an abortion on a married woman without receiving a signed statement from the woman that she has notified her spouse that she is about to undergo an abortion. The woman has the option of providing an alternative signed statement certifying that her husband is not the man who impregnated her; that her husband could not be located; that the pregnancy is the result of spousal sexual assault which she had reported [or that she fears bodily harm from him.] A physician who performs an abortion on a married woman without receiving the appropriate signed statement will have his or her license revoked, and is liable to the husband for damages.

. . . In well-functioning marriages, spouses discuss important intimate decisions such as whether to bear a child. But there are millions of women in this country who are the victims of regular physical and psychological abuse at the hands of their husbands. . . . Many may have a reasonable fear that notifying their husbands will provoke further instances of child abuse [or psychological abuse]. . . .

. . . [A]s a general matter . . . the father's interest in the welfare of the child and the mother's interest are equal. Before birth, however, the issue takes on a very different cast. It is an inescapable biological fact that state regulation with respect to the child a woman is carrying will have a far greater impact on the mother's liberty than on the father's. [That is why the Court has already ruled that when the wife and husband disagree on the abortion decision, the decision of the wife should prevail.]

... There was a time, not so long ago, when a different understanding of the family and of the Constitution prevailed. In *Bradwell* v. *Illinois*, three Members of this Court reaffirmed the common-law principle that "a woman had no legal existence separate from her husband." ... Only one generation has passed since this Court observed that "woman is still regarded as the center of home and family life," with attendant "special responsibilities" that precluded full and independent legal status under the Constitution (*Hoyt* v. *Florida*). These views, of course, are no longer consistent with our understanding of the family, the individual, or the Constitution.... [The Pennsylvania abortion law] embodies a view of marriage consonant with the common-law status of married women but repugnant to our present understanding of marriage and of the nature of the rights secured by the Constitution. Women do not lose their constitutionally protected liberty when they marry.

CHIEF JUSTICE REHNQUIST, WITH WHOM JUSTICE WHITE, JUSTICE SCALIA, AND JUSTICE CLARENCE THOMAS JOIN:

The joint opinion ... retains the outer shell of *Roe* v. *Wade* ... but beats a wholesale retreat from the substance of that case. We believe that *Roe* was wrongly decided, and that it can and should be overruled consistently with our traditional approach to *stare decisis* in constitutional cases. We would ... uphold the challenged provisions of the Pennsylvania statute in their entirety.... [B]y foreclosing all democratic outlet for the deep passions this issue arouses, by banishing the issue from the political forum that gives all participants, even the losers, the satisfaction of a fair hearing and an honest fight, by continuing the imposition of a rigid national rule instead of allowing for regional differences, the Court merely prolongs and intensifies the anguish.

We should get out of this area, where we have no right to be, and where we do neither ourselves nor the country any good by remaining.

BY JUSTICE BLACKMUN CONCURRING IN PART AND DISSENTING IN PART:

Three years ago, in Webster v. Reproductive Health Serv., four members of this Court appeared poised to "cas(t) into darkness the hopes and visions of every woman in this country" who had come to believe that the Constitution guaranteed her the right to reproductive choice. All that remained between the promise of Roe and the darkness of the plurality was a single, flickering flame. Decisions since Webster gave little reason to hope that this flame would cast much light. But now, just when so many expected the darkness to fall, the flame has grown bright.

I do not underestimate the significance of today's joint opinion. Yet I remain steadfast in my belief that the right to reproductive choice is entitled to the full protection afforded by this Court before Webster. And I fear for the darkness as four Justices anxiously await the single vote necessary to extinguish the light. . . .

In brief, five members of this Court today recognize that "the Constitution protects a woman's right to terminate her pregnancy in its early stages." A fervent view of individual liberty and the force of stare decisis have led the Court to this conclusion.

At long last, the Chief Justice admits it. Gone are the contentions that the issue need not be (or has not been) considered. There, on the first page, for all to see, is what was expected: "We believe that Roe was wrongly decided, and that it can and should be overruled consistently with our traditional approach to stare decisis in constitutional cases." If there is much reason to applaud the advances made by the joint opinion today, there is far more to fear from the Chief Justice's opinion.

The Chief Justice's criticism of Roe follows from his stunted conception of individual liberty. While recognizing that the Due Process Clause protects more than simple physical liberty, he then goes on to construe this Court's personal-liberty cases as establishing only a laundry list of particular rights, rather than a principled account of how these particular rights are grounded in a more general right of privacy. . . .

While there is much to be praised about our democracy, our country since its founding has recognized that there are certain fundamental liberties that are not to be left to the whims of an election. A woman's right to reproductive choice is one of those fundamental liberties. Accordingly, that liberty need not seek refuge at the ballot box.

In one sense, the Court's approach is worlds apart from that of the Chief Justice and Justice Scalia. And yet, in another sense, the distance between the two approaches is short—the distance is but a single vote. I am 83 years old. I cannot remain on this Court forever, and when I do step down, the confirmation process for my successor will may focus on the issue before us today. That, I regret, may be exactly where the choice between the two worlds will be made

"JUST ANOTHER LIFESTYLE CHOICE"
VICE PRESIDENT DAN QUAYLE

In a speech intended to lecture the nation and also invigorate his party's 1992 presidential campaign, in which he and incumbent President George Bush were running for reelection, Vice President Dan Quayle caused a national uproar by linking what he perceived to be a decline in moral values to a fictional television character's decision to bear a child out of wedlock. Speaking before the Commonwealth Club of California on May 19, 1992, Quayle linked a devastating riot in Los Angeles to the breakdown of the American family. The riot, which claimed over fifty victims, occurred in Los Angeles after police officers were acquitted in the brutal beating of Rodney King, an African American man. After first condemning both the treatment of King and the violence that followed after outraged blacks learned about the acquittal, Quayle then launched into a sermon on the "poverty of values" in America, including the decline of the traditional nuclear family. He defined the American family as "two parents married to each other" and accused Hollywood of mocking moral values by creating such "prime time" television characters as Murphy Brown, a high-powered journalist played by Candace Bergen, who chose to bear a child out of wedlock.

Newspapers and commentators across the country seized on Quayle's words about the character Murphy Brown and ignored the rest of his speech. While some pundits chastized the vice president for attacking a woman who chose to keep her baby rather than have an abortion, thus upholding the Bush Administration's antiabortion stance, others had a field day with the humorous possibilities inherent in Quayle's speech. Declared the Philadelphia Daily News: *"Murphy Has a Baby . . . Quayle Has a Cow." Accepting an Emmy Award as best television actress for her role in "Murphy Brown," Candace Bergen said in her acceptance speech, "I would like to thank the vice president."* And when the show launched its new season on September 21, 1992, the opening episode began with news clips of Quayle's speech, then switched to scenes of an exhausted Murphy Brown, having just given birth, staring in disbelief at a television screen showing the vice president. "Glamorize single motherhood?" Brown asks incredulously. "Look at me . . . am I glamorous?"†*

---

* Quoted in *Historic Documents of 1992* (Washington, D.C.: Congressional Quarterly, Inc., 1993), pp. 446–48, 450.
† Ibid.

But beyond the unintended humor that his speech inspired, Quayle generated a good deal of public debate and commentary on the situation of single mothers, who make up a growing portion of the population. Following are excerpts from Quayle's speech; the document "Few Generalizations to Be Made about Single Mothers," which follows this one, explores the complex reasons and realities of single mothers' lives.

SOURCE: In the public domain.

. . . WHEN I HAVE BEEN ASKED during these last weeks who caused the riots and the killing in L.A., my answer has been direct and simple: Who is to blame for the riots? The rioters are to blame. Who is to blame for the killings? The killers are to blame. Yes, I can understand how people were shocked and out-raged by the verdict in the Rodney King trial. But there is simply no excuse for the mayhem that followed. To apologize or in any way to excuse what hap-pened is wrong. It is a betrayal of all those people equally outraged and equal-ly disadvantaged who did not loot and did not riot—and who were in many cases victims of the rioters. No matter how much you may disagree with the verdict, the riots were wrong. And if we as a society don't condemn what is wrong, how can we teach our children what is right?

But after condemning the riots, we do need to try to understand the under-lying situation.

In a nutshell: I believe the lawless social anarchy which we saw is directly re-lated to the breakdown of family structure, personal responsibility and social or-der in too many areas of our society. For the poor the situation is compounded by a welfare ethos that impedes individual efforts to move ahead in society, and hampers their ability to take advantage of the opportunities America offers.

If we don't succeed in addressing these fundamental problems, and in restoring basic values, any attempt to fix what's broken will fail. But one rea-son I believe we won't fail is that we have come so far in the last 25 years.

There is no question that this country has had a terrible problem with race and racism. The evil of slavery has left a long legacy. But we have faced racism squarely, and we have made progress in the past quarter century. The landmark civil rights bills of the 1960's removed legal barriers to allow full participation by blacks in the economic, social and political life of the nation. By any meas-ure the America of 1992 is more egalitarian, more integrated, and offers more opportunities to black Americans—and all other minority group members—than the America of 1964. There is more to be done. But I think that all of us can be proud of our progress. . . .

But as we all know, there is another side to that bright landscape. During this period of progress, we have also developed a culture of poverty—some call it an underclass—that is far more violent and harder to escape than it was a generation ago.

The poor you always have with you, Scripture tells us. And in America we have always had poor people. But in this dynamic, prosperous nation, poverty has traditionally been a stage through which people pass on their way to joining the great middle class. And if one generation didn't get very far up the ladder—their ambitious, better-educated children would.

But the underclass seems to be a new phenomenon. It is a group whose members are dependent on welfare for very long stretches, and whose men are often drawn into lives of crime. There is far too little upward mobility, because the underclass is disconnected from the rules of American society. And these problems have, unfortunately, been particularly acute for Black Americans. . . .

It would be overly simplistic to blame this social breakdown on the programs of the Great Society alone. It would be absolutely wrong to blame it on the growth and success most Americans enjoyed during the 1980's. Rather, we are in large measure reaping the whirlwind of decades of changes in social mores.

I was born in 1947, so I'm considered one of those "Baby Boomers" we keep reading about. But let's look at one unfortunate legacy of the "Boomer" generation. When we were young, it was fashionable to declare war against traditional values. Indulgence and self-gratification seemed to have no consequences. Many of our generation glamorized casual sex and drug use, evaded responsibility and trashed authority. Today the "Boomers" are middle-aged and middle class. The responsibility of having families has helped many recover traditional values. And, of course, the great majority of those in the middle class survived the turbulent legacy of the 60's and 70's. But many of the poor, with less to fall back on, did not.

The intergenerational poverty that troubles us so much today is predominantly a poverty of values. Our inner cities are filled with children having children; with people who have not been able to take advantage of educational opportunities; with people who are dependent on drugs or the narcotic of welfare. To be sure, many people in the ghettos struggle very hard against these tides—and sometimes win. But too many feel they have no hope and nothing to lose. This poverty is, again, fundamentally a poverty of values.

Unless we change the basic rules of society in our inner cities, we cannot expect anything else to change. We will simply get more of what we saw three weeks ago. New thinking, new ideas, new strategies are needed. . . .

We can start by dismantling a welfare system that encourages dependency and subsidizes broken families. We can attach conditions—such as school attendance, or work—to welfare. We can limit the time a recipient gets benefits. We can stop penalizing marriage for welfare mothers. We can enforce child support payments.

Ultimately, however, marriage is a moral issue that requires cultural consensus, and the use of social sanctions. Bearing babies irresponsibly is, simply, wrong. Failing to support children one has fathered is wrong. We must be unequivocal about this. . . .

It doesn't help matters when prime time TV has Murphy Brown—a character who supposedly epitomizes today's intelligent, highly paid, professional woman—mocking the importance of fathers, by bearing a child alone, and calling it just another "lifestyle choice."

I know it is not fashionable to talk about moral values, but we need to do it. Even though our cultural leaders in Hollywood, network TV, the national newspapers routinely jeer at them, I think that most of us in this room know that some things are good, and other things are wrong. Now it's time to make the discussion public.

It's time to talk again about family, hard work, integrity and personal responsibility. We cannot be embarrassed out of our belief that two parents, married to each other, are better in most cases for children than one. That honest work is better than hand-outs—or crime. That we are our brothers' keepers. That it's worth making an effort, even when the rewards aren't immediate.

So I think the time has come to renew our public commitment to our Judeo-Christian values—in our churches and synagogues, our civic organizations and our schools. We are, as our children recite each morning, "one nation under God." That's a useful framework for acknowledging a duty and an authority higher than our own pleasures and personal ambitions.

If we lived more thoroughly by these values, we would live in a better society. For the poor, renewing these values will give people the strength to help themselves by acquiring the tools to achieve self-sufficiency, a good education, job training, and property. Then they will move from permanent dependence to dignified independence. . . .

"FEW GENERALIZATIONS TO BE MADE
ABOUT SINGLE MOTHERS"
ROBERTO SURO

In the wake of Vice President Dan Quayle's family values speech, in
which he lambasted television character Murphy Brown's decision to have a child
out of wedlock (see the preceding document), social historians, sociologists, and
family advocates around the country debated whether his words pointed to truths
about a relationship between the breakdown of moral values and the rise of single-
mother households. In the following article from the New York Times, *Roberto*
Suro interviewed a cross-section of academics and single mothers around the na-
tion and discovered that single women bore children because of a complex mix of
practical and emotional reasons, and oftentimes out of little choice at all, especial-
ly when male partners reneged on their responsibilities. But for some women it was
indeed a "lifestyle choice," as Quayle put it, an opportunity to experience mother-
hood in the absence of a partner. Whatever the reasons, as the article points out,
the percentage of families headed by single women was the fastest growing catego-
ry of family groupings in the 1980s and 1990s and has forced people to redefine their
notion of family.

SOURCE: Roberto Suro, "For Women, Varied Reasons for Single Motherhood," *New York*
Times, 26 May 1992, p. A-12. Copyright © 1992 by The New York Times Company. Reprinted with permission of Roberto Suro.

HOUSTON—Vice-President Dan Quayle issued a blunt reminder last week that
after 25 years of cultural warfare over the American family, single mothers were
likely to remain a divisive topic because their lives illuminate unresolved differences between the races and the sexes.

In a speech on Tuesday, Mr. Quayle argued that the riots in Los Angeles
were "directly related to the breakdown of family structure, personal responsibility and social order in too many areas of our society."

But his remarks will be best remembered for the connection he drew between poor, unmarried black mothers and Murphy Brown, an affluent, white
television character who he said mocked "the importance of fathers by bearing
a child alone and calling it just another 'life style choice.'"

Census Bureau statistics and studies by social scientists suggest that there are
few generalizations to be made about single mothers except that their numbers
have been increasing for 20 years, although at a slower rate recently.

VARIED NEEDS, VARIED CHOICES

Interviews conducted around the country with single mothers of varying races and economic conditions suggested that the decision to bear a child involves a mixture of practical, emotional and spiritual considerations and is usually not a straightforward moral choice.

For Jean Pollard it was not a matter of choice at all. "He wasn't a planned child," Ms. Pollard, 34 years old, said of her 3-month-old son who lives with her in a shelter for homeless families in Houston. She was laid off from work, she said, and then the child's father reneged on a promise to marry her.

"I wanted kids, but I always figured when I had a child I would be married, the typical American dream," she said. "Sometimes it doesn't work out like that."

Like many single mothers, Ms. Pollard acknowledges the value of marriage. But she went on, "Marriage doesn't guarantee anything anymore because it's not like it used to be with our parents."

For Debbie Spain, staying married was not an option.

A 32-year-old medical secretary in Boston, Ms. Spain was beaten by the father of her first child and ended a brief marriage to her second child's father, who was an alcoholic. "Just because you have someone's last name doesn't mean that's going to solve any problems," she said.

Both of her children remain in close contact with their fathers, but Ms. Spain finds they are happier now that she is raising them alone. "I just decided I'm going to do it right as much as I can," she said.

For Patty Friedmann, having a child was more important having a husband.

Ms. Friedmann, a 45-year-old writer in New Orleans, deliberately became pregnant when she was single and 28 because she wanted a child. In an autobiographical novel published last year by Viking. "The Exact Image of Mother," Ms. Friedmann, who is now married, described how women can assert their identities by making such choices.

Of her protagonist, Ms. Friedmann wrote, "She is unfocused in life and in conflict with her mother, and her decision to have a child brings her strength and her resources together and defines her.

The many different reasons that women give for being single mothers suggest that their lives reflect a variety of trends in American life.

"You can't isolate single parenting by women as a discrete phenomenon," said Barrie Thorne, a professor of sociology at the University of Southern California. "You have to see it in the context of an overall change in attitude towards many sexual and family issues including the status of women, divorce and premarital sex."

Census Bureau statistics show a period of turmoil in the American family beginning in the mid-1960's, although the rate of change in family composition slowed markedly in the 1980's. Married couples with children, for instance, made up 40 percent of all households in 1970 but only 26 percent last year.

Single parenthood by unwed mothers rose quickly, and is still increasing. The number of families headed by mothers who have never married increased at annual rate of nearly 15 percent in the 1970's. Although the rate dropped to just under 10 percent from 1980 to 1991, this now constitutes the fastest growing category of family groupings.

Single mothers now head a quarter of all families with children, counting those [who] have never married along with women who are divorced, widowed or are living apart from a spouse for any other reason. (There are single fathers, too, of course, but they head fewer than 4 percent of all families.)

Experts say that although economic circumstances have changed since the 50's, the "Father Knows Best" family—two parents with only the husband working—that typified that decade still exerts a powerful pull on American values and emotions. Large majorities in opinion polls consistently say they are committed to conservative views of the family like those articulated by Mr. Quayle, and the vast majority of children continue to live in households with two parents.

But, said Arlene Skolnick, a research psychologist at the University of California at Berkeley, "People often care deeply in opposing directions, such as believing in the 1950's family but also accepting the value or the necessity of women working outside the home."

Aside from this complex cultural context, Professor Thorne said, "there are structural and circumstantial problems that go beyond individual choices that help explain why families headed by single parent mothers are not only the most rapidly growing type of household but also the type most associated with poverty."

Felicia Bryant, 19, of Chicago spoke of the devastating impact an unwanted pregnancy can have on a poor woman.

On learning she was pregnant, Ms. Bryant said: "I was upset and shocked. I wanted to commit suicide. I felt that I was too young to have a child." Then 15 years old, she dropped out of school and went on welfare.

Although Mr. Quayle asserted that "marriage is probably the best anti-poverty program of all," Ms. Bryant did not see it as an antidote.

"Many of the homeless are whole families—men, women and children—and they are still in poverty," she said. "A man can lose a job anytime. A man is not always the best means of support. A woman can be just as independent as a man." . . .

In America the issue is complicated by race. While single parenting by mothers has increased quickly among both whites and blacks, it is far more prevalent among blacks. In 1991, women headed 58 percent of all black families with children, as against 19 percent among whites.

And there are major differences between blacks and whites in the reasons women head families.

Among white mothers, the major reasons are divorce and separation, although the number who have never married has increased rapidly, from less than 3 percent of one-parent families in 1970 to 19 percent last year.

Among black mothers, divorce and separation also used to be the major causes for single parenthood, but no more. Last year 54 percent of one-parent black families were headed by women who had never married. This was up from just 15 percent in 1970, according to the Census Bureau.

"Poverty, unemployment, welfare programs that penalize families: these things explain a major portion of the variance between blacks and whites in the number of female headed households, but not all of it," said Bonnie Thornton Dill, a professor of women's studies at the University of Maryland in College Park.

One explanation may lie with changes in the nature of urban poverty that have led to an increasing number of people cut off from the education or employment that might allow them to improve their status or give them the impetus to marry.

"Teen-age pregnancy among blacks has not increased so much, but the rate of marriage among teen-agers has dropped and the number of children born to married couples has dropped," Professor Dill said. "These things are related to perceptions of opportunity."

Perceptions of another sort also emerged as a major theme in interviews with single mothers, who argued that although their households may not be considered conventional they are nonetheless real families.

Grace Cox, a 35-year-old typographer in Houston, has one child from an early marriage that ended in divorce and another born to her as a single mother.

"When you have kids by yourself, you have to work harder at making sure they have what they need and at keeping the family together," she said.

Like several other women, Fran Ramer, a 42-year-old Chicago businesswoman who is a single mother, said she was deeply committed to the family as a social ideal and saw herself adapting that ideal to reality.

She said, "I don't disagree with Quayle about family values, but I think he is a little behind the times about what a family is."

CHAPTER 5

THE THIRD WAVE:
FEMINISM AND FAMILY VALUES IN THE 1990s

During the 1992 presidential campaign, both the Republican and Democratic parties rallied around the concept of family values, but their conception of just what family values entailed differed dramatically. The Republicans trumpeted the vision of a traditional nuclear family, with a breadwinning husband and father, and enlisted Marilyn Quayle, the vice president's wife, to remind Americans, in a televised speech at the Republican National Convention, that "most women do not wish to be liberated from their essential nature" as full-time homemakers. The Democrats, who nominated Governor Bill Clinton of Arkansas as their candidate, also made family values a cornerstone of their campaign platform and offered proposals such as the Family and Medical Leave Act to help working mothers and fathers cope with family medical needs and an initiative of tax credits to encourage adoption by American families.

Economic issues played a key role in Bill Clinton's victory; voters were dissatisfied with incumbent President George Bush's prescriptions for boosting an anemic economy and did not believe that he fully understood the day-to-day struggles of low- and middle-income Americans. Clinton came across as a far more empathetic candidate for low-income and minority voters, even though he positioned himself as a new centrist Democrat who championed moderate social values and fiscal accountability. He supported safe, legalized abortion, but he also supported capital punishment; he supported gun control, including background checks on prospective owners, but he also supported a strong military. He supported tax cuts but gave lip service to creating a safety net of social programs that would help the aged, disabled, and indigent. This adroit political positioning helped him reach out to a broad constituency, including moderate Republicans disillusioned with the conservative social and political policies of their own party. But the gender gap first seen in the 1980 presidential election—the difference between men's and women's perceptions of the issues and their responses to the candidates—also played a significant role in Clinton's victory, as "It Was Payback Time," included in this chapter, illustrates. Women voted for Clinton by a slightly higher margin than men— 46 percent to 41 percent—and more women supported Clinton than Bush, in part because of their outrage over the scourging of Anita Hill by the all-male members of the Senate Judiciary Committee during the televised hearings of Judge Clarence Thomas's nomination to the Supreme Court.[1]

Clinton rode into office on a wave of support from American women, and the decisions he made early in his administration did not disappoint his female voters. His first significant piece of legislation was the Family Medical Leave Act (included in this chapter), which required companies with fifty or more employees to grant up to twelve weeks unpaid leave to employees facing the birth or adoption of a child or coping with the illness of a spouse or other immediate family member. Some family advocates charged that the act did not go far enough and should have mandated paid leave, but the legislation was nevertheless an important first step in developing public policies to make the workplace more responsive to family needs.

Women in the military received a significant boost when Clinton's secretary of defense, Les Aspin, signed a directive to all military branches to reverse restrictions banning women from combat duty (see the defense department directive in this chapter). Although Aspin allowed some gender-based restrictions to remain in place, his directive went far toward creating a gender-integrated armed services.

And feminists across the country celebrated Clinton's nomination of Ruth Bader Ginsburg to the U.S. Supreme Court. Though she was not the first woman to join the High Court—that distinction belonged to Sandra Day O'-Connor, appointed by President Ronald Reagan in 1981—her nomination ensured that policies favorable to women, such as legal access to abortion and laws preventing gender discrimination in the workplace, would have a forceful advocate: Ginsburg had enjoyed a distinguished legal career as a law professor and judge and as a pioneer in the realm of sex equity cases pertaining to the workplace and to the distribution of medical and insurance benefits. Ginsburg's moving acceptance speech on the occasion of her nomination appears in this chapter.

Clinton also appointed a number of women to high-level positions in his administration, including Janet Reno, his attorney general, and Donna Shalala, his secretary of health and human services. As attorney general for the state of Florida, Reno had a strong record of prosecuting domestic violence offenders, and Shalala set the goal of combating domestic violence as a top priority of her department. During Clinton's second administration, he appointed Madeleine Albright, the former U.S. ambassador to the United Nations, to be secretary of state, making her the third-highest-ranking official in the executive branch of the federal government.

As the first presidential spouse to have pursued a high-level career of her own, Clinton's wife, Hillary Rodham Clinton, a highly successful lawyer, symbolized a new kind of first lady, not one who had simply been a helpmate to her husband but an accomplished professional in her own right. She also emerged as the most powerful first lady in the history of the republic. Eleanor Roosevelt had wielded considerable informal power in her husband's administration, serving as an ad hoc counselor and advisor on social policy. But shortly after taking office, Clinton appointed his wife as head of his twelve-member Task Force on National Health Care Reform. In this position she directed a staff of over five hundred people and chaired some fifty Congressional meetings in an effort to restructure the country's delivery of health care. Although the health reform measures that she recommended were not adopted, Hillary Rodham Clinton continued to serve as an informal advisor to her husband and turned her attention to issues pertaining to women and children.

Throughout the 1990s she seemed to be a lightning rod for the public's ambivalence toward a first lady who wielded so much power and, in a larger sense, toward women who placed priority on careers as well as on marriage and motherhood. During her husband's impeachment trial that followed the exposure of his affair with a White House intern, she was repeatedly accused of staying with him because she wanted to protect her access to presidential power and the prospects for her own political future. Detractors ascribed the most nefarious motives to her, including murder and the cover-up of financial improprieties. Yet, after a bitterly fought campaign, Clinton emerged as a public figure in her own right when she was elected to Congress in 2000 as the junior senator from New York. Once again, she made history, this time as the first former first lady to secure elected office, and her election gave notice that she would continue to advocate for issues of importance to women and children. Her victory speech is reproduced in this chapter.

In 1993 journalist and author Naomi Wolf published a call to arms for women to spurn what she called "victim feminism"—a preoccupation with persistent inequalities and problems in women's lives—and embrace "power feminism," a strategy of focusing on what they had already achieved and building on those achievements. (See document "We Won't Stop Fighting" in this

chapter.) She hoped both to inject new ideas and energy into what she perceived to be a movement demoralized by infighting and a narrowing agenda
and also to reach out to new constituencies. Wolf's appraisal for the future of
feminism was ebullient and was credited with drawing scores of younger women into the movement.

The buoyant spirit of her book was everywhere in evidence at the United
Nations World Conference on Women in Beijing in 1995. This conference
turned out to be the largest international gathering of women to date and produced a wide-ranging platform of action, which is reproduced in this chapter.
American women actively participated at the conference, both as official delegates from the United States and as representatives of nongovernment agencies
(NGOs). Because of the breadth of international representation and the goals
and ideas that came out of it, the Beijing conference symbolized a pinnacle of
female solidarity and empowerment.

But there were fissures in the pathways of progress for American women
during the last decade of the twentieth century—cracks in the social, economic, and political foundations of American life that threatened to engulf
low-income women and women of color in particular. By the year 2000, 40
percent of African American women comprised part of the female middle
class and had entered such professions as law, medicine, and business. But another 40 percent were trapped in an ever widening net of poverty, unemployment, and welfare. The impact of race and ethnicity was particularly evident
in the rising poverty rate among American women. Throughout the decades
after 1960 the number of female-headed households surged as a result of divorce and lower rates of marriage. By the 1990s one-fifth of white families
were headed by women, but among Latino and African American families, almost one-third and three-fifths, respectively, were female-headed. In 1998,
28.8 percent of white households headed by single mothers lived below the
poverty line, but the numbers jumped to 47.5 percent for black single-mother
families and 52.2 percent for Latino single-mother households.[2] The document by Virginia Schein in this chapter, "You Gotta Do What You Gotta Do,"
a profile of thirty impoverished and single mothers, poignantly captures the
realities—the setbacks and humiliations—of women struggling to climb out
of poverty and welfare dependence during the 1990s.

Clinton had campaigned on a pledge to end welfare "as we know it," and the
Personal Responsibility and Work Opportunity Act, which he signed in 1996,
dealt a particularly harsh blow to single mothers. Proclaiming the superiority
of two-parent families, the act ended sixty-one years of federal assistance to

single mothers with children by putting a time limit on welfare eligibility and by requiring all "welfare mothers" and fathers to seek employment or job training—despite providing little or no assistance to impoverished mothers who could not afford day care. The Personal Assistance Act both narrowed the definition of family to a two-parent nuclear family and further penalized poor, single mothers who were already living on the edge. It also helped to draw a clear distinction between professional middle-class women who were benefiting from continued access to skilled work and changing cultural attitudes and impoverished women who could not reap the benefits of opportunities available to their more privileged sisters.

African American and Hispanic women were also the prime victims of a growing epidemic of AIDS (auto-immune deficiency syndrome), which, during the 1990s, spread far more quickly among women than among men. As David Anthony Forrester's piece in this chapter illustrates, many of these victims were from a low-income background and often lacked the health insurance and social support needed to combat this vicious disease.

The issue of domestic violence continued to be a significant social concern. As noted above, Attorney General Janet Reno and Secretary of Health and Human Services Donna Shalala targeted the reduction of domestic violence as a high priority of their tenures. Several states also began to prosecute domestic violence offenders more vigorously or passed legislation commuting the sentences of women who had been convicted of killing or injuring their batterers out of self-defense. The publication of a landmark study on the prevalence of family violence, commissioned by the Family Violence Prevention Fund (included in this chapter), also helped to put the crisis of domestic violence on the national radar screen. Among those surveyed, almost twice as many respondents had witnessed domestic violence in their homes, in which women were victims, compared to those who had seen a robbery or mugging. These statistics suggested that domestic violence was, and remained, far more pervasive than law-enforcement officials had previously acknowledged.

Although Clinton supported access to safe, legal abortions and appointed judges and other officials who shared his views, reproductive choice continued to be an issue of heated dispute. Antiabortion groups kept up a vigorous campaign of targeting physicians and clinics that performed abortions, and several abortion providers lost their lives at the hands of violent abortion opponents who thought it Christian to commit murder in the defense of "unborn children." As the number of abortion providers diminished in response to the illegal and often violent tactics of antiabortion groups, women who lived in remote geographic regions and were unable to travel to urban areas for treatment had little recourse but to carry an unwanted pregnancy or resort to medically unsound methods to end their pregnancies. But an important victory for reproductive choice came when the Food and Drug Administration (FDA), after a long and contentious struggle, approved RU-486, a drug that enables women to end an unwanted pregnancy without the invasive surgical techniques of abortion. Although the drug has potentially serious side effects and must be closely monitored by a physician—and also has been targeted by antiabortion groups as another wrongful form of abortion—it does provide women with an alternative to surgical abortions. The FDA's official approval of the drug appears in this chapter.

At the other end of the reproductive spectrum, women faced a bewildering array of choices to help them conceive or maintain a pregnancy. By 1995, nine million women had used the services of fertility specialists, and in that year 2.1 million couples were classified as infertile.[3] Research and the availability of assisted reproductive techniques (ART) to treat women who could not get pregnant on their own increased dramatically between the 1980s and 1990s. In 1986, for example, only about forty-one clinics offered infertility treatments, including in vitro fertilization (IFV), a process by which a number of eggs are fertilized outside of the womb and the resulting embryos are implanted in the uterus; by 1996 more than three hundred clinics offered this and a variety of other treatments for infertility.[4] These treatments involved expensive drugs and invasive procedures—often paid for out of pocket because few medical insurance policies covered the costly treatments—and were typically sought after by married, older, better-educated, and more affluent women. These sophisticated reproductive technologies raised complex ethical questions about when life begins and who holds parental rights over contested embryos. As "Our Biology Hasn't Changed One Bit," in this chapter, points out, they also contributed to raising perhaps unrealistic expectations among women that they could afford to delay pregnancy and rely on ART in their less fertile years to help them get pregnant.

Issues of elder care, especially for aging women, also took on new importance as baby boomers increasingly shared a new designation: the in-between generation, those caring for children as well as elderly parents. As Virginia Macken Fitzsimmons, in "Our Society's Ugly Secret," points out, aging women often outlive their spouses and rely on their families for their care—and more often than not that task falls to women. In nursing homes as well as in private homes, elderly women and their female caretakers are locked into a tragic cycle of dependency and resentment that may lead to violence when a caretaker becomes overwhelmed or simply fed up with the demanding task of caring for an aging adult.

If Hillary Rodham Clinton represented the public face of American women in the late 1990s—the accomplished career woman who is also a devoted wife and mother—Martha Stewart, the high queen of homemaking, represented the private face, or at least what so many American women aspired to be in the privacy of their homes: talented, resourceful, creative homemakers who, after a long day at the office, cook, clean, and entertain with effervescent ease. In numerous surveys of American women during the 1990s, Martha Stewart emerged as one of the most admired women, and people flocked to read her magazine, watch her television show, and purchase her home-decor products. As Molly O'Neill's piece in this chapter reveals, Stewart is the perfect Betty Crocker for the nineties: a savvy businesswoman, she has made domesticity her dominion and, in the process, created a multimillion-dollar empire of consumer goods and advice for making homes and family life more cozy and inviting. With seemingly effortless charm, she symbolizes the successful synthesis of home and career that women, at all income levels, are struggling to make.

IN THE FAMILY MEDICAL LEAVE ACT and in the Clinton Administration's initiatives to encourage adoption and combat domestic violence and to develop more resources for child care, feminism and family values seemed to achieve a kind of synthesis. But the administration's sponsorship of harsh welfare reform policies and Clinton's refusal to recognize same-sex marriages as legal unions that entitle their partners to social security and other federal benefits (see President Clinton's remarks in this chapter) indicated that the administration hewed to a narrow and traditional definition of family that undercuts the feminist view of inclusion. Thus issues of gender, race, and class continued to shape the public discourse on social policy. And both the beneficiaries as well as the victims of that discourse were, in large part, women.

NOTES

1. Naomi Wolf, *Fire with Fire: The New Female Power and How It Will Change the 21st Century* (New York: Random House, 1993), p. 307.

2. William H. Chafe, "The Road to Equality," in *No Small Courage: A History of Women in the United States*, edited by Nancy Cott (New York: Oxford University Press, 2000), p. 579.

3. Vital and Health Statistics, Series 23, Number 19, U.S. Department of Health and Human Services.

4. Elizabeth Hervey Stephen and Anjani Chandra, "Use of Infertility Services in the United States: 1995," in *Family Planning Perspectives* 32, no. 3 (May/June 2000).

"IT WAS PAYBACK TIME"
ELOISE SALHOLZ ET AL.

Since the passage of the Nineteenth Amendment to the Constitution, which granted women the right to vote, state and federal politicians have made sporadic attempts to "win the woman's vote" by passing legislation that, they believed, would appeal to women. Examples are the 1921 Sheppard-Towner Act, which appropriated funds for the improvement of maternal and infant health; the Cable Act of 1922, which allowed women to retain their U.S. citizenship if they married foreigners; and other laws pertaining to child labor, family welfare, and gender issues.

In the 1984 presidential campaign, as the document below points out, Walter Mondale tried but failed to marshal women's support by picking Geraldine Ferraro as his running mate (see Ferraro's acceptance speech in chapter 4). In 1992, however, in the aftermath of the Clarence Thomas hearings (see Anita Hill's testimony in chapter 4), the "Year of the Woman" finally did arrive, as women voters put their money and votes behind female candidates. Emily's List, a political action committee, or PAC, founded in 1984 to finance the campaigns of Democratic female candidates, raised 6.2 million dollars—more than any other PAC in America—from approximately sixty-three thousand people, who each donated about one hundred dollars. This money helped to underwrite the campaigns of nineteen newly elected congresswomen, bringing the total in the House of Representatives to forty-eight, and four new female senators, more than doubling the number of women senators to six. As this article makes clear, women voted along gender lines in outrage over Hill's treatment and over the reality of sexual harassment in women's lives. They also voted for Bill Clinton because he seemed to represent women's concerns more clearly than his opponent, President George H. Bush. In 1992 women made history, as candidates and as voters who demanded that politicians respond to the issues that were important to them.

SOURCE: Eloise Salholz, Lucille Beachy et al. "Did America 'Get It'?," in *Newsweek* 120/26 (December 28, 1992): 20–22. Copyright © 1992 by Newsweek, Inc. All rights reserved. Reprinted by permission.

THERE THEY STAND, two caryatids at the portals of 1992: Anita Hill, who ushered in the year, and Hillary Clinton, ushering it out on her way to the White House. Two women, both Yale-educated lawyers. One black and single, the other white and married. One a picture of powerlessness, trapped before a committee of uncomprehending men who just "didn't get it," the other a powerhouse First Lady-in-waiting—credentialed, outspoken and, up until now, a bigger breadwinner than her husband. In their way, Hill and Hillary—*the* woman of the year in this year of the woman—embody the debate about the political and social significance of 1992: when the ballots were tallied and the accomplishments ticked off, was the glass half empty or half full?

Pundits had confidently promised "The Year of the Woman" before this, only to find that the real political gains never quite matched the hopeful expectations of women's advocates. By most measures, however, 1992 has come closer to living up to the advance billing than '88 or '90 or even '72, when a Life Magazine cover story featuring Bella Abzug opened with the proviso "It may not quite be the year of the . . ." Four freshwomen will enter the Senate in January (half full), bringing the grand total up to six (half empty); 24 new women will join 23 veterans in the House (full), accounting for 11 percent of the votes (empty). Emily's List, the Democratic women's fund-raising group, fed approximately six million dollars into House and Senate campaigns this year, making it the biggest congressional PAC—a clear victory in a process where nothing confers influence as much as money in the (very full) war chest.

Judging the meaning of '92 merely in terms of winners and losers or dollars and cents, however, may ultimately be another way of not *getting it*. The fact is, women's issues dominated political discourse in a dramatic new way. The sexual assaults at Tailhook[*] might have been dismissed as the peccadilloes of boys being boys, but—in the year of the woman—they instead triggered one of the worst scandals in naval history. Susan Faludi's "Backlash,"[†] a feminist call to arms, and Gloria Steinem's "Revolution from Within" rode the best-seller list.

---

[*] At a convention of the Tailhook Association, an organization composed primarily of navy and marine corps aviation officers, held in Las Vegas, Nevada, in early September 1991, eighty-three women and seven men were assaulted by drunken, unruly fellow attendees. Female victims were attacked, groped, and grabbed by a throng of men as they made their way through a hallway toward one of the convention-sponsored social events. The ensuing government investigations focused public attention on the Pentagon's careless investigative methods and culture of sexism as well as on the incident itself.

[†] *Backlash: The Undeclared War Against American Women* (1991) by journalist Susan Faludi chronicled what Faludi perceived to be the many social, cultural, and institutional forces trying to undermine the achievements of the women's movement. The book provoked considerable debate throughout the early 1990s and became a bestseller. Gloria Steinem's *Revolution from Within: A Book of Self-Esteem* (1992) explored the need to formulate an internal feminist revolution of consciousness to augment external feminist social activism.

When Marilyn Quayle stood before the GOP convention, lecturing women about their "essential natures,"she proved how out of touch the GOP was with the reality of their lives. Soon it was payback time: female voters, says "Megatrends for Women" author Patricia Aburdene, "elected Bill Clinton."

There are certain events whose historic significance emerges only bit by bit. Rosa Parks's refusal to give up her seat on the bus was one such seminal moment; the rioting at a Greenwich Village gay bar called Stonewall was another. Last fall's Judiciary Committee hearings transfixed the public; but given the nation's sound-bite attention span, it was by no means clear that Hill's testimony about Clarence Thomas would have such an extraordinary shelf life. Yet it not only has continued to matter, it is a still-evolving event: a *Newsweek* Poll last week found that 51 percent of the women surveyed now believe Thomas sexually harassed Hill, compared with only 27 percent in October '91. Carol Gilligan, a feminist psychologist at Harvard, believes the image of Hill and those men will define this age the way Nick Ut's searing photo of a napalmed child captured the Vietnam era.

If Hill's witness had come at another time, her legacy might have been confined to consciousness-raising—and '92 might have been just another year that wasn't. But the election season was moving into high gear, and women like Carol Moseley Braun in Illinois were quick to capitalize on the deep outrage over Hill's treatment. In an attempt to mine public disgust with politics as usual, some women made much of their outsider status. But while female candidates were able to seize the moment, many—notably Senator-elect Dianne Feinstein of California—had been toiling in local vineyards for decades. "These women did not jump full blown on the political stage," says Ruth Mandel, director of the Center for the American Woman and Politics at Rutgers. "This [was] a year when opportunity [met] preparedness, a well-deserved reward after 20 years of work."

The candidates weren't the only women making history for the first time, women voted the gender line. As recently as 1984 women sent Geraldine Ferraro contributions and little notes saying, "I don't want my husband to know, but I'm supporting you ." Then, on Election Day, says Ferraro (who lost her bid for the U.S. Senate this year), they "voted the same as men." But in the 1992 primaries, all the women winners except Feinstein owed their victory to a disproportionate number of female votes. "Women were gatekeepers," says political consultant Ethel Klein. "This was an election where women said, 'We're going to respect ourselves—and we're going to demand that you respect us.'"

The message got across, partly because the terms of the debate had changed so drastically. In other elections, Democratic presidential candidates had to prove they could push the button as well as any Republican. Since the fall of communism, there was no button. Instead, voters wanted to know what the candidates were going to do about unbalanced budgets, education and health insurance—"soft" issues often associated with women. So 1992 wasn't the year that the electorate abandoned stereotypes about who was fit to handle the nation's problems. Instead, says California pollster Mark DiCamillo, "gender stereotypes worked to [women's] advantage." Patty Murray of Washington state ran for the U.S. Senate as the "mom in tennis shoes," a slogan suggesting she knew all about schools, medical expenses and, of course, supermarket scanners.

Arguably, the person who did the most to feminize political rhetoric in '92 was Hillary's husband. Bill Clinton became the Oprah of presidential politics, embracing not only women's issues but womenspeak. "It became clear at the Democratic convention that most of the good that had come to Clinton had come through women, his mother and others," says poet Robert Bly, a founder of the men's movement. "This is a man who got up there," adds consultant Klein, "and told a personal story about putting himself bodily in front of a raging stepfather who was about to hurt his mother. That is at the core of the vulnerability women feel in this society." . . . Clinton, says sociologist Michael Kimmel, is "Anita Hill's revenge."

It is clear that women have had tremendous impact on the political process this year; less clear is the impact of the political changes on the lives of American women. Most of the respondents in the *Newsweek* Poll believe women either made progress or held their ground in 1992; only 14 percent say women lost ground. While a majority of the women surveyed say that the men they know personally have become more sensitive to the needs and problems of women, 68 percent replied that most American men do not understand the issues that concern women most. Bill and Hillary Clinton may represent a generational shift from old-fashioned First Couple to postmodern partnership, but the sexes obviously find themselves still talking at cross-purposes.

Thanks to the confirmation hearings, there's far less static on the line when the subject is sexual harassment. "Every time a man and a woman meet at the water cooler now, Anita Hill [is] right there between them," says Andrea Sankar, an anthropologist at Wayne State University in Detroit. After the hearings, many firms reviewed existing sexual-harassment policies or implemented new ones. A survey in *Working Woman* magazine last June found that 81 percent of Fortune 500 companies offer sensitivity-training programs, up from 60 percent in 1988. According to the Equal Employment Opportunity Commission, where Hill and Thomas worked together, 10,522 people filed sexual-harassment complaints this year, compared with 6,883 in fiscal 1991. Following Maine's lead, Connecticut passed a law requiring that employers provide a harassment policy and sensitivity training for workers; similar statutes are pending in several other states. . . . Taking no chances, Senator-elect Murray promises to introduce a bill making Congress accountable to the same sexual-harassment laws as everybody else.

Members of both sexes are waiting to see whether Washington's newest women will indeed bring a unique sensibility to the task of government. Clinton appointee Donna Shalala, who served as an assistant secretary of HUD under Jimmy Carter, noted that women looked at public housing differently than men. "It's not just strategy," she told *Newsweek* before her appointment. "It's that we know you don't [put in] showers when you have little kids and need bathtubs." After an hourlong meeting, incoming women representatives quickly settled on four priorities: fully funding Head Start, passing family-leave legislation, codifying legal abortion and rescinding Congress's immunity to sexual harassment laws. Will there be power in numbers? Colorado Rep. Patricia Schroeder recalls her pioneer days in the early '70s, when she found herself changing her children's diapers on the House floor. Now carpenters are busily remodeling the Capitol to add a ladies' room off the Senate floor. While they're at it, maybe they should put in a changing table—and another, for good measure, in the men's room. Now, that would be a sign of changing times.

"THE MILITARY SERVICES SHALL OPEN UP
MORE SPECIALTIES AND ASSIGNMENTS TO WOMEN"
DEFENSE DEPARTMENT DIRECTIVE, 1993

Throughout American history, women have contributed significantly to military preparedness both in time of war and peace. During the Civil War they served as military spies, scouts, and battlefield nurses, and some four hundred women even disguised themselves as soldiers to fight on both the Union and Confederate sides. During World Wars I and II, they served as battlefield nurses and as administrative support. World War II also brought the entry of women into every part of military service, except combat, in separate women's units, as Jacqueline Cochran's oral history in chapter 1 illustrates. By 1978 all of these separate women's corps—the WACs, WAVEs, SPARs, and the women's reserve of the Marine Corps—had been abolished, and though women were integrated into the armed forces, they were still barred from combat duty.

In 1977 Congress enacted a compulsory draft registration system that excluded women because of this gender-based prohibition against combat duty, and four years later the U.S. Supreme Court upheld that exclusion. But women's substantial combat support in the 1989 war against Panama and again in the 1991 Gulf War against Iraq, in which women flew reconnaisance planes and shot down incoming SCUD missiles, prompted the government to rethink the ban on women's participation in combat. After the Gulf War, both the House of Representatives and the Senate passed legislation that ended restrictions against women flying combat missions. As Representative Patricia Schroeder, sponsor of the combat measure in the House, said, "The Persian Gulf helped collapse the whole chivalrous notion that women could be kept out of danger in a war. We saw that the theater of operations had no strict combat zone, that SCUD missiles were not gender-specific—they could hit both sexes and, unfortunately, did."*

The following document is a directive by then Secretary of Defense Les Aspin to all three military branches to implement congressional measures against gender-based combat restrictions. He also instructs military commanders to review other remaining restrictions against women in the armed forces. But note that he allows some restrictions to remain in place.

SOURCE: Secretary of Defense Les Aspin, Memorandum of April 28, 1993, concerning "Policy on the Assignment of Women in the Armed Forces," United States Department of Defense.

---

* Quoted in Kathryn Cullen-Dupont, *The Encyclopedia of Women's History in America* (New York: Facts on File, 1996), p. 132.

AS WE DOWNSIZE the military to meet the conditions of the post–Cold War world, we must ensure that we have the most ready and effective force possible. In order to maintain readiness and effectiveness, we need to draw from the largest available talent pool and select the most qualified individual for each military job. . . .

Accordingly, I am directing the following actions, effective immediately.

A. The military services shall open up more specialties and assignments to women.

1. The services shall permit women to compete for assignments in aircraft, including aircraft engaged in combat missions.
2. The Navy shall open as many additional ships to women as is practicable within current law. The Navy also shall develop a legislative proposal, which I will forward to Congress, to repeal the existing combat exclusion law and permit the assignment of women to ships that are engaged in combat missions.
3. The Army and the Marine Corps shall study opportunities for women to serve in additional assignments, including, but not limited to, field artillery and air defense artillery.
4. Exceptions to the general policy of opening assignments to women shall include units engaged in direct combat on the ground, assignments where physical requirements are prohibitive and assignments where the costs of appropriate berthing and privacy arrangements are prohibitive. The services may propose additional exceptions, together with the justification for such exceptions, as they deem appropriate.

B. An implementation committee shall be established to ensure that the policy on the assignment of women is applied consistently across the services, including the reserve components.

The first piece of legislation that President Bill Clinton signed into law was this act, which requires companies with fifty or more employees to grant up to twelve weeks of unpaid leave for the birth or adoption of a child or to care for a seriously ill spouse or other immediate family member. The act also applies to employees themselves who are unable to work because of a serious health condition.

Originally drafted in 1984, the bill was passed by Congress and vetoed twice by President George Bush, first in 1990 and then two years later, just before the 1992 presidential election, which he lost to Clinton. The act has had an enormously beneficial impact on pregnant female employees, who, until its passage, were seldom granted maternity leave by employers. Organizations as diverse as the National Organization for Women (NOW) and the U.S. Catholic Conference supported family leave legislation, as did a large percentage of Americans polled on the issue. But for some feminists and family and workplace advocates, the act does not go far enough because it fails to require paid leave—the only way that many workers, especially single parents, can afford to take advantage of it.

SOURCE: Public Law No. 103-3, 107 Stat. 6 (1993)

Sec. 102.

(a) In General.—

(1) Entitlement to Leave.—Subject to section 103, an eligible employee shall be entitled to a total of 12 workweeks of leave during any 12-month period for one or more of the following:

(A) Because of the birth of a son or daughter of the employee and in order to care for such son or daughter.

(B) Because of the placement of a son or daughter with the employee for adoption or foster care.

(C) In order to care for the spouse, or a son, daughter, or parent, of the employee, if such spouse, son, daughter, or parent has serious health condition.

(D) Because of a serious health condition that makes the employee unable to perform the functions of the position of such employee.

(2) Expiration of Entitlement.—The entitlement to leave under sub paragraphs (A) and (B) of paragraph (1) for a birth or placement of son or daugh-

ter shall expire at the end of the 12-month period beginning on the date of such birth or placement. . . .

Sec. 104.

(a) Restoration to Position.—

(1) In General.—Except as provided in subsection (b), any eligible employee who takes leave under section 102 for the intended purpose of the leave shall be entitled, on return from such leave—

> (A) to be restored by the employer to the position of employment held by the employee when the leave commenced; or
>
> (B) to be restored to an equivalent position with equivalent employment benefits, pay, and other terms and conditions of employment.

(2) Loss of Benefits.—The taking of leave under section 102 shall no result in the loss of any employment benefit accrued prior to the date on which the leave commenced.

"WE WON'T STOP FIGHTING"
NAOMI WOLF

Naomi Wolf, a journalist and lecturer on women's issues, interviewed women from across the country to try to understand why, at a time when the basic principles of feminism had taken root in the American mainstream and when women had achieved political and economic clout, so many women continued to resist the label "feminism" or view themselves as victims. What she found was that the problem lies not only with the conservative opponents of feminism but with the movement itself—with what she perceived to be its infighting, narrow vision, and failure to reach beyond the already converted. In the book based on this research, Fire with Fire: The New Female Power and How It Will Change the 21st Century, *Wolf exhorts the movement's leaders to move beyond what she calls "victim feminism" to "power feminism"—from a preoccupation with the continuing inequalities in women's lives to a new focus on the movement's achievements, energy, and profound impact on American history. She urges the movement to reach out to new constituencies and use the most potent tools at hand—women's votes and money—to continue transforming women's lives.*

Wolf's book received much media attention and was credited with attracting younger women to the movement. Following is an excerpt, in which she presents her vision of power feminism and urges women to harness the victories they've already achieved—reproductive choice and political and economic clout—to form coalitions and alliances, focus on achieving practical results, and move forward from a collective perception of doubt and weakness to one of strength and confidence. Although Wolf's sanguine perception of the genderquake, as she calls it, is somewhat simplistic because of her boundless faith in the power of self-confidence to overcome serious institutional obstacles to women's equality, her honest criticism of the movement and her clarion call to capitalize on the political and economic power women have achieved is a buoyant and useful road map to feminist action in the twenty-first century.

SOURCE: Naomi Wolf, *Fire with Fire: The New Female Power and How It Will Change the 21st Century* (New York: Random House, 1993), pp. 48–54. Copyright © 1993 by Naomi Wolf. Used by permission of Random House, Inc.

THE LESSONS OF THE GENDERQUAKE

Recently, women became comfortable with telling their opponents to "get it" about their victimization, but American women are slower to get it about their might.

The lesson of the genderquake is this: Women of all races are not a minority. Our numbers are 10 percent shy of the total number of votes cast in the last election [1992]. We can cast seven million more votes than men. Insofar as we are still tangled up in a rhetoric in which others grant us the "Year of the Woman," and can take such treats back at any time depending on their whim and our behavior, we still don't understand.

Women don't need to beg anyone for a ride. We can't even hope to stay safely in the copilot seat. Whether we are ready to face it or not, in electoral terms, women are flying this plane.

Our opponents have understood that fact better than we have ourselves, and their control of events depends only on how long they can keep us from grasping this.

In 1992, seventy-two years after women won the vote, we finally dared to use it properly. We achieved an unprecedented roster of victories.

The lesson? Women made this happen. Women elected the president. Insofar as the majority of citizens—women—used their ballot-box clout to elect a president on his commitment to serve the majority, our democracy has worked effectively for the first time. Our power, harnessed as the majority, is virtually unstoppable. We didn't quit with the White House. We showed our clout in Washington State, Texas, California, and Illinois. We did it from the Senate down to the school boards. It was no fluke; we weren't lucky; no one sent victory to us gallantly, wrapped in ribbons and tissue like a dozen long-stemmed roses. There's no point in looking distractedly around us, or playing demurely with our handbags, or saying, as sweetly grateful as we were raised to be, "Oh, sir, you're too kind!" Because no one else did it for us. We did it.

And since women are used to running with ankle weights—maintaining work, home, and family on two thirds the income we deserve—*it wasn't even that hard.* As one new representative said, Congress is child's play if you've organized a birthday party.

The ease with which women's irritation brought about political change in 1992–1993 underscores the single most puzzling condition of women's lives: Why is it, after all, that a demographic majority that overwhelmingly favors women's rights is still subordinate? The primary reason is that this majority has never, until now, had a cogent demonstration of the effectiveness of its use of political power, and so did not really believe in it.

Women tend, in the dreamy, feminine way in which we have been taught to think about our own volition, to have a kind of rescue fantasy about our rights: Eventually, when we are somehow made equal—by the unfolding of time, or by government edict, or by whatever means—we can expect to get what we need.

But it is not until we take what we need that we can make our opportunities equal. As British Attorney Helena Kennedy once observed, waiting for women to obtain equality "when the time is right" is like waiting for a fish to grow feet.

In other words, women are suffering from much subordination for no more pressing reason than that we have stopped short of compelling it to end. In the bad old days, when women could not vote, we were helpless indeed. When we could not earn our own money, independence was a cruel mirage for all, as it still is for so many women struggling financially. When we lacked reproductive choice, civil rights were only partly within our possession. Under those conditions, women were not really living in a representative democracy.

Today, we still have enormous burdens. Subsidized child care is a rarity; most women have been sexually harassed at work; the court system is almost useless in deterring rape and domestic violence; and women are paid less than men for doing the same jobs. But we tend to talk about these obstacles as if they were insurmountable, as if we lived under a fascist state in which women can neither earn money nor vote.

Now that reproductive choice and the right to a wage are minimally secure, and now that we have a clear demonstration of the simplicity with which we can bring about the changes that the polls show most of us desire, we must realize that democracy puts our fate squarely in our own hands. If we are slow in lifting those obstacles, it will be for many good reasons, as we acclimatize to our strength. But unless the country suffers a coup d'état, if we do not manage to move them significantly by the millennium, and reach parity in the twenty-first century, it will be because women on some level have *chosen* not to exert the power that is our birthright. When we tell ourselves that we are, as women, helpless and at the mercy of events, we are telling ourselves a comforting fable left behind from a world that is already gone.

When I argue that women have enormous unclaimed power, I am not pretending that women are not harmed and held back in every way, or that "everything's all right now" so we can relax and stop fighting. I am saying rather, that if we understand the events of the recent past and act on that understanding, and if we undergo a sea change in our own self-image, matters will become increasingly "all right." Feminists, including myself, are often anxious when commentators focus on women's achievements, because we fear a return to apathy. My hope is that if we interpret the genderquake rightly, we won't stop fighting. We will fight more intelligently and more elegantly. And we will suffer less of the wear and tear of anger and helplessness while having a lot more sheer fun.

When I say that the genderquake has potentially changed forever what it means to be female, I mean this: *It is no longer necessary for women to ask anyone's permission for social equality.*

Women feel they need to spend a lot of time doing PR for their own equality, but it is no longer necessary to focus primarily on appealing to the opposition for justice. In other words, whether it is ready or not, "society" no longer has the power to keep women in their place. For women now have the electoral clout to create the conditions they need for equality. The question to ask is not whether society is ready to yield to women their rightful places, but whether women themselves are ready to take possession of them.

Equality is no longer something we need to beg for from others. This paradigm shift demands that women begin to see themselves as potent agents of change with many resources, rather than as helpless victims. Indeed, what is the point of settling for equality when women are entitled to true democracy, in which the advantage of our numbers makes us the single strongest force on earth? As Western women, we are, in fact, not just in charge of our own countries, but are also, whether we like it or not, and as truly unjust as it is, in a position to affect what becomes of most of the rest of the world.

This exhilarating, terrifying responsibility for the fate of nations is not waiting to descend on us someday, in some smoky, hazy future of a feminist science-fiction novel. It's not even around the corner. It's already here. You've been living it.

If we stay hunkered down, defensive, and angry, we waste our energies. We act effectively now if we learn to relax into our power, stand upright, and leave the foxholes that we have almost begun to consider a permanent home. We must stand in a new posture, walking with a loving heart, an open mind, and a very big stick called clout. If we do that, then we can live to see the start of the Egalitarian Era: a reality in which women become something there is no word for—that is, not unequal by virtue of gender.

Today, after thirty years of education against racism have left racial barriers substantially intact, many African-American civil rights activists are turning to the strategies of Malcolm X and the Reverend Jesse Jackson. Their approach mobilizes people's will to self-determination and consolidates their money and influence to force change where antiracist education and appeals to justice have failed. This approach pressured corporations to divest in South Africa, urges African-Americans to support black-owned businesses, and seeks out public-private partnerships. Gay and lesbian groups are making similar shifts, trading in the plea for tolerance and compassion in favor of PR campaigns, high-profile fund-raising, and a show of political influence. Women, as a group, must make the same psychic transition.

Now that women have begun to steal fire from the gods and use it; it is time to abandon orthodoxy, sloganeering, ideological posturing, and life lived on the margins for marginality's sake. It is time to turn outward in a fair and goal-oriented way, time to trade in preaching to the converted for negotiating with the opposition from a position of strength. And time to forge a new link between sisterhood and capital that offers women the encouragement to get more and the responsibility to give more.

For now is a time in which real change for women depends upon a willingness to engage with power with its seductions and responsibilities, democracy with all its open conflicts, and money with all its pleasures and dangers.

What is power feminism? It means taking practical giant steps instead of ideologically pure baby steps; practicing tolerance rather than self-righteousness. Power feminism encourages us to identify with one another primarily through the shared pleasures and strengths of femaleness, rather than primarily through our shared vulnerability and pain. It calls for alliances based on economic self-interest and economic giving back rather than on a sentimental and workable fantasy of cosmic sisterhood.

Power feminism can, without compromising its principles, be reclaimed by the majority. It is flexible enough to make use of its temporary peace dividend: It can adapt much of its wartime economy, based on the struggle for abortion rights, into a peacetime economy, centered on money and work. It welcomes men and honors their place in the lives of women, straight and gay; and it has no difficulty telling the difference between hating sexism and hating men.

I am not asking us to delude ourselves with the thought that we can move out of victimization into confidence by some sort of individualistic positive thinking. We can only do so by uniting toward more power. Frederick Douglass said, "If there is no struggle there is no progress. . . . Power concedes nothing without a demand. It never did and it never will."

The late feminist poet Audre Lorde wrote that the master's tools would never dismantle the master's house. But the electoral process, the press, and money are among the master's tools. The genderquake should show us that it is *only* the master's tools that can dismantle the master's house; he hardly bothers to notice anyone else's.

Now that some women have access to some of his tools, the master has yielded to women the instruments that can rearrange and even open up his stronghold. The question for women now is, "Do we dare to escalate our use of them?"

"DOMESTIC VIOLENCE IS A STAGGERING SOCIAL PROBLEM"
FAMILY VIOLENCE PREVENTION FUND

On April 19, 1993, the Family Violence Prevention Fund, based in San Francisco, released a study on the prevalence of domestic violence across the nation. This study, the first of its kind, was based on a national survey of nineteen hundred people conducted by EDK Associates, a New York public opinion research firm. The survey found that 34 percent of those questioned claimed to have witnessed domestic violence—in contrast to 19 percent who said they had witnessed a robbery or mugging. The survey also found that respondents, picked randomly as a cross-section of the population, did not shy away from talking about domestic violence in their own lives and regarded it as a major social problem.

Released at a hearing of the House Subcommittee on Health and the Environment, the survey was intended to provide further ammunition in support of President Bill Clinton's proposal to give the Federal Centers for Disease Control ten million dollars for a national domestic violence prevention program. Clinton had earlier raised the issue of domestic violence by speaking about his abusive stepfather in his acceptance speech at the 1992 Democratic National Convention, and two of his cabinet secretaries—Secretary of Health and Human Services Donna Shalala and Attorney General Janet Reno—made curbing domestic violence a priority of their respective departments. Almost half the nation's states also instituted programs to prosecute wife batterers or overturn the convictions of women who had killed or injured abusers out of self-defense. The Family Violence Prevention Fund used the study to launch a national campaign against domestic violence. Esta Soler, executive director of the fund, declared in congressional testimony that "more women are seriously injured by beatings than by car accidents, muggings, and rape combined."* Following are excerpts from the report.

SOURCE: This material was adapted from the publication entitled "Men Beating Women: Ending Domestic Violence," produced by the Family Violence Prevention Fund: www.endabuse.org.

DOMESTIC VIOLENCE is a staggering social problem with far-reaching consequences in every sector of American life. The Federal Bureau of Investigation

---

* Quoted in *Historic Documents of 1993*, copyright © 1994 Congressional Quarterly, Inc., p. 287.

estimates that every 15 seconds a woman is beaten by her husband or boyfriend. More women are injured or killed by being beaten than in car accidents, muggings and rapes combined. Juvenile delinquents are four times more likely to come from homes in which their fathers beat their mothers.

In the course of the past two decades the movement to end domestic violence has succeeded in raising public consciousness about male violence toward women. The movement has exposed the violence and made it clear that women don't ask for it. However, domestic violence incidents are still seen as isolated events. The blame is placed on the failures of individual men. To some extent it is still a "private problem."

The Family Violence Prevention Fund has launched the "There's No Excuse" National Domestic Violence Media Campaign to significantly reduce the incidence of violence against women in intimate relationships and to promote women's right to safety in the home by changing the attitudes of the American public and increasing their involvement in the issue.

Before launching this campaign, The Family Violence Prevention Fund set out to answer a variety of questions to help determine the current shape of public understanding of domestic violence. The objectives of the research were to assess how receptive or resistant people are to talking about domestic violence, to determine how much they already know and the perceived seriousness of the problem and to determine what people are willing to do to help end violence against women. . . .

VIOLENCE AS PART OF EVERYDAY LIFE

Our personal lives are not free from violence or fear of physical harm from the people we love. Americans acknowledge a pervasive amount of violence in private relationships.

Getting people to talk about domestic violence was seen as a major obstacle to conducting both the focus groups and survey research. Experts believed that people would refuse to open up in the groups or stay on the phone once they understood the topic.

We were wrong. One of the most striking findings of this research is that Americans across all race and ethnic backgrounds are both ready and willing to discuss this issue. People in the focus groups and on the phone discussed domestic violence as a real problem that they have seen in their own lives. And they want it to end.

WE HURT THE ONES WE LOVE

Shoving, pushing and throwing objects are not a rare occurrence when a man and a woman have a fight, according to this research. The public is not willing to draw a line where women are always good and men are always bad. When it comes to fighting, both men and women shove, push and throw objects during the course of an argument. But, as the level of physical violence escalates, both men and women acknowledge that men harm women more than women harm men. One in two women believes that battering is not an uncommon experience in women's relationships with men.

When it comes to physical blows: men beat women. And men *do* beat women—44% of Americans report that when a man and a woman have a fight he could wind up hitting her. Some people say he does it often (19%), but more likely it happens sometimes (25%). Given the extreme nature of this behavior, the noteworthy point is that less than half say it rarely happens (43%).

Men also physically restrain or push women. Six out of 10 Americans believe that when a man and a woman have a fight there is a good chance he will grab and shove her to make his point (57%—24% often and 33% sometimes). A woman is less likely to get this physical with him (40%—11% often and 29% sometimes). This is not to say that women never express rage or anger. She is more likely to throw something at him (55%—26% often and 29% sometimes) than he is at her (39%—13% often and 26% sometimes).

Moreover, abusive behavior isn't only physical. Men and women are often nasty to one another. Almost half say that he often says nasty things to hurt her (48% say often and only 11% say this rarely happens). She also says nasty things to hurt him (44% say often and 13% say rarely).

IT HAPPENS TO US

Public recognition of the seriousness of domestic abuse reflects the violence people acknowledge in their own lives. The majority of Americans have witnessed potentially violent circumstances (57%). *More people have directly witnessed an incidence of domestic violence (34%) than muggings and robberies combined (19%).*

One out of three American men and women have stared domestic violence in the face. Fourteen (14%) percent of American women acknowledge having been violently abused by a husband or boyfriend. Almost half of these are women who acknowledge having been abused. While domestic violence is not completely limited to men beating women—two out of 10 men report having witnessed a woman beating up on her husband or boyfriend—most Americans identify the case of men beating women as a very serious problem.

The survey results corroborate the surprising prevalence of experience with domestic violence found in the focus groups. Given that the people attending these groups were not selected on the basis of their exposure to incidents of violence nor were they told that the subject matter was domestic violence, the number of people who volunteered personal stories was quite striking. . . .

"WE'RE COMING HOME, AMERICA"
TORIE OSBORN

Nearly thirty years after the historic March on Washington, in which a quarter of a million African Americans marched to the Lincoln Memorial to hear the Reverend Martin Luther King, Jr.'s eloquent appeal for social and political justice, another march for justice took place in the nation's capital on April 25, 1993. This time three hundred thousand lesbian women and gay men marched through downtown Washington and ended their protest with a rally at the Mall. Along the way they encountered angry demonstrators who chanted slogans such as "God hates fags," "fags burn in hell," and "fag equals AIDS." The marchers, waving a sea of rainbow flags, banners, signs, red ribbons, and pink triangles, had as their goal passage of a civil rights bill including provisions for homosexual rights, increased funding for AIDS research, and an end to the exclusion of gay and lesbian teachers and administrators in the public school system and in the military. Although a few political leaders participated in the march, President Bill Clinton chose not to attend and instead sent a message of support for the marchers' overall goal of equality.

Torie Osborn, executive director of the Gay and Lesbian Task Force, gave the keynote address. Her use of the metaphor "coming home" is a poignant reminder of how gays and lesbians have felt excluded not only from their communities and country but also from their own families.

SOURCE: Reprinted by permission of the National Gay and Lesbian Task Force

MY NAME is Torie Osborn. I'm here to talk about the future—our future—but to do that, I need to start with the past. Not so long ago, people actually believed that in order to have power in America, you had to be white. You had to be a man. And you had to be straight. All lies. In the sixties, the civil rights movement fought the lie that you had to be white.

The women's movement of the '70s revolutionized the very concept of power—and let us remember today that it was lesbian leadership that created that new vision.

And in 1969, those brave drag queens and working class dykes at Stonewall laid seige to that last lie—and catapulted us toward this moment—into this movement that proclaims our right to love and desire whom we choose.

By 1980 our movement was growing. We had begun to come out and we had begun to fight for our rights.

And then we began to die. At first, just a few, and then in terrifying numbers. Thousands, then tens of thousands, shunned by society, betrayed by America's leaders. At the beginning of the 1980's, we stood alone, outcasts, forsaken by family, lacking community. Frightened. Frustrated. Furious.

We were fighting for our very lives—and we began to link arms—around bedsides, in street demonstrations, in service organizations, before committees of Congress,and yes, at thousands of wakes, and funerals and memorial services that should have driven us insane—but only drove us closer together.

And, so the sorrow and the rage of AIDS propelled us out of the closets of fear and denial into the sunlight of community, and we came out in greater numbers than ever before—and each person who came out—every single one of you—added to the strength of this new community.

Well, my friends, if the '80's was the decade of coming out—the nineties will be the decade of coming home.

We're coming home, America—with our heads held high, not as strangers, but as the people we are—your daughters and sons. Your carpenters and teachers, captains of industry and captains in the Army—we're coming home.

We're coming home for Christmas and Hanukah and Kwanzaa, Easter and Passover, Ramadan and Solstice, Thanksgiving, and the Fourth of July. America, this brave community is coming home.

We're walking home. We're flying home, and we're going to drive home our powerful message: that in the midst of unrelenting hate and the agony of AIDS, we've had the power to move through anger to love and hope. And now we're bringing it home. We're coming home.

So, listen to us, America, you the divided country, a country with too little hope—just look at these faces, look at our diversity, look at our unity. America, if we could find hope and optimism, everyone can. America—we're coming home to help bring this country together. To make it whole, we're coming home.

We're coming home so everyone who isn't out can come out. I say to those still trapped in the prisons they call closets, we are here, waiting for you—a community of support—gay men and lesbians and bisexuals—and friends who are "straight but not narrow."

And come out you must. Your secrecy is killing you; it's killing us. We're coming home to lend you shoulders of support so you can tell your story without fear, so you can put your lover's picture on your desk at work, so you can finally find freedom in your lives. We're coming home.

We're coming home because the truth of who we are obliterates the lies of the religious right. Today, together, we say to those sexophobic, homophobic neopuritans—you have fair warning: We're coming home.

In order to survive, we built a community separate from the rest of society. But the ideal of America—a democracy that includes everyone—cannot be realized without us. So, we're coming in from the outside, to take our place at the table as equals, no more, no less. We're coming home.

And, America, do not be fooled by our loving spirit. Let no one doubt from this day forward our determination to take what is rightfully ours. We will drive that message home again and again and again. Are you listening, Pat Robertson and Pat Buchanan?* Do you get the message, Sam Nunn?†

Yes, we're coming home to Army bases in Georgia and to living rooms in California and to community centers in Vermont and to farms in Kansas and to factory floors in Ohio. . . . America, are you listening? We are your family too, and we are everywhere—and we're finally coming home. We're coming home.

---

* Right-wing religious and political leaders who have equated homosexuality with immoral behavior.

† Senator from Georgia who supported a ban against gays in the military.

"THIS EXTRAORDINARY CHANCE AND CHALLENGE"
RUTH BADER GINSBURG

Ruth Bader Ginsburg was not the first woman to be appointed to the United States Supreme Court. That distinction belonged to Sandra Day O'Connor, who was appointed by President Ronald Reagan in 1981. But Ginsburg's appointment had special resonance for women because of her path-breaking legal work on behalf of women. In fact, when President Bill Clinton formally nominated her on June 14, 1993, he declared, "She is to the women's movement what former Supreme Court Justice Thurgood Marshall was to the movement for the rights of African Americans."

Born in 1933 in Brooklyn, New York, Ginsburg attended Cornell University, where she studied prelaw, and received her law degree from Columbia Law School, though she had also spent two years at Harvard Law School. Despite making law review at both of these top-rated law schools, she was unable to find employment at any prestigious law firm in New York City. Even Supreme Court justice Felix Frankfurter, one of the most liberal judges on the Court, refused to interview her for a clerkship, explaining to the New York Times *that he "just wasn't ready to hire a woman." Ginsburg found her first job with a U.S. district court judge and went on to teach law, first at Rutgers University Law School and then at Columbia. In the early 1970s she founded and directed the Women's Rights Project of the American Civil Liberties Union. She argued six women's rights cases before the Supreme Court and won five of them. Like an earlier generation of women's rights advocates, Ginsburg drew on the Fourteenth Amendment's equal-protection clause to seek redress for gender discrimination; she declared that laws that treat women differently from men violate women's right to protection under that Constitutional clause.*

Ginsburg was serving on the U.S. Court of Appeals in Washington, D.C., when President Bill Clinton nominated her for the High Court. At her confirmation hearing before the Senate Judiciary Committee, she paid homage to previous champions of equality. "I surely would not be in this room today," she observed, "without the determined efforts of men and women who kept dreams alive— dreams of equal citizenship in the days when few would listen—people like Susan B. Anthony, Elizabeth Cady Stanton, and Harriet Tubman come to mind. I stand on the shoulders of those brave people."*

---

* Quoted in the *New York Times*, 25 June 1993, p. A-19.

Following are excerpts from Ginsburg's response to her formal nomination by Clinton. Here, too, she pays homage to the civil rights and women's movements and, most poignantly, to her late mother for bringing her to this historic occasion.

SOURCE: In the public domain.

THE ANNOUNCEMENT the President just made is significant, I believe, because it contributes to the end of the days when women, at least half the talent pool in our society, appear in high places only as one-at-a-time performers. Recall that when President Carter took office in 1976, no woman ever served on the Supreme Court, and only one woman . . . then served at the next Federal court level, the United States Court of Appeals.

Today Justice Sandra Day O'Connor graces the Supreme Court bench, and close to twenty-five women serve at the Federal Court of Appeals level, two as chief judges. I am confident that more will soon join them. That seems to me inevitable, given the change in law school enrollment.

My law school class in the late 1950s numbered over 500. That class included less than 10 women. . . . Not a law firm in the entire city of New York bid for my employment as a lawyer when I earned my degree. Today few law schools have female enrollment under 40 percent, and several have reached or passed the 50 percent mark. And thanks to Title VII, no entry doors are barred. . . .

I am indebted to so many for this extraordinary chance and challenge: to a revived women's movement in the 1970s that opened doors for people like me, to the civil rights movement of the 1960s from which the women's movement drew inspiration. . . .

I have a last thank you. It is to my mother, Celia Amster Bader, the bravest and strongest person I have ever known, who was taken from me much too soon. I pray that I may be all that she would have been had she lived in an age when women could aspire and achieve and daughters are cherished as much as sons. I look forward to stimulating weeks this summer and, if I am confirmed, to working at a neighboring court to the best of my ability for the advancement of the law in the service of society. Thank you.

Like Reaganomics, AIDS (acquired immune deficiency syndrome) sadly made its debut in this country in the early 1980s. A disease of the human immune system, it is caused by the human immunodeficiency virus (HIV) and is commonly transmitted in blood and bodily secretions, such as semen. The disease is increasingly treatable, but to date there is still no cure for AIDS. In the early 1980s the primary victims of AIDS were homosexual and bisexual men and intravenous drug users who injected themselves with infected needles. Until blood samples were tested, beginning in the late 1980s, patients receiving intravenous blood infusions were also at risk of contracting AIDS from infected blood.

By the early 1990s the scourge of AIDS had spread to women as well, and, as the following selection indicates, AIDS began to spread far more quickly among women than men during the mid-1990s, with black and Hispanic women most at risk. In the following selection, twelve urban black, Hispanic, and white women living in the mid-Atlantic region of the United States, diagnosed with AIDS for at least one year, speak about the impact of living with the disease. In addition to the physical symptoms—the continual fatigue and debility, the disfigurement from sores and scarring, and their increased susceptibility to other diseases—they describe their profound sense of powerlessness, their experience of rejection and discrimination, and their fears for themselves and the children whom they will leave behind. They speak of fear but also of hope and determination.

SOURCE: David Anthony Forrester, "Women Living with HIV/AIDS: The Third Wave," in *The Emergence of Women into the 21st Century*, edited by Patricia L. Munhall and Virginia M. Fitzsimmons (New York: NLN Press, 1995), pp. 131–40. Reprinted by permission of Jones and Bartlett Publishers, Sudbury, MA. www.jbpub.com.

WOMEN MEET many complex challenges in their search and struggle for peace, equality, and personal development. It is within their situated contexts that women must strive to meet their personal challenges and obtain their future fulfillment. There is no greater challenge than living day-to-day within the context of a terminal illness. In fact, there can be no greater threat to the "personhood" of women than a stigmatized illness that destines them for eventual death. And yet, every day women meet this challenge with grace and dignity. They prevail—they must.

BACKGROUND AND SIGNIFICANCE

The human immunodeficiency virus (HIV) and the acquired immune deficiency syndrome (AIDS) it causes clearly pose some of the most compelling challenges imaginable. Some are unique to HIV/AIDS; some are common to other serious illnesses as well. For women, the issues raised by HIV/AIDS are amplified by the urgency associated with this rapidly evolving global pandemic and the complex psychological, political, legal, and social problems it engenders. For this and future generations of women, the ultimate challenge of HIV/AIDS will be to provide sensitive, compassionate care while balancing individual rights and liberties against issues of public health.

In the United States, following gay men and intravenous drug users, women represent the third and most far reaching epidemiological wave of the evolving global HIV/AIDS pandemic. AIDS is spreading almost six times as quickly among women as it is among men, and disease transmission is fastest among black and Hispanic women. Worldwide, 50% of all new HIV infections are among women. New AIDS diagnoses are increasing at an annual rate of 17% among American women, compared to 3% for the nation's population as a whole.

DESIGN AND SAMPLE

This study is an exploration of some issues of importance to women with HIV/AIDS. Its existential/phenomenological design entailed investigator-conducted, confidential, unstructured, audiotape interviews of a racially diverse sample of 12 urban women either alone or in groups for no more than one hour's duration. These women were contacted through the investigator's nursing practice and community service activities. Physical and psychological safety, informed consent, and confidentiality were guaranteed.

These 12 urban women, living in the mid-Atlantic United States, were HIV-infected and had been diagnosed with AIDS for at least one year. Their ages ranged from 20 to 59 years with a median age of 28.9. Their ethnicity was black (8; 67%), Hispanic (3; 25%), and white (1; 8%). Their exposure categories were intravenous drug use combined with heterosexual contact (8; 67%), intravenous drug use only (2; 17%), heterosexual contact only (1; 8%), and other/unknown (1; 8%). Ten (83%) of these women had dependent children living in their home. . . .

The following are some of the salient themes and issues identified by the women participating in this investigation. They are accompanied by interview exerpts. For these women, issues of concern were an outgrowth of the psychologic and social stresses of living with HIV/AIDS.

Psychologic Stresses

Perhaps the major *psychologic stress* expressed by these women living with HIV/AIDS is their knowledge that they have an incurable illness that holds the potential for rapid decline and death. Their expressions of fear, anxiety, loss and grief, guilt, dependence, depression, and powerlessness and vulnerability were compounded by the uncertainty of the course of their disease.

Fear was universal among these 12 women with AIDS. Generally, expressions of fear centered around disease progression and diminished capacity. Specific expressions of fear were associated with fear of contagion, disfigurement, and death.

The progressive effects of HIV/AIDS, including symptoms, debilitation, and disability, figured prominently in almost all of these women's expressions of fear. One woman said, "I'm tired all the time—even on my 'good days.' I'm so afraid that I won't be able to get out anymore—afraid I won't be able to take care of my kids." Another woman said, "Every day that passes brings new worries. I'm afraid of every infection . . . I'm afraid every time that this may be the one that kills me."

A number of the women in the study expressed fear of contagion, and usually related to contracting opportunistic infections from others. For example, "I'm afraid everywhere I go that someone will sneeze or cough on me and that I'll get sick again. I don't go out a lot of times because of this." Occasionally their fears had to do with infecting others, even if they believed these fears were irrational. For example, "I've had other friends with AIDS and I haven't been afraid of them. But now that I have it [AIDS], I think sometimes that I'm afraid I'll give it to somebody else . . . I worry about my kids. I worry about using the same shower as them . . . using the same soap . . . letting them drink after me. I know I shouldn't worry about this, but I can't help it."

Fear of disfigurement for themselves and others was also mentioned. "I'm afraid every time I look in the mirror about what I might see. Every change is worse. My clothes don't fit . . . I don't look like me anymore," said one woman. And, "Other people I see [in the clinic] are changing too. I see it almost every time I go. So many people I don't even know begin to look like living skeletons. Sometimes it goes for a long time and then I don't see them . . . they just evaporate."

Whether overtly or covertly, fear of death was expressed by several of these women. One woman said, "When I first found out I was HIV-positive, I thought . . . Oh my God, I'm going to die!" Another woman reported, "Sometimes I feel like I'm already dead. Things move so fast—with or without me. I'm scared!"

Anxiety was expressed by almost all of these women. "I'm always nervous . . . nervous about everything, my health, the bills, the kids . . . everything. I'm never alone that I'm not worrying about something to do with AIDS."

Ambivalence was a feature of the psychologic stress expressed by a number of these women. One woman said, "It's hell if I do and hell if I don't . . . I don't know what's better, being sick—getting the treatments and taking my medicine, or being well [symptom free] and worrying about what's next." Another said, "Sometimes I'm actually glad I have it [AIDS]—at least I know. But then I think—no, nobody wants this . . . I hate it."

Loss and grief, including denial, anger, bargaining, resolution, and mortality awareness and value of life were common features of these women's experiences with HIV/AIDS. This grief was for perceived losses already experienced and anticipated losses. There seemed to be dimensions of both anticipatory and post mortem grief. For example, one woman said, "It seems so long ago that I was normal—healthy . . . I miss just being normal. I'd give anything if I could go back to just being normal." And, "I've had so many people [friends] die. I haven't been able to think about them so much now . . . I used to think about them a lot—before I got sick. Now I think about my kids. I don't want to lose them. I don't want to be taken away from them."

One woman described her shock and disbelief and subsequent denial upon learning of her HIV-positive status by saying, "How could this happen? There must have been some mistake!" Later, upon learning of her AIDS diagnosis, "I just couldn't believe my ears . . . I was numb—still am. I still just can't believe it!"

Frank anger was expressed by several of these women. It was sometimes expressed as time-limited and undirected anger leading to social isolation such as, "I went for a while there when I was mad at everyone and everything. I've never been so mad—and I didn't really know why. I just knew I was mad and that everybody should stay away from me. And they pretty much did [stay away]." Some of these women also expressed anger as being vague and ever present. For example, "I walk around tied up in knots about half the time. I want to hit something . . . hurt someone, but I don't know what or who."

At least one woman expressed anger and feelings of inner turmoil that were self-directed, "I hate my body for betraying me. I hate myself sometimes for giving in . . . for being weak." Yet another woman reported feelings of anger toward others, "I really hate other people sometimes just for being healthy. I'm jealous of them for that and I get mad at them."

Bargaining was a feature of at least one woman's experience of living with HIV/AIDS. She said, "I used to pray for Jesus to give me the strength to get off drugs . . . [I used to] think that if I could only get straight, maybe he would let me keep my life like it used to be. Now, I pray every day that he'll let me live. I try to make little deals with him every day if I can stay well, get better and live longer."

Resolution regarding their diagnosis and the probable eventuality of death was mentioned by several of these women living with AIDS. One woman said, "Once other people knew about my sickness, it was easier for me to accept it. It was like telling my secret [and] getting this huge weight off my shoulders. I was relieved and now I live with it [AIDS] better." Another woman said, "I know I'm going to die. I don't know really when or how, but I know I'm going to die of AIDS. Of course it bothers me, but not like it did at first. I've just come to accept it . . . I'm not giving up though. I'm still fighting it."

Increased mortality awareness and value of life were also of concern to several of the women in the study. "I'm just glad to be alive. I looked out my window last night at the moon through the trees and I was overwhelmed by the beauty and how lucky I am to be here to see it. Even though it hasn't been a hard winter . . . not like last winter—I still want to see spring. Life is so beautiful; it just means so much more to me now."

A number of these women living with HIV/AIDS expressed feelings of guilt. Some were experiencing guilt over behaviors which, as they perceived them, had placed them at risk of contracting HIV. For example, one woman with a history of intravenous drug use said, "I try to remember to be mad at the virus, but it doesn't always work. I keep thinking that it's my fault I have AIDS. If I had been able to get straight maybe this wouldn't be happening." Another woman expressed guilt over transmission of HIV to her children, "Now my babies have it. I don't know what to do for them. I feel like it's my fault; I don't know what to do."

Dependence, especially regarding care givers, health professionals, and the health care delivery system as a whole, was also mentioned. Comments often had to do with their perception that the "system" was in some way failing them. "Sometimes I don't think they [health professionals] know how much we [people with AIDS] are depending on them. I feel like I'm at their mercy for everything. I try not to let them know [that I feel this way] because I'm afraid they might use it against me . . . I know this is paranoid. I don't think they can really do very much for me anyway . . . I'm always hearing why this or that can't happen. Sometimes I want to shake them so they'll know that I'm counting on them. I have to count on them a lot."

Depression, episodic or continuous, was described by every woman interviewed. Expressions of depression included the entire continuum ranging from a sense of discouragement, to sadness, to impulsive thoughts and behavior such as suicidal ideation. One woman said, "I try to 'have good days' like you hear about—but I can't. I can't get away from having AIDS—it doesn't go away. There are no 'good days' because you can't forget you have AIDS. I'm so depressed; it's been that way for a long time." Another woman reported, "Once I finally got tested and found out I really had AIDS, I couldn't stand it . . . I just wanted to kill myself. If it hadn't been for my kids, I think I would have."

Powerlessness and vulnerability were expressed by these women in virtually every aspect of their lives. Feelings of helplessness, hopelessness and loss of control were frequent. These not only had to do with their health but their day to day lives. "It feels like I'm always the last to know what's going on in my life . . . When I see the doctor, sometimes I'm almost home before I think, 'I don't really know what she's doing to take care of me.' I mean, I'm out of the room and talking to the nurse before I'm told what the plan is. Most of the time, I just do what they tell me. I think a lot of other people [with AIDS] do better at telling the doctors and nurses what to do instead of [it being] the other way around like it is with me. I think they may do better . . . you know, get more and stay better."

Social Stresses

The major social stresses expressed by these women with HIV/AIDS included disclosure, stigmatization, prejudice, discrimination, alienation, and rejection and abandonment. These social stresses seemed to be subjectively experienced as fear, anger, and guilt as previously described, as well as human reduction and suspicion as described below.

A number of the women in the study expressed social concern regarding their disclosure of having HIV/AIDS in the community. Their concerns had to do with both self-disclosure and fear of others' disclosure of their illness within their family, friends, health care providers, and their larger social community. Their expressions of these concerns included a full spectrum, ranging from personal relief of finally being able to openly discuss their situations with others, to frank fear of the real or imagined repercussions of others' knowledge of their diagnosis. "When I first found out about my HIV, I didn't want anyone to know . . . and then, more and more, I just had to tell them—I couldn't keep it in anymore."

Several of these women felt that due to the physical changes they had experienced, they simply had no option as to whether or not they disclosed their illness to others. "My mother saw how much weight I lost and she would look at me funny . . . and ask me why. I didn't have any choice; I didn't have the energy not to tell her I had HIV."

Public identification as a person with HIV/AIDS also invites stigmatization. A number of the participants in the study were concerned about the social stigma associated with their illness. Comments such as, "I didn't think of myself as 'disabled' until I heard the social worker refer to my 'disability.' I don't like being thought of as disabled. I know that, technically—legally, I am [disabled]; but I still don't like it." And, "I don't always think of myself as a person with AIDS. Usually it's other people who think of me as an 'AIDS patient.' And always, they want to know how I got it. Some people ask about it in a round about way, but it always comes up . . . and soon. Sometimes I tell them I'm a gay man just to see what they'll say. It's surprising how many people pause. Some even say OK."

All of the women participating indicated that they felt that they had born the burden of HIV/AIDS prejudice of others. One woman reported, "I even feel it [HIV/AIDS prejudice] here [in the AIDS support group]. It's like it's the IV drug users versus the 'innocent' hemophiliacs or the straight sex partners versus the gay men. We even do this to ourselves and each other . . . If the 'IVDUs' take too much from the clothing bank or get ahead in the dinner line, we're looked down on." Another woman said, "Everyone I know with AIDS has lost something more than their health. They've lost friends, families, their homes, their jobs . . ."

Almost all of these women said that they had experienced some form of HIV/AIDS discrimination. This discrimination was not always directed at these women alone. For example, one participant said, "When my little girl's friends found out that her mother has AIDS, they were mean to her. You know how they [children] can be. Even her friends were ridiculed by the other children just for staying friends with my daughter. My little girl even thinks the teachers at her school reinforce this negative attitude. They may not say anything bad directly to my little girl, but I don't always think they try to help her either."

Social alienation in some form or other was a frequent complaint. "I've noticed in the hospital and in the clinic that the nurses and doctors don't really want to touch me. They don't ever ask how I feel about anything." And, "Sometimes people I know, who know [about my diagnosis] are overly happy to see me—sort of too friendly but stand-offish at the same time. It's really weird, like they're trying too hard to be nice to somebody they really wish would go away." One woman put it this way, "I don't relate to people the way I used to. I'm not sure if it's me or them . . . probably it's both."

In at least two extreme instances, the prejudice, discrimination, and alienation experienced by women in this study resulted in actual rejection and abandonment by family, friends, and/or co-workers. At a time when these women most needed social support, comfort, compassion, and closeness, they felt alone and isolated. One 20-year-old woman, who was now sleeping on a friend's couch, said, "When my family found out [that I have AIDS], they just shut me out. They just didn't want anything to do with me anymore. I don't know if it will ever get better." Another woman said, "The only people who will really have anything to do with me now are here [in the AIDS support group]."

All of these women expressed some sense of human reduction. Typically their sense of diminished self had to do with feelings of devaluation, and perceived weakness or worthlessness. They blamed themselves as well as others for their feelings of being diminished. "Sometimes I want to hide under the covers and play like this isn't happening to me. I feel dirty . . . damaged—like I'm less than human." Another woman said, "A lot of times I think it's other people that make me feel bad about myself . . . like I'm not a real person . . . like I'm a third class citizen." These women's feelings of devaluation, whether arising from the self or others, frequently were related to expressions of anger and feelings of inner turmoil.

Suspicion was expressed by some of the women in the study. For example, "I don't think they [health providers] tell me everything. Oh, I don't mean they lie to me—I just don't always think they tell me the whole truth about how I'm really doing." One woman was suspicious that her family members weren't being completely honest with her, "They [my mother and children] sometimes stop talking when I come around. They just stop—like they're keeping secrets from me. Sometimes I ask what they're talking about; sometimes I don't." . . .

Women represent the third and perhaps most far reaching epidemiological wave in the global HIV/AIDS pandemic. The resonating themes regarding these women's search and struggle for peace, equality, and development have been made more evident through this investigation. These women, living with HIV/AIDS, share with all women the same fundamental needs for hope, safety and security within their environment. Unique to these women's experiences, however, are the contingencies and situated contexts within which they attempt to meet their personal challenges for present and future self-fulfillment.

These women's desire to maintain their sense of "personhood" and "normalcy" in their daily lives may make them reluctant to share expressions of their psychological stresses (including fear, anxiety, loss and grief, guilt, dependence, depression, and powerlessness and vulnerability) and social stresses (including disclosure, stigmatization, prejudice, discrimination, alienation, rejection and abandonment, human reduction, and suspicion). For example, for these women living with HIV/AIDS, the first and perhaps most difficult psychological and social issues had to do with their children and their childbearing potential. Fear and grief for the physical and psychological health of their children combined with the social stigma they and their children bear may keep women silent and, therefore, invisible in their struggle.

A global HIV/AIDS research, care and educational agenda must be established which acknowledges women's perspectives, experiences and contexts. Gaps in knowledge regarding women's situations who are living with HIV/AIDS should be made a top priority. The totality of the context within which these women live their daily lives needs to be identified, described, and integrated into an agenda which has three main objectives: (1) to prevent further HIV infection among women; (2) to provide humane care for women already living with HIV/AIDS; and (3) to engage women in national and international efforts to fight HIV/AIDS and its associated stigma.

"WOMEN'S RIGHTS ARE HUMAN RIGHTS"
BEIJING DECLARATION AND
PLATFORM FOR ACTION, 1995

Fifty years after the founding of the United Nations, women from across the world gathered in Beijing, China, in September 1995 to discuss the current status of women and set goals for the future. It was the fourth world conference on the status of women and the largest international gathering of women on record, an ebullient but down-to-business convocation on women's advancement. The "Platform of Action" that came out of the conference did not have he force of law, but it was a powerful tool in setting forth global standards for women's rights across the spectrum of political, economic, educational, health-related, and social issues. Marjorie Margolies-Mezvinsky, former congresswoman from Pennsylvania and deputy chair of the U.S. delegation, compared the platform to the document that came out of the previous UN World Conference on Women in Nairobi, Kenya, in 1985. "People are going to look back and say it all began in Beijing," she commented later. "If Nairobi was a compass, then Beijing is a detailed map."*

The document that came out of Beijing declares that the human rights of women and girls are "an inalienable, integral, and indivisible part of universal rights" and that these rights are in the "interest of all humanity." The document establishes that such sexual abuses as systematic rape, which the Serbians used as an instrument of war against Bosnian women in the ethnic conflict that engulfed the former Yugoslavia in 1993, and forced pregnancy as well as forced sterilization and abortion are "grave violations" of women's human rights. The document is both detailed and wide-ranging in the goals it sets forth to combat female poverty and violence against women, improve women's access to education and health care, promote their participation in the economies and institutions of their respective countries, and promote the welfare of girls. It is an extraordinary road map to women's advancement, which came from an extraordinary global gathering of women.

SOURCE: From United Nations (U.N.) "Beijing Declaration and Platform for Action, 1995," from the fourth United Nations Conference on Women. Reprinted by permission from the United Nations.

---

* Quoted in Kathryn Cullen-Dupont, *The Encyclopedia of Women's History*, rev. ed. (New York: Facts on File, 2000), p. 24.

DECLARATION

1. We, the Governments participating in the Fourth World Conference on Women,

2. Gathered here in Beijing in September 1995, the year of the fiftieth anniversary of the founding of the United Nations,

3. Determined to advance the goals of equality, development and peace for all women everywhere in the interest of all humanity,

4. Acknowledging the voices of all women everywhere and taking note of the diversity of women and their roles and circumstances, honouring the women who paved the way and inspired by the hope present in the world's youth,

5. Recognize that the status of women has advanced in some important respects in the past decade but that progress has been uneven, inequalities between women and men have persisted and major obstacles remain, with serious consequences for the well-being of all people,

6. Also recognize that this situation is exacerbated by the increasing poverty that is affecting the lives of the majority of the world's people, in particular women and children, with origins in both the national and international domains,

7. Dedicate ourselves unreservedly to addressing these constraints and obstacles and thus enhancing further the advancement and empowerment of women all over the world, and agree that this requires urgent action in the spirit of determination, hope, cooperation and solidarity, now and to carry us forward into the next century.

We reaffirm our commitment to:

8. The equal rights and inherent human dignity of women and men. . . .

9. Ensure the full implementation of the human rights of women and of the girl child as an inalienable, integral and indivisible part of all human rights and fundamental freedoms. . . .

11. Achieve the full and effective implementation of the Nairobi Forward-looking Strategies for the Advancement of Women;

12. The empowerment and advancement of women, including the right to freedom of thought, conscience, religion and belief, thus contributing to the moral, ethical, spiritual and intellectual needs of women and men, individually or in community with others and thereby guaranteeing them the possibility of realizing their full potential in society and shaping their lives in accordance with their own aspirations.

WE ARE CONVINCED THAT:

13. Women's empowerment and their full participation on the basis of equality in all spheres of society, including participation in the decision-making process and access to power, are fundamental for the achievement of equality, development and peace;

14. Women's rights are human rights;

15. Equal rights, opportunities and access to resources, equal sharing of responsibilities for the family by men and women, and a harmonious partnership between them are critical to their well-being and that of their families as well as to the consolidation of democracy;

16. Eradication of poverty based on sustained economic growth, social development, environmental protection and social justice requires the involvement of women in economic and social development, equal opportunities and the full and equal participation of women and men as agents and beneficiaries of people-centered sustainable development;

17. The explicit recognition and reaffirmation of the right of all women to control all aspects of their health, in particular their own fertility, is basic to their empowerment;

18. Local, national, regional and global peace is attainable and is inextricably linked with the advancement of women, who are a fundamental force for leadership, conflict resolution and the promotion of lasting peace at all levels;

19. It is essential to design, implement and monitor, with the full participation of women, effective, efficient and mutually reinforcing gender-sensitive policies and programmes, including development policies and programmes, at all levels that will foster the empowerment and advancement of women;

20. The participation and contribution of all actors of civil society, particularly women's groups and networks and other non-governmental organizations and community based organizations, with full respect for their autonomy, in cooperation with Governments, are important to the effective implementation and follow up of the Platform for Action;

21. The implementation of the Platform for Action requires commitment from Governments and the international community. By making national and international commitments for action, including those made at the Conference, Governments and the international community recognize the need to take priority action for the empowerment and advancement of women.

WE ARE DETERMINED TO:

22. Intensify efforts and actions to achieve the goals of the Nairob Forward-looking Strategies for the Advancement of Women by the end of this century;

23. Ensure the full enjoyment by women and the girl child of all human rights and fundamental freedoms and take effective action against violations of these rights and freedoms;

24. Take all necessary measures to eliminate all forms of discrimination against women and the girl child and remove all obstacles to gender equality and the advancement and empowerment of women;

25. Encourage men to participate fully in all actions towards equality;

26. Promote women's economic independence, including employment, and eradicate the persistent and increasing burden of poverty on women by addressing the structural causes of poverty through changes in economic structures, ensuring equal access for all women, including those in rural areas, as vital development agents, to productive resources, opportunities and public services;

27. Promote people-centered sustainable development, including sustained economic growth, through the provision of basic education, life-long education, literacy and training, and primary health care for girls and women;

28. Take positive steps to ensure peace for the advancement of women and, recognizing the leading role that women have played in the peace movement, work actively towards general and complete disarmament under strict and effective international control, and . . . the prevention of the proliferation of nuclear weapons in all its aspects;

29. Prevent and eliminate all forms of violence against women and girls;

30. Ensure equal access to and equal treatment of women and men in education and health care and enhance women's sexual and reproductive health as well as education;

31. Promote and protect all human rights of women and girls;

32. Intensify efforts to ensure equal enjoyment of all human rights and fundamental freedoms for all women and girls who face multiple barriers to their empowerment and advancement because of such factors as their race, age, language, ethnicity, culture, religion, or disability, or because they are indigenous people;

33. Ensure respect for international law, including humanitarian law, in order to protect women and girls in particular;

34. Develop the fullest potential of girls and women of all ages, ensure their

full and equal participation in building a better world for all and enhance their role in the development process. . . .

MISSION STATEMENT

1. The Platform for Action is an agenda for women's empowerment. It aims at accelerating the implementation of the Nairobi Forward-looking Strategies for the Advancement of Women and at removing all the obstacles to women's active participation in all spheres of public and private life through a full and equal share in economic, social, cultural and political decision-making. This means that the principle of shared power and responsibility should be established between women and men at home, in the workplace and in the wider national and international communities. Equality between women and men is a matter of human rights and a condition for social justice and is also a necessary and fundamental prerequisite for equality, development and peace. A transformed partnership based on equality between women and men is a condition for people-centered sustainable development. A sustained and long-term commitment is essential, so that women and men can work together for themselves, for their children and for society to meet the challenges of the twenty-first century.

2. The Platform for Action reaffirms the fundamental principle . . . that the human rights of women and of the girl child are an inalienable, integral and indivisible part of universal human rights. As an agenda for action, the Platform seeks to promote and protect the full enjoyment of all human rights and the fundamental freedoms of all women throughout their life cycle. . . .

44. To this end, Governments, the international community and civil society, including non-governmental organizations and the private sector, are called upon to take strategic action in the following critical areas of concern:

- The persistent and increasing burden of poverty on women
- Inequalities and inadequacies in and unequal access to education and training
- Inequalities and inadequacies in and unequal access to health care and related services
- Violence against women
- The effects of armed or other kinds of conflict on women, including those living under foreign occupation

- Inequality in economic structures and policies, in all forms of productive activities and in access to resources
- Inequality between men and women in the sharing of power and decision-making at all levels
- Insufficient mechanisms at all levels to promote the advancement of women
- Lack of respect for and inadequate promotion and protection of the human rights of women
- Stereotyping of women and inequality in women's access to and participation in all communication systems, especially in the media
- Gender inequalities in the management of natural resources and in the safeguarding of the environment
- Persistent discrimination against and violation of the rights of the girl child.

"YOU GOTTA DO WHAT YOU GOTTA DO"
VIRGINIA SCHEIN, ED.

In 1992, the year that Vice President Dan Quayle gave his famous "Murphy Brown" speech, in which he lambasted Hollywood for portraying single motherhood as just "another lifestyle choice" (see his speech excerpted in chapter 4), the Census Bureau counted 10.1 million single mothers—including only fifteen thousand single mothers who, like the fictional Murphy Brown, were between the ages of thirty-five to forty-four and had family incomes of fifty thousand dollars or more. The year before, a U.S. General Accounting Office Report found that many single mothers remain near or below the poverty level even while holding down full-time jobs, because they lack medical insurance and paid sick leave and must pay high costs for child care.*

With these facts in mind, Virginia E. Schein, an organizational psychologist and professor of management at Gettysburg College in Gettysburg, Pennsylvania, interviewed thirty single mothers from a variety of communities—rural villages, small and medium-sized towns, and large metropolitan areas—who had been on some form of public assistance and also had some work experience. Their average age was 31.6; approximately half of them had one or two children, and the other half had three to five children. Eighteen of the women had been married, and twelve had never married. Some had left abusive, alcoholic, or addicted husbands, while others had been abandoned by their mates. Schein wanted to dispel the myth of the "welfare mother" who allegedly has more children in order to increase her welfare payments and avoid work. More important, she wanted to explore the reasons why most single mothers remain impoverished and what can be done, in her words, "to help poor single mothers move out of poverty and into lives with opportunities for themselves and their children."†

Following are excerpts from her interviews with some of the women about their work and welfare experiences. It is clear that the women certainly do not regard welfare as "just another lifestyle choice"; rather, they see it as a degrading, unsatisfying last resort. Also striking is how rigid and strenuous their paid work is, especially for the near-minimum wages that they earn. As these first-person narratives show, women who have little training or education and are the breadwinners

---

* Cited in Virginia E. Schein, Working from the Margins: Voices of Mothers in Poverty (Ithaca: ILR Press, an imprint of Cornell University Press, 1995), p. 5.
† Ibid., p. 8.

for their families are often caught between a rock and a hard place—between low-paying, dead-end factory work or welfare.

SOURCE: Reprinted from Virginia E. Schein, *Working from the Margins: Voices of Mothers in Poverty* (Ithaca, N.Y.: ILR Press, an Imprint of Cornell University Press, 1995), pp. 70–73, 106–7. Copyright © 1995 by Cornell University. Used by permission of the publisher, Cornell University Press.

TOO MANY RULES

Jean, the mother of five children, completed her GED after leaving her abusive husband and now works in a food-processing plant. "I work in Ruttle Food Company. I tray pack. What you do is trim the meat, the drumsticks or whatever, put them on trays, package them up, and box them. I really don't mind the job. We do different things—anywhere from trimming the meat to packing it up. It is not one dull boring job the whole day long. You are jumping around from one thing to another and it's interesting. The people I work with are great. They are fun to get along with. We carry on. It makes the day go faster. It's like a family.

"I just had a performance evaluation by the lead person and she is pleased with my job performance. I'm going to do something else now, clipping wings. Right now I'm getting $6.05 an hour. I started out at $5.80 an hour. After thirty days you get a quarter raise and after sixty days another quarter raise.

"I don't like my supervisor. He can't look you in the eye and say 'hi' to you. Even if you say hello to him, he won't look you in the eye. The only time he talks to you is if he has a problem with you.

"All the rules really get to me. During the first sixty days, your probationary period, you are not allowed to miss two days. Well, I missed two days. My car broke down. I couldn't find one over the weekend, so I had to take Monday off to get a car. Then I missed another day and left work ten minutes early one day because I was sick. Now they have extended my probationary period. They say if I miss one more day, come in late, or leave early during the next month, you're terminated and they will do it.

"Last Tuesday I made it by a hair. My car was being worked on again and my brother's girlfriend forgot to pick me up. I got there two minutes before seven. A girl who started with me was five minutes late, and she was fired. But if I get a phone call and one of my kids is sick, you better believe I'm out of here. Let them fire me, that's ridiculous. Kids get contagiously sick and you cannot take them to child care."

Marilyn is the mother of two teenagers and a young boy with medical problems. She left school after completing the tenth grade and has worked in a variety of jobs ever since. "I worked for four years in a foundry. They made anything from cast-iron doorstops to manhole covers. It's good money. I made $8.45 an hour and I went from $7.02 to $8.45 in three months. That's good money. Normally I would work from three in the afternoon until midnight. But sometimes you had to work a lot more. It is nonunion so you have to do it. Many times we worked from one in the afternoon until three in the morning. And that was six days a week.

"I worked on the sorting line. You have to break castings off of the molds. Like, if it's a barbell, we made barbells, you pick the weight up, slam it on the side of the line to break the mold casting off. You take an air gun, sort of like a dentist's drill with a sander on it, and sand the barbell down smooth. Then you take it over and slide it down a chute. I would do like three or four of these a minute. The work can be hard, lifting all night. I got tendinitis in both of my arms.

"There are about five people on a sorting line. It's very noisy and very dirty. You have to take a shower before you leave there. It's black sand and oil, pieces of cast-iron metal. You get it in your hair. You are all black. You look like you came out of the coal mine.

"They really don't train you. You just put your ear cuffs on, you wear your safety glasses and steel-tip shoes, and go down the stairs. I had a super boss. His boss would come out and yell at him. Then he would come over and say 'Hey, look, you did this wrong but I am supposed to really yell at you, so bear with me.' Then he would scream at the top of lungs at you, so the big guys would understand that he was yelling at you. Then he would say, 'I'm sorry I had to do that.'

"You get two fifteen-minute breaks and thirty-five minutes for lunch. They shut down two weeks in the summer. Once you've been there a year, you get paid one week, and the other you don't get paid. After five years you get a whole whopping two weeks. That's still during the shutdown weeks.

"I don't know if I could have gone any further. You work there. That's it. That's as far as you go. After five or six months you might get a quarter raise. But I started to get more raises, almost up to $2.80 through my work. I probably would have worked my way up, probably to the weighing scale. They bring the parts over, you weigh them, and that's how they can determine how many parts are in or how many parts are missing."

WORKING ON THE LINE

Renata, the mother of two teenagers, has held a variety of factory jobs. "I worked on the assembly line at the lighting company for six years. We made lightbulbs. These long lights would come down the line. they would be open and we would have to put the ballast in. The ballast is like a big battery. It goes in first and then we would have to wire the batteries to where the lightbulbs would hook in. The lights would go on down the line and somebody would put the cover over the battery and at the end someone would put the glass over it.

"I learned how to do each one of the jobs so if someone didn't come in or there was a new person, I would do the most important job. I was most proud of learning how to ballast because that was the fastest position there. You really didn't have time to think when the lights started coming down the line. I lost a lot of weight. I was mostly twisting all day long. It was great exercise.

"I felt good on that job. I knew what I was doing and I could explain it to someone else. I could show it to someone else. I never had a problem. I made $6.35 an hour. We had good benefits—hospitalization, dental, all of that.

"I made supervisor a couple of times. When the supervisor for our belt didn't come in, I would supervise. I get along very well with people. I liked being the supervisor. If the supervisor didn't come in, I would go to the supervisor over me and tell him that I needed someone to take my spot, while I took the supervisor's spot.

"There wasn't any opportunity for me to be a permanent supervisor. The place was full. If someone didn't come in, then I was on the list to take that position for that day. But to be permanent, someone would have to quit and then I would have to move up a ladder. It would make me one more step closer to being a permanent supervisor, but they always had enough supervisors. Nobody quit. If I had been a supervisor I wouldn't have had to stand on my feet as much. Working on the line, I had to stand on my feet all day, every day, for six years."

LaVerne, never married, a high school graduate and the mother of one child, has worked in restaurants, factories, and construction. "I worked at a dog-bone factory. They would bring in big sheets of rawhide. Then they would rinse them off because they have bleach and stuff on them. Then they would give you some little squares and we had to roll them up and tie knots in them.

"My boss was okay, but I didn't like the girls on the line. It was minimum wage and piece rate. The girls were really nasty. You are standing beside someone and they are bitching because you have a little bit more work than they did. I don't enjoy that. We are all there for the same purpose, to work."

Vicki is divorced and the mother of two children. "The worst job I ever had was in a cookie factory. It was an assembly line. The cookies came down the line and you had to be super fast. These older women had been there for years and they could do it. It was terrible. You just had cookies flying everywhere. I was up to my knees in cookies. It was animal cookies. I won't forget that."

LIFE IN THE SEWING FACTORIES

LaVerne: "I worked at the coat sewing factory for almost two years. Everything had to be perfect, not a stitch could be out of place. The small parts had to be perfect too. I had to outline a small part and it would go on to the next lady. She could tell if you made a stitch out and then they would bring it back. It was really nerve-racking. You weren't allowed to talk to the people who sat beside you. And you were sitting pretty close to them. The ladies would cry if you got more work than they got. Then they would end up arguing. It was crazy.

"It was a forty-hour-a-week job and then I worked half-time on Saturday. It was a good-paying job. I made pretty good money. It started out minimum wage, but it was piece rate. If you sat there all day long, except for your half-hour break, you'd make seven or eight dollars an hour.

"I think most of the same people are still there. I guess it's the money. Constantly they just sit there all day long. They don't even get up and go to the bathroom. They get up and eat their lunch, and that's it. It was mostly women that did the sewing. They had bundle boys that bring you the work."

SURVIVAL, NOT LIVING

None of the women described being on welfare as a satisfactory way to five and raise a family. Indeed, the cash grant, and even the grant and the food stamps, cannot bring a woman and her family up to the poverty level. The cash and food stamp allowances are about 70 percent of the poverty level, providing just bare subsistence for the families.

Renata: "The hardest part about living on welfare and juggling money is paying the bills. They give you enough to survive on but they don't give you enough to live on. There is a difference. They don't think so, but there is."

Susan: "Welfare is designed to keep you where you were ten years earlier."

Marilyn: "My main thing with welfare is, it's not hard to get on it and it's not hard to go off it, but it's hard to get something out of it while you are on it."

Carol: "Between the food stamps and the cash grant, I just about make it. If you make partial payments on your bills, you can manage. Other than that, there is no way it covers other things you need, especially when the kids need clothes for school."

Some, like Arlene and Amelia, see welfare as a dead-end system.

Arlene: "I went into the system and it's like, you can't get ahead. If you earn money, they lower your benefits, and you are just not getting anywhere."

Amelia: "When I was working, at five dollars an hour, they prorated my AFDC checks down to seventy-nine dollars a month. But this is what I don't understand. When they prorate your check down, your food stamps go way up. I don't understand. I can't pay my bills, but my food is there."

But there are no other options for the women.

Connie: "If it hadn't been there, I would have been in a very desperate situation. I don't know what I would have done. You need the assistance."

Anita: "I get a medical card for her and I get food stamps. If it wasn't for them, I wouldn't be able to do it, to tell you the truth."

Vicki: "I had to leave my job because of medical problems. I tried to get on unemployment, but I couldn't. So I've been looking for work. I had no choice but to go on assistance."

FEELINGS OF SHAME AND DEGRADATION

Many of the women talked about how badly they feel about themselves for being on welfare.

Ursula: "I used to feel downcast for being on welfare. It was something I felt low-rated about. It felt degrading. They want to know who is giving you this or who is helping to send your child to school. If I had to stop paying the water bill this month to keep them in school for the next month, I would do that. But that's my business. I don't like them prying into what somebody may give me or who is paying something for me."

Joy: "When you are on public assistance, it's like you're going to pick up someone else's money that you didn't work for. You didn't make it yourself. When I got my first welfare check it felt odd, because I could compare it to receiving my work check. I knew what it was like to have both. I used to hear people say, 'Well, you are taking money from people that work and you are not working.' It felt kind of funny to be a person on the other side this time. This is my first experience with welfare. Nobody in my household had ever been on public assistance but me. My mother worked for the government and so did my grandmother. I was the first person that ever needed welfare.

"I don't like the people who work in the welfare offices. They are nasty to me. They have a bad attitude. They act real snooty and they really don't want to do the work. They act like the money is coming right out of their pockets. I figure, if I go in there with a nice attitude, because I know some people are nasty with them, too, then they will be different. But it doesn't help. They still are nasty."

Susan: "I used to feel like I was just this tall. I just felt like I just was wee little. It was being on welfare plus everything that I've been through. Like the welfare image. If you take food stamps to the store, you get looks like, 'Oh my God.' I'm glad that I'm done with all of that."

Marie: "You get this little card and then you show it and you get your food stamps. It's kind of degrading. When you go into the grocery store you hope nobody from work sees you standing in the line with food stamps. But then, on the other hand, I do work. It's not like I'm sitting at home and taking handouts. I do work. If I didn't work, I would feel like it's a handout. But I do work and I can't make it, so I deserve to have that help. That's the way I feel. And my kids deserve that."

LaVerne: "I really don't care anymore about being on welfare. You gotta do what you gotta do. I have a child to take care of and if I have to do that to take care of her, then I'm going to do it.

"I HAVE LONG OPPOSED GOVERNMENT RECOGNITION OF SAME-GENDER MARRIAGES"
PRESIDENT BILL CLINTON

Despite his support for gay rights and his strong standing among gay and lesbian voters, Bill Clinton signed a bill on September 26, 1996, that barred federal recognition of same-sex marriages. The bill also stipulated that no state was required to recognize the validity of another state's laws allowing same-sex marriages, even though the Constitution allows states to give "full faith and credit" to the laws of other states. More important, the legislation defined legal marriage in the eyes of federal law to be a union between a man and a woman, which would prevent gay or lesbian couples from receiving federal benefits, such as social security, even if their marriages were recognized by individual states.

Conservative lawmakers pushed through the legislation because of a pending court case in Hawaii that could have led to legalizing same-sex marriages, thus forcing other states to honor them. Despite the blow to same-sex marriages dealt by the new law, gay and lesbian Americans have achieved important rights at the state level. In May of that same year, the Supreme Court overturned an amendment to Colorado's Constitution that would have barred any state efforts to protect homosexuals against discrimination, and several states, including New York State, now extend health-care coverage to domestic partners, a designation that legally includes gay and lesbian unions. In addition, major corporations such as IBM, American Express, Eastman Kodak, and Walt Disney also extend employee benefits to the partners of homosexual employees. While the federal government hews to a traditional definition of marriage and family, some states and private corporations are expanding their vision of what constitutes a family.

SOURCE: In the public domain.

THROUGHOUT MY LIFE
I have strenuously opposed discrimination of any kind, including discrimination against gay and lesbian Americans. I am signing into law H.R. 3396, a bill relating to same-gender marriage, but it is important to note what this legislation does and does not do.

I have long opposed governmental recognition of same-gender marriages and this legislation is consistent with that position. The Act confirms the right of each state to determine its own policy with respect to same-gender marriage and clarifies for purposes of federal law the operative meaning of the terms "marriage" and "spouse."

This legislation does not reach beyond those two provisions. It has no effect on any current federal, state or local anti-discrimination law and does not constrain the right of Congress or any state or locality to enact anti-discrimination laws. I therefore would take this opportunity to urge Congress to pass the Employment Non-Discrimination Act, an act which would extend employment discrimination protections to gays and lesbians in the workplace. This year the Senate considered this legislation contemporaneously with the Act I sign today and failed to pass it by a single vote. I hope that in its next Session Congress will pass it expeditiously.

I also want to make clear to all that the enactment of this legislation should not, despite the fierce and at times divisive rhetoric surrounding it, be understood to provide an excuse for discrimination, violence or intimidation against any person on the basis of sexual orientation. Discrimination, violence and intimidation for that reason, as well as others, violate the principle of equal protection under the law and have no place in American society.

On August 22, 1996, President Bill Clinton signed into law legislation that ended the sixty-one-year guarantee of federal welfare aid to all eligible families with dependent children. Like Ronald Reagan before him, Clinton, in his 1992 presidential campaign, made welfare a campaign issue by promising to end the cycle of dependence caused by the "welfare state" and replace the complex and costly system with a more efficient program that puts able-bodied women and men to work. And like the centerpiece of President Reagan's overhaul of welfare, this new legislation shifted the responsibility for dispensing welfare from the federal government to the states by creating block grants for states to use in operating welfare programs as they saw fit.

Although Clinton had campaigned on a promise to "end welfare as we know it," in 1995 he twice vetoed legislation drafted by a Republican majority in Congress to replace the welfare system with federal block grants, calling each measure extreme and harmful to the poor. But by 1996 both he and the Republicans saw political advantages to fashioning a welfare overhaul bill that all parties could agree upon.

Although the final bill, which emerged after months of compromise and concession by both Clinton and the Republican-controlled Congress, was still too extreme for Clinton's moderate preferences, he announced that he would sign the bill; shortly after his announcement both houses of Congress voted for and passed the legislation. Clinton signed the legislation into law on August 22, just three months shy of the presidential election of 1996, in which he won an historic second term.

The law included several controversial and hugely money-saving components. The most controversial was the end of the sixty-one-year-old Aid to Families with Dependent Children, a program of cash grants to low-income mothers and their children; in its place a new system of block grants called Temporary Assistance for Needy Families was instituted. This system of block grants also imposed more stringent guidelines for eligibility, including a requirement that adults who receive welfare benefits begin working within two years, a five-year time limit on supporting each recipient with federal money, and a stricter definition of disability for children eligible under Supplementary Security Income (SSI), a cash program for low-income, blind, aged, and disabled persons. The food stamp program reduced individual allotments and imposed a new work requirement as well. Finally, over Clinton's strongest objections, legal immigrants would be barred from receiving benefits

*under the SSI and food stamp program until they became citizens or had worked
in the United States for at least ten years, and states could also deny them welfare,
Medicaid, and other forms of social services. Clinton promised to work with Congress to reverse some of the food stamp cuts and the prohibition against aid to legal
immigrants. Following are excerpts from a summary of the bill's provisions.*

SOURCE: *1996 Congressional Quarterly Almanac* (Washington, D.C.: Congressional Quarterly, Inc., 1997), pp. 6–13—6–15. Reprinted by permission.

WELFARE

The new law ended the federal guarantee of providing welfare checks to all eligible mothers and children. Instead, states were allowed to create their own
welfare programs within certain federal restrictions, such as new work requirements and time limits on welfare benefits. The bill contained provisions to:

State Plans

Create block grants for temporary assistance for needy families (TANF) to
replace Title IV-A of the Social Security Act, which provided Aid to Families
with Dependent Children (AFDC). Individuals and families were no longer entitled to benefits if they met the existing eligibility requirements.

Each state was required to file a plan with the secretary of Health and Human Services (HHS) every two years that:

- Explained how it would serve all of the state's political subdivisions.
- Explained how it would require and ensure that parents and caretakers who
  received block grant assistance engaged in work activities within two
  months of receiving benefits.
- Established goals to prevent and reduce out-of-wedlock pregnancies.
- Explained whether and how the state intended to treat families moving into
  the state differently from other residents.
- Explained whether it intended to provide aid to non-citizens.
- Established criteria for delivering benefits and determining eligibility, and
  for providing fair and equitable treatment. The plan also had to explain how
  the state would provide an administrative appeals process for recipients.
- Required a parent or caretaker who was not engaged in work or exempt
  from work requirements and who had received assistance for more than two

months to participate in community service. A state could opt out of this requirement if the governor sent a letter to the HHS secretary.

- Provided education and training on statutory rape, and expanded teenage pregnancy prevention programs to include men.

Each state also was required to certify that it would:

- Operate a child support enforcement program.
- Operate a foster care and adoption assistance program and ensure medical assistance for the children involved.
- Specify which state agencies would administer the welfare plan, and provide assurances that local governments and private sector organizations had been consulted on it.
- Provide Indians with equitable access to assistance.
- Establish standards to combat fraud and abuse.
- At state option, establish procedures to identify recipients with a history of domestic violence, and refer them to counseling and supportive services.

Funding

Federal Funds. Authorize $16.4 billion annually from fiscal 1996 through fiscal 2001 for the new block grant to states. States were required to convert to block grants by July 1, 1997, and could choose to do so earlier.

Money was to be distributed to each state based on its federal funding for AFDC benefits and administration, emergency assistance, and the Job Opportunities and Basic Skills (JOBS) program in either fiscal 1995, fiscal 1994 or the average of fiscal 1992–94, whichever was higher.

State spending. Require that to receive their full share of federal welfare funds in fiscal 1997–2001, states spend at least 75 percent of the state funds they spent in fiscal 1994 on AFDC benefits and administration, emergency assistance, JOBS, AFDC-related child care, and at-risk child care. States that did not place the required percentage of welfare recipients into the work force as stipulated by the legislation would be required to spend at least 80 percent of the funds spent in fiscal 1994. States would lose $1 in federal funding for each $1 they fell short of this requirement. . . .

Work Requirements

Adults receiving benefits under the block grant were required to begin working within two years of receiving aid.

States could develop individual responsibility plans that set employment goals, the individual's obligations and the services the state would provide. States could reduce assistance to families that included an individual who did not comply with these plans.

Work participation rates. Require states to have a certain percentage of their welfare caseload participating in work activities, starting at 25 percent in fiscal 1997 and rising to 50 percent in fiscal 2002.

A state's annual participation rate would be set at the average participation rate for each month in the fiscal year. The state's monthly participation rate would be the number of families receiving assistance that included an adult or minor head of household who was working, divided by the number of families receiving assistance (excluding those who had been subject to a recent penalty for refusing to work).

A state's required participation rate for a year would be reduced by the same percentage that it reduced its average monthly welfare caseload below fiscal year 1995 levels. However, those caseload reductions would not be considered if they were required by federal law—such as when recipients exceeded the five-year time limit on benefits—or resulted from changes in state eligibility criteria.

The work participation rates for the entire caseload were:

- Fiscal 1997: 25 percent.
- Fiscal 1998: 30 percent.
- Fiscal 1999: 35 percent.
- Fiscal 2000: 40 percent.
- Fiscal 2001: 45 percent.
- Fiscal 2002 and thereafter: 50 percent.

States also had to meet higher participation rates for two-parent families that received cash assistance, as follows:

- Fiscal 1996: 50 percent.
- Fiscal 1997–1998: 75 percent.
- Fiscal 1999 and thereafter: 90 percent.

State options. Allow states to:

- Count those who received assistance under tribal family assistance in the work participation calculation.
- Count toward meeting the work requirement single parents with a child under age 6, if the parent worked at least 20 hours per week.

- Exempt from the work requirement and the participation rates a parent of a child under age 1. However, a parent could receive this exemption only for a total of 12 months, regardless of whether they were consecutive.

Work activities. Require that individuals engage in one or more of the following activities for a state to count them toward the work participation rate:

- Unsubsidized employment.
- Subsidized private sector employment.
- Subsidized public sector employment.
- Work experience if sufficient private sector employment was unavailable.
- On-the-job training.
- Job search and job readiness assistance for up to six weeks, no more than four weeks of which could be consecutive. Individuals in states with unemployment rates at least 50 percent above the national average could engage in these activities for up to 12 weeks.
- Community service programs.
- Vocational educational training, for up to one year. (No more than 20 percent of all families could count toward the work rate by participating in vocational education.)
- Jobs skills training directly related to employment.
- Education directly related to employment, for a recipient who lacked a high school diploma or equivalency and was under age 20.
- Satisfactory attendance at a secondary school, for a recipient who had not completed high school and was under age 20.
- Providing child care to another welfare recipient who was engaged in community service programs.

No more than 20 percent of all families could count toward the work rate by participating in vocational education, education directly related to employment, or secondary school.

Hours. Require that to count toward the work participation rate, individuals work a minimum number of hours per week, as follows:

- Fiscal 1996–1998: 20 hours.
- Fiscal 1999: 25 hours.
- Fiscal 2000 and thereafter: 30 hours.

The primary wage earner in a two-parent family was required to work at least 35 hours per week to count toward the work participation rate.

Both parents in a two-parent family were required to engage in work activities if they also received federally funded child care. Exceptions would be granted in cases where one parent was disabled or caring for a severely disabled child.

Individual penalties. Require a state to reduce assistance to a family by at least the same pro rata percentage that an adult family member refused to work as required under the welfare block grant. Thus, someone who missed work 20 percent of the time would receive 20 percent less aid. A state could waive the penalty for good cause and other reasons established by that state.

A state also could terminant assistance to adults who refused to work, and end their Medicaid coverage—though Medicaid coverage would continue for their children.

A state could not penalize a single parent caring for a child under age 6 if the parent proved he or she failed to work because child care was unavailable.

State penalties. Reduce a state's block grant by 5 percent if it failed to meet the work requirements. Subsequent failures would result in an additional 2 percent reduction per year, reaching 7 percent the second year and 9 percent the third year, rising to a maximum deduction of 21 percent. However, the HHS secretary could reduce the penalty based on the degree of non-compliance, or if the state had a high unemployment rate or rapidly growing food stamp rolls as defined in criteria for the contingency fund.

Restrictions on Aid

Children. Specify that only families with a minor child (who resided with a custodial parent or other adult relative) or a pregnant woman could receive assistance from the grant.

Time limit. Prohibit the use of block grant funds for adults who had received welfare for more than five years, although those who exceeded the time limit could still qualify for other federal, state and local funds. The time limit applied only to those who were the head of a household or the spouse of a household head. (Children could qualify later for five years of aid as parents, no matter how many years they got as children.)

The time limit also applied only to benefits received after the state accepted its welfare block grant.

States could exempt up to 20 percent of their caseload from the five-year time limit. They also could opt to impose a shorter time limit.

Paternity. Reduce a family's benefits by at least 25 percent if parents did not cooperate in establishing paternity or in assisting a child support enforcement agency. States could choose to eliminate their benefit entirely. States also could exempt parents from these responsibilities for good cause.

Drug abuse. Deny welfare benefits and food stamps to individuals convicted of a felony offense for possessing, using or distributing an illegal drug. Family members or dependents of the individual would still be eligible for aid. Those penalized for drug abuse would still be eligible for emergency benefits, including emergency medical services. States could opt out of this prohibition if they passed legislation to do so.

Fraud. Deny aid from the family assistance grant for 10 years to any person convicted of fraudulently misrepresenting his or her residence to obtain benefits in two or more states from the welfare grant, Medicaid, food stamps, or Supplemental Security Income.

Unwed teenagers. Allow unmarried parents under age 18 to qualify for block grant funds only if they attended high school or an alternative educational or training program and if they lived with a parent or in an adult-supervised setting.

State options. Give states the option of choosing to:

Deny welfare assistance to children born to welfare recipients.

Deny welfare to all unwed parents under age 18.

Provide newcomers from another state the same benefits the families would have received from their former state for up to 12 months.

State Penalties

If a state's welfare block grant was reduced because of one of the following penalties, it would have to replace the penalized federal funds during the next fiscal year with state funds. The penalties were:

- Unauthorized use of block grant funds: repay amount used and, if the violation was intentional, repay an additional 5 percent of the state's quarterly block grant payments.
- Failure to submit a required report within one month of the end of each fiscal quarter: 4 percent of the annual block grant, to be rescinded if the state submitted the report before the end of the next fiscal quarter.
- Failure to satisfy minimum work participation rates: 5 percent of the block grant, plus an additional 2 percent each year for consecutive failures, up to a maximum of 21 percent.

- Failure to use an income and eligibility verification system: up to 2 percent of the annual block grant.
- Failure to enforce penalties sought by a child support agency: up to 5 percent of the block grant.
- Failure to repay a federal loan in a timely fashion: a reduction of the block grant by the amount of the outstanding loan, plus interest.
- Failure to maintain the proper percentage of state spending as required by the legislation: $1 reduction in the block grant for each $1 the state fell below the requirement for state spending.
- Failure of a state child support enforcement program to comply with federal law: for the first finding of noncompliance, a reduction of between 1 and 2 percent of a quarterly block grant payment; for the second consecutive finding of noncompliance, between 2 and 3 percent of the next quarterly payment; for the third or subsequent findings, between 3 and 5 percent.
- Failure to maintain 100 percent of state fiscal 1994 welfare expenditures when receiving money from the contingency fund: repay money received.
- Failure to provide benefits to single adult parents who had custody over their children but could not obtain child care for them, up to age & up to 5 percent of the block grant.
- Failure to comply with the five-year time limit on benefits: 5 percent of the annual block grant.

Related Provisions

States also had to continue to provide Medicaid to those who would have been eligible for AFDC if that program were still in effect.

Federal waivers. Allow states that previously received waivers of federal laws and regulations to conduct experimental welfare programs to continue those programs until the waivers expired.

Work force reduction. Require HHS to reduce the number of positions within the department by 245 full-time equivalent positions—including 60 managerial positions—related to the conversion of several federal programs into the block grant.

Charitable and religious organizations. Allow states to provide family assistance services (as well as services under SSI, foster care, adoption assistance and independent living programs) by contracting with charitable, religious, or private organizations.

SUPPLEMENTAL SECURITY INCOME

The bill made it more difficult for disabled children to qualify for Supplemental Security Income (SSI), which provided cash assistance to the low-income aged, blind and disabled. The Congressional Budget Office estimated that about 315,000 children, or 22 percent, who would otherwise be receiving SSI in 2002 would lose their eligibility as a result of the legislation.

The SSI section of the bill contained provisions to:

Disabled Children

Definition. Deny SSI eligibility to a child under age 18 with an impairment of "comparable severity" to what would be considered a work disability in an adult.

The bill redefined a childhood disability to require that the child have a "medically determinable physical or mental impairment, which results in marked and severe functional limitations." As in prior law, this disability had to be expected to result in death or to last more than 12 months.

Assessments. Eliminate an Individualized Functional Assessment (IFA) as a standard by which children could qualify for SSI.

Under prior law, the Social Security Administration first determined whether a child was eligible for SSI by deciding whether he or she met or exceeded a "Listing of Impairments." A child who did not meet that test could still qualify for SSI through an easier-to-reach determination, known as an IFA, that analyzed whether a child's mental, physical and social functioning was substantially lower than children of the same age.

With elimination of the IFA as a standard, children could qualify for SSI only through the more stringent "Listing of Impairments." The legislation also eliminated references to "maladaptive behavior" when determining a child's personal and behavioral functioning. . . .

"OUR SOCIETY'S UGLY SECRET"
VIRGINIA MACKEN FITZSIMMONS

By the mid-1990s a new term of reference came into the social lexicon: the in-between generation—the generation of people, including but not restricted to baby boomers, who are responsible not only for their children but also for elderly parents. And the responsibility to care for elderly parents, as the following article makes clear, often falls on women who are already struggling to balance paid work outside of the home with domestic responsibilities. Virginia Macken Fitzsimmons, a nurse and nursing educator, discusses the unique stresses that female caregivers experience and the signs of elder abuse, which can result from the frustrations and problems of caring for an elderly parent. Elderly women who outlive spouses are often the victims of abuse. The statistics that Fitzsimmons cites—as of 1995, up to one million women a year were the victims of abuse and mistreatment—are shocking and cry out for policies and legislation to redress this deplorable situation.

SOURCE: Virginia Macken Fitzsimmons, "Pain in the Golden Years," in *The Emergence of Women into the 21st Century*, edited by Patricia L. Munhall and Virginia Macken Fitzsimmons (New York: NLN Press, 1995), pp. 290–96. Adapted from a paper presented at the United Nations, april 1995. Reprinted by permission of Jones and Bartlett Publishing, Southbury, MA. www.jbpub.com.

"YOU CRAZY OLD BATTLEAX," Louise screamed at her mother Martha, "How many times have I told you that I don't care what you think. Now shut up and don't bother me." Martha, 82 years old, cried as she walked slowly up the stairs to her hot attic bedroom. The pain of her arthritis and osteoporosis was awful and she really did need a ride to her doctor, but Louise her 58-year-old daughter had no patience for her suffering. Louise had troubles of her own. In another era, it would have been Louise who was considered to be old. But in these times, Louise is still young. We have a myth of the "golden years" of untroubled retirement and relaxation. A troubled family moves the bad feelings to all of its members, including the old. Because this family is struggling with difficulties, its members feel considerable pain. Martha was filled with physical and psychological pain. Instead of a life in the sheltering, loving arms of a caring family, she found herself in the middle of a conflicted, troubled family. She felt abandoned and abused. If only her two other children didn't live so far away, she could ask them for help, she thought.

Martha has been widowed for seven years now and living with Louise and her family far from the town where she had raised her own family. Louise had no patience for her. Louise had enough problems managing to cope with her own husband and three grown children. And Martha's story is far from unique.

SOCIETY'S UGLY SECRET

Behind apparently lovely closed doors is housed our society's ugly secret: violence against the elderly.

Abuse and mistreatment is something that affects up to one million elder women a year. Detection is difficult because the woman is isolated in her home. Case finding, reporting, and intervention are needed and the general members of a community, as well as its public and health-related officials are all in a position to help. Data clearly show that persons from all races, ethnic, and socioeconomic groups are included as both the abusers and the abused.

Elder abuse is the least known form of domestic violence. The entire topic is hindered by disbelief. "This can't be?" a neighbor or fellow church member thinks when confronted by a bruised or withdrawn aging person.

Misinformation prevails and underdetection is a major issue in the problem. In sharp contrast to child abuse awareness, elder mistreatment is seen in up to 4% (1 in 25) of the older female population. The overall prevalence rate of abuse in the presence of Alzheimer's Disease is a dramatic and shocking 18% (4 in 25).

Caroline sits gazing out of her 11th floor window. She remembers the days when she was an active community member, participating in her church and sending her children off to school. For all of her 70 years she cared for her house, spoke with her neighbors, and tended to her garden. Now she can hardly see the street. Few visitors come to see her in this high-rise senior citizen housing unit. Her family had convinced her to sell her home and to move here. It seemed like a good idea initially. At first it seemed to be a pleasant and safe place to live. Recently, however, the rules at this senior housing project had changed. Now in addition to seniors, "displaced" people were allowed to move in. Caroline sees men who hang around drinking and she suspects of taking drugs. There is a clear smell of urine in the room with the incinerator. Lightbulbs are broken and not replaced. Caroline feels abandoned and alone. She is right. Her family and friends have either moved away or are dead now. Like Martha, Caroline is one of the many millions of older women who are invisible in our society and who are suffering. Only 5% of all older people are in nursing homes. Many millions of seniors are safe and live independent and comfortable lives. These seniors we see in active roles, enjoying themselves, and having vacations. But, that is the visible part of our picture.

RAISING OUR CONSCIOUSNESS

Neglect and verbal mistreatment are far more common manifestations of elder abuse than are actual physical beatings. The senior women in these situations, however, feel terrified and in despair.

Psychological abuse in the form of verbal aggression, denigration, harassment, intimidation, and threats of punishment or deprivation are all abuse on a psychological level. The most common form of abuse, however, and the most open to community recognition and resolution is psychological neglect. It is a failure to provide social stimulation; it is social isolation. The family is at work and school all day and the elder person is unattended for long periods of time. In periods of family stress, verbal threatening to abandon the elderly or threats to place them in nursing homes constitute clear abuse. . . .

IDENTIFYING PHYSICAL ABUSE

Physical abuse can be severe. Out of 1000 older women, 32 are beaten physically and hospitalized each year. Abuse ranges from subtle and insidious to blatant. There is a lack of clear and consistent definitions. Nevertheless, we should be concerned for the safety and well-being of older women. All women will be a part of that population someday. And while there are ethnic variations of behaviors, respect for women of all ages will assist a society to value and respect its older women. As an entire nation, we must come to a place of common understanding of what is acceptable behavior toward women. . . .

It is estimated that 13 cases of abuse go unreported for each case that comes to light. By law, health professionals are required to report cases. Family, friends, and community persons are morally obliged to report suspected or witnessed abuse or mistreatment.

Why the under reporting? There is a lack of recognition of cases. There is a lack of awareness of laws on reporting. There are poor expectations as to outcome. Neighbors and friends ask, "What good will it do?" There is a belief that reporting may actually harm the person. "They'll be mad," the neighbor will say, and the mistreatment and suffering continues. There is a reluctance to report abuse because of the fear of liability despite immunity provisions of the law. Always there is a fear of damage to relationships within the family.

WOMEN ABUSE OLDER WOMEN

It is women who abuse older women. The abuser is often heavily dependent on the woman being abused either financially or has housing or child-care needs from the woman. Frustration increases the anger level. The abuser often has an addiction, and lives with the woman herself. The abuser often controls access to family and friends and imposes a social isolation on the older woman. It is always an issue of control. Often, there is a history of intrafamilial violence and feelings of powerlessness.

The abuser seeks to counterbalance the situation and so strikes out with harmful acts toward the woman. Caregiver depression is often a variable. Low self-esteem is always correlated with violent feelings. A shared living situation increases tension and fatigue and can be a precipitating factor in abuse.

Mistreatment is categorized as physical violence, chronic verbal aggression, physical neglect, financial exploitation, and/or acts of omissions.

WHAT TO DO

Women are usually cast in the role of caregiver to family members. How can we protect both the caregivers and the cared for woman? What can we do?

I teach my groups these things: We can avert potentially risky situations. Plan with families of patients with dementia and Alzheimer's disease. Reduce stressors. Plan for caregiver relief. Time can be given—called respite care—when the caregiver is herself given time off.

In case finding, speak with the elder woman and caregiver separately. Be sympathetic to each. Ask the older woman: Has anyone at home ever hurt you? Has anyone ever scolded or threatened you? Have you ever signed a document you didn't understand? Are you afraid of anyone at home? Ask the caregiver: What would you like me to know about (state the woman's name)? Have you ever felt frustrated with her? How do you suppose she got the bruise on her arm? Look for unexplained delay in seeking health treatment, injuries inconsistent with medical findings, poor personal hygiene, dehydration and malnutrition. Look for fractures, falls, dislocations, or evidence of physical restraints. Be suspicious.

What skin signs will you see? There might be bruises, hematomas, welts, lacerations, and/or abrasions. Medication related signs include symptoms of over or under medication, loss of memory, dizziness, excessive sleeping, or changes in personality. Neglect is seen as decubitus ulcers, absence of needed eyeglasses, dentures, and prostheses. Is there evidence of poor hygiene? Look for signs of withdrawal, depression, agitation, low self-esteem, infantile behavior, mental status changes, and sleep disorders.

Does the caregiver refuse to let the woman see you alone? Are there unusual behavior patterns between the older woman and her caregiver. Is there a history of spousal abuse?

WHAT CAN BE DONE?

Communities and professionals from a wide range of fields can be a part of the solution. Reliable studies are needed to fully understand the problems. Anticipatory guidance for caregiver/family starts in the community. Identify caregiver depression. Encourage support groups for family members. Day care for the elder woman has great advantages. Plan for interventions to address ambivalence on the part of client and family members, refusal of services, denial, caregiver stress, and feelings of being overwhelmed.

Reduce psychological abuse. Caregiver burden is a major contributory factor. Stress and conflict may be most likely to emerge when a single relative has been designated as the primary caregiver, when there is little support from the rest of the family, when the caregiver and elder woman have had a strained relationship in the first place and when caregiving needs are great.

The stressed caregiver may have financial or other needs that keep him/her from exploring alternatives. Or the caregiver is living up to a promise never to let the elder woman go to a nursing home.

Caregivers of the chronically ill older woman have high rates of depression and low self-esteem. It is a difficult job with little recognition or appreciation. Stress increases and should not be overlooked because it is this which leads to inadequate care and then outright neglect.

Evaluate the caregiver. Ask, How many hours a day do you spend caring for her? Do you get enough sleep at night? (It is not uncommon to be disturbed 2 or 3 times a night and have sleep deprivation and the changes that go with it.) Ask, How do you feel about your caregiving responsibilities? Are there times when you feel you cannot meet her needs? Do you feel angry or frustrated? How do you deal with these feelings? Ask about the caregiver's financial status, health status, and ask are there family support systems for the caregiver? Plan for the caregiver.

Plan interventions to decompress caregiver stress, treat depression, and care for the caregiver. Acknowledge the difficulties of the overburdened caregiver. Interview therapeutically. Use community groups and resources. Use spiritual resources. Use periodic relief opportunities. Care about the caregiver. Women are usually the caregivers.

"ALL MOMMIES ARE MONSTERS"
ERICA JONG

In 1997 Louise Woodward, a nineteen-year-old nanny from England, was convicted of murder for shaking her eight-month-old charge, Matthew Eappen, to death. Her trial created such an international sensation that the judge overturned the jury's verdict of guilt. Woodward returned to England, but the debate over her guilt and the larger issue of hiring young, inexperienced women for such demanding work continued on talk shows and in the media.

Poet and novelist Erica Jong, who first gained notoriety when she wrote Fear of Flying *(1973), a raucous novel about a woman's sexual liberation, explores who the real villain is in the public's eye—Deborah Eappen, the baby's mother, who chose to continue working part-time after her son was born. In pungent, provocative prose, Jong raises compelling questions: why do women, and not men, bear all the responsibility for their children's welfare and the blame when a child is injured or killed? And what impact will the public tarring of Deborah Eappen have on the next generation of women, who may be reluctant to pursue careers along with motherhood?*

SOURCE: "Monster Mommies," in Erica Mann Jong, *What Do Women Want?* (New York: HarperCollins, 1998), pp. 29–32. Copyright © 1998 by Erica Mann Jong. Reprinted by permission of HarperCollins Publishers Inc.

MOMMY GUILTIEST? So reads the headline in the *New York Daily News's* rehash of the "Nanny Case," which has riveted the media's public since everybody overdosed on treacly elegies to Diana, Princess of Wales. The *Daily News* has proved once again the old saying "*Vox populi* is, in the main, a grunt." The *News* is supposed to cater to the downmarket crowd that doesn't read the *New York Times* or the *Wall Street Journal*, but in truth most people in the word biz read *all three*, as well as the *New York Post* and the *New York Observer*. But without the *News*, you can't possibly know all that's *not* fit to print. And, of course, that's what tells you about the vacillations of the zeitgeist. And the zeitgeist is currently into blaming mommies for the deaths of their kids.

For *this* is the lesson of the nanny trial: Louise Woodward may have been nineteen, inexperienced, drowsy in the mornings and moonfaced at night, but Dr. Deborah Eappen was *really the one at fault*, because she worked three days a week as an ophthalmologist rather than staying at home full-time with her baby. Never mind that she came home at lunch to breast-feed on the days she worked. Never mind that she pumped out breast milk on the *other* days. Never mind that she was an M.D. working a drastically reduced schedule—a schedule no intern or resident would be *permitted* to work. *She* is the one to blame for the heinous crime of baby murder.

In an age when most mothers work because they *have* to, it is nothing short of astounding that this case resulted in raving callers to talk shows who scream that Dr. Deborah Eappen *deserved* to have her baby die because she left him with a nineteen-year-old nanny.

So much for twenty-five years of feminism. So much for smug commentators who say we live in a "post-feminist age." The primitive cry is still "Kill the mommy!" She deserves to be stoned to death for hiring a nanny.

Of course, we Americans already knew that *welfare* mothers were monsters. Dear Bill Clinton, champion of women and children, signed the most disgusting welfare bill in American history—a bill more appropriate to Dickensian England, a bill basically reinstating the workhouse in millennial America. But, of course, we *know* the American poor deserve nothing. Poverty is, after all, un-American. America has abolished any definition of the worthy poor (children, mothers, the blind, the lame) and decided that *they* alone shall pay for the budget deficit run up by male politicians. After all, children have no votes—unlike savings and loan officers. Besides, the latter have lobbyists, and poor children naturally can't afford them. So we have no worthy poor in the country I so lavishly fund with my taxes, but neither have we any child care initiatives—let alone child care.

Even some *reactionary* countries—*La Belle France*, for example—have mother care, crèches, kindergartens, but in America we rely on nature red in tooth and claw, so crèches are seen as "creeping socialism," and nobody's allowed to have creeping socialism except the army and the non-tax-paying superrich.

Okay—welfare mommies are monsters, but what about *entrepreneurial M.D.* mommies? What about women who *delayed* childbearing to finish school, had babies in their thirties and forties, and work part time? Well, now we learn that they, also, are monsters. Why? Because they don't *stay home* full time. Apparently *all* mommies are monsters—the indigent *and* the highly educated both deserve to watch their babies die.

Wait a minute. What happened here? Is this 1898 or 1998? It doesn't seem to matter. Where motherhood is concerned we might as well be in Dickens's England or Ibsen's Norway or Hammurabi's Persia. Mothers are, by definition, monsters. They're either monsters because they're poor or monsters because they're rich. Where mothers are concerned, *everything* is a no-win situation.

Poor Louise was nice but somewhat incompetent. Maybe she *did* shake poor little Matty—the medical evidence is inconclusive. After all, she was a Brit, and Brits *love* caning kids; shaking is *nothing* to them. But Deborah was even *worse* than Louise. She was a doctor's wife (and a doctor, but who cares?) who chose to work.

Both women have been thoroughly trashed. Nobody inveighs against the *other* Dr. Eappen—the one with a penis—and nobody screams that *his* baby deserves to die. Nobody talks about Matty either. He's just a dead baby. Dead babies have no votes and no lobbyists. No—what everyone carries on about is which *woman* is at fault.

The mommy or the nanny? The lady or the tiger? Women, by definition, are *always* guilty. Either they're guilty of neglect or they're guilty of abuse. Nobody asks about the father's role or the grandparents' role. If it takes a village to raise a child, as Hillary Clinton's bestseller alleges, then that village consists of only *two* people: monster mother and monster *au pair*. Everyone else is off the hook. (Including a government that penalizes working moms in its tax policies, its immigration policies, and its lack of day care.)

How must Dr. Deborah Eappen feel, first losing her son and then facing this chorus of harpies (for the women-haters are often women)? Imagine the trauma of losing your baby, the trauma of reliving the pain at the trial, only to face the further trauma of trial by tabloid. Dr. Deborah *chose* her job because it allowed flexible hours. So did her husband, Dr. Sunil Eappen. But nobody's blaming *him*. If we have come so far toward the ideal egalitarian marriage, then why does nobody discuss the *couple*? Only the women are implicated. Both nanny and mommy face death by tabloid firing squad.

If the nanny trial is used as a litmus test for social change, then we must conclude that very little change has occurred. No wonder generation Y is full of young women who want to stay home with their babies! They saw what happened to their weary boomer mothers, and they don't *like* what they saw. If all feminist progress is dependent on the mother-daughter dialectic (as I believe it is), then we are in for a new generation of stay-at-home moms, whose problems will be closer to our grandmothers' than our own. Betty Friedan's *Feminine Mystique* will be as relevant in 2013 as it was in 1963—and our granddaughters will have to regroup and start feminist reforms all over again.

No wonder feminism has been ebbing and flowing since Mary Wollstonecraft's day. We *have never* solved the basic problem that afflicts us all—who will help to raise the children?

"A WIFE IS TO SUBMIT HERSELF TO HER HUSBAND"
BAPTIST FAITH AND MESSAGE

*At its annual meeting in June 1998, the Southern Baptist Convention, which represents the largest Protestant denomination in the United States, issued a statement on the family calling for a wife to "submit herself graciously to the servant leadership of her husband." The statement, which made front-page coverage in newspapers across the country for its starkly traditional view of gender roles, became part of the "Baptist Faith and Message," a body of basic beliefs to be observed by the sixteen million members of the church. The statement is an outgrowth of conservative Baptists' opposition to abortion, divorce, and homosexuality and also to their growing power within the denomination. At the 1997 annual convention, delegates requested a statement on the role of the family, and a panel of seven church leaders, including two women, drafted the statement for adoption at the next convention. When asked about the statement, President Bill Clinton, a practicing Baptist, threw up his hands and said, "What can I do?," but other moderate Southern Baptist members were more vocal and disavowed the statement as a misrepresentation of the Bible and as socially regressive. At the convention a handful of delegates tried to modify the statement. One delegate tried to soften the language by suggesting the passage read that the husband and wife "are to submit graciously to each other," and another delegate tried to expand the definition of a family to include single adults, childless couples, and widows and widowers. But delegates overwhelmingly rejected both proposals and adopted the family statement by acclamation. Church leaders were undaunted by the controversy surrounding the statement and vigorously defended it. Declared Richard Land, president of the Southern Baptist Ethics and Religious Liberty Commission: "Some things are always wrong and some things are always right. That automatically puts us in direct confrontation with this culture. We're not trying to be politically correct, but biblically correct."**

How does the role of women articulated in this statement compare to Pope John Paul's view of women in his apostolic letter included in chapter 4?

SOURCE: "The Family," from the Baptist Faith and Message. Copyright © 2000 Southern Baptist Convention. Used by permission.

GOD HAS ORDAINED the family as the foundational institution of human society. It is composed of persons related to one another by marriage, blood, or adoption.

---

* Quoted in *Historic Documents of 1998*, Congressional Quarterly, Inc., copyright © 1999 by Congressional Quarterly, Inc., p. 335.

Marriage is the uniting of one man and one woman in covenant commitment for a lifetime. It is God's unique gift to reveal the union between Christ and His church, and to provide for the man and the woman in marriage the framework for intimate companionship, the channel of sexual expression according to biblical standards, and the means for procreation of the human race.

The husband and wife are of equal worth before God, since both are created in God's image. The marriage relationship models the way God relates to His people. A husband is to love his wife as Christ loved the church. He has the God-given responsibility to provide for, to protect, and to lead his family. A wife is to submit herself graciously to the servant leadership of her husband even as the church willingly submits to the headship of Christ. She, being in the image of God as is her husband and thus equal to him, has the God-given responsibility to respect her husband and to serve as his helper in managing the household and nurturing the next generation.

Children, from the moment of conception, are a blessing and heritage from the Lord. Parents are to demonstrate to their children God's pattern for marriage. Parents are to teach their children spiritual and moral values and to lead them, through consistent lifestyle example and loving discipline, to make choices based on biblical truth. Children are to honor and obey their parents.

Gen. 1:26–28; 2:15–25; 3:1–20; Ex. 20:12; Deut. 6:4–9; Josh. 24:15; 1 Sam. 1:26–28; Ps. 78:1–8; 127; 128; 139: 13–16; Prov. 1:8; 5:15–20; 6:20–22; 12:4; 13:24; 14:1; 17:6; 18:22; 22:6, 15; 23:13–14; 24:3; 29:15, 17; 31:10–31; Eccl. 4:9–12; 9:9; Mal. 2:14–16; Matt. 5:31–32; 18:2–5; 19:3–9; Mark 10:6–12; Rom. 1:18–32; 1 Cor. 7:1–16; Eph. 5:21–33; 6:1–4; Col. 3:18–21; 1 Tim. 5:8, 14; 2 Tim 1:3–5; Titus 2:3–5; Heb. 13:4; 1 Pet. 3:1–7.

In 1903 Mary Harris "Mother" Jones, a dressmaker and labor reformer, led a contingent of child mill workers on a weeklong march from the textile mills of Kensington, Pennsylvania, to President Theodore Roosevelt's summer home in Oyster Bay, New York, to protest their exploitive working conditions and rally support for child labor legislation. Almost a hundred years later, on February 29, 2000, ninety-year-old Doris "Granny D" Haddock completed a fourteen-month walk from Los Angeles to the steps of the Capitol in Washington, D.C., to promote the need for national campaign finance reform. A social activist and former shoe-factory worker from New Hampshire, she walked through 105-degree deserts, skied cross-country through heavy winter snowstorms, and stopped all along the way during her thirty-two-hundred-mile trek to address Americans in outdoor gatherings and town hall meetings.

As Granny D describes it, the inspiration for her walk originally came from her Tuesday Morning Academy, a study group made up of women who undertook a petition campaign to lobby for campaign finance reform. When they received form letters from their senators in response to their petitions, Granny D decided to undertake the cross-country walk to dramatize their cause. In the post–Civil War period, American women formed study clubs across the country for self-education and self-improvement; many of these clubs transformed themselves into social welfare and reform groups that achieved remarkable results for their communities and for the nation, from better libraries and municipal sanitation facilities to consumer-protection and labor legislation. Thus, at the end of the twentieth century, Granny D carries on a long-standing tradition of social protest and political reform born out of women's grassroots organizing.

SOURCE: Doris Haddock and Dennis Burke, *Granny D: Walking Across America in My Ninetieth Year* (New York: Villard, 2001), pp. 6–11, 13. Copyright © 2001 by Doris Haddock and Dennis Burke. Used by permission of Villard Books, a division of Random House, Inc.

"MOTHER, what are you thinking about?" my son, Jim, said as we were driving toward Florida a year earlier. It was February 1998. I was looking in the side mirror at an old man beside the road—we had just sped past him. My son was headed for a three-week camping trip in the Everglades and had agreed to drop me off at my sister Vivian's house in Pompano Beach. I had just returned from my best friend Elizabeth's funeral.

The old man on the road, wearing a black watch cap and a full-length mackintosh, learned against his cane and blew his nose with his bare fingers. He was miles and miles from any town or house, carrying only a paper bag. "What's with the old man, do you suppose—way out here?" I said.

"Looks like he's on the road again, Mother," Jim replied.

We talked for a few miles about Jack Kerouac's life and sang a few bars of Willie Nelson's song. That sounds cheery, but I was quite melancholy.

This old man mesmerized me. His image resonated with something very deep. Now that Elizabeth and my husband no longer needed me, I had been worrying about how I might use what remained of my own time. As we drove further, there seemed to be some connection with this man on the road and that slow-boiling question.

I had been on the road with my husband nearly forty years earlier when we worked to stop the Alaska bombs. This old man was perhaps some ghost of those days, still out there like a part of me. He was calling, as might my Jim be calling. That is rather what it felt like.

Something else had also been eating at me: In the 1960s during the Alaska project, we were able to appeal to the sense of fair play of U.S. senators and representatives. They listened to our appeal and made a decision they thought best. They did not have to consult with their campaign contributors, nor did they care that we had not given money to them. I felt a real sense of belonging as an American back then, in the early sixties. There was a sense that we were adults who respected each other and listened to each other. I don't mean to overidealize it, for politics is often a dirty business underneath. But the backroom scandals we heard about back then, where cash was traded for votes, are now the front room norm. There is no room for regular citizens in that front room, and there is no shame.

I had been watching the change. During my husband's final years, in the early nineties, I had worked hard and successfully to bring some modest respite services to the families in our area who were caring for Alzheimer's patients. The logic of these programs was obvious, yet our only way of getting funding was to raise money privately, which we did. From what I was hearing in the community, and from my own experience fighting the interstate highway system, which had threatened to destroy our little town of Dublin, New Hampshire, congressmen were no longer interested in what some person or village might need if they were not major campaign donors. For the first time in my life I felt politically powerless—something no American should ever feel. It was like living in some other country.

My women friends in our Tuesday Morning Academy, which is a little study group in New Hampshire, had looked at the campaign finance situation in detail over the previous few years. We had become quite knowledgeable about it, just as we had studied many other issues.

Our group had its origin in 1984, when the Extension Service canceled an adult study class for lack of students. Nineteen of us—mostly retired—were nevertheless set on the idea of learning something new, so we accepted the leadership of Bonnie Riley, a retired teacher whose passions are poetry, drama, and history. . . .

At her invitation, we began meeting at her house in Francestown. We continue there today after fifteen years—occasionally picking up a new student and burying an old. Bonnie decides what we will study next, as she has a good radar for issues and knows well our interests and gaps. A new subject always begins with a provocative book on a good topic. We studied China in great detail for a full year and then the Middle East. We never stop with just the book: We find related books and articles and we each make reports. Our Tuesday meetings begin around 8:30 A.M. with some ballet exercises to get the blood moving and our brains in gear. We hold our class in her living room until noon.

We are good followers because Bonnie is a good leader—we trust her because her commitment to us is unselfish, skillful, and generous. It is easy to be a good follower when you have unselfish and competent leaders.

When Bonnie's husband leaves town from time to time for a conference, we ladies have a night out. During one of these evenings—on the same day when the newspaper reported the Senate's failure to pass Senators John McCain and Russ Feingold's campaign finance reform bill—I said, "I am terribly distressed about what is happening to our government. It seems to me that the rich are taking over and that you can't get elected unless you have a million dollars!"

Bonnie, the wonderful leader, said, "Well, Doris, what are you going to do about it?"

"Me? For heaven's sake, what can I do?"

"Well, what *can* you do?"

So I thought it over and remembered what Jim and I did during the Alaska campaign in the sixties. At the next meeting of the Tuesday Academy, I had a plan ready.

"We can make up a petition and send it out to all our relatives and friends throughout the whole fifty states. When we get them back, we will send them to our senators and ask for a meeting to discuss what should be done. What do you think, girls?"

I was still naive enough to think that today's senators and congressmen care what people think and would even look at our petition. Times had changed more than I realiz?d, and politics had become far more "hardball." But we hadn't fully learned that lesson yet, so the ladies agreed to my plan. It took us two years, but we organized tens of thousands of petitions demanding campaign finance reform. We each sent them to our two senators and waited for replies.

What I got back from one of my senators was a form letter quite like the letters senators in other states were sending to others of us, saying that spending money was a form of political speech protected by the Constitution. My other senator didn't respond at all, and when I contacted him he said he never received the petitions. I sent him fresh copies of all of them. Again no response.

I had spent many rainy afternoons standing in parking lots around New Hampshire to talk about campaign reform and get those signatures. The form letter response and total refusal to look seriously at reform sickened me and embarrassed me in front of my friends. I was an old Yankee accustomed to calling up her congressman and getting things moving. To not have proper representation! It was deeply disturbing. That wonderful feeling of belonging, of being a valued participant, was jerked away. I fully understood: I was no longer a village elder at the council fire. Those places were reserved for wealthy campaign contributors. I was a woman scorned.

This was part of the despair I was suffering as I traveled with my son down to Florida. I was in quite a deep pit of it.

A few minutes after I saw the old man on the road, it occurred to me that I should go on the road for my reform issue. A silly idea, but how else might I better spend my remaining days? Think of the adventure it would be! How my late husband, that dear old reformer, would surely cheer me from the other side! It would be a memorial walk dedicated to my love for him and for Elizabeth.

I looked at my son as he drove us along—tough in his Greek fisherman's hat and his scruffy brown and gray beard. I knew I was about to change our lives when I spoke.

"I would like to walk all the way across the United States for campaign finance reform," I said to him. I explained that I would talk to people along the way about how our democracy is being bought out from under us. I would round up some votes for reform in Congress. Perhaps I could help create a modest groundswell to demand action.

Poor Jim. Here is a sixty-four-year-old man driving with his wheezing, eighty-eight-year-old, arthritic mother, and she says something like that. If you would like to know what a remarkable man Jim is, listen to his response.

First of all, of course, he said, "Oh, boy." That was a natural reaction, along with the quick, severe stare through his eyebrows. But he didn't dismiss me. He thought about it for a few miles. He knows who I am, what I have done in life. . . . So he silently drove and thought. . . .

Back home in Dublin, New Hampshire, which snuggles next to Peterborough, west of Manchester, I began walking my ten miles with a heavy backpack. I am already a little stooped over, which the pack didn't help, but it was manageable. There are lovely roads and hills in my town, and I became something of a constant fixture upon them. Through all of 1998 I walked and walked, probably about eight hundred miles in all, wearing out one good pair of hiking shoes.

I practiced sleeping on the ground, especially in the spring weather. I mapped out my cross-country trek with the help of the auto club. A geology professor revised it for me, routing me away from cold country and steep climbs. In July, I mailed a thousand letters of introduction to police chiefs and churches along my route, plus newspaper offices and radio and television stations.

In the autumn of 1998, after all my hard tramping around my town, and even once walking and hitchhiking sixty miles to hear presidential candidate Bill Bradley speak (it was a good speech, but perhaps only about ten miles' worth), I felt that I was ready. I told my son that it was now or never.

"THE MODERN DIVA OF DOMESTICITY"

MOLLY O'NEILL

For many American women, Martha Stewart is an American icon—a woman who not only has it all but does it all. Stewart first insinuated herself into America's kitchens and consciousness in 1982 with her first book Entertaining, *followed by a succession of how-to cooking, gardening, and home decor volumes. By the mid-1990s she had her own television show and magazine, along with a multimillion-dollar empire of books and home-decor products carrying her name, and popped up on countless lists of the "most admired" women in America. As the writer Joan Didion perspicaciously observed, "Stewart's success lies not in her mastery of traditional skills but in her skillful blend of business savvy and Betty Crockerlike resourcefulness. The dreams and the fears into which Martha Stewart taps are not of 'feminine' domesticity but of female power, of the woman who sits down at the table with the men and, still in her apron, walks away with the chips."** In 2002, however, Stewart's brand-name image and reputation was considerably tarnished when she became the subject of a congressional investigation into allegations that she had engaged in insider stock trading.*

In the following article, Molly O'Neill humorously skewers the Martha mystique while showing Stewart's irresistible impact on couples who strive to emulate her ideas and create the domestic idyl that Stewart preaches.

SOURCE: Molly O'Neill, "But What Would Martha Say?" *New York Times Magazine*, 16 May 1999, section 6, pp. 145–6. Copyright © 1999 by Molly O'Neill. Reprinted with permission of The Wylie Agency, Inc.

I WANT TO BE Martha. What married working woman with a family has remained untouched by the modern diva of domesticity?

One minute, she's creating canapés in her East Hampton home on Long Island. A moment later, Martha Stewart is stitching cocktail napkins while discussing gardening in the huge white kitchen of her home in Westport, Conn.

Not one strand of her hair is ruffled. She changes her Oxford-cloth shirts—each one a hue from the same palette of paint colors she designed for K Mart—before they have a chance to wrinkle. Occasional brushes of powder conceal the sweat on her brow.

---

* Joan Didion, "Everywoman.com: Getting Out of the House with Martha Stewart," *New Yorker* (February 21 and 28, 2000), p. 279.

She moves like Miss Rogers, my cool and purposeful seventh-grade home-ec teacher, back in Ohio. But unlike Miss Rogers, Martha is sexy. Martha is powerful. Martha is rich. For one hour a day, five days a week, plus a half-hour on weekends, she leads an estimated 49 million monthly viewers through her hobbies, her obsessions, her virtual life. She is America's superego. The mother. The lover. The coach. The boss. The woman who can shingle the chicken coop as tastefully as she can cook the *petit poulet*.

It all began in 1982, when her first book, "Entertaining," taught Americans how to be their own caterers; then she taught them how to get married in her book "Weddings." Twelve more books have coaxed and trained time-pressed Americans—most recently the fastidious working couple of the late 90's—through cooking, gardening and decorating.

Which doesn't mean everyone likes Martha. Even Martha acolytes make fun of her. Ann Antoshak, a graphic designer who lives Jersey City with her husband, Gerry Gallagher, a broadcast technician who works nights, says that she and her husband "aren't going to decorate flowerpots the one day we have to spend together." Even so, she finds Martha mesmerizing: "I love seeing the domestic life that we don't have time to live." Couples like the Antoshak-Gallaghers don't worry too much about keeping up with the Joneses, since the Joneses, of course, are busy working day and night to buy those flowerpots. But the Antoshak-Gallaghers do nervously wonder what Martha would say about the way they manage their domesticity, especially in the kitchen, where couples have been experiencing power struggles in the last few decades. Martha, you see, is more of a moralist than the Joneses. She is the ultimate all-competent and ever-watchful neighbor.

Her company, Martha Stewart Living Omnimedia, is the Jones family gone monolithic. Altogether, Omnimedia is a conglomerate that includes the monthly magazine Martha Stewart Living, with a circulation of 2.35 million; 110 one-hour television shows a year; daily "Ask Martha" radio spots; Martha by Mail, the catalogue she rolled out last month; a Web site, and 26 books. This great big enterprise touches about 91 million people every month, and according to a 1998 article in The New York Times, the company was worth $250 million. All by taking the public into her private domain. The funny thing is, Martha doesn't really live there.

Which must make the Antoshak-Gallaghers sleep better at night (or during the day). Martha's homes, for one, have been reconstructed in her television studio—a 30,000-square-foot former greeting-card company in Westport, which became functional last year.

In a sprawling craft shop, test kitchen, woodworking shop and acres of offices, more than 80 people carry out the details of Martha's pretend life in print as well as on radio and cable television. The staff seems happy merely to work for Martha.

But I don't want to just work for Martha. I want to be a patch of perfectly modulated periwinkle blue in the button-down, gray workaday world. I want to supply a regular fix of cheerful, efficient domesticity.

Like Martha, I won't take it personally when someone like Marella Consolini, a 38-year-old vice president of the Knoedler Gallery in Manhattan, simply tries to incorporate her ideas "on a reasonable level."

Let Consolini take what she wants and leave the rest. Indeed, she and her husband, James Rodewald, have found that Martha is big enough for the two of them. Consolini uses Martha's recipes as springboards to make the comfort food she loves, and Rodewald, whose cooking is more spontaneous and relies less on recipes, culls Martha's books for ideas on pairing up certain foods.

Other couples find that Martha's clear, can-do directions in recipes help them resolve those territorial battles that have arisen since two-income households have sprouted two-cook kitchens. But couples are so tired of fighting, they're now trying to get along in the kitchen, to move marriage into the next century. "I study her recipes and use them as a shopping list," says Camille Guthrie, a 28-year-old professor of poetry at New York University. "Then my husband uses the same recipe to chop stuff and get it ready." Martha, in other words, helps dual-income families live off the same page. Well, almost. Take Serena Jost, a cellist, and Dan Machlin, who is a copy-writer on the Internet. They split the cooking chores down the middle but still grapple with control. She chops the vegetables with surgical precision, and he uses every pot in the house to make spaghetti.

"I stepped into the void and have always been perfectly clear about my intention of filling that void," Martha says, sipping Pellegrino between takes during a show and referring to her original intent of filling in the hole women left after entering the work force en masse.

Before sliding up to a conference table in her TV studio, Martha clears the remains of several lunches, uttering a tsk-tsk-tsk. "I shoot here in Connecticut three days a week and commute into the city the other four days," she says. "I run seven businesses. I'm starting seven others."

Why? "Because that's the fun part!" Martha says, her voice gaining a Julia Child-like boom as steadily as her enterprises are professionalizing the traditional sphere of "women's work" into an even bigger and more demanding arena: "couples' work."

The single bad part about being Martha, she admits, is that the only time she can do the hobbies she promotes is on her set. "I'm always trying to find time to really cook, garden, be with my friends."

And therein lies Martha's conundrum. (Does she need a Martha?) Still, the Martha fantasy endures. Like Mrs. Isabella Beeton and Irma Rombauer—and the whole line of American women who systematized cooking and homemaking and created successful public personas from their private lives—Martha is about wishful thinking.

Rising to return to take 50 of the day, Martha sighs, "I'd be very happy to kick everybody out of here and sew napkins for the rest of the day."

"OUR BIOLOGY HASN'T CHANGED ONE BIT"

CLAUDIA KALB ET AL.

Throughout the 1980s and 1990s a growing phenomenon, along with cell phones, SUVs, and telecommuting, was the medical practice of assisted reproduction (AR). As thousands of women discovered they were having difficulty getting pregnant, they turned to lengthy, invasive, and costly forms of medical treatment to help them conceive and/or carry a pregnancy. These treatments, which usually included several cycles of injectable drugs along with blood tests and other forms of monitoring, cost thousands of dollars and were often not covered by medical insurance. In many instances, however, women who were unable to get pregnant on their own, because of age or specific medical conditions interfering with fertility, did produce healthy babies with the intervention of AR.

But, as the following article points out, the intractable reality of the biological clock—the role that aging plays in declining fertility—has run up against the high hopes raised both by these technological advances and by women's expectations that they could defer motherhood after establishing careers or achieving other goals. Alarmed that women are overlooking the role of age in declining fertility, the American Society for Reproductive Medicine (ASRM) and other fertility advocacy groups launched a campaign to alert women to the limitations of their biological clock. Are such warnings a form of responsible medical practice or undue intrusion and pressure in one of the most important personal decisions that a woman will make?

SOURCE: Claudia Kalb, et al., "Should You Have Your Baby Now?" From *Newsweek*, 13 August 2001, pp. 40–48. © 2001 Newsweek, Inc. All rights reserved. Reprinted by permission.

NANCY WEIL, 44, always knew she wanted kids—but the timing was never quite right. In her 20s and 30s, she was intoxicated by her career as a television producer—she worked late nights, she traveled. A social life? She squeezed it in between assignments. "I thought, 'Hey, I can do my career and have children later,'" she says. At 42, Weil met her soulmate and decided it was time. For two years, they've been trying, first naturally, now with fertility drugs. A year ago she conceived, then miscarried. Last month alone, she spent $3,300 on injections. "If you ever told me I'd be having this kind of difficulty, I would have laughed in your face," she says. "I exercise, I eat well, I keep better work hours, but I'm really not in control of what's happening with my little eggs. It's devastating. It's a terrible sense of failure."

These are the dilemmas of babymaking in the 21st century. Women are de-laying childbearing as never before: the rate of first births for women in their 30s and 40s has surged in this country—quadrupling since 1970. At the same time, rates for women in their early 20s have dropped by a third. Glamorous celebrity moms like Jane Seymour, Cheryl Tiegs and Mimi Rogers are setting a trend in 40- and even 50-plus motherhood. And headlines touting the latest technological advances (just last month: Australian research fertilizes eggs without sperm) are making it all sound so easy. But our biology hasn't changed one bit. Only about 2 percent of all babies are born to women over 40 every year, and yet every day, doctors say, fortysomething women arrive at their of-fices pleading to be the exception to the rule—and then are crushed when tech-nology cannot help them.

Alarmed by what they view as a widespread lack of understanding about ag-ing as a risk factor for infertility—and a false sense of security about what sci-ence can do—infertility groups have decided to turn up the heat on public awareness. This fall the American Infertility Association, a patient-advocacy group, will pepper doctors' offices with pamphlets educating women about how age can affect fertility—and what can go wrong. And next month the American Society for Reproductive Medicine, the nation's largest professional organization of fertility specialists, will launch a bold ad campaign that will de-but on buses in New York, suburban Chicago and Seattle. The headline: Ad-vancing age decreases your ability to have children. The message: women "in their twenties and early thirties are most likely to conceive." The image: an up-side-down baby bottle in the shape of an hour-glass. "It's kind of like issuing a warning," says ASRM president Dr. Michael Soules, who spearheaded the cam-paign. "It's our duty to let people know."

That warning strikes at the heart of a complex web of emotional issues in women's lives. Women today have grown up with the expectation of "having it all": material wealth, career success, marriage and children. But many find the yellow brick road to motherhood littered with obstacles: lack of a partner, husbands who aren't ready, financial insecurity, divorce. "The idea that you can choose what age you'll be to have your children is a ludicrous proposition for most women," says Kim Gandy, president of the National Organization for Women, who delivered the first of her two daughters when she was 39, "as though you can simply snap your fingers and say, 'OK, I'm the right age,' and then have all the accouterments magically appear—the stable relationship, fi-nancial stability, life stability." For those who find themselves wanting children in their lifetime but are unable to envision having them now, the pressure and the anguish can be unbearable. Throw a tick-tock ad into the mix and it is bound to stir up controversy. Cindy O'Keefe, 28, who is single and wants to have kids, had a visceral reaction to the ad. "That's pressuring women in their 20s and 30s to conceive," she said, shouting over the lounge music at a trendy New York City bar. "That's sick!"

Women have had strong reasons to believe in the promise of technology, which has worked wonders for tens of thousands since test-tube baby Louise Brown's birth 23 years ago. Researchers can now not only mix egg and sperm in a petri dish, they can genetically test embryos for certain abnormalities, then weed them out before implantation. Science has made enormous strides in treating male infertility, which accounts for nearly half of all fertility problems: a single, sluggish sperm can be hunted down, then injected directly into an egg. Surrogates can carry babies for women who can't. And now donor eggs can be sucked out of one woman's ovaries and transferred to another's, giving life to couples who might have had no chance at all. . . .

And there's more going on in the lab, where scientists have been looking for new ways to attack the most frustrating problem in infertility today: the older woman's egg. Freezing eggs on college graduation day might seem like an ideal solution, but the success rate of that technique so far has been dismal because eggs tend to crystallize in sub-zero temps, disrupting their chromosomal integrity. Now researchers are experimenting with a variation on the theme: freezing slices of ovarian tissue, which contain thousands of eggs in an immature state. The procedure is being done for chemotherapy patients who hope one day to restore their fertility. It's far too soon to know if it will ever work, but the most optimistic doctors speculate that in the future some kind of freezing technique could be available for healthy young women who just want to wait. . . .

For women like Lindy Faier of Chicago, who is single and "old enough to be president," the future of assisted reproduction holds enormous promise. Faier spent her early adult life studying to be a lawyer; she's about to graduate from medical school. She'd like a baby, and while she knows she's pushing the odds, she still has hope. "I often think technology is going to rescue me," she says.

But the odds, say doctors, are that it probably won't. These experimental technologies are just that, experimental, and may never be available to humans. . . . What's more, success rates decline significantly as women age: for women in their 30s, about 33 percent; after 43, they drop to well under 10 percent. As wonderful and improved as science is, says Dr. Mark Sauer, of Columbia University's Center for Women's Reproductive Care, "we haven't seen any real improvements in treating women over 40. You can't change biology."

Biology has always made fertility a delicate proposition. A woman is born with a finite number of eggs, which gradually get ovulated or die off as she ages. And older eggs, which are less energetic than younger ones, have a harder time making it through the fertilization process. Among healthy couples in their mid-20s who are not using birth control—at a time when most American women have babies—about one in four will get pregnant each month. By 30, fertility rates begin to slowly decline. But the greatest risk, say doctors, is pushing child-bearing to the late 30s and 40s, when the chance of conception drops by 5 to 10 percent a year. By 43, when older eggs are far more likely to develop chromosomal abnormalities, the odds of getting pregnant through fertility treatments are so grim that most clinics strongly resist performing IVF with a woman's own eggs—they don't want to offer an ineffective option, nor do they want to drag down their own success rates. Miscarriage soars as women age—from about 15 percent in women aged 25 to 30, to about 40 percent in women over 40.

Statistics, however, never tell the whole story, and fertility doctors see a skewed population of patients. Some women conceive easily after 40, and others in their 20s struggle for years unsuccessfully. That margin for hope has convinced June Cohen, 31, that she can wait. Single and loving it, Cohen is aware that it may get harder for her to conceive later in life—"I don't know that there is a woman alive who isn't aware of her biological clock," she says—but she also wants to be the kind of supporting, devoted parent her mother was to her. "I'm not there yet," she says. "I know I want to have kids but I know I want to have them later. And I'm really, absolutely, not worried about that."

Fertility doctors *are* worried—so worried, in fact, they have decided to warn women that science can't always beat the biological clock. The ASRM says its $50,000 campaign, paid for by the group's annual budget, is aimed at educating women just like Cohen. Called "Protect Your Fertility," the campaign—which is linked to a Web site to be unveiled this week—will also highlight three other risk-factor public-service announcements: smoking, sexually transmitted diseases and body weight. The aging issue is clearly the most sensitive. Early on, the association had trouble finding a creative agency to design the campaign—some wouldn't touch it—and there were internal debates about whether the ad could be presented "without beating up women or encouraging adolescent pregnancy," says Soules. At one point, the group had pulled aging out of the mix altogether. But in the end, says Soules, "we feel it's the responsible thing to do." Support groups for infertility patients, like Resolve, which has chapters nationwide, agree wholeheartedly. "Aging is the issue that is coming up time and time again," says executive director Joan Bowen.

Ads are not the only answer, say fertility specialists—obstetrician-gynecologists should be doing more to educate young women during regular exams. Baby boomers' parents may have had kids in their 20s, but boomers themselves—the birth-control-pill generation—entered adulthood confident that they could schedule their reproductive lives. Many, like Nancy Weil, believed that staying fit and healthy would keep them young, not realizing that their ovaries were aging much faster than the rest of their bodies. A new Internet survey of thousands of women, to be reported at a scientific meeting this fall, found that while women have an excellent understanding of birth control, they tend to "overestimate the age at which fertility declines," says Dr. Richard Scott, of Reproductive Medicine Associates in New Jersey, who analyzed the findings. Dr. Jane Rosenthal, a psychiatrist at Columbia University, says she counsels infertility patients in their 40s who feel betrayed by the medical profession for not telling them more. "Many women are angry at their gynecologists who they feel didn't talk turkey with them about what's going to happen as they get older," she says.

Pamela Madsen, executive director of the American Infertility Association, wants to try to change that. She's hoping her educational pamphlets about infertility . . . will not only educate women, but empower doctors to raise the issue. "It's great that we have birth control and that women have a choice," says Madsen. "But part of that choice and reproductive freedom is the freedom to have a baby. What we've done is fed women this myth that they are in complete control of their reproductive lives and they can do it all. We fed them a fairy tale."

Afraid to offend or intrude, most doctors don't raise the question of fertility unless asked. The American College of Obstetricians and Gynecologists has no standard policy. . . . Other obstetricians say it's important to make the first move—even if it means stepping over the boundary of personal choice. Dr. Robert Gunby, of the Baylor University Medical Center in Dallas, says he begins asking women about having children when they're around 32. "I start saying, 'I'm not trying to pry into your business, but as women mature, their eggs aren't as fertile,' " says Gunby. "Some women take offense at that, like I'm trying to push them into being pregnant, but I feel obligated to explain that to them. Otherwise they reach the age where they have no choice."

Many women say they have absolutely no regrets about waiting—whether it's a conscious choice or life circumstances—even if they end up having no children or choosing to adopt. Others are thrilled to be older mothers. Karen Eubank, 45, of Dallas, had no trouble getting pregnant with her son, Rowan, at

40. She devoted her 30s to her career and her marriage. Now she has the patience for a child. "I'm more generous with my time now," she says. "Being older allows me to be a better mother."

Some question the motives of the fertility doctors. They wonder whether the ASRM may just be launching a public-relations campaign, to make themselves look responsible when they are also the ones helping to raise false hopes by creating headlines about 63-year-old moms. Amy Allina of the National Women's Health Network, a nonprofit advocacy group in Washington, D.C., says the skeptic in her wonders if the group may even have a financial stake in raising worries about getting pregnant. "If women are more anxious about pregnancy, they may be more likely to seek medical help earlier, which would be in the interest of fertility doctors," she says. "I hope that's not what the campaign is about." The ASRM says absolutely not. The fertility business has boomed from about 40 clinics in 1986 to 360 today. "We're overwhelmed with patients already," says Soules. "This truly is altruistic."

One day down the road, scientists say they hope to figure out a way to determine each woman's reproductive age: she could take a test at 23 to predict how fertile she'll be at 40. Or science will unravel the mysterious molecular process that makes eggs age, then slow down the process. And, yes, researchers are working on both. But no matter how astonishing these advances, the human body, which hasn't changed in thousands of years, will stay fundamentally the same. And as long as it does, when, and how, to have children will remain the most personal of all life's choices.

After sixteen years of testing, accompanied by a long and contentious debate between supporters and opponents of abortion, the drug RU-486, or mifepristone, was approved by the Food and Drug Administration (FDA) on September 28, 2000. Developed in France in 1980, the RU-486 drug can induce abortion without the standard invasive surgical procedure. In 1989, during George H. Bush's presidency, the FDA banned the drug after six years of testing yielded unsatisfactory results. Four years later Bush's successor, President Bill Clinton, ordered the Department of Health and Human Services to launch proceedings for renewed testing of the drug.

In October 1994 new clinical trials began, and in September 1996 the FDA gave conditional approval for the drug. By then more than one hundred thousand women had used the drug in clinical trials, and a group of investors formed a company, Danco Laboratories LLC, in New York City, to market and distribute it. The Population Council, a nonprofit research group that supports the legal availability of birth control and abortion, held the U.S. patent rights to the drug. But as of late 2000, the company has refused to identify the manufacturer, and a number of pharmacies are refusing to carry RU-486 for fear of repercussions from antiabortion groups.

When the FDA approval was finalized, abortion proponents praised the drug for enabling women to end an unwanted pregnancy safely and legally in the privacy of their own homes, and antiabortion advocates predictably feared the drug would make abortions too easy to obtain. Gloria Feldt, president of the Planned Parenthood Federation of America, hailed the drug as "the most significant technological advance in women's reproductive health care since the birth control pill," while Jodie Brown, of the American Life League, declared, "We will not tolerate the FDA's decision to approve the destruction of innocent human persons through chemical abortion." *Several antiabortion organizations that routinely picketed abortion clinics threatened to pressure doctors not to use the drug.*

As it turns out, both sides were wrong, because RU-486 is wrought with complications; it requires at least three trips to the doctor's office and may result in unpleasant side effects, including bleeding, cramping, and headaches. In addition, the

---

* Quoted in *Historic Documents of 2000*, copyright © 2001 by Congressional Quarterly, Inc., pp. 783, 784.

drug can be used only during the first seven weeks of a pregnancy. These compli-cations have discouraged women, and also many doctors, from embracing the drug. At least initially, the drug appeared to be used primarily in clinics such as Planned Parenthood of America. But that outcome has not silenced the ongoing debate over use of the drug and, despite the controversy and medical complexities involved, it offers to American women a safe, private, and less physically invasive form of abortion.

SOURCE: The Food and Drug Administration

THE FOOD AND DRUG ADMINISTRATION today approved mifepristone (trade name Mifeprex) for the termination of early pregnancy, defined as 49 days or less, counting from the beginning of the last menstrual period.

Under the approved treatment regimen, a women first takes 600 milligrams of mifepristone (three 200 milligram pills) by mouth. Two days later, she takes 400 micrograms (two 200-microgram pills) of misoprostol, a prostaglandin. Women will return for a follow-up visit approximately 14 days after taking mifepristone to determine whether the pregnancy has been terminated.

Because of the importance of adhering to this treatment regimen, each woman receiving mifepristone will be given a Medication Guide that clearly ex-plains how to take the drug, who should avoid taking it, and what side effects can occur.

"The approval of mifepristone is the result of the FDA's careful evaluation of the scientific evidence related to the safe and effective use of this drug," said Jane E. Henney, M.D., Commissioner of Food and Drugs. "The FDA's review and approval of this drug has adhered strictly to our legal mandate and mission as a science-based public health regulatory agency."

FDA based its approval of mifepristone on data from clinical trials in the United States and France.

The labeling for mifepristone emphasizes that most women using the prod-uct will experience some side effects, primarily cramping and bleeding. Bleed-ing and spotting typically last for between 9 and 16 days. In about one of 100 women, bleeding can be so heavy that a surgical procedure will be required to stop the bleeding.

The drug's labeling also warns that it should not be used in women with the following conditions:

- Confirmed or suspected ectopic ("tubal") pregnancies
- Intrauterine device (IUD) in place
- Chronic failure of the adrenal glands
- Current long-term therapy with corticosteroids
- History of allergy to mifepristone, misoprostol or other prostaglandins
- Bleeding disorders or current anticoagulant (blood-thinning) therapy.

Under the terms of the approval, mifepristone will be distributed to physicians who can accurately determine the duration of a patient's pregnancy and detect an ectopic (or tubal) pregnancy. Physicians who prescribe mifepristone must also be able to provide surgical intervention in cases of incomplete abortion or severe bleeding—or they must have made plans in advance to provide such care through others.

To gather additional data about the use of mifepristone, the Population Council (sponsor of the product) has made a commitment to conduct post-marketing studies. These include a study comparing patient outcomes among physicians who refer their patients needing surgical intervention, compared to those who perform surgical procedures themselves; an audit of prescribers that will examine whether patients and their physicians are signing the patient agreement and placing it in the patient's medical record, as required; and a system for surveillance, reporting and tracking rare ongoing pregnancies after treatment with mifepristone in the U.S.

"I WILL WORK MY HEART OUT FOR YOU"
HILLARY RODHAM CLINTON

After a bruising senatorial campaign against her opponent, Congressman Rick Lazio, in November 2000, First Lady Hillary Rodham Clinton achieved a historical first: she became the first first lady to enter public office, this time as the junior senator from New York State. Not since Eleanor Roosevelt has a first lady proved to be as controversial as Clinton. Equally outspoken and visible as Roosevelt, Clinton, a lawyer by profession, made political enemies from the start of her husband's presidential campaign when he boasted that if voters chose him, they'd get "two for the price of one." Hillary Rodham Clinton further alienated the public and many members of Congress, when, at the beginning of her husband's first term, she chaired a national commission to overhaul the nation's delivery of health care. Although some of her recommendations have since become public policy, she was bitterly criticized at the time for creating a health-care delivery system that was allegedly mired in red tape and government interference. She and her husband were also the subjects of a criminal investigation into a questionable real estate deal, and she was further scrutinized for her role in summarily firing the entire White House travel office. When President Clinton's affair with a White House intern was first made public and subsequently led to impeachment proceedings, his wife, as usual, garnered extreme public reactions: sympathy for being the "wronged" woman as well as criticism for remaining in her marriage simply to preserve her own power.

In February 2000 Clinton announced her candidacy for the seat of retiring New York State senator Patrick Moynihan—and immediately came under attack as a carpetbagger and opportunist for planning to use the seat as a potential presidential run in 2004. Even white, professional baby-boomer women—her logical supporters—were ambivalent about supporting her. But during a bitter campaign in which her opponent tried to exploit the scandals that had clouded her husband's two administrations, she proved her mettle by standing up to the mudslinging—and by thoroughly educating herself in the issues of concern to New York State voters. She went on to defeat Lazio, winning 55 percent of the popular vote, and has proved to be a highly capable, dedicated advocate for the people of New York State. Following is her victory speech in New York City on November 7, 2000.

SOURCE: In the public domain.

THANK YOU. Thank you so much. I mean, wow, this is amazing. Thank you all. You know, we started this great effort on a sunny July morning in Pinders

Corner on Pat and Liz Moynihan's beautiful farm and 62 counties, 16 months, three debates, two opponents, and six black pantsuits later, because of you, here we are.

You came out and said that issues and ideals matter. Jobs matter, downstate and upstate. Health care matters, education matters, the environment matters, Social Security matters, a woman's right to choose matters. It all matters and I just want to say from the bottom of my heart, thank you, New York.

Thank you for opening up your minds and your hearts, for seeing the possibility of what we could do together for our children and for our future here in this state and in our nation. I am proudly grateful to all of you for giving me the chance to serve you. I will do everything I can to be worthy of your faith and trust and to honor the powerful example of Senator Daniel Patrick Moynihan.

I would like all of you and the countless New Yorkers and Americans watching to join me in honoring him for his incredible half century of service to New York and our nation. Senator Moynihan, on behalf of New York and America, thank you.

And I thank [New York senator] Chuck Schumer for his generous support and friendship. He has been and will be a great champion for the people of New York and I very much look forward to fighting by his side in the United States Senate.

I want to thank both of my opponents, Mayor [Rudolph W.] Giuliani and Congressman [Rick A.] Lazio. Congressman Lazio and I just spoke. I congratulate him on a hard-fought race and I thank him for his service to the people of New York and Long Island and I wish him, Pat, and their two beautiful daughters well.

I promise you tonight that I will reach across party lines to bring progress for all of New York's families. Today we voted as Democrats and Republicans. Tomorrow we begin again as New Yorkers.

And how fortunate we are indeed to live in the most diverse, dynamic and beautiful state in the entire union.

You know, from the South Bronx to the Southern Tier, from Brooklyn to Buffalo, from Montauk to Massena, from the world's tallest skyscrapers to breathtaking mountain ranges, I've met people whose faces and stories I will never forget. Thousands of New Yorkers from all 62 counties welcomed me into your schools, your local diners, your factory floors, your living rooms and front porches. You taught me, you tested me and you shared with me your challenges and concerns—about overcrowded or crumbling schools, about the struggle to care for growing children and aging parents, about the continuing challenge of providing equal opportunity for all and about children moving away from their home towns because good jobs are so hard to find in upstate New York.

Now I've worked on issues like these for a long time, some of them for 30 years, and I am determined to make a difference for all of you. You see, I believe our nation owes every responsible citizen and every responsible family the tools that they need to make the most of their own lives.

That's the basic bargain I'll do my best to honor in the United States Senate. And to those of you who did not support me, I want you to know that I will work in the Senate for you and for all New Yorkers. And to those of you who worked so hard and never lost faith even in the toughest times, I offer you my undying gratitude. I will work my heart out for you for the next six years.

And I wouldn't be here if it weren't for the steady support of so many people. I want to thank . . . the entire New York Democratic Congressional delegation, my future colleagues. I'm very grateful for the support of our Democratic statewide elected officials. . . .

I want to thank . . . all the Democratic assembly members and all the Democratic members of the state Senate.

I want to thank all of my upstate friends who couldn't be here tonight, . . . all the county chairs and other elected officials. And thank you to all of my downstate friends. . . . And particularly my friends right here in New York City, the citywide officials, the borough presidents, the city council members and two great friends: former mayors, Ed Koch and David Dinkins.

And somebody just yelled, "Don't forget Long Island, we got beat up out there!"

And I am grateful to everybody from Long Island. And I want to thank all my friends in the state Democratic party leadership, . . . all the hardworking labor leaders who really helped turn out the vote today, . . . and the other local, state and national labor leaders whose support was so crucial.

And I want to thank all of the people who started volunteering with me from the very beginning. You knocked on doors, you raised funds, you built rallies, you did everything necessary to bring us to this point and today I want to thank the 25,000 volunteers from all across the state who started phone banking, knocking on doors, giving out palm cards the minute the polls opened at 6 a.m. and didn't stop until the last voter left. You made a difference in this race and I'm very grateful to you.

And I want to thank Harold Ickes, my campaign chairman, Bill DiBlasio, my campaign manager, and Gigi George, the coordinated campaign director, and I want to thank the best, hardest working campaign staff any candidate has ever had.

And finally, I want to echo Chuck Schumer in saying that I know I would not be here without my family. And I want to thank my mother and my brothers, and I want to thank my husband and my daughter.

You know, because this campaign was about ideas and issues, we have a lot of work to do and I am looking forward to doing that work with all of you from one end of the state to the other. I tonight am just overwhelmed by the kindness and support that I've been given and I will work my heart out for the next six years for all of you.

Thank you, thank you, thank you and God bless you all.

CHAPTER 6

SHAPING A NEW MILLENNIUM:
OLD PROBLEMS AND NEW VISIONS

September 11, 2001, dawned bright and balmy in New York City and along the Eastern seaboard. In Manhattan millions of people got up as usual to commute to work, and there was no reason to think that this day would be different from any other workday. But by 10:30 that morning, any thoughts of normality had been cruelly shattered. In an unprecedented terrorist attack, two airplanes, hijacked by terrorists of the Al Qaeda organization, a shadow network of terrorists operating throughout the Middle East and Europe, slammed into the World Trade Center, the mighty symbol of New York's financial preeminence. A similar attack took place at the Pentagon in the nation's capital, and another attack was narrowly averted by the courageous passengers on a fourth airplane, who overtook their terrorist hijackers. Although that plane crashed into the Pennsylvania woods, killing everyone on board, its passengers had prevented a more devastating loss of life by steering the plane away from populous metropolitan centers.

New York bore the brunt of the destruction; the two majestic towers of the World Trade Center, structurally overcome by the heat and flames of the airplanes that had rammed into their top floors, crumpled to the ground in an inferno of smoke and flames, taking with them nearly three thousand office workers and rescuers. Never before had the nation endured an assault of this magnitude on its own shores with such an enormous loss of life. Altogether, the number of victims from these horrific attacks amounted to over three thousand—more than the number of sailors and civilians killed at Pearl Harbor when Japanese warplanes bombed a fleet of American warships on December 7, 1941. The terrorist attack on the World Trade Center and the Pentagon was different in one other respect as well; it was an equal-opportunity attack, taking the lives of women and men alike who worked at these citadels of military and financial power. And among the rescue and recovery teams who came to search through the rubble for any survivors and begin the enormous and heartbreaking task of clearing away debris were scores of female iron-workers, fire fighters, police officers, cable splicers, and carpenters who worked alongside their male colleagues. Sharon Sellick, a cable splicer for the Consolidated Edison electric company in New York, described her work: "We're cross-trained, so we can function as mechanics and splicers. We go into manholes and piece cables together. We can do welding. I feel like we're the Marines of Con Ed because we're all over." At "ground zero," the embattled site of the former World Trade Center, she and others spent sixteen-hour shifts crawling gingerly along the jagged shards of steel and concrete remaining from the 110-story towers, "laying cables over the ground and building shunt boxes to protect them."[1]

Although women worked in shipyards and munitions factories during World War II, performing such untraditional female labors as welding and construction, it was not until the late seventies, as a result of the heightened awareness of gender discrimination in the trades, that women began to perform this work in peacetime and were therefore poised to participate in one of the biggest recovery efforts in American history. It is a tragic but highly significant barometer of the progress that American women have made in the last half century that, at the site of the worst terrorist attack in American history, women shared in the grueling and dangerous physical work of recovery and reconstruction, equipped with flashlights, torch guns, shovels, and hardhats. This scenario would not have been possible fifty years ago.

Whether or not all or most American women share the values and worldview of feminism, the women's movement has indeed had a profound impact upon all women's lives by challenging traditional gender norms and expanding the range of life choices available to them. For better or for worse, depending upon one's viewpoint, the women's movement has offered new visions for women's lives and, in the process, changed the social landscape of the nation over the past four decades.

But the work of equality and democracy is not finished. Even before the millennium was upon the country, old problems in new forms stubbornly persisted, and against the promise of a new millennium they appear in even starker relief. The workplace still remains an arena of inequality and struggle for women, whether they work in the trades or the professions. As late as 1995 more than 96 percent of top corporate executives in the United States were white males.[2] Previously all-male bastions as finance and law, as Reed Abelson's piece in this chapter shows, have proven to be intractably inhospitable to female advancement, yet when women adopt behaviors that would be acceptable in men, such as aggressiveness and ambition, they're seen as "bully broads" who need help with their interpersonal skills at work. (See the selection by Neela Bannerjee in this chapter.) And, if women are to excel in their careers, they must still bend to the demands of the office at the expense of home life, as Diane K. Shah's document in this chapter illustrates. Most American companies simply aren't prepared to help their employees, especially their female employees, advance to the top while offering the kind of enlightened policies that "Best Practices" in this chapter proposes. Concludes Robin Ely, a professor at Columbia University who specializes in gender and race relations: "To be successful in a lot of companies, a woman has to conform to the image of someone who doesn't have an outside life, who doesn't have a family, and who doesn't have any interests outside of work. We're not much better on this than we were a few years ago."[3]

Most working women, however, are still clustered in low-paying, sex-segregated jobs and have more immediate concerns than penetrating the glass ceiling. They need programs and initiatives to help them break out of living from paycheck to paycheck and get the education and training they need for higher-skilled and better-paying work. They also need adequate, affordable child care, which would enable them to pursue decent jobs while their children are getting the proper medical care, nutrition, and educational stimulation needed to improve their own prospects for a productive life. In 1972 Congress passed the Comprehensive Child Development Act, which mandated a federally subsidized system of day-care centers throughout the country, available to all children regardless of a family's income level. But President Richard Nixon vetoed the measure because he felt it would undermine the strength of the nuclear family. The need for quality, affordable day care remains, especially for low-income families, but it is unlikely that the government will champion such a program anytime soon.

Nor does the implementation of affirmative action, a once potent tool of advancement for women and minorities, offer much hope. Starting in the 1990s, the nation's commitment to affirmative action policies that benefit women and minorities in higher education and the workplace has diminished significantly. A series of court cases and legislative initiatives has weakened the enforcement of these policies. In 1996 voters in California voted for Proposition 209, which prohibits the consideration of race or gender in college admissions and in all municipal and state government hiring policies. Although there have been challenges to this law and attempts to circumvent it, it has severely undermined women's ability to surmount barriers against educational and professional advancement in that state. In the 1995 to 1996 academic year, before Proposition 209 took effect, women comprised 35.8 percent of all new faculty hired in the statewide University of California system; by the 1999 to 2000 academic year, only 25.1 percent of new faculty hired were women.[4] There will, no doubt, be other challenges to affirmative action policies—challenges that can only serve to slow down the educational and professional progress that women, in large measure because of these policies, have made thus far.

The institution of welfare, like affirmative action, also faces an uncertain future. The current welfare system had its origins during the Great Depression and the New Deal's safety net of social welfare programs for the poor and unemployed. During President Lyndon B. Johnson's administration, the delivery of welfare along with Medicare and Medicaid—government-subsidized medical benefits for the elderly and indigent—was a cornerstone of his Great Society host of programs to curb poverty. Few would dispute that the nation's current welfare system is unwieldy and creates almost as many problems as it solves—chief among which are low subsidies that keep recipients at near poverty level and policies that end up penalizing those who try to work by taking away their government-subsidized medical coverage. During Ronald Reagan's two administrations and again during Bill Clinton's second term in office, the federal government reexamined its obligation to provide a safety net for those who are unable to support themselves and scaled back its level of commitment toward the poor, turning much of the responsibility over to the states. This is a dangerous precedent that has created uneven and usually inadequate levels of support across the country. Many states are experimenting with new ideas, such as putting a limit on the length of time that recipients can collect benefits, requiring recipients to perform some type of work in return for their benefits, and imposing harsh eligibility measures for receiving welfare. Women, and especially women of color, along with their children, have historically comprised welfare's major constituency. Whatever changes the welfare system undergoes will have a direct and immediate impact on their ability to meet their basic needs for food and shelter and, beyond that, on their capability of breaking out of the cycle of dependency to get the education, training, and child-care assistance they need for a better way of life.

Another critical area of concern for American women lies in the realm of reproduction and sexuality. As the twenty-first century gets under way, American women's access to safe, legal abortions remains under assault. Through demonstrations and by political pressure, and also through the calculated use of violence, a highly cohesive network of religious-right groups has managed to intimidate both state legislators and physicians from making access to abortion more readily available. In many cities across the country, women can no longer obtain an abortion at a doctor's office or hospital and must travel long distances for the procedure. And though RU-486, the "abortion pill," is now legally available, militant antiabortion groups have again marshalled their resources to discourage physicians and clinics from prescribing it.

Nearly every state has some form of law limiting abortion, including waiting periods, parental consent for minors, enforced notification of alternatives to abortion, and record keeping that can undermine a woman's right to privacy. State and federal courts have upheld these and other restrictions, and a continuing conservative majority on the Supreme Court does not bode well for expanding rather than contracting a woman's access to abortion. After a hotly contested presidential election in 2000, in which the Supreme Court stepped in and stopped a series of recounts, thereby opening the Court up to allegations that it had short-circuited the democratic process, George W. Bush became the forty-third president. His strong antiabortion stand, coupled with the prospect that he would have an opportunity to replace at least two Supreme Court judges during his administration with conservative jurists who share his views, indicates that the struggle to preserve the right to a safe, legal abortion as delineated in *Roe v. Wade* will not be won any time soon. If women are to have full power over their lives, they must have control over their reproduction through safe, legal contraceptive measures and access to abortion.

They must also be protected, legally and otherwise, from harassment or abuse because of their sex. In October 1991, during the televised Senate confirmation hearings of Judge Clarence Thomas's nomination to the U.S. Supreme Court, the nation was transfixed by the testimony of Anita Hill, who recounted past instances of his inappropriate behavior toward her. Although Thomas's nomination was eventually approved by the full Senate, Hill's testimony gave other women the courage to reveal their own experiences of sexual harassment in the workplace. Women in the military also overcame their fear of speaking out and exposed major incidents of sexual harassment by male superiors against female enlistees and officers. In September 1997 the U.S. army published its findings from a widespread investigation into sexual misconduct by male army officers and found that "sexual harassment exists throughout the Army, crossing gender, rank, and racial lines."[5] Although uncovering such abuses is a necessary first step, both the federal government, the private sector, and women themselves have much work to do to implement policies and change cultural attitudes to eradicate sexual harassment in the workplace.

Violence against women is another major social concern. While other forms of crime—homicide, burglaries, assaults—have diminished somewhat, domestic violence and sex-related crimes have skyrocketed. Between 1976 and 1984, sex-related murders rose 160 percent, and from 1983 to 1987 domestic violence shelters recorded a greater than 100 percent increase in the numbers of women who took refuge in them.[6] Women's groups have formed hotlines and sponsored "take back the night" rallies to protest the growing violence, but sex-related assaults continue to be one of the fastest growing forms of crime. Across the country, rape crisis centers, domestic violence shelters, and other social service organizations help women and their children cope with an ongoing epidemic of violence, but what is needed in addition is the commitment of law enforcement agencies and, harder yet, a sea change in attitudes that dismiss violence against women as merely a private family matter.

Older women—who are often the victims of violence by overtaxed caregivers—face a different kind of crisis. Over the past several decades women have increasingly outlived their male partners or spouses and are often ill-prepared to support themselves financially on limited incomes. The federal government has tried to tackle the rising cost of health care for elders, and debates about the government's role in subsidizing expensive prescription drugs for the elderly figured hugely in the 2000 presidential campaign. By 2010 baby boomers will start to draw on social security and medicare. Although this generation has grown up in prosperity and has continued to generate wealth through investment or inheritance, the same problem of rising living and health-care costs—and the extent to which social security and medicare can help defray these costs—will follow both female and male baby boomers into their twilight years. The government must begin now to put into place social and economic policies that will protect these programs and accommodate the shifting demographics.

These are just a few of the issues facing American women as they enter the new millennium. But ours is an open moment. Will women embrace a renewed sense of historicism, as Naomi Wolf urges in her piece in this chapter, to guide them into the future? Will they draw inspiration from the creative and courageous female leaders and movements of the past to develop new strategies for dismantling the remaining barriers to full freedom and equality? And will they pursue their goals with the zeal and passion that earlier generations of American women have shown? From raising "successful" daughters to developing new coalitions and communities of common interest to tackle the problems that still divide this country, the writers of the documents in this chapter seek to raise enduring questions, reframe issues in new ways, and provide a compass for the future.

NOTES

1. Quoted in "The Women of Ground Zero," New Jersey *Star Ledger*, 25 October 2001, p. 25.
2. Kathleen C. Berkeley, *The Woman's Liberation Movement in America* (Westport, Conn: Greenwood Press, 1999), p. 105.
3. Quoted in "Somber News for Women on Corporate Ladder," *New York Times*, 6 November 1996, pp. D1, D19.
4. The Affirmative Action and Diversity Project, English Department, University of California at Santa Barbara. A timeline of events and actions related to Proposition 209 can be found on the World Wide Web at http://aad.english.ucsb.edu/pages/prop.209.html.
5. "Army's Leadership Blamed in Report on Sexual Abuses," *New York Times*, 12 September 1997, pp. A1, A22.
6. Susan Faludi, *Backlash: The Undeclared War Against American Women* (New York: Crown, 1991), p. xvii.

"TO BE KNOWN ON OUR OWN TERMS"
KATE SHANLEY

Kate Shanley, an Assiniboine Indian with Irish blood, grew up on the Fort Peck reservation in Montana. At the time she wrote this essay, she was a single mother of an adolescent son and was working on her Ph.D. in literature at the University of Michigan. Shanley astutely identifies the issues on which Native American feminists and the "majority women's movement," as she calls it, agree and disagree. Reproductive freedom, child health and welfare, and equal pay for equal work are issues that both Native American feminists and mainstream feminists can rally around, but for Native American feminists the notions of equality and feminism carry different meanings. The continuity of tradition and affirmation of tribal integrity and sovereignty are a vital part of the Indian feminist's worldview, and dovetail well with the feminist vision of unity within diversity, of a global community of different peoples practicing respect for their own members and for others.

SOURCE: Kate Shanley, "Thoughts on Indian Feminism," in *A Gathering of Spirit: Writing and Art by North American Women*, edited by Beth Brant (Degonwadonti) (Rockland, Me.: Sinister Wisdom, 1984), pp. 213–15. Reprinted by permission of Kate Shanley.

TWO YEARS AGO, after the Ohoyo Conference in Tahlequah, Oklahoma, the Ohoyo Resource Center put together a book titled, *Words of Today's American Indian Women: Ohoyo Makachi.* Among the addresses included is Rayna Green's speech, "Contemporary Indian Humor." A mixture of anecdote and tribute to Indian women, Green's talk addresses with humor the serious problems facing Indian women in America today. Of the relationship of the Indian women's movement to the majority women's movement, however, she writes:

> Many people want to know why the Indian women's movement didn't really join the majority women's movement in this country. I've come up with a new theory of why they have not joined the women's movement. You've all heard that one of the first things people in the movement did was to burn their bras. I've decided why Indian women didn't do that. Being the shape most of us are in, we were afraid they'd have to bring the fire trucks in from ten miles around. So you can understand why we were reluctant. We figured we stopped air pollution in Eastern Oklahoma by not doing that kind of burning.

Aside from the obviously funny reference to the large-chestedness of Indian women, Green plays off the popular mistaken notion that "the first thing" feminists did to protest women's oppression in this country was to burn their bras—a weak, if not self-trivializing gesture—and she jokingly cites bra-burning as the point where Indian and "majority" women depart from each other. Of course, humor is humor—and what could be worse than taking a joke seriously? Then again, what could be more foolish than denying the serious assumptions that underlie most humor, assumptions as commonly-held beliefs. The American women's movement historically has been and continues to be more than a weak protest against the notion of woman as sex symbol, but the questions remain: why do Indian women seem reluctant to join the majority women's movement? Or do they?

Toward the end of the 1983 Ohoyo Indian Women's Conference on Leadership, I began to notice that the participants were not referring to themselves as feminists, although the group of women present are as strong and committed as any group of women in America today who are working for change. Why, then, do Indian women avoid the designation "feminist?" The more I thought about it, the more that question began proliferating into many questions: how many other women (of all colors and creeds) have I encountered in my travels (plenty!) who do not choose to identify as feminists? What do they have in common with Indian women? What is a feminist, anyway?

My thoughts on the questions raised thus far by no means represent a consensus among Indian women; in fact, before I could begin to deal objectively with the subject of Indian feminism, I had to come to terms with my own defensiveness about representing other women, particularly other Indian women. On the one hand, I am a woman who refers to herself as a feminist. If most Indian women do not refer to themselves as feminists, does that fact make me somehow *less* representative, *less* Indian? On the other hand, does the theoretical feminism of the university constitute something different from (though, perhaps giving it the benefit of the doubt, correlated to) the "grass-roots" feminism Ohoyo represents? To some extent I know that I suffer the conflicts of an "academic squaw" (to borrow a term from poet and educator Wendy Rose), a certain distance from the "real world."

Attending the Ohoyo conference in Grand Forks, North Dakota was a returning home for me in a spiritual sense—taking my place beside other Indian women, and an actual sense—being with my relatives and loved ones after finally finishing my pre-doctoral requirements at the university. Although I have been a full-time student for the past six years, I brought to the academic experience many years in the workaday world as a mother, registered nurse, volunteer tutor, social worker aide, and high school outreach worker. What I am offering in this article are my thoughts as an Indian woman on feminism. Mine is a political perspective that seeks to re-view the real-life positions of women in relation to the theories that attempt to address the needs of those women.

Issues such as equal pay for equal work, child health and welfare, and a woman's right to make her own choices regarding contraceptive use, sterilization and abortion—key issues to the majority women's movement—affect Indian women as well; however, equality *per se*, may have a different meaning for Indian women and Indian people. That difference begins with personal and tribal sovereignty—the right to be legally recognized as peoples empowered to determine our own destinies. Thus, the Indian women's movement seeks equality in two ways that do not concern mainstream women: (1) on the individual level, the Indian woman struggles to promote the survival of a social structure whose organizational principles represent notions of family different from those of the mainstream; and (2) on the societal level, the People seek sovereignty as a people in order to maintain a vital legal and spiritual connection to the land, in order to *survive* as a people.

The nuclear family has little relevance to Indian women; in fact, in many ways, mainstream feminists now are striving to redefine family and community in a way that Indian women have long known. The American lifestyle from which white middle-class women are fighting to free themselves, has not taken hold in Indian communities. Tribal and communal values have survived after four hundred years of colonial oppression.

It may be that the desire on the part of mainstream feminists to include Indian women, however sincere, represents tokenism just now, because too often Indian people, by being thought of as spiritual "mascots" to the American endeavor, are seen more as artifacts than as real people able to speak for ourselves. Given the public's general ignorance about Indian people, in other words, it is possible that Indian people's real-life concerns are not relevant to the mainstream feminist movement in a way that constitutes anything more than a "representative" facade. Charges against the women's movement of heterosexism and racism abound these days; it is not my intention to add to them except to stress that we must all be vigilant in examining the underlying assumptions that motivate us. Internalization of negative (that is, sexist and racist) attitudes towards ourselves and others can and quite often does result from colonialist (white patriarchal) oppression. It is more useful to attack the systems that keep us ignorant of each other's histories.

The other way in which the Indian women's movement differs in emphasis from the majority women's movement, lies in the importance Indian people place on tribal sovereignty—it is the single most pressing political issue in Indian country today. For Indian people to survive culturally as well as materially, many battles must be fought and won in the courts of law, precisely because it is the legal recognition that enables Indian people to govern ourselves according to our own world view—a world view that is antithetical to the *wasicu* (the Lakota term for "takers of the fat") definition of progress. Equality for Indian women within tribal communities, therefore, holds more significance than equality in terms of the general rubric "American."

Up to now I have been referring to the women's movement as though it were a single, well-defined organization. It is not. Perhaps in many ways socialist feminists hold views similar to the views of many Indian people regarding private property and the nuclear family. Certainly, there are some Indian people who are capitalistic. The point I would like to stress, however, is that rather than seeing differences according to a hierarchy of oppressions (white over Indian, male over female), we must practice a politics that allows for diversity in cultural identity as well as in sexual identity.

The word "feminism" has special meanings to Indian women, including the idea of promoting the continuity of tradition, and consequently, pursuing the recognition of tribal sovereignty. Even so, Indian feminists are united with mainstream feminists in outrage against woman and child battering, sexist employment and educational practices, and in many other social concerns. Just as sovereignty cannot be granted but *must be recognized* as an inherent right to self-determination, so Indian feminism must also be recognized as powerful in its own terms, in its own right.

Feminism becomes an incredibly powerful term when it incorporates diversity—not as a superficial political position, but as a practice. The women's movement and the Indian movement for sovereignty suffer similar trivialization, because narrow factions turn ignorance to their own benefit so that they can exploit human beings and the lands they live on for corporate profit. The time has come for Indian women and Indian people to be known on our own terms. This nuclear age demands new terms of communication for all people. Our survival depends on it. Peace.

"NO ONE TEACHES WOMEN
HOW TO KNOW PLEASURE"
AMY LAROCCA

Consciousness-raising, a widely practiced tool for personal empowerment and social change in the early years of the women's movement (see Vivian Gornick's "Consciousness-Raising" in chapter 3), takes new form here for a new millennium. As this article about a "school" dedicated to teaching the art of self-pleasure among New York City's privileged women shows, Mama Gena, the "instructor" adopts a prime strategy of consciousness-raising groups—that of sharing personal experience to help restructure consciousness, in this case for the pursuit of sexual and other pleasures. Note how the participants refer to themselves as "sister goddesses" who have the ability to "conjure" desired results. Radical feminists also used such rich imagery to establish their shared and special qualities as women. Is Mama Gena's School of Womanly Arts a new way to exploit women as sex objects, or is she helping her students achieve a higher level of personal power and satisfaction?

SOURCE: Copyright *New York Magazine*, 23 July 2001, 39–41. Reprinted by permission.

"WE LIVE IN A CULTURE that doesn't acknowledge the importance of appetite," complains Mama Gena the proprietress of Mama Gena's School of Womanly Arts. Mama Gena sports a head of very blonde Shirley Temple curls and a gold lamé suit at home one recent afternoon. "Nobody," she says, "teaches us to really examine or explore the details of what creates a totally succulent, gratified, dewy, fabulous, lubricated life!" New York women are experts at denying themselves—depending on the month—carbs, sugar, dairy, fruit. They wear tall, spindly heels that uncomfortably cramp calves overdeveloped by so many hours with the personal trainer. There is very little that's pleasant about a Brazilian bikini wax, and not much to recommend the absence of stockings on bitter winter mornings. Mama Gena's devotees—boldface models doted on by paparazzi, business women with big titles and bigger offices, chic creative types with hunky husbands and cute children—know all of this. "Even when you go to a party, it's like work," one best-dressed glamazon sighs. "Everything is about success and about fame, and that's great, but after a while, you start to feel like you're lacking."

What does Mama Gena have to say to these high achievers with existential angst? You're just underlubricated. Have ice cream. Have orgasms. Tell your man to touch you right *there*.

"I think a lot of women just have their lights off," she says. "I'll see women on the street and say, 'Look at that beautiful woman. There's no reason for her lights to be off.' These women need to learn to trust their pussies. Not their vaginas, their coochies, their down-theres, but their pussies. Vagina is the wrong word, because it's referring to your internal cavity."

Mama Gena explains that using the word vagina is not unlike calling your penis your prostate. "When women use the word *pussy*, it sets them free. They flush, they get all crazy. They feel all wild. It snaps a woman into her sassiness."

So, on a typical weekday evening twenty New York women pack up their pussies in La Perla thongs and make their pilgrimage to Mama Gena's brownstone in the West Eighties to learn to say the word ("They shout it!" Mama Gena swears. "We have to restrain them sometimes!") and to take classes with titles like "Training Your Man," "Power Play: The Art and Science of Hexing," and, of course, "Trust Your Pussy." While at school, they call themselves sister goddesses.

Mama Gena's students are not unusual or eccentric—you'd find the same cross-section of New Yorkers in a spin class at Equinox. A few lawyers, some Upper East Side moms, a debutante, some jewelry designers. They dress in Sigerson Morrison mules, Diane Von Furstenberg wrap dresses, Earl jeans. They dabble in yoga; they love sushi. They are toned and plucked and blown dry. And they are absolutely willing to share with one another, in graphic detail, tips on masturbating.

Mama Gena, whose real name was Regena Thomashauer back when she was an actress-teacher-waitress type, has devoted the past ten years to being mother figure to the lost, pleasure-challenged female population of Manhattan. She is their ur-goddess, their Eros enabler, their heroine. . . . "No one teaches women how to know pleasure. We aren't educated into the womanly arts. Nobody teaches us how to flirt, how to own our own sensuality. We're always looking to our husbands and our boyfriends to make us gratified and happy.

"My school is really about dipping your toe into the waters of womanhood; it's a courtesan academy. Selfishness is our ultimate goal, because what no one teaches us is that if you're not pleasuring yourself, you don't have the surplus to take care of anyone else. But if you learn how to take exquisite care of yourself, you're like, *Give me your tired, your poor!*"

Mama Gena, who's now 44, offers herself as living proof: She has a beautiful 4-year-old daughter and a happy marriage. She works with her (well-trained) husband at home. "I can have sex whenever I want!" she brags. (She favors, for the record, late morning.) And she can get up afterward and put on her gold lamé suit, which makes her feel very "pussified."

Her students start as the inverse of this model—better trained in deprivation than in indulgence—and her formula for reversing the balance involves introducing them to their crotches, to the sensual pleasures, like Brie cheese and aromatherapy candles, to their dark sides (the bitch, after all, is just another face of the goddess).

"Before the class I would intellectualize decisions," one sister goddess explains. "I would make choices based on data and facts. Now I make choices based on what turns me on. Mama Gena would say, what makes your pussy wet. I pay attention to my desire now. You have to be trained to do that. It doesn't come naturally."

They also learn to make their men do whatever they want, just like Sister Goddess Nancy Reagan did. "That man would have never made it to the White House without her," Mama Gena says appreciatively, "so she really got the ride she wanted."

A group of women gather in a circle on the parlor floor of Mama Gena's house to brag. They introduce themselves; they lead sort of dreamy New York lives. Most are married or in relationships. They are thin, pretty, fashionable. They go to L.A. for the weekend, and even though it's only early spring, a number of them look rather tan. "I am Sister Goddess So-and-so," they begin. And then they brag. "This week, men at work called me beautiful," says a women in a rosy Agnès b. top. "Well bragged!" raves Mama Gena. Auntie Beth, her pretty, bright, leggy protégée—a refugee from corporate America who asks herself when shopping, "Would the Charlie's Angles wear this?"—agrees.

Another sister goddess boldly ignored her date at Bouley Bakery and flirted with everyone else at the party. One "held court" (a popular sister-goddess term) over her entire table at a benefit. Lots of women took bubble baths. One sister goddess stopped her husband in the middle of hotel sex, turned on the lights, and said, "Would you like to see my clitoris?" (He would.) One woman brags that upon seeing a "gross" woman scarf down sushi on the subway, she did not feel disdain; she did not give her a mental fashion makeover. She sent out a little prayer for her instead. This sister goddess won best brag that night and was rewarded with a pink feather boa and a drugstore tiara.

Mama Gena's suggested curriculum begins with a seven-week, $650 sister-goddess boot camp called the Foundation Course. The class meets weekly for three hours at a time. In addition to the brag, each class has a theme. Pussify your wardrobe, for example (that is, throw out anything that makes you feel less than foxy), or dress up as your favorite woman from history or fiction (several Jackie O's, a Princess Di here, an Auntie Mame there).

There is homework, too, such as watching Mae West movies, or practicing Pussy Appreciation. "Look at your crotch every day," reads a handout. "Write in a journal three things you like about it. Touch your crotch in different places and see what feels good, write in your journal and bring it to class."

And there is reading: A favorite text is called *Extended Massive Orgasm* and promises, much like a cookbook, fantastic results to anyone who can follow directions. Mama Gena herself doesn't teach the mechanics of masturbation, although she does encourage and even assign it. She calls in her expert friends from California, Steve and Vera Bodansky (the married doctor-authors of *Extended Massive Orgasm*), who demonstrate during special, one-day weekend courses that cost $300.

After boot camp, the more specific classes open up (like the "Power Play" how-to-hex session, which is less about witchcraft than cultivating sassiness). "What I love about it," says one client, "is that it's not about suffering through the course so you can get results. It's not just about having another therapist." And Mama Gena believes that her goddesses can conjure up things. She has many tales of this female power: the sister goddess who wanted to show in a gallery but didn't know how conjured a dealer during a party at Mr. Chow. Another sister goddess left for L.A. with nowhere to stay and conjured an old friend on her flight. (The old friend had, naturally, a large room at the Standard.)

You can also send your man to class—Mama Gena will teach him how to kiss, how to wrangle a bitch, where, exactly, to find your clitoris, and what to do with it when he does. The philosophy behind the men's courses is that men inherently want to make their women happy, they just need to be told how. "Men love to date my goddesses," Mama Gena boasts.

There are many things sister goddesses are looking for when they enroll: courage, raises, relationships. "They want to feel like they can get any guy they want," Mama Gena says, "and they can." But what they walk away with is another ritual to integrate into their maintenance routine: pleasure. Naps. Massages. Pedicures.

"I'm much more disciplined about my pleasure now," one graduate says. "If I haven't done something pleasurable for myself by the end of the day, I make sure I get it in. I think of it as like going to the gym."

Almost a century after Virginia Woolf wrote "A Room of One's Own," a treatise on the conditions required for women to write—money and privacy—and, in a larger sense, to live as independent human beings, Lynne Hektor, a writer from New York City, revisits the issues that Woolf raised: what are the conditions needed for creativity, for pursuing a life that is consonant with internal needs and aspirations? She writes in praise of the single life, of women who have defied social norms to marry and rear children by creating a rich, fulfilling life as a family of one. But she also exhorts women who live as wife or partner (of which, she is among the latter) to embrace solitude when they can in order to pursue their own pleasures. They, too, must, in her words, "learn to hear one's own voice . . . to feel one's own desire." As women approach the new millennium, she urges them to contemplate a range of choices for their lives—to shape, like a sculptor, lives of beauty and grace.

SOURCE: Lynne Hektor, "A Room of One's Own: Revisited," in *The Emergence of Women into the 21st Century*, edited by Patricia L. Munhall and Virginia M. Fitzsimmons (New York: NLN Press, 1995), pp. 266–75. Reprinted by permission of Jones and Bartlett Publishers, Sudbury, MA. www.jbpub.com.

FOR WOMEN, unrelentingly socialized over centuries to needs of home and hearth, there continues to be far too little societal recognition and validation of the need of all women for a "room of one's own," be it a physical or psychic space. The purpose of this chapter is to revel in the delights of solitude, to sing the praises of time alone and unfettered, to cast out notions of obligations and responsibilities to others in favor of the unabashed joys of a cup of tea in the early morning, before anyone else is stirring, by oneself; in the secretive pleasure of an afternoon movie, a slip into a cool and dark cinema off an urban street to see a film no one *we* know would even want to see; that cool spring evening in the country, right before dark, when, sure that the baby is asleep, there is the furtive stroll, by oneself, down the lane, sky changing colors, wildflowers and weeds on the side of the road, riotious and collective, the crickets just beginning their June chirp.

Allusions to times alone are often conceptualized, for women, as "stolen." Stolen from whom? And for what? These are questions I pose that demand answers. For I would advocate that the capacity to be alone is vital to health and happiness. I quote Montaigne, "We must reserve a little back-shop, all our own, entirely free, wherein we establish our true liberty and principle retreat and solitude." Although I would agree that in infancy and early childhood that attachment to parents and/or parent substitutes is essential if the child is to survive, and that such secure attachments are indeed necessary for the child to develop into an adult capable of making intimate relationships with other adults on equal terms, I would speculate that intimate attachments to other human beings, while important, are nonetheless highly over-rated, especially for women. Attachment theory, a popular cornerstone of conventional, although largely unexamined, wisdom, gives shortshrift to the value of work, as well as to the emotional importance of what goes on in the mind of the individual when alone; in short, the *imagination*. In the words of Samuel Johnson, "Were it not for imagination, Sir, a man would be as happy in the arms of a chambermaid as of a Duchess." Intimate attachments are a center around which the life of the individual revolves, not necessarily *the* center.

How that center is defined will vary from person to person, culture to culture, historical time and place, inevitably the mixture of individual interaction with an ever-evolving context. I enter into this dialogue on behalf of all women; the busy young mother is as in need of a sip of the cool glass of solitude as the Ivory Tower academic—perhaps more so. And those who drink of that glass—especially those requiring long droughts, are frequently perceived as greedy, perhaps anti-social, or ultimately, mad. Women as artist, women as writer, women as poet, women as social activist—any women whose life includes risk and the desire for individual achievement in the public world, as well as, or worse yet, in place of, marital love, is often still villified, as frequently by her own cultural expectations as those of others. A collection follows of thoughts and writings of and about women who have chosen and relentlessly pursued their solitary visions and lives, as well as a celebration of choices too seldom celebrated.

I myself currently write from the perspective of a ten-year, live-in, heterosexual relationship. Perhaps my thoughts on, and memories of my single life are romanticized, sanitized, and ultimately idealized. But, I have resisted the legal sanctions of marriage, in part, I think, because of these memories, and because of my view of myself as a single and solitary being, free, unencumbered, autonomous. "Free, white, and twenty-one" as the old, racist saying used to go, implying all the perogatives of full citizenship and responsibilities, rights, and yes again, autonomy.

And so I am still single (legally, at least) and also childless. A true creature of the twenty-first, uniquely American century, replete with Planned Parenthood and free birth control since before I was 18. And now nearing 50, birth control is no longer needed; children are a moot issue. Regrets? Not at the present. Maybe regrets will come; maybe they won't. As far as I'm concerned, we all take our chances, make our choices, cut our losses.

In actuality, I revel in my freedom, in a bath of frequent self-indulgence, and disclaim most responsibilities to my fellow creatures. Ultimately selfish, I suppose, I arise early to savor hot coffee, alone. To enjoy the house with no one else stirring. To see the sun come up, alone. To sniff the air with my cats (Of course, there are cats in my life!) and gird myself for the coming onslaught of interaction with the rest of humanity that life in 1995 brings on a daily level. I yearn for the nineteenth century—a slower pace, time to appreciate subtleties, of texture, of food, of discourse. On the week ends, I sleep late sometimes. Or don't get out of bed at all! Wickedly—for I always *feel* wicked—I peruse the paper—or worse yet read a novel! I don't answer the phone. And I don't feel obliged to have dinner parties, either. I view attachment as highly over-rated.

I guess at a different point in time, historically, or in a different culture, I could be burned at the stake. Or stoned. Or perhaps, merely viewed as mad. At best, unabashedly anti-social. Children in restaurants disturb my sense of propriety.

I remain convinced there is a vast cultural apparatus to convince us otherwise. That a life without children is unlived. That a life without a marriage, for a woman, is unfulfilled. That a divorced woman is unwanted, rejected, neglected, ultimately unlovable. That the widowed are to be pitied, forever. That their life is over. Dead and buried with their dead husband. Rubbish! Garbage! That any relationship is better than waking up alone, on sheets wet and drenched from tears, touseled and wrinkled from a night of wrestling with the devil of loneliness and need.

The "nineties" woman that I know, the one with a full-time job, and a full-time husband, and full-time children, and a full-time house is not a happy camper. The ones I know are stressed—can't find the time for any quality of life; can't find the time to enjoy the house, the husband, the kids, the job. I speak in generalities. Do I think women should just stay home and raise children? That is not my point.

My point, instead, is to say the things that are not said enough, to celebrate an alternate choice, to say some of the things we frequently dare not say aloud because of "family values"; because of the newly elected, majority Republican Congress; because of the Clarence Thomas on the Supreme Court; because of "Christianity"; because of the nature of what it means to be a woman; because of the "Pro-Lifers" who shoot doctors in cold blood, planned and executed; because of our husbands and mates; because of *our* mothers and fathers; because of convention; because of all the "shoulds" in our lives; because of *notions* of feminity; because of *ideas* of love and marriage, and relationships; because of *pictures* in our heads of what our home *should* look like; because of *mental images* of what the perfect female body *should* be; because of how we *should* feel; because of encrusted and outmoded definitions of *the family*.

I write instead to acclaim a different voice, and a different life. I write to remember the delight of slipping into an afternoon movie in New York City by oneself, the cool and dark interior of the cinema like a caress. (You can do what you want. Your time is your own.) The extravagence! I write to recall staying up late at night, jazz playing on the stereo, or is it the CD (you can pick what you want, with no excuses), sipping wine and savoring old pictures. Pulling out old journals. Reading. Looking. Remembering. Musing. Dreaming. Commemorating. The time to write a letter. To write in a journal. To learn to hear one's own voice. Time to feel one's own desires. Time to dream one's own dreams.

I write instead to celebrate the lives of other women who have made the choice to be themselves. Who have made the choice, in this case, not to marry. Listen to the words of Oriana Fallaci, for starters, acclaimed, albeit controversial journalist. She claims she chose against marriage because ". . . marriage is an expression that to me suggests 'giving up,' an expression of sacrifice and regret . . . The solitude [I needed] wasn't a physical solitude . . . It was an internal solitude that comes about from the fact of being a woman—a woman with responsibilities in the world of men . . . Today, I need that kind of solitude so much—that sometimes I feel the need to be physically alone. When I am with my companion, there are moments when we are two too many. I never get bored when I'm alone, and I get easily bored when I am with others."

I write instead to commemorate the life of scientist Barbara McClintock, noted geneticist, another woman who listened to her own voice, another woman who has lived her life alone. Her biographer, Evelyn Fox Keller, called the second chapter of her recounting of McClintock's life, *A Feeling for the Organism: The Life and Work of Barbara McClintock*, "The Capacity to Be Alone." Keller recalls a summer many years before that she spent as a graduate student at a laboratory where McClintock was working and describes her memories of the scientist, whom she had never met. "I remembered seeing her—contained, aloof, perhaps even eccentric—going to and from her laboratory or on solitary walks in the woods or by the beach" (p. 16). Years later, when Keller approached McClintock about the proposed biography, McClintock resisted. She did not see how her life could be of interest, and certainly not of value, to other women. After all, and she was adamant on this, she was too different, too much of a "maverick" to be of any conceivable interest to other women. She had never married, never had children. She had never had any interest in what she called "decorating the torso." Keller's argument was that her story was of interest precisely for these reasons.

Keller recounts McClintock's years as an undergraduate at Cornell, in particular her relation to men. In the first two years, she had lived the life of a coed, going out on many dates. "Then," she said, "Then I finally decided I had to be more discriminating. I remember being emotionally fond of several men . . . they were not casual involvements." But she continued, these attachments could never have lasted. "I was just not adjusted," she explained, "never had been, to being closely associated with anybody, even members of my own family . . . There was not that strong necessity for a personal attachment to anybody. I just didn't feel it. And I never could understand marriage. I really do not even now . . . I never went through the experience of requiring it."

Keller associates McClintock's stance with the word "autonomy," with its attendant indifference to conventional expectations. Noting that McClintock has lived most of her life alone—physically, emotionally, and intellectually—Keller also states that no one who has met her could doubt that it has been a full and satisfying life, a life well-lived.

For example, in McClintock's view, conventional science fails to illuminate not only "how" you know, but also and equally, "what" you know. A true naturalist in approach, she sees the need to not press nature with leading questions but to dwell quietly and patiently in the variety and complexity of organisms. Keller speculates that this is a worldview frequently unique to a woman scientist. The recent discoveries—largely led by McClintock—of genetic liability and flexibility forces us to recognize the magnificent integration of cellular processes—a kind of integration that McClintock says is "simply incredible to old-style thinking." This major revolution in thought will completely re-organize things and the way we do research. She adds, "I can't wait. Because I think it's going to be marvelous, simply marvelous. We're going to have a completely new realization of the relationship of things to each other" (p. 207). Certainly not the words of an embittered and frustrated woman, but rather the words of a woman who has trailblazed, usually alone, to reach new heights, and certainly someone who has enjoyed the ups and downs of the journey.

Unfortunately, the single-mindedness of a Fallaci or a McClintock is all too rare. What is more common is the many voices we never get to hear—women's voices hobbled by circumstances of class, color, sex, and the times into which they are born, the cultural and political apparatus that still operates to maintain the *Silences* that writer Tillie Olsen so eloquently and poignantly describe[d] . . .

This was what Virginia Woolf addressed in 1928, when she presented two papers that ultimately became *A Room of One's Own*. She straightforwardly presented the facts as she saw them: for a woman to write fiction she must have money and a room of her own. And therein lies the ultimate rub of the true question of a life lived alone even now for women in 1995. For, as we approach the next millenium, how much have things in actuality changed?

Woolf's solution came in the form of a lifelong legacy bequeathed to her. She remembers, "The news of my legacy reached me one night about the same time that the act was passed that gave votes to women. A solicitor's letter fell into the post box and when I opened it I found that she [Woolf's aunt, who died by a fall from her horse when she was riding in the night air of Bombay] had left me five hundred pounds a year forever. Of the two—the vote and the money—the money, I own, seemed infinitely the more important (Woolf, 1929, p. 37).

There is no doubt about it. The money, the economic freedom, is not always available to women. But again, I write here to celebrate the victories of women, to acknowledge the ability, sometimes against all odds, external and internal, of women to create their own, unique lives. I write to cherish the words of the woman who chooses *against* the conventional wisdom of attachment to others, who structures her life independent of family obligations, the woman who honors her own sensibilities. . . .

I remember my completely single, free, and unencumbered days in New York City with longing. I especially remember my days in graduate school, working on my thesis, a piece of work that intellectually and psychically absorbed me, which my single lifestyle permitted. I re-arranged my one bedroom East side apartment to accommodate my work. I set up a large, aluminum folding picnic table to have the space on which to spread out my books and papers. It was autumn; I had visited the country and returned with drying snowball flowers. Ivory and fat, they hung over my papers, dried and drooping. Doing work on an historical figure, I papered my apartment with pictures needed for inspiration. In a conceptual and methodological daze, I worked, in relative oblivion to life around me. I remember certain Saturday nights; I would work. My respite would be a stroll to the corner deli—a purchase of hot coffee in a paper Blue Acropolis cup that all New Yorkers of certain years can recall. Crossing First Avenue to the corner Newsstand to purchase the Sunday *New York Times* on Saturday night. The pleasure of the stroll home. I remember walking home from the typist, completed thesis in hand. It was a warm New Year's evening, I recall, and nighttime, but the walk was wonderful. No manic exhilaration, but contented sense of achievement. My journal for that January 1 reads:

> *Somehow it seems fortuitous to have ended up*
> *in bed writing tonite*
> *to start tonite Anew, as my thesis winds*
> *down freeing up time & energy—*
> *I truly do feel a sense of achievement*
> *Janet, the typist, has been great*
> *walking down First Avenue to Hunter*
> *foggy, misty, weirdly warm January nite*
> *past the UN, looming in the dark*
> *the River*
> *a New Year, 1985*

Major life changes ensued for me that year.

Despite the advancement of the status of the unmarried female at the conclusion of the nineteenth century, strong sanctions in new forms continued to emerge against those women who lived their lives as they chose—the "new woman," unmarried, and committed to political and social causes. These were the suffragettes, the women of the Settlement House movement, the fighters for fair labor practices and decent treatment of children. This was the first appearance of a new breed of distinctly American womanhood: the single, highly educated, economically autonomous New Woman. This New Woman threatened existing gender relations and challenged distributions of power. And, significantly, they failed. By the 1930s, women and men alike disowned the New Woman's brave visions.

As progressive women reformers had increased their political power in the years immediately preceding the First World War, and as the suffrage movement reached its crescendo, articles complaining of lesbianism in women's colleges, clubs, prisons—wherever women gathered—became common. By the 1920s, charges of lesbianism had become a common way to discredit women professionals, reformers, and educators—as well as the institutions they had founded and run. Women's rights became divorced from their social and economic context. What was the mothers demand for political power and autonomy, was recast as the daughter's quest for heterosexual pleasures. The feminist modernists rejected an older, Victorian or Edwardian female identity, tied as it was to sexual purity and sacrifice. They wished to free themselves from considerations of gender. Victories won by earlier generations of New women in educational and professional arenas had made an androgynous world possible. However, modern women shed their primary identity as woman before the world they inhabited accepted their legitimacy. It is a struggle that continues.

I currently live in tandem; I live with another. But it is not a conventional marriage. I count myself lucky. And still free, unbound, unconstrained. I attribute it to years of single living and a singularly unusual man and partner.

Ultimately, I am compelled to continue to celebrate the alternate, the other, the life as woman lived alone, childless, seemingly rootless, yet reminiscent of Tennyson's experience-hungry Ulysses, scorning family ties to take his being from his world: "I am part of all that I have met." And moreso. All that I dream, all that I imagine, all that I touch, on this journey of a life lived alone, freely chosen.

Founded in 1962 as a nonprofit research and advocacy program to promote women's advancement in corporations and professional firms, Catalyst engages in a variety of activities to put more women in the boardroom. It conducts surveys to determine what barriers lie in the way of women's advancement, advises CEOs and senior partners at law firms, and sponsors an annual Census of Women Corporate Officers and Top Earners, *which quantifies women's progress in achieving top corporate and professional positions. Catalyst's goal is to get women to the top by advocating strategies and identifying workplace environments and policies that promote women's advancement without fundamentally changing the definition and rules of corporate success—that is, by working in the system to make the system more responsive. Following are excerpts from the first edition of a guidebook for corporate leaders that showcases the most effective initiatives and practices.*

SOURCE: Catalyst, *Advancing Women in Business—The Catalyst Guide* (San Francisco: Jossey-Bass, 1998), pp. 59–68. Copyright © 1998 by Catalyst. This material is used by permission of John Wiley and Sons, Inc.

THIS PORTION OF THE BOOK is dedicated to descriptions of best practices that Catalyst has selected, based on benchmarking activities carried out through our basic research activities, proprietary research, and advisory services in individual companies and firms, as well as extensive involvement with corporate change initiatives nominated for the Catalyst Award. These best practices have been demonstrated to improve women's advancement at the organizations where they are used, and they have produced measurable results. They provide examples of approaches that have been used in a wide array of industries and professional services firms.

Initiatives, programs, and processes—rather than companies—are profiled because they can be replicated, with appropriate modifications, in companies seeking to improve their diversity performance. The Catalyst Award focuses on gender initiatives rather than "the best companies for women" because we know there are no perfect companies. Companies approach women's advancement and development in a variety of ways; no one way would be right for every company. Each practice could potentially stand on its own, and it may make sense for a company to begin with one program it can use as a platform to build on. A corporate culture cannot be replicated, whereas these component parts of existing initiatives for advancing women can be. We present these best practices with thanks to the companies whose generative leadership brought them into being and whose commitment sustains them. . . .

Some of the best practices described here may seem obvious or appear to be simple to implement—until one examines the context in which they have been developed and operationalized. Some industries have been difficult if not hostile business environments for women to enter and advance: mail-package-freight delivery, securities, computer software, food services, airlines, engineering, construction, computer data services, trucking, and pipelines. The annual *Catalyst Census of Women Board Directors of the Fortune 500* reports that certain industry areas continue to show the lowest representation of women at the board table, as well. Companies in these industries are starting at a different level of performance; it follows that their best practices may appear rudimentary, that is, focused on programmatic approaches to issues like recruitment or child care as opposed to more comprehensive initiatives. . . .

Most companies that have implemented leadership development programs for women use at least one, and often more than one, of the following:

- Flexibility in arranging work schedules and sites (flexible work arrangements)
- Removal of cultural and environmental barriers to women's advancement
- Early identification of high-potential women
- Leadership development for women that emphasizes lateral moves and line experience

. . .

WOMEN'S ADVANCEMENT

Leadership development is the process by which individuals are provided with the training and experiences needed to assume increasing levels of responsibility within their company. Key leadership development experiences include profit and loss responsibility, learning to direct and motivate subordinates, gaining lateral cooperation, learning how the business works, standing alone, building and using structure and control systems, learning to be tough, persevering under adverse conditions, learning strategies and negotiation tactics, finding alternatives in solving and framing problems, and managing former peers or supervisors.

Upward mobility in corporations involves being selected for and performing successfully in a series of positions that involve increasing responsibility and accountability for business results. There is considerable variation in the way companies approach leadership development and upward mobility for women. Some companies believe that ensuring that women have equal access to training and other corporate development programs will suffice. Other companies have designed programs specifically for women, and still other companies have designed programs that address specific needs of women (and often minorities as well) but make them available to all employees whose performance and tenure qualify them for participation.

Many of the initiatives include explicit provision for formal mentoring arrangements. The word *mentor* is generally understood to mean a trusted counselor or guide. With mentoring's application to business, however, its definition and significance have grown more complicated. The classic mentor-protégé relationship in business is hierarchical in both age and experience. Generally, the responsibility of a mentor is to provide the protégé with the recognition, attention, and guidance she needs for optimum personal and professional growth.

A mentor may serve as a sponsor who nominates and helps advance the candidacy of a protégé for a promotion, pulling the protégé up through the organization. A mentor may also act as a coach, instructing the protégé on the training she needs to accomplish her career objectives and the skills her competition possesses. At times, the mentor may perform the role of protector, intervening or providing guidance to help the protégé avoid difficult situations.

WORK-LIFE PRACTICES

Among the work-family initiatives that have been implemented in companies and professional firms are parental and other dependent care-related leaves, sick leave for dependent care, adoption assistance, flexible spending accounts, domestic partner benefits, child care centers, family day care networks, emergency child care, preschool programs, after school programs, training and support groups, dependent care resource and referral, relocation assistance, and elder care programs.

Implementation of work-family programs is often the first step in a company's development of programs to attract, retain, develop, and advance women. Such programs are fundamental to women's retention and upward mobility, since most women in the U.S. labor force are in their prime childbearing years.

The impact of work-family programs on measurable phenomena such as absenteeism and tardiness and retention are clear. A 1990 study by the Urban Institute showed that 35 percent of mothers with children under twelve years old had a sick child in the last month; 51 percent of them missed work to care for their sick child. A 1987 *Fortune Magazine* study reported that 25 percent of employees with children under twelve years old experienced child care breakdowns two to five times in a three-month period.

Breakdowns were linked to higher absenteeism and tardiness, as well as lower concentration on the job and less marital and parental satisfaction. Aetna increased its retention rate for women from 77 percent to 88 percent when it instituted a six-month leave program with flexible return-to-work possibilities. Based on a cost-of-turnover study that found employee replacement costs 193 percent of annual salary, Aetna estimates its savings to be $1 million per year.

A positive impact of work-family programs on less easily measured factors such as productivity, morale, and loyalty has also been suggested by responses to opinion surveys: six studies have found lower absenteeism and improved productivity to be the most important benefits reported by employees who were surveyed (Conference Board, 1991). Eight studies of manager perceptions of the impact of child care assistance found the major benefits were better morale and lower absenteeism (Conference Board, 1991). A large study that examined corporate responses to maternity found pregnant employees who worked for more family-responsive companies were more satisfied with their jobs, felt sick less often, missed less work, spent more uncompensated time working, worked later in their pregnancies, and were more likely to return to their jobs (National Council of Jewish Women, 1987, 1993).

While work-family programs are necessary and fundamental steps for companies that are concerned about recruitment, retention, development, and advancement of women, they are not sufficient to guarantee women's career advancement, nor are they universally applicable: women with children do not all have the same level of need for corporate-sponsored work-family benefits, and neither do women who never had children. . . .

Corporate best practices in the area of work-life balance run the gamut from child care centers to leaves for elder care to flextime (altering the hours at which one begins and ends the work day while maintaining an eight-hour schedule), part-time, job sharing (two employees jointly fulfill the responsibilities of one position) telecommuting and maternity leaves.

WOMEN'S WORKPLACE NETWORKS

Corporate women's networks provide an opportunity for management as well as a career development resource for women. Catalyst's research on these networks shows that there is no typical group; they vary in terms of membership, structure, and reason for origin. However, most share the same basic goals of encouraging women's professional business objectives. Most groups focus on career and skills development, promotion of networking, and improvement of communication between women and management, or some combination of these activities. Some extend their scope to examine corporate policy issues such as career mobility, managing diversity, and child care. Groups pursue their objectives through a variety of channels, such as speaking engagements, workshops, task forces, and published reports.

GENDER AWARENESS TRAINING AND SAFETY TRAINING

A 1996 article in *Across the Board* pegged the amount companies invest in training at over $30 billion annually. Historically, most training by companies has focused on skills development or enhancement related to production and sales of products and services. Today, companies also provide a range of training opportunities focused on interpersonal competencies like communication and conflict resolution and on human resources management activities such as recruiting, coaching and performance appraisal, and feedback. And manager training is critical to effective implementation, utilization, and evaluation of diversity initiatives.

Training has become increasingly important in companies that are downsizing and restructuring, where a smaller employee base requires a broader skill set. In addition to the original purpose of skills building, training today is used to build teams, change cultures, and communicate company values. Most companies with which Catalyst is familiar have embarked on some form of training around gender awareness and broader diversity awareness programs, as well as activities more focused on sexual harassment or work-life conflicts of employees. . . .

Catalyst's experience shows that training is a necessary component of successful corporate leadership development initiatives, but does not suffice as a stand-alone approach to individual and organizational growth. More and more corporations and firms are including training as part of their overall initiatives to recruit, retain, and advance women. These vary from sexual harassment training and gender awareness training to programs to enhance safety.

"TO RAISE A SUCCESSFUL DAUGHTER"
NICKY MARONE

During the 1990s books and studies such as the American Association of University Women's "How Schools Shortchange Girls" (see their report in chapter 4) and Reviving Ophelia: Saving the Selves of Adolescent Girls *by Mary Pipher, which traced a decline in adolescent girls' self-confidence, documented an alarming rise in feelings of self-doubt, anxiety, and inferiority among American girls. Social scientists, educators, and psychologists offered a battery of proposals to curb this collective decline in self-esteem among the next generation of American women. One such prescription for positive upbringing came from Nicky Marone, a lecturer and workshop leader, who wrote a guide addressed to mothers who want to raise "successful" daughters.*

Marone's definition of success is based primarily on internal notions of resiliency and resourcefulness and less on the usual external measures of achievement and performance. She offers age-appropriate advice for preschool, elementary-grade, and teenage girls. For Marone, nurturing self-efficacy—a belief in one's self and an ability to seize opportunities and achieve desired goals—is key to nurturing successful daughters: daughters who respect themselves and are able to take responsibility for their own choices in life.

SOURCE: From *How to Mother a Successful Daughter* by Nicky Marone (New York: Harmony, 1998), pp. 15–20, 79–92. Copyright © 1998 by Nicky Marone. Used by permission of Harmony Books, a division of Random House, Inc.

AS YOUR DAUGHTER ATTEMPTS to incorporate femininity into her self-image she is likely to experiment with many different aspects of a feminine personality, one which is nice, sweet, passive, small, quiet, polite, deferential to the needs of others, and above all, nonthreatening. She is encouraged to do so by society. "Every time I'm in a bad mood my mother says, 'Jennifer, nobody likes a sad face. Smile!' " volunteered a teenager in one of my workshops for girls. "The thing is, she never says that to my brother, and he's always grouchy." As you already know if you are a woman in this culture, the desire to please, to be polite and inoffensive (feminine), can be the root of many problems women encounter, especially when confronted with the harsher realities of ambition, achievement, and business, not to mention technology, science, and math—in other words, those risky highly competitive arenas that men have already defined.

Right about now a lot of you are undoubtedly feeling pained indignation at the suggestion that we must train femininity out of our daughters if they are to compete with men in the workplace. Mothers in my seminars constantly voice concern that the traditional feminine traits of consensus-building, consideration, and sensitivity to the needs of others are devalued in our culture; yet they represent our last glimmer of hope for a society in which caring for others is a cultural norm.

I agree wholeheartedly. These feminine traits are the glue the holds together relationships, nurtures self and others, and creates consensus in a divided world. Besides, femininity has a fun side. It's exciting to discover the alluring and sexy aspects of oneself. This, too, is part of the experience of puberty, but girls must learn how to handle the powerful forces of their own youthful femininity.

Because this period of oceanic change with regard to sex roles is still in progress at the cultural level, however, enough of the old feminine stereotype remains alive to cause confusion. When deference to others is not a cultural value for all members of the society, an opportunity exists for exploitation. Suffice it to say that strengthening your daughter's achievement-related behaviors and resiliency responses will achieve the goal of creating a strong, hardy, decisive young woman who gets her needs met.

A couple of girls in one of my intervention groups said it best.

"My boyfriend likes me to act all sweet and nurturing," said an African-American girl, "so I do. But I don't confuse it with other stuff."

"Like what?" inquired another.

"Like if I have to ask for a raise," she continued, "my boss couldn't care less how sweet and nurturing I am."

Another girl, a high school senior, chimed in with her variation on the same theme when she recollected the events around a recent audition. "I went back to find out if I made the cut," she began. "I found out I didn't."

"Ahh," everyone murmured, genuinely sympathetic.

"Thanks," she said, "but my point is, I acted like such a *girl*. I sat down on the steps and cried. There was a bunch of guys around who didn't make the cut either. They must have been as disappointed as I was, but they didn't *cry*."

"Well, that's all right," I said, in my most nurturing tones. "Your response was probably healthier. They were just holding their feelings inside."

"Yeah, but that can be a good skill to have when you need it," she observed.

Her point is well taken. When traditional feminine responses are inappropriate—when the moment to ace one's physics exam, run for class president, or annihilate the opposing basketball team has arrived—traditionally feminine behavior can be ineffectual. In situations where even more intense action is required, such as defending oneself against physical abuse, an assault, or a hostile environment, it can be downright dangerous.

RECONCILING SUCCESS AND FEMININITY

If our daughters are to experience the broadest range of success we can envision for them, which means achieving the seemingly dissimilar goals of being self-sufficient *and* attracting a life mate, they must reconcile and bring balance to the shifting, ambiguous, and often conflicting concepts of femininity and achievement. The only reconciliation that makes any sense and gives girls the options they deserve is to teach them how and when to adapt their behavior appropriately so as to do whatever they must do in order to get what they want. That is the only way to prepare them for something even more important than success—*life*.

That old rogue, life, the most demanding of teachers, is supremely indifferent to sex. Life places us in situations that demand great compassion, sensitivity, and the other nurturing qualities associated with femininity. The successful individual, male or female, will respond appropriately. By the same token, life places every individual, male or female, in situations that demand assertiveness and, yes, perhaps even aggression and intimidation—if one is attacked in a dark parking lot in the middle of the night, for example. Again, the successful individual will respond appropriately. For our purposes, then, we shall define the successful individual, male or female, as one who adapts his or her behavior appropriately in each and every circumstance. Such an individual is not hampered by cultural definitions of either femininity (often tainted with helplessness and passivity) or masculinity (competitive and often lacking in compassion).

Successful people are able to modify their behavior and employ a set of responses over the course of a lifetime that enables them to reach desired outcomes—a definition that is synonymous with self-efficacy, achievement, and mastery behavior. Whether they choose to challenge the dominant paradigm or function within it, be employed by a corporate giant or paint watercolors in the garage, enjoy the stimulation of an urban setting or walk the earth in a rural community, raise a family, pursue a career, or none of the above, the common thread is that all successful endeavors, indeed life itself, require a set of skills that remain the same. These skills include taking positive risks; staying resilient and persistent through difficulty, obstacles, and setbacks; and being a creative and strategic problem-solver who copes effectively with change.

THE POWER OF DEEP BELIEFS

At a still deeper level, there must exist a foundation upon which one's behavior rests. It is the belief that one will achieve one's goals. While to some it may seem that a belief is simply too insubstantial to be effective, the truth is that persistent people are persistent because at the deepest level they believe in their ability to bring about whatever future they may envision, regardless of how long it may take or how difficult it may be.

The women in history we venerate today had this sense of self-efficacy and displayed it for all the world to see. They overcame great obstacles, suffered setbacks, knew hardship, and endured public scorn and ridicule. But they were not deterred from their belief in themselves and their mission. The suffragists, the abolitionists, the prohibitionists, the early labor activists who helped establish child labor laws, the pioneers of birth control and women's reproductive rights, the women of the frontier who scratched out an existence in a hostile land, the garment workers in turn-of-the-century sweat-shops, even the southern belles fainting, not from the delicate state of their womanhood, but because they were so tightly corseted that they couldn't breathe—all required belief in themselves, all required self-efficacy to survive in a difficult world.

In the formative and developmental years, girls are immersed in this profound task of building their self-efficacy. The premise of this book is that raising successful daughters is really the challenge to preserve and increase self-efficacy. I will be taking you through these processes step by step, but remember that *in life*, these processes are like a fabric, a tapestry, in which each thread helps to maintain the whole cloth. Your job as a mother is to

- Strengthen and increase your daughter's self-efficacy—that is, the belief in herself that will enable her to see opportunity and bring about desired outcomes.
- Strengthen resiliency so that she can persist through hardships and difficulty.
- Teach and train your daughter in the attitudes and responses that will enable her to adapt her actions and modulate her behavior appropriately to various circumstances.

To raise a successful daughter, every caring mother must ask herself these questions:

- Is my daughter learning the life skills of positive risk taking, resilience, and persistence? Do I model these skills myself?
- Am I teaching my daughter that success and achievement are a set of behaviors rather than a set of goals, processes rather than products, verbs rather than nouns?
- Am I teaching her how to be strong and capable and how to stay safe and secure?
- Am I preparing my daughter to be economically self-sufficient in the twenty-first century?
- Is she receiving the formal education she will need to be competitive in a highly technological society—is she taking math, science, and computer courses?
- Am I teaching her how to vary her behavior according to circumstances?
- Am I helping her to see herself doing important work?
- Am I helping her to believe that the future holds promise for her?
- Am I training her to be a good problem-solver?
- Am I training her to manage change?
- Am I teaching her to cope effectively with doubt, fear, frustration, and disappointment?
- Am I teaching her how to make her own decisions?
- Am I teaching her how to play hard but fair?
- Am I helping her to recognize and appreciate her own unique gifts, regardless of society's opinions?
- Am I helping to create a society that will accept the contributions of my daughter, whatever they may be?

This approach takes nothing away from our daughters. On the contrary, it adds to their behavioral repertoire, putting more tools at their disposal. It opens them up to the full range of their human potential, offering them the full spectrum of behavioral choices from the uninhibited expression of compassionate, intuitive, nurturing femininity to the rugged and hardy display of persistent mastery behavior.

Finally, raising successful daughters is not about coercing them to jump through hoops of our devising. It is about giving our daughters the mastery skills to make their own choices and to be successful at whatever they choose over the course of a whole lifetime. Only in this way can we be sure they will be adequately prepared for the next century.

MOTHER-DAUGHTER MASTERY PROJECTS

Choosing a Learning Goal

Your first task in modeling mastery is to choose learning goals over performance goals. The possibilities are endless. Have fun!

Physical Learning Goals

1. Take a ropes course or wilderness survival course together.
2. Learn to Rollerblade.
3. Learn to dance.
4. Join a team sport you have never played before such as volleyball, soccer, touch football, or basketball.
5. Start a competitive mother-daughter racquetball team.
6. Learn a martial art.
7. Take a self-defense course.
8. Go on an extended backpacking trip.
9. Learn to ski.
10. Learn to water-ski.
11. Learn to snowboard.
12. Take yoga or Tai Chi classes.
13. Get certified in scuba-diving.
14. Go snowmobiling.
15. Go sailing, wind-surfing, or sky-diving.

Intellectual and Financial Learning Goals

16. Take a computer class together.
17. Play the stock market.
18. Start a mother-daughter poker night.
19. Do some household repairs.
20. Change the oil in the car.
21. Learn to play an instrument.
22. Learn a foreign language or visit a foreign country together.
23. Join an animal rights group or some other controversial group together.
24. Build something out of wood.
25. Learn a game of strategy such as chess, Go, or backgammon.
26. Start a reading group.
27. Take a course at a university or museum.

28. Create a Web site.
29. Make a financial plan for a small business.
30. Do a science experiment, using one of the kits available at museums or through environmental organizations.

Avoid Inappropriate Comparisons

The second mastery behavior to model is to avoid making inappropriate comparisons. In fact, avoid comparisons altogether. They do not promote a mastery attitude, and they can damage self-esteem.

Comparisons often inadvertently model a negative aspect of femininity. Trivializing one's own accomplishments by comparing them to someone else's can masquerade as humility—a culturally sanctioned feminine behavior. In fact this kind of humility borders on self-deprecation. Avoid it. Model femininity for your daughter in other ways.

Comparing yourself to others sets up the dangerous dynamic of judging your worth based on accomplishments and success only. As we saw earlier, success can ebb and flow. Judging your worth based on these inconstant factors will not sustain self-esteem during the rough periods of life. Therefore, to properly model mastery for your daughter, you must not undermine your own self-esteem by engaging in comparisons.

As the two of you learn a new game, sport, instrument, or subject, do not compare yourselves to gold medal Olympians, Pulitzer and Nobel Prize winners, supermodels, millionaires, elected officials, or celebrities. In fact, do not compare yourselves to anyone, even each other. The only valid comparison might be to your own progress. For example, it's okay to make the observation that two weeks ago you could barely manage to stand up on your new in-line skates, but now you are able to teeter along for a few yards, wildly flailing your arms and screaming. Acknowledge this breakthrough! Be playful. Don't be heavy-handed about success. Be happy for your own and your daughter's progress, especially the first small steps. Take yourself lightly and have fun.

Be Strategic and Creative

Modeling strategic and creative thinking for your daughter means allowing her to see you make, change, and execute plans, change them again, and then execute your new plan. Involve her whenever possible. Let her observe you and work with you as your assistant or apprentice as you make out a budget, organize a committee, plan a fund-raiser, mobilize a political campaign or local legislative reform, acquire a sponsor, develop a church seminar, figure out how to afford the new addition to your home, argue a case with your boss, write a grant, or present your point of view before a board or even your own husband. Witnessing you in the process of strategizing, and even participating where and when she can, will be invaluable lessons for her future, regardless of whether that future entails painting water-colors in the garage or running for public office. The ability to strategize is a key component of persistence in reaching any goal.

Remember to be creative in developing alternative strategies. For example, be creative about money, since it is easy to use lack of money as an excuse for not trying something new. Suppose you can't afford to take tennis lessons from a pro, for example. Barter for the lessons with something you know how to do. Suppose you can't afford a computer. Rent or trade a bicycle, guitar, lawn mower, or something else you have lying around the house unused for a computer.

Sometimes being creative in developing alternative strategies involves an apparent change of direction. Although persistence is a mastery-oriented behavior, there are no formulas. Take an honest look at the situation to determine if you and your daughter have been persistent. If so, then perhaps taking an alternative tack is the more mastery-oriented approach. My mother, the musician and music teacher, taught me that some people will take naturally to one instrument but not to another. Therefore, sometimes the most creative alternative strategy is simply to pick a different instrument, metaphorically speaking. If the violin is not your daughter's style, have her try the piano, flute, cello, or guitar or something nontraditional for girls like the trumpet, drums, or saxophone. (Next to President Clinton, Lisa Simpson is the most famous amateur saxophone player in the country.) If she doesn't like soccer, try volleyball. If she doesn't like chess, try backgammon or Go.

Because there are many exciting ways to break through problems and develop a variety of routes toward a goal, let your daughter experience the thrill of strategizing and problem-solving. That's how she will learn. Besides, it will be fun for both of you.

"IT'S EXTREMELY DISHEARTENING
TO SEE HOW FAR WE HAVE NOT COME"
REED ABELSON

Perhaps one of the last bastions of gender discrimination in the corpo-rate world is Wall Street. Although women have moved up into middle- and up-per-management on the Street, as it is commonly called, the following article from the New York Times *about a survey conducted by Catalyst of employees at sev-eral major securities firms suggests that female employees are still running up against a glass ceiling or, at the very least, a corporate climate that is not hos-pitable to female advancement. From enduring crude comments by male col-leagues to being excluded from male-dominated networks that are crucial for achieving professional success, the women surveyed indicated that their work-places were not making progress quickly enough to eradicate discriminatory atti-tudes and practices.*

According to the article, this is the first comprehensive survey of women work-ing on Wall Street, and it came at a time when the nation's economy was just be-ginning to falter after eight years of surging prosperity. If women are still facing discrimination during prosperous times, the prospects for female advancement in a weaker economy are even more uncertain.

The survey also reveals that only half of the women questioned have children, compared with about three-quarters of the men surveyed, thus suggesting that wo-men have a harder time—or believe that they will have a harder time—juggling family needs with workplace demands. Together, this document and the one that follows it reveal the double standards and different rules that women must play by in the corporate world.

SOURCE: Reed Abelson. "A Survey of Wall Street Finds Women Disheartened," *New York Times*, 26 July 2001, pp. C1, C15. Copyright © 2001 by the New York Times Co. Reprinted by permission.

WOMEN ON WALL STREET have a hard time arguing with the money to be made, but a survey released yesterday of men and women at seven major secu-rities firms suggests that many women are dissatisfied with the extent of progress that has been made to help women advance in the securities industry.

The findings reaffirm an impression by many women on Wall Street that the industry remains inhospitable.

"It's extremely disheartening to see how far we have not come," said Alexandra Lebenthal, who heads her family's Wall Street firm and has been in the business for about 15 years.

Most of the nearly 500 women who responded to the survey conducted by Catalyst, a nonprofit research and advisory organization in New York, say they are happy with their jobs, citing the challenging work and generous compensation.

But they also describe an industry where it is difficult to get ahead. Two-thirds say that they must work harder than men for the same rewards, and a third report a hostile environment where crude or sexist comments are tolerated, they are treated unfairly or are subject to unwanted sexual attention.

The survey, which is the first extensive look at the experiences of women working on Wall Street, also suggests that many women are making significant sacrifices in their personal lives, similar to the ones made by lawyers and other professionals. Only half of the women surveyed have children, compared with about three-quarters of the men surveyed. In a 1996 survey of senior women at Fortune 1000 companies, about two-thirds had children. Two-thirds of the Wall Street women were married or living with a partner, compared with 86 percent of the men.

While women praise the efforts of the securities firms generally to promote an atmosphere of respect, they say this has not yet translated into a workplace free of harassment or one that can be seen as a true meritocracy. Fewer than half of both men and women said they thought that promotion decisions were made fairly at, their firm. "Cultural change is very tough to make happen," said Sheila Wellington, the president of Catalyst.

Catalyst sent surveys to 2,200 women and men, both in senior and junior positions, at seven firms, the names of which it agreed not to disclose. All the findings were reported anonymously. Some 38 percent, 482 women and 356 men, responded. Catalyst also conducted nine focus groups in New York, Chicago and San Francisco.

About a quarter of the women who responded held the title of managing director or higher, with the typical respondent having worked at her current firm for 10 years and in the industry for 14 years.

The report is part of the settlement of a sex-discrimination lawsuit brought against Smith Barney, now part of Citigroup, in which women charged that there had been a "boom-boom room" in one of the firm's offices, where male managers would harass female employees.

While the leaders of many Wall Street firms are committed to change many in their organizations are not, Ms. Lebenthal said, adding, "I think there are a lot of people on Wall Street who do not see the need to change."

And only a fifth of the women surveyed say that the opportunities to advance have increased greatly in the last five years.

Given the resources many of the firms are pouring into efforts to diversify their work forces and given the large number of women on Wall Street, the lack of progress is surprising, said Dee A. Soder, an executive coach in New York who is managing partner in the CEO Perspective Group. "It's gotten much better," she said, "but there is still a glass ceiling with less reason for a glass ceiling."

There needs to be a greater commitment by the leadership at many Wall Street firms agreed Janice Reals Ellig, an executive recruiter in New York and the co-author of "What Every Successful Woman Knows," which offers advice from senior women executives about how to get ahead. "The progress is so slow," she said. "By the year 3000, we're going to get there."

But some argue that the securities industry is difficult for both men and women. "Wall Street, in general I believe, is undeservedly maligned," said Cristina Morgan, a senior investment banker at J. P. Morgan, the investment banking arm of J. P. Morgan Chase. Many women, and men, choose to leave Wall Street because of the hours and the travel required, she said. The clients "pay us lots and lots of money to be at their disposal 24 hours a day, 7 days a week," she said.

And juggling the demands of a family with the work is extraordinarily hard, Ms. Morgan said, adding: "I am filled with admiration for my women partners who are successful and have children, I am mystified to how they do it." She indicated that she thought Wall Street was indeed a meritocracy.

But many of the women who remain in the business are deciding to forgo having children. "I cannot imagine ever having children and doing this business," a senior-level woman told Catalyst.

Men, of course, are also aware of the sacrifices required to rise on Wall Street, particularly in investment banking. "It's hard to be a middle-level vice president and not spend 90 hours a week at the firm," one man said. "That just doesn't jibe with trying to raise a family."

As a result, many women simply leave, as Janet Tiebout Hanson did when she departed from Goldman, Sachs to create her own firm, Milestone Capital Management. An adviser to Catalyst on the study, Ms. Hanson has also worked to improve the ability of women to network by creating 85 Broads, an Internet-based network of women who work or used to work at Goldman, Sachs. The name refers to the firm's famous address.

Ms. Hanson, for one, is optimistic that securities firms will be forced to change as women, especially those coming out of business school, leave Wall Street for friendlier, if not greener, pastures. Many, she thinks, will go elsewhere in corporate America. "It's a much bigger problem than they think," Ms. Hanson said.

Ms. Soder, the executive coach, agreed, saying, "Corporations are now losing many of the best and the brightest."

Many of the women cited as a barrier to their moving up exclusion from important networks. "Well, it was every broker but me that got invited," a senior-level woman told Catalyst. "So they all got input as to maybe what they were doing wrong, or how they could improve their business, but me."

The survey also offers a glimpse into the continued problem of sexual harassment on Wall Street, which continues to surface from time to time. While sexual harassment is difficult to define and to measure with any precision, with little comparative data in private industries, the survey suggests that many women think that inappropriate or crude comments continue to be tolerated where they work. Some men agree. "In my experience," one said, "brokers are the raunchiest people that you'll ever meet."

About 13 percent of the women surveyed say they receive unwelcome sexual attention at work.

The impetus now, according to Susan Chadick, an executive recruiter who works with Ms. Ellig at Gould, McCoy & Chadick in New York, is to take some of the findings and look deeper. "It requires a lot more probing," Ms. Chadick said.

And she worries that the downturn in the economy may make the future, especially for senior-level women, more bleak. "Not only hasn't there been any progress," she said, but "I'm concerned we're going backward."

"WHEN WOMEN SPEAK THEIR MINDS, THEY'RE SEEN AS HARSH"
NEELA BANERJEE

In the 1980s books such as the best-selling How to Dress for Success *instructed aspiring professional women to look and act the corporate rising star by dressing in conservative gray suits and projecting an image of no-nonsense corporate team player in interviews and on the job. Twenty years later the rules have changed: though in many industries and on Wall Street, women are expected to work the same long, punishing hours as men and produce as much, they are also expected to project a different, softer image from that of their male counterparts— a kinder, gentler corporate demeanor.*

The following article from the New York Times, *about a session of Bully Broads, an executive retraining program designed to "soften" up intimidating women executives, raises interesting questions about double standards for male and female behavior in the corporate workplace and the mixed signals for professional conduct that corporate women must still grapple with.*

SOURCE: Neela Banerjee, "Some 'Bullies' Seek Ways to Soften Up," *New York Times*, 10 August 2001, pp. C1 and C2. Copyright © by the New York Times Co. Reprinted by permission.

MOUNTAIN VIEW, CALIF.—The first Thursday of every month, about a dozen women executives gather in this Silicon Valley town to repent and change their ways.

They sit in a ring, the picture of corporate propriety in their suits and low-heeled mules, turning off cell phones before the confessions begin. "I'm Suzann," says Suzann Manteufel, a financial executive at Sun Microsystems, "and I'm a recovering bully broad." She slumps in her chair. "Or maybe I should say, a relapsing one."

They continue around the circle. "I came here—excuse me, I was sent here—two years ago because of my intolerance for incompetence," says Debra Martucci, vice president for information technology at a software design firm, "and for having a level of passion for my job that scared people to death."

By many measures, these women would seem to need little help. They are experienced executives who have pushed their companies to higher profits and wooed the most clients. But nearly all have been told that the toughness that made them six-figure successes has become a liability, preventing them from rising higher. Their no-nonsense ways intimidate subordinates, colleagues and, quite often their bosses, who are almost invariably men.

And so they have ended up here for an unusual kind of executive coaching, a program called Bully Broads that offers a new set of rules for getting ahead. For women to succeed now, they must become ladies first, says the program's founder, Jean A. Hollands, who has coached hundreds of executives over the last 15 years. Ditch all that hardball stuff from the 80's—being assertive, standing firm—and learn to hold your tongue, stammer and couch what you say. Don't choke back tears if you start to cry at a meeting. . . .

Such advice, needless to say, raises the hackles of any number of women executives and management experts; life and work are more complicated, they say, than a stark choice between being tough and being tearful. Still others note that being tough certainly seems to have worked well for men. "I think women in many cases need to be more aggressive," said Alexandra Lebenthal, chief executive of the brokerage firm Lebenthal & Company.

Yet in training female executives, Ms. Hollands realized that she was repeatedly tackling the same problem: their companies found them scary. Two-years ago, she gathered 30 women for what was to be a one-time meeting. But the women, she says, wanted it to be continuing, and 17 have stayed with the program from the start.

Nobody defends abusive behavior by top executives, male or female. But men, Ms. Hollands says, seldom hear that vulnerability is the route to power. Few men who come to her coaching firm, the Growth and Leadership Center, are labeled bullies, with the vast majority sent to learn how to delegate or handle stress better. But of the women who come, 95 percent, she says, are sent because of "intimidating styles."

"Many of the things these women do would not be as inappropriate in a man," Ms. Hollands said. "We want these women to be more powerful and not feel more victimized, thinking, 'We don't get the same consideration men do.' We don't. So what? We've only been in the work force as leaders for 50 years. Men have a 600-year head start on us."

Nearly all the women who attend Bully Broads were sent to Ms. Hollands by their companies, and most, at the beginning, rolled their eyes like they do when they hear dumb things at staff meetings.

"I feel like I've landed at an A.A. meeting," said a distressed Kyung Yoon, a first-time participant who runs the North Asia operations for her executive search firm. "I'm not a bully; I'm not obnoxious; I'm not unreasonable," Ms.

Yoon says, chopping one hand into another for emphasis and looking around for backup.

"Where'd you get that gesture?" asks Laura Steck, one of the group's facilitators.

Ms. Yoon will probably come around. The first stage in the Bully Broad makeover is always denial Ms. Hollands says. Some longtimers are still shaken from hearing what others at work think of them, information culled from so-called 360-degree job reviews that allow not just superiors, but colleagues and subordinates, to assess one's performance.

Helen Kinnaman still thinks that maybe she rubs colleagues the wrong way because she is an over-caffeinated New Yorker in laid-back California. . . .

Her clients loved her. Her co-workers didn't. She didn't say please and thank you or greet everyone as she walked down the hall. Many men at her company don't either, but she was sent to Ms. Hollands for her "intimidating style."

"Some of the, um, modifications Jean suggested have helped me," Ms. Kinnaman says. "I just said 'um.' I never used to say 'um.' But I'll pause more now. I'll pause after a stressful call before sending off an e-mail or talking to someone about getting something done."

As he tries to tiptoe out of the office, Ron Steck, a vice president at the Growth and Leadership Center and Ms. Hollands's son-in-law, is summoned to the meeting to offer a man's insight—the prevailing insight—into the ways of powerful women.

"With a male executive, there's no expectation to be nice," he said. "He has more permission to be an ass. But when women speak their minds, they're seen as harsh."

"Well, I'd tell the men to get over it," says Julia Campbell, who recently stepped down as the head of information technology at a company because, she suspects, she could not hide her lack of respect for the founder.

Ms. Hollands counters: "Can you get over your DNA? This is a deeply embedded thing in them."

One new arrival to the Thursday meeting this month recalled telling a colleague, a favorite of her bosses, that she was "disappointed" he had usurped her professional turf. Some women praised her for staying calm and using the word "disappointed."

But Ms. Hollands worried she had burned her bridges with a rising star. "Did you use any foreplay?" she asked.

"Foreplay?"

"When you deliver bad news, you have to give foreplay," she said. "You know: 'I know you must be busy, and I know this is a big field, and it's been hard for me to accept others on it, so I might get a bit testy as I talk about this.' " . . .

Ms. Hollands says that about 25 of the 30 participants in Bully Broads have received better job reviews, more responsibility or promotions.

Management experts agree with Ms. Hollands that expectations for office behavior are changing, but they are concerned that her advice reinforces a longstanding double standard at work.

Joyce K. Fletcher, a professor at the Simmons Graduate School of Management in Boston, which offers the nation's only women-only M.B.A. program, said the new corporate approach favors using more inclusive, softer language to coax employees to speak up. But women who talk that way, she said, are seen as lacking in confidence.

It is the Catch-22 of that corporate mindset that needs to change, she said, more than the personalities of individual women. "I have no problem sending women to executive training to deal with a hostile environment," said Professor Fletcher, "but not if you aren't doing something to address that environment."

Still, the Bully Broads premise seems to reflect the moment. Whether in love or work, it can seem these days that the most acceptable woman is the nice girl. The woman whose playbook is "The Rules," the bestselling throwback guide to playing hard to get, stands the best chance of snaring her dream man. The spouse who cedes control to her husband, as prescribed in another best seller, "The Surrendered Wife," stands the best chance of keeping him.

The cultural message sent to women "is confusing," said Jean Baker Miller, a professor of psychology and organizational training at Wellesley College. "Should you be like men? No, you shouldn't be like men." And so women figure, "Oh well, let's just go back to the old ways."

The desire to climb higher on the corporate ladder—and perhaps a longing to be liked—keep most of the executives in Bully Broads coming back to their new finishing school. But if the women manage to get over their disbelief at being labeled bullies, acceptance of ladylike ways is harder.

Michelle Whiting, 42, is one of the few women to enroll herself in Bully Broads. From 1993 to 1997, she nurtured a start-up, as its controller, into a $178 million company that she helped take public. Despite her success, she knew she had a reputation for being tough.

"I'd talk to people and make them cry, and then I'd become more infuriated because I thought they were weak," she tells the group. "God, I can't imagine what they were saying about me behind my back."

For the last 18 months, she has worked hard at letting go of the daily battles at work to build lasting good will. But Ms. Whiting says she's "in crisis" now, having spent the last three days arguing with her boss over pay and other issues.

"Have I told Jean this? No!" she said in an interview. "She would tell me never to yell at a manager. But damn it, if I hadn't yelled at him, I would never have gotten this meeting to sort out the situation. You need an act of civil disobedience to get any attention at that firm. . . . I know I'm not supposed to say this," she says, "but I like the fact that the women in our group are proud, have strong convictions and aren't afraid to speak their minds."

She considers her own transgressions and finally adds, "Do I feel bad that I yelled? Well, yeah. But, hell, maybe we can't be reformed after all."

"OUT OF OUR SHEER HUMANITY
COMES COMMON GROUND"
ELIZABETH BIRCH

*In September 1995 the Christian Coalition, a nationwide grassroots po-
litical movement of fundamentalist Christians who oppose homosexuality, abortion, and many tenets of the feminist movement, held a conference in Washington,
D.C. Elizabeth Birch, director of a national nonprofit organization called the Human Rights Campaign (HRC), appealed to the Christian Coalition's director,
Ralph Reed, for an opportunity to speak at the conference. Her request, not surprisingly, was refused; the HRC is one of the country's most powerful gay rights organizations, and Birch herself is a lesbian. Undaunted, Birch went to the hotel
where the conference was being held and gave a speech, which drew a few members of the press and some curious Christian Coalition members. Birch's speech
was an eloquent plea for tolerance and for working to establish common ground
between the two organizations. Despite the temperate tone of the speech, Birch
makes it clear that gay and lesbian Americans will continue to defend their fundamental right to exist and will not be intimidated by hostile opposition.*

SOURCE: Reprinted by permission of the Human Rights Campaign.

Dear Members of the Christian Coalition:

An open letter was not my first choice as a way of reaching you. I would have
preferred speaking to all of you directly, and in a setting where you would
be most comfortable.

That was my motivation some weeks ago when I asked your executive director, Ralph Reed, for the opportunity to address the Christian Coalition's
"Road to Victory" conference. It is still my motivation today. And it is supported by a single, strong belief that the time has come for us to speak to
each other rather than past each other.

It took Mr. Reed very little time to reject my request. Perhaps he misunderstood my motivation. But I can assure you that what has driven my request is this: I believe in the power of the word and the value of honest communication. During my years of work as a litigator at a major corporation,
I was often amazed at what simple, fresh, and truthful conversation could
accomplish. And what is true in the corporate setting is also true, I'm convinced, in our communities. If we could learn to speak and listen to each
other with integrity, the consequences might shock us.

Although your podium was not available to me, I am grateful for those who have come today and will give me the benefit of the doubt and be willing to consider what I have to say. I will be pleased if you are able to hear me without prejudging either the message or the messenger. And I will be hopeful, most of all, if you respond by joining me in finding new ways to speak with honesty not only *about* one another, but also *to* one another.

If I am confident in anything at all, it is this: Our communities have more in common than we care to imagine. This is not to deny the many differences. But out of our sheer humanity comes some common ground. Although the stereotype would have us believe otherwise, there are many conservative Americans within the nation's gay and lesbian communities. What's more, there are hundreds of thousands of Christians among us—Christians of all traditions, including those represented in the Christian Coalition. And, like it or not, we are part of your family. And you are part of our community. We are neighbors and colleagues, business associates and friends. More intimately still, you are fathers of sons who are gay and mothers of daughters who are lesbians. I know many of your children very, very well. I work with them. I worry with them. And I rejoice that they are part of our community.

Part of what I want you to know is that many of your children who are gay and lesbian are gifted and strong. Some are famous. Most of them are not. But many are heroic in the way they have conquered barriers to their own self-respect and the courage with which they've set out to serve a higher good. All were created by God. And you have every right to be proud of each of them.

I begin by noting the worthiness of the gays and lesbians in your family and our community for a reason: It's hard to communicate with people we do not respect. And the character of prejudice, of stereotype, of demogoguery, is to tear down the respect others might otherwise enjoy in public, even the respect they would hold for themselves in private. By taking away respectability, rhetorically as well as legally, we justify the belief that they are not quite human, not quite worthy, not quite deserving of our time, of our attention, of our concern.

And that is, sadly, what many of your children and colleagues and neighbors who are gay and lesbian have feared is the intent of the Christian Coalition. If it were true, of course, it would be not only regrettable, but terribly hypocritical. It would not be worthy of the true ideals and values based in love at the core of what we call Christian.

The reason I have launched this conversation is to ask you to join me in a common demonstration that this is not true. I make my appeal as an individual, Elizabeth Birch, and also as the executive director of the Human Rights Campaign Fund, America's largest policy organization for gay men and lesbian women.

This is such a basic appeal to human communication and common decency that I do not even know how to distinguish between what is personal and what is professional. But my appeal is sincere. I am convinced that if we cannot find ways to respect one another as human beings, and therefore to respect one another's rights, we will do great damage not only to each other, but also to those we say we represent.

I recognize that it is not easy for us to speak charitably to each other. I have read fund-raising letters in which people like me are assigned labels which summon up the ugliest of dehumanizing stereotypes. Anonymous writers have hidden under the title of "Concerned Christian" to condemn me with the fires of God and to call on all of you to deny me an equal opportunity to participate in the whole range of American life. I have heard of political agendas calling not merely for the defeat of those I represent, but for our eradication.

Such expressions of hatred do not—cannot—beget a spirit of trust. Nor do they pass the test of either truthfulness or courage. They bear false witness in boldface type. And I believe that they must embarrass those who, like me, heard of another gospel—even the simple Gospel taught me as a child in Sunday School.

I would not ask that you, as members of a Christian group, or as supporters of a conservative political cause, to set aside either your basic beliefs or your historic commitments. The churches which many of you represent—Baptist, for example, and Pentecostal—were also the churches I attended as a young woman. In those days, I heard sermons about justice and sang songs about forgiveness. My greatest hope is not that you will give up your faith, but that it will work among all of us.

Neither of us should forsake our fundamental convictions. But we could hold those convictions with a humility that allows room for the lives of others. Neither of us may be the sole possessors of truth on every given issue. And we could express our convictions in words that are—if not affectionate, and if not even kind then at least decent, civil, humane. We need not demonize each other simply because we disagree. . . .

Many of us in this community have a long history with the church. . . .

For some, the deepest agony of life is not that they risk physical abuse or that they will never gain their civil rights, but that they have felt the judgment of an institution on which they have staked their lives: the church. What they long for most is what they once believed was theirs as a birthright: the knowledge that they are God's children, and that they can come home.

And it is not only those of us who are gay or lesbian who have suffered on the doorstep of some congregations. Parents, fearing what others at church might whisper, choose to deny the reality that their son is gay or their daughter is a lesbian. Brothers and sisters suffer an unhealthy, and unwarranted, and un-Christian shame. They bear a burden that cripples their faith, based on a fear that cripples us all.

This means, I think, that we are still a long way from realizing the ideal of America as a land of hope and promise, from achieving the goal of religion as a healing force that unites us, from discovering that human beings are, simply by virtue of being human beings, deserving of respect and common decency.

And so, I have come today—in person, bearing this letter, and in writing, to those who will only receive it—to make three simple, sincere appeals to those of you who are members of the Christian Coalition.

The first appeal is this: Please make integrity a watchword for the campaigns you launch. We all struggle to be people of integrity, especially when we campaign for funds. But the fact that we are tempted by money is no excuse. We need to commit ourselves to a higher moral ground.

I do not know when the first direct-mail letter was issued in your name that defamed gay men and abused gay women, that described us as less than human and certainly unworthy of trust. Neither do I know when people discovered that the richest return came from letters that depicted gays and lesbians with intentionally dishonest images. But I do know—and I must believe that you know too—that this is dishonest, this is wrong.

I can hardly imagine that a money machine is being operated in your name, spinning your exaggerations as if they were truths and that you do not see it. But perhaps you do not. In which case, I ask that you hear my second appeal: I ask that, as individuals, you talk to those of us who are gay or lesbian, rather than succumb to the temptation to either avoid us at all cost, as if we are not a part of your community, or to rant at us, as if we are not worthy of quiet conversation.

We are, all of us and those we represent, human beings. As Americans, you will have your political candidates; we will have ours. But we could, both of us, ask that our candidates speak the truth to establish their right to leadership, rather than abuse the truth in the interest of one evening's headline. We may work for different outcomes in the elections, but we can engage in an ethic of basic respect and decency.

Finally, I appeal to you as people who passionately uphold the value of the family. You have brothers and sons who have not heard a word of family affection since the day they summoned the courage to tell the simple truth. You have sisters and daughters who have given up believing that you mean it when you say, "The family is the basic unit of society," or even, "God loves you, and so do I."

Above all the other hopes with which I've come to you hovers this one: that some member of the Christian Coalition will call some member of the Human Rights Campaign Fund and say, "It's been a long time, son," or "I'm missing you, my daughter," and before the conversation ends, someone will hear the heartfelt words, "Come home. Let's talk to each other."

In that hope, I appeal to each of you.

"I FEEL I'M NEITHER HERE NOR THERE"

DIANE K. SHAH

*Women professionals, like their male counterparts, often endure a great
deal of traveling for their jobs. Business and corporate women on the road face special problems in juggling work demands with family needs, not least of which is
feeling even more cut off from family crises and exigencies, as the following document illustrates. Note, too, how hoteliers have begun to accommodate women
travelers, indicating they recognize that female travelers are now a steady and vital part of their business.*

SOURCE: Diane K. Shah, "A Suitcase Full of Guilt," *New York Times Magazine*, March 8,
1998, section 6, pp. 57–8. Reprinted by permission of Diane K. Shah.

4:45 A.M. It's pitch black out as Eileen Oswald, like a thief in the night, wheels
a carry-on bag out the front door and heaves it into the trunk of her silver 1989
BMW. Moments later, her car steals down the drive while upstairs, in the spa-
cious two-story brick colonial, her husband and two children sleep.

5:10 A.M. Oswald arrives at O'Hare International Airport in Chicago. Entering precisely the right ramp and winding up to precisely the right level—four—
she parks in a row leading out of the garage (all the better for a fast getaway).
Then she wheels her bag 30 feet to a door that goes straight into the American
Airlines terminal.

5:20 A.M. The man behind the counter chats with Oswald as he automatically upgrades her to first class. Now, heading for the gate, she scans the passengers for familiar faces. "It's like taking a bus to work," she says with a smile.
"You get to know the people on the route."

6 A.M. Strapped into her seat, Oswald awaits takeoff to La Guardia in New
York. "Five hours," she announces cheerfully, "from my house to my office.
That's my commute."

With the timed precision of a blast-off from Cape Canaveral, Eileen Oswald
travels every Tuesday from her home in Lincolnshire, Ill., to her office in Nor-
walk, Conn., where, as vice president and general manager of Ullo International, a high-tech marketing and communications company, she's boss to 30
men and women in the trade-show division. By sunrise on Thursday, she's
checking out of her no-frills (no room service) hotel and—luggage in rental
car—heading for the office. Thursday nights she leaves at 6:30 for the hourlong
drive to La Guardia, where she boards the 8 P.M. flight to O'Hare. If all goes

without a hitch, she'll get home shortly after 10, look in on her sleeping children, chat with her husband, Timothy, then walk the dog before tumbling into bed. At 7:30 Friday morning, as Tim leaves for work, Eileen walks into her home office, just as the Connecticut folks arrive at work, to telecommute at the end of another typical week.

When there is one. A perky 43-year-old with curly blond hair and a dimpled smile, Oswald orchestrates a dozen or so of the 80 exhibitions that Ullo mounts yearly. During a show—like the one for boat builders in Fort Lauderdale in February, followed days later by the wine show in Sacramento—she's on scene, making sure things run smoothly. "I'm probably on the road 70 percent of the year," she says.

Oswald's work life is not more physically taxing than that of many others, but it takes an emotional toll. "I feel I'm neither here nor there," she laments. "Where's home? I worry that I'm not in any place long enough to have an impact on either one."

Oswald is far from alone with her frequent-flier life or the suitcase of guilt she, like other mothers, totes with her. By the year 2000, according to travel-industry projections, female foot soldiers will make up half of the nation's army of business travelers. Many have children and come wired to precise calendars noting activities while Mommy's away—Susie's book report due; Billy's Cub Scout meeting; Dad's two-day trip, and, oh, God, the dishwasher repairman on Wednesday. And unlike traveling dads who "try to," traveling mothers always call home at night. Yet despite her protective reach from the road, Oswald confesses, "It doesn't remove the tremendous guilt I feel for my children."

Life on the road has noticeably improved in recent years as hotels, airlines and car-rental agencies scramble to accommodate the growing numbers of cash-bearing female business travelers, currently estimated at 17.2 million. Not that women weren't "accommodated" in the past. Until 1924, the Palmer House in Chicago had a separate entrance that unescorted women were required to use—and a ladies' floor complete with matrons to strap them into their corsets. In the 60's, Hiltons provided "pink" rooms for women. Even throughout the 70's, women alone were often greeted with a wink and a leer.

Now, regarded not so much as anomalies as potential gold mines, women are under the microscope of every major hotel chain. For instance, last summer Hyatt Hotels and Resorts commissioned a study of business travelers and, from 500 responses, gleaned that the average female traveler is 43 and that 69 percent are married or living as married. And while most married men rely on their spouses to take care of the children and run the house in their absence, women often rely on family members or hired help.

Security, a major concern of female travelers, has been given top priority. Better lighting, indoor courtyards instead of exterior ones, electronic-key systems and peepholes have become the norm. Most hotels will also provide an escort to anyone nervous about parking in the garage or walking to a room. But Chad Callaghan, Marriott's senior director of loss prevention, warns: "More and more, we're seeing acquaintance assault. It's difficult for hoteliers to prevent that."

Mostly, women brush off unwanted advances themselves. Jillian Hoffman travels twice a month selling a New York-based hedge fund. In her mid-20's and standing 5 foot 4, she says: "I wear very high heels, but I still come across as little. My boss gave me a body alarm, which I keep in my purse. Yes, I get hit on a lot. But any woman in the financial industry is going to have that. You deal with it." Or, as Alison Dohring, 36, a stockbroker turned money manager, puts it: "If you're attractive, you're going to get hit on. I grew up in New York. I can handle men."

Eyes fixed on the bottom line, hotel marketing executives are clambering to provide other amenities they think women want. Thus the sudden appearance of hair dryers, coffee makers, ironing boards and irons. ("Are they kidding?" snorts Jamie Fragen, a Microsoft saleswoman. "I don't even iron at home.") Tim Sullivan, area director of marketing for the Pavilion Marriott in St. Louis, boasts: "One woman complained there was nowhere to put her hanging bag when she was checking in. So we attached a hook to the reception desk." Hot on the trail, too, is Morris Lasky, C.E.O. of Lodging Unlimited, who has begun marketing to hotels a kind of bathroom minibar stuffed with stockings, blowup pillows for the bathtub, tampons, emery boards—everything but the kitchen sink.

Meanwhile, all manner of surveys fly out of the fax machines. In one, Marriott discovered that 7 percent of all business travelers—mark this down—never leave home without a stuffed animal, the teddy-bear-toters equally divided between women and men. And, oh, yes: 1 percent of men say the single personal "item" they can't do without is their wife. None of the nearly 100 women polled mentioned husbands.

LIKE MANY SEASONED TRAVELERS, Oswald knows the hotels, the airlines and most of the folks along the way. "I thought you were going to Paris," she says to the Avis guy at La Guardia. Rarely does she feel slighted by flight attendants who dote on men and ignore her. "The only horror stories I have about travel," she notes, "is the travel." Rather, like many of her colleagues, she grapples with the dicier issues that come with leading two lives. "Our conversation tends to be, What do you do about child care?" she says.

The Oswalds seem to be doing everything possible for Tom, 11, and Sarah, 7. Tim Oswald, an intense, taciturn man of 43, works for Abbott Laboratories, and he has tailored his schedule to fill Eileen's gaps. The couple employ a baby sitter who arrives each morning at 7:30 and leaves at 6 when Tim walks in the door to cook dinner and help with the homework. But even though his office is a short distance from school, it is Eileen whom the baby sitter calls first, whether to report a sniffle or to make sure it's O.K. for Sarah to visit a friend after school. On weekends, Eileen pays the bills, does laundry and goes grocery shopping. "I try to overcompensate," she says. "I don't want to put extra pressure on my husband."

When Eileen was offered the Ullo job two years ago, Tim was reluctant to give up his career at Abbott, and the onus shifted to her. A math major who left Michigan State University without a degree, Eileen has always worked, climbing the corporate ladder once before making her latest move. "I like to work," she says. "And as long as I have the support of my family, I'm going to continue to do what I do."

Still, it's a life fraught with anxiety. Jamie Fragen, 33, the single mother of a 4-year-old daughter, at times feels as if she's doing a high-wire act. As a "sales evangelist" for Microsoft, Fagen, based in Los Angeles, is on the road each week teaching the ignorant the marvels of the Internet. "There's nothing worse," she says, "than sitting on a runway, realizing you won't be home in time for your child's play at school." Fragen has learned to make every minute count. Make-up is applied on the plane, hotel rooms better have two phone lines—three's ideal—not to mention a massage service and a gym down the hall. "Traveling dads aren't as sensitive to their kids as moms," she says. "After a meeting, they'll want to have a drink. Me? I want to exercise, do a few hours of work, talk to my daughter and enjoy the only free time I have for myself."

When all support systems fail, Fragen takes her daughter on the road. "My daughter's already got a frequent-flier number, and when I open my laptop on the plane, she whips out her toy laptop," she says. But the nagging guilt never subsides. "Is she going to be independent—or a head case?"

Some of these women eventually decide enough is enough. Five years ago, at age 38, Pat Dolson was promoted to regional president of Reed Exhibition Companies, where she managed about 50 shows a year. "I traveled to board meetings, our trade shows, our competitors' shows, to Germany, France and Asia," she says. "I had superior child care, high compensation and no guilt. But increasingly, I felt a need to be home. My kids are so interesting. I wanted to be with them." Last summer she resigned. "I had been able to achieve what I'd wanted to," she theorizes. "So I thought: What do I want to do now? Be chairman and never get off the plane?"

5:15 P.M. Tuesday. since arriving at her Connecticut office, Oswald has reviewed plans for two shows, talked to outside reps who sell booth space and handled personnel problems. Only right now, she is on the phone dealing with a family crisis 750 miles away. Eyes wide with fright, she explains, "My son didn't get off the school bus."

When Tom hadn't come through the front door at the usual time, the baby sitter, panicked, phoned Oswald. While the baby sitter took the cell phone and went searching, Oswald called a neighbor thinking that maybe Tom went home with a friend. No answer.

Minutes later, Oswald phones again, this time reaching the other boy's mother. It turned out that she had gone looking for the boys in her car and found them playing nearby. "Send Tom home," Oswald says woodenly. "I want to talk to him. Privately."

Twenty minutes later, Oswald is explaining to Tom why he must check in at home first. Assuring the boy that she'll phone later, she hangs up with a sigh.

6:20 P.M. Oswald leaves the office and drives a mile to her hotel. She carries no mementos from home, only pictures of her children in her checkbook, "'Cause I always have that with me."

7:10 A.M. Wednesday. Coffee in hand, she unlocks the office door. Today there will be no crisis calls, just the normal workload.

It's 5 o'clock before Oswald remembers that she hasn't had lunch.

The expression "soccer mom" came into vogue in the early 1990s to de-
scribe mothers, who, in the nineties version of the family station wagon, the mini-
van, spent their days chauffering their children from one activity to another. Of
course, as the following article points out, not only stay-at-home mothers but also
working mothers, and fathers, are kept busy chauffering their children to sports ac-
tivities, music lessons, and other extracurricular activities. Here is a glimpse of life
in the fast lane for families who want their children to have it all.

SOURCE: Barbara Kantrowitz and Pat Wingert, "The Parent Trap," *Newsweek*, January 29, 2001, pp. 49–53. Copyright © 2001 Newsweek, Inc. All rights reserved. Reprinted by permission.

ALL FALL, Suzanne Upton of Ann Arbor, Mich., struggled to manage her children's demanding schedule: homework plus soccer and hockey for Sam, 9, and piano, soccer and ballet for Annie, 7. It wasn't easy, especially with Sam's required practices—three days a week for soccer and five days for hockey. The Christmas season, filled with school parties, threatened to be even more hectic. Then the snow started falling . . . and falling . . . and falling. Four housebound days later, the family had baked cookies and generally mellowed out. Those snow days, Upton says, "were God's way of telling us to slow down."

But that's not likely. These days, raising kids is like competing in a triathlon with no finish line in sight. Millions of parents around the country say their lives have become a daily frantic rush in the minivan from school to soccer to piano lessons and then hours of homework. But they're trapped, afraid to slow down because any blank space in the family calendar could mean their off-spring won't have the résumés to earn thick letters from Harvard—and big bucks forever after. And a busy schedule at the office only adds to the pressure. . . .

Although the current generation of parents is the richest and best educated in history, they are particularly apprehensive because they're raising their kids in an uncertain time. In a world where a high divorce rate and job hopping are the norm, "parents themselves are more insecurely placed in life," says Arlie Hochschild, a sociologist at the University of California, Berkeley, who studies modern family life. Rapid technological change has contributed to that sense of instability, says Stephanie Coontz, a professor of history and family studies at Evergreen State College in Washington. She thinks today's middle-class parents are reacting to the aftershocks of the seismic shift to the digital economy, just as blacksmiths and farmers in the 1820s worried that *their* kids wouldn't make it through the Industrial Revolution. "Parents today are having a comparable anxiety crisis," says Coontz. "What do you do to protect your child and secure them a good future?" No one really knows the answer to that question. Thirty years ago a college degree was the key to the good life. Today's parents fear that a B.A. isn't good enough, but they're not sure what's better. So they try to give their kids a little of everything that's available.

Parents sacrifice their dwindling free time (and their own social lives) to make sure their kids are safe and want for nothing. It starts off innocently enough, with playdates for their toddlers set up weeks in advance. Then it snowballs to the point where everyone is overwhelmed—and bragging about it. In elementary school, many youngsters attend activities every afternoon because their parents are afraid to let them ride bikes down the street. Workdays end with frenzied trips to pick up the kids; no one wants to leave a 6-year-old alone on a soccer field in the dark. . . .

For many parents, activities that used to be just for fun now seem to have lifelong consequences. Sports are particularly fraught; no one wants to raise a loser. Brad Bole, a stockbroker who volunteers as the coach of his sons' soccer and hockey teams in Marietta, Ohio, says he's constantly trying to get the "really intense" parents to calm down. But he's not always successful. "I had a mother come over to me and tell me she thought Brad really needed to push the kids more," says his wife, Babette. "They want that intensity. They want their children to be fighters. They want them to be hustling."

That intensity is fueled by stories about champions like Venus and Serena Williams or Tiger Woods, whose very involved parents were key to their success. The message: champions are made, not born. That message is reinforced by childbearing advice in books and magazines that stresses the importance of stimulating developing young brains. Parents think they can't let up; every minute of the day has to have a purpose. That's why Angela Collins, 40, a mother of four in La Grange, Ill., a Chicago suburb, says she spends so much time driving her three older kids to activities that her 1-year-old, Malachy, is practically being raised in the family minivan. "When he's not in the van, he's somewhat disoriented," she says. "It's funny, but kind of sad, too." Caileen, 10, is signed up for Irish dancing, church choir, soccer and Girl Scouts; Quinn, 8, has soccer, baseball, basketball and Boy Scouts, and Kristen, 5, has Irish dancing, soccer and Daisies (the youngest rank of Girl Scouts). "Our parents think we're insane because we're flying all over the place," says Collins. "My husband

[Patrick, 40] is one of 13 kids, and I don't think his parents did as much running around as we do with four. But I feel it's part of my job, my obligation, to expose my children to the arts, sports, various activities." But while parents believe they need to be constantly on top of things at home, the corporate culture is demanding that they put in longer hours at the office as well. Americans are working harder than anyone else in the world, including the Japanese. According to a 1997 study by the International Labor Organization, fathers were working an average of 50.9 hours, while mothers were working 41.4 hours. So you have the spectacle of parents on their mobile phones taking care of business while they're cheering their kids on the football field, and parents working late at the office correcting their kids' homework by e-mail and fax. Even if parents wanted to cut back at work, they couldn't afford it. They need the big paycheck to foot the bill for tutoring or tennis lessons.

Jane Sullivan, the mother of 6-year-old Jack and 1-year-old Bridget, performs what she describes as a "daily ballet" taking care of her family and staying on top of her job as the director of public relations for San Francisco International Airport. Her husband, John, runs his own graphics business. "I say that we are a working family; we all kind of work," says Jane. "We cook, cook, cook through the day. And it's not just me and my husband. The kids are on a treadmill, too." Still, she tries to make time for Jack's weekly swim lessons. "I carve out a slice of my day so I can take him," she says, "but just because I'm there doesn't mean I can switch from working woman back to Mom. There are all these nonworking moms looking at me as I get calls on my cell phone." Jack, a first grader, is already showing signs of burnout. Homework that should take no longer than 20 minutes to complete often takes an hour or more to get through. "He doesn't see us much, and this is his time to act out," she says. "We have battles in which he tests us. Maybe this is his way of getting us to fully focus on him." . . .

Even as they struggle to get through the day, many parents know that on some level all this overscheduling could be harmful. They just aren't sure how to cut back without depriving their kids. Take, for example, the Hagner family in Boston, N.Y., outside Buffalo. A day with mom Cathy Hagner makes those opening-credit shots on "ER" look like slow motion. The kids—Brenden, 12, Matthew, 10, and Julie Ann, 8—are signed up for hockey, soccer, basketball, flag football, skiing and piano. And that's on top of a full load of schoolwork and assorted extra projects. "My whole day, from the time they come home to the time they go to bed, is spent doing homework and running them around," says Hagner. "Yesterday I spent four solid hours in the car. First Brenden had to go to basketball, then I took Julie to a soccer game, then I went back to the basketball game to get Brenden and take him to the flag-football game, while my husband went and got Julie, and it just went on from there. By the time it was all over, all I had done other than drive around was stop at the store to get a gallon of milk."

Last year Hagner quit her job as a paralegal because there were too many conflicts with her children's schedules. Now she's a substitute teacher, working on call about 35 hours a week. Her husband, Dennis, a truckdriver, is on the road 60 hours a week delivering gas, oil and asphalt. Cathy Hagner, who never played organized sports as a child, says she often longs for a simpler life with more time for picnics, reading by the fire and even schoolwork. "Sometimes I question the value of all this," she concedes. But there's no time for more reflection: she has to take Matthew to a soccer game.

In a few communities, parents are organizing to find ways to stop the madness. A group called Family Life 1st!, based in the affluent Minneapolis suburb of Wayzata, has asked coaches, teachers and leaders of youth groups to cut back on required games and practices—especially during holidays and vacations. But most parents who buck the trend are just taking action on their own. . . .

Many parents use grades as a test of how much is too much. Kim and Jerry Larance of The Woodlands, Texas, say that they make their three very active sons scale back on sports if there are conflicts with schoolwork. "If push comes to shove, academics are their first priority," Jerry Larance says.

Others set a rule of only one major activity per child. Lynn Reed of Downers Grove, Ill., says she's determined to control the schedules of her two kids, Aileen, 10, and Andrew, 9. "When they were younger, they wanted to try everything," she says. "Andrew had basketball, baseball, soccer, swimming. But he has found a love for soccer. He made a traveling soccer team, so we cut back on his other sports activities." Aileen has made a similar commitment to swimming, with practices for her private swim team four days a week, 60 minutes per day.

Still, it's not easy to keep the family functioning smoothly, says Reed, who runs a part-time business out of her home. Though they're only in third and fifth grade, the children have at least an hour of homework daily, plus 20 to 30 minutes of mandatory reading. Reed has a strict routine; homework is the first order of business when the kids come in from school. "Trying to juggle the homework is tough," says Reed. "I joke that if I knew about homework, I would have reconsidered this kid thing!"

Homework is a major battleground for many families. Parents think they are giving their children a tactical advantage by closely supervising their assignments, often to ensure that their children get the best possible grades. Students today have lots of homework at earlier and earlier ages, even though many educational researchers say homework in elementary school has almost no effect on student achievement. As assignments get more complex, parents find that a huge chunk of the "quality time" they could be spending with their children is devoted to untangling algebra. . . .

Students who've never learned to make their own choices can feel lost and confused once they get to college. Even then, parents aren't letting go. With e-mail and mobile phones, parents can keep in constant touch with their kids—a dramatic change from their own college years, when a weekly call home was considered more than adequate. "I had a student crying in my office the other day," Coontz recalls, "who said, 'I know how to write a paper, taking any position, but I have no idea what I believe in myself' . . . There's a significant minority of kids who have shut down emotionally because they've tried so hard to achieve."

The best way to prevent that, child-rearing experts say, is to pare down the family calendar and remember that downtime can be the most productive of all. That's a lesson Houston mother Cindy Cicio is trying to teach her three kids—ages 10, 6 and 4. They're all involved in sports, music and church activities, but she's constantly on the watch for burnout. When any of them shows signs of stress, she reminds them that their activities are just intended to be fun, and that they shouldn't worry about how well they do. She also tries to leave a little space for just hanging out. "I make sure they have time in their day when they can go outside for 45 minutes to an hour and just be a kid." She and her husband, Patrick, try to give themselves the same gift of time every night. Around 9, after all the homework is done and the kids are in bed, they make it a priority to just be together. "If there are clothes that need to be put away, they just sit there," she says, "because I have to chill out." And, of course, gather strength for another round in the minivan.

"THE FRUIT OF A PATRIARCHAL SYSTEM"
BARBARA NEWMAN

Founded in 1972, Feminists for Life of America (FFLA) has aroused the wrath of NOW and other feminist organizations for calling itself feminist. In the following article from one of its newsletters, Barbara Newman, a well-respected scholar and professor of medieval women's literature, argues that abortion, far from being "pro-choice," often becomes an act of last resort for pregnant women who have no other options because they lack the emotional and economic support of their partners, the confidence to refuse aggressive sexual advances by lovers that lead to unwanted pregnancies, and workplace policies that will accommodate the needs of working parents. To her way of thinking, social attitudes and policies must change dramatically before women can exercise the freedom to conceive and bear children on their own terms.

SOURCE: Barbara Newman, "Why Postmodern Patriarchy Loves Abortion," *Sisterlife* 13, no. 1 (Winter 1993): 3, 5. Reprinted by permission of Feminists for Life of America.

THE LEADERS of organized American feminism have unfortunately defined "reproductive rights" as *the* fundamental issue of equality. But although NOW and NARAL [National Abortion Rights Action League] maintain that abortion is liberating, they have failed to persuade the majority of American women, and for good reason. For abortion is in reality the fruit of a patriarchal system that is still unable to accept either the human dignity or the mature sexuality of women.

The appealing rhetoric of "choice" proves, on closer inspection, to conceal a dangerous double bind. Abortion advocates cite a woman's "right to privacy," claiming that no parent or boyfriend or husband—much less the state—has the right to intervene in her private reproductive decisions. Yet this logic implies that if abortion is a woman's "private choice," then so is child-rearing. The woman who seeks to raise a child despite economic hardship is frequently abandoned by her child's father and finds little help from society. Since she refused the easy choice of abortion, she alone must bear the burden of her difficult and courageous choice. Thus privatizing the sphere of reproduction leaves women, especially poor women, more vulnerable to exploitation than before. Many young mothers seek abortions precisely because they feel they have no "choice"—a feeling of powerlessness, not control, which is too often reinforced by parents, boyfriends, doctors, social workers, and of course, abortion counselors. As the

Chicana activist Graciela Olivarez says plaintively, "The poor cry out for justice and equality, and we respond with legalized abortion."

It is not enough to look at the "problem of unwanted pregnancies" unless we ask *why* so many women become pregnant against their will. In many cases, that means asking why so many men do not want pregnant women in their lives. My own belief is that, despite a generation of propaganda about women's "freedom of choice," women and especially teenaged girls in America are still far from being sexually free, but feel pressured into having sexual relationships they don't really want with men they don't really love because having a boyfriend, even an abusive one, is the only form of security they know. And if a woman is not afraid or ashamed to say "no," it is a rare boyfriend who will respect that choice.

In a society where rape and sexual assault are endemic, few unmarried men are willing to take responsibility for either contraception or child care. When their partners become pregnant, they believe they are being moral and responsible if they offer to pay for the "termination." But such morality is self-serving and shallow: It allows men to go right on being manipulative playboys while leaving women to suffer all the pain and guilt of abortion. Too often, young women expose themselves to the anguish of sacrificing a wanted child in order to "save their relationship" with a man who was not mature enough to use a condom, let alone assume the burdens of fatherhood.

There is yet another reason why so many pregnancies are unwanted: Our patriarchal society does not want, and cannot cope with, mothers in the workplace. The sexual liberation of women is no threat to men as long as we are willing to model our sexuality on theirs, especially that of the least mature. Postmodern patriarchy can accept the women whose sexuality conforms to the consumerist model—sex for fun, pleasure, and profit with no strings attached. Abortion now "liberates" this woman to be just as irresponsible as male playboys have always been. Society can also accept the increasingly rare woman who chooses—and is wealthy enough—to be a full-time wife and mother. But the woman who works in the marketplace *and* bears children, the so-called "working mother" who is in fact the average American woman, still faces discrimination in the workplace and demands on her time and energy so severe that it is no wonder if she greets the news of another pregnancy with horror, even if she is married and affluent.

It is understandable, but unfortunate, that so many men have taken up the easy view of abortion as "a woman's issue." Abortion, like childbearing, *is* a woman's issue in the sense that only women are physically at risk. But if both partners are equal in the act that began the pregnancy, they share an equal responsibility for its outcome. American society is still a long way from recognizing this basic principle of justice. Shared parenting remains a utopian feminist ideal, not a reality, and rare indeed is the workplace that offers parental leave to new fathers. At the university where I teach, in the supposedly enlightened world of academia, even maternity leaves are still granted under the rubric of "sick leave" and "disability." But pregnancy is not a sickness; it is a natural and healthy condition of the female body. The capacity to bear a child is no disability, but the reverse; it is men who are "disabled" in this sphere. Patriarchy, as usual, turns reality on its head and defines the "disability" as ours, punishing it with stiff economic penalties and then defining the conflicts that result as a "women's problem" rather than a problem that affects us all.

Given an economic system that inflicts a penalty on motherhood and refuses to recognize fatherhood at all, it is no wonder that so many pregnancies are unwanted. Changing the system to accommodate the reality of working parents would require an enormous investment of thought, creativity, commitment, and of course, money. So it is no wonder that we prefer to take the cheap and time-honored way out. Resolve the dilemma with an act of violence; reduce the woman to a surrogate man, tough and competitive and untroubled by fertility. Then deny that her fertility has any emotional consequences or imposes any responsibilities, least of all on the man who fertilized her. Once this is done, it is easy enough to "terminate" the pregnancy and justify this violence in the usual way, by denying humanity to the "terminated" person.

What, then, is the way out of the abortion impasse? Changing the laws is important, and providing direct support for pregnant women in trouble is even more important. But there are still more fundamental changes we must make. We must do everything we can to oppose violence against women, sexual exploitation, and rape, for until men are willing to take full responsibility for their sexual behavior, including the children they beget, there will be a demand for abortion. We must change the way we do business in order to recognize the needs and responsibilities of all working parents, for until employers are willing to adopt more flexible work schedules, provide on-site day care, and stop penalizing women for motherhood, there will be a demand for abortion. We must support a public policy that promotes high-quality health care, education, housing and jobs for all people, for until our society is willing to invest as much annually in child care as it invests daily in weapons, the plague of unwanted pregnancies will be with us.

It is far cheaper to abort the next generation than to nurture it; it is far easier to subject women's bodies to surgical violence than to provide the economic and emotional support that would make our fertility a blessing rather than a curse. As long as patriarchy insists on business-as-usual—in the bedroom, the board room, and the operating room—women's "right" to abortion will be a pitiful surrogate for freedom from the sexual and economic exploitation that compels this oppressive "choice."

"WE MUST FIND COMMUNITY
OUT OF DIFFERENCES"
GERDA LERNER

The Schlesinger Library at Radcliffe College, one of the premier research libraries in women's history, celebrated its fiftieth anniversary in March 1994 with a conference dedicated to presenting papers and panel discussions on new scholarship in the field. The conference brought together several generations of women's historians, including one of the founding mothers of the field, Gerda Lerner, whose research and theoretical insights have been a guiding force for the past four decades. (See an early article of hers on methodological goals of women's history in chapter 3.) At the end of the two-day conference, Lerner gave an eloquent appraisal of the intellectual growth and contributions of the field of women's history and offered her vision of how feminist scholarship can contribute to building a global community of social equality and respect for difference. Her speech underscores the political mission of feminist scholarship—to create social change for the present and future by understanding and exposing the social inequities of the past.

SOURCE: Gerda Lerner, " 'Many Shinings of Truth' in a Time of Transition," in *Working Papers from the Schlesinger Library 50th Anniversary Conference*, edited by Susan Ware (Cambridge, Mass.: Arthur and Elizabeth Schlesinger Library, 1994), pp. 254–58. Reprinted by permission of Schlesinger Library, Radcliffe Institute, Harvard University.

CERTAINLY OUR MOST IMPORTANT accomplishment is to have challenged the traditional male-focused and male-centered paradigm for historical scholarship, in fact for all scholarship. That our challenge has power and that it has been heard is evidenced by the increasingly acrimonious debate, the veritable cultural war, now taking place inside and outside the academy. In a sense this is a continuation of the 600 year long "querelle des femmes" debate begun by Christine de Pizan, only this time it is the patriachal position which is on the defensive, even as it still holds on to power. The so-called "backlash" against feminism, so often and repeatedly misread by the media as signifying the demise of feminism, is only one aspect of this debate. The other aspect is expressed by new attitudes toward rape, sexual violence, sexual harassment, family violence and the civil and moral rights of homosexuals. It is expressed by law courts and juries, by new corporate practices and by increasing media attention (though not always favorable attention) to these issues. That we have succeeded in our challenge is clear, but it is far less clear where this challenge is going to take us.

It is not so very long ago, perhaps no more than ten years ago, that the mere existence of conflict among women was something that filled most of us with profound bewilderment, regret and confusion. Those days seem simple in comparison with what followed. Certainly, we have lost our innocence, and perhaps our "dream of a common language." At this time, judging from published articles and from current discourse, what looms largest before our eyes is disunity, splintering, discontinuity, disconnection. The postmodernist world seems fragmented into a thousand uncertainties, cut loose from the past without a vision of the future, free of illusions but also devoid of hope.

When we started to attack the seemingly impenetrable fortress of patriarchal thought and patriarchal power, this is not where we hoped to end. Nor is this, I think, where we will end.

To say that we are in the spasms of a process, caught in whirlpools of a river flowing across resistant obstacles, is to merely describe our experience without illuminating it. We need some historical perspective to help us across the whirls and chasms.

Patriarchy, a system of social organization well established for over 2500 years, is dying. Whether modern feminism is its gravedigger or merely a response to its death spasms is a matter of opinion. There is no question in my mind that the end of the hierarchical, exploitative, competitive system, based on militarism and intergroup rivalry, which pitted man against nature, is doomed. The nuclear revolution ended social relations which originated in Bronze Age militarism and patriarchal social structures well adapted to its needs. We no longer live in the Bronze Age, and militarism, in the nuclear age, has proven incapable of finding solutions to the most urgent problems of humanity. We may, as the human race, make the wrong choices and fail to survive. I am not an absolute optimist; I concede that that may happen. But if we are to survive, it will have to be with a social organization better adapted to the 21st century than is patriarchy. Of this I am certain.

And if that is so, patriarchal ideas are obsolete and powerless. Feminist ideas, conversely, are future-oriented and powerful. And we, in Women's Studies, are at the frontier of feminist ideas. If, at the moment, we are uncertain of our directions, and see few hopeful signs for the future, let us regain our perspective by considering our historical situation.

Up to this time, as long as we have any record of human endeavor, the world has been run on the intellectual power of half the human race, or perhaps much less than half the human race when one considers all the disadvantaged, excluded and oppressed groups of humanity. Now, these groups, all of them, and chief among them women, are reclaiming their place in history.

Whatever differences there are among us, what we share is our being outside of power, outside of the power to make political and economic decisions, outside of the power to define what is human discourse. Now, at this historic moment, we, the female majority, are moving from the margins to the center, an unprecedented event in history.

We are not united, as we present this challenge to patriarchy. I would like to suggest that we cannot expect to be united. Men, so long dominant in human affairs, are not united among themselves. They do not speak in one voice, they do not represent one interest. Why should we expect that of women? Women are half of humankind and we come in every shape, form, type and identity. We are no more going to be united than men have been. So losing our innocence should mean losing the simplistic belief that we can ever speak in one voice.

We will be different, one from the other. We will represent differences among women. We will differ in how we relate to that other half, men. We will be different in how we relate to the men of our own identity group, again, depending on many factors such as class, ethnicity, religion, even age.

What I think is emerging, is a holistic concept of society as a functioning organism. To use the analogy of the human body: the muscle system, the skeletal structure, the nervous system, the lymph, the neurological system all function holistically in one organism, the human body. We separate them out for purposes of analysis and to better understand them, but unless we represent them each as interconnected in a functioning system, we miss the truth.

Society, as we try to reconstruct it in history, is a functioning holistic system. All the various tools for analysis we have identified, offer us at best a two-dimensional representation. The great importance of feminist scholarship is that it called attention to the hidden dimensions of gender and sexuality in the formation of systems of power and dominance. Now we must find ways of presenting holistic pictures of the functioning social organism. Or, to put it in plainer terms, we must find community out of differences. Unless we do, we, as the human race, will not survive. If we do, feminist scholarship and feminist political thought will be an important aspect of our survival.

"WE WILL KEEP MOVING FORWARD"
NATIONAL ORGANIZATION FOR WOMEN (NOW)

In July 1998, one hundred and fifty years to the month after Elizabeth Cady Stanton, Lucretia Mott, and three other women launched the organized American women's rights movement at Seneca Falls, New York, the National Organization for Women (NOW) issued a Declaration of Sentiments. Like the Declaration of Rights and Sentiments, which came out of the Seneca Falls Convention and charted the course of the nineteenth-century women's rights movement, this declaration presents the unfinished work that lies ahead to achieve full gender equality. While celebrating the many advances that women have made in their personal lives and in American society, the document restates NOW's commitment to, in its words, "equality, empowerment, and justice." The declaration is solemn but joyful in tone, clear-eyed about the obstacles ahead but also hopeful and visionary, a fitting charter for the next millennium.

SOURCE: Reprinted by permission of the National Organization for Women (NOW).

On this twelfth day of July, 1998, the delegates of the National Organization for Women gather in convention on the one hundred and fiftieth year of the women's rights movement.

We bring passion, anger, hope, love and perseverance to create this vision for
the future:
We envision a world where women's equality and women's empowerment to
determine our own destinies is a reality;
We envision a world where women have equal representation in all decision-
making structures of our societies;
We envision a world where social and economic justice exist, where all people
have the food, housing, clothing, health care and education they need;
We envision a world where there is recognition and respect for each person's in-
trinsic worth as well as the rich diversity of the various groups among us;
We envision a world where non-violence is the established order;
We envision a world where patriarchal culture and male dominance no longer
oppress us or our earth;
We envision a world where-women and girls are heard, valued and respected.

Our movement, encompassing many issues and many strategies, directs our love for humanity into action that spans the world and unites women. But our future requires us to know our past.

One hundred fifty years ago the women's rights movement grew out of the fight to abolish slavery. Angered by their exclusion from leadership and public speaking at abolitionist conventions and inspired by the power of the Iroquois women, a small dedicated group of women and men built a movement. After its inception, the movement was fractured by race. Our history is full of struggle against common bonds of oppression and a painful reality of separation. Nevertheless, these activists created a political force that achieved revolutionary change. They won property rights for married women; opened the doors of higher education for women; and garnered suffrage in 1920.

In 1923, on the seventy-fifth anniversary of the historic Seneca Falls convention, feminists led the demand for constitutional equality for women to win full justice under the law in order to end economic, educational, and political inequality.

Our foremothers—the first wave of feminists—ran underground railroads, lobbied, marched, and picketed. They were jailed and force fed, lynched and raped. But they prevailed. They started with a handful of activists, and today, the feminist movement involves millions of people every day.

Standing on their shoulders, we launched the National Organization for Women in 1966, the largest and strongest organization of feminists in the world today. A devoutly grassroots, action-oriented organization, we have sued, boycotted, picketed, lobbied, demonstrated, marched, and engaged in non-violent civil disobedience. We have won in the courts and in the legislatures; and we have negotiated with the largest corporations in the world, winning unparalleled rights for women.

The National Organization for Women and our modern day movement have profoundly changed the lives of women, men and children. We have raised public consciousness about the plight of women to such an extent that today the majority of people support equality for women.

In the past 32 years, women have advanced farther than in any previous generation. Yet still we do not have full equality.

We have moved more feminists than ever before into positions of power in all of the institutions that shape our society. We have achieved some measure of power to effect change in these institutions from within; yet still we are far from full equality in decision-making. We demand an equal share of power in our families and religions, in law, science and technology, the arts and humanities, sports, education, the trades and professions, labor and management, the media, corporations and small businesses as well as government. In no sphere of life should women be silenced, underrepresented, or devalued.

Today, we reaffirm our demand for Constitutional equality for women and girls. Simultaneously, we are working with sister organizations to develop and pass a national women's equality act for the twenty-first century. And we participate in and advance a global movement for women and demand that the United States join the overwhelming majority of nations of the world in ratifying the United Nations Convention on the Elimination of All Forms of Discrimination Against Women without reservations, declarations, or understandings that would weaken this commitment.

We reaffirm our commitment to the power of grassroots activism, to a multi-issue, multi-tactical strategy.

We are committed to a feminist ideology and reaffirm our historic commitment to gaining equality for women, assuring safe, legal and accessible abortion and full reproductive freedom, combating racism, stopping violence against women, ending bigotry and discrimination based on sexual orientation and on color, ethnicity, national origin, economic status, age, disability, size, childbearing capacity or choices, or parental or marital status.

We will not trade off the rights of one woman for the advancement of another. We will not be divided. We will unite with all women who seek freedom and join hands with all of the great movements of our time and all time, seeking equality, empowerment and justice.

We commit to continue the mentoring, training, and leadership development of young and new activists of all ages who will continue our struggle. We will work to invoke enthusiasm for our goals and to expand ownership in this movement for current and future generations.

We commit to continue building a mass movement where we are leaders, not followers, of public opinion. We will continue to move feminist ideals into the mainstream thought, and we will build our media and new technology capabilities to control our own image and message.

How long and hard a struggle it was to win the right for women to vote. Today, we fight the same reactionary forces: the perversion of religion to subjugate women; corporate greed that seeks to exploit women and children as a cheap labor force; and their apologists in public office who seek to do through law what terrorists seek to accomplish through bullets and bombs. We will not submit, nor will we be intimidated. But we will keep moving forward.

   Those who carried the struggle for women's suffrage through to its end were not there at the start; those who started the struggle did not live to see the victory. Like those strong feminist activists, we will not let ourselves be dispirited or discouraged. Even when progress seems most elusive, we will maintain our conviction that the work itself is important. For it is the work that enriches our lives; it is the work that unites us; it is the work that will propel us into the next century. We know that our struggle has made a difference, and we reaffirm our faith that it will continue to make a difference for women's lives.

   Today, we dedicate ourselves to the sheer joy of moving forward and fighting back.

In the 1990s Naomi Wolf, author and journalist, was quite sanguine about the power of women's collective efforts to achieve feminist social change. (See her remarks in chapter 5.) She urged women to exercise "power feminism"—to marshal their political and economic power to achieve further gains. On the precipice of the new millennium, Wolf now laments what she perceives to be a lack of historical awareness among American women. Without this historical aware-ness, she eloquently argues, women will forget that the achievements of the past, such as the ballot, the right to earn their own salaries, and the right to exercise re-productive freedom, were hard-won by women who organized on their own behalf and that the preservation of these and other rights depends on continued vigilance, collective action, and political and economic leverage. American women can sleep-walk their way into the twenty-first century in a haze of complacent ignorance, claims Wolf, or they can draw on the lessons and heroines of the past to use their voices, their will, and their collective strength to keep the revolution alive.

SOURCE: Naomi Wolf, "The Future Is Ours to Lose," *New York Times Magazine*, May 16, 1999, section 6, pp. 134–35, 154. Reprinted by permission of Naomi Wolf.

STANDING AT THE TURN of the millennium, how odd it seems that women, the majority of the human species, have not, over the course of so many cen-turies, intervened successfully once and for all on their own behalf. That is, un-til you consider that women have been trained to see themselves as having no relationship to history, and no claim upon it. Feminism can be defined as wo-men's ability to think about their subjugated role in history, and then to do something about it. The 21st century will see the End of Inequality—but only if women absorb the habit of historical self-awareness, becoming a mass of people who, rather than do it all, decide at last to change it all. The future is ours to lose.

Since there has always been some scattered awareness that women's low sta-tus was unfair, you could say that there has always been a women's movement. And just as you could say that there has always been a women's movement, you could also say that there has always been a backlash. It is truly striking how of-ten Western humanity has taken the leap forward into more egalitarian, ra-tional and democratic models of society and government, and made the deci-sion—for a decision it had to be—to leave women out. At every turn, with a

heroic effort of the will to ignore the obvious path of justice, men were granted, and granted themselves, more and more equality, and women of all races
were left in history's tidewater.

Once again, we are at a turning point. This decade has seen one new landmark after another: the Family and Medical Leave Act; a feminist sitting on the
Supreme Court; a woman in charge of American foreign policies that now include opposition to clitoridectomy. Indeed, feminism has become mainstream:
Betty Friedan has met Betsy Ross; Barbie's ads now read "Dream With Your
Eyes Wide Open" and "Be Your Own Hero." Oprah* is talking about how to
walk out of an abusive marriage, and Tori Amos and Fran Drescher* speak out
in the celebrity press about sexual assault. This flood tide could either crest further to change the landscape forever, or it could recede once again. This is what
historians call an "open moment," and women have blown such moments in
the past. What determines the outcome is the level of historical awareness we
reach before the tide inevitably turns.

There are four ways that our culture militates against historical consciousness in women. One is the steady omission of women from history's first draft,
the news. Women, Men and Media, a national watchdog project, reports that
women are featured in only 15 percent of the front-page news—and then usually as victims or perpetrators of crime or misconduct. It is not because no one
is interested in what women are doing that this ceiling of visibility is kept so
low; nor is it a conscious conspiracy. But if tomorrow the editors in chief and
publishers of national news media were to see front sections dominated by 53
percent female newsmakers, they would not shout, Stop the presses! Too many
women! Rather, there would be the impression that somehow these publications had, by featuring newsmakers who are part of a majority, marginalized
themselves. So women's advances take place with little day-by-day, let alone
month-by-month, popular analysis.

The second pressure, which complements the omission of women from historical culture, is the omission of history from women's culture. One example:
under its previous editor, Ruth Whitney, *Glamour* magazine ran a political column. Bonnie Fuller, a new editor fresh from *Cosmopolitan*, has deleted this
monthly column and added a horoscope. It's a shift from real-time—historical-
political time—back into that dependent, dreamy, timeless state of Women's

---

* *Editor's note:* Oprah Winfrey, a popular talk show host
* *Editor's note:* Television celebrities.

Time. In Women's Time, your fate is not in your own hands as an agent of historical change. Rather—Hey, are you a Pisces? Why bother running down your Manolo Blahniks to do something as *mousy* as voting? Your fate is in your cleavage, and in the stars.

Emerging naturally from this is the third pressure: the recurrent ideological theme that if women take themselves seriously they will lose femininity and, therefore, social status. If what they do, think, worry about and long for doesn't matter, surely it's not important that history pays them attention.

The fourth pressure is forgetfulness. Young women I have met on real college campuses think sex discrimination is a thing of the past. Or that the struggle for the vote lasted maybe 10 years, not more than 70. Or that women got the vote when African-Americans did. Or that it has always been legal to get an abortion in America. They are stunned to discover that in their mothers' lifetimes women could not get credit on their own. They are amazed to learn that it was African-American middle-class women's clubs that led the movement against lynching. They didn't know that women chained themselves to the gates of Congress, or went on hunger strikes and were force-fed—so that young women far into the future could take their rights for granted. These young women are shocked, in other words, to find that they have a history.

As a result, women remain dependent on other models of "revolution" for their own. They must catch the taste and techniques of activism like a hit song of the month wafting through the air. So one sees women slumbering and then "waking up" every 30 years or so; periods of feminism always follow periods of agitation by women on behalf of other, more respectable causes.

This past century shows how fragile conscious feminism has been. The 1910's, with their wave of populist reform, saw the crescendo of women's push for the vote. But the year before it was granted, in 1919, the term "post-feminist" had already expediently been coined. By the 20's, pop culture was once again ridiculing the suffragists' generations as being man-hating old battle-axes, irrelevant and out of touch with "today's women."

A long sleep followed, with fitful waking. After Betty Friedan's 1963 book helped middle-class white women identify the causes of their deeper malaise, the magical 15 years, from 1965 to 1980, began, representing a high point of historical self-awareness for Western women. Again, other movements had to set the stage: the anti-war movement, the free-speech movement and the hippie movement all contributed to the idea that it was all right to break free of social roles. The civil rights movement trained a generation of African-American activists. The 70's were astonishing: the statutes against sex discrimination labeled

Title VII and Title IX; Shirley Chisholm's 1972 race for the Democratic Presidential nomination. That era, personified by Steinem and Jong, NOW and the National Women's Political Caucus, showed what could happen for women when, as an energized mass in a democracy, they wanted change badly enough to make noise about it.

The predictable backlash came, as it always does; the evil 80's were a time of shoulder pads, silicone and retrenchment. Again—so quickly, so thoroughly— women "forgot." A Time/CNN poll found that only 33 percent of women called themselves feminists—and only 16 percent of college-age women. "Guilt" and "the Mommy Track" were the catchwords of the day. Once again, feminists were represented as hairy-legged man-hating shrews.

The heartbreak of those times was in seeing newly clueless young women come of age. Once, when I visited Yale as a speaker, a brilliant young Asian-American student joined her male debating society peers in loudly ridiculing feminism. Later, when we were alone for a moment, she confided that she didn't really believe what she said—but the guys were in charge of the club and she just wanted to get along with them. "Besides," she had said, as if parroting some women's magazine, "women my age just have to accept that we can't have it all." It was as if all those words—flextime, family leave, egalitarian marriage—had vanished, taking with them the ways in which that young woman could have reconsidered her life.

Enter the explosive 90's. Women are now the most important voting mass in America. "Women's Issues" dominate the agenda. The word "feminism" is as taboo as ever, but does it matter if you call yourself a feminist if you are living feminism? And American women are doing that, considering the number of their new businesses, and their new judgeships, new elected officials and new spending power. Feminism today is not a label; it's a way of life.

But here's the catch: if we remain indifferent to history, we risk losing it all. The bad old days are always ready to knock at your door, sisters: while you're packing your briefcase or getting into your truck, feeling confident, having thrown out the mailing from that advocacy group, you could just find that you can't get a legal abortion anymore; or that your boss knows that those sexual harassment statutes can be managed with a wink and a nod.

Women who are ignorant of their own history forget the main lessons, like: Here's how you mobilize; being nice is never as good as getting leverage; the nature-nurture debate has been going on forever, and neither side is going to win; your representatives pay attention when you use your money, your voice and your will. And voting millions can provide the will.

Maybe we will learn at last. Maybe we will create institutions that are will-ing to share influence with younger women coming up, rather than hoarding power for one generation. Maybe we will learn to honor our heroines and role models while they are still alive: maybe Gloria Steinem and Shirley Chisholm will get their commemorative stamps and parades in their own lifetimes, so our daughters will grow up with some one to turn to more powerful in their imag-inations than Kate Moss and Calista Flockhart. Maybe we will learn at last that dissent and disagreement among women across the political spectrum is a sign of our diversity and strength. Maybe we will turn from the horoscope page to the Congressional Quarterly, and understand at last that our salvation lies not in our stars, but in ourselves.

In this beautifully rendered poem, rich with imagery, Japanese American poet Janice Mirikitani speaks to the specific ethnic aspects of Japanese women's suppression, from the cultural admonitions to be humble and submissive to the very tangible oppression of being interned in detention camps during World War II. But she also speaks of crippling gender roles that transcend ethnic boundaries— the "hospitals and forceps and kitchens" that have circumscribed women's lives. Just as she wants to free herself from the negative and limiting self-perceptions of her mother's generation, she urges her daughter to break the emotional shackles passed down from her own generation and live bravely and adventurously.

SOURCE: Reprinted with permission from *Shedding Silence,* copyright © 1987 by Janice Mirikitani. Reprinted by permission from Celestial Arts, P.O. Box 7123, Berkeley, Calif. 94707.

BREAKING TRADITION

For my daughter

My daughter denies she is like me,
her secretive eyes avoid mine.
  She reveals the hatreds of womanhood
  already veiled behind music and smoke and telephones.
I want to tell her about the empty room
  of myself.
This room we lock ourselves in
where whispers live like fungus,
giggles about small breasts and cellulite,
where we confine ourselves to jealousies,
bedridden by menstruation.
This waiting room where we feel our hands
are useless, dead speechless clamps
that need hospitals and forceps and kitchens
and plugs and ironing boards to make them useful.
I deny I am like my mother. I remember why:
She kept her room neat with silence,

defiance smothered in requirements to be otonashii,*
passion and loudness wrapped in an obi,**
her steps confined to ceremony,
the weight of her sacrifice she carried like
a foetus. Guilt passed on in our bones.
I want to break tradition—unlock this room
where women dress in the dark.
Discover the lies my mother told me.
The lies that we are small and powerless
    that our possibilities must be compressed
    to the size of pearls, displayed only as
    passive chokers, charms around our neck.
  Break Tradition.
    I want to tell my daughter of this room
    of myself
    filled with tears of shakuhachi,†
    the light in my hands,
    poems about madness,
the music of yellow guitars,
sounds shaken from barbed wire and
goodbyes and miracles of survival.

My daughter denies she is like me
  her secretive eyes are walls of smoke
  and music and telephones.
  her pouting ruby lips, her skirts
  swaying to salsa, Madonna and the Stones.
  her thighs displayed in carnivals of color.
  I do not know the contents of her room.
She mirrors my aging.

She is breaking tradition.

---

* Ootonashii: humble, unselfish, submissive.
** A wide, heavy, constricting sash worn with a kimono.
† Shakuhachi: a bamboo flute that makes a breathy, haunting sound.

FURTHER READING ABOUT
TWENTIETH-CENTURY AMERICAN WOMEN

GENERAL STUDIES AND DOCUMENTARY COLLECTIONS IN
RECENT AMERICAN WOMEN'S HISTORY

Banner, Lois. *Women in Modern America: A Brief History*. New York: Harcourt Brace Jovanovich, 1984.

Baxandall, Rosalyn, Linda Gordon, and Susan Reverby, eds. *America's Working Women: A Documentary History–1600 to the Present*. New York: Vintage, 1976.

Chafe, William H. *The Paradox of Change: American Women in the Twentieth Century*. New York: Oxford University Press, 1992.

Cott, Nancy F., ed. *No Small Courage: A History of Women in the United States*. New York: Oxford University Press, 2000.

———, et al., eds. *Root of Bitterness: Documents of the Social History of American Women*. Rev. ed. Boston: Northeastern University Press, 1996.

Dubois, Ellen Carol, and Vicki L. Ruiz, eds. *Unequal Sisters: A Multicultural Reader in U.S. Women's History*. New York: Routledge, 1994.

Evans, Sara M. *Born for Liberty: A History of Women in America*. Rev. ed. New York: Free, 1997.

Friedman, Jean E., William G. Shade, and Mary Jane Capozzoli, eds. *Our American Sisters: Women in American Life and Thought*. Lexington, Mass.: D. C. Heath, 1982.

Gatlin, Rochelle. *American Women Since 1945*. Jackson: University Press of Mississippi, 1987.

Hine, Darlene Clark, ed. *Black Women in United States History: From Colonial Times to the Present*. 16 vols. Brooklyn, N.Y.: Carlson, 1990.

James, Edward, Janet Wilson James, and Paul Boyer, eds. *Notable American Women, 1607–1950: A Biographical Dictionary*. 3 vols. Cambridge: Harvard University, Belknap, 1971.

Kerber, Linda, and Jane Sherron DeHart. *Women's America: Refocusing the Past*. 5th ed. New York: Oxford University Press, 2000.

Lerner, Gerda, ed. *Black Women in White America: A Documentary History*. Rev. ed. New York: Vintage, 1992.

Rosenberg, Rosalind. *Divided Lives: American Women in the Twentieth Century*. New York: Hill and Wang, 1992.

Ware, Susan. *Modern American Women: A Documentary History*. New York: McGraw-Hill, 1997.

Woloch, Nancy. *Women and the American Experience*. 3d ed. New York: McGraw Hill, 2000.

1940s

PRIMARY SOURCES

Chadakoff, Rochelle, ed. *Eleanor Roosevelt's "My Day": Her Acclaimed Column, 1936–1945*. New York: Pharos, 1989.

Gluck, Sherna. *Rosie the Riveter Revisited: Women, the War, and Social Change*. Boston: Twayne, 1987.

Klein, Yvonne M., ed. *Beyond the Home Front: Women's Autobiographical Writings of the Two World Wars*. New York: New York University Press, 1997.

Litoff, Judy Barrett, and David C. Smith, ed. *American Women in a World at War: Contemporary Accounts from World War II*. Wilmington, Del.: Scholarly Resources, 1997.

——. *Since You Went Away: World War II Letters from American Women on the Home-front*. New York: Oxford University Press, 1991.

Sone, Monica. *Nisei Daughter*. Boston: Little, Brown, 1953.

Terkel, Studs. *"The Good War": An Oral History of World War II*. New York: Pantheon, 1984.

SECONDARY SOURCES

Anderson, Karen. *Wartime Women: Sex Roles, Family Relations, and the Status of Women During World War II*. Westport, Conn: Greenwood, 1981.

——. "Last Hired, First Fired: Black Women Workers During World War II." *Journal of American History* (June 1982).

Berube, Alan. *Coming Out Under Fire: The History of Gay Men and Women in World War II*. New York: Free Press, 1990.

Campbell, D'Ann. *Women at War with America: Private Lives in a Patriotic Era*. Cambridge: Harvard University Press, 1984.

Frazer, Heather T. *"We Have Just Begun to Not Fight": An Oral History of Conscientious Objectors in Civilian Public Service During World War II*. New York: Twayne, 1996.

Goossen, Rachel Waltner. *Women Against the Good War*. Chapel Hill: University of North Carolina Press, 1997.

Hartmann, Susan M. *The Home Front and Beyond: American Women in the 1940s*. Boston: Twayne, 1982.

Honey, Maureen. *Creating Rosie the Riveter: Class, Gender, and Propaganda During World War II*. Amherst: University of Massachusetts Press, 1984.

Matsumoto, Valerie. "Japanese-American Women During World War II." *Frontiers* 8 (1984).

Milkman, Ruth. *Gender at Work: The Dynamics of Job Segregation by Sex During World War II*. Urbana: University of Illinois Press, 1987.

Rupp, Leila J. *Mobilizing Women for War: German and American Propaganda, 1939–1945*. Princeton: Princeton University Press, 1978.

Weatherford, Doris. *American Women and World War II*. New York: Facts on File, 1990.

1950s

PRIMARY SOURCES

Barnard, Hollinger F., ed. *Outside the Magic Circle: The Autobiography of Virginia Foster Durr*. University: University of Alabama Press, 1985.

Bates, Daisy. *The Long Shadow of Little Rock: A Memoir*. New York: David McKay, 1962.

Beals, Melba Pattilo. *Warriors Don't Cry: A Searing Memoir of the Battle to Integrate Little Rock's Central High*. New York: Pocket, 1994.

Garrow, David J., ed. *The Montgomery Bus Boycott and the Women Who Started It: The Memoirs of JoAnn Gibson Robinson*. Knoxville: University of Tennessee Press, 1987.

Gladney, Margaret Rose, ed. *How Am I to Be Heard? Letters of Lillian Smith*. Chapel Hill: University of North Carolina Press, 1993.

Hampton, Henry, ed. *Voices of Freedom*. New York: Bantam, 1990.

Harvey, Brett. *The Fifties: A Women's Oral History*. New York: HarperCollins, 1993.

Lundberg, Ferdinand, and Marynia Farnham. *Modern Woman: The Lost Sex*. New York: Harper, 1947.

Mead, Margaret. *Male and Female: A Study of the Sexes in a Changing World*. New York: William Morrow, 1975 [1949].

Moody, Anne. *Coming of Age in Mississippi*. New York: Dial, 1968.

Motley, Constance Baker. *Equal Justice—Under Law: An Autobiography*. New York: Farrar, Strauss and Giroux, 1998.

Raines, Howell, ed. *My Soul Is Rested: Movement Days in the Deep South Remembered*. New York: Penguin, 1983.

SECONDARY SOURCES

Crawford, Vicky L., et al. *Women in the Civil Rights Movement: Trailblazers and Torchbearers, 1941–1965*. New York: Carlson, 1990.

Hayden, Dolores. *Redesigning the American Dream: The Future of Housing, Work, and Family Life*. New York: Norton, 1984.

Higginbotham, Evelyn Brooks. *Righteous Discontent: Women in the Black Baptist Church*. Cambridge: Harvard University Press, 1993.

Kaledin, Eugenia. *Mothers and More: American Women in the 1950s*. Boston: Twayne, 1984.

Komarovsky, Mirra. *Blue-Collar Marriage*. New York: Random House, 1987 [1964].

May, Elaine Tyler. *Homeward Bound: American Families in the Cold War Era*. New York: Basic, 1988.

Meyerowitz, Joanne, ed. *Not June Cleaver: Women and Gender in Postwar America,
1945–1960*. Philadelphia: Temple University Press, 1994.

Mills, Kay. *This Little Light of Mine: The Life of Fannie Lou Hamer*. New York: Dutton, 1993.

Robnett, Belinda. *How Long? How Long? African-American Women in the Struggle for Civil
Rights*. New York: Oxford University Press, 1997.

Rupp, Leila J., and Verta Taylor. *Survival in the Doldrums: The American Women's Rights
Movement, 1945 to the 1960s*. New York: Oxford University Press, 1987.

Wright, Gwendolyn. *Building the American Dream: A Social History of Housing in America*. New York: Pantheon, 1981.

1960s AND 1970s

PRIMARY SOURCES

King, Mary. *Freedom Song: A Personal Story of the 1960s Civil Rights Movement* New York:
William Morrow, 1987.

Mead, Margaret. *American Women: The Report of the President's Commission on the Status of Women and Other Publications of the Commission*. New York: Charles Scribner's
Sons, 1965.

Murray, Pauli. *Song in a Weary Throat: An American Pilgrimage*. New York: Harper and
Row, 1987.

SECONDARY SOURCES

Gitlin, Todd. *The Sixties: Years of Hope, Days of Rage*. New York: Bantam, 1987.

Isserman, Maurice, and Michael Kazin. *America Divided: The Civil War of the 1960s*. New
York: Oxford University Press, 2000.

Linden-Ward, Blanche, and Carol Hurd Green. *Changing the Future: American Women
in the 1960s*. New York: Twayne, 1992.

Rubin, Lillian B. *Worlds of Pain: Life in the Working-Class Family*. New York: Basic, 1976.

Swerdlow, Amy. *Women Strike for Peace: Traditional Motherhood and Radical Politics in
the 1960s*. Chicago: University of Chicago Press, 1993.

Wandersee, Winifred. *On the Move: American Women in the 1970s*. New York: Twayne,
1988.

1980s AND 1990s

PRIMARY SOURCES

Miedzian, Myriam and Alisa Malinovich. *Generations: A Century of Women Speak About
Their Lives*. New York: Atlantic Monthly Press, 1997.

SECONDARY SOURCES

Helgesen, Sally. *Everyday Revolutionaries: Working Women and the Transformation of American Life*. New York: Doubleday, 1998.

McLaughlin, Steven D., et al. *The Changing Lives of American Women*. Chapel Hill: University of North Carolina Press, 1988.

Morrison, Toni, ed. *Race-ing Justice, En-gendering Power: Essays on Anita Hill, Clarence Thomas, and the Construction of Social Reality*. New York: Pantheon, 1992.

EDUCATION

American Association of University Women. *How Schools Shortchange Girls: Executive Summary*. Washington, D.C.: American Association of University Women Foundation, 1992.

Solomon, Barbara. *In the Company of Educated Women: A History of Women and Higher Education in America*. New Haven: Yale University Press, 1985.

EMPLOYMENT, ECONOMIC ISSUES, AND THE FEMINIZATION OF POVERTY

Evans, Sara, and Barbara Nelson. *Wage Justice: Comparable Worth and the Paradox of Technocratic Reform*. Chicago: University of Chicago Press, 1989.

Goldin, Claudia. *Understanding the Gender Gap: An Economic History of American Women*. New York: Oxford University Press, 1990.

Gordon, Linda, ed. *Women, the State, and Welfare*. Madison: University of Wisconsin Press, 1990.

Groneman, Carol, and Mary Beth Norton. *"To Toil the Livelong Day": America's Women at Work, 1780–1980*. Ithaca, N.Y.: Cornell University Press, 1987.

Howe, Louise Kapp. *Pink Collar Workers: Inside the World of Women's Work*. New York: Putnam, 1977.

Jones, Jacqueline. *American Work: Four Centuries of Black and White Labor*. New York: Norton, 1998.

Kessler-Harris, Alice. *In Pursuit of Equity: Women, Men, and the Quest for Economic Citizenship in Twentieth-Century America*. New York: Oxford University Press, 2001.

———.*Out to Work: A History of Wage-Earning Women in the United States*. New York: Oxford University Press, 1982.

Ogden, Annegret S. *The Great American Housewife: From Helpmate to Wage Earner, 1776–1986*. Westport, Conn.: Greenwood, 1986.

Pearce, Diana. "The Feminization of Poverty: Women, Work and Welfare." *Urban and Social Change Review* 11 (February 1978).

Sidel, Ruth. *Women and Children Last: The Plight of Poor Women in Affluent America.* New York: Viking, 1986.

Stallard, Karen, et al. *Poverty in the American Dream: Women and Children First.* Boston: South End, 1983.

Van Horn, Susan Householder. *Women, Work, and Fertility, 1900–1986.* New York: New York University Press, 1988.

Weiner, Lynn. *From Working Girl to Working Mother: The Female Labor Force in the United States, 1820–1980.* Chapel Hill: University of North Carolina Press, 1985.

FAMILY LIFE AND HOUSEHOLD LABOR

Coontz, Stephanie. *The Way We Never Were: American Families and the Nostalgia Trap.* New York: Basic, 1992.

Cott, Nancy F. *Public Vows: A History of Marriage and the Nation.* Cambridge: Harvard University Press, 2000.

Cowan, Ruth Schwartz. *More Work for Mother: The Ironies of Household Technology from the Open Hearth to the Microwave.* New York: Basic, 1983.

Degler, Carl. *At Odds: Women and the Family in America from the Revolution to the Present.* New York: Oxford University Press, 1980.

Gordon, Linda. *Heroes of Their Own Lives: The Politics and History of Family Violence.* New York: Viking, 1988.

Hewlett, Sylvia Ann and Cornel West. *The War Against Parents: What We Can Do for America's Beleaguered Moms and Dads.* Boston: Houghton Mifflin, 1998.

Hochschild, Arlie. *Second Shift: Working Parents and the Revolution at Home.* New York: Viking, 1989.

Matthews, Glenna. *"Just a Housewife": The Rise and Fall of Domesticity in America.* New York: Oxford University Press, 1987.

May, Elaine Tyler. *Barren in the Promised Land: Childless America and the Pursuit of Happiness.* New York: Basic, 1985.

Mintz, Steven, and Susan Kellogg. *Domestic Revolutions: A Social History of American Family Life.* New York: Free, 1988.

Pleck, Elizabeth. *Domestic Tyranny: The Making of Social Policy Against Family Violence from Colonial Times to the Present.* New York: Oxford University Press, 1987.

Skolnick, Arlene. *Embattled Paradise: The American Family in an Age of Uncertainty.* New York: Basic, 1991.

Strasser, Susan. *Never Done: A History of American Housework.* New York: Pantheon, 1982.

Weitzman, Lenore J. *The Divorce Revolution: The Unexpected Social and Economic Consequences for Women and Children in America.* New York: Free, 1985.

FEMINISM AND THE WOMEN'S MOVEMENT

PRIMARY SOURCES

Baxandall, Rosalyn, and Linda Gordon. *Dear Sisters: Dispatches from the Women's Liberation Movement.* New York: Basic, 2000.

Boris, Eileen, and Nupur Chaudhuri, eds. *Voices of Women Historians: The Personal, the Political, The Professional.* Bloomington: Indiana University Press, 1999.

Brown, Rita Mae. *Rita Will: Memoir of a Literary Rabble-Rouser.* New York: Bantam, 1997.

Brownmiller, Susan. *Against Our Will: Men, Women, and Rape.* New York: Simon and Schuster, 1975.

———. *In Our Time: Memoir of a Revolution.* New York: Dial, 1999.

Bunch, Charlotte. *Passionate Politics: Feminist Theory in Action.* New York: St. Martin's, 1987.

Crow, Barbara A. *Radical Feminism: A Documentary Reader.* New York: New York University Press, 2000.

Daly, Mary. *Beyond God the Father: Toward a Philosophy of Women's Liberation.* Boston: Beacon, 1973. Rev. ed., 1976.

Duplessis, Rachel Blau and Ann Snitow, eds. *The Feminist Memoir Project: Voices from Women's Liberation.* New York: Three Rivers, 1998.

Dworkin, Andrea. *Heartbreak: The Political Memoir of a Feminist Militant.* New York: Basic, 2002.

———. *Pornography: Men Possessing Women.* New York: Plume, 1981.

———. *Woman Hating.* New York: Dutton, 1974.

Feigen, Brenda. *Not One of the Boys: Living Life as a Feminist.* New York: Knopf, 2000.

Firestone, Shulamith. *The Dialectics of Sex: The Case for Feminist Revolution.* New York: Morrow, 1970.

Firestone, Shulamith, and Anne Koedt, eds. *Notes from the Second Year: Major Writings of Radical Feminists.* New York: Radical Feminist Publications, 1970.

Friedan, Betty. *The Feminine Mystique.* New York: Norton, 1963.

———. *It Changed My Life: Writings on the Women's Movement.* New York: Random House, 1976.

———. *The Second Stage.* New York: Summit, 1981.

Gornick, Vivian, and Barbara Moran. *Woman in Sexist Society.* New York: Basic, 1971.

Greer, Germaine. *The Female Eunuch.* New York: McGraw-Hill, 1971.

———. *The Whole Woman.* New York: Knopf, 1999.

hooks, bell. *Ain't I a Woman: Black Women and Feminism.* Boston: South End, 1981.

———. *Feminist Theory: From Margin to Center.* Boston: South End, 1984.

———. *Talking Back: Thinking Feminism, Thinking Black.* Boston: South End, 1989.

Lerner, Gerda. *Fireweed: A Political Autobiography.* Philadelphia: Temple University Press, 2002.

Millet, Kate. *Sexual Politics.* Garden City, N.Y.: Doubleday, 1970.

Morgan, Robin. *Going Too Far: The Personal Documents of a Feminist.* New York: Random House, 1977.

———, ed. *Sisterhood Is Powerful: An Anthology of Writings from the Women's Liberation Movement.* New York: Vintage, 1970.

Plant, Judith, ed. *Healing the Wounds: The Promise of Ecofeminism.* Philadelphia: New Society, 1989.

Redstockings. *Feminist Revolution.* New York: Random House, 1978.

Reuther, Rosemary Radford. *Sexism and God Talk: Toward a Feminist Theology.* Boston: Beacon, 1983.

Rich, Adrienne. *Of Woman Born: Motherhood as Experience and Institution.* London: Virago, 1986.

———. *On Lies, Secrets, and Silence: Selected Prose, 1966–1978.* London: Virago, 1980.

Richardson, Diane, and Vicki Robinson, eds. *Thinking Feminist: Key Concepts in Women's Studies.* New York: Guilford, 1993.

Schlafly, Phyllis. *The Power of the Positive Woman.* New Rochelle, N.Y.: Arlington House, 1977.

Schneir, Miriam, ed. *Feminism in Our Time: The Essential Writings, World War II to the Present.* New York: Vintage, 1994.

Smith, Barbara, ed. *Home Girls: A Black Feminist Anthology.* New York: Kitchen Table/Women of Color, 1983.

Steinem, Gloria. *Outrageous Acts and Everyday Rebellions.* New York: Holt, Rinehart and Winston, 1983.

Thom, Mary, ed. *Letters to Ms., 1972–1987.* New York: Henry Holt, 1987.

Walker, Alice. *In Search of Our Mother's Gardens.* San Diego, Calif.: Harcourt, 1982.

Watkins, Bonnie, and Nina Rothchild. *In the Company of Women: Voices from the Women's Movement.* St. Paul: Minnesota Historical Society Press, 1996.

Wells, Diane, ed. *Getting There: The Movement Toward Gender Equality.* New York: Carroll and Graf, 1994.

SECONDARY SOURCES

Cohen, Marcia. *The Sisterhood: The Inside Story of the Women's Movement and the Leaders Who Made It Happen.* New York: Fawcett Columbine, 1988.

Cott, Nancy F. *The Grounding of Modern Feminism.* New Haven: Yale University Press, 1987.

Davis, Flora. *Moving the Mountain: The Women's Movement in America Since 1960.* New York: Simon and Schuster, 1991.

Dubois, Ellen Carol, et al. *Feminist Scholarship: Kindling in the Groves of Academe.* Urbana: University of Illinois Press, 1985.

Echols, Alice. *Daring to Be Bad: Radical Feminism in America, 1967–1975.* Minneapolis: University of Minnesota Press, 1989.

Eisenstein, Zillah. *The Radical Future of Liberal Feminism.* White Plains, N.Y.: Longman, 1981.

Evans, Sara. *Personal Politics: The Roots of Women's Liberation in the Civil Rights Movement and the New Left*. New York: Knopf, 1979.

Faludi, Susan. *Backlash: The Undeclared War Against American Women*. New York: Crown, 1991.

Firestone, Shulamith. *The Dialectic of Sex: The Case for Feminist Revolution*. New York: Bantam, 1979.

Fox-Genovese, Elizabeth. *Feminism Without Illusions: A Critique of Individualism*. Chapel Hill: University of North Carolina Press, 1991.

Freedman, Estelle B. *No Turning Back: The History of Feminism and the Future of Women*. New York: Ballantine, 2002.

Freeman, Jo. *The Politics of Women's Liberation*. New York: David McKay, 1975.

Hewlett, Sylvia Ann. *A Lesser Life: The Myth of Women's Liberation in America*. New York: William Morrow, 1986.

Hole, Judith, and Ellen Levine. *Rebirth of Feminism*. New York: Quadrangle, 1971.

Horowitz, Daniel. *Betty Friedan and the Making of "The Feminist Mystique": The American Left, the Cold War, and Modern Feminism*. Amherst: University of Massachusetts Press, 1998.

Roiphe, Katie. *The Morning After: Sex, Fear, and Feminism on the American Campus*. Boston: Little, Brown, 1993.

Rosen, Ruth. *The World Split Open: How the Modern Women's Movement Changed America*. New York: Viking, 2000.

Shreve, Anita. *Women Together, Women Alone: The Legacy of the Consciousness-Raising Movement*. New York: Viking Penguin, 1989.

Weigand, Kate. *Red Feminism: American Communism and the Making of Women's Liberation*. Baltimore: Johns Hopkins University Press, 2001.

Wolf, Naomi. *Fire with Fire: The New Female Power and How It Will Change the 21st Century*. New York: Random House, 1993.

HEALTH AND PSYCHOLOGY

PRIMARY SOURCES

Boston Women's Health Book Collective. *Our Bodies, Ourselves*. New York: Simon and Schuster, 1973.

———. *Our Bodies, Ourselves for the New Century*. New York: Simon and Schuster, 1998.

Gilligan, Carol. *In a Different Voice: Psychological Theory and Women's Development*. Cambridge: Harvard University Press, 1982.

Miller, Jean Baker, M.D. *Toward a New Psychology of Women*. Boston: Beacon, 1986.

White, Evelyn C. *The Black Women's Health Book: Speaking for Ourselves*. Seattle, Wash.: Seal, 1990.

RACE, CLASS, AND GENDER

PRIMARY SOURCES

Abbott, Shirley. *Womenfolks: Growing Up Down South*. New Haven, Conn.: Ticknor and Fields, 1983.

Anzaldua, Gloria, ed. *Making Face, Making Soul (Haciendo Caras): Creative and Critical Perspectives by Women of Color*. San Francisco: Aunt Lute, 1990.

Asian Women United of California. *Making Waves: An Anthology of Writings by and about Asian Women*. Boston: Beacon, 1989.

Bambara, Toni Cade, ed. *The Black Woman: An Anthology*. New York: New American Library, 1970.

Brant, Beth (Degonwadonti), ed. *A Gathering of Spirit: Writing and Art by North American Women*. Rockland, Me.: Sinister Wisdom, 1984.

Castillo-Speed, Lillian, ed. *Latina: Women's Voices from the Borderlands*. New York: Touchstone, 1995.

Hull, Gloria, et al. *All the Women Are White, All the Blacks Are Men, But Some of Us Are Brave*. New York: Feminist Press, 1982.

Lorde, Audre. *Sister Outsider: Essays and Speeches*. San Francisco: Crossing, 1984.

Moraga, Cherrie, and Gloria Anzaldua, eds. *This Bridge Called My Back: Writings by Radical Women of Color*. New York: Kitchen Table/Women of Color, 1984.

Rader, Jacob Marcus, ed. *The American Jewish Woman: A Documentary History*. Cincinnati: American Jewish Archives, 1981.

Vidal, Mirta. *Women: New Voice of La Raza*. New York: Pathfinder, 1971.

Yung, Judy. *Unbound Feet: A Social History of Chinese Women in San Francisco*. Berkeley: University of California Press, 1995.

SECONDARY SOURCES

Amott, Theresa, and Julie Matthaei. *Race, Gender, and Work: A Multicultural Economic History of Women in the United States*. Boston: South End, 1991.

Andersen, Margaret L., and Patricia Hill Collins, eds. *Race, Class, and Gender: An Anthology*. Belmont, Calif.: Wadsworth, 1992.

Antler, Joyce. *The Journey Home: Jewish Women and the American Century*. New York: Free Press, 1997.

Davis, Angela Y. *Women, Culture, and Politics*. New York: Random House, 1989.

———, *Woman, Race, and Class*. New York: Random House, 1981.

Dill, Bonnie Thornton. "Race, Class, and Gender: Prospects for an All-Inclusive Sisterhood." *Feminist Studies* 9 (Spring 1983): 131–50.

Giddings, Paula. *When and Where I Enter: The Impact of Black Women on Race and Sex in America*. New York: Bantam, 1984.

Glenn, Evelyn Nakano. *Issei, Nisei, War Bride: Three Generations of Japanese American Women in Domestic Service*. Philadelphia: Temple University Press, 1986.

Jones, Jacqueline. *Labor of Love, Labor of Sorrow: Black Women, Work, and the Family from Slavery to the Present*. New York: Basic, 1985.

Polakow, Valerie. *Lives on the Edge: Single Mothers and Their Children in the Other America*. Chicago: University of Chicago Press, 1993.

Rubin, Lillian B. *Families on the Fault Line: America's Working Class Speaks About the Family, the Economy, Race, and Ethnicity*. New York: HarperCollins, 1994.

Ruiz, Vicki L. *From Out of the Shadows: Mexican Women in Twentieth-Century America*. New York: Oxford University Press, 1998.

Schein, Virginia E. *Working from the Margins: Voices of Mothers in Poverty*. Ithaca, N.Y.: Cornell University Press, ILR Press, 1995.

Sidel, Ruth. *Women and Children Last: The Plight of Poor Women in Affluent America*. New York: Penguin, 1986.

Weinberg, Sydney Stahl. *The World of Our Mothers: The Lives of Jewish Immigrant Women*. Chapel Hill: University of North Carolina Press, 1988.

SEXUALITY AND REPRODUCTION

PRIMARY SOURCES

Adelman, Marcy, ed. *Long Time Passing: Lives of Older Lesbians*. Boston: Alyson, 1986.

Wattleton, Faye. *Life on the Line*. New York: Ballantine, 1996.

SECONDARY SOURCES

Bailey, Beth. *Sex in the Heartland*. Cambridge: Harvard University Press, 1999.

D'Emilio, John, and Estelle B. Freedman. *Intimate Matters: A History of Sexuality in America*. Chicago: University of Chicago Press, 1997.

Dworkin, Andrea. *Right-Wing Women: The Politics of Domesticated Females*. London: Women's Press, 1983.

Faderman, Lillian. *Odd Girls and Twilight Lovers: A History of Lesbian Life in Twentieth-Century America*. New York: Columbia University Press, 1991.

Ginsburg, Faye D. *Contested Lives: The Abortion Debate in an American Community*. 2d ed. Berkeley: University of California Press, 1998.

Gordon, Linda. *Woman's Body, Woman's Right: A Social History of Birth Control in America*. New York: Grossman, 1976.

Joffe, Carole. *Doctors of Conscience: The Struggle to Provide Abortion Before and After "Roe v. Wade."* Boston: Beacon, 1995.

Luker, Kristin. *Abortion and the Politics of Motherhood*. Berkeley: University of California Press, 1984.

Petchesky, Rosalind Pollack. *Abortion and Woman's Choice: The State, Sexuality, and Reproductive Freedom*. New York: Longman, 1984.

Solinger, Rickie. *Beggars and Choosers: How the Politics of Choice Shapes Adoption, Abortion, and Welfare in the United States*. New York: Hill and Wang, 2001.

————, ed. *Abortion Wars: A Half Century of Struggle, 1950–2000*. Berkeley: University of California Press, 1998.

———. *Wake Up Little Susie: Single Pregnancy and Race before "Roe v. Wade."* New York: Routledge, 1992.

SOCIAL AND POLITICAL REFORM

PRIMARY SOURCES

Abzug, Bella S. *Bella!: Ms. Abzug Goes to Washington.* New York: Saturday Review Press, 1972.

Adams, Judith Porter, ed. *Peacework: Oral Histories of American Women Peace Activists.* Boston: Twayne, 1991.

Chisholm, Shirley. *The Good Fight.* New York: Harper and Row, 1973.

Smith, Lillian. *The Journey.* Cleveland: World, 1954.

———. *Killers of the Dream.* New York: Norton, 1961.

SECONDARY SOURCES

Berry, Mary Frances. *Why the ERA Failed: Politics, Women's Rights, and the Amending Process.* Bloomington: Indiana University Press, 1986.

Burkett, Elinor. *The Right Women: A Journey Through the Heart of Conservative America.* New York: Scribner, 1998.

Cantarow, Ellen, et al., eds. *Moving the Mountain: Women Working for Social Change.* Westbury, N.Y.: Press, 1980.

Harrison, Cynthia. *On Account of Sex: The Politics of Women's Issues, 1945–1968.* Berkeley: University of California Press, 1988.

Hartmann, Susan M. *From Margin to Mainstream: American Women and Politics Since 1960.* New York: Knopf, 1989.

Hewitt, Nancy A., and Suzanne Lebsock, eds. *Visible Women: New Essays on American Activism.* Urbana: University of Illinois Press, 1993.

Hoff-Wilson, Joan, ed. *Rights of Passage: The Past and Future of the ERA.* Bloomington: Indiana University Press, 1986.

Klatch, Rebecca. *Women of the New Right.* Philadelphia: Temple University Press, 1987.

Kornbluh, Joyce L., and Mary Frederickson, eds. *Sisterhood and Solidarity: Workers' Education for Women, 1914–1984.* Philadelphia: Temple University Press, 1984.

Lynn, Susan. *Progressive Women in Conservative Times: Racial Justice, Peace, and Feminism, 1945–1960.* New Brunswick: Rutgers University Press, 1992.

Mansbridge, Jane J. *Why We Lost the ERA.* Chicago: University of Chicago Press, 1986.

Mathews, Donald, and Jane Sherron DeHart. *Gender and Politics: Cultural Fundamentalism and the ERA.* New York: Oxford University Press, 1990.

Matthews, Glenna. *The Rise of Public Woman: Woman's Power and Woman's Place in the United States, 1630–1970.* New York: Oxford University Press, 1994.

Ruddick, Sarah. *Maternal Thinking: Toward a Politics of Peace.* New York: Ballantine, 1990.

WEB SITES FOR THE STUDY OF
RECENT AMERICAN WOMEN'S HISTORY

Listed below are some major Web sites that include archival and bibliographic resources in recent American women's history. Many of these sites offer links to additional Web sites.

AMERICAN WOMEN'S HISTORY: AFRICAN-AMERICAN WOMEN
www.mtsu.edu/~kmiddlet/history/women/wh-afam.html

AMERICAN WOMEN'S HISTORY: ASIAN-AMERICAN WOMEN
www.mtsu.edu/~kmiddlet/history/women/wh-asian.html

AMERICAN WOMEN'S HISTORY: HISPANIC WOMEN
www.mtsu.edu/~kmiddlet/history/women/wh-hispanic.html

AMERICAN WOMEN'S HISTORY: JEWISH WOMEN
www.mtsu.edu/~kmiddlet/history/women/wh-jewish.html

FEMINIST RESEARCH CENTER
http://www.feminist.org

GENERAL HISTORY OF FEMINISM
http://www.nau.edu/~wst/access/fhist/fhistsub.html

A GEOGRAPHIC GUIDE TO UNCOVERING WOMEN'S HISTORY
IN ARCHIVAL COLLECTIONS, UNIVERSITY OF TEXAS, SAN ANTONIO
http://www.lib.utsa.edu/Archives/WomenGender/links.html

INTERNATIONAL INSTITUTE OF SOCIAL HISTORY: WOMEN'S HISTORY
http://www.iisg.nl/~womhist/index.html

THE LESBIAN HISTORY PROJECT
http://isd.usc.edu/~retter/main.html

NATIONAL MUSEUM OF WOMEN IN THE ARTS

www.nmwa.org

REDSTOCKINGS WOMEN'S LIBERATION STUDIES ARCHIVES FOR ACTION CATALOG

www.afn.org/~redstock/

A catalog containing ordering information for the Redstockings Manifesto, which appears in chapter 3, and other documents from the 1960s rebirth years of feminism is available from the Project at P.O. Box 2625, Gainesville, Fla. 32602-2625, or, without graphics, on the above Web site.

SCHLESINGER LIBRARY AT THE RADCLIFFE INSTITUTE CAMBRIDGE, MASS.

www.radcliffe.edu/schles/libcolls/index.htm

SOPHIA SMITH COLLECTION AT SMITH COLLEGE, NORTHAMPTON, MASS.

www.smith.edu/libraries/ssc/home.html

WOMEN'S ARCHIVES AND SPECIAL COLLECTIONS ON THE WORLD WIDE WEB

http://scriptorium.lib.duke.edu/women/article.html

WOMEN'S COLLECTION ROUNDTABLE, DIRECTORY

http://www.archivists.org

Search: women's collections roundtable.

WSS LINKS: GENERAL WOMEN'S SITES, ASSOCIATION OF COLLEGE AND RESEARCH LIBRARIES, WOMEN'S STUDIES SECTION

www.libraries.psu.edu/crsweb/docs/women/general.htm

INDEX